EXTERNALLY GENERATED TENSIONS:
CREATED BY OR RELATING TO CONDITIONS OF

The external marketplace—Tensions can arise or be imposed by general market conditions or economic forces from outside the firm or industry. Chapter 14 examines the venture capital/Initial public offering model of new firm development and whether it was used to build firms or to build stock market value.

Governmental policy, legal, technical or social forces—This final group of tension sources lists those noneconomic forces that pull the development of e-commerce and the Internet in opposing directions. For example, Chapter 5 examines the economic implications of keeping the Internet an open technology as opposed to one that is walled off in part by a system of proprietary patents.

At times, the tensions appear as the result of conflicts between elements of the five sources. For instance, Chapter 5 looks at the struggle between structure and performance, with the Internet organized as a vehicle for easy entry creating in conflict with the need for e-commerce firms to earn normal or perhaps even economic profits. Likewise, Chapter 7 examines the struggle between law and economic performance inherent within the digital conflict—between protecting intellectual property rights and the desire to promote innovation. In these situations, two numbers will accompany the tension icon. In many cases, these inter-origin tensions prove to be the most interesting to observe and discuss, although they may prove to be the most difficult to resolve.

The Economics of
e-Commerce
and the Internet

The Economics of
e-Commerce
and the Internet

Edward J. Deak, Ph.D.
Fairfield University

THOMSON

SOUTH-WESTERN

Australia · Canada · Mexico · Singapore · Spain · United Kingdom · United States

THOMSON
SOUTH-WESTERN

The Economics of e-Commerce and the Internet
Edward J. Deak

Vice-President/Editorial Director:
Jack Calhoun

Vice-President/Editor-in-Chief:
Mike Roche

Publisher of Economics:
Michael B. Mercier

Acquisitions Editor:
Michael W. Worls

Developmental Editor:
Jennifer E. Baker

Senior Marketing Manager:
Janet Hennies

Production Editor:
Tamborah E. Moore

Media Technology Editor:
Vicky True

Media Development Editor:
Peggy Buskey

Media Production Editor:
Pam Wallace

Manufacturing Coordinator:
Sandee Milewski

Production House/Compositor:
DPS Associates, Inc.

Printer:
Phoenix Color
Hagerstown, Maryland

Design Project Manager:
Bethany Casey

Internal Designer:
Bethany Casey

Internal Photography:
PhotoDisc, Inc.

Cover Designer:
Bethany Casey

Cover Photography:
Digital Vision, Ltd.
PhotoDisc, Inc.

Library of Congress Control Number:
2002116008

ISBN: 0-324-13381-2
(InfoTrac + core text + Econ Apps
package)

ISBN: 0-324-13381-2
(core text + Econ Apps package)

ISBN: 0-324-27340-1
(core text only)

This book is dedicated to my wife Alice and my family, including P.J., Bryan, Jennifer, Carolyn, Cole, and Pablo, whose encouragement and support made possible the writing of the text.

B R I E F   C O N T E N T S

CONTENTS

The Economics of e-Commerce and the Internet is truly a student-driven accomplishment. In the mid- to late 1990s many Fairfield University economics and business majors were both fascinated at the growth of the new Internet technology and enamored of the instant riches that it seemed to bestow upon even college-aged participants who were part of the burgeoning e-commerce marketplace. In response to a desire for more information on the topic, a colleague, Dr. Robert Kelly, and I created a course entitled "The Economics of Entrepreneurship and e-Commerce." While the course was well received by the students, the e-commerce topic caught the eye of Keith Chassé, the Regional Sales Representative for South-Western Publishing, who brought it to the attention of Michael Worls, a textbook editor in the firm's Cincinnati headquarters. Together with my longtime friend Orville Haberman, who is a market consultant with the firm, we were able to put together an agreement to write this book. I have no doubt that this text could never have been delivered on time without the support from my home institution, Fairfield University, where the members of the Research Committee awarded me the Dr. Robert E. Wall Research Sabbatical for the Fall of 2001. I am grateful to them beyond words for the time and trust that they offered in aiding the development of the project.

This book was classroom tested in an earlier version with numerous student comments—most positive and some critical—dealing with the clarity of the prose, the vividness of the examples, and the value of the information. From among these student "beta testers," I would especially like to single out and thank Benjamin Erling and Dimitrios Koutmos for their insight, range of comments, and dedication to the evaluation process. The approach of the text reflects many of the creative insights that I gained as an Eli Lilly Visiting Faculty Fellow at Yale University a number of years ago. In particular, the focus on tensions as a way to highlight and organize the alternative forces within each topic area had its origins as part of the courses taught by Professor Merton Peck, who sponsored my time at Yale. By examining e-commerce through the lens of economic tensions I hope to help you organize your thinking about the similar nature of conflicting goals or tradeoffs as they relate to the development of both e-commerce and the Internet. The inside front cover of this text details a numbered system of economic tensions that are developed into specific examples throughout the book. I focus on five types of common tensions. Three of these tensions are internal (Firm or Industry Structure, Competitive Behavior, and Economic Performance), while the other two tensions have external origins (The External Marketplace, and Government Policy, Legal, Technical or Social Forces).

An instructor's manual to accompany this text is available for download from the book's Web site at **http://deak.swlearning.com**. In addition, you'll also find links to South-Western's many economics resources, such as EconDebate Online, EconNews Online and EconLinks Online.

There are many people to acknowledge and thank at South-Western, such as Jennifer Baker, my Developmental Editor, whose comments kept me on track and on time, Cheryl Wilms, the copyeditor, who had great patience and the dedication to catch numerous small flaws and errors, and Tamborah Moore, the Production Editor, who turned a raw manuscript into a presentable and readable text.

As is customary with academic texts, I retain the responsibility for any errors and omissions that might appear in the text despite the outstanding help of the above-named individuals. If any reader wishes to contact me with comments or criticisms, you may do so via e-mail at deak@fair1.fairfield.edu. I eagerly solicit all comments, both positive and negative, and will return a quick and pleasant response. I trust that you will find the following chapters both interesting and informative. Enjoy!

REVIEWERS

Eric Abrams	*Hawaii Pacific University*
Kregg Aytes	*Idaho State University*
James Barnes	*James Madison University*
Eric Darbkin	*Hawaii Pacific University*
Wafa Elgarah	*University of Central Florida*
John H. Gerdes, Jr.	*University of California, Riverside*
Henry Ingle	*University of Texas, El Paso*
James Koch	*Old Dominion University*
Joshua Livnat	*New York University*
Laurence J. Malone	*Hartwick College*
Shaheed N. Mohammed	*Marist College*
Norbert Mundorf	*University of Rhode Island*
Hong V. Nguyen	*University of Scranton*
Neil B. Niman	*University of New Hampshire*
Mahesh S. Raisinghani	*University of Dallas*
Joseph Stawicki	*Central Connecticut State University*
William J. Trainor, Jr.	*Virginia State University*
William C. Ward	*Kent State University, Trumbull*
Rolf Wigand	*Syracuse University*

ABOUT THE AUTHOR

Edward J. Deak is Professor of Economics at Fairfield University in Connecticut. Professor Deak received his Bachelor's and Master's degrees in economics from the University of Connecticut in 1965 and 1966, respectively. He received his Ph.D. in economics in 1974, also from the University of Connecticut. Dr. Deak is the co-author of *Environmental Factors in Transportation Planning*, and has published articles on a wide range of topics in *Growth and Change*, *The New England Journal of Business and Economics*, *Social Science Journal*, *Aging*, and *The Savings Bank Journal*. He co-authored a chapter entitled "Outmigration as Adjustment in New England" in the book *New Urban Strategies in Advanced Regional Economics*, and has testified before a number of Congressional subcommittees on issues ranging from the economic problems facing the elderly to the condition of the regional economy and potential economic consequences resulting from the Y2K conversion effort. Dr. Deak has served since 1983 as the Connecticut Model Manager for the New England Economic Project, where he has produced and published a semiannual economic forecast of the Connecticut economy. He has taught courses in antitrust and regulation, industrial organization, and global competition and competitiveness at Fairfield University since 1970. He is the Governor's appointee to the Connecticut Economic Conference Board, where he has served as a past chairman. Dr. Deak has served as a consultant to the Connecticut Department of Economic and Community Development, as well as a number of regional agencies, local governments, and private law firms. He is a member of the Board of Directors of Coastline Terminals and served as the publicly elected Chairman of the Stratford Town Council. He currently serves as a member of the Board of Police Commissioners in Monroe, Connecticut, where he lives with his wife, Alice, and family.

PART

1

Introduction and Background Topics

CHAPTER

1

Introductory Case

DISTANCE IS DEAD!¹

What do George Washington, Babe Ruth, and the physical concept of distance have in common? The answer is simple: they are all dead. The human life cycle caused the demise of Washington and Ruth. Science and the Internet revolution killed the concept of distance as it has been known in business, commerce, and our personal lives. It is difficult to fully understand and appreciate the extent to which commerce and human interaction have been and will be changed by the Internet without recalling some basic facts about science and the physical environment. The following question-and- answer approach establishes a basis for our comparison.

1. *How fast does light travel?*
   It travels at the incredible speed of 186,000 miles per second. The science of physics postulates that nothing travels faster.
2. *What is the circumference of the earth?*
   It's approximately 24,000 miles, or 1,000 linear miles for each of the 24 time zones that the earth spins through to create one day.
3. *Given the answers to questions 1 and 2, about how long would it take for a beam of light to travel around the earth?*
   This last question is more mathematics than it is pure science. The answer is, less than one-seventh of a second. In other words, the light beam would circumnavigate the earth approximately seven times each second. Now that's fast!

Great review of basic science and math you say, but what do these facts have to do with the idea that distance is dead? Well, thanks to the **science of photo optics**, or light management, just about anyone can converse with anybody else, anywhere in the world, over the **Internet**, at the speed of light. Not only is Internet communication fast, but it is reliable, efficient, and cheap as well. If the individual who initiates a communication is physically in Chicago, she can contact customers, suppliers, retailers, or friends in Cairo or Calcutta as fast and as easily as those in Cleveland or Chula Vista. She can actually speak to them for about two cents per minute (and sometimes for free) as long as she doesn't mind a grainy tone. She can *instant message* (IM) them online and conduct a running keyboard conversation. She can also "pick" their brains (i.e., access information and help files) and ask electronic questions to be answered later with e-mail. She can use the speed of the Internet to buy products and have them gift wrapped (with a card²), as well as shipped overnight (FedEx). She can make a conditional offer to buy (eBay), or leave product specs and an e-mail address along with an offer to sell. All of these tasks can be accomplished without leaving the security and convenience of home. Distance is dead!

---

1 This phrase is credited to management guru Tom Peters, who uses it as part of his opening narrative in *The Circle of Innovation* (Random House Audiobooks, 1997). He applies it to the general topic of firm organization and technological change. Here it is used within the specific context of e-commerce. Tom Peters is among the very best at articulating and assessing the constant change that takes place in global business. Accenture, the global consulting and management solutions firm, ranked him as the second most influential "business intellectual" in a 2002 survey. The full results of the survey are available at **http://www.accenture.com/xd/xd.asp?it=enWeb&xd=_dyn/dynamicpressrelease_487.xml**.

2 Actually, consumers can send electronic greeting cards with animation and music, in a foreign language if desired, all free of charge, at least for the first month, from **http://free.bluemountain.com/**.

An Introduction to the Economics of
e-Commerce and the Internet

E-COMMERCE IS A FORCE FOR CHANGE

e-Commerce Brings Empowerment

Not only can individuals accomplish all these actions, but they are also empowered do them at a time of their choosing. The Internet is always open, 24 hours a day, seven days a week, 52 weeks per year. It is the first truly global 24/7 business model. The amazing part is that this communications access can be achieved with a limited amount of equipment, including a multipurpose computer, modem, telephone line, and Internet service provider.[3]

When the first 7-Eleven convenience store opened, it introduced a revolution in food retailing. The consumer was empowered, no longer constrained by the daylight business hours of traditional grocery retailers. A sudden, late night case of the "munchies" could be cured by driving to the local 7-Eleven and paying an outrageous price for the right to buy a bag of Doritos chips or a pint of your favorite ice cream.

The Internet revolution conveys a degree of personal **empowerment**, or the ability to act and control transactions, many times greater than what is generated by a 7-Eleven. The Internet empowers the consumer by *time* because it is available at 4:00 A.M. (even the local 7-Eleven isn't that accessible). It empowers consumers *economically* because they can comparison shop to their heart's content for the lowest price, the best quality, or most generous warranty conditions on a car, a book, or even that pint of Chunky Monkey. Considering the travel costs and the value of the time spent on physical shopping, the prices and convenience of Internet purchases made at home are potentially less expensive, even including shipping.[4] It empowers consumers with *knowledge* by allowing them, for example, to search for information on medical care or government services and to take college classes electronically. These opportunities allow individuals better control of their own health care and economic destiny.[5]

e-Commerce Changes the Economics of Search

The **economics of search** is a branch of economics that identifies both clock time and distance as two of many market frictions that hold implications for consumer behavior

---

3 Users are also able to access the Internet through a cell phone or a personal digital assistant (PDA) such as a Blackberry or Palm Pilot. In fact, a user doesn't even need to own any of this equipment if he or she can gain Internet access for an hourly fee at a local cybercafe or for free at many public libraries. This latter public access linking method is popular in Eastern Europe, the Middle East, Asia, and Africa, where lower incomes limit private access.

4 A few (now defunct) e-firms even tried to give one-hour guaranteed delivery in certain cities on orders for books, videos, and snack items.

5 Many of the historical and scientific facts mentioned in this chapter were checked at the search engine **http://www.AskJeeves.com**. The ability to find information and check facts is a form of Web empowerment.

and market efficiency.[6] **Market frictions** interfere with the assumption of *perfect information* that yields a smooth, continuous, and efficient exchange process. For example, market participants usually possess only *imperfect information* about key exchange variables such as the location of buyers and sellers, the range of prices offered for the same product, and the quality of the goods and services being traded. As a consequence of these frictions, traders are willing to spend some of their time and other resources to conduct a limited search of the marketplace prior to engaging in an exchange. The expenditure of resources on the search effort involves the implicit assumption that acquiring more information will improve the level of satisfaction that a trader receives as a result of an exchange.

Information acquisition usually displays diminishing returns relative to the increased expenditure on the search effort. Consequently, a tradeoff or tension exists between the value of the resources spent to acquire additional information and the value of the additional information acquired. Recognizing this tension, the economics of search postulates the existence of some **optimal level of search** up to the point when the value of the additional resources spent on the search process just match the value of the information obtained. This optimal search calculation is shown in Figure 1-1. The marginal or incremental value curve (MV) is downward sloping and reflects the declining reward from searching for and acquiring additional information. The marginal cost curve (MC_1) is upward sloping indicating the increasing cost of searching for and acquiring incremental amounts of harder-to-obtain information. The optimal level of search (OLS_1) appears at the intersection point of the two curves. Beyond the optimal point, additional search would be uneconomic or inefficient, as the added cost (MC) would exceed the added gain (MV). Part of the search literature involves the development of search rules that aid traders in determining when that optimal point has been reached.

As noted previously, the combination of the Internet and e-commerce empowers the consumer by both helping to destroy distance and working to eliminate clock time as frictions in the exchange process. It also improves market efficiency by reducing the cost of information search and widening the scope of the search process. The Internet allows consumers to get more information, faster, at a lower cost in terms of time and effort spent on the search activity. As such it works to benefit the consumer by tilting the exchange process in favor of the buyer. In Figure 1-1, buyer access to e-commerce information on the Internet has the potential of shifting the marginal cost curve down and to the right to MC_2. The optimal level of search expands to OLS_2 allowing the buyer to efficiently obtain additional amounts of information, thereby improving the results of the selection process.

Before the Internet, an individual who wanted to purchase a book had a limited number of bookstores in the neighborhood from which to choose. He could also go into the next town or state to widen his search area and make a purchase, but the cost of travel in time and gasoline would make overcoming distance uneconomic except in the rare instance where the extra search costs would be exceeded by the extra benefits. Now, not only can consumers buy books from a Barnes & Noble or Borders store, but from BarnesandNoble.com or Borders.com. The virtual bookseller, Amazon.com, sells books only in cyberspace, and offers books at prices that are usually below those at physical stores, with a wider selection and without sales taxes. If these options are not enough, the potential buyer can consult search engines, such as Yahoo.com or Google.com among others, to find dozens or hundreds of potential sellers not just on the East or West Coast of the United States but anywhere in the world. Not only is distance dead, but its demise radically changed the cost and calculus of the search process.

Still, book sales are child's play compared to the Internet's effects on the search costs and sales of other products. Suppose a potential car buyer wants to purchase a Honda

---

6 The economics of search owes its origin as a branch of inquiry to George Stigler "The Economics of Information," *Journal of Political Economy*, 69 (1961), pp. 213–225.

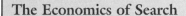

The Economics of Search	**FIGURE 1-1**

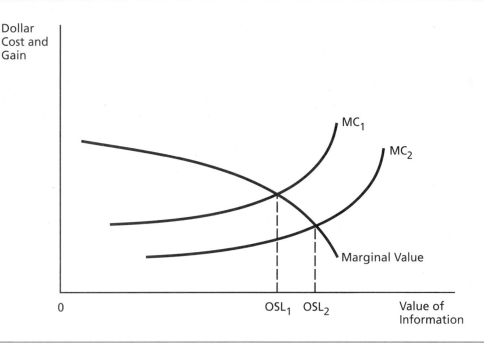

Accord. If the consumer is lucky, three or four Honda dealerships operate within a 15-mile, local search radius. Traveling to each and getting prices is an expensive and time-consuming activity. It might also be possible to contact them through their e-commerce site on the Web and get a cyber quote from each in less than 30 minutes. Consider the Honda dealers upstate or out-of-state as well. Would a buyer travel two hours round trip, just once, to a dealer fifty miles away to pick up the vehicle if he could buy the car over the Internet for $300 to $500 less? Most of us would at least consider this option. Distance is indeed dead!

e-Commerce Turns Differentiated Products into Commodities

If potential buyers conduct their e-commerce searches through the Internet, not only is distance dead and time irrelevant, but also products that were previously differentiated become more like commodities. In **competition through product differentiation**, producers spend a lot of time and money creating a distinct image or brand for their product. A Honda Accord is different from a Toyota Camry and from a Ford Taurus. These cars are differentiated not just by nameplate, but also by styling, features, quality and reliability, as well as dealer service reputation. The makers of different brands compete vigorously among themselves to attract your interest, create brand loyalty, and sell you their cars at a profitable price for themselves and for their dealers. This work is the essence of competition through product differentiation.

Commodities, on the other hand, are sold differently by producers and treated differently by potential buyers. Take, for example, the bananas being sold at several fruit stands as part of some farmers market. Bananas are a homogeneous product in that they are all the same within reason. United Fruit can put the "Chiquita" brand name on their product, advertise it, and try to convince you that it is better than the bananas sold by others, but most consumers aren't fooled. Buyers can tell almost everything they want to know about the bananas offered for sale just by looking at them. How big are they?

How much do they weigh? Are they green, yellow, or overly ripe? Given satisfactory answers to the preceding questions, the only distinguishing feature now is the price. Generally, the consumer will buy from the seller at the farmers market with the lowest price per pound for bananas. This process is good for the consumer because it forces the seller to charge the lowest possible price. Price competition restrains the seller, however, because the lowest price slices away any excess profits that the seller might enjoy, which is the essence of **competition through price**.

So, what does this traditional economic tension between competition through differentiation versus competition through price have to do with cars and e-commerce? Again, the answer is fairly simple. Buyers can get information on Accords, Camrys and Tauruses from *Consumer Reports* or other sources. They can look at, test drive, and select options for the different brands at their local dealer. Once they decide to buy an Accord rather than a Taurus, they can go to the World Wide Web and contact any number of Honda dealers who sell an identical product.[7] They can get cyberquotes, dicker with the lowest-priced two or three sellers, and buy the car from the online dealer with the cheapest price. E-commerce empowered the buyer by turning a differentiated product into one with more of a commodity character. It is a matter of the *large number of firms, selling the same product,* that are two of the essential characteristics of competition through price. Lastly, if the buyer doesn't like contacting dealers and haggling over price directly, she can always go to one of the cyberdealers, such as Autonation.com, to conduct the purchase. E-commerce intensifies economic competition. E-commerce and the Web help to turn brands into commodities.

SOME DOT-COMS AND INTERNET FIRMS ARE DYING TOO

Not only has the technology of the Internet led to the death of distance in e-commerce, but the explosive growth of the Internet and e-commerce in the decade of the 1990s also contributed to the rapid demise of many of these nascent firms in the early years of the twenty-first century. For example, ten firms carry the majority of the nation's high speed Internet traffic. Six of these **Internet backbone carriers** are facing serious financial trouble, with WorldCom, Global Crossing, and Metromedia Fiber Network having already filed for bankruptcy.[8] Three others, including Qwest Communications, Genuity, and Level 3 Communications are struggling to keep their financial heads above water.[9] Even though some of the firms have been tainted by accounting scandals and financial mismanagement, the simple truth is that backbone capacity built to carry Internet traffic grew at a rate far in excess of the actual level of traffic growth. Fierce price competition for the existing business erupted and carrier revenues fell, leaving them unable to service the multibillion-dollar debt levels that most had incurred during the expansion phase.

These examples do not mean that the Internet as a technology is disintegrating and will fade from view as quickly as the pet rock craze. As the discussions in the next section and Chapter 3 show, the Internet is the latest permanent step in the evolution of communications technology. As with any new technology, however, the imagined value of the advance can create an initial investment bubble that over-extends the capacity in the early stages. For example, the combination of irrational optimism and fraudulent behavior led to excessive expansion of the U.S. railroad system in the 1800s. Some railroad firms failed, while others merged to form stable profit-generating enterprises. Also, the invention of the automobile saw the birth of dozens of car manufacturing firms

---

7 Taking up a dealer's time with test drives and information gathering and then buying elsewhere online involves an economic concept called the *free rider problem*, which will be detailed in greater depth as part of the discussion in Chapter 5.

8 "Net Carriers' Struggles Could Cost Consumers," *USA Today*, August 13, 2002, p. 1B.

9 Others include AT&T, Sprint, and Global Center.

USA Today Internet Index Companies July 6–7, 2000 and August 13, 2002		**TABLE 1-1**
Survivors	**Eliminated**	**Additions**
Amazon.com	At Home	Internet Security
E*Trade	CMGI	NetIQ
EBay	Emusic	Hotels.com
Earthlink	Etoys	Net2Phone
Priceline.com	TheStreet.com	University Phoenix Onln
Yahoo	NorthPoint	WebEx
Broadcom	PSINet	
Cisco System	Teligent	
Verisign	Rhythms NetConn	
Realnetworks	Winstar	

Source: Adapted from *USA Today*.

in the early years of the twentieth century. Many of these firms disappeared outright, such as Locomobile, Stanley Steamer and Pierce-Arrow. Some were absorbed into larger auto firms, including Oldsmobile, Buick, and Chevrolet, which became part of General Motors. Others, such as Kaiser, Willys, and Nash changed corporate identities several times, first forming American Motors, which later became part of Daimler-Chrysler. The lesson is that being first with a new technology does not always guarantee long-term survival. Conversely, the competitive demise of firms does not mean that the technology itself won't survive and thrive.

The problems of the backbone carriers can also be traced to the demise of a number of the dot-com firms that were expected to provide the volume of e-commerce traffic. In 1999, *USA Today* initiated an Internet index to track the equity value of 50 e-commerce and 50 e-business firms. The index reached a peak value of approximately 210 in late March 2000 and declined fairly steadily thereafter. The index was reconstituted in December 2001, with 25 e-business firms and 25 e-consumer firms. Only 22 of the firms in the revised index were part of the original 100 Internet companies. Some of the original firms merged or changed their focus, but a significant number either failed outright or shrank in value to the point where they were no longer appropriate for inclusion in the index. Table 1-1 contains a partial list of firms found in the July 2000 index and those in the August 2002 listing. Survivors are firms found in both time periods: the Eliminated heading includes firms that failed or still live but post a near-zero per-share market value; and the Additions listing contains some firms that have grown to the point where they deserve inclusion as part of the *USA Today* Internet 50 index.

Some 700 dot-com firms failed due to lack of customers, insufficient profits on customer volume, or a poorly conceived business plan in general. These firms received the bulk of attention in the period subsequent to the general collapse of Internet stock values. However, some 56 percent of the 109 largest online retailers reported profitable online operations in 2001, up from 43 percent in 2000.[10] Several of the Table 1-1 survivors were part of this profit list, including eBay, Priceline.com and E*Trade. The inclusion of new dot-coms in the *USA Today* Internet index lends support

---

[10] See the press release for the 2002 version of the annual study "The State of Retailing Online 5.0," available at **http://www.shop.org/press/061202.html**.

to the proposition that **e-tailing**, or online retailing, shows sufficient traction to be a permanent addition to the list of consumer point-of-purchase options. Have no fear that time spent learning about the economics of e-commerce and the Internet might be wasted. Rather, it should pay handsome dividends as these two technologies expand at a more sustainable pace in the foreseeable future.

THE INTERNET AS PART OF THE COMMUNICATIONS REVOLUTION

Taken together, the Internet, the World Wide Web, and e-commerce are just the latest phase in a long line of historical changes in the way the humans communicate and do business.

The Introduction of a Spoken Language. The first revolution occurred when prehistoric humans first learned to speak. Language is not just about "one grunt go left, two grunts go right," although that step was at least some help in human survival and progress. The key is the development of language sufficiently complex enough to convey sophisticated ideas. Language development must have been an extremely important concept for early humans, because it happened in almost every society in every part of the world. Complex language most likely conveyed an enormous strategic and economic advantage. First and foremost, the tribe could construct an oral history about practical things such as the seasons, hunting, gathering, and planting techniques. They might also have accumulated oral knowledge about building techniques, diseases, and threats to safety. This knowledge provided an advantage to the tribe in the struggle for survival and perhaps helped them to advance their standard of living. Lastly, tribal members may have used language to plan their adventures into new areas or organize their reactions as they encountered other humans.

Creating a Symbolic Language Through Writing. Speaking is one thing, but oral traditions can get lost in time or become altered as each storyteller embellished the tale with personal interpretations. A written or symbolic language can be more permanent if the material on which the concepts are written survives over time. Today, archeologists know a great deal about the Egypt of the pharaohs even though almost all of the information about them and their society was originally lost in antiquity. The knowledge of ancient Egypt comes from the ability to decipher the hieroglyphs chiseled into the clay tablets, stonewalls of tombs, and monuments that survived more than 4,000 years.[11] The hieroglyphs allowed the Egyptians to keep track of their most important accomplishments, religious rituals, and business transactions. Call this *s-commerce* as in "written in stone." In contrast, we know comparatively little about the rather sophisticated society of the Eutruscans who did not leave behind a written language. They inhabited Italy around the time of the later Egyptian pharaohs, just prior to the appearance of the Romans.[12]

The Printing Revolution. Fast-forward about 2,000 to 2,500 years or so to 1456 in Germany with Johannes Gutenberg, the inventor of the printing press. No longer did the world depend upon the tedious efforts of scribes or monks who painstakingly copied

---

11 It was the finding of the Rosetta Stone, with similar inscriptions written in hieroglyphs, Latin, and Greek languages that provided the key to unlocking the Egyptian code. The stone was chiseled circa 196 B.C., and discovered in 1799 A.D. It is on permanent display at the British National Museum and is contemporary testimony to the value of sheer luck.

12 Of course, the chiseling of words or symbols into stone is a lengthy process requiring physical as well as language skills. Thank goodness for the Chinese who invented paper. Paper writing not only made the process of communicating ideas a lot easier and cheaper, but also allowed the written word (such as this book) to become more plentiful.

and preserved by hand, the great (and lesser) works of their time. Now words and ideas could be set as movable type in a printing press and distributed on paper to all readers both efficiently and cheaply. In 1517 Martin Luther nailed his 95 Theses, in protest of papal indulgences, on the door of Wittenberg Castle Church. Perhaps, if his disciples had to distribute this document in written rather than printed form, the words might have had less of an impact. Set in type and distributed quickly as printed material throughout the land, it led to the Protestant Reformation with monumental effects that changed forever the religious and political landscape of Europe. Apart from religious and political revolt, the printing press was a boon to commerce. Even though the records of individual business transactions were still kept in writing for another four centuries, business contracts, laws, and other documents were now easier to produce. You may call this printing press or *pp-commerce* if you need a name to keep straight the timeline of this communications history lesson.

The Telegraph and Telephone Revolutions. Fast-forward again about 375 years to America. Samuel Morse figures out how to send messages in dots and dashes over an electric impulse mechanism, and the telegraph system, along with Morse code, is born. Now information of all types can be sent quickly over long distances through metal wires, but the transaction requires a person skilled in telegraphy on each end. Wouldn't it be nice if ordinary people could just speak to each other over a similar wired system? That was most likely what Alexander Graham Bell thought as he labored to invent the telephone and started what was to become the corporate institution of American Telephone and Telegraph, or AT&T. His invention gave rise to what we might call *t-commerce*, with all forms of business transactions taking place over the wired telephone system.

The Wireless Revolution. Communication by telephone and telegraph are great and can go anywhere as long as you have the wire connections. Communication *without* wires? Now that's a real innovation. Not surprisingly, about the same time that primitive, commercial telephone systems began to appear in America, an Italian inventor by the name of Guglielmo Marconi created his own communication revolution by receiving a wireless signal sent across the Atlantic Ocean to St. Johns in Newfoundland, Canada, from a transmitter in Poldhu, England. This technology was refined and became known as radio. It quickly evolved into our first medium of mass entertainment.[13] National audiences laughed at Jack Benny over advertiser-sponsored network radio. Baseball fans heard the baseball game live and cheered for the Boston Red Sox even without paying for a seat at the ballpark. The nation listened intently as President Roosevelt explained that the United States was entering into World War II against Japan as a result of the bombing of Pearl Harbor.

Wireless voice is nice but wouldn't it be really great to see Jack Benny's performance or watch the game as it unfolded as well as hearing it live? Hence, television broadcasting was born. Philo Farnsworth sent the first television signal in 1927.[14] David Sarnoff and the scientists at NBC perfected the concept, and commercial broadcast television was born just after WWII. Howdy Doody, Ed Sullivan, and Jack Benny came into the private entertainment hall or living rooms in animated black and white. Bobby Thomson's 1951 playoff home run and Willie Mays' catch off the bat of Vic Wertz in the 1954 World Series really looked great on TV. And the Kennedy-Nixon debates in 1960 permanently altered the character of American presidential politics. The addition of color, narrow-casting via cable, and now high-definition television simply enhanced the quality of the greatest communications medium up to the time of the Internet.

---

13 It was also used to send business and emergency messages. Recall the movie *Titanic* in which the brave radio operator feverishly tried to send an SOS message over the airwaves on the new wireless transmitter.

14 Believe it or not, the first televised image was a dollar sign just like this $.

The Internet Revolution. For all the reasons discussed in the opening pages of this chapter, the Internet and the World Wide Web are the latest (and unlikely to be the last) stage in the evolution of communications technology. They kill distance, they empower the user, they facilitate commerce by making commodities out of brands, they are fast, cheap, reliable, and efficient. The Web is a destroyer of old ways of doing business and the father of new business forms. The Web is the vehicle of choice for a new era of global competition where firms located anywhere sell to end-users (**business-to-consumer,** or **B2C**) and to other businesses (**business-to-business,** or **B2B**) located everywhere. It is also a technology that allows individuals to do business with each other (**peer-to-peer** or **P2P**) to converse, swap items, or trade digital signals containing music, movies, or books.

This book is about the e-commerce component of the Internet revolution. It is selective, with a narrow focus that looks mostly at the economic aspects of e-commerce. Even though it may face a pretty broad task given the general scope of economic inquiry, this book attempts to get a pair of academic arms around the e-commerce topic.[15] The text may contain substantial information, but it has only a limited ability to expound on the future of e-commerce. Both the rapid spread of the e-commerce concept, along with its broad failure as a profitable business model to date, make prophecy in this area a risky business at best. Besides, it is doubtful that individuals in Egypt, Germany, Newfoundland, or at NBC knew where their part of the communications evolution would lead and the changes they would bring. Despite the limitations mentioned, the e-commerce topic is an important one. It is of considerable public as well as academic interest, as well as being fun to think about. So sit back, read with an open and creative mind, and trust that you will enjoy the journey.

INTERACTION OF ECONOMICS AND E-COMMERCE

For purposes of this book **electronic commerce**, or e-commerce, is defined as the act of doing business electronically over the Internet. The two key distinguishing features of this e-commerce definition are first, the phrase "over the Internet." The **Internet** is an electronic entity that links individual networks of computers together. Therefore, by limiting the definition of e-commerce to transactions over the Internet, the scope of activity is a bit narrower than might be found in other studies. For example, an automatic teller machine (ATM) allows users to conduct financial transactions electronically (withdraw funds, make deposits, shift balances) by means of an ATM network. Because the ATM transactions do not take place over the Internet, however, they are excluded from the definition. Conversely if a consumer accesses a bank account using a Web browser on a computer and performs the same functions, this is e-commerce. By the same logic, using an electronic retail credit or debit card to purchase goods at a gas station or a local merchant would be excluded as well, but it would be e-commerce if the same consumer paid by credit card for an airline or hotel reservation over the Internet at a travel site such as Orbitz.com.

The **World Wide Web** is the most popular and common application for making use of the Internet technology. It provides a way to access e-commerce sites quickly with a minimal demand for technical skill on the part of the user. The Web allows for color, graphics, animation, and sound, all of which make the e-commerce event a more entertaining and potentially informative experience. The material in Chapter 3 provides more information on the history and technology of both the Web and the Internet.

---

15 Search Amazon.com for books on "economics and e-commerce" and the pickings are mighty slim. Most of the responses contain information about how to start an e-commerce Web site rather than an examination of the economic consequences of the e-commerce phenomenon itself.

The second distinguishing feature of the e-commerce definition involves the interpretation of the phrase "doing business." This phrase has traditionally been associated with the acts of buying and selling a product or service. However, supplying Internet-based information, free of charge, might also be considered as part of "doing business" through e-commerce. This interpretation would hold if the information supplier acted with the intent of making a current or future profit on the transaction by, for example, hosting paid advertising on the site or by linking the free service to a fee-based one. Yahoo.com provides free search information and a number of free services, including e-mail accounts, with the hope of attracting viewers to support banner advertising and possibly to access some of its fee-based services.

The Internet first came to life in 1969, and originally served as a vehicle for transmitting mostly scientific information among university and government computer networks. The introduction of the Internet as a vehicle for e-commerce dates back only to the early 1990s. Conversely, **economics** as a social science first appears in 1776, according to conventional wisdom, with roots that reach back in antiquity to the time of the Greeks and Romans.[16] Economic analysis starts from the reality of *scarcity*. It is based upon the fact that the physical resources, which supply goods and services to fulfill human wants, are limited relative to those wants. Therefore, life is always about material choices in terms of what and how to produce, how much should be produced and who should get what share. Every act of using scarce resources has an economic cost, called an opportunity cost. **Opportunity cost** reflects the cost of using scarce resources in the current use and is measured in terms of the value of the best alternative forgone or what must be given up. For example, the cost to a student of reading this book may be forgoing the mystery and fright of reading the latest Stephen King novel.[17]

Discussing e-Commerce in Economic Terms

If resources are relatively scarce, what is the best way to use them as efficiently as possible? Economics postulates that unhindered, competitive markets are the most efficient resource users. Competitive markets respond to the signals sent by product prices, resource costs, and firm profits or losses to offer the best, but not perfect, solution to getting the greatest value from the resources at the lowest possible cost. These key economic concepts of markets, competition, price signals, and efficiency help to identify and organize the topics of this book as economic analysis is applied to the phenomenon of e-commerce. First, the Internet provides the technology to construct an electronic market, or *virtual market*, where goods and services can be exchanged. Second, the e-market contains *e-firms* that compete with each other electronically and with the brick-and-mortar firms that are part of the *physical market*. Third, the e-firms deal with prices, costs, profits, and losses just as the *physical firms* do. Fourth, structural characteristics of e-markets affect the e-firm's competitive behavior. And last, business plans or strategies of e-firms affect their survival and growth.

A sampling of questions arising from this marriage of economics and e-commerce issues would include the following:

---

16 Adam Smith, the father of economics, published his seminal text *The Wealth of Nations* in 1776. But the Greek philosopher Aristotle raised questions about the value of things and the "just price." The Mosaic law of the Old Testament, which among other things prohibited the charging of interest or usury for the lending of money, created a moral code to limit the conduct of economic behavior. It is almost certain that the ancient Egyptians had economic concerns, but they may have been just too difficult to summarize into hieroglyphs and chisel into stone.

17 Stephen King has joined the e-commerce age. *The Plant*, a recent novel, was sold directly to readers on a pay-per-chapter basis by King at **http://www.stephenking.com**. In March 2000, 500,000 fans bought and downloaded King's e-novella, *Riding the Bullet*, over the Internet during the first two days of sale. The Internet is substantially changing the book business.

- What is (are) the structure(s) of an electronic market(s)?
- Do the number and size of the e-firms in a given market make a difference in terms of how resources are used? If so, how?
- What barriers to entry and exit might new firms encounter? Are these barriers technical or strategic?
- How do e-firms price their product?
- How do e-firms differentiate their products and add sufficient value to create loyalty?
- How do the e-firms interact with one another and with physical firms?
- How do e-firms react to the competitive initiatives of their rivals?
- How efficient are e-firms in controlling costs and using resources?
- Are e-firms able to generate a profit?
- Are e-firm profits sufficient to reward those who took the risks and invested in the start-up of the e-firm?
- Will the e-firms be able to grow over time, anticipate gaps or changes in the market, and adopt new technology?

In working to answer these and other questions about the economics of e-commerce and the Internet, it is important to keep two qualifiers in mind. First, one goal is to identify and apply a general set of economic principles for analyzing e-commerce activity. Keep in mind that the text examines the behavior of individual and diverse e-commerce firms operating in different e-commerce industries and markets. It may be that market structure, behavior, and efficiency differ in some key ways among B2B as opposed to B2C firms or industries. Even within B2C, the economics of selling books might differ in some important ways from the model constructed to sell cars, consumer electronics or travel. Therefore, what may be acquired is a tool kit of economic concepts that can be drawn upon and applied judgmentally to help understand the operation of and anticipate the future for a particular e-commerce firm or industry.

Second, economics has evolved a body of theory called **microeconomics**. This branch of economics looks at the behavior of individual units, including firms and consumers as they deal with the scarcity problem. In terms of e-firm behavior, just how different is e-commerce from other types of economic activity? Although it may trigger a revolution in the way business is done, the competitive actions of e-commerce and the tool kit to analyze them may not be unique, but rather just part of traditional microeconomics. Therefore, the discussion can profit by devoting a part of Chapter 2 to an examination of standard microtheory principles and concepts.

TEXT ORGANIZATION: TOPICS, CASES, AND TENSIONS

The text covers some 18 topics, which are contained in five major divisions. These divisions are loosely organized along the lines of a traditional case study in the branch of economics called industrial organization. As such, they form a logical progression in determining the economic consequences of e-commerce and the Internet. The first part covers background topics including this chapter and the following two, which discuss microeconomic models and the technology of the Internet. Part 2 examines topics dealing with the structure of the e-commerce marketplace, including economic concentration and entry barriers such as patents and copyrights, as well as mergers in e-commerce. Part 3 looks at issues dealing with firm strategy and competitive behavior. The chapters identify strategies to achieve or challenge dominance in e-commerce markets, pricing and revenue strategies, and B2C behavior designed to differentiate as well as promote e-commerce products and Web sites.

Part 4 assesses how well or how poorly e-commerce firms are doing in terms of using scare resources efficiently. Chapters here include discussions of individual firm and industry profitability, B2B productivity, the role of venture capital and IPOs in fostering development of e-commerce and the Internet, an analysis of e-commerce failures, and an examination of some key service areas in which e-commerce prompted important changes in the way that business was being conducted. The fifth and final part looks at important issues, both economic and otherwise, dealing with e-commerce and the Internet. The topics of the taxation of e-tail transactions, the threat to Internet privacy and security, along with the role that the e-commerce and the Internet play in changing society are examined.

Most of the chapters begin with a brief introductory case focusing upon the behavior of a particular e-firm, key issue, or e-commerce problem. For example, this chapter began with an issue-oriented case detailing how the Internet contributed to the death of distance. The demise of distance benefited consumers by eliminating one barrier to conducting more efficient commercial transactions. The cases are designed to give readers a quick introduction to the topic area as well as get them actively involved in the subject matter. In most instances, the subject matter of the introductory case is revisited later in the chapter. This approach allows the analytical material to be applied to the case, which can aid in resolving the issue or problem facing the e-firm. Not all of the case problems or e-firm challenges conclude with a happy and definitive ending. The analysis often displays the types of competitive problems and frustrations that face not only e-commerce entities, but almost all economic firms of any competitive form. It is essential to keep that economic similarity in mind. It supports the hypothesis that even though the Internet and e-commerce possess some unique and revolutionary characteristics, they are also evolutionary in nature and extend the form of economic behavior, in addition to transforming certain parts of the competitive landscape. From the perspective of economic analysis, e-commerce may prove itself to be a case of "old wine in a new bottle."

Lastly, each chapter contains one or more pairs of **economic tensions**. The tensions help to define the competitive pressures that are pulling e-firms in different and sometimes mutually exclusive directions. Frequently, the key tension is identified as part of the challenge outlined in the introductory case. Some of these tensions involve traditional economic controversies with a long and unresolved economic history that is playing out in the newest context of e-commerce. For example, earlier this chapter identified the tension that exists between competition through product differentiation as opposed to competition through price. Some e-firms, such as Amazon.com, spent considerable effort and money to differentiate their firm and products, developing a brand name and business model that emphasizes customer ease of use, reliability, and quality service. Although they frequently offer lower prices, Amazon is much like Wal-Mart in that the e-firm shies away from advertising that they sell any product at the lowest price. Any firm must make a profit on its sales in order to survive in the long run, and Amazon.com has made considerable strides toward that end.

Certain characteristics of e-commerce and retail in general drive competitors, such as Buy.com, to undercut the Amazon.com business model. They advertise that they sell products at prices below that of Amazon and offer other services, such as free shipping, as well.[18] With this strategy the low-price sellers, including Buy.com or Southwest Airlines, offer a business model that emphasizes competition through price, turning the buying experience into more of a commodity activity. Whether fierce e-tail price competition will permit the survival of any or all e-firm competitors is an important question arising from the identification of the competitive tension. The answer to that question is still open to debate.

Understanding the Origins of a Specific Tension

Identifying the tensions that are part of commerce and growth plays a key role in this text's overall approach. An icon shown in the margin accompanies the identification of each tension discussed. This icon includes a number that identifies a common type or origin for each tension. The goal is to help you organize your thinking about the communal nature of conflicting goals or trade-offs as they relate to various chapter topics

---

18 Louis Lavelle, "The High Cost of Free Shipping", *BusinessWeek*, July 22, 2002, pp. 60–61.

and the development of e-commerce and the Internet. The numbering system identifies five common types of tensions. Three of these tensions are internal and arise from or are related to conditions within the firm or industry under discussion. The other two tensions develop out of an external origin related to or imposed upon the firm or industry by outside forces. The tension origins and icon numbers are organized as follows. (For easy reference, you can also find a listing of these tension descriptions and numbers inside the front cover of your textbook.)

Internally Generated Tensions

1. *Firm or industry structure*. These tensions appear as a result of conflicts between current or evolving characteristics of the firm or industry. For example, in Chapter 11, the text looks at the consequences of e-commerce activity being conducted by a market made up of virtual e-tailers as opposed to one where firms are structured to take advantage of a variety of channels to reach the customer.

2. *Competitive behavior*. These tensions arise from choices regarding the ways in which rival firms vie with one another to increase customer sales. For example, the discussion in Chapter 1 shows that firms can elect to attract buyers on the basis of product differentiation or on the basis of price.

3. *Economic performance*. These tensions come from differences in the ways that industries should be judged or firms may choose to report how well they are doing as part of the competitive struggle. For example, Chapter 12 looks at the profit reporting tension between those firms that follow conventional accounting and net income rules compared with those that elect a pro forma reporting standard. The pro forma approach spotlights specific revenue measures that might be considered to be more germane to an understanding of the growth of e-commerce firms.

Externally Generated Tensions

4. *The external marketplace*. Tensions can arise or be imposed by general market conditions or economic forces from outside the firm or industry. Chapter 14 examines the venture capital/IPO model of new firm development and whether it is used to build firms or to build stock market value.

5. *Governmental policy, legal, technical, or social forces*. This final group of tension sources lists those noneconomic forces that pull the development of e-commerce and the Internet in opposing directions. For example, Chapter 5 examines the economic implications of keeping the Internet an open technology as opposed to one walled off in part by a system of proprietary patents.

At times, the tensions appear as the result of conflicts between elements of the five sources. For instance, Chapter 5 looks at the struggle between structure and performance, with the Internet organized as a vehicle for easy entry that creates conflict with the need for e-commerce firms to earn normal or perhaps even economic profits. Likewise, Chapter 7 examines the struggle between law and economic performance inherent within the digital conflict between protecting intellectual property rights and the desire to promote innovation. In these situations, two numbers will accompany the tension icon. In many cases, these interorigin tensions prove to be the most interesting to observe and discuss, although they may also prove the most difficult to resolve.

Individual Chapter Topics, Cases, and Tensions

What follows is an outline of the 18 subject matter chapters focusing on topics, cases, and tensions. The purpose of this summary is to introduce you to the broad range of Internet, e-commerce, economic and social material presented within the text. The survey allows you to appreciate the scope of the material as well as the complexity of the issues that make e-commerce an interesting area of applied economic analysis and study.

Chapter 2   *Topic:* Survey of microeconomic models as applied to e-commerce
Case: The intensely competitive nature of online banking
Tension: Equilibrium versus disequilibrium approaches to microeconomics

Chapter 3   *Topic:* Examining the technology of e-commerce and the Internet
Case: Using the Internet and Web technology for an e-commerce activity
Tension: The future direction of fiber-optic research and Internet delivery

Chapter 4   *Topic:* Measuring e-commerce concentration
Case: Numbers and size dispersion among Internet service providers (ISPs)
Tension: The competitive benefits of many small versus a few larger firms

Chapter 5   *Topic:* Entry barriers
Case: AOL and instant messaging
Tension: Protecting economic profits versus promoting easy entry

Chapter 6   *Topic:* Legal/institutional entry barriers (patents and copyrights)
Case: Amazon.com: One-click ordering versus two clicks
Tension: Patents as a reward for innovation versus an entry barrier

Chapter 7   *Topic:* Copyrights: Protecting intellectual property in the digital age
Case: Metallica versus the digital world of Napster et al.
Tension: Protecting intellectual property versus protecting individual rights

Chapter 8   *Topic:* Structural change through mergers
Case: AOL merges with Time Warner
Tension: Mergers driven by efficiency versus market power motives

Chapter 9   *Topic:* Creating + Sustaining + Challenging market dominance
Case: Microsoft bundles up against the competition
Tension: Protecting private property and innovation versus preserving competition and the ability to compete

Chapter 10   *Topic:* e-Commerce pricing and revenue strategies
Case: Salon Magazine, not so free at last
Tension: Cost-of-service versus value-of-service pricing

Chapter 11   *Topic:* Strategic behavior: Product differentiation and promotion
Case: Estyle.com is in style, at least for a while
Tension: Virtual e-tailers versus physical retailers

Chapter 12   *Topic:* e-Commerce profitability
Case: Priceline versus Amazon: Reaching + Measuring profitability
Tension: GAAP profits versus pro forma profits

Chapter 13   *Topic:* e-Commerce efficiency and productivity
Case: Covisint and supply-chain management
Tension: Distributing the B2B efficiency gains

Chapter 14   *Topic:* Venture capitalists and IPOs
Case: Loudcloud goes public
Tension: The VC-IPO Model: Builder of companies versus builder of stocks

Chapter 15   *Topic:* Learning from dot-com failures
Case: Selling groceries via the Web
Tension: Forces of e-commerce success versus forces of failure

Chapter 16   *Topic:* e-Commerce industry applications
Cases: Health care, education, financial services, and real estate
Tension: The forces of intermediation versus disintermediation

Chapter 17   *Topic:* The taxation of e-tailing
             Case: Taxing retailers versus taxing e-tailers
             Tension: Federal moratorium versus state tax policy

Chapter 18   *Topic:* Economics of Internet privacy and security
             Case: The dual problems of Internet privacy and security
             Tension: Internet privacy versus Internet security

Chapter 19   *Topic:* The Internet and society
             Case: The Internet brings change
             Tension: Benefits of change: Populist myth versus monopolist myth

SOME IMPORTANT INTERNET AND E-COMMERCE DATA

Before the data flow begins, past experience suggests that even though some readers love seeing lots of data, others quickly get lost and are turned off by lengthy statistical presentations. Figures can help tell a story, but only if the numbers are understandable, and the audience is receptive to as well as appreciates the value of the message being sent. The following numbers are offered to provide a feel for the size of the Internet and e-commerce without causing the classic phenomenon known as *mego*.[19]

Internet Access Estimates: Global, Regional, and National

Just how big is the Internet in terms of U.S. and global connections? The answer is that it is already enormous, with access spreading worldwide since 1991 when it was made available to the public. Even though no one knows the precise number of persons who can enter the Internet, several survey "guesstimates" use a variety of methodologies to determine the number of persons with Internet access. The nature and degree of access vary widely. Access ranges from the use of home or office computers connected by either dial-up or broadband service, to connections made available at Internet cafés or commercial kiosks, to villages where one or two computers serve the entire community from a school or public building. The keys to accepting any of the estimates include the reputation and impartiality of the surveyor, the consistency of the survey method, and the regularity of reporting. These characteristics allow for both an appreciation of the absolute size of the Internet universe and the rate of growth over time. Two Internet survey firms, Nua.com and Nielsen-Netratings.com, publish publicly available, online, regional user access data on a regular basis. The Nua.com global and regional access estimates as of May 2002 are shown in Table 1-2. They indicate that roughly 580.78 million persons, or just 9.5 percent of the global population, have access to the Internet.

Europe is the region with the largest absolute number of individuals having Internet access with 185.82 million persons, or 25.6 percent of the total population. North America, including the United States and Canada, contains 182.67 million persons with Internet access, or 57.8 percent of the population. The combined area of Asia and the Pacific region holds 167.86 million persons with Internet access, but this amount is only 4.7 percent of the region's vast population base. Latin America has a smaller number of persons online at 32.99 million, which represents 6.3 percent of the population and is a bit larger than that for the Asia/Pacific region. Lastly, in both the Middle East and Africa, a much smaller percentage of the total population has Internet access. Because the Internet originated in the United States, Americans made up a high percentage of early users. Therefore, English has become the de facto language of the Internet. Also, North America and Europe combined account for nearly two-thirds of the current users. Consequently, the Web displays a decidedly Western culture and character. However, the data indicate that if Internet

---

19 Mego is the acronym for "my eyes glaze over."

| Global and Regional Internet Access Estimates of May 2002 | | | | **TABLE 1-2** |

Geographic Division	Number of Persons with Internet Access (mil)	Percentage of Persons with Internet Access	Number of Persons in the Geographic Division (mil)	Percentage of Population with Internet Access
Global	580.78	100	6,137.0	9.5
Europe	185.83	32.0	727.0	25.6
U.S. + Canada	182.67	31.5	316.0	57.8
Asia/Pacific	167.86	28.9	3,558.0	4.7
Latin America	32.99	5.7	525.0	6.3
Africa	6.31	1.1	818.0	0.8
Middle East	5.12	0.9	193.0	2.7

Sources: Internet access estimates and population estimates were obtained from **http://www.nua.com/surveys/ how_many_online/index.html**, and **http://www.prb.org/Content/NavigationMenu/Other_reports/ 2000-2002/sheet1.html**. Accessed on July 2002.

access is to expand in the future, the majority of new users will be located outside of North America and Europe. Whether this expansion brings language and cultural diversity to the global community of Web users is a topic to be addressed in Chapter 19, which deals with the Internet and society.

In a related study, the Internet research firm of Nielsen NetRatings estimated that 553 million persons worldwide had access to the Internet in the second quarter of 2002, up by 4 percent from the previous quarter. On a country basis, 166.4 million Americans were projected to have Internet access, of which 52 percent are female.[20] Globally, the Internet is available to 51.3 million Japanese, 32.6 million Germans, 29 million in the United Kingdom, and 22.7 million in Italy.[21] The firm estimated that in China, the at-home Internet user population totaled 56.6 million, placing it second behind the United States in at-home access. The Nielsen NetRatings survey data, displayed in Table 1-3, shows that the fastest growing U.S. segment of at-home Internet users was among the Hispanic population, with year-over-year growth of 13 percent from June 2001 to June 2002. In total, the U.S. unique audience grew from 107.2 million to 111.8 million persons for a 4.3 percent year-over-year gain.

Where Internet Surfers Go and What Surfers Do

More than four billion Web pages as of 2001 provide a lot of places to go and information to access on the Internet.[22] Researchers at Stanford University conducted a survey of some 4,000 U.S. Internet users to see which of some 17 activities they undertook on the Internet.[23] The responses showed that e-mail was the most common activity with 90 percent participation. Some 77 percent secured general information, using the Internet as a convenient electronic library. Information about specific products or travel was accessed by 62 percent and 54 percent respectively. Using the

---

20 "Number of Female Web Surfers Grow Faster Than Overall Internet Population, According to Nielsen NetRatings," **http://www.nielsen-netratings.com/pr/pr_020118_monthly.pdf**.

21 "Nielsen//NetRatings Finds China Has the World's Second Largest At-Home Internet Population," **http://www.nielsen-netratings.com/pr/pr_020422_eratings.pdf**.

22 "More Useless Info: 2 Billion Web Pages," *USA Today*, July 11, 2002, p. 3D.

23 Survey available at **http://www.stanford.edu/group/siqss/Press_Release/press_detail.html**.

TABLE 1-3	Nielsen//NetRatings Online Population by Race (U.S. Home) June 2002		

Ethnic Group (mil)	June 2001 Unique Audience	June 2002 Unique Audience	Year-over-Year Growth
Hispanic Origin	6.7	7.6	
Percent Composition	6.60	7.2	13%
Asian or Pacific Islander	2.2	2.4	
Percent Composition	2.20	2.30	6%
White (Caucasian)	90.8	94.0	
Percent Composition	89.5	89.6	4%
African American	7.5	7.8	
Percent Composition	7.40	7.40	3%
Total U.S. Audience	107.2 mil	111.8 mil.	4.3%

Source: "Hispanics Are the Fastest Growing Ethnic Group Online," **http://www.nielsen-netratings.com/pr/ pr_020716.pdf.**

Internet for work related activities was cited by 46 percent, while 36 percent said they used it for buying or e-commerce. The respondents indicated that 27 percent used the Internet to obtain stock quotes, while 26 percent used it as a tool to aid in a job search. Participating in chat room activity was cited by 24 percent, while 12 percent engaged in online banking, and just 7 percent used it for online stock trading. Similar results were found outside the United States. For those who were 16+ years of age in 10 European nations plus Hong Kong and Brazil, sending and receiving e-mail was the most common activity for 75 percent of households with Internet access. On average, 25 percent participated in chat room discussions, 28 percent engaged in instant messaging, 31 percent looked at audiovisual content, and 23 percent used the radio via the Internet.[24]

Where do people go when they log onto the Web? As of July 2002, the data from comScore Networks, shown in Table 1-4, indicates that two Internet service providers held the top spots for surfers to visit, with 98 million surfers stopping by the collection of AOL Time Warner sites and 89.8 million visiting the set of Microsoft Network (MSN) sites.[25] The next three most commonly accessed sites were the Web search engine/portal sites of Yahoo, Google, Terra Lycos, while information gathering about products and places attracted visitors to About/Primedia. The most popular commercial activity would appear to be selling your unwanted stuff to someone else, or buying theirs on eBay, with 33 million unique visitors. Buying books, CDs and electronic equipment at Amazon.com attracted almost 28 million visitors, while sites helping surfers to look for lost classmates or gather information about Internet and electronic products rounded out the top 10 sites visited. These site visit numbers along with the rankings are calculated monthly with the results being important to the participants. With millions of potential buyers showing up every month, the space on the screen at each site becomes extremely valuable real estate for the sale of profit-generating banners or other forms of advertising.

---

24 "European Newsletter," available at **http://www.nielsen-netratings.com/newsletter/newdesign/ global/global.htm**. Accessed August 2002.

25 "U.S. Top 50 Internet Properties," available at **http://www.comscore.com/news/csmmx_july_ top50_081902.htm**. Link to the comScore Media Metrix home page at **http://www.comScore. com** for the most recent top 50 list and data.

ComScore Media Metrix, U.S. Top 50 Internet Properties	TABLE 1-4
July 2002	

Rank		Unique Visitors (mil)
	All Web and other Digital Media	121.758
1	AOL Time Warner Network – Proprietary & WWW	97.995
2	MSN-Microsoft Sites	89.818
3	Yahoo! Sites	83.433
4	Google Sites	39.460
5	Terra Lycos	36.173
6	About/Primedia	35.297
7	Ebay	33.370
8	Amazon Sites	27.753
9	Classmates.com Sites	24.163
10	CNET Networks	22.762

Source: comScore Media Metrix, "U.S. Top 50 Internet Properties," July 2002, **http://www.comscore.com/news/ csmmx_july_top50_081902.htm.**

e-Commerce Activity: B2C

One popular Internet activity is e-tailing, or the purchase of retail products on the Web. The U.S. Census Bureau has been tracking e-tail (business-to-consumer) e-commerce sales beginning with data for the fourth quarter of 1999. Both the quarterly and annual totals are shown in Table 1-5. The census sales estimates do not include figures for travel agencies or ticket sales, purely financial transactions such as stock sales, or quasi-illicit activities such as e-gaming or e-sex.[26] Given these omissions, on average, e-commerce sales amounted to just over one percent of all retail sales. They totaled $35.9 billion in 2001, up by 24.3 percent from the sales amount for 2000.[27] Although the historical quarterly data is limited, the year-over-year percentage gains have been solidly in the double-digit range, with some gains per quarter topping 20 percent.

What do online buyers spend their money on? The answer to this question is tracked on a monthly basis by the Internet research firm comScore Media Metrix. Their survey for July 2002, which includes online expenditures for travel and tickets, revealed a total of $6 billion in consumer purchases, excluding sales made via auction sites.[28] This figure was up by 24 percent from the amount estimated for July of 2001. Expenditures on nontravel goods accounted for $3.1 billion, with computer and hardware sales amounting to $927 million. The comScore nontravel total approximates the numbers estimated by the Census Bureau. Media sales, including books, music, and videos are another significant online sales category with a monthly value in excess of $1 billion. Sales of online travel services totaled $2.9 billion. Economy.com projected that all forms of e-tailing

---

[26] For a discussion of the focus of the Census Bureau Index and how it compares to some other popular e-commerce dollar estimates see Yochi J. Dreazen, "U.S. Unveils New Quarterly Index to Track E-Commerce," *The Wall Street Journal*, March 3, 2000, p. A2.

[27] The census e-commerce data are reported quarterly at **http://www.census.gov/mrts/www/ current.html**.

[28] Available at **http://www.comscore.com/news/csmmx_july_top50_081902.htm**. The survey results were reported by Bob Tedeschi, "Online Sales Grew Slightly in July," *The New York Times*, August 22, 2002, p. C9. A summary of the monthly results can usually be accessed at **http://www. comscore. com.**

TABLE 1-5	Estimated Quarterly U.S. E-commerce Sales ($mil)

Year/Quarter	E-commerce Sales ($ mil)	E-commerce Sales as % of Total Retail Sales	Year-to-Year % Change in E-commerce Sales
1999: 4th Quarter	5,481	0.7	n.a.
2000: 1st Quarter	5,814	0.8	n.a.
2nd Quarter	6,346	0.8	n.a.
3rd Quarter	7,266	0.9	n.a.
4th Quarter	9,459	1.2	72.6
Total 2000	28,885		
2001: 1st Quarter	8,256	1.1	42.0
2nd Quarter	8,246	1.0	29.9
3rd Quarter	8,236	1.1	13.3
4th Quarter	11,178	1.3	18.2
Total 2001	35,916		24.3
2002: 1st Quarter	9,880	1.3	19.7
2nd Quarter	10,243	1.2	24.2

Source: **http://www.census.gov/mrts/www/current.html**.

sales should grow to exceed $80 billion by 2003, up nearly fourfold from the $22.5 billion in sales that they estimate took place in 2000.

A seamier side creeps into the e-commerce boom. Vice is a big B2C seller on the Web. More than 1,500 Internet casinos as of 2002 represented a 230 percent jump from 650 in 2000.[29] All of these sites currently originate outside of the United States. Roughly 4.5 million persons worldwide gambled and lost some $4.5 billion via the Internet, up from $2.2 billion in 2000. U.S. residents accounted for slightly more than one-half of those placing online wagers, with some 80 percent of the bets being technically illegal in the state where the gambler resides.[30] PayPal is the major credit card intermediary for the processing of all types of Internet transactions. The firm earned 8 percent of its revenue, or $8.2 million, from the processing of Internet wagering transactions in 2001.[31] If PayPal takes an average of 2.5 percent of the value of the transactions as its fee, then it alone would have processed in excess of $325 million in fund transfers in support of Internet wagers. These wagering and profit numbers rival the $20 billion in profits earned at 450 U.S. commercial casinos and the $7.2 billion in profits made by 160 domestic Indian casinos in 2000.

Adding to the volume of e-gaming revenues are the dollar flows resulting from the trade in cybersex. Plug in any variation on the Web address of sex, from sex.com to xxx.com and see the number of sites selling downloadable pornographic material, including pictures and video, as well as personal chat and live sex shows. Locate one site, and it is linked to dozens of others in the United States, Canada, Denmark, Australia, Poland, wherever. The perceived user anonymity of the Internet means that sex sells on the Web; it's B2C and really big business.[32] Little is available in the way

29 Ira Sager, Ben Elgin, Peter Elstrom Faith Keenan, and Pallivi Gogoi, "The Underground Web," *BusinessWeek*, September 2, 2002, pp. 67–74.

30 Ibid, p. 70.

31 "PayPal Inc. to Stop Processing Payments from New Yorkers", *The Wall Street Journal*, 8/22/02, p. B8.

32 Users may think that their sex site visits are anonymous, but the existence of "cookies" belies that assumption. For more on tracking cookies, see Chapter 18, which deals with issues of Internet privacy and security.

Value of U.S. Firm Shipments/Sales by Major Sector, 2000			**TABLE 1-6**
Sector	**Value of 2000 E-Commerce Shipments/Sales (mil)**	**Year-to-year Percentage Change E-Commerce**	**E-Commerce as % of Total Shipments/Sales**
Manufacturing (B2B)	$776,942	6.5	18.4
Wholesale Trade (B2B)	212,842	10.2	7.5
Services (B2B) (B2C)	37,312	47.6	0.8
Retail Trade (B2C)	28,829	92.1	0.9
$ Ratio: B2B/B2C	21:1		

Source: U.S. Census Bureaus available at **http://www.census.gov/eos/www/ebusiness614.htm**.

of reliable data on usage and dollars spent to define the extent of e-sex as part of e-commerce. However, it is a profitable, if exploitative, activity, judging by the proliferation of adult sites.

e-Commerce Activity: B2B

Even though B2C e-commerce rang up impressive numbers in a short period of time, the current level and potential growth for B2B sales dwarf the B2C dollar data. As with B2C e-tailing, the U.S. Census Bureau attempted to estimate the dollar size and industry distribution of B2B activity. The most recent results are for the year 2000 and are summarized in Table 1-6. The value of e-commerce-contracted manufacturing shipments totaled nearly $777 billion, or a substantial 18.4 percent of all manufacturing shipments. E-commerce-generated wholesale activity totaled almost $213 billion, or 7.5 percent of total sales. Some of the manufacturing and wholesale numbers may represent a double counting of the same item, but the total for e-commerce-generated transactions amounted to nearly $1 trillion in 2000. Service related e-commerce sales totaled $37 billion, while retail sales neared $29 billion. Assuming that one-half of the service sales were to final consumers, the dollar ratio of B2B to B2C sales exceeded 21:1. Despite the heavy concentration of public attention on B2C markets, the numbers clearly indicate that overwhelmingly, business-to-business transactions have quickly come to dominate e-commerce.

For example, as of 1999, Intel, the maker of the Pentium and other computer chips, was selling $1 billion a month in chips over the Web to computer makers, and it expected to sell all of its $30 billion in 2000 chip production that way.[33] Projections by Forrester Research estimate B2B sales of some $900 billion in 2003, rising to just a bit less than $1.5 trillion in 2004.[34] Who's selling what to whom? In 2004 sales are estimated to be $437 billion in computing and electronic items, $243 billion in gas and electricity utilities, $210.6 in motor vehicles, $147.1 billion in petrochemicals, and $138.1 billion in paper and office products. It represents a tremendous volume flowing over a combination of firm-specific sites and cooperative business-to-business exchanges that have been put in place. The expectation is that a small percentage of

[33] Associated Press, "Intel Sells Half Its Chips on the Web," *The Connecticut Post*, October 7, 1999, p. E5.
[34] "Reality Bytes," *The Wall Street Journal*, April 17, 2000, p. B10.

these large dollar numbers will be left on the table as profit for those who run the exchanges. In Chapter 13, the text explores the potential for B2B exchanges.

Managing financial assets online is also big business. It ranges from online banking at a local institution to banking with a virtual bank such as Netbank.com. It includes the online trading of stocks through a virtual broker such as E*Trade.com, the discount broker CharlesSchwab.com, or the ultra discount broker Scottrade.com. Twelve million households had an online banking account as of 2000 with 27.5 million expected by 2003.[35] In 2000, more than 7 million online brokerage accounts totaled in excess of $500 billion in assets. Despite the dramatic fall in equity values from March 2000 to July 2002, these online brokerage numbers are expected to rise as the equity markets recover.

SUMMARY AND PROSPECTS

Together, the Internet and Web based e-commerce are changing both individual consumer behavior and the ways in which firms do business. They erase distance and time as barriers in the exchange process. They empower consumers by reducing search costs and tilting the information gathering process more in favor of the buyer. The ready availability of information and the demise of distance also influence the balance between competition through product differentiation and competition through price. Together, they work to turn differentiated products into commodities, which can lead to lower prices that benefit consumers. The Internet is the latest step in a long history of communications revolutions. However, e-commerce is less of a revolution that transforms markets, and more of an evolutionary force that provides an added distribution channel that extends the range of transactions options. The data show that the volume of e-commerce business being done via the Internet is large and growing. Therefore, while many of the original dot-com firms have died as quickly as they were born, others have survived and begun to make profits. For that reason it is not surprising to see a number of new e-firms rising up to take the place of their fallen predecessors. Both the Internet and e-commerce are here to stay.

The tools and rigor of economic analysis provide a useful approach to examining the nature, behavior, and consequences of e-commerce and the Internet. Competitive market standards, the formation of and reaction to price signals, strategic behavior, and notions of efficiency in the use of scarce resources are all valuable economic concepts that work to explain electronic exchange. These tools help their users to formulate and perhaps answer some key questions about e-firms, e-markets, and e-commerce in general. They also guide the reader in developing and understanding specific trade-offs, controversies, and tensions. Some of these tensions are unique to e-commerce, while others are extensions of old economic debates in a new market setting.

The introduction to the economics of e-commerce and the Internet continues in the following two chapters. They detail the building blocks of microeconomic theory followed by a nontechnical survey of the structure and operation of the Internet as well as the World Wide Web. The Web is a tool for managing volume and complexity in the Age of Information. It brings order out of chaos by helping users locate knowledge within a mass of detail. The Internet and e-commerce are innovations with the potential for generating economic, social and humanistic change on par with the introduction of electricity, the telephone, or the automobile. Luckily, they are open to the power of economic inquiry, which is where the text points in the following chapters.

---

35 "Going Online With Personal Finance," *The New York Times*, December 20, 1999, p. C18.

KEY TERMS AND CONCEPTS

business-to-business e-commerce (B2B)
business-to-consumer e-commerce (B2C)
commodities
competition through price
competition through product
  differentiation
economic tensions
economics
economics of search
electronic commerce (e-commerce)
empowerment
e-tailing

externally generated tensions
internally generated tensions
Internet
Internet backbone carriers
market frictions
microeconomics
opportunity cost
optimal level of search
peer-to-peer e-commerce (P2P)
science of photo optics
World Wide Web

DISCUSSION AND REVIEW QUESTIONS

1. What does it mean to say that distance is dead? How have e-commerce and the Internet contributed to the death of distance?

2. What is empowerment? How have e-commerce and the Internet worked to empower the consumer?

3. Define the branch of economic inquiry known as the "economics of search." How do the Internet and e-commerce alter the behavior and efficiency of the search process?

4. What is the nature of the tension that exists between the value of conducting additional search and the cost of acquiring additional information? Is it irrational for a consumer to acquire all of the information that exists before entering into a transaction? Why?

5. Distinguish between the consequences of perfect versus imperfect information as each affects the efficiency of exchange. What kind of imperfect information is typically found in the marketplace for final goods and services?

6. Describe the nature of the tension that exists between competition through product differentiation and competition through price. Why would Buy.com challenge Amazon.com using competition through price? Won't this approach just lead to lower prices and profits for both firms? Why?

7. When does a differentiated product become a commodity? Is it advantageous for a firm to have its product regarded as a commodity by consumers? Why?

8. What are Internet backbone carriers? Why did so many of them experience financial problems? Are these kinds of problems unusual in the early stages of a new technology? Why?

9. Why did so many dot-coms die an early economic death? Does the demise of hundreds of dot-com e-tailers necessarily mean that the commercial value of e-commerce is a failure? Why?

10. Explain how the Internet is just the latest stop on the evolutionary road tracing changes in communications technology.

11. Define the term *electronic commerce* (e-commerce) and identify the two distinguishing features of this definition.

12. Define the term *Internet* and explain how it relates to the concept of the World Wide Web.

13. Distinguish between a virtual market and physical market. Why must e-firms recognize that they are really competing in both of these markets?

14. Define *economics*. What are some of the issues and questions raised by economics as it looks at the operation of e-commerce?

15. What is an economic tension? How helpful is it to frame the discussion of Internet and e-commerce issues in the form of a tension?

16. How many people have access to the Internet globally, and by region? Where do users go and what do they do when they are online?

17. How large is the dollar volume of B2C and B2B e-commerce activity? Explain the disparity in the dollar volumes of the two activities.

WEB EXERCISES

1. Link to the Web site created by Professor Hal Varian, Dean of the School of Information Management and Systems at the University of California at Berkeley. The site is located at **http://www.sims.berkeley.edu/resources/infoecon/**. Browse through the information on the site. It contains one of the most comprehensive lists of economic and other Web sites dealing with a range of Internet, intellectual property, and information-related issues.

2. To see the full list of the Accenture top 50 business intellectuals, link to their site **http://www.accenture.com/xd/xd.asp?it=enWeb&xd=_dyn/ dynamicpressrelease_487.xml**.

3. Link to Nua at **http://www.nua.com/surveys/how_many_online/index.html** to see their current estimate of the number and location of individuals who have Internet access.

4. Link to the Nielsen//NetRatings site at **http://www.nielsen-netratings.com** to check their latest data and stories on Internet usage. Which firms are on their list of top Internet properties? Compare this list and visitor numbers to the one at **http://www.comscore.com**.

5. Link to the U.S. Census Bureau data on quarterly e-commerce sales at **http://www. census.gov/mrts/www/current.html**. What was the total value of e-commerce sales for 2002? How did this figure compare with 2001?

6. To see whether the government updated the B2B E-Commerce Multi-Sector Report numbers beyond those for 2000, link to the Census Bureau's E-stats homepage at **http://www.census.gov/eos/www/ebusiness614.htm**.

CHAPTER

2

Introductory Case

ONLINE BANKS IN CYBERSPACE

The discussion of economics as it applies to e-commerce begins with an exercise using one of the popular Web search engines. The purposes of this introductory case are to serve as a departure point for a review of the four microeconomic theoretical market models and to highlight some of the differences among these models. Open any browser, and type in the address or URL[1] of the search engine Google.com, which claims to be able to search some 1.4 billion Web pages. The task of the case is to identify the number of financial firms that supply the e-commerce service of online banking. Be aware that creating key words for the search engine to link to is an art in its own right, and a collection of trial-and-error searches is always in order.

To start the search, type in the keywords "online bank."[2] The response yields nearly 34,000 sites that contain the phrase *online bank*. These sites are listed in the order of their relevance to the keywords and their ability to supply useful information. The first page holds links to NetBank, Bank One and directbanking.com, which are all located in the United States. It also contains a link to simile.co.uk, which offers online banking services from within the United Kingdom. In addition, sponsored links, including Citibankonline.com and ingdirect.com, will appear.[3] Most, but not all, of the 34,000 listings are for banks, especially in the first 10–20 of some 3,400 pages. If you click on the Directory tab in the upper center left of the screen, the result is a set of 50+ banks with online services that list themselves with Google. Many of these are pure-play Internet banks, operating only in cyberspace and without retail branches. If 34,000 undifferentiated sites are too many links to wade through, the search can be narrowed by adding in the name of a home state and/or city at the end of the keywords. If Texas and Dallas are the state and city of choice, the search using the four key terms without parentheses returns almost 78,000 links, with the first 3–4 pages listing Dallas, Texas-based banks with online services.

Undoubtedly, these results will vary over time as Web listings for online banks come and go. This exercise shows that a large number of banks list online services. Some are pure-play, while others are traditional retail banks with an online product delivery channel. Thousands are located within the United States with thousands more located outside of the country, some displaying languages other than English. A quick perusal of the banking sites shows that

---

1 A **uniform resource locator** or URL serves as a filename and allows access to a particular site on the Web.
2 The keywords within the quote marks ask Google to find and display all sites containing the exact phrase in that order. If the key phrase "Internet bank" had been entered, a different listing of some 31,000 sites would have appeared, but many would have been the same institutions as shown in the first search. If the keywords "Internet bank online banking" were entered without the parentheses, the search would be asking Google to find any site containing any of those words in any combination. The result here would contain some 650,000 links. Link to **http://www.searchenginewatch.com** for more information about searches and search engines.
3 Sponsored links are really paid advertisements that are designed to show up on the opening page, and Google freely acknowledges them as such. Paid ads are one way that Google covers its costs and can offer free Web searches to the public.

Microeconomic Models of e-Commerce

most offer checking and savings accounts, certificates of deposit, credit cards, mortgages, student loans, and so on. Be aware that local banking laws may keep the user from accessing all online services in every state, and that offshore banking activities, outside of the United States, may greatly increase the complexity of the typical U.S. income tax form. For the most part, however, the online banks are all offering the same services with minor variations.

Economics holds that with many firms in the same market, offering the same product, the consumer benefits by receiving the product at the lowest possible price. It is the essence of competition. Competition in its purest sense is only one of four possible theoretical market models. The three other market structures deviate in important ways and in varying degrees from the competitive norm. On the one hand, some models may yield potentially less efficient results in both the physical and virtual worlds. Conversely, other deviations from the competitive structure may actually be beneficial and improve upon the degree to which the results satisfy consumer desires. The task for this chapter is to identify these four static structures and to compare them in terms of their potential consequences for e-commerce. Their comparison raises some important questions about the adequacy of these models as the sole basis for evaluating real-world behavior. Consequently, the discussion turns to additional dynamic aspects of market structure analysis as a way to expand the review of e-commerce and the Internet. The expectation is that the theoretical models, including both their static and dynamic aspects, will aid in the description of the nature and evolution of e-commerce. This discussion should also help to frame the statement and analysis of many of the market tensions as they pull and shape the future development of e-commerce.

MICROECONOMIC THEORY—EQUILIBRIUM ANALYSIS[4]

Microeconomic theory is the study of how markets work to organize and influence the actions of consumers and firms, helping them to get the most out of the relatively limited supply of resources. Over the past 200 years microtheory developed as a powerful set of tools and models capable of analyzing and predicting competitive behavior in the marketplace. Two important aspects of economic markets include the competitive structure of the firms and the nature of the equilibrium result. Firms and industries are defined in terms of their characteristics, such as the number of competitors, the nature

---

4 The following brief summary of standard microeconomic theory can be found in most of the popular introductory economics texts including William A. McEachern, *Economics: A Contemporary Introduction*, 6th ed. (Cincinnati: South-Western Publishing, 2002).

of the product, the degree of price control, the extent of nonprice competition, or the ease with which resources enter or leave the market. These characteristics lie at the heart of the **structural approach** to the examination of markets. The structural approach typically involves a discussion of **equilibrium analysis**, or the examination of markets at rest. The approach strives to identify the pressures that move the market toward **equilibrium**, where opposing forces are in balance. Once markets are at rest, an assessment is made of the **efficiency consequences** of that equilibrium in terms of how well the scarce resources are being used in both the short and long runs. Lastly, equilibrium analysis examines the reactions to any external shock that permanently disturbs the existing condition, creating a new equilibrium or balance point toward which the market gravitates. This **comparative static technique** involves taking one equilibrium position and comparing it to another. Within comparative statics, little or no discussion focuses on how the adjustment process takes place, such as the path that it follows or the length of time needed to move between the two equilibrium points.

Given the theoretical discussion of structure and equilibrium, microanalysis helped to create the applied field of industrial organization (IO). IO researchers developed a particular view of how to interpret the results of the theoretical discussion within the context of real world firms and industries. What emerged was the **structure-conduct-performance (SCP) paradigm** that looked at competition and efficiency as flowing in a fairly linear and deterministic way.[5] The SCP approach started from the structural characteristics of the firms within a given industry, which in turn influenced the competitive behavior of the firms, which worked to determine the performance results. These real-world outcomes were then tested against the static microeconomic efficiency criteria. The purpose here was to assess how different the structural and behavioral characteristics contributed to the best use of scarce resources. Today, the field of IO recognizes that real-world markets and firms are much more complex, aggressively interactive, and subject to far greater external competitive pressures.[6] These complexities limit the ability to allow for just a single linear view of competition. However, the SCP approach allows for the organization of key economic variables in ways that hold potential value for the study of e-commerce. The approach asks important economic questions and highlights key market tensions or diverging forces. These organizational aids to the analysis of e-commerce are helpful as long as they don't lead the discussion into the trap of imposing a one-way flow of causality. With these facts, history, and cautions in mind, the next sections briefly review standard microtheory and offer a few hints as to how it might be applied to the study of e-commerce.

Pure Competition: Many Firms and a Commodity Product

The term **pure competition** describes a collection of firms that form an industry defined by the following structural characteristics. First, it is made up of a *large number*, typically thousands, of similarly sized firms. Second, each firm produces an identical or *homogeneous product*. Here, all that the consumer needs to know about the product is readily available on the basis of inspection. Therefore, the consumer need not know the identity of the producer. Third, given these factors, the firm has no ability to set the price for its product. Purely competitive firms are *price takers*, with product price being determined in the larger market by the competitive forces of supply and demand. Fourth, there is *no nonprice competition*. Consumers make their purchase decisions solely on the basis of price and their personal inspection of the product. Identical products prevent the opportunity for product differentiation or advertising to sway the consumer. Lastly, resources flow freely into and out of the industry. *Entry and exit are easy* with an absence of barriers to hinder the flow. **Consumer sovereignty** dominates in purely competitive

---

5   A seminal work in this area would be Joe S. Bain, *Barriers to New Competition* (Cambridge: Harvard University Press, 1956).

6   For example, see Lynne Pepall, Daniel J. Richards, and George Norman, *Industrial Organization: Contemporary Theory and Practice*, 2nd ed. (Cincinnati: South-Western Publishing, 2002).

markets. Firms acquire resources and produce products because buyers want the item, and relative prices signal which items are of greatest value to the consumer.

In microtheory, time is divided into the **short run** where at least one resource is fixed in supply while others are variable, and the **long run** where all resources are variable. In the short run, the production process is governed by the physical **law of diminishing marginal returns**. This law states that as an extra unit of the variable resource (usually labor) is added to the fixed input (usually capital), the size of the resulting addition to output will eventually decline. Marginal product declines in the short run because each unit of the variable input labor has less of the fixed capital to work with. Microtheory also assumes that firms are primarily motivated by the goal of profit maximization. They are in business to maximize the total dollar amount of their profits, measured in terms of total revenue minus total costs. For the firm, this goal translates into the **short run profit maximizing rule**, which is to produce to the point where marginal cost is equal to marginal revenue (**MC = MR**). Here the added cost of producing one more unit of output (marginal cost) is just covered by the added revenue (marginal revenue) received from the sale of that unit. These short-run cost and revenue relationships for pure competition are shown in Figure 2-1. The steep positive slope for the marginal cost curve (MC) demonstrates that, even with a constant wage rate for additions to the variable input labor, the force of diminishing marginal returns will come to dominate the short run production process, leading to a rising marginal production cost. In turn, the steep rise in marginal costs will pull the per-unit cost curves upward, including average total cost (ATC) and average variable cost (AVC). On the revenue side, the purely competitive firm is a price taker. Therefore, it can sell all that it wishes at the equilibrium price Pe, which is determined in the market for the product according to the forces of demand and supply. Both the price and the marginal revenue that the firm receives from selling one more unit of output are equal and remain constant. These concepts can be shown by a single horizontal line such as $Pe_1 = MR_1$, which is also equal to both the demand

---

Firm Short-Run Revenue and Cost in Pure Competition   **FIGURE 2-1**

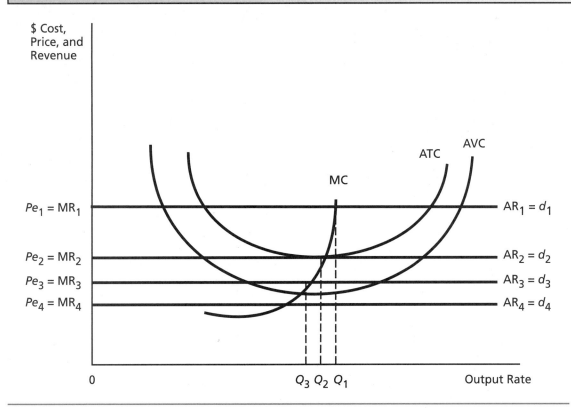

curve facing the firm (d_1) and its average revenue (AR_1). As a result, the decision as to what output level will maximize profits is made on the basis of rising marginal costs, which will eventually intersect with and then exceed the marginal revenue line.

Alternative Short-Run Outcomes in Pure Competition

Now that the firm is in short-run equilibrium, producing an output where MC = MR, the attention turns to determining whether the firm is making a profit. If at this output level the firm's revenue per unit, or average revenue (AR), exceeds its total cost per unit, or average total cost (ATC), as measured in terms of opportunity cost, then the firm is making an **economic profit**. In this desirable position for the firm, **opportunity cost** measures the value of the resources in their next best alternative use, including a sufficient return to compensate and retain the services of the entrepreneur. The situation is shown by the intersection of the MR_1 line and the marginal cost curve. Here the firm sells its Q_1 amount of its product at the equilibrium price of Pe_1. The firm is happy with this situation, because with $AR_1 > ATC$, the profit results are better here than it can achieve anywhere else. It earns a return greater than what is needed to retain resources in their current use. In the long run, when all resources are variable and entry can take place, the existence of economic profits will attract new firms into the industry. Entry occurs because the owners of these external resources perceive that they can do better (make higher profits) here than in their current activity. As entry takes place the new firms will increase product supply, lower the market price and compete away the excess profits.

Economic profits are not the only possibility in the short run, however. If average revenue (AR) falls short of average total cost (ATC), the firm is making an **economic loss**. In this case, the firm is failing to cover all of its opportunity costs. The resources could be earning more money if they were active in the next best alternative use. This situation is shown by the intersection of the MR_3 line and the marginal cost curve. Here the firm sells its Q_3 amount of product at the equilibrium price of Pe_3. It is not happy with this money-losing result. However, as long as the average revenue exceeds the firm's average variable costs (AR > AVC), it will continue to produce in the short run despite the loss. Short-run production despite losses is the correct choice because the sale of the output contributes some revenue above variable cost. This revenue covers a portion of the firm's fixed costs, which can't be avoided in the short run. Therefore, short-run production will allow it to minimize its losses. If the average revenue falls below average variable costs (AR < AVC), such as with line MR_4, the firm would shut down in the short run and produce nothing. The absence of production in this case would be the correct choice because losses here would be limited to the amount of the firm's fixed costs. Persistent short-run losses will be corrected in the long run as firms and resources exit the industry for more profitable activities elsewhere. The departure of firms decreases product supply, raises the market price, and eliminates the losses.

A fourth short-run equilibrium possibility exists, when average revenue just equals average total cost (AR = ATC). Here, the firm is earning a **normal profit** for the entrepreneur, which is just equal to what could be earned in the next best activity. This situation is shown by the intersection of the MR_2 line and the marginal cost curve. Here the firm sells its Q_2 amount of its product at the equilibrium price of Pe_2. The firm is satisfied with this position, because it is doing as well here as it can do anywhere else. This situation can serve as both a short- and long-run equilibrium, if the firm is unable to lower its production costs by changing its size of plant to capture additional **economies of scale**. At this point both entry and exit are discouraged, because no redistribution of resources can improve the profit picture. All purely competitive firms and industries will gravitate to this equilibrium point in the long run.

Pure Competition: Efficient Resource Use in the Long Run

This position of long-run rest, as shown in Figure 2-2, yields some important efficiency consequences for the use of resources. First, the long-run equilibrium is **productively efficient** in that the firm adopts the best technology to produce the product at the lowest possible production cost. In addition, the pressure on the firm from the competitive

| Long-Run Equilibrium and Efficiency in Pure Competition | **FIGURE 2-2** |

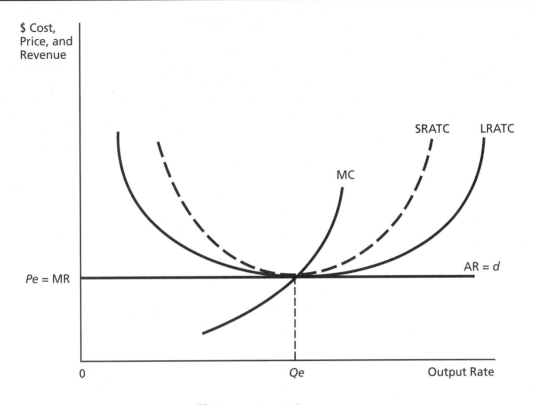

Productive Efficiency: $Pe = LAC_{min}$

Allocative Efficiency: $Pe = MR = MC$

market ensures that all of the cost reduction resulting from efficiencies of increased scale will be passed along to the consumer in the form of the lowest possible price for the product ($P = LAC_{min}$). Second, the equilibrium result is **allocatively efficient**. Here, the price that the consumer pays for the marginal unit is just equal to the extra costs the firm must pay to attract the resource away from its next best use ($Pe = MC$). The value of the last unit (Pe) that society demands is just equal to the value of the last unit of the next best product (opportunity cost) that society must give up if the resources are transferred into the current use. On balance, when a purely competitive industry is in long-run equilibrium, society achieves the most efficient distribution of scarce resources, resulting in just the right mix of products (allocative efficiency) that are produced using the best technology at the lowest possible resource cost (productive efficiency). This equilibrium result provides one way of addressing the basic economic problem regarding how best to use scarce resources.

One possible inference that may be drawn from the preceding analysis is that large numbers of small firms, without control over prices and with vigorous competition, will yield a long-run equilibrium that meets certain efficiency tests for the best use of resources. However, a number of limitations are associated with the reliance upon pure competition as the predominant means to efficiently use scarce resources. First, either persistent economies of scale, or the presence of severe inequities in the distribution of income distribution will block the link between pure competition and the best use of resources. Second, purely competitive markets may ignore **spillover costs**, such as adverse environmental consequences, resulting from the production process. Third, consumers may desire some product variety and want more than one way to satisfy the unique characteristics of their demand. Lastly, risk taking aimed at enhancing technological progress may be under-rewarded and discouraged by easy imitation and quick entry that eliminate the source of economic profits. Despite these limitations and qualifiers, the opinion persists that competitive markets are capable of yielding desirable results.

Pure Competition and the Internet Banking Case Revisited

Pure competition may be of considerable value to the consumer, who receives an **undifferentiated commodity product** at the lowest possible cost. However, the competitive pressure poses a problem for and threat to the purely competitive firm. Unrelenting pressure drives prices down to their absolute minimum level, yielding the potential for the slenderest of profit margins. It is a manifestation of **economic Darwinism**, where only the fittest survive. Either be the low-cost, low-price firm or suffer the wrath of the fickle consumer. This lack of apparent differentiation creates a problem for the pure-play online banking firms, making the Internet banking-only model a difficult one in which to earn even a normal profit. Competitive pressures drive pure-play online banks to offer checking and savings accounts with the highest interest rates, accompanied by rock-bottom monthly service fees for the use of the accounts.[7] In March 2001, the average yield on an interest bearing checking account was 3.78 percent, which was a premium of 2.61 percentage points above the rate offered by their brick-and-mortar competitors. Monthly service fees in turn averaged $5.25 at the typical Internet bank and $10.77 at a retail bank.[8]

Internet-only banks are supposed to be more efficient because of the absence of expensive branches and the prevalence of low-cost electronic transactions. Nevertheless, the combination of high interest payments and low fees, along with minimal customer acceptance, leaves most of them unprofitable. Consequently, the market responded in predictable ways. Some online banks had to exit the market; others, including NextBank, were closed by federal regulators,[9] while a third group, including Wingspan.com, sought out consolidation with a brick-and-mortar counterpart. Given the competitive pressures and the strategic response, the pricing trend moved toward lowering interest rate payments and raising fee charges at most online banks. Interest rates in March 2002 were lower in general throughout the economy, relative to March 2001. However, the spread on interest-bearing checking accounts between rates at e-tail and retail banks narrowed to just 1.23 percentage points. In addition, the average monthly service fee for e-tail checking accounts rose by $2.11 as opposed to falling by $0.10 at retail banks. Although individual online banks lack the pricing power to enact these changes alone, the situation of losses leading to consolidations in the market allow them to act simultaneously, in a noncollusive manner, to improve their collective profit position. The Internet banks still give the consumer a better deal than the retail banks, but the spread is narrowing. In Chapter 16, the text revisits the issues surrounding the topic of online banking as part of a larger inquiry into the economics of electronic finance.

Monopoly: A Single-Firm Industry in the Short and Long Runs

Monopoly is the polar extreme from pure competition both in terms of structural characteristics and usually in terms of efficiency outcome. A **monopoly** is a *single-firm industry*, where the producer makes a product for which *no good substitutes* are available. The monopolist faces the entire market demand curve and exercises *total control over the price* of the item. Therefore, it can exploit consumer preferences by charging a price that proves most advantageous to the firm rather than the buyer. Of course, the consumer can always respond by not buying the product. The absence of adequate

---

7 Michelle Higgins, "Internet-Bank Customers Pay Up," *The Wall Street Journal*, April 24, 2002, p. D2.

8 The data cited here are taken from the semiannual survey of bank interest payments and fee charges available at **http://www.bankrate.com**.

9 "Feds Shut Down Internet NextBank," available at **http://www.mail-archive.com/e-gold-list @talk.e-gold.com/msg08977.html**.

substitutes, however, makes the decision not to buy a painful choice. Electricity would be a good example of a product that until recently was produced and distributed under monopoly conditions. The act of turning on the TV could have been much more expensive without the presence of regulatory price controls. The absence of competitors today means there is *little need for nonprice competition* or product differentiation. And future competitors are barred given the *existence of entry barriers*. **Entry barriers** can arise because of cost-reducing economies of scale, ownership of key resources, government patents or franchise grants, product differentiation that creates unwavering brand loyalty, and so on. These barriers prolong the monopolist's grip on the market. They prohibit the flow of new firms into the industry regardless of the existence of positive profit incentives.

In the short run, the possession of a monopoly position does not always guarantee the existence of an economic profit. Even though a monopoly producer of buggy whips may have made a fortune in the nineteenth century, the technological advance that created the horseless carriage (car) changed consumer demand for different modes of travel. Even a monopolist needs a sufficiently strong demand for the product to allow total revenues to equal or surpass total economic costs (TR > TC). Regardless of the fact that they are the sole producers of a unique product, monopolists, like purely competitive firms, also abide by the profit maximizing rule MC = MR to identify the best output level. However, because the monopolist enjoys pricing power over a desired product, it can choose a price on the market demand curve that will often yield a short-run economic profit. This relationship is shown in Figure 2-3, where average revenue

---

| **Short-Run and Long-Run Equilibrium in Monopolies** | **FIGURE 2-3** |

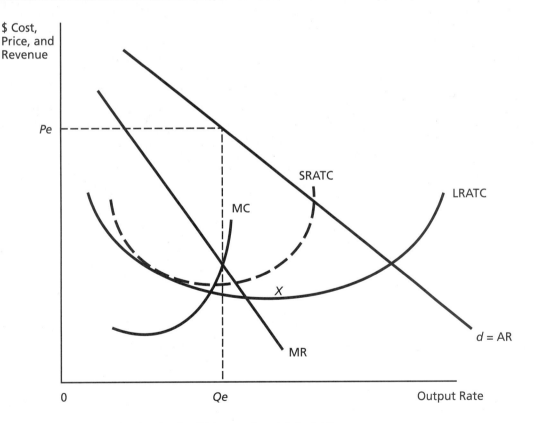

Productive Inefficiency: *Pe* > LAC > LAC$_{min}$

Allocative Inefficiency: *Pe* > MC

exceeds average total cost at the equilibrium price *Pe* and quantity *Qe*. Short-run economic profits exhibit some valuable efficiency consequences, such as *compensating the entrepreneur* for risk taking, or signaling the rewards for *competitive entry* in the long run. Because entry barriers exist and preclude entry into the monopolistic industry, the profits persist into the long run and distort the efficiency-creating aspects of the market. **Persistent economic profits** also work to distort the distribution of income, which further undermines market efficiency. Higher monopoly prices are extracted from consumers with the income accruing to the owners of the monopoly, which yields to the owners a greater level of control over the mix of consumer goods produced by the market. In this situation, the market may produce extreme luxuries for the wealthy monopolists, while others have a hard time acquiring the basic necessities of life.

Monopoly: Resource Inefficiency in the Long Run

In the long run, monopolies are typically *productively inefficient*, such that $Pe > LAC_{min}$. The firm does not necessarily seek out the scale of plant that will yield the lowest long-run production cost, shown at point X. Monopolists undertake a careful weighing of the added revenues and costs resulting from an increase in their output level. Usually they find that, even though average total cost diminishes as output rises, the average revenues fall faster because of the need to lower price in order to sell more output.[10] Therefore, increasing output in the long run reduces overall profits. This decline in profits eliminates any desire on the part of the firm to experience greater scale efficiencies through cost reductions in the absence of competitive pressures.

Monopoly production is also *allocatively inefficient*, because the price charged for the last unit sold is above the marginal cost of producing it ($Pe > MC$). Society values the monopolist's product far more than the next best use of the resource, and consumers would like to see more of the monopoly product made available. The monopolist ignores this desire and restricts output below the socially optimum level so as to raise price and maximize its own profits. A monopolist may also be *dynamically inefficient* as the pace of technological change may lag in monopoly markets in the absence of constant competitive pressures. Without a compelling profit result, the firm is reluctant on its own to introduce new technologies that will outmode the existing capital structure before the equipment is fully depreciated. Lastly, a monopolist may experience **X-inefficiency** by becoming "fat, dumb and lazy" in daily production and control over operating expenses. As a result, he or she may function at a cost level that is above the minimum unit cost associated with the current output rate.

Overall, microeconomic analysis supports the view that pure competition is efficient and good, while monopoly is inefficient and bad. Given the structural focus of both market definitions, it's not too much of a leap to infer that when an industry is closer to being competitive in structure, it may be more efficient than when it more closely resembles a monopoly market.

Monopoly and e-Commerce: The Case of Internet Explorer

It's a bit unusual to find an example of pure monopoly in any real-world setting. The market power held by Microsoft in market for personal computer operating systems comes close. The MS-Windows product was found in an antitrust trial court to control some 95 percent of the market for personal computer operating systems, which is as close as any firm has come in monopolizing an important, contemporary marketplace. Keep in mind that proving a firm is a monopoly isn't by itself a violation of the antitrust law. Rather, the government or private plaintiff must also prove that the firm acted in some anticompetitive way, to either achieve or maintain that monopoly position. A number of aspects are important in the Microsoft antitrust trial, but the one that bears notice here is how Microsoft leveraged its dominant position in the operating system market to also achieve a dominant position in the Internet browser market.

---

10 The relative rates of decline in cost and revenue can be seen in Figure 2-3, given that the negative slope of the AR curve is greater than the negative slope of the ATC curve.

In what may seem like eons ago in Internet time, a blossoming firm called Netscape, which had developed Netscape Navigator by the early 1990's, became the first commercially successful **Internet browser**. A browser is the software package that links a personal computer to the Internet and allows the user to carry on e-commerce transactions. With a browser, the user is able to easily access a specific site and hyper-link to other sites, all in living color and accompanied by sound. Netscape's share of the browser market was 73 percent in the fourth quarter of 1996.[11] However, allegedly illegal actions by the monopolist Microsoft vaulted the various versions of its browser, Internet Explorer, into the number one position as of April 2002, with 90 percent of the market. The Netscape product, which was acquired by AOL-Time Warner, has been reduced to a minor player in the browser field, with just a 7 percent market share.[12] The issue of the browser wars and what Microsoft did to win them is covered in Chapter 9, later in this book. However, at this point it is sufficient to note that monopoly is not just a tired theoretical discussion. Rather, it has an important application in the world of e-commerce and the Internet.

Monopolistic Competition: Product Differentiation and Nonprice Competition

These conclusions and inferences regarding the efficiency aspects of pure competition and monopoly become less definite in the presence of our third market structure, **monopolistic competition**. This model blends economic characteristics, some resembling those of pure competition, while others approach the condition of monopoly. First, many firms still operate within a monopolistically competitive industry, perhaps not the thousands of pure competition, but hundreds at least. Second, the output of each of these hundreds of firms demonstrates some form of **product differentiation**; the product is or is perceived to be slightly different from that of competitors. Product differentiation is the key to understanding the behavior of monopolistically competitive firms because, as a third characteristic, it gives them some degree of pricing power over the amount that they can charge for their product.

Figure 2-4 shows that, if the consumer believes the product of one monopolistically competitive firm is somewhat unique relative to the products of other firms, or that the products of other firms are inferior substitutes, then the firm with the unique product can exploit this belief. It can raise its price above the level of other competing firms, such as from Pe_1 to Pe_2, without losing all of its customers, as it would if it were a pure competitor. For example, legions of consumers accept that Perdue chickens are more tender, plumper, or generally of better quality than store brand chickens. Therefore, Purdue is able to charge pennies more per pound for whole roasters, breasts, and cut parts, selling tens of millions of chickens to satisfied customers. Even though many consumers still buy the cheaper brands, Perdue does well in the profit area. Just multiply $0.05 times 200 million pounds of chicken, which equals $10 million, and you begin to see how lucrative monopolistic competition can be. Of course, by raising its price, the monopolistically competitive firm would lose more customers than would a monopoly. Firms involved in monopolistic competition must deal with substitutes, even though the substitutes might be perceived as being inferior. The customer of a monopoly finds no reasonable alternative products. The choice is either to continue to buy from the monopoly at the higher price or do without the product entirely.

Fourth, the potential return on investment in product differentiation motivates each firm to engage in aggressive and extensive **nonprice competition**. This differentiation can take one of many forms including accentuating differences in quality, styling, color,

---

11 "Browser War Heats Up During the Third Quarter of 1997, According to Dataquest," available at **http://gartner11.gartnerweb.com/dq/static/about/press/pr-b9759.html**. Accessed August 2001.

12 Dick Kelsey, "Netscape Share Hits All-Time Low-User Survey," available at **http://www.washtech.com/news/software/15907-1.html**. Accessed August 2001.

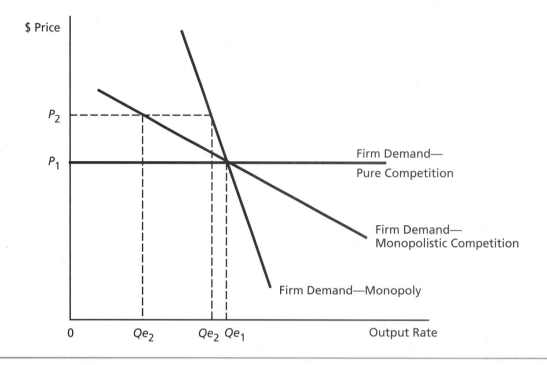

FIGURE 2-4 — Pricing Power in Different Market Structures

$ Price

P_2

P_1

Firm Demand—
Pure Competition

Firm Demand—
Monopolistic Competition

Firm Demand—Monopoly

0   Qe_2 Qe_2 Qe_1 Output Rate

shape, brand name, logo, service, location of sale, warranty conditions, and so on. Each firm can design its own *promotional policy* to create buyer perceptions or a recognized brand through advertising. Each firm can undertake its own *product development policy*, spending money on R&D or design changes. The goal of nonprice competition is to create **customer loyalty** to the product, rendering the buyer less sensitive to price increases. The purpose here is not to sell more units, because a purely competitive firm can already sell all that it produces. Rather the target is to sell the units at a higher price, resulting in a greater level of total profit.

Fifth, just as in pure competition, entry and imitation are easy. Therefore, the existence of short-run economic profits attracts new firms to the industry, The new firms compete away most if not all of the economic profits in the long run. This tendency leaves the majority of firms with close to normal profits. The profits at McDonald's hamburger franchises encouraged others to open up competing fast-food services. The entrants delivered slightly differentiated products, from flame-broiled hamburgers to foot-long subs, deep-dish pizzas, and crispy fried chicken. In terms of a luncheon menu, each of these food items provides a tasty if calorie-laden alternative to a Big Mac®. They also provide the customer with the opportunity for choice, which is absent in a purely competitive industry. Choice is valuable to the consumer because it allows the buyer to tailor the product purchase more closely to individual tastes and preferences.

Monopolistic Competition: Efficiency Questions in the Long Run

In terms of the two long-run efficiency criteria, the results for monopolistic competition are potentially better than monopoly but less desirable than pure competition. Figure 2-5 shows that the firms in a monopolistically competitive industry are productively inefficient ($Pe > LRATC_{min}$). This result appears for two reasons. First, market demand is so fragmented among the array of sellers, with each offering a slightly differentiated product, that optimal firm scale in the long run isn't possible. Second, the existence of individual

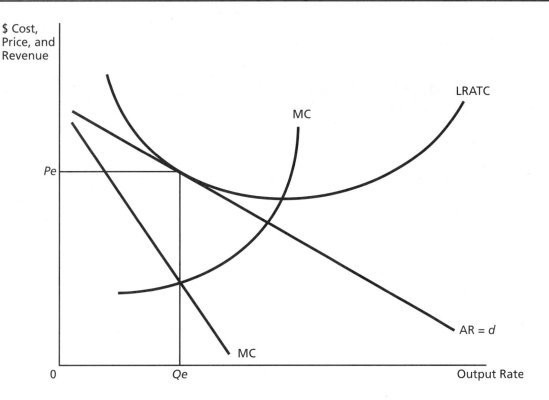

Long-Run Equilibrium in Monopolistic Competition   **FIGURE 2-5**

Productive Inefficiency: $Pe > LRATC_{min}$

Allocative Inefficient: $Pe > MC$

product uniqueness among an array of substitutes means that some consumers will stick with their favorite product even in the face of a slight increase in price. Consequently, the negatively sloped demand curve makes it impossible for the firm to achieve a long-run tangency solution at the $LRATC_{min}$.

This failure to achieve productive efficiency is an important and frequent criticism of monopolistic competition in that it supports a surplus of firms that mostly underutilize their capacity. For example, it is a rare filling station that has all of its gasoline pumps going simultaneously throughout the day. Production by monopolistically competitive firms is also *allocatively inefficient* because $Pe > MC$. Easy entry, motivated by the lure of economic profits, divides up the market demand among an ever-increasing number of suppliers. Entry also drives price below the monopoly level, leaving only normal profits at the tangency point between the firm demand and long-run average total cost curves. However, the equilibrium price is still above marginal cost. The absence of normal profit (AR < LRATC) at any output level above Qe keeps the firm from expanding. The absence of expansion occurs even though society pays a price above marginal cost, and would like to see more output made available.

So monopolistic competition appears to be an inferior market structure expect for one important consequence, the opportunity for an enriched range of choice. A purely competitive world is a dull environment where everything looks, smells, feels, and sounds the same. A monopolistically competitive world allows buyers to tailor their purchases to their individual and frequently changing tastes and preferences. On some days a consumer may prefer Raisin Bran cereal for breakfast. On other days an individual's tastes may turn to Froot Loops, Cap'n Crunch, or even Grape Nuts. The fact that consumers don't have to eat Cheerios every day has great value to them. Suffering a little waste in the form of excess capacity or paying a slightly higher price so a that buyer can indulge personal whims would seem to be a small loss in exchange for variety and choice. Other things being equal, the opportunity for choice leads to greater satisfaction being attached to the purchase of an item.

Product Differentiation and e-Commerce: Wireless Telephony

If choice is what the consumer wants, then the cell phone industry, which offers the potential of wireless connection to the Internet, is determined to supply that variety. Telephone service, even in its wireless form, comes close to being a purely competitive business. As long as the connections are safe and reliable, little distinguishes the service provided by one company from that of another. The same can be said of airline flight service, commercial trucking, and common stock transaction services offered by stock-brokers. These services become *undifferentiated commodities*, with only the price separating the service of one provider from that of its competitors. This characteristic of product homogeneity helps to explain why the competing providers work as hard as they can to differentiate themselves from one another, so as to tap unique segments of the buying public. For AT&T Wireless, it even undertook an extensive, and a bit confusing, branding campaign to attach the trade name of "mlife" to its service, hoping to distinguish it from the service offered by competing providers.[13]

Apart from branded service, the bulk of the differentiation comes in the form of a variety of unique calling plans offering differing levels of service and discounts on the purchase of the cell phone. For example, as of the spring 2002, for a monthly charge of $39.99 VoiceStream offered 500 whenever minutes, including long distance, and unlimited weekend calling time. For the same fee, AT&T Wireless offered 400 any-time minutes and unlimited night and weekend minutes for life. For $10 more, Cingular offered 500 anytime minutes and 3,500 night and weekend minutes. Lastly, Verizon Wireless offered a "Family SharePlan" with 4,000 minutes shared over two cell lines for a joint fee of $55. The key here is that not all buyers are the same, with the identical communication needs or calling patterns for their cell phone service. If the wireless provider tailors the plan to the common characteristics of a significant segment of cell phone uses, then the provider is likely to capture a substantial portion of that segment, thereby creating a potentially profitable customer base. For consumers, the trick is to know their own potential usage pattern, and to pick the plan with the characteristics that best fit the personal calling profile. With this strategy, wireless firms differentiate what is generally a commodity product, while making consumers a bit better off with a plan that meets their needs. Later, in Chapter 11, the text explores the topic of product differentiation, where the discussion examines the theory and e-commerce applications of product attributes and the tailoring of products to variations in consumer demand.

Oligopoly: Rivalry and Resource Efficiency Issues Among a Few Firms

The last of our theoretical market structures is **oligopoly**, an organization that offers us greater diversity in both characteristics and in strategic market behavior. It is an industry *dominated by a few large rivals.* Numerous other firms may be operating in the industry as well, but they are smaller and survive either by following the lead of the dominant firms or by pursuing their own niche strategy that has little effect on the larger leaders. The products can be *homogeneous,* as with steel (U.S. Steel, Bethlehem,

---

13 Christopher Saunders, "AT&T Wireless' mLife Campaign Enters Phase Two," available at **http://www.internetnews.com/IAR/article/0,,12_979021,00.html**. Accessed August 2001.

National), differentiated through branding, as with beer (Anheuser Busch, Phillip Morris, Coors), or *differentiated* by style and design, as with automobiles (Ford, Honda, Volkswagen). The key characteristic of an oligopoly is **mutual interdependence**. Here, an action taken by one firm has a direct, immediate, and perceptible effect on the sales and revenue received by the firm's rivals. Because the action poses a potential threat to the profitability and possible survival of the rival, the rival can be expected to react quickly in one of a number of ways. This process of strategic action and reaction is especially true with respect to *product pricing* and gives oligopoly its real-world richness in terms of analytical complexity. Oligopolistic firms are no longer *impersonal competitors* as in pure competition. Rather, their actions invoke *intense rivalry* and are focused in nature. Think of Coke versus Pepsi or McDonald's Big Mac versus Burger King's Whopper.

Figure 2-6 shows that the threat posed by aggressive price competition and the recognition of their mutual interdependence may lead the few firms in an oligopoly to prefer a quiet life rather than engaging in mutually self-destructive price competition. The demand curve facing each firm is perceived to have a kink in it at the existing market price (Pe), rather than being smooth and continuous as it might be in the other theoretical market structures. The kink arises because the firm fears that if it lowers price to P_2, it will precipitate a price war, with rivals having no choice other than to immediately match the price cut. Therefore, the firm will not be able to steal customers away from its rivals and the added demand ($0Q_1 - 0Qe$) will be less responsive, or elastic, than it might otherwise be. Under most demand and revenue conditions, the firm triggering the price war will see its profits diminish. Consumers will be the prime beneficiaries of the price war, by receiving the product at a lower cost. Conversely, if the firm raises its price from Pe to P_2 and its rivals fail to follow, then it will loose a considerable volume of sales ($0Qe - 0Q_2$), as customers are attracted to the products of rivals to the extent that they are good substitutes.

Oligopolistic Short-Run Pricing: Kinked Demand	**FIGURE 2-6**

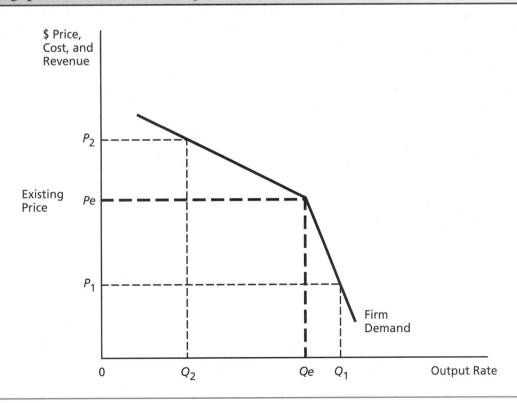

The potentially unfavorable consequences of price competition within an oligopoly lead the firms to favor nonprice competition as a method for stimulating sales and creating customer loyalty. Nonprice competition tends to vary with the character of the product itself, and whether the product is sold to other producers or directly to the public. Auto firms (GM, Ford, Toyota) engage in extensive advertising and styling behavior while selling their product to an impressionable public. Conversely, aluminum firms (Alcoa, Reynolds, Kaiser) sell a standardized product, aluminum sheets or ingots, to professional buyers and therefore engage in minimal nonprice competition. Entry, while not impossible, is usually made difficult by a combination of technical and strategic barriers such as pricing, design, scale economies, R&D policies, or government manipulation. Still, successful entry can occur in U.S. industries over time. Foreign firms, including Toyota, Nissan, and Honda, entered the U.S. auto industry, originally by supplying products in market segments that were being ignored by U.S. car firms. U.S. mini mills entered the domestic steel industry by employing a better technology, which relies on electric furnaces to melt new steel from steel scraps, rather than the older open hearth furnace technology that makes steel from iron ore.

Economic efficiency is not a common result emanating from an oligopoly. The significance of the threat posed by price competition often leads them to try to find ways to avoid it and to coordinate pricing behavior rather than using it as a competitive weapon. Periodic price wars can and do break out, especially in the soft drink or airline industries (American, United, Delta), but the principle gainers are the consumers, not the producers, hence the desire on the part of the firms in an oligopoly for a quiet life of cooperative behavior with respect to pricing. This goal leads the firms to search for ways (some legal, some illegal) to coordinate pricing behavior. The firms are content to rely on nonprice means to defend and expand market shares. So price is greater than marginal cost, creating allocative inefficiency, and firms may operate at a scale of plant other than that which is most efficient.

Oligopoly and e-Commerce: Internet Travel Sites

In the early days of e-commerce, some hoped that independent travel sites would spring up and offer consumers greater opportunities for a wider selection of travel services offered at lower prices. These sites would be direct competitors to the large number of physical travel agents, whose competitive but relatively expensive services dominated the highly localized travel booking industry. The online sites might also serve to limit some of the market power held and exercised by the large travel service providers, including airlines and hotel chains. Several independent sites did appear, including Priceline.com, Getaway.com, Travelocity.com, and SuperClubs.com, which offered travel services and packages put together across a wide spectrum of service providers. Often these sites bought deeply discounted bulk and distressed travel services from original providers and repackaged them to price-conscious Internet buyers.

A strange thing happened on the way to the low-cost world of commodity travel marketing. Within the $14.2 billion online reservations market, the oligopoly purveyors of travel services began to integrate forward into the online travel market.[14] The giant travel distribution firm Sabre Holdings purchased both Travelocity.com and the last-minute e-travel firm Site59.com. Orbitz.com, the third largest e-travel booking agent, is owned by the five largest airlines. Four of these firms also have a stake in the deep discount e-travel site Hotwire.com. Expedia.com was owned by Microsoft, but was sold to the cable TV conglomerate USA Networks. Recently, Cendant, which owns a time share service as well as franchising the services of Ramada Inns, Travelodge, Avis car rental, Howard Johnson, and Days Inn, began Trip.com, its own proprietary Internet e-travel booking service. In addition, Cendant also owns CheapTickets.com, the tenth-largest seller of deep discount airline fares. Lastly, the

---

14 Motoko Rich, "Trip.com Starts Tough Trek to a Top Spot in Online Travel," *The Wall Street Journal*, April 29, 2002, p. B1.

hotel giants Hilton, Hyatt, Marriott, Starwood and Six Continents combined to form a firm called Hotel Distribution System. Their intent is to launch a Web site that will jointly offer hotel space in a manner similar to the way that Orbitz sells plane seats from its airline owners.[15]

With all of this forward integration creating an oligopolistic back end to the apparently competitive front end of the e-travel industry, considerable legitimate concern centers on just how vigorous the future competition will be.[16] Will the travel providers who own one site give the same access to travel deals to rival travel sites owned by rival service providers? Will different site owners demand reciprocity in the exchange and listing of travel deals? Will independent sites, without a travel service provider owner, get equal access or even any access to discounted travel services? And if they do, will they have to abide by certain conditions limiting discount pricing and availability so as not to spoil the market for the travel service providers? The market for e-travel services is an evolving one, and no one knows the correct answers to these questions. Still, oligopolists like the quiet life of live and let live, especially with respect to price competition, which threatens profit margins and ultimately survival. As a result, the future world of e-travel service booking, which involves an oligopoly component, may not be as vigorously competitive and inexpensive as it might otherwise have been.

MICROECONOMIC THEORY: DYNAMIC COMPETITION

Despite the generally accepted nature of the microeconomic models, industry theory also encompasses a number of concepts that don't fit as neatly within the traditional equilibrium and comparative static frameworks. Some of these concepts raise doubts about the structural or behavioral assumptions that helped to define our theoretical markets. For example, are one or a few large firms *always* less efficient than a great number of smaller ones? Do forces in competitive markets sometimes dictate the existence of a few larger firms? If so, what are these forces and how might they play out in markets for e-commerce firms? Other concepts raise challenges to the idea of equilibrium as the appropriate place to be looking at the results of the competitive struggle. They raise questions as to value of economic conclusions that are drawn within the context of a comparative static world, where the market is held constant and the consequences of incremental steps can be employed to evaluate the efficiency of resource use. For example, what forces trigger economic change and how do real firms wrestle with these challenges? Are static market models, judged in equilibrium, the best place to analyze and evaluate the economic consequences of a complex and ever-changing real world? How are firms able to overcome external challenges and shape them to their own advantage? The following sections look at these kinds of questions, and use them to help frame the discussion e-commerce and the Internet.

Criticisms of the Static Market and Efficiency Assumptions

Recall that consumer sovereignty was an important assumption helping to justify the inference that competitive markets yield the best use of scarce resources. After all, firms use resources only to produce the goods most valued by consumers. Production follows consumer demand, case closed. Not so fast! Suppose that firms and technology are able to produce items that consumers never previously thought of. After all, who ever heard of a Furby or a Razor scooter, let alone a DVD player or personal digital assistant, before they were put up for sale by their creators. The creators of these kinds of products assume

---

15 Motoko Rich, "Hotels Launch Price Wars," *The Wall Street Journal*, May 8, 2002, p. D1.

16 "Airline ticket site object of Senate scrutiny: Committee points, clicks at Orbitz.com," available at **http://www.cnn.com/2000/TRAVEL/NEWS/07/20/congress.orbitz/**.

that they will be able to shape consumer tastes and preferences through clever marketing and advertising, so that buyers can't live without the item. The economist John Kenneth Galbraith called this the "dependence effect."[17] It disrupts our rationale for resource distribution led by consumer-based competitive markets. The reversal of cause and effect undermines the subsequent efficiency analysis, throwing the results into a quandary. Now consumer desires follow the ability to produce an item, not the other way around. So is the production of goods to satisfy consumer demand really yielding the best use of resources, or is the set of consumer desires just the figment of some clever marketer's manipulation? Without doubt, the owners of many now defunct e-commerce firms question the assertion that marketing can manipulate consumer tastes. For example, how many pet owners ever bought dog food from pets.com, even after seeing the urgings of that engaging sock puppet?

The existence of economies of scale and scope pose other challenges to the static conclusion that many small firms are more efficient users of resources than one or a few large ones. Economies of scale appear because the technology of an industry allows firms to reduce their production costs as they increase their size of plant. Even though rising plant scale increases productive efficiency, it also reduces the number of possible competitors vying to satisfy a given level of demand. When each firm is capable of producing a larger volume of lower-cost output, fewer firms will survive in that fixed market. The extreme case is **natural monopoly**, such as a public utility that distributes electricity, where one firm can satisfy the entire market at the lowest possible cost. In this instance, the introduction of competition actually raises the product price for buyers. Economies of scope involve situations in which the value of an item to an individual user increases depending upon the number of total users. **Networks** are particularly good at generating economies of scope. The value to the user of a telephone system or network grows more than in proportion to the number of customers added. If only two phones use the network, the user can talk to a best friend, which has some value. If consumers can connect to millions of other global phone users, they can do many more things with their phones, boosting the productivity and value of their membership in the network. These network economies lower the possibility of multiple independent networks unless they can somehow be interconnected seamlessly, perhaps by an Internet.

The discussion of equilibrium analysis introduced the static resource use criteria of productive and allocative efficiency. These criteria focus primarily on how skillfully private markets can divide up an existing resource pie. What about criteria that look at how the market changes the size, composition, or quality of the pie over time? Aren't these important elements of resource use as well? For example, **technological change** can mean either **product innovation** that yields new products and services for consumers, or **process innovation** that creates new ways of performing existing activities more efficiently, thereby lowering the overall costs of production. Does a market of many small firms or a few large ones foster these changes best? And how should society weigh the benefits from technological change relative to the static criteria if the two come into conflict? These and other questions are not easy issues to deal with in the physical world. Their complexity is magnified as they migrate into the fast-growing and rapidly changing virtual environment.

The champion of the disequilibrium approach to competition was the economist Joseph Schumpeter.[18] His view was that the essence of competition is a process of **creative destruction**. Markets are places of constant turmoil and threat where new firms, ideas, products, and ways of doing business arise to replace old ones. Disequilibrium is the norm and the process of competition is best analyzed as a reaction to turmoil rather than as part of a static equilibrium state.

---

17 John Kenneth Galbraith, *The Affluent Society* (New York: The New American Library, 1958), Ch. 11.
18 Joseph A. Schumpeter, *The Theory of Economic Development*, (New York: Oxford University Press, 1961).

The Schumpeterian perspective sees existing positions of market power as being under relentless attack from the forces of change. These forces include alterations in consumer tastes and preferences, new technological capabilities, changes in the relative availabilities and prices of resources, and globalization that encourages competition from firms in new geographic areas and opens new market possibilities. Within each of these threats lies an opportunity created by gaps in the market. The gaps are unlikely to be filled by current firms who are satisfied with and wedded to existing products, processes, or conditions.[19] Rather, it is the **entrepreneur**, an outsider and risk taker, who perceives the market gaps and seizes the opportunity for a profitable response to the forces of disequilibrium. What emerges from Schumpeter is a dynamic entrepreneurial model of competition. This **dynamic competition**, or the value of a competitive market, is as an engine of growth and change where consumers benefit far more by their exposure to new products, processes, and ideas than they can ever gain from a plodding, incremental assessment of productive and allocative efficiency.

Applying Dynamic Disequilibrium Analysis to e-Commerce

In the static world, dominant firms may prove to be abusive, inefficient, and technologically sluggish, but in the world of the Internet and e-commerce, other forces render dominance as a tolerated and sometimes preferred method for conducting business. For example, consider the case of eBay, the enormously popular and profitable e-commerce firm. It was just in 1996 that eBay began as a Web-based trading site for Pez candy dispensers. Today it is one of the most profitable sites on the Web, with nearly 29.3 million unique visitors in March 2002.[20] Not only does eBay facilitate trades of treasures and trifles among individuals, but it is increasingly becoming an outlet for the sale of surplus commercial products as well.[21] Its size and reach overwhelm that of its nearest competitors. If not a pure monopoly, eBay is at least the dominant firm in the market for e-auctions, but is it an inefficient user of resources, as the monopoly model would predict? Not hardly, for it couldn't survive in the fast changing e-commerce world if it wasn't highly efficient. If eBay is so efficient, however, how did it get to this point and why doesn't it become "fat, dumb and lazy" like the static model would predict? Instead of feeling exploited by eBay, most traders are repeat users, who seem to be overwhelmingly satisfied with the service. Why haven't the participants perceived that they are being abused by a price-gouging dominant firm? These kinds of disequilibrium questions and issues enter into the discussion of e-commerce in the subsequent chapters. Forces of discontinuous change and disequilibrium keep markets in flux, such that performance criteria other than just the static efficiency tests might be needed to evaluate the market behavior of e-commerce firms.

This tension between the **equilibrium** and **disequilibrium approaches** to microeconomic analysis provides considerable relevance for our discussion of e-commerce. For instance, returning to the example of Microsoft, should the firm be applauded and encouraged for its aggressive technological innovation and focus on increasing the value-added of its computer software? Or should Microsoft be punished under the antitrust laws for its dominance of the markets for browsers and operating systems? The answers to these important questions depend at least in part upon the approach that is chosen to undertake the microanalysis and efficiency evaluation. With the cases of eBay and Microsoft, it is apparent that when questions surrounding the appropriate approach to efficiency are examined in combination with the focus on other tensions, the organizational topics of competitive structure, behavior, and performance provide a rich and varied tool kit for the analysis of e-commerce.

---

19 In one of his most famous observations, Schumpeter notes, "In general it is not the owner of stagecoaches who builds railroads." Ibid, p. 66.

20 "U.S. Top 50 Web and Digital Media Properties," available at **http://www.comscore.com**.

21 Nick Wingfield, "Corporate Sellers Put the Online Auctioneer on Even Faster Track." *The Wall Street Journal*, July 1, 2001, p. A1.

SUMMARY AND PROSPECTS

The chapter began with a brief survey of both equilibrium analysis and the industry models that populate a basic course in microeconomics. The review showed four different theoretical models of industry organization, including pure competition, monopoly, monopolistic competition, and oligopoly. Each model differs from the others in terms of its structural characteristics and the ultimate degree of efficiency with which it uses scare resources. These structural differences are summarized in Table 2-1. The performance efficiency is measured in terms of the two prominent static criteria of allocative and productive efficiency. Both criteria accept as fixed, for the moment, the tastes of consumers, the amount of resources available, and the technology, which defines how these resources are capable of being combined with one another. The introductory Internet banking case highlighted the vast number of banks, both pure e-tail and retail, that now offer services over the Web. These larger numbers, along with the relatively undifferentiated nature of their product offerings, resulted in online banks being most closely associated with the purely competitive model, where price is the key distinguishing variable. It created short-run profit and long-run survival problems for many of the Internet banks.

Given this static moment, the task of efficiency evaluation becomes analogous to the equitable division of a predetermined pie, among a stable and unchanging number of consumers. What if the size of the pie or its quality is changing over time? What if the tastes and preferences of consumers are evolving so that today's pie division reflects the outmoded tastes of yesterday? What if the nature of today's pie can itself alter the consumer's tastes and preferences? Lastly, what if external pressures are constantly changing the nature of the pie, making it impossible to ever reach a point of stability, which would allow for the division of the pie in a static sense?

These kinds of questions show that static efficiency might not be either the best nor the only way to judge how well markets are performing. If markets such as the Internet and e-commerce are continually in flux, their performance should be judged in terms of criteria that recognize and incorporate the change in their evaluative scheme. Such criteria might include how well the market adapts to and uses changing technology, how well it promotes technological change, and how well it extends the economies brought about by network externalities and economies of scope. It is just

TABLE 2-1   Theoretical Market Models: Distinguishing Economic Characteristics

Economic Characteristics	Pure Competition	Monopoly	Monopolistic Competition	Oligopoly
Number of firms	Many thousands	Single firm	Several hundreds	Dominated by a few large
Nature of product	Homogeneous	Unique	Differentiated	Similar or differentiated
Degree of price control	None: Firm is price taker	Total	Some	Mutually interdependent
Extent of nonprice competition	None	Very little	Extensive	Some if differentiated
Ease of entry/exit	Very easy	Entry barrier	Fairly easy	Difficult
Industry example	Agriculture	Desktop operating system	Apparel	Automobile

these kinds of interesting if unstable conditions that make the ensuing economic assessment of the Internet and e-commerce so interesting and challenging. These dynamic possibilities set up the identification and discussion of the chapter tension between applying an equilibrium versus a disequilibrium approach to the evaluation of Internet efficiency.

This chapter placed the discussion of e-commerce within the context of economic theory as it reviewed and introduced key concepts that will be part of the analysis of later chapters. By extension, the material in Chapter 3 discusses the e-commerce topic within the context of the history and technology of both the Internet and the World Wide Web. Anyone who wishes to fully comprehend the topic of e-commerce should be familiar with the technology that both supports its expansion and works to define its functional limits as well as its future potential.

KEY TERMS AND CONCEPTS

allocative efficiency
comparative static technique
consumer sovereignty
creative destruction
customer loyalty
dynamic competition
economic Darwinism
economic profit and loss
economies of scale and scope
efficiency consequences
entrepreneur
entry barriers
equilibrium
equilibrium analysis
equilibrium and disequilibrium
  approaches
Internet browser
law of diminishing marginal returns
long-run and short-run
microeconomic theory
monopolistic competition
monopoly
mutual interdependence

natural monopoly
networks
nonprice competition
normal profit
oligopoly
opportunity cost
persistent economic profits
process innovation
product differentiation
product innovation
productive efficiency
pure competition
short-run profit maximizing rule
  (MC = MR)
spillover costs
structural approach
structure-conduct-performance (SCP)
  paradigm
technological change
undifferentiated commodity product
uniform resource locator (URL)
x-inefficiency

DISCUSSION AND REVIEW QUESTIONS

1. Identify and explain how and why firm control over product price differs among the four theoretical market models.

2. In what ways are the pure competition and monopoly models polar extremes to one another? How are some of their characteristics blended within the model of monopolistic competition?

3. Why is the demand curve for monopolistic competition negatively sloped? Is it more or less steep than the slope of the typical monopolist's demand curve? Why?

4. What is an economic profit and why does it stimulate entry? Would entry occur if the firms in an industry were earning a normal profit? Why?

5. Discuss the nature of the tension that exists between the equilibrium and disequilibrium approaches to microeconomic analysis.

6. What characteristics make individual products and markets the most susceptible to the type of dynamic competition embodied within Schumpeter's concept of creative destruction? For example, list the five following industries in order from the most to the least susceptible to creative destruction and explain why you did so: Furniture, Computers, Textiles and apparel, Telephony, and Banking.

7. Why have the wireless phone companies worked so hard to differentiate their products?

8. If search engines such as Google.com list all of the *online banks* when a user searches with those keywords, why would a firm pay for a sponsored link?

9. Overture.com is also a major search engine, which provides its services to Yahoo, among other clients. But it lists the search results in terms of the amount of money that the owners of the site pay to Overture in order to secure a premier listing. The highest-paying site gets the first listing on the opening page. Why would a search engine list responses primarily by the amount of money paid? Why would a site pay to be listed?

10. From an economic efficiency perspective, what is to be gained by allowing product differentiation in any market, such as the wireless phone industry?

11. Locate and examine Figure 2-4. What happens to sales for a purely competitive firm if it raises its price from Pe_1 to Pe_2? Why? Will the same result occur if the firm is monopolistically competitive? Why? How do the results for the first two models compare to the results for a monopolist who raises price? What accounts for this difference?

12. In the section on monopoly and inefficiency the text states that "the pace of technological change may lag in monopoly markets." Has this proven to be true in the browser market dominated by the Microsoft Internet Explorer product? Why?

13. In the section on monopolistic competition and efficiency, the text notes that monopolistic competition "supports a surplus of firms that mostly underutilize their capacity." Has this generalization proven to be true for the cell phone industry? Why? How do the various pricing plans try to overcome the underutilization of capacity?

14. To a greater or lesser extent, all firms within any industry are mutually interdependent, regardless of the market structure. What makes firms within the oligopoly model so unique in being able to recognize their mutual interdependence? What makes the interdependence so problematic in this market structure?

15. Consider the problem of consumers regarding your product as an undifferentiated commodity. How does this perception affect the firms in that industry? What might the online banking firms do to get around this problem?

16. If the oligopolistic purveyors of travel services are successful in integrating forward into the online travel business, how might the oligopoly model predict the level and type of rivalrous behavior?

WEB EXERCISES

1. Link to the Internet survey data site **http://www.comscore.com**, and see how many unique visitors eBay had in the latest month. How fast is the growth in the use of eBay's service? What were the three most commonly visited sites according to MediaMetrix? Do you have any thoughts as to why they might have been so popular?

2. Link to any search engine and look for the key words *online bank* and the name of your *home state*. Is your own personal bank on that list? Next, do the same search, but use the keywords *Internet bank* along with the name of your *home state*. Does the search engine generate the same list of banks? Why? What kind of problems does this difference in lists or placement within each list pose for a bank that wants a potential customer to find it?

3. Make up an airline trip plan from Chicago to Los Angeles for exactly two months from today's date. Go to Orbitz.com, Travelocity.com, and Trip.com to see any variations in the cost of the trip or the identity of the carrier among the different sites. Were the prices the same or different? What does this comparison tell you about competition in among e-travel sites?

4. Link to **http://www.overture.com** and read about their pay-for-listing service. Is this type of search service necessarily deceptive and harmful for consumers? Under what economic conditions would a pay-for-listing service be beneficial to the consumer?

5. Link to **http://www.searchenginewatch.com** and check out their Reviews, Ratings, and Tests department to see which are the top five search engines. Where did Google.com and Overture.com rank?

6. Link to **http://www.Bankrate.com** and select their Online Finance information directory located in the left column headed Rates and News. Select the link to a comparison of checking account rates and see which institutions offer the best deals for online interest-bearing checking accounts. The sight also lists rates for certificates of deposit for up to one year or greater than one year. Which Internet banks offer the best rates here? You might also want to consult their semiannual survey on earnings and fees for online checking accounts.

CHAPTER

3

Introductory Case

THE TECHNOLOGY OF "GOING AND DOING"

This case involves an e-commerce activity that most Web surfers try successfully without thinking much about the technology behind the result. Connect to an Internet service provider such as Earthlink or the Web connection at school, and type in the URL of Sonypictures.com. The result takes you to the Sony Pictures Entertainment homepage. Once on the site, click to view a video clip from a current or upcoming movie, or access information from one of the Sony's other entertainment properties, including TV shows or VHS/DVD products. If you wish to know movie theater locations and show times, or prepurchase tickets, you simply click on other links at the site. Depending upon the ISP connection speed, usually expressed in kilobits per second, each link probably took 10 seconds or less to complete. Usually, the streaming video movie trailer is viewable and entertaining, although the signal maybe a bit short of cable TV quality.

So how did it all happen? How did the computer find Sonypictures.com? How did Sonypictures.com send the signal back to you? These questions are much like the ones that millions of Americans asked some 50 years ago, when people wondered how Lucy and Desi Arnaz got into the little box in their living rooms. For its day, TV was the entertainment marvel of the nation, but the technology of television in its early years was child's play compared to the sophisticated connections that are part of this chapter's e-commerce story.

Was the connection with Sonypictures.com made using the Internet or the World Wide Web? This question, which asks the respondent to separate the Internet from the World Wide Web, is not a trivial one. Some surfers may ask, "What's the difference?" but the difference is both substantial and important.[1] The origin of the Internet preceded that of the World Wide Web by about 20 plus years. The **Internet** is a network of networks and is structured as a set of computer and cable connections. The purpose of the Internet is to allow for communications between the otherwise independent computers on different networks. It functions to send and receive messages including text, data, voice, and images. As such, it is primarily a **message-based system**. The **World Wide Web** is the most common application carried by the Internet, and is structured to provide a system of multimedia links to different nodes on the network. The purpose of the Web is to organize and manage information, allowing the creator of the information to render it easier to access and available to others on the Internet. The Web accomplishes these tasks by searching, linking, and accessing specific facts located at the Web nodes. Therefore, the Web is an **information-based system**.

When Web surfers type in Sonypictures.com they are connected to the Sony Web site (node) via the Internet. They search for and receive information from Sony regarding

---

1 Sometimes the best answer to this question is neither, especially if the ISP also serves as a portal providing its own service connections in response to clicking a keyword link. Depending upon how a surfer looks for sites, he or she might never leave the portal or enter the Web on his or her own.

The Technology Behind e-Commerce and the Internet

current movies and are linked to another site for a list of local theaters and times, and to undertake the e-commerce transaction of ticket purchase. Any surfer who stops and thinks about it will realize how amazing it is, with considerable user value added. How does it all work? What is the technology that lies behind this electronic transfer of information? The remainder of this chapter looks briefly at the answers to these questions. It examines the "how and why" of the Internet and Web technologies that support the flow of information and e-commerce.

THE ORIGINS AND DEVELOPMENT OF THE INTERNET[2]

The impetus for the Internet can be traced back to October 4, 1957, when the Soviet Union launched the small, beeping satellite called Sputnik I into orbit around the earth. This event challenged the assumption that the United States had a technology lead over the Soviet Union and made the Cold War seem potentially a lot hotter for people who were responsible for the defense of the United States. One result was the creation of the Advanced Research Projects Agency (ARPA) within the Defense Department. Its job was to stimulate and support scientific research designed to ensure the military preparedness and superiority of the United States. In 1962, ARPA began to fund research designed to link geographically dispersed computers together using an experimental **packet switching technology** to transmit messages. Packet switching would break a computer message up into separate parts or "packets" using an interface message processor (IMP). The IMP would then send the packets individually through a network, using *multiple channels*, toward a predetermined **Internet address**, where the message was to be received and acted upon. An IMP at the address end would then reassemble the packets into the original message and display it over a computer. Packet switching would be a flexible substitute for **circuit routing**, which, like a telephone signal, would send the message in one continuous link over a single open line.[3] A packet system offered two distinct military advantages. First, by using multiple delivery pathways, it would not depend upon any specific circuit link that might be knocked out in time of war. Second, by breaking the message up into individual packets and sending them by different routes, it would be much more difficult for an enemy or unauthorized party to intercept and decode the message.

By 1969, the timeline shown in Figure 3-1 indicates that technological capability caught up with theoretical possibility and the first simple signal was sent from a computer at UCLA to another computer at the Stanford Research Institute over a network

---

2 Much of this brief historical discussion is adapted from the Internet Society available at **http://www.isoc.org/internet/history/**. The definitive timeline for major events in the development of the Internet and World Wide Web can be found at Robert H. Zakon, "Hobbes's Internet Timeline," available at **http://www.zakon.org/robert/internet/timeline/**. A substantially condensed version of this timeline is shown in Figure 3-1.

3 Even today, some of these packets get lost on route and have to be resent. This helps to explain why voice signals such as telephone calls sent via Internet packet switching have a lower quality than calls sent over a traditional direct line circuit.

FIGURE 3-1	Time Line of Key Internet and Web Events

1961   Leonard Kleinrock, MIT, publishes first paper on packet switching theory.

1966   Lawrence G. Roberts, MIT, develops first ARPANET plan.

1968   Request for proposals for ARPANET sent out.

1969   First four nodes established: UCLA, Stanford Research Institute, UC Santa Barbara, U. of Utah.
First packets sent by Charley Kline at UCLA as he tried logging into SRI.

1972   Ray Tomlinson (BBN) modifies email program for ARPANET using @ sign.
First computer-to-computer chat takes place at UCLA.

1973   First international connections to the ARPANET: University College of London England.
Vinton Cerf and Bob Kahn present basic Internet ideas.

1974   First public packet data service Telnet begins (a commercial version of ARPANET).

1981   BITNET and CSNET University computer research networks created.

1982   Transmission control protocol (TCP) and Internet protocol (IP) established as protocol suite.

1984   Domain name system and county tags appear, including .com, .org, .gov, .edu, .uk, and .fr.
Number of hosts exceeds 1,000.

1986   NSFNET created by the United States National Science Foundation.

1988   First Internet worm burrows through the Net, affecting approximately 6,000 of the 60,000 hosts on the Internet.

1991   World Wide Web released by CERN; Tim Berners-Lee is developer.
PGP (pretty good privacy) message encryption system released by Philip Zimmerman.
NSF stimulates commercial use of Web by allowing private connection to its backbone servers.

1992   Number of hosts exceeds 1,000,000.

1994   First Virtual, the first cyberbank, opens up for business.
The first banner ads appear on hotwired.com.

1995   WWW becomes the service with greatest traffic on NSFNET.
Traditional online dial-up systems, AOL, Compuserve, Prodigy begin to provide ISP service.
A number of Net-related companies go public, including Netscape.

1998   Technologies of the Year: e-commerce, e-auctions, portals.
Emerging Technologies: e-trade, XML, intrusion detection.

2000   Massive denial-of-service attack is launched against major Web sites: Yahoo, Amazon, and eBay.
Web size estimates surpass 1 billion indexable pages.
Emerging technologies: Wireless devices, IPv6.
Lawsuits of the Year: Napster, DeCSS.

Source: Hobbes' Internet Timeline. Copyright (c)1993–2002 by Robert H Zakon. Available at **http://www.zakon.org/robert/internet/timeline/**.

that became known as **ARPANET**. By 1972, ARPANET had linked computers at some 40 different locations. In the same year, the concept of e-mail incorporating the @ command was created, which allowed for direct person-to-person messaging over ARPANET. In 1974 ARPANET researchers "developed a common language that would allow different networks to communicate with each other. The language was known as **transmission control protocol/internet protocol (TCP/IP)**."[4] When universally adopted in 1982, the TCP/IP standard allowed for the creation of the Internet,

---

4 R.T. Griffiths, "Internet for Historians," **http://www.let.leidenuniv.nl/history/ivh/frame_theorie.html**.

or network of networks.[5] TCP/IP was based upon the concept of an "open architecture" that allowed free passage of packets, through always-open gateways, without retaining or censoring the information in the packets, and with the operating principles being freely available for access by all networks.[6]

Upper level **domain name suffixes** appeared in 1984, including .com, .edu, .gov, and .org, to signal that messages were being sent to commercial, educational, governmental, or international organizations.[7] In addition, two-letter suffixes were added to designate the country location of the address, such as .uk or .fr for Britain or France.[8] It is important to realize that all of this technology was created without the use of proprietary patents, the reaping of individual profits, or much thought about the commercial as opposed to scientific applications of the technology.

By the end of 1989, the number of host computers on the Internet surpassed 100,000, with the number of new hosts appearing at an almost exponential rate. Most of the contacts were either at scientific locations or governmental in nature, with few e-commerce uses. Access to the Internet was arcane and required the typing of long nonsensical addresses. The sites were unattractive, without sound, color, or animation. Finding material was disorganized and message times were slow. "The main attractions for the commercial sector (were) the e-mail facilities and access to e-mail, newsgroups, 'chat' facilities and computer games."[9] Everything was about to change, however, with the introduction of a new Internet application that refocused the use of the Internet from a message-based system to one that was information based.

THE WORLD WIDE WEB: HISTORY, TECHNOLOGY, AND OPERATION

Tim Berners-Lee and the Origin of the World Wide Web

The origin of the World Wide Web is most closely associated with the actions of **Tim Berners-Lee**, a physicist working at the Centre European pour la Recherche Nuclearire (CERN), in Geneva, Switzerland.[10] In 1989 Berners-Lee set out to create an easier way to share and manage the information associated with large, complicated research projects within an organization. With multiple computer systems working on the same project, finding and connecting to important information was difficult, resulting in the potential loss of relevant documents. His genius was in combining two known concepts: the Internet and **hypertext**, which is a method for presenting information in a nonsequential manner, in a unique and highly productive fashion. The result was the creation of a special search and retrieval protocol named **hypertext transfer protocol (HTTP)**. HTTP did three things: first it made it easier to write Internet addresses. Second, it automatically

---

5 The IP protocol is the standard for breaking information into packets for transmission over the Internet, while the TCP protocol is the standard that controls the transmission and reception of the IP packets.

6 "Internet for Historians," Ibid.

7 In 2000, seven new upper-level domain names were added, including .name for personal Web sites, .pro for professionals, .museum for museums, .aero for airline groups, .coop for business cooperatives, along with .biz and .info for general use. See, Chris Gaither, "7 New Domains Are Chosen to Join the Popular .com," *The New York Times*, November 17, 2000, p. C4.

8 Tuvalu, a small, impoverished Pacific Island nation had the good fortune of being assigned the domain suffix of .TV. They sold the rights to .TV to a commercial venture for $20 million and an annual payment of $4 million for 12 years, doubling their annual GDP. The new owner sold some 200,000 Internet addresses using the .TV suffix. Chris Gaither, "For Tiny Pacific Nation, Its Domain Is Its Treasure, *The New York Times,* July 16, 2001, p. C5.

9 "Internet for Historians," Ibid.

10 Anick Jesdanun, "The Web Turns 10," *Concord Monitor*, December 16, 2000, p. D1.

scanned the Internet for the site associated with the address. Third, it automatically retrieved the document(s) at the address for viewing.[11] Within a year, Berners-Lee had created a rudimentary browser/editor, labeled his creation the World Wide Web, and released the programs free of charge for anyone to use.[12] The browser employed an easy to use, text-based, computer language called **hypertext markup language (HTML)** to write material to Web pages. HTML also allowed a code writer to create with ease the links that connected one Web page to another in cyberspace. By clicking on URL address links, Web surfers could go where they wanted in a nonsequential fashion. Even though users could go anywhere, they had few places to go initially. The Web concept was a bit slow to catch on. Toward the end of 1992, only 50 Web sites were available, with a 150 at the end of 1993.[13]

Better Browsers and the Growth of the Web

In 1993 a more sophisticated browser, *Mosaic*, was created at the Illinois National Center for Supercomputing Applications. It proved so highly productive and wildly popular that Marc Andreessen and the Mosaic team quickly converted it into a commercial product call **Netscape Navigator**. This commercial browser combined text and graphics on the same page, made the software simple to install, and opened the Web to the world. In addition to the birth of the new browser, a second series of events in the 1990s triggered the explosive growth of the Web. They involved the increase in computing power associated with desktop computers, the simultaneous decline in the cost of manufacturing that power, and the rise in the connection speed or baud rate that links the computer to the Internet. Gordon Moore, one of the founders of Intel, articulated what has become known as **Moore's Law**, which predicts that the computing power on each microprocessor would double approximately every 18 months.[14] This law held true for almost 35 years. As the processing power of each logic chip grew, the technology of chip making drastically lowered the cost of fabricating the chip. The result was a more powerful processor that was faster, could do more, and was cheaper to sell to the public.

These twin forces of technology and economics created more computing power and at lower cost, leading to a rapid rise in the number of computer owners, especially at home among nontechnical consumers. Before the introduction of the Web, the Internet was available mostly to scientists, governmental agencies, and computer savvy *netizens*, or citizens of the net, for e-mail or chat. Now the combination of Web and browser technology along with powerful, low cost computers and faster connection speeds gave the average person both the hardware and the software to achieve functional access to the Internet. The Web and browser combination gave individuals something useful to do. They could search, store, retrieve, copy, view, transmit, manipulate, and receive information of all types including text, data, video, sound, and images. Therefore, it was not surprising that the e-commerce possibilities for the Web began to open up, given the public's ability to easily access a rapidly growing number of sites. In the words of

---

11 "Internet for Historians," Ibid.

12 It is one of the most truly altruistic (unselfish) gifts to society, on par with the discovery of penicillin, the first antibiotic, by Sir Alexander Fleming. Fleming and subsequent scientists declined to patent the discovery so that it could be distributed widely at low cost to save the lives of Allied soldiers in WWII. Berners-Lee remains as an unwavering advocate for unrestrained access to the Web and its use to speed the free flow of information. See "Penicillin: The First Miracle Drug," available at **http://www.herb.lsa.umich.edu/kidpage/penicillin.htm** and "Could Patents Have Sped Penicillin Development?" available at **http://www.biotech.about.com/library/weekly/ aa_penicillinpatent. htm**.

13 Ibid.

14 Gordon Moore (1965), available at **http://www.intel.com/intel/museum/25anniv/hof/moore. htm.** The microprocessor is the chip, such as a Pentium® 4, which controls the math, logic, and data transfer functions of the computer. Accessed July 2001.

Berners-Lee, "The Web made the net useful because people are really interested in information (not to mention knowledge and wisdom!) and don't really want to know about computers and cables."[15]

What makes the Web so valuable for e-commerce? To appreciate the importance of this connection, start by thinking about the difference between live theater and a play that is broadcast over a television network. In the theater world, for everyone in the United States to see Shakespeare's classic play *Macbeth* simultaneously, it would require that a theater company be present in each and every city and town in all 50 states. Television, on the other hand, allowed a single production company to perform the play in one location. Television stations across the country, linked together to form a network, allowed everyone in the United States to tune in at once and see the same performance. From an economic perspective, the producer of the play dramatically reduced the performance cost of the play per viewer by using the television network rather than the individual live theaters. In addition, the revenue potential is greater per performance, because more viewers can be reached with the same program. From an advertising perspective, the ability of the network performance to aggregate viewers also greatly reduces the cost of getting the same commercial message to as many viewers as possible. This notion explains why the price charged per minute of advertising during the widely watched annual Super Bowl game is both so outrageously expensive in the absolute sense, but so cost efficient in terms of expenditure per viewer reached.

The Web advances this analogy even one step further. Not only can everyone tune into the play, but also they can tune in at any time. The play starts wherever the audience decides show up (or in this case log on). From a business perspective, the theatre company can now supply thousands of renditions of the same play, starting and ending at the convenience of the individual audience members, all for the cost of a single performance. Under most conditions, the existence of a computer network makes Web delivery of e-commerce an enormously profitable operation.

BEHIND THE INTERNET: THE TECHNOLOGY OF FIBER OPTICS

Any functional understanding of the operation of contemporary e-commerce needs at least some grounding in the technology of today's Internet. The science of **fiber-optic technology** lies at the heart of the advances in the speed and low cost of Internet connections. It rests on the leading edge of complex physics research, but its basics are fairly easy. Fiber optics starts with multiple strands of tiny, hair-thin, glass wires bundled together into a cable. Each wire has a solid core of ultratransparent glass, surrounded by a covering, or cladding, made up of a mixture of other types of glass and insulating materials. The purpose of the cladding is to retain as much of the light as possible inside of the core, keeping the signal from deteriorating as it moves along. Each glass strand carries a light impulse created by a **laser**, or switch, that is blinking millions of times per second. The impulses carry encoded messages representing text, data, sound, and images. Different colors of light can carry different encoded messages in the same strand. Each strand has the potential to carry millions of telephone conversations or billions of bits of Internet information over long distances. Periodically, the light encounters amplifiers or signal repeaters that capture the impulses, strengthen the signal, and send the light farther along the cable. It is the need for amplifiers and repeaters that makes sending fiber-optic signals an expensive process that is efficient (cost effective) only at high traffic volumes.

Located at the transition points at the beginning and end of the cable are converters and transmitters called **routers** that transfer the signals to and from light impulses. At their origin, converters take the raw data or sound signals and convert them into an electronic digital format (0,1). From there, the digital signals are further transformed

15 Available at **http://www.w3c.org/people/Berners-Lee/FAQ.html**.

into light impulses to be sent through the glass fiber cables by lasers. Converters at the reception end take the light impulses and transform them back into digital signals, which are then decoded into the original sound or data format for viewing or listening over your computer. Even though each step involves complex physics, it is not too hard to understand.

Key Issues in Fiber Optic Technology: Challenges at the Frontiers of Optical Physics Research

One challenge facing the research physicists is to how to make the communication process even faster and cheaper? For starters, scientists are looking into the possibilities for developing **all-optical Internet systems** that would eliminate the need for costly and bulky converters or routers when the signal changes direction.[16] It might be possible to insert tiny mirrors, crystals, bubbles, or acoustical devices in the cable to deflect the signal in a new direction. If and when optical switches do appear, the high cost of these switches will require even greater traffic volumes and revenues to justify the added expense.

The Technology and Usage of Bandwidth

A second research challenge looks to determine how best to use the abundance of fiber **bandwidth** that is already in place. Bandwidth is a measure of the carrying capacity of the transmission system. It determines the amount of information that the system can handle per unit of time.[17] The objective for the signal transmission (backbone) firm is to send the largest volume of information across long fiber distances as quickly and cheaply as possible, while yielding the greatest possible profit for the provider.[18] The analysis of the bandwidth optimal use challenge begins with an important economic concept.[19] In most production situations, some economic resources are relatively abundant (A) in supply, rendering them lower in cost, while other resources are relatively scarce (S), making them more expensive. Through the application of the **cost-minimizing rule**, economic theory recognizes these cost and availability differences and offers some production guidance to the firm regarding the appropriate ratio for the combined employment of the abundant and scarce inputs. The rule states that, to produce a targeted level of output at the lowest cost, the firm should employ each resource up to the point were the marginal product (extra output) added from using one more unit of the abundant resource, divided by the marginal cost of employing the extra unit of the abundant resource, just equals the same ratio for the scarce resource. In equation form, the cost minimizing resource combination would be where:

$$\frac{\text{Marginal Product of Resource A}}{\text{Marginal Cost of Resource A}} = \frac{\text{Marginal Product of Resource S}}{\text{Marginal Cost of Resource S}}$$

Numerically, the rule would be applied as follows. Assume that workers per unit are abundant and are paid low wages, while capital is scarce and results in a high cost for the employment of an extra unit. Assume further that the next worker hired produces just 12 units of output per hour, but carries a wage rate of $3 per hour, while the next unit of capital produces 600 units of output but at a cost of $200 per hour. The application of

---

16 Mark Heinzl, "All-Optical Telecom Network Faces Slowing Economy, Excess Capacity," *The Wall Street Journal*, February 23, 2001, p. B1.

17 To appreciate the concept of bandwidth, fill an empty soda can and a 12-ounce drinking glass with 12 ounces of water. Turn them both upside down. The one with the greatest bandwidth empties first.

18 Heinzl, "All-Optical Telecom . . . ," p. B1.

19 Bret Swanson, "Bad Bets on Bandwidth," *The Wall Street Journal*, June 19, 2001, p. A22.

the cost-minimizing rule dictates that adding the low-productivity, low-wage additional worker is a less costly and more efficient way of producing the extra output than adding the extra unit of capital.

Wisely or not, the intensely competitive, private suppliers of fiber cable systems installed more than 39 million miles of fiber-optic cable in the United States from 1996 to 2000, enough cable to circle the globe 1,566 times, and costing some $90 billion to place underground.[20] Originally, Internet traffic was projected to grow at 50 percent annually, but it expanded at only a little more than 20 percent of late. So less than 3 percent of the fiber-optic cable capacity, or bandwidth, is in present use. Bandwidth is clearly the resource that is in current abundant supply. Economics predicts that when an item is in excess supply, its price will fall. Therefore, not unexpectedly, data transmission prices fell on average by 45 percent in 2000 and another 65 percent in 2001. Therefore, the cost-minimizing rule says that Internet technology should be using cable capacity as much as possible, almost up to the point of waste. The reality is that it is not always the direction in which Internet research and technology have moved.

The next step in resolving the bandwidth optimal use challenge lies in an important Internet technology called **wave division multiplexing**. This technology involves the "process of combining many colors of light, each carrying separate streams of data, onto a single fiber-optic strand and sorting them at the other end."[21] The process "has increased the carrying-capacity—the bandwidth—of a single optical fiber strand to almost 3 terabits (3 trillion bits) per second."[22] In addition, the carrying capacity per fiber-optic strand is also being increased even further over time as a result of two other forces. First, approximately every six to nine months the number of colors per strand doubles, with the number having gone from four in 1996 to 320 in 2001. Second, the amount of data that can be sent over each color of light is growing as well, but at the slower rate of just one-third or one-half as fast as the rise in the color expansion. This issue sets the stage for the following fiber-optic research tension: should fiber-optic research focus on increasing the volume and speed of data flow over each wavelength of light, or should it focus on increasing the number of wavelengths with each carrying more data but at a slower speed? Which technique is more cost effective and therefore potentially more profitable; increasing the number of wavelengths or intensifying the use of each wavelength?

Increasing data speed and packing more dissimilar data bits on the same fiber-optic strand skimps on the use of an already abundant (cheaper) resource, bandwidth, while requiring the addition of more costly equipment to electronically process the information and direct the results to the correct end-user. Conversely, increasing the number of colors per strand and using them to provide greater direct end-to-end connectivity allows for cheaper and more individual light flows, without the use of expensive microchips to disassemble and reroute the data signal. Color multiplexing uses the more abundant (cheaper) bandwidth more efficiently, while conserving on the use of the more costly routing equipment.

The efficiency and manageability issues within this tension are revealed by the analogy of shipping surface freight using trains versus trucks.[23] Trains carry huge amounts of freight efficiently on long-haul routes. Packing more cars on the train is like increasing the amount of data per fiber strand, but trains become inefficient and unmanageable if they must make many stops to remove cars from the train and direct them onto sidings for delivery. Trucks individually carry far less freight, but are much more efficient at routing the freight for door-to-door delivery. Just as trucks divert surface traffic from trains, increasing the number of wavelengths appears to be the economically correct optical answer.

---

20 "Overbuilt Web," *The Wall Street Journal,* June 18, 2001, p. A1.

21 Swanson, "Bad Bets on Bandwidth," p. A22.

22 Ibid.

23 Ibid.

The Last Mile Problem: Linking Optical Fiber to the End-User

A third challenge in fiber-optic technology is the **last-mile problem**, which defines the painfully slow connection of the computer to the Internet, which is found in the majority of homes and some office locations. Today, most last-mile connections are dial-up, analog links, made over copper wires that are a legacy from the construction of the telephone system. While fiber-optic connections travel at light speed, the limited bandwidth on the last-mile, copper wire connections are like an eyedropper supplying data one bubble at a time. The connection weakness created by the last-mile problem poses real obstacles for e-commerce. **Killer apps**, such as videoconferencing, commercial movie, or music distribution and interactive games, which use lots of bandwidth and hold the promise of high profits, require high-speed Internet connections well beyond the 56 kilobit speed of today's dial-up modems. T-1 lines are dedicated telephone connections that that support 1.544 megabits of data transmission per second, supplying enormous last-mile bandwidth, but they are costly. Their prices are beyond the reach of all but the largest corporate, government, or institutional users.

Most residential users are left with a choice between obtaining high-speed Internet connections either over cable Internet access or through **digital subscriber line (DSL)** service provided through the existing telephone system. Currently, fewer than 5 million home and business subscribers connect through cable modems, while fewer than 3 million link up through DSL lines. These numbers are expected to rise to 13.8 million and 11.2 million respectively by 2005.[24]

Each technology has its own limitations, including speeds that are still below those that would allow for the transmission quality of today's TV signals. It limits the type and range of e-commerce products that can be sent via the Web. The delivery of profitable and high-quality streaming video for business and home entertainment applications appears limited by last-mile technology at least in the near term.

THE WIRELESS WEB: THE FUTURE OF E-COMMERCE AS M-COMMERCE?

The History of Cell Phone Technology

A curious person might ask how the topic of cell phones fits into a technology discussion of the Internet, the Web, e-commerce, and fiber optics. It is a good question until one realizes that the evolutionary track of mobile telephony is converging with the other areas to create an "ever-in-touch" era of multichannel communications. In fact, the expansion of the wireless Web offers a possible solution to the last-mile problem just described, potentially transforming e-commerce into mobile or m-commerce. But the story is getting a bit ahead of itself at the moment.

The discussion of the history of the cell phone comes in two segments, starting in the early 1980s with the first generation of cell phone services (**1G**). This technology allowed a user to make a simple telephone call using wireless, cell-based, analog connections. Cell antennae were set up close together, at locations in major cities, to receive the calls for service. That call was handed off to other cells on the same system as the caller moved (drove, walked) about the area while completing the conversation. Dropped calls were common as the caller traveled outside of the range of the cell transmission system. Despite its limitations the cell phone was so revolutionary and productive at the time that people almost forgot that you needed to carry a heavy and bulky bag phone, about the size of a shoebox, to make the connections.

Now, fast-forward about a dozen years to the mid- to late 1990s, where cell phones were reduced in size and weight to about the size of an eyeglass case and a small digital screen was added that could carry up to four lines of text at 22 characters per line. Now

---

24 Simon Romero, "High Technology Stew," *The New York Times*, December 28, 2000, p. C3.

the cell phone could serve to communicate information as well as voice signals. It had the potential to exchange text messages including e-mail and instant messaging (IM), to offer limited Web access, and to receive important news alerts. It is basically the second generation (**2G**) service that we enjoy today and all for the price of a telephone call. Among the problems with using the 2G phone as an Internet connection device, however, is that the speed of the Internet connection, at 9.6 to 14.4 kilobits per second, is slow and limiting, which makes the call expensive.[25] The high cost limits the number of Web calls, restricting them to only the quickest and most valuable connections. Second, although the caller may not notice it directly, three technologies compete for the cell wireless radio spectrum among multiple users. **Code division multiple access (CDMA)** " . . . translates voice conversations into tiny packets of data and sends them out over the airwaves."[26] Verizon Wireless and Sprint PCS use this Qualcomm-created technology in the United States, and it is commonly used in Japan and South Korea. **Time division multiple access (TDMA)** " . . . slices up a phone conversation into segments of time on a given frequency and pieces it back together when it reaches its destination."[27] AT&T Wireless and Cingular Wireless in the United States were the original champions of the TDMA standard. It does not, however readily support data transmission, which requires the overlay of another, older format for Internet access.[28] Lastly, the **global system for mobile communications (GMS)** is a "distant cousin" to the TDMA technology. GMS is employed by VoiceStream in the United States, Deutsche Telecom in Germany, and available in some 131 nations globally.

So what's the difference? Must everyone conform to the same standard? Isn't variety the spice of life, and competition the driver of efficient markets? On the one hand, the strict answer to the standards conformity question is no.[29] Still, uniform standards can help in the intra-industry competitive race by forging technology leadership. The Scandinavian nations, other European countries, and parts of Asia have each more or less settled on a single standard and are far more advanced in terms of cell phone usage and technology than is the United States. Part of the reason is that landline technology is less reliable in other nations, rendering cell phones as a superior communication tool. Also, landline calls are often charged by the minute even for local calls. So the cost of a cell call rivals that of a landline call, making it more convenient and cost effective to have a cell phone as the only means of communication. Combine these facts with the problem of multiple United States standards and the consequences are significant.

Two of the leading manufacturers of cell phones are the Scandinavian firms Nokia and Ericsson. Go to any large European or Asian city and see the incredible volume of cell phone usage. And if you really want to see the future of the cell phone go to Japan. The wireless firm NTT DoCoMo introduced its wildly popular **i-mode** service, which had 36.8 million subscribers at the end of 2002. It captured the imagination of Japanese teenagers and adults alike. Teens type out quick e-mails, or IMs, and access games or cartoon images. Adults retrieve information on weather, travel, restaurants, news, stock prices, and travel schedules, and perform mobile banking. Clearly, i-mode users have the highest volume of usage per subscriber of any system in the world, and this has transformed DoCoMo into Japan's largest firm, as measured by equity value.[30]

---

25 Remember, at 56 kilobits, even dial-up modems operate four to five times faster.

26 Nichole Harris, "The Basic Question: Which Wireless Standard Is Best? A Lot Hangs in the Balance," *The Wall Street Journal,* September 18, 2000, p. R30.

27 Ibid.

28 Both firms are moving toward the GMS standard. Shawn Young, "Cingular Wireless Sets Overhaul To Offer Next Generation Services," *The Wall Street Journal*, September 30, 2001, p. B6.

29 Even though this answer may be true for voice-based signals, the difference in standards can limit the ability to send text messages between rival systems. See Almar Latour, "Wireless Operators Pitch Fancier Services," *The Wall Street Journal*, January 4, 2002, p. A11.

30 Robert A. Guth, "DoCoMo Minimizes Delay on Cutting-Edge Phones," *The Wall Street Journal*, April 27, 2001, p. A17.

The Future of the Wireless Web

The Japanese experience with i-mode convinced many wireless firms that cell phone users want more and faster Web services, even though it isn't always clear as to what kinds of services users want, how they want them delivered, or how much they are willing to pay for them. European telephone companies (telcos) took a bold step by acquiring $100 billion worth of radio spectrum, at auction, to supply the next generation of cell service, known as **3G**, or third generation. The 3G cell system is intended to offer transmission speeds 40 times faster than those of today. Therefore, it is potentially capable of supporting a wide range of e-commerce transactions, including fast Internet connections and streaming video for entertainment and business conferencing, along with quick downloads of music and games. These spectrum purchases already imposed crushing debt burdens on the European telcos, and system build-out is projected to cost another $100 billion.[31] Not surprisingly, DoCoMo is striving to be the first wireless firm to offer 3G cell service globally, having already begun service in Japan as of October 2001. Unfortunately, the consumer response proved to be lukewarm, at least through mid-2002.[32] In Europe, the launch date for 3G service is not expected before 2003. In the United States, the nationwide launch date is potentially even further away because of concerns about the availability of sufficient radio spectrum for government auction in support of the service.[33] Although 3G may or may not succeed as the next wave of Internet technology, delays in United States' implementation mean that domestic firms risk being technology followers rather than leaders.

All is not a total competitive loss for U.S wireless telcos, however. An interim solution, dubbed **2.5G**, has been introduced by AT&T Wireless and Cingular Wireless.[34] It offers improvements in cell network technology, advances in data compression, and faster data transfer speeds at up to three times dial-up modem rates. In addition, the introduction of 2.5G service is thought to be considerably less expensive than 3G, to both the telcos and the cell users. However, each existing United States wireless transmission standard has its own form of 2.5G upgrade, which does nothing to resolve the uniform standard problem.

Lastly, the question arises as to whether consumers actually want to conduct high volumes of Internet transactions using small cell phone screens and paying by the minute for cell phone calls. The benefits of cell phone convenience and portability may come in conflict with issues of screen size and call costs. Perhaps the Web's wireless future lies in contact using handheld **personal digital assistants (PDA)** made by Palm, Handspring, or Blackberry. Perhaps wireless laptops are the answer, connected to the Internet through short-wave radio technology and subscription services. Wired fidelity, or Wi-Fi, systems currently light up the airwaves in some individual hotels, airports, corporate office buildings, academic campuses, coffeehouses, and so on. Short-wave connections bypass the vexing last-mile problem and are even faster than 3G.[35] Each of these alternatives is possible, but which one(s) will emerge? No one knows for sure, but the beauty of economics is that consumer choice working through the marketplace will generally determine the outcome.

---

31 Almar Latour, "Disconnected: How Europe Tripped Over the Wireless Phone Made for the Internet," *The Wall Street Journal*, June 5, 2001, p. A1.

32 Robert A. Guth, "NTT DoCoMo Says Profit Slumped," *The Wall Street Journal*, May 9, 2002, p. B5.

33 Stephen Labaton, "Studies Find Scant Availability of Spectrum for Wireless Internet," *The New York Times*, March 31, 2001, p. C1. Verizon Wireless began limited 3G service in early 2002. See Simon Romero, "Fast Hookup With Cellphone Is Expected from Verizon," *The New York Times*, January 28, 2002, p. C6.

34 "Fast Hookup...," Ibid.

35 The text takes a second look at short-wave wireless or Wi-Fi 802.11b Internet connections in Chapter 20, which deals with the future of the Internet.

SUMMARY AND PROSPECTS

This chapter presented, in brief, the origins and workings of the Internet, the World Wide Web, and their associated technologies. Keep in mind that much of this advance in communications was accomplished by voluntary effort, in the name of scientific progress, with the adoption of open rather than proprietary standards, and without a great deal in the way of motivation based upon personal profit. One of the prospects for the Web that worries Tim Berners-Lee is the potential for fragmentation of the Web as firms innovate first without agreement on standards.[36] The current keys to Web freedom and universal access are that the computers understand the Web address system (IP), that they understand the markup language, and that they understand the Internet transmission scheme (TCP). **Java** and other languages can make the Web less accessible to older computers when scripting languages change. Also, some commercial browsers contain unique features that are exploited by individual Web sites, making Web access less universal. Creators of commercial browsers who further differentiate their products in an attempt to "lock-in" users and boost profits may fragment the Web even further.

A second challenge involves the potential shortage of user Internet addresses. As more people around the world go online, and more hardware, including computers, cars, cell phones, and even appliances seek to acquire an Internet address, the 4 billion or so potential addresses will become exhausted. One solution is to introduce an enhanced version of the existing Internet Protocol, dubbed IPv6.[37] Cisco introduced Ipv6 technology in its routers, and Microsoft needs to do the same in the next version of its operating system. The appearance of 3G cell phone technology will help to raise the demand for the conversion of phone numbers into Internet addresses, thereby accelerating the introduction of IPv6.[38] Lastly the disparity between the number of existing IP addresses in North America (74%) versus Europe (17%) and Asia (9%) means that the latter regions of the world will be pushing for the adoption of the new IP standard to allow address expansion outside of North America.

A third prospect for the Web harkens back to the original intent of the Internet as a place to carry on scientific research. On one research front, several @home research projects are looking at using the Web as a vehicle to access surplus computer time at thousands of computers across the world. The names of some of the more prominent Web sites and their causes are listed in Table 3-1. The projects, known as **distributed computing,** break complex problems up into smaller parts that can be worked upon independently and recombined later. They usually involve sifting through mountains of data in search of an outcome designed to advance the public good. On another front, CERN, the original research home of Berners-Lee and the birthplace of the Web, is structuring the development of a European DataGrid to "harness together research computers in four European countries to crunch the river of data the (Hadron) Collider will generate."[39] Rather than entering a post-PC age, the DataGrid will allow the power of geographically diverse PCs to be bundled together to form a global computer that could potentially save billions of dollars in computing costs. The structure of this DataGrid will be an advance beyond current unidirectional distributed-computing projects, because it will allow any user to access the power of the new supercomputer.

---

36 "The Web turns 10," Ibid.

37 Dan Goodwin, "New Internet Protocol Still Has Many Hurdles to Clear," *The Wall Street Journal*, May 14, 2001, p. B5.

38 Thomas E. Weber, "How a Phone Number May One Day Become Your Internet Address," *The Wall Street Journal*, January 18, 2001, p. B1

39 Ben Vickers, "Europe's Grid Gives Glimpse of Web's Future," *The Wall Street Journal*, March 1, 2001, p. B8. The Hadron Collider is a super-collider that allows for the extremely fast acceleration and collision of physics particles, possibly leading to the discovery of new physical elements.

TABLE 3-1	Prominent @home Research Sites

Project Internet Address (URL)	Distributed Computing Research Focus
http://setiathome.ssl.berkeley.edu/	Search for extraterrestrial life
http://folding.stanford.edu/	Discover how and why proteins fold
http://gah.stanford.edu/	Research genetic mapping
http://www.evolutionary-research.net/	Study transmission of genetic mutations throughout a species
http://www.parabon.com/cac.jsp	Compute Against Cancer Research Project
http://www.fightaidsathome.org/	Model drug resistance and the development of anti-HIV drugs
http://www.mersenne.org/prime.htm	Search for mathematical prime numbers
http://www.distributed.net/	Crack cryptographic codes

Source: George Johnson, "Supercomputing '@Home' Is Paying Off," *The New York Times*, April 23, 2002, p. F1.

As a final thought, it is helpful to visualize the Web and Internet as being similar to living organisms. They will grow and change over time as ideas for use and technological capabilities allow for new ways to employ the system. Therefore, it can be expected that the application of the economic topics, as well as the e-commerce examples described within the ensuing chapters, will change over time as well. The central proposition of this text will remain the same, however, namely that the Web and the Internet are amazing new technologies. They open up a wide range of opportunities for the efficient, fast, and low-cost flow of information and the development of commercial uses. It is here that the principles of economics offer a valuable way to organize, as well as analyze, the commercial opportunities for the Web.

KEY TERMS AND CONCEPTS

all-optical Internet systems
ARPANET
bandwidth
Berners-Lee, Tim
cable Internet access
circuit routing
code division multiple access (CDMA)
cost-minimizing rule
digital subscriber lines (DSL)
distributed computing
domain name suffixes
fiber-optic technology
global system for mobile communications (GSM)
hypertext
hypertext markup language (HTML)
hypertext transfer protocol (HTTP)
i-mode
information-based system (Web)

Internet
Internet address
IPv6
Java
killer apps
laser
last-mile problem
message-based system (Internet)
Moore's Law
Netscape Navigator
packet switching technology
personal digital assistant
routers
time division multiple access (TDMA)
transmission control protocol/Internet protocol (TCP/IP)
wave division multiplexing
World Wide Web
1G, 2G, 2.5G, 3G

DISCUSSION AND REVIEW QUESTIONS

1. Identify and explain the significance of the technical and functional differences and interdependencies that exist between the Internet and the World Wide Web.

2. Initially, the United States government funded the research, development, and operation of the Internet. Would funding from the private sector have been as efficient or even better as an incubator source for the Internet? Why?

3. The initial development of the World Wide Web was undertaken primarily by private research and commercial enterprises. Was this source the most efficient support for the Web? Why?

4. How did Moore's Law and the economics of chip making combine to speed the spread to personal computers, as well as the urge to connect to the Internet and Web?

5. How did the Web reinforce the spread of personal computers?

6. How does the technology of a computer network expand upon and improve the economics of a television network? What characteristics of a network help to make the Web such a valuable vehicle for conducting e-commerce transactions?

7. What is the last-mile problem? How does this problem affect the spread of e-commerce and the profitability of Internet infrastructure investments?

8. Refer to the capital and labor example that illustrates the cost-minimizing rule. If the sample numbers hold for the extra worker, why would any firm wish to ever employ an extra unit of capital? [*Hint:* Return to Chapter 2 and the discussion of diminishing marginal returns to find the answer to this question.]

9. State the cost-minimizing rule. Explain how this rule helps to resolve the fiber optic research tension.

10. How does competition in product diversity usually affect the efficiency of the marketplace? Does this conclusion necessarily hold true for the technical diversity of cell phone connection standards in the United States. Why?

11. How does the diversity of cell phone connection standards in the United States affect the global competitive position of United States wireless service providers?

12. Distinguish between 1G, 2G, and 3G in terms of wireless telephone services.

13. What are the obstacles to the expansion of 3G cell phone service in the United States?

14. Assume for the moment that you are the chief executive of a major wireless phone company such as AT&T Wireless. What conditions or characteristics might make the delivery of 3G wireless Internet service via cell phones more popular? What might you do to enhance the number of 3G subscribers?

15. What might be the economic worth of the Web to Berners-Lee if he had decided to patent the technology and code? Would the growth of the Web have been so rapid if it was a patented product for sale? Why would someone give away such a valuable idea? Why do thousands of people participate, for free, in the various @home computer research projects?

WEB EXERCISES

1. Link to "Hobbes's Internet Timeline," at **http://www.zakon.org/robert/internet/timeline/**, and identify the five most important events affecting the Internet and/or the Web during the past three years.

2. Link to the Web site maintained by Tim Berners-Lee at **http://www.w3.org/People/Berners-Lee/FAQ.html**, and see how the creator of the Web sees the difference between the Internet and the Web.

3. Link to either the extraterrestrial search project at **http://setiathome.ssl.berkeley.edu/**, the Compute Against Cancer research project at **http://www.parabon.com/cac.jsp**, or one of the other sites in Figure 3-2, and see whether you would like to donate some of your spare computer time to help either of these worthy, distributed computing research causes.

4. Link to Richard T. Griffiths' "History of the Internet Site," at **http://www.let.leidenuniv.nl/history/ivh/frame_theorie.html**, click on the Chapter 2 link "From ARPANT to World Wide Web," and read the final paragraph of the chapter. What is the difference between the homepage as shown in the current Internet Explorer browser and the original CERN and Mosaic browsers? Which homepage is more visually appealing and why?

Market Structure Topics

CHAPTER 4

Introductory Case

ISP MERGERS AND INTERNET COMPETITION

In Chapter 2, the discussion emphasized competition as a key factor in determining the amount and distribution of consumer benefits to be derived from the market. The markets for e-commerce and the Internet are no exception to this observation. The essence of competition contains both behavioral and structural elements. To be competitive in the behavioral sense, firms must be constantly striving to improve their product, lower their price, and act aggressively to attract buyers to their goods and away from those of their rivals. The degree of competition can also be influenced by some important market structure characteristics, including the number of firms in the industry along with their relative size distribution. An industry with a large number of similarly sized, small firms tends to yield a market that provides only minimal economic power to control price. Thus, the benefits arising from competition as defined in the structural sense are more likely to be passed along to the consumer in the form of the lowest possible price for the product. Although the science of economics offers no specific guidance on a precise quantitative rule linking the vigor and benefits

of competition to firm numbers and relative size, the size and numbers statistics can be valuable in examining the efficiency of any market.

A key link in the e-commerce chain of electronic interconnection is the **Internet service provider (ISP)** industry. An ISP firm provides the Web user with the connection to the Internet, perhaps with other services. These firms are potentially powerful and stand as gate-keepers to the Internet, controlling what subscribers see on the ISP screen, and precisely how users access the Internet. Internet users would most likely benefit from as much competition as possible in this market segment. Table 4-1 contains the names of the largest U.S. ISPs, ranked by their self-proclaimed number of subscribers, as well as their share of the total market.

One might expect data of this importance would be centrally collected and readily available, but it isn't. The ISPs regard subscriber data as proprietary and competitive information to be released only when it is of advantage to the ISP. Also, the data can be suspect at times, not always revealing the technical nature of the subscriber connection (dial-up or broadband), the geographic service area, or what fraction of the subscribers are paying full price versus discount fees, or even receiving free service. Therefore, the figures, developed from a number of sources[1] include the estimate the Internet subscription market in the United States at approximately 70 million unique subscribers.[2]

---

1 One of the better sources for ISP subscriber information was created by Nick Christenson at **http://www.jet-cafe.org/~npc/isp/large.html**. Accessed September 2002.

2 Nielsen//NetRatings estimated that some 104.7 million people logged onto the Internet from the United States in December 2001, up from 98.6 million in December 2000. However, they also estimated that some 176.5 million persons, or 62 percent of the population had Internet access either at home or at work. See Susan Stellin, "More Americans Online," *The New York Times*, November 19, 2001, p. C7, and "Logging On Coast to Coast," *The New York Times*, January 28, 2002, p. C10. Multiple users can log on through a single ISP subscription account. The Internet research firm ARS estimates approximately 50 million dial-up Internet subscribers as of the first quarter of 2002. Mark Kersey, "AOL Time Warner is at a Crossroads," available at **http://www.serverworldmagazine.com/ars/2002/1q/0123_aolbroadband.shtml**. Estimates of household broadband connections range from 10.7 to 13.4 million connections. See Saul Hansell, "Demand Grows For Net Service At High Speed," *The New York Times*, December 24, 2001, p. C1

Measuring e-Commerce Concentration:

A Characteristic of Market Structure

Table 4-1 holds several points to note. First, the largest ISP is America Online (AOL), with 26.1 million U.S. subscribers and an estimated global count of 34.4 million, including 5.9 million in AOL Europe and 2.6 million elsewhere. With an estimated subscriber share of 37.3 percent, AOL is more than three times the size of its nearest competitor, the Microsoft Network, or MSN, which has 7.7 million subscribers and a market share of 11.0 percent. From there, the market share percentages decline rapidly, such that the 14th and 15th largest ISP firms, with approximately 750,000 subscribers each, claim approximately a 1 percent market share. Second, the type of Internet connection service can vary by firm. The first six firms listed mostly provide service through relatively slow **dial-up connections** using standard telephone lines. Other providers are telephone companies themselves that offer faster service through **direct subscriber line (DSL)** connections. Finally, cable TV systems such as Comcast, Cox, and Charter provide another type of faster, always-on Internet connection through their cable TV connections.

Third, the data in Table 4-1 show national numbers under the assumption that all of the connections are available to every consumer in each region of the country. This assumption is clearly not true for DSL and cable connections, which are more localized in their offerings. Fourth, AOL also owns two of the lesser ISP services Compuserve and Road Runner. Therefore, the market reach of AOL is larger than the data for AOL's flagship service alone would tend to indicate. Fifth, the remaining number of interconnection firms include thousands of very small ISPs spread across the county, most of which can be accessed only from a local phone either free or via a toll charge. A quick Web search may turn up a few within your local area code.[3]

In June 2001, NetZero.com and Juno Online, two of the largest ISPs, agreed to merge their services under the banner of United Online.[4] One year later, United Online ranked as the third largest ISP with 5.2 million subscribers. Prior to the merger, the two firms operated independently, with NetZero being fourth in size at 4.4 million subscriber accounts and Juno holding the fifth position with 2.6 million accounts. Both NetZero and Juno originally offered a free ISP access service, supported by revenues generated through client advertising. The free ISP approach was a distinct alternative to the fixed monthly fee-for-service plans offered by both AOL and MSN. As such, the NetZero and Juno were aggressive competitors to each other and to the market leaders. Unfortunately, the free ISP business model proved to be unprofitable. Therefore each firm began independently to offer a fee-based subscription service as an enhanced version of their free access service, which in turn was made more restrictive.

What makes the market share and merger information so important is that the merger of NetZero and Juno Online changes the market share rankings. It decreases the number of firms overall, while it increases the number of large firms. Depending upon how these firms see the new market, the merger potentially alters the level as well as the nature of the competition among ISPs. Subsequent to the merger, the financially revitalized United Online service shrank in size from 7 million to 5.2 million subscribers, with a combined market share of 7.4 percent. The combined firm

---

3 To see whether a small independent ISP operates near you, link to "The Definitive Internet Service Buyer's Guide" at http://thelist.internet.com/ and locate your area code. Sixteen listings found for area code 203 in June 2002 included 11 that weren't part of those listed in Figure 4-1.

4 Julia Angwin, "NetZero and Juno Online Agree to Merge, Uniting 4th-, 5th-Biggest Web-Access Firms," *The Wall Street Journal*, June 8, 2001, p. B6.

further deemphasized the free Internet access service, while reducing the number of major competitors. These changes hold potential consequences for Internet service pricing, competition, and market power. For example, will the merger of these two major services pose a stronger competitive threat to AOL?

Will AOL see the absence of a free service alternative as a license to raise its own prices? Will the combined United Online exhibit more market power to raise prices (from a still low $9.99) to some higher level? Which alternative or other outcome is most likely, and is there any way to tell?

TENSION ① These questions set the stage for the identification of the following tension involving industry numbers and size dispersion within economic concentration. Does the dispersal of market share among a large number of similarly sized firms improve the vigor of competition of Internet and e-commerce firms, or does the existence of a few, large, well-capitalized firms allow for greater e-commerce competitive survival, creativity, and adaptability to change? Where is the dividing line between an industry with too many small firms or too few large ones, where the line influences the degree of resource efficiency? Where does the consumer tend to receive the greatest benefit, from a industry with large numbers of small firms, or one with fewer numbers and larger firm size? The

TABLE 4-1		Leading U.S. Internet Service Providers, June 2002	
Internet Service Provider	**Claimed Number U.S. Subscribers (mil).**	**Type of Service**	**Market Share %**
America Online	26.1	Dial-up	37.3
MSN	7.7	Dial-up	11.0
United Online	5.2	Dial-up	7.4
Earthlink	4.9	Dial-up	7.0
Prodigy (w/SBC Narrowband)	3.6	Dial-up	5.1
Compuserve (AOL owned)	3.0	Dial-up	4.3
Road Runner (AOL owned)	2.4	Cable	3.4
SBC (w/Prodigy Broadband)	1.5	DSL	2.1
AT&T WorldNet	1.4	Dial-up	2.0
AT&T Broadband	1.4	DSL	2.0
Verizon	1.4	DSL	2.0
Comcast	1.0	Cable	1.4
Cox	1.0	Cable	1.4
Charter	0.75	Cable	1.1
BellSouth	0.73	DSL	1.0
Subtotal top 15 ISPs	62.08		88.7
Other U.S. ISPs	7.92		11.3
Estimated Number of U.S. Internet Subscriber Accounts	70.0		100%

remainder of this chapter may provide some insight into this tension, but its resolution on a case-by-case basis may not always yield one definitive answer.

THE CONCEPT OF MARKET CONCENTRATION

The number of firms is a key structural characteristic that distinguishes the four theoretical market structures discussed in Chapter 2. The term **economic concentration** is a concept that helps to define and quantify the number or relative size dispersion of the firms in a given product market. The *number of firms* in an industry is important because, if they are few in number and large in size, the market leaders may find it easier to coordinate their pricing behavior and limit price competition. Conversely, the existence of many small firms makes the coordination of behavior more difficult, even if the advantages of such cooperation are apparent. Substantial *size dispersion* may allow the giants to dominate the competitive behavior of an industry, with smaller firms having little or no competitive impact.

Measures of economic concentration usually have an industry focus. An **economic industry** is a collection of firms producing products that consumers regard as similar to one another and serve as good substitutes. The *definition of the product* itself and the *boundaries of the product market* in terms of buyer perceptions and purchase behavior must be very precise. For instance, common terminology refers to a group of firms linked together in what is called the automobile industry. Is a Lexus, Cadillac, or Acura in the same product market as a Kia, Cavalier, or Sentra? Is an SUV in the same market as a minivan or a two-door sports coupe? Do buyers examine the entire range of vehicle styles and brands when they go car shopping? Or are they looking at just a limited subset of vehicles in terms of performance, style, appearance, and price? The auto firms think they know the answers to these questions. They design different products for different **market segments** that are likely to be distinct in terms of age, income, sex, driving habits, and other characteristics. All cars may provide transportation, but they do so in vastly different ways at widely varying price levels. Therefore, considerable care must be taken in looking at the degree of product similarity and substitutability in order to define an industry such as automobiles.

Care must also be taken in defining the *geographic scope* of the product market. Some products are marketed and purchased only locally or regionally, such as food or appliances. Freshness and bulk are among the product characteristics that tend to limit the search radius for certain items. How many times might a consumer be in another part of the country and scan a TV or newspaper ad for a product that he wants to buy. Perhaps he finds one offered for sale at a price lower than the one quoted by the hometown supplier. Would he react by purchasing the item at the distant location? Or would the hassle of out-of-state purchase and lugging the item home be too much, relative to the dollars saved? For refrigerators and lettuce, the out-of-town purchase is unlikely. For a car or a consumer electronics product, a distant purchase may be made. Some products with high value and relatively low shipping charges can be marketed and sold nationally or even globally. Books, DVDs, some clothing and software, or branded items, have a known quality, are easily identified, and can be shipped anywhere at minimal expense relative to their purchase price. These kinds of differences in product characteristics, geographic boundaries, prices, and shipping charges define some of the more successful forays into **business-to-consumer (B2C) e-commerce**.

THE CONCENTRATION RATIO:
A PARTIAL INDEX OF CONCENTRATION

The **concentration ratio** is one quantitative approach to the measurement of the number of firms and their size within an industry. It indicates the percent of market share for final sales or some other share measure (i.e., data for assets, employees, or value added)

FIGURE 4-1	Formula for the Four-Firm Concentration Ratio

$$CR4 = \frac{\displaystyle\sum_{i=1}^{i=4} \text{Total Sales}_i}{\displaystyle\sum_{i=1}^{i=n} \text{Total Sales}_i} \times 100\%$$

where n equals the number of firms in the industry

that is held by a subset of firms in the industry. The formula for calculating the typical grouping is displayed in Figure 4-1, and shows aggregates market share for the four largest firms (**CR4**). Other common aggregations include the largest eight (CR8) and sixteen firms (CR16), where data are available and relevant. The U.S. Census Bureau conducts a periodic count of firms and data sufficient to permit the calculation of concentration ratios for census firms. These firms are organized into **census industries** according to the **Standard Industrial Classification (SIC) code**.[5] This classification process uses a supply rather than a demand focus. The SIC code groups firms by their technical process of production or the raw materials used to make the finished good. Therefore, it may or may not capture all of the firms that produce substitute products or compete with each other in the eyes of the consumer.

Given the supply focus of the census survey and the newness of most of the Internet and e-commerce industries, the SIC data are of minimal use for the purpose of calculating industry concentration. Rather, to demonstrate key points, the estimates must rely on privately collected and often incomplete data, such as was shown in Table 4-1. Table 4-2 contains subscriber data for cell phone service. Recall from Chapter 3 that wireless phone connection and 3G technologies offer the potential for greatly expanded Web access in the next round of Internet innovation.

Calculating the value for the CR4 yields a concentration ratio of 69.3 percent, using the number of subscribers as a measure of market share. Traditionally, if somewhat arbitrarily, oligopoly has been defined to begin when the CR4 reaches 40 percent, which has the **CR4 numbers equivalent value** of four firms with a 10 percent share each. It is thought that firms begin to recognize their mutual interdependence at this point. **Tight oligopoly** is similarly defined as occurring when the CR4 reaches or extends beyond 60 percent, the equivalent of four firms with a 15 percent share each. Here, firms are thought to be able to begin to act on their mutual interdependence, to coordinate their competitive behavior, and to potentially limit the extent of price competition. In the wireless market, the number-one firm, Verizon, holds 28.5 percent of the market, while number four Sprint PCS has 7.3 percent, or just one-fourth of the subscribers of the largest firm. Without access to the size dispersion data found in Table 4-2 this important detail on relative size is masked by CR4 focus only on the sum total of the shares for the four largest firms. Also, in the Census SIC data, the identities of individual firms and their market shares are kept hidden.

So, do the results indicate that the U.S. Department of Justice's Antitrust Division should be concerned about the potential for anticompetitive behavior in the wireless phone market? Most likely not. Supplemental economic conditions such as firms aggressively fighting for market share, rapid technological change, and substantial price-cutting by smaller firms ensure the vigor of competition, at least for the moment. Also, the eighth-largest U.S. firm, VoiceStream, was purchased by the German firm Deutsche Telekom, the world's second largest phone company. This act reinforces the competitive assessment based upon the ease of foreign entry and the potential for wireless competition on a global

---

5 The SIC system is in the process of being replaced by a broader coding system to be known as the *North American Industrial Classification System*, or *NAICS*.

Wireless Telephone Market Share Data: First Quarter 2000			TABLE 4-2
Wireless Provider	**U.S. Subscribers (mil)**	**Market Share %**	**HHI Value**
Verizon Wireless	25.9	28.5	812.25
SBC/Bell South	17.5	19.3	372.49
AT&T Wireless and affiliates	12.9	14.2	201.64
Sprint PCS and affiliates	6.7	7.3	53.29
Alltel	5.9	6.5	43.56
Nextel Communications	5.1	5.7	32.49
United State Cellular	2.7	3.0	9
VoiceStream	2.4	2.7	7.29
Western Wireless	0.9	1.0	1
Dobson Communications	0.8	0.8	0.64
Top 10 Total	80.8	89.1	
Total U.S. Carriers			
HHI est. other U.S. Providers			7.51
HHI Value			1541

Source: Adapted from Simon Romero, "Deutsche Telekom Stands to Gain a U.S. Foothold," *The New York Times*, July 25, 2000, p. C10.

rather than just a national scale. After all, wouldn't the cell phone customer like to use the same wireless connection anywhere in the world? The wireless providers, too, would be pleased to see this global spread of wireless connections, because they would experience both a rise in usage and revenue growth from their cell infrastructure investments.

THE HERFINDAHL/HIRSCHMAN INDEX: A SUMMARY INDEX OF CONCENTRATION

The CR4 is one way to look at the issue of concentration, but it leaves out potentially useful and interesting information. Therefore, it is referred to as a *partial index of concentration*. The **Herfindahl/Hirschman Index (HHI)** makes use of market share data for all of the firms in the industry and incorporates information on their relative size dispersion as well. Therefore, it is characterized as a *summary index of concentration*. The formula for the HHI involves summing the squares of the individual firm market shares (See Figure 4-2). Notice that by squaring each market share value, the index gives greater weight to industries where one or two firms tower above all the others. Squaring 2 yields a value of 4 or a number twice as large, but squaring 4 yields a value of 16 or a number four times as large. Size dispersion matters in the area of economic concentration, and the HHI gives that dispersion greater weight.

Herfindahl/Hirschman Index of Economic Concentration	FIGURE 4-2

$$HHI = \sum_{i=1}^{n} (\text{Market Share}_i)^2$$

where n is the number of firms in the industry

The wireless provider data in Table 4-2 present a problem in calculating the HHI. Subscriber data are available for only the top 10 wireless firms. The figures and names are missing for the remaining firms in the industry. Fortunately, enough information is available to infer some market shares for the remaining firms, which account for a total of 9.9 million domestic users. All of the firms must have fewer than 800,000 subscribers or they would surpass Dobson for tenth place on the list. If we make the assumption that each has about 760,000 subscribers, we get an additional 13 wireless providers. Verizon would have a squared market share and HHI value of 812.25, SBC/BellSouth, now known as Cingular, would have a value of 372.49, and so on. The 13 smallest would each have an HHI value of .5776 which, when summed 13 times, would yield a combined impact of 7.51. In total, the HHI value for the set of firms in the wireless phone industry would be no more than 1541.

As with the CR4 value, the interpretation of the HHI number is somewhat arbitrary. The HHI formula indicates that in a situation of *atomistic competition*, with thousands of similarly sized small firms, the HHI value approaches 0. Conversely, in a *pure monopoly*, where one firm has a 100 percent market share, the HHI has a value of 10,000. So how are HHI numbers in between these two extremes to be interpreted? The Antitrust Division of the U.S. Department of Justice determined that an industry with an HHI value of 1,000 is not a problem. It would generate an **HHI numbers equivalent value** of 10 firms each with 10 percent of the market, yielding a potentially vigorous competitive market.[6] However, an HHI value such that $1,600 < HHI < 1,800$ would be regarded as problematic. An HHI of 1,700 would yield a numbers equivalent of fewer than six firms with a market share of slightly less than 17 percent each. Mutual interdependence would be recognized with the potential for it being acted upon. Lastly, an HHI value greater than 1,800 would signal a tight oligopoly and be a cause for concern as the industry evolved over time. An HHI value of 2,000 could support at most five firms with a 20 percent market share each. This structure might yield an even greater temptation, as well as ability for the firms to coordinate their behavior.

So where does HHI = 1,541 leave us in the discussion of the wireless providers? It says that the industry could lie on the border of some concern. However, the HHI number is less ominous than the CR4 value of 69.3 percent. The existence of a large fringe of smaller firms outside of the big four implies the increased possibility of competitive vigor that is not captured by the partial index. Size dispersion, as well as numbers and market shares matter in the judgment as to competitive vigor.[7]

REVISITING THE ISP SUBSCRIBER DATA

Let's revisit the ISP data in Table 4-1 to perform a similar set of economic concentration calculations. As of June 2002, the top four ISPs yielded a CR4 of 62.7 percent, just above the borderline for traditional tight oligopoly concern. To get a rough HHI value it is again necessary to make some assumptions regarding the market shares for the firms that hold the remaining subscribers. The top 15 ISPs captured 62.08 million of the total of 70.0 million subscribers, or 88.7 percent. The smallest listed firm was BellSouth with 0.730 million subscribers and a 1.0 percent market share. Therefore, the remaining ISPs must have a subscriber base and market share no larger than that of BellSouth. At the worst, let's assume that the remaining 7.92 million subscribers are served by 11 equally sized firms, with 0.73 million customers per ISP. This allocation would yield a market

---

6 The numbers equivalent figure equals 10,000/HHI and yields the maximum number of firms of equal size that can exist in the industry with the corresponding HHI value.

7 With heavy debt loads and intense competitive pressures relentlessly driving down wireless calling rates and profits, the financial community is pushing for consolidation that will raise the HHI through mergers within the wireless phone sector. See Matthew Karnitschnig, "VoiceStreams's Outlook Rules Sommer's Fate," *The Wall Street Journal*, June 18, 2002, p. B6.

Leading U.S. Internet Service Providers June 2000				TABLE 4-3

Internet Service Provider	Claimed Number U.S. Subscribers (mil).	Type of Service	Market Share %	HHI Value
America Online	26.1	Dial-up	37.3	1,391
MSN	7.7	Dial-up	11.0	121
United Online	5.2	Dial-up	7.4	55
Earthlink	4.9	Dial-up	7.0	49
Prodigy (w/SBC Narrowband)	3.6	Dial-up	5.1	26
Compuserve (AOL owned)	3.0	Dial-up	4.3	18
Road Runner (AOL owned)	2.4	Cable	3.4	12
SBC (w/Prodigy Broadband)	1.5	DSL	2.1	4
AT&T WorldNet	1.4	Dial-up	2.0	4
AT&T Broadband	1.4	DSL	2.0	4
Verizon	1.4	DSL	2.0	4
Comcast	1.0	Cable	1.4	2
Cox	1.0	Cable	1.4	2
Charter	0.75	Cable	1.1	1
BellSouth	0.73	DSL	1.0	1
Subtotal top 15 ISPs	62.08		88.7	1,694
Other U.S. ISPs	7.92		11.3	121
Total HHI Value				1,815
Numbers Equivalent Value				5.5
Estimated Number of U.S. Internet subscriber accounts	70.0		100%	

share of 1.0 percent for each of the 11 firms, for a combined HHI of 11, or 11 times 1.0.[8] The HHI for the ISP industry after the merger of NetZero and Juno would equal 1,815. See Table 4-3. This HHI yields a numbers equivalent value of 5.5 equally sized firms for the industry. These numbers appear to be within the boundary of market power concern. Also, keep in mind that these are national HHI numbers for all ISPs, which will yield an HHI that may be less than the HHI values for any given local market.

Prior to the merger, Juno Online and NetZero posted subscriber numbers of 2.6 and 4.4 million respectively, with corresponding market shares of 3.9 percent and 6.3 percent. Splitting the two firms and subtracting out the current share for United Online yields a pre-merger HHI of 1,815. The merger led to essentially no change in the HHI. Is the post-merger HHI sufficiently high enough to serve as a cause for alarm? It's too early to tell. AOL raised its price by $1.95 per month, or 8 percent, right around the time of the merger.[9] Most of the other leading ISPs held their prices steady and continued to

---

8   As with the wireless data, this assumption yields a slightly higher estimated value for the HHI than may appear in real life. Nevertheless, note how insignificant the market shares of the fringe firms are in calculating the industry HHI value.

9   Saul Hansell, "AOL Raising Monthly Rate 9%; Rival May Follow Suit," *The New York Times*, May 23, 2001, p. C12.

FIGURE 4-3   e-Commerce Service Delivery Pyramid

e-Commerce Firms
Direct sites vs. exchanges; B2B, B2C, P2P

Internet Service Providers
CLECs: Competitive local exchange carriers
cable TV, direct subscriber lines (DSL), dial-up

Backend Architecture and Software Firms
Web hosting and data center storage
Software vendors: Procurement, Content +
Data Base Mgt + Personalization + Customer Relationship

Internet Hardware and Infrastructure Firms
Optical fiber makers and fiber network firms
Telecommunications and optical equipment firms

aggressively encourage AOL subscribers to leave AOL for equivalent service at lower costs.[10] However, Earthlink, the number three ISP, increased its dial-up connection charges by $2 per month to $21.95 toward the end of June 2001.[11] Was this act a coincidental change brought about by a rise in the cost of providing the service, or an act of conscious parallel behavior designed to exploit consumers and generate greater economic profits?

Looking to the vigor of competition in the ISP industry, one must ask and answer a series of questions. For example, does the existence of an aggressively competitive set of fringe firms restrain the pricing power of AOL, the market leader? Are AOL subscribers likely to change to a competing ISP?[12] And, if so, will the drain on subscribers be sufficient to hurt AOL's revenues? These are questions that will be looked at with an attempt to answer them in Chapter 5, when the issues of entry barriers and product differentiation are addressed. But it appears at this point that competition among the ISPs is vigorous and capable of restraining coordinated price increases designed to exploit the consumer.[13]

TAXONOMY OF E-COMMERCE INDUSTRIES AND INTERNET MARKETS

In any attempt to be vigilant regarding economic concentration in e-commerce, just what industries should be tracked? As it turns out, a lot more is involved in e-commerce than simply typing in the URL for Priceline.com on your Web browser. The delivery of e-commerce products and services is best thought of as a technology pyramid, as shown in Figure 4-3.

The delivery of an e-commerce service begins with a broad base of Internet hardware and infrastructure firms, followed by a layer of project specific **business-to-business**

---

10 See Catherine Greenman, "Is There Life After AOL?," *The New York Times*, June 21, 2001, p. G1.

11 "Earthlink Raises Prices," *The New York Times*, June 27, 2001, p. C4.

12 Catherine Greenman, "Is There Life After AOL?" *The New York Times*, June 21, 2001, p. G1.

13 The subscriber data was further in flux when Excite@Home lost its exclusive ISP provider status on the Cox and Comcast cable systems. This event contributed to the demise of the ISP and a redistribution of its 3.2 million cable-based subscribers. See Kara Swisher and Deborah Solomon, "Excite @Home Loses Two Cable Partners," *The Wall Street Journal*, September 4, 2001, p. B8.

(B2B) service software or service providers. Next comes the layer containing the interconnection services, or ISPs. Finally, with the Internet foundation layers in place, we are ready to identify the inhabitants of the pyramid's top layer, those who deliver the e-commerce services. They include B2B sales from firm sites and exchanges, B2C sales of products and services, and the range of **peer-to-peer (P2P)** exchanges. It is readily apparent that e-commerce is complicated business, which explains the need for an e-commerce taxonomy, or organizational system, to name the various layers, classify their components, and identify some key firms.

Basic Infrastructure Firms

The **Internet hardware and infrastructure firms** are at the base of the pyramid and carry out a number of functions. First, firms such as Corning Glassworks make the optical fiber cable, which carries the light impulses that comprise the traffic on the Internet. Next, fiber network firms lay the fiber cables, maintain the connections, and provide wholesale, long-haul Internet backbone services. Some of these firms are fairly well known, such as Global Crossing, WorldCom, Qwest, and Williams Communications Group. These firms, and about 1,500 more, cause part of the current problem. Together they laid 39 million miles of fiber-optic cable, enough to circumvent the globe 1,566 times.[14] With Internet traffic growing less than 20 percent per year rather than the expected 40 percent to 50 percent, only 3 percent of the cable is operable. The supply overhang is causing cable access fees to fall by 60 percent annually, threatening the profitability and survival of many of the network firms. The third layer of infrastructure is made up of the optical equipment firms such as JDS Uniphase, Lucent Technologies, and Nortel Networks. They make the lasers that blink billions of times per second, sending the light signals, in varying colors, through the fibers. The final block in the infrastructure layer contains the firms providing the routers, switches, and servers, such as Cisco, Juniper Networks, and Sun Microsystems, that move the traffic over the Internet.

In the midst of the dot-com frenzy during the 1990s, financial analysts suggested that the safest place for equity investors to place funds was in the infrastructure firms rather than trying to pick an individual dot-com winner. They drew an analogy to the Gold Rush of 1849 to remind investors that it wasn't just the few lucky prospectors who were the most likely to become rich, but rather it was the merchants who sold the shovels, jeans, and food supplies to all of the prospectors. For a while, these advisors proved to be right. Cisco was, at one point, the most valuable firm on Wall Street, as determined by the worth of its equity shares. Its stock value exceeded the worth of perennial giants including General Electric, Exxon-Mobil, and General Motors. Then, the drop in the growth of Internet traffic, the rising number of dot-coms who became not-coms, and the financial problems at many upstart telecommunications firms fed back rapidly to the infrastructure leaders, who fell on hard times in 2001–2002. Sales were down, big losses mounted quickly, and some infrastructure firms may fail before Internet growth rates resume a faster pace. So much for the value of even a good analogy.[15]

Backend Architecture Firms

The next layer of the pyramid includes the **backend architecture firms** that provide a range of essential e-commerce services, which are generally unseen by the user.[16] First, web-hosting and data center firms, such as Exodus Communications and Globix, serve

---

14 Rebecca Blumenstein, "Overbuilt Web: How the Fiber Barons Plunged the Nation into a Telecom Glut," *The Wall Street Journal*, June 18, 2001, p. A1.

15 Simon Romero, "Telecommunications Outlook: First the Bad News, Then the Bad News," *The New York Times*, June 18, 2002, p. C6. Telecommunications firms and related industries lost some $2 trillion in market value from March 2000 through June 2002, with the prospects for more losses as additional firms fail.

16 "How Killer B-to-B's Slid to the Endangered List," *The New York Times*, May 7, 2000, p. 3–1.

as the repository for a commercial Web site, receive and deliver customer communications, and hold customer data in e-warehouses called **server farms**. These farms are so large and numerous that their growing demand for electricity to run the computers and air conditioning systems were a contributing factor in the 2001 rolling blackouts experienced in California.[17] Next in line are the firms that produce the data storage capacity equipment and the software to manage commercial transactions. For airlines and travel reservation sites such as Orbitz.com or Travelocity.com, billions of bits of information must be handled quickly, stored securely, and retrieved flawlessly. Firms such as EMC offer the data storage equipment and systems, while Oracle or Sybase are leaders in the database management software field. Also included here are the firms that provide e-commerce firms with niche-oriented software products. These would include the following:

- *Procurement software*, such as Oracle's Internet Procurement Suite, to manage the buying and selling of products or supplies
- *Content management and database management software*, from Interwoven, to analyze and present content on company Web sites
- *Personalization software*, from Broadvision, that tailors Web-site content to different users, including customers, suppliers, partners, or employees
- *Customer relationship software*, from Vignette, which consists of customer-centric products that establish life cycle relationships and boost sales from customer data analysis

Lastly, if the owners of a potential commercial Web site aren't quite sure what all of these firms do or how to integrate their "e-ssential" software into a business, they have a couple of choices. First, they can call on any number of e-guidance or consulting firms, including Scient or Viant. The e-guidance firms help the commercial site owners to develop an e-business strategy, put them in touch with the necessary B2B suppliers, and either get them started or increase their competitiveness on the Web. Second, if the owners want all of their e-business software services and more from a single firm, they can contact Sap.com and their suite of e-business management products.

The purpose of this discussion isn't to make you expert in the various niches of e-commerce or to confuse you to the point of frustration. Rather, it is intended to alert those interested to the complex reality of e-commerce, and show how many individual industries and services it takes to get a sophisticated e-business effort off the ground. And the story isn't complete yet.

The Interconnect and Internet Service Provider Pyramid Layer

The information in the opening case introduced the names of a number of familiar ISPs, so they won't be repeated here. The Internet linking and service process is really much larger, starting with the broadband interconnect firms, focusing on businesses, and offering high-speed T-1 or T-3 Internet access lines costing thousands of dollars or more. They are included within the 300-plus **competitive local exchange carriers (CLECs)**, such as Covad and XO Communications, who grew out of the Telecommunications Deregulation Act of 1996.[18] Next in line are the cable systems with high-speed, always-on access through cable TV lines. Lastly, regional phone companies such as SBC, Bell South, and Verizon provide their own interconnect technology called **digital subscriber line** or **DSL** service. They also provide the potential for wireless Internet connections using a cell phone, hand-held personal digital assistant (PDA), or even a wireless laptop. Today, only romantics or "old fogies" have rotary dial telephone service. In the not-too-distant future, most phone users will have cell technology and only the "old fogies" will

---

[17] Meal Templin, "Power-Hungry Web 'Server Farms' Find Cooler Reception in California," *The Wall Street Journal*, February 28, 2001, p. B1.

[18] "Broadband Failure Has a Political Cause," *The Wall Street Journal*, June 21, 2001, p. A18.

have hard-wired phones. "Dark" laptops will be a thing of the past as cell nodes allow total, mobile Internet connections, creating "always lit" laptops.[19] Of course, this mobile Internet service will give rise to mobile content providers, service firms, and so on, further increasing the complexity of e-commerce.

The e-Commerce Site Layer

Once the potential e-commerce seller resolves the hardware, software, content, interconnect, and strategy problems, it must figure out how best to make the site available to potential customers. If the e-commerce firm involves B2B contact, will it set up its own unique sales-oriented site modeled after those created by Cisco, Intel, or General Electric? Will it join an **industry-created exchange** to buy resources and sell products, like eSteel or Covisint? Perhaps it will join an independent exchange organized by VerticalNet, Vmarkets, or eMerge, among others. **Independent exchanges** aggregate otherwise fragmented firms into centralized buying and information networks covering business activities as diverse as energy, health care, cattle and farm products, or food products. Of course, a whole array of firms would like to sell software and other services to these exchanges, including Ariba, Commerce One, and FreeMarkets.

If the firm has a B2C focus, will it be an Internet-only seller such as Amazon.com or Priceline.com? If it follows this route, then brand awareness and customer service satisfaction are crucial to its long-run survival. B2C firms may be inclined to combine **clicks-and-bricks**, such as Wal-Mart or Barnes & Noble, or **clicks-and-catalog**, as does the clothing retailer Lands' End. Perhaps the firm is looking to be a full, **multichannel seller,** where e-commerce is just one point of potential buyer contact along with stores and catalog sales. The lingerie firm, Victoria's Secret, and the giant office products firm, Staples, fit into this category. Staples claims to successfully sell by physical site, Web, and phone, while avoiding both channel conflict and the cannibalization of store sales.[20] Lastly, the firm might want be a **niche seller** offering a highly specialized product, such as out-of-print books, as does Austin's Antiquarian Books in Wilmington, Vermont; fly fishing equipment at Creekside Flyfishing in Salem, Oregon; or masquerade costumes at Costume Universe in Atlanta, Georgia.

Will the firm offer financial services, ranging from banking through real estate, to loans and credit cards, home, auto, and life insurance, or opportunities to buy common stocks, bonds, mutual funds, or treasury obligations? Will it be a source of investment information, such as Motley Fool, or a conduit to other sites organized by topic, such as Apple Books? Will the business be a self-organizing site such as eBay, where your customers do most of the work, or will you make music or other forms of entertainment available, such as Napster or MP3? Will the firm offer adult entertainment, like Whitehouse.com, or e-gambling, such as LuckyDragon.com? The possibilities, opportunities, and challenges are endless, and so are the potential pitfalls.

One last range of choices would be Peer-to-Peer (P2P) e-commerce. The music exchange site, Napster, popularized this approach, but the technology has much greater potential application in the area of distributed computing, as discussed in Chapter 3. The concept involves linking two or more independent computers together for purposes of file sharing. Napster linked files by way of a central information storage system. Other file sharing systems, such as Gnutella and Freenet, are free standing and allow files to be shared anonymously, without a central connection. In the distributed computing mode, the technology allows for thousands of computers to combine their power and search for extraterrestrial intelligence through the SETI@home project. P2P is fascinating stuff, open to imagination, with many potential applications.

---

19 "Wireless Laptops Links Still Slow, Costly," *Connecticut Post*, June 24, 2001, p. F4.

20 Glenn Rifkin, "The Staples Merger of Its Web Site and Catalog Business Offers a Lesson in How to Reevaluate Online Strategies," *The New York Times*, June 25, 2001, p. C4.

SUMMARY AND PROSPECTS

This chapter on concentration began with some data on ISPs and the wireless phone industry. It then showed how the data might be analyzed and interpreted in terms of numbers as well as relative size distribution using either the concentration ratio or the Herfindahl/Hirschman index. The discussion raised the potential for an efficiency tension between an industry comprised of many small firms and one made up of a lesser number of larger firms. Mergers among smaller firms were shown to have little impact on the concentration within the industry, but may have had some influences upon behavior. From the perspective of consumer benefit or exploitation, it was ambiguous at best to infer efficiency consequences from numbers and size dispersion alone. More information about market structure and behavior is needed to judge the vigor of competition within a given industry.

From there, the discussion identified the range of markets and industries involved in the e-commerce effort. It noted that many of these firms fell on hard times as overbuilding created excess capacity leading to falling prices and losses. This type of turmoil is not unusual in new markets.[21] Innovative technologies, including the telegraph, railroads, car manufacturing, and personal computers, all experienced similar fates in the early going, followed by bankruptcies and mergers. They all survived as new industries and prospered after the initial period of "irrational exuberance." The lesson for the future is simple. Individual firms may come and go, but efficiency-creating new technologies persevere.

The one certain thing about this book is that the landscape of e-commerce is changing so fast that any sample data or taxonomy of e-business firms is outdated almost before the ink is dry. All of the firms mentioned were alive and their site URLs worked at the time of this writing, but firms fail, merge, or in other ways change their missions or names rapidly in e-time. So the lasting value of this chapter is not in the specific firm names and data mentioned. Rather, the value lies in the appreciation that the chapter provides of the breadth and interconnectedness of e-commerce, along with the view that economics plays a role in analyzing those relationships. Lastly, the discussion should have stirred an understanding that the birth and growth as well as the application of e-commerce entail an interdependent "e-volution" of extensive and complex technologies.

KEY TERMS AND CONCEPTS

backend architecture firms
broadband interconnect firms
business-to-business (B2B) e-commerce
business-to-consumer (B2C) e-commerce
census industries
click-and-brick
click-and-catalog
competitive local exchange carriers
　(CLECs)
concentration ratio (CR4)
dial-up connections
digital subscriber lines (DSL)
e-Commerce taxonomy
economic concentration
economic industry

Herfindahl/Hirschman Index (HHI)
independent exchanges
industry-created exchanges
Internet hardware and infrastructure
　firms
Internet service providers (ISPs)
market segment
multichannel sellers
niche sellers
numbers equivalent value: CR4, HHI
peer-to-peer (P2P) e-commerce
server farms
Standard Industrial Classification (SIC)
　code
tight oligopoly

21 Daniel Gross, "Creative Destruction and the Web," *The Wall Street Journal*, June 20, 2001.

DISCUSSION AND REVIEW QUESTIONS

1. Distinguish between a partial index and a summary index of industry concentration. Which index does a better job of portraying information about the number and size dispersion of firms within an industry? Why?

2. What is the difference between a census industry and an economic industry? Which is more relevant to the calculation of economic concentration? Why?

3. Explain why the precise definition of the product and the specification of the exact geographic area of service are so vital to the correct identification of an economic industry.

4. Why did the merger between NetZero and Juno Online have almost no impact on either the CR4 or the HHI?

5. What information is shown by the numbers equivalent value for the CR4 and the HHI? What does this statistic tell us about the potential for competition or collusion within a given industry?

6. What effect does the squaring of the market share value for firms within the HHI have on the interpretation of economic concentration?

7. Does AOL have market power? Why? What factors might affect its degree of market power?

8. Does Verizon Wireless have market power? Why? What factors might affect its degree of market power?

9. Tight oligopoly is assumed to begin with a CR4 of 60 percent or higher. This number could be reached in an industry with four equally sized firms with a 15 percent market share each. What would be the corresponding highest possible value for the HHI in such an industry?

10. The following table provides data for the top 10 firms in the cable TV industry as of spring 2001. These firms are capable of bringing high-speed Internet access to residential customers through their cable lines. The total number of U.S. cable subscribers is estimated to be 64 million. Calculate the CR4 and the HHI for the cable industry. When Comcast acquires AT&T Broadband, how will this merger affect both the CR4 and the HHI? Will the merger give the larger Comcast more market power relative to consumers? Why?

Cable TV Subscriber Data, Spring 2001	
Cable Firm	**Number of Subscribers (mil)**
AT&T Broadband	16.09
Time Warner Cable	12.75
Comcast	7.60
Charter Communications	6.35
Cox Communications	6.19
Adelphia Communications	5.29
Cablevision Systems	2.83
Insight Communications	0.92
Mediacom	0.78
CableOne	0.73
Estimated number of U.S. cable subscribers	64 million

Source: Deborah Solomon and Robert Frank, "Comcast Deal Cements Rise of an Oligopoly in the Cable Business," *The Wall Street Journal*, December 21, 2001, p. A1.

11. Review the tension within the topic of economic concentration. Are many small firms or fewer large firms of greater benefit to consumers in the ISP, wireless phone, and cable TV markets? Why?

WEB EXERCISES

1. Go to the Web and contact each of the four top ISP sites, AOL.com, MSN.com, NetZero.com, and Earthlink.com. Check out their prices and terms for unlimited use, monthly dial-up service. Are the prices the same or different? Which firm charges the most and which charges the least? Why might the prices for the same service be different, if the firms are in the same industry?

2. Go to the site that lists the names of ISPs listed by local area code at **http://thelist. internet.com/**. Type in your local area code and determine the number of ISPs that provide service in your area. How many are not in the top 15 list shown in Table 4-1? Which one offers the lowest price for unlimited use, monthly dial-up service?

3. Access ISP-Planet at **http://www.isp-planet.com/research/rankings/usa.html**. Look for the ISP ranking data for the most recent quarter. Assume that the total number of U.S. Internet subscribers is now 72 million. Calculate the CR4 and the HHI for the most recent data. How have the ISP concentration numbers and rankings changed relative to the data in Table 4-3?

4. Go to the ISP data Web site maintained by Nick Christenson at http://**www.jetcafe. org/~npc/isp/large.html**. Again assume that the total number of U.S. Internet subscribers is 72 million. Use Christenson's data to calculate the CR4 and the HHI for the top 15 ISPs. How do these numbers compare to those published by ISP-Planet?

5. Type in the URL for at least two of the following e-commerce support firms: Cisco.com, Vignette.com, EMC.com, Oracle.com, and Covad.com. Examine the site for the kinds of e-commerce support service that each firm offers.

CHAPTER 5

Introductory Case

AOL AND INSTANT MESSAGING

The discussion in Chapter 4 detailed the intricacies of economic concentration as they may relate to Internet and e-commerce industries. If you found the material interesting you might wish to share this newfound knowledge with a distant friend. Ten years ago, an enthusiastic student might have called that friend on the telephone. However, today the trend is to sign onto the computer and send the friend an e-mail message detailing the "joy of discovery." An e-mail message gets to the destination quickly enough, but it has a serious drawback. E-mail doesn't provide the same interactive experience that a telephone call might offer. A better choice is to use the computer to carry on an electronic **instant message (IM)** conversation with the friend. IM is a software technology that allows two or more persons to carry on a real-time discussion, sending notes to each other that are delivered directly to the computer screen, as soon as they are sent. It is a close cousin to talking on the phone.

To carry on this IM conversation, all parties must be at their computers and logged on to the Internet. Each potential "talker" must know that the others are available. Here is where a list of friends and their Internet identities comes in handy. AOL has a screen window called a Buddy List, where subscribers can type in the names of friends and family members to know when they are online. All that the potential user needs to do is to click on the name and send a message, which pops up on the friend's screen. The friend can then continue the conversation.

Can a subscriber IM all of his or her friends and family this way? The answer is yes if all parties to the conversation are using the same IM system. The answer is no, or not always, if the friends are using a different IM system. IM systems use differing codes and standards. Therefore, they don't always "talk" to one another. To speak between differing systems requires **interoperability**, and the owners of the varying IM systems have not all agreed on a standard set of protocols and codes. Interconnection is technologically possible and valuable to the IM user. If phone companies can interconnect, why can't providers of IM services link up? The answer to that question leads into the subject matter of this chapter, which identifies the nature, purpose, and various forms of entry barriers.

THE CONCEPT OF ENTRY BARRIERS

The economist Joe Bain conducted early research focused on the role entry barriers might play in affecting the structure, conduct, and performance of an industry. To Bain, a **barrier to entry** involved any economic factor that yielded an advantage to "established sellers in an industry over potential entrant sellers, these advantages being reflected in the extent to which established sellers can persistently raise their prices above a competitive level without attracting new firms to enter the industry."[1] In other words, entry barriers are obstacles that allow existing firms to earn economic profits, while keeping potential competition at bay. These same obstacles may also work to make the competitive playing field uneven among firms already in an industry, yielding a persistent, profitable, competitive edge for one firm relative to another.

---

1 Joe S. Bain, *Barriers to New Competition* (Cambridge, MA: Harvard University Press, 1956), p. 3.

Entry Barriers:

A Structural Factor Limiting e-Competition

A curious student might ask what the topic of entry barriers has to do with e-commerce. After all, as was pointed out in the opening chapter, entry onto e-commerce via the Internet is easy. Anyone or any firm can become an e-commerce competitor. However, most existing e-commerce firms still want to protect themselves and their profits against the ravages of competition, from either new or current rivals. This quandary sets up the basic tension that lies at the heart of this chapter's discussion: How can an e-commerce firm, faced with conditions of easy entry, sustain the earning of economic profits over an extended period of time?

Bain and others identified three broad sources of entry-barring obstacles. The first involves **technical barriers to entry** associated with the supply or production of the product. These include (1) absolute cost advantages, (2) economies of scale, (3) economies of scope, and (4) capital cost barriers. The second set of entry barriers is based upon **strategic behavior**. These barriers are artificial in nature, created by the deliberate actions of the firm. This grouping includes (1) product differentiation, (2) the creation of a "credible threat" against entrants, and (3) the maintenance of excess capacity. Lastly, obstacles to entry can be created by **legal or institutional entry barriers**, which are barriers created by government power that either deliberately or inadvertently hinders entry. These barriers include (1) patents or copyrights, and (2) government granted franchises.[2] The following pages investigate the causes and consequences of the technical and strategic barriers, while the examination of the role of patents, copyrights, and government franchises will be the subject matter of Chapters 6 and 7.

TECHNICAL BARRIERS TO ENTRY

Absolute Cost Advantage

An **absolute cost advantage** appears when an existing firm is able to produce and sell the product or service at a lower average cost than any potential entrant or existing firm. This ability allows the holder of the cost advantage to earn a persistent economic profit. It does so by charging a price premium above the holder's average cost, equal to the height of the cost advantage. This situation is shown in Figure 5-1. Compare the height of the long-run per-unit cost line (LAC) for the existing firm with the higher LAC for the potential entrant.[3] The entrant experiences some cost disadvantage relative to the existing firm. For example, the entrant's disadvantage may result from higher resource costs, an inferior sales location, or the fact that it must use a less-efficient production technique. The market demand curve is the negatively sloped line *DD*, located up and to the right. If the existing firm is a monopolist, then Chapter 2 showed that to maximize short-run profits, it would charge the price on the demand curve at the output level

---

2 For an extended list of these and other possible entry barriers, see, William G. Shepard, *The Economics of Industrial Organization*, 4th ed. (Prospect Heights, IL: Waveland Press, 1999), p. 210.

3 Both of the long-run cost curves are assumed to be constant for this example to facilitate the comparison. Given that the average cost is constant, the cost of each extra unit, or marginal cost, is also constant and equal to average cost.

FIGURE 5-1 — Absolute Cost Advantage Barrier

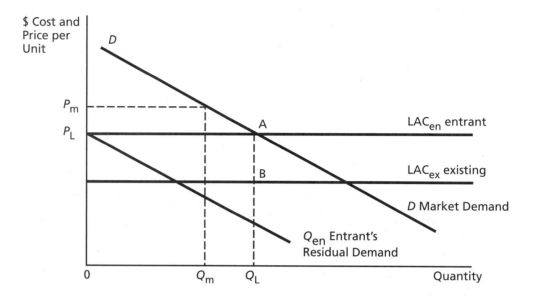

where marginal cost would equal marginal revenue (P_m and Q_m, for example). If the monopoly price yields economic profits in the short-run, it would encourage entry in the long run, if P_m is above the entrant's long run average cost (LAC_{en}). Entry should compete away the economic profits in the long run. Therefore the existing firm may alter its profit goal to one of maximizing a combination of short and long run profits. The revised goal might require the firm to price the product to forestall entry, thereby sustaining monopoly control as long as possible. As such, the monopoly would charge a **limit price** (P_L), which is just equal to the potential entrant's long-run average cost ($P_L = LAC_{en}$).

The purpose of the limit price is to discourage long-run entry in a static market. Entry is discouraged because it splits the market demand between the existing firm and the entrant. If the entrant assumes the existing firm will maintain its Q_L limit price sales level, even in the presence of entry, then the entrant is left with the remaining or residual demand beyond Q_{ex}. To facilitate easy interpretation, the entrant's **residual demand curve** Q_{en} is moved to the left, such that it intersects the vertical axis. It signifies that production will start at unit 1 for the entrant. However, at no output level, except $Q = 0$, is the entrant's price or average revenue (AR) at or above its long-run per-unit production cost (LTC_{en}). Therefore the entrant does not see the potential for profitable entry into the market, even though the existing firm is earning an economic profit per unit equal to the distance AB. In a competitive industry, Bain saw the price premium, AB, as a way of measuring the height of the entry barrier facing the potential entrant.

An Internet Example of an Absolute Cost Advantage

To consider a possible application of this absolute cost barrier within e-commerce, recall that the discussion in Chapter 3 stated the CDMA technology for sending wireless phone messages was created and owned by Qualcomm. At one time the firm produced and sold its own wireless phones using CDMA, while simultaneously licensing the technology to other phone firms for a fee. By having this absolute cost advantage, Qualcomm could either extract economic profits from rival phone producers, or keep them from using the CDMA technology in the wireless market. So why did Qaulcomm choose instead to exit the market for the sale of phones? The answer is that Qualcomm wanted to maximize the value of its technology to itself (i.e., the profits over time), rather than its control over the technology.[4] The firm saw the maximum value was in licensing the CDMA technology and having it become the standard for wireless signal sending. If other phone producers perceived Qualcomm as being in competition with them, they would readily see their competitive disadvantage and switch their technology choice to TDMA or GMS. So to engage in **competition to become the** wireless **standard**, Qualcomm exited the phone market and now licenses its technology to some 75 communications manufacturers worldwide.[5] This broad market penetration might have been unlikely if Qualcomm had enforced its absolute cost advantage and retained exclusive control over the CDMA technology.

Economies of Scale and the Learning Curve

Two mantras of many e-tailers have been "get big fast" and "get the revenues first and work out the cost structure later."[6] Why is there such an emphasis on size? What positive value does size convey? After all, doesn't bigger size mean bigger risk? Why not follow a more conservative policy of "launch and learn"? Start quickly, start small, see the market reaction to your initial offering, and modify your e-commerce product as you grow in measured steps over time.

Part of the reason for the get-big-fast mania in e-commerce may lie in the existence of supply side **economies of scale**. Economies of scale exist when the per-unit cost of production (LAC) declines as the firm increases its production volume or scale of output. Some examples of scale-based cost reductions include the benefits from specialization and division of labor, the use of more efficient technologies, the ability to access more cost-effective national as opposed to regional advertising, and more efficient use of management skills.

The existence and nature of economies of scale can give an existing firm, or a *first mover*, the ability to forestall entry on the part of other firms, shown in Figure 5-2. The long-run average cost curve (LAC) demonstrates a segment of sharp decline in unit cost as output grows up to the point of **minimum efficient scale (MES)**.

At MES, the firm achieves all of the possible scale economies, and beyond this point, costs are assumed to remain constant for additional units of production in this example. *DD* is the market demand curve, which is currently served by the existing firm at P_{ex} and Q_{ex} yielding an economic profit to the firm. However, if entry takes place in response to these profits, the market demand may become evenly divided up between the two firms, with each facing one-half of the market at demand curve *dd*. With *dd*, neither firm can find a price that will cover full unit cost (LAC). The result is that the potential entrant is discouraged from risking actual entry. This conclusion is based upon the perception that it will be unprofitable to share the market, even though the incumbent demonstrates some positive and persistent level of economic profit.

Several important keys to successfully enjoying this entry barrier result from economies of scale. First, the level of demand must be limited to the extent that sharing the market would result in a mutual loss. If the entrant can somehow grow the market, shifting *DD* out to the right, the strategy is less effective. Second, the scale economies must exist over an extended volume of output. If scale economies are quickly exhausted at a low output volume relative to market demand, many firms can exist at a small scale. Lastly, the *cost gradient* must be sufficiently steep to ward off entry. If scale economies are present but minimal as output grows, few penalties faces entrants at a scale less than MES. The conclusion is that a **get-big-fast strategy** is most effective for a market first mover when it can capture most of the market demand, in an industry with substantial,

---

4 This important point is skillfully made by Carl Shapiro and Hal R. Varian in their book, *Information Rules* (Boston: Harvard Business School Press, 1999), pp. 97–98, 198.

5 See **http://www.qualcomm.com** for more on this firm.

6 An interview with Jeff Bezos, CEO of Amazon.com, "The Company Is Not the Stock," *BusinessWeek*, April 30, 2001, pp. 94–96.

FIGURE 5-2   Scale Economies Creating an Entry Barrier

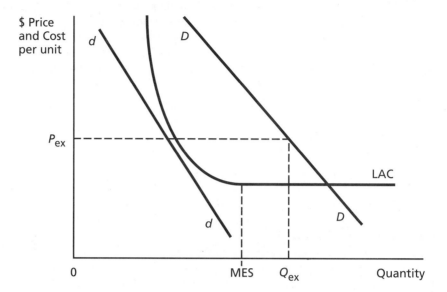

steep scale economies and at a price to the customer that will allow the firm to achieve at least minimum efficient scale.

Another cost phenomenon that could justify getting big fast may be to experience the cost reductions associated with the **learning curve**. As a new process begins, the first few units are usually produced at a high cost per unit. Workers are unfamiliar with their tasks, equipment must be debugged, and the flow of the production process is uneven. In general a lot of trial and error goes on. As the cumulative level of output grows over time, however, worker skills and dexterity improve, shortcuts appear, equipment begins to run smoothly, and flow of the production process is modified to incorporate newly discovered efficiencies. The effect of the learning curve concept is to shift the entire LAC curve downward over time.

e-Commerce Applications of the Scale and Learning Curve Concepts

In e-commerce, order fulfillment, site recognition, and branding are scale elements that may justify the get-big-fast strategy, especially at the B2C level. *Order fulfillment* involves the process of picking, packing, and shipping an order once it has been placed. From a customer service/satisfaction perspective, it is essential to accomplish fulfillment and delivery as quickly and accurately as possible. The fulfillment function also encompasses dealing with the inevitable problem of receiving, handling, restocking, or disposing of product returns from unhappy customers.

For Web-only firms, a large supply scale may appear to be necessary in support of the fulfillment infrastructure and to allow efficient advertising at minimum cost per customer reached. When the product is sold through a virtual as opposed to physical store, the only sales access to customers is via the Web. Therefore, high-volume advertising is essential to familiarize potential buyers with the firm's Web address and product line, along with establishing a brand or quality image. E-commerce firms such as Amazon.com., Webvan, and eToys built large and costly regional distribution centers to carry out fulfillment and as support for their advertising campaigns.[7] The firm must then capture a large enough share of the market to make these centers operate at peak efficiency. It can lower the price enough to attract an efficiency-enhancing level of customers. If the firm's size and

---

7 Being large-scale does not necessarily guarantee Web success or survival. If you doubt this observation, try looking for either Webvan or eToys.

demand are large enough to capture all of the potential scale economies, with prices above the variable costs of production and with a sufficiently large enough share of the market, then it may eventually be successful in making a profit and perhaps keeping others from entering the market as well.

Of course, all is not necessarily lost for the smaller firms. Sam Adams proved to be a successful competitor to Budweiser. Volvo thrives as a car company despite competition from General Motors. A local lumberyard earned its owner a good living located less than five miles from the nearest Home Depot. How do they and thousands of other firms do it? Simple again! They exist or entered into the market following a **niche strategy**. The entrants look for a segment of the market that is not being satisfied by the market leader and then tailor their product, pricing, and promotion strategies to entice the underserved consumers. No firm can sell more products cheaper than Wal-Mart or Home Depot, and yet low price and economies of scale are not the only competitive answers. Service, convenience, upscale image, quality, safety, location, filling customer orders, friendliness, and so on, are other ways to compete. Consumers are not a homogeneous lot. They do not all value the same attributes equally. Any seller who can put together an attractive mix of attributes has the potential to live side-by-side with the low-cost firm. After all, how frequently does the media carry ads lampooning the apparently cavernous, confusing, and time-consuming interiors of any number of "big box" stores. What is true in traditional retailing is true in e-tailing. Niche strategies can be winning strategies.

Economies of Scope

In addition to the efficiencies introduced by economies of scale and the learning curve, another set of efficiencies, when successfully employed by the existing firm, can keep others from either entering the market or diminishing the profits of a market leader. These efficiencies involve the concept of **economies of scope**. In one variant, producers found it is often less costly for the firm to provide multiple products within a single firm rather than splitting the production among several, single-product firms. These scope economies usually arise as the result of having some fixed resource where the productive value cannot be fully exploited by a single activity. Therefore, a second or third product is introduced whose activity will also employ the fixed resource. Telephone poles carry separate wires conveying electricity, telephone, and cable connections. Railroad tracks carry both passenger and freight trains. Colleges use their campus facilities for higher education nine months per year and then rent them out for summer sports or cheerleading camps, corporate meetings, or even to serve as NFL training sites.

Examples of these kinds of scope economies abound in e-commerce. For instance, Amazon.com started life as an inexpensive Internet new bookseller. The Web site hardware and software, along with the fulfillment system, can easily handle more than just books. Therefore, Amazon quickly added CDs and VHS and DVD videos, along with video games, to their list of products. Eventually, they expanded further to offer consumer electronics, photography equipment, tools, hardware, outdoor living products, auctions, and storefront sites for other merchants. They even began to market used books from secondhand book dealers and signed an agreement to handle the Web marketing of toys from Toys "R" Us. Whether offering all of these products at one Web site is a profitable undertaking, guaranteeing long-run survival, is still in doubt. However, it is clear that the proliferation of products at the site is an example of economies of scope.

Ebay, which originally billed itself as "the worlds largest garage sale," is another Web example of a firm enjoying economies of scope. Go to eBay today and the person-to-person *auction* is still there, but the site is also selling products at fixed prices through its subsidiary half.com, and auctioning used cars as well as professional services such as accounting, Web and graphics design, or legal work. Click on their items for sale site, half.com, and the screen shows an array of products that mirror many of the items offered at Amazon. Although person-to-person auctions are still its thing, eBay now earns a substantial part of its revenue from business firms disposing of surplus stock at auction. For example, the amount of IT hardware being auctioned on eBay really accelerated as the asset disposals from the "tech wreck" began to take hold.

Network Externalities in e-Commerce

A second variation of economies of scope involves **network externalities**, which are an important concept for many firms engaged in e-commerce. In economics, the term **externality** refers to a situation in which a normal market transaction between two individuals has either positive or negative third-party consequences. One example of *negative externality*, or spillover cost, is pollution. A pollution externality can arise from the dumping of untreated, production-created wastewater into a river. Water users, located downstream, are forced to spend their own money to clean up the effluent. The example of a lighthouse serves to demonstrate the nature of a *positive externality* or spillover benefit. Once a lighthouse is built, anyone can use the beam at night to warn of danger, or determine her location, regardless of whether she contributed to the construction of the facility.[8]

Networks involve a situation in which diverse consumers, groups, or locations are served by the same connection. Airlines, using the hub-and-spoke system to assemble and transport passengers, are an example of a network. Telephone systems, electricity grids, and assemblages of broadcast TV stations to show programs simultaneously on ABC, CBS, NBC, or Fox, are other examples of networks in the physical world. The Internet is an example of a network in the virtual world.

So how do networks operate to create externalities? Network externalities convey positive benefits on both the supply and the demand sides of the marketplace. Trash hauling is a particularly instructive example in understanding the *supply side benefits* of network externalities. Trash haulers cover specific routes, passing perhaps hundreds of potential residential and commercial stops. Providing service to one more stop is profitable for the hauler given that the stop requires no greater fixed cost and little marginal cost. Therefore, it is to the advantage of each hauler to sign up as many stops as possible on a given route, thereby benefiting from the increased density of demand. Where network externalities are present, competition tends to be unstable and perhaps impossible. It is not unknown for nominally competitive haulers to engage in cartel-like behavior, entering into secret and illegal agreements to divide up a city or residential suburb into noncompeting spheres of monopoly control. Alternatively, they might engage in price discrimination, or charging different customers different prices for the same service, to entice potential users to join the service. Markets where competition is unstable can also lead to the emergence of either a dominant firm or even a monopoly.

The e-commerce firm eBay enjoys strong supply side network economies. It is in eBay's best interest to have every potential auctioneer list products on the eBay Web site. The additional listings both enhance the use of the site and boost profits at almost zero marginal cost. As commercial use of the site grows, eBay is said to be offering special pricing deals to attract high-volume listers. The forces resulting from the supply side network economies helped eBay become the dominant firm in the online auction market, both in the United States and increasingly worldwide.

Demand side network externalities appear when the addition of an extra or marginal network member increases the value of the network for all of the participants. Physical world examples include almost all communications networks, including telephone and fax networks, along with the software network created by the Microsoft PC operating system. When Alexander Graham Bell invented the telephone, his assistant, Thomas A. Watson, had the only other phone, located in the next room. It was useful for summoning Watson

---

8 The lighthouse example also encompasses the **free rider problem**, such that it is difficult to get shippers to pay for construction if they can use the facility for free. Therefore, governments, relaying on taxes levied on all potential users, are the usual builders of lighthouses rather than entrepreneurs relying on markets.

but not for much else. As more phones were hooked up and the first commercial phone exchange system was opened in New Haven, Connecticut, in 1878, the value of the network grew exponentially with the number of installations.[9]

Prior to Microsoft becoming the de facto operating standard in the PC market, desktop computing was an electronic tower of Babel. Desktop computers such as the Apple IIe, TRS-80, Commodore 64, and Altec, each had their own operating system, with unique codes that did not allow for the easy exchange of files among them. Also, printers and other peripherals had to be configured to each operating system. The productivity of the PC was severely restricted, limiting it in most cases to word-processing tasks, as a more advanced form of electronic typewriter.

The growth and acceptance of Microsoft's Disk Operating System (MS-DOS) and later Windows as the common operating system for IBM compatible computers, created a network among its users. As more members joined the network, the greater scope of usage magnified its value. Data and text documents could be shared seamlessly among the community of Windows users. Software programmers, drawn by the potential for increased sales and profits, began to write business utilities and games for the larger number of users in the Windows market. In turn, the larger number of applications programs made being a member of the Windows network even more valuable. Peripherals could be installed almost effortlessly as the plug-and-play technology within Windows encouraged peripheral producers to adopt a Windows standard. Because of these network economies, the Windows operating system became the **de facto standard** for the vast majority of desktop and laptop computers. Today, it would take nothing less than a major upheaval for Microsoft to be dislodged from its current dominant position.[10] Economies of scale and scope, independently and together, create a formidable entry barrier protecting the dominant position of MS-Windows operating system.

In the area of e-commerce, eBay again provides an insightful example of how these demand side network externalities can come into play. Auction listers want to place their products on the sites that will yield the highest price for the item. Generally, that means the site with the most visitors. Conversely, bidders want to visit sites that have the largest number and greatest variety of listings in the hope of getting the item at the lowest possible price. The more listers a site has, the greater is the value of the site to each potential bidder, while the larger the number of potential bidders, the higher the worth of the site to each lister. These bidder and lister forms of demand-based network externalities reinforce one another, jointly working to create the e-commerce powerhouse eBay. Add to them the supply side network externalities, along with the benefits of traditional economies of scale and you can easily see why it will be difficult for any potential rival to dislodge eBay from its dominant position. Other sites, including Yahoo!, uBid.com, and AOL, have auction components. You will often see more items with high minimum bids on these sites, as listers guard against selling the item too cheaply in the absence of a sufficient number of bidders. Of course a preponderance of high minimum bids discourages potential bidders from visiting the site at all. The eBay example shows that entry barriers based upon economies of scale and scope can arise just as easily in the e-commerce world as they can in physical retailing.

---

9 Metcalfe's Law holds that "If there are *n* people in the network and the value of the network to each of them is proportional to the number of other users, then the total value for the network (to all the users) is proportional to $n \times (n - 1) = n^2 - n$. If the value of a network to a single user is \$1 for each other user on the network, then a network of size 10 has a total value of roughly \$100. In contrast, a network of size 100 has a total value of roughly \$10,000. A tenfold increase in the size of the network leads to a hundredfold increase in its value." Shapiro and Varian, *Information Rules*, (Boston: Harvard Business School Press, 1999), p. 184.

10 This choice-based acceptance by the market of MS-Windows as the de facto standard conveyed a great deal of power and wealth to Microsoft. The potential for a radical change in technology serves as a external source of disruptive change, which is constantly threatening Microsoft's operating system dominance. Also, the firm's use and possible abuse of that dominance has attracted a lot of competitive and regulatory attention. More of that topic is discussed in Chapter 9.

Capital Cost Barriers

Even though the act of *physical entry* into e-commerce by setting up a Web site is easy, *effective entry*, which is entry at sufficient scale and profit to justify the risks, is not. Effective entry requires financial backing, or capital as it is called on Wall Street.[11] The "tech wreck" of 2001–2002 led to the demise of more than 500 fledgling e-commerce sites, with a considerable loss of capital. Financial markets underestimated exactly how risky this type of venture really was. This lesson has not been lost on the venture capitalists who provided the early financing for this kind of risky investment. From 1996 to 2000, the capital spigot was wide open for dot-coms. The role of venture capital and IPOs as they relate to e-commerce is examined in Chapter 14, but it seems apparent for now and the foreseeable future that the availability of funds for new e-commerce start-ups is going to be severely restricted, if in fact it is available at all. Here the maxim "once bitten, twice shy" comes into play.

What the withdrawal of capital does is to create another form of entry barrier, forestalling the appearance of new firms, while protecting the position of those already within an industry. Existing firms will not necessarily have an easy time acquiring more funds now. However, as going concerns they face a lowered threat of entry (protection from higher entry barriers) if they can hang on. Finance professionals often argue the perfectly competitive nature of capital markets, with funds being freely available to any and all borrowers on a risk-adjusted basis. The track record of dot-com failure, combined with the *uncertainty* as opposed to *risk* associated with the application of Web technology to individual e-commerce efforts, creates a unique barrier for new e-commerce entrants. Investors can insure or hedge against risk because, while the exact outcome isn't known, the range of outcomes and their probabilities *are* known. With uncertainty, either the range of outcomes and/or their probabilities of occurrence are unknown. Loans and equity capital investments will be extended only at relatively higher costs to tomorrow's entrants as opposed to firms already in the marketplace. In some instances, investors in existing dot-com firms may decide to extend additional rounds of financing to weak firms at terms they would not grant to new entrants. They would do this in the hope of seeing the existing firm become profitable, thereby protecting their original investment. Of course, in doing so, they encounter the danger of throwing good money after bad. Remember also, that e-commerce firms potentially face steep scale economies that require high current fixed costs to be spread over a large volume of future users, triggering low variable costs. As a result, the more expensive capital charges for tomorrow's entrants will reflect a combination of impediments, including the following:

1. The heightened investment risks from large, up-front capital costs
2. The recent history of dot-com failures
3. The risks normally associated with being small, start-up entrants
4. An uncertainty premium

Is it any wonder that e-commerce start-ups will find the financing of their entry into the market that much more difficult, now and in the future?

STRATEGIC BARRIERS TO ENTRY

Product Differentiation

Recall that strategic entry barriers are primarily an artificial creation. Existing firms erect strategic barriers as a means of protecting their market position and profits from being challenged by new or existing firms. One form of strategic barrier is **product differentiation**, which involves building a distinction, either real or imaginary, in the

---

11 The term capital in economics is often confused with its usage in finance. In finance capital means money, while in economics it refers to the physical resources, made by humans, that go into the production process. Although this text focuses on economics, it will adopt the finance interpretation for the term capital in this section.

mind of the consumer, between your product and the product produced by your actual or potential rivals. The purpose is to reduce the degree of perceived substitutability, rendering your product unique up to the point of establishing a monopoly position. This process will have the effect in the market of increasing the slope of the demand curve facing the firm, rendering it relatively less price elastic, or even inelastic. When demand is price inelastic, the firm is able to raise the product's price without losing a disproportionately large number of customers. Differentiation can be achieved by any number of means, including variations in product quality, packaging, design, warranties, reputation, advertising, location, brand name, the use of logos, and so on.

These distinguishing characteristics help to create an entry barrier for several reasons. First, no other firm is allowed to use the firm's brand name or logo. If the firm is lucky enough to have the product's brand name become synonymous with that of the generic item, then this confusion will inhibit the ability for others to enter and attract customers. For example, if a person has a cold, he may go to buy a box of Kleenex to wipe his nose. Only Kimberly-Clark can sell a Kleenex brand product. Everyone else offers just facial tissues. On a hot day a consumer may want to cool off by drinking a Coke, and only Coca-Cola can sell that product. Competitors quench the buyer's thirst with a Pepsi, 7-Up, or Dr. Pepper. Lastly, when a person has an injury that needs covering, she may look for a BAND-AID, which is available only from Johnson & Johnson. Everyone else sells adhesive bandages. Tabasco, Xerox, Brillo, and A-1 provide other examples where the brand name of a product has become synonymous with the generic product. For some users, the name Yahoo! may have become synonymous with that of the search process in e-commerce. Therefore, when they need a search engine they type in the URL Yahoo and begin the information hunt. "Do you Yahoo"?

No one can use the logo of five interlocking Olympic rings to sell merchandise unless authorized by the International Olympic Committee. No one, except Ralph Lauren, can place the logo of a mallet-wielding rider astride a polo pony on the upper front of his shirts.[12] However, you can locate an alligator in the same spot, as does Izod. No other sports affiliation can call itself Major League Baseball or the National Football League. These are brand names that are carefully developed and guarded. They are intended to convey a unique level of professional performance and to help identify any potential entrant as not living up to that standard. Remember the XFL? In e-commerce, one of the best-known logos was the sock puppet representing pets.com. Unfortunately even popular logos can't keep bad business models from going "belly up."

Brand Proliferation

Another method of using product differentiation to preclude entry involves the concept of **brand proliferation**. Here the firm "stuffs the product space" with as many variations on the central product as possible. This process is designed to preclude rivals from finding an attribute combination that will attract consumers for a new product and allow them to achieve a toehold. In the 1970s the U.S. Antitrust Division unsuccessfully accused the cereal manufacturers, including Post, General Mills, and Kellogg's, of pursuing brand proliferation by adding sugar, honey, fruit, or vitamins to the half dozen basic forms of breakfast cereals. A specific example of brand proliferation in e-commerce is not readily available. Some specialty clothing firms such as Victoria's Secret and J.Crew might be "stuffing the distribution space" using a combination of physical stores, outlets, catalogs, and Web sites to achieve somewhat the same result. For an entrant to compete successfully against these existing apparel firms, it might have to at least consider bearing the expense of opening up each of these distribution channels simultaneously. This requirement could raise the cost of entry and serve as a barrier to the appearance of new competition.

---

12 Even the U.S. Polo Association is barred from using the term polo and using some representation of a polo rider as its logo. "In Polo (the Players) v. Polo (the Shirt), Lauren Is in the Lead," *The New York Times*, July 26, 2001, p. D2.

Establishing a Credible Threat

Sometimes a firm may keep others from entering if it can establish a reputation as a vicious and nasty competitor. All entry efforts pose some degree of risk, while at the same time, the markets being entered have only a finite level of profits. If, apart from the normal challenges of entry, a potential entrant also must face an existing rival with the personality and behavior record of a pit bull, it may conclude that the potential risks aren't worth the uncertain gain. Therefore, in the face of a **credible threat** it walks away from entry into an otherwise inviting market and seeks out an easier challenge. By behaving in this manner, the existing firm created a strategic entry barrier in the form of a credible threat. It promised to act in such an unreasonable manner that it appears willing to experience its own financial losses or physical demise in launching an all out attack on the potential entrant.

Some major airline carriers have been accused of this kind of behavior in response to entry on the part of low-price regional competitors. Specifically, American Airlines was charged by the U.S. Department of Justice with using "predatory" tactics designed to drive three small, low-cost airlines out of the Dallas-Fort Worth International Airport, where American maintains a large hub operation. American allegedly lowered prices and flooded the market with additional flights as a way of disciplining the competitors and forcing them out of business. When the rivals departed or otherwise capitulated, American raised prices back to or higher than the original level and scaled back the number of flights.

The case was dismissed in April 2001. In his decision, Judge Martin noted, "There is no doubt that American may be a difficult, vigorous, and even brutal competitor. But here it engaged only in bare, but not brass, knuckle competition."[13] The dismissal reaffirmed the view that competitive prices as low as average variable cost are justifiable and immune from antitrust attack. This conclusion may unleash a torrent of otherwise vicious behavior in markets like the airline industry that have high fixed costs in combination with low variable costs.[14] Who would want to enter such a market if they were to face a "brutal competitor" such as American Airlines, which had posed a credible threat?

Recollect that most e-commerce markets fit this cost description. Their high fixed costs provide the ability to serve a marginal customer at little or no additional cost. At some point, when the current shakeout among e-commerce firms subsides, the number of surviving suppliers in each e-commerce market may decline to a core of one to three profitable firms. Then, entry with the intent of competing directly with the market leaders could become exceedingly difficult. The dominant firm(s) could temporarily cut prices, ramp up advertising campaigns, or create attractive bundles of products that would overwhelm the entrant. Evidence of this kind of behavior, or any threats to react in this manner, might be enough to scare away the financial support needed by the potential entrant.

Maintaining Excess Capacity

One interesting variant on the "credible threat" strategy is the tactic of **maintaining excess capacity** as a deterrent against entry. This strategy has a long, if somewhat checkered, history in antitrust enforcement, going back to the Supreme Court's Alcoa monopolization case in 1945.[15] Here, the lead jurist, Judge Learned Hand noted, "It was not inevitable that it (Alcoa) should always anticipate increases in the demand for ingot and be prepared to supply them. Nothing compelled it to keep doubling and redoubling its capacity before others entered the field. It insists that it never excluded competitors; but we can think of no more effective exclusion than progressively to embrace each new

---

13 "American Airlines Is the Winner in a U.S. Antitrust Case," *The New York Times*, April 28, 2001, p. C1.

14 "Predatory Pricing: Cleared for Takeoff," *BusinessWeek*, May 14, 2001, p. 50.

15 *U.S. v. Aluminum Company of America*, 148 F.2d 416 (2d Cir. 1945). Because the U.S. Supreme Court could not secure a quorum of judges to hear the case, it was sent to the 2nd Circuit Court of Appeals for a final decision.

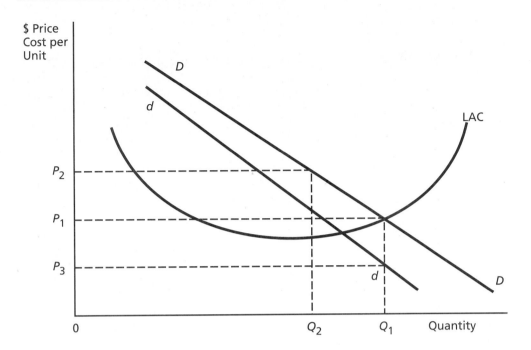

opportunity as it opened, and to face every new comer with new capacity already geared into a great organization."[16]

The economist Michael Spence later provided a theoretical explanation for the effectiveness of this preemptive behavior.[17] As shown in Figure 5-3, Spence started with the assumption that the existing firm builds output capacity beyond its current needs and up to the point Q_1, where price just equals long-run average cost (P_1=LAC). It can then restrict its current output and raise price above the competitive level to, say, P_2 and Q_2, creating economic profits, without encouraging entry. The potential entrant is drawn by the economic profits, but entry will divide up the market yielding a *dd* level of demand to each firm. However, the potential entrant will also see the unused capacity and realize that if it enters, the existing firm will raise output to its maximum capacity. This added output, when combined with the new production of the entrant, will cause the price to fall below LAC to at least P_3, creating losses for both firms. This credible entry-deterring threat arises because the existing firm has already made the capital investment. Given a reputation as a vicious competitor, it has *less to lose* by carrying out the threatened action. Conversely, the entrant has yet to make its investment and therefore has *more to lose*. If it enters, it faces a mutually destructive price war that would jeopardize the ability to recoup its investment or earn a return on its committed resources. Therefore, it backs away and looks for an easier target to challenge.

Although e-commerce is still in the shakeout stage, the original philosophy of "get big fast" makes even more strategic sense given the entry-deterring potential of excess capacity. The economies of scale discussion demonstrated the rationale for a quick expansion to the low-cost volume of production. Why not build at an even bigger scale than the firm might need in the foreseeable future if the added capacity gave it protection against potential entrants? Excess capacity would allow the firm to pounce immediately upon

---

16 Ibid.

17 Michael A. Spence, "Entry, Capacity, Investment and Oligopolistic Pricing," *Bell Journal of Economics* 8 (Autumn 1977), pp. 534–544.

every increase in demand, leaving the perception of no profitable unfulfilled opportunities for the entrant. Size in many ways does indeed convey the potential for entry-deterring advantages. All of this entry-deterring strategy assumes that the existing firm, as big as it is, can find a profitable level of demand and scale of output.

REEXAMINING AOL'S INSTANT MESSAGING SYSTEM

How does this discussion of entry barriers assist in understanding the strategy behind AOL's instant messaging system (AIM)? What advantage, if any, does AIM convey to AOL? Recall that AOL is the largest ISP with 26.1 million subscribers in the United States and 34.4 million worldwide. Both AIM and the Buddy List are totally internal to AOL and are proprietary systems. It means that they are wholly owned and available exclusively to AOL subscribers or others at the discretion of AOL. Many AOL subscribers regard this feature as one of the biggest benefits of membership. Now reflect for a moment on the fact that AIM is a form of communications network. As such, it demonstrates all of the economies of scope characteristics, including the network externalities already noted. AIM and the Buddy List have value to subscribers only if their "buddies" are on the same IM system. If they are, then the more buddies that subscribe, the more valuable the system becomes to each individual subscriber, and the more that each subscriber is willing to pay to belong.[18] This point is not lost on AOL! It also helps to explain why IM interoperability has been slow in coming.[19]

As of August 2001, AOL's three versions of instant messaging had a total of 54.7 million users, with the free AIM Web version attracting 27.3 million users, the AOL subscriber service at 19.9 million, and ICQ at 7.5 million users.[20] AIM is a stand-alone program that users can load onto any computer for free. It allows individual access to the subscriber IM service over a marginally slower Internet, as opposed to an internal, connection. Therefore, AOL subscribers are not cut off from IM if they happen to be away from their AOL connections at work, school, or an Internet café. Also, individual nonsubscribers can converse using AIM as well. The patrons of all three AOL IM services account for approximately 60 percent of all IM users. MSN's Messenger is second with 19.9 million users and Yahoo's Messenger has 13.5 million users. The current market involves mainly the exchange of personal conversations, but the expectation is that the next big explosion in IM traffic will be at the corporate level. Therefore, from an efficiency perspective, the introduction of **universal interoperability standards** is essential.

Why does AOL jealously guard this proprietary system? The answer is twofold. First, it helps AOL attract new paying customers. After all, subscribers want to be where their buddies are, and they want to know when their buddies are online in order to IM them. Second, the proprietary system raises a barrier to new entrants by creating a **lock-in effect** that deters customers from transferring to another ISP. Even if another ISP, such as ATTWorldNet, comes along with a lower-priced service, including IM, chat rooms, and Internet access, who cares? The **customer switching costs** associated with dropping AOL and signing up with ATTWorldNet could be substantial. The switchers will lose their AOL e-mail addresses, their buddy lists, their direct connections to IM, and the company of the millions of other potential AOL participants in various AOL chat rooms. Would teenage subscribers really want to chat with the subscribers to ATTWorldNet?

---

18 This point appears to have been missed by Shapiro and Varian, who state that ISPs are a high-tech industry that "does not experience large network effects." "The availability of standardized protocols or menus/browsers, e-mail, and chat removed the advantage of being a larger ISP and led to the creation of thousands of smaller providers." *Information Rules*, pp. 186–187.

19 Denise Caruso, "Digital Commerce, The battle over instant messaging is another case of a company clinging to customers like flypaper," *The New York Times*, August 2, 1999, p. C4.

20 Julia Angwin, "AOL to Test Compatible Instant Messaging," *The Wall Street Journal*, August 15, 2001, p. B5.

Despite its protestations to the contrary, AOL has been the biggest obstacle to the adoption of universal interoperability standards leading to an open IM system. MSN, ATTWorldNet, and some 40 other firms supplying IM systems are more than willing to develop a standard for exchanging IM transmissions. Only AOL says "yes, but go slow," and understandably so. In fact, it has worked diligently to keep outside suppliers of rival IM systems from accessing AIM en masse by writing code to interconnect with AIM through Instant Messenger.[21] Individual connection is fine according to AOL, but a mass link-up with subscribers at MSN, for example, is not. Universal interoperability would remove one strong reason for staying with AOL as opposed to subscribing to a cheaper service. In fairness to AOL, they cite the protection of their customers' privacy and security as the basic reasons for blocking interconnection with other IM systems. They fear that open access will result in AOL IM users being bombarded with advertising or having their e-mail addresses sold.

AOL faces a regulatory challenge to keeping AIM and the Buddy List proprietary. When the Federal Communications Commission (FCC) approved the merger of AOL with Time-Warner, it did not order the immediate opening up of the AOL IM system. Rather, the FCC introduced an **advanced-services rule**, which said that before additional capabilities were added to AIM, AOL must make its system accessible to other IM services.[22] Providing video clips of new movies or sample music bytes through AIM could prove to be a valuable way for AOL to leverage its Time-Warner entertainment content properties. Look for the profit motive to compel AOL to more forward in the development of interoperability standards. Just how much of its AIM treasure will AOL give away? Will it make self-serving choices, selecting the interoperability standard, and what will be the degree or quality of the interconnections? Stay tuned for the next round of the IM economic strategy saga.

The Question of AOL and Market Power

Recall a question that was asked in Chapter 4: Does AOL have market power? Certainly, the concentration data showed that they possessed a substantial share of the market. Could either an existing firm or a new entrant pose a potential challenge to AOL's market dominance? Looking at the concentration data alone did not provide enough information to conclusively answer that question. The numbers in isolation were insufficient to offer an explanation as to how AOL achieved its dominance, or how it was being maintained. The discussion of entry barriers helped to clarify the picture a bit. AOL was an early mover that created attractive product differentiation and sufficient scale to allow for both a low-cost operation as well as network externalities. It capitalized on these externalities through its proprietary control over an IM system that binds millions of users to AOL's communications system. New users are attracted to AOL's broad range of services including IM, because AOL offers the potential for contact with the largest number of other users. Once on board, subscribers become locked in, because customer-switching costs raise a potentially significant obstacle to leaving AOL for another ISP.[23]

If reliable, flat rate, Internet interconnection is all that the subscriber wants, then that service is available at many competing ISPs, at a much lower monthly charge. If the subscriber seeks additional value added services associated with belonging to the largest community of ISP users, then AOL provided them with a related product that is difficult to

21 Jason Blair, "On Internet, David-and-Goliath Battle Over Instant Messages," *The New York Times*, June 24, 2000, p. B3.

22 The FCC gave AOL three options: (1) open its AIM system to at least one rival IM provider before introducing any advance services and two more within six months of introducing the services, (2) accept an industry-approved standard for open IM access, or (3) prove that open access is not in the public interest.   Stephen Labaton, "F.C.C. Approves AOL-Time Warner Deal, With Conditions," *The New York Times*, January 12, 2001, p. C1.

23 John Schwartz, "The Land of Monopolies," *The New York Times*, July 1, 2001, p. WK-3.

acquire from competing ISPs. As the reach of AOL grows, it may be able in the future to exercise its market power more boldly in terms of extracting higher prices for its stable of products. For now at least, the package of product differentiation and network externalities creates a barrier to new firms that want to challenge AOL, and limits the likelihood of AOL losing customers to other existing services.

SUMMARY AND PROSPECTS

The chapter began by highlighting the tension between easy e-commerce entry on the one hand and the desire on the part of existing firms to create persistent profits on the other. The discussion revealed that in the physical world, firms can call upon numerous techniques to forestall entry. Some are technical and reflect the nature of the production process, the market, or the characteristics of the product. Others are strategic and result from existing firms creating obstacles or hurdles that rivals must overcome. Technical barriers, especially economies of scale and scope, appear to have multiple areas of application in e-commerce. The instances of strategic barriers at the e-commerce level are less obvious, at least at present. It may well be because of the relative newness of the enterprises. As e-commerce outlives the present turmoil and establishes itself as a potent sales force in certain markets, look for the reduced number of survivors to at least attempt to develop strategic barriers that fit their own unique circumstances. Remember AOL and the proprietary IM system. It is there for a strategic reason and is unlikely to be surrendered without a fight. Economic history and the imperatives of the market process indicate that others will try to do the same.

KEY TERMS AND CONCEPTS

absolute cost advantage	learning curve
advanced-services rule	legal or institutional entry barriers
barriers to entry	limit pricing
brand proliferation	lock-in effect
competition to become the standard	maintaining excess capacity
credible threat	minimum efficient scale (MES)
customer switching costs	network externalities
de facto operating standard	networks
economies of scale	niche strategy
economies of scope	potential competition
externality	product differentiation
free-rider problem	residual demand curve
get-big-fast strategy	strategic behavior
instant message (IM)	technical barriers to entry
interoperability	universal interoperability standards

DISCUSSION AND REVIEW QUESTIONS

1. Distinguish between the origin and consequences of structural versus strategic entry barriers. Which of the two would appear to be the most harmful to economic efficiency and competition? Why?
2. Review the discussion of absolute cost advantage and the information in Figure 5-1. Explain why a dominant firm may choose to keep its price at the monopoly level P_m and attract entry rather than establish the limit price P_L and possibly preclude entry.
3. Why did Qualcomm elect not to exercise its absolute cost advantage in the cell phone market? Was this decision efficient and rational? Why?

4. Identify the nature of the get-big-fast strategy that was followed by a number of prominent dot-com firms. Why might this strategy be economically rational? What events or conditions might render the strategy as a complete economic failure?

5. What are network externalities? How can they affect the structure and competitive behavior of certain e-commerce industries?

6. Some philosophers say that "timing is everything." How does this observation contribute to an understanding of the capital cost barriers faced by today's new e-commerce start-up firms?

7. Explain the nature of the tension that exists in e-commerce between easy entry and persistent profits. How can product differentiation and the creation of a credible threat work to resolve this tension?

8. How has AOL used its proprietary IM technology to establish and sustain its profitability and position as the leading ISP?

9. How do customer lock-in and customer switching costs work to limit challenges to the dominant position of AOL?

10. Does AOL have market power? Why?

WEB EXERCISES

1. Check out the Web site **http://www.pbs.org/newshour/media/dotcom/index.html** and learn the identity of the latest firms to face the threat of economic extinction.

2. Link to the Internet and e-commerce survey data firm Jupiter Media Metrix (JMM) at **http://netratings.com/**. Call up their list of the top 25 U.S. Internet properties listed in terms of the number of unique monthly visitors. Identify the firms in the top 10 places on the list and see whether you can identify how and why they achieved and maintained this position using the concepts developed in this chapter.

3. At the **http://www.jmm.com/** site, call up their industry projections and focus on the data for anticipated broadband growth over the period 1999-2006. If this technology shift holds true, how might it affect the market position and power of AOL, which is primarily a dial-up ISP?

4. At the JMM site, call up their data for online advertising indicators. How do AOL, and MSN compare in terms of the number of impressions for Web sites hosting ads? Do you find this numerical disparity surprising? Why might this wide disparity exist?

CHAPTER

6

Introductory Case

AMAZON.COM: ONE-CLICK ORDERING VERSUS TWO

Some customers who previously purchased books via the Internet may notice subtle, but potentially significant, differences associated with the e-commerce act of buying a book at the Amazon.com site compared to other Web booksellers. To experience this difference, type in the URL for Amazon.com. Any customer who has been to Amazon before and bought an item, or otherwise gave them some information, such as name, credit card number, or shopping preferences, is automatically remembered by the Web site. Amazon.com recognizes visitors by name and provides a personalized greeting. It may also list some suggested purchases on the opening screen that are similar to one or more of the items purchased during the last visit at the Amazon site. Smart people, these Amazon.com marketers! Of course, this incredible memory all has to do with **cookies**—not the kind baked by the Keebler elves, but the kind that Web sites place on a computer as part of customer's visit. Cookies are digital identifiers triggered when the computer revisits the site; they help to let Amazon know who you are. The topic of "good cookies versus bad cookies" is an important part of the discussion concerning Internet privacy and security in Chapter 18.

Here, though, we are about some serious business: we want to buy a book. Let's look for a copy of *The Grapes of Wrath* by John Steinbeck. It is one of the great pieces of American literature, detailing the economic and social hardships of the Great Depression. The tale is told through the eyes of the Joad family, whose travels are documented after they are displaced from their Oklahoma farm during the Dustbowl days of the 1930s. Type in the title and up pops a list of hardcover and paperback, as well as new and used, editions that are available. Select the first available hardcover edition, and add it to the shopping cart. If it is the only item you wish to purchase, you have the option of clicking on the Proceed to Checkout button to access Amazon.com's speedy **one-click ordering** and checkout system. It combines the use of a password with the previously obtained information to save as much time and typing as possible to complete the order and speed customers on their way.

Now let's try the same thing at an Amazon.com competitor, Barnes&Noble.com (BN). Type in its URL. Next, type in the book title in the keyword area and click on search. Up pops a listing of copies. Add the first hardcover edition to the shopping cart and click on Checkout. Notice that something slightly different happens next at BN, as opposed to Amazon. The BN home screen takes you to another screen containing your shopping cart, which lists all of your purchases and may offer some helpful suggestions. You must click again on Checkout Now to trigger the actual checkout process.

What's the big difference, one click or two? The customer wanted the book, and perhaps the information on the shopping cart page at BN had something useful to say. Frequently, in the past, this page told potential customers that BN was running a special. For example, if a second book were purchased, BN would ship both for free. The difference in the checkout process is subtle, but it is of such potential importance to Amazon.com that it patented the one-click process and defended that patent vigorously.[1] Herein lies the

---

1 Barnes&Noble.com raised a legal challenge to Amazon.com's patent, which gives them exclusive control over the one-click shopping technology. Carol King, "Court Hands Barnes&Noble.com a Legal Victory," available at **http://www.atnewyork.com/news/article.php/589701**.

Legal/Institutional Entry Barriers:

Patents, Copyrights, and Government Franchises

subject matter of this chapter. What is a patent and how does the protection that it affords differ from a copyright or trademark, or the rights granted by a government franchise? What role do these tools play in the topic of e-commerce? How can these legal and institutional tools be used to differentiate a product, or to convey a distinct advantage to a firm that is already in an industry, or serve as a barrier to the entry of new firms?

THE BASICS OF LEGAL/INSTITUTIONAL BARRIERS TO ENTRY

Patents and the Patent System

Legal/institutional entry barriers are created by various levels of government and can lead to monopoly control over a specific piece of potentially valuable "property." These barriers may arise in any of three guises, including patents, copyrights, or government-granted franchises. Patents and copyrights have a prominent place in U.S. history. The framers of the U.S. Constitution felt so strongly about the importance of encouraging and protecting creativity that they specifically designated to Congress the power "To promote the Progress of Science and useful Arts, by securing for limited Times to Authors and Inventors the exclusive Right to their respective Writings and Discoveries."[2] **Patents** are a way to achieve this goal and are granted by the U.S. Patent and Trademark Office. They provide protection for inventions including machines, products, and processes, with the process component having been interpreted to include **methods of doing business**. This interpretation presents numerous potential problems as the techniques of patent approval and protection are applied to e-commerce activity.

In 1995, the United States changed the way it calculates the **legal life of a patent**, going from the former 17 years after the *date of issuance* of the patent to the current 20 years from the U.S. *filing date* for the patent. Existing patents can be renewed on the basis of the holder making a further advance based upon the technology within the original patent. For many years, Polaroid was able to extend its monopoly control over the instant developing picture market in this fashion.

In order for the Patent Office to approve a patent, it must fulfill three **patent criteria**. First, the proposed invention must be *useful*. It can't be just a theoretical proposition. Second, the invention must be *novel*. It must be something original, that no one has thought of or done before. This criterion usually involves a lengthy search to establish the **prior art** in the area of the patent. Lastly, the invention must be *unobvious* to "a person having ordinary skill in the art to which said subject matter pertains."[3] In this area, questions regarding the validity of a patent application can arise, because what may be unobvious to one may be plainly obvious to another.

---

2 U.S. Constitution, Art. I, Sect. 8.

3 Quotation available at **http://www.patents.com**.

The Interaction of Economics and Patents

In economics, existing knowledge is regarded as a **public good**. Subsequent to initial discovery, it is most efficient to make information available to everyone at zero additional cost. After all, as the old adage goes, keeping information secret or otherwise unavailable would be an inefficient use of resources. It would require potential users to spend the time and effort to "reinvent the wheel" each time someone need to use the technology. If information, once discovered, is best made freely available to all, how does society motivate the inventor to spend the time and take the risks associated with the process of creation? After all, not all inventive efforts are a success. Here is where the patent system comes into play. It assumes that new ideas or technologies must be nurtured, protected, and induced. It also assumes that the actions of inventors respond most strongly to the profit motive, such that gains in the form of potential monopoly rewards are needed to set in motion the creative juices of inventors. Of course these assumptions ignore the fact that many of the most useful inventions, including penicillin and key elements of the Internet, were developed in the name of scientific research or simple inquiry, without the stimulus of monetary reward.[4]

From an economic perspective, any firm that applies for a patent is entering into a **Faustian bargain**, which conveys both a benefit and a burden.[5] On the one hand, the firm is exchanging information that it currently holds in the form of a **trade secret**, which might be stolen or copied at any time, for the *benefit* of government-sanctioned protection that can last as long as 20 years. To make the patent as defendable as possible, the firm must spell out, in great detail, all of the intricacies of the invention being patented. The *burden* appears at the end of 20 years when, as the patent protection expires, anyone is free to use the information as he sees fit, without compensating the original patent holder.[6]

The patent system is not necessarily an unquestionable economic benefit to society, however. First, the 20 years of monopoly control may do more harm to the forces of creativity and innovation than can be overcome by the social good resulting from the broad dispersal of information. Competition is a powerful force and patents stifle competition for a long period of time. The absence of competition may choke off alternative research avenues. If the patent holder can achieve scale economies prior to the termination of the patent, it may develop such a market position that it becomes highly invulnerable to competition, even without the patent. Alcoa, the giant aluminum firm, experienced this kind of size-based protection subsequent to the expiration of its bauxite processing patents. Second, the potential rewards resulting from a patent may be so great that it stimulates wasteful **racing behavior** among inventors or possible patent holders. Only one firm can hold the patent and reap the rewards, but several firms may spend resources, in an extravagant manner, to become the successful patent holder. The inventor who wins the patent succeeds, while the quest by the others fails and they fade back into the shadows along with Elijah Gray, who also invented a telephone device and appeared at the Patent Office just hours after Bell filed his application for the telephone.

---

4 Recall the discussion in Chapter 3 of the contributions of Tim Berners-Lee. How rich might he be today if he had patented the technology of the Web? It was not a mistake or oversight by Berners-Lee, but a conscious decision to keep the Web open for the free flow of information. It is a goal he continues to champion today.

5 James Gleick, "Patently Absurd," *The New York Times Magazine*, March 12, 2000, p. 44. Faust was the character who sold his soul to the devil in exchange for the knowledge of all things in the play *Faust: A Tragedy*, by Johann Wolfgan von Goethe.

6 Pharmaceutical firms must deal with this issue as rival labs make generic versions of the branded, but no longer patent-protected, prescription drugs. In turn, the brand-name drug companies have been using tactics of dubious legality to prolong their monopoly control. See Robert Pear, "Drug Makers' Generic Tactics Criticized," *The New York Times*, April 24, 2002, p. C6.

Copyrights Protect Intellectual Property

The U.S. government also carries out its mandate to promote and protect the creative efforts of its citizens through the issuance of **copyrights**.[7] Copyrights focus on protecting the **intellectual property** created by authors, composers, photographers, filmmakers, and writers. Most books (including this one), films, music (including performances by artists or in sheet composition form), photography stills, trademarks, graphic arts, architectural designs, computer code, as well as other forms of creative effort may secure copyright protection. This protection can last as long as the life of the author plus 50 years, or up to 100 years from the date of creation. Note that the length of copyright protection is substantially in excess of the 20-year protection granted to an inventor by a patent.[8] The U.S. Copyright Office, a service unit of the Library of Congress, assists in the administration of copyright laws and the registration of copyright claims.

Once a copyright is registered, the owner has the exclusive right to perform, distribute, reproduce, display, or license the work. Therefore, the holder may require permission to be granted or payment made before any other person may make use of the copyrighted work. The owner also receives the exclusive right to produce or license derivatives of his or her work.[9] Limited exceptions to this exclusivity exist in the form of the **fair use doctrine**.[10] This exception allows for such things as properly attributed quotes, book reviews, teaching, scholarship, and research. It includes certain uses of a copyrighted piece, such as a music CD held by a rightful owner who purchased the work from the copyright holder. The combination of the digital age and the widespread use of the Internet make it difficult for copyright holders to protect their work from illegal duplication and distribution. This conflict between copyright protection and the illegal digital reproduction and distribution of the material is the topic for discussion in Chapter 7.

Barriers Created by Government Franchises

The third source of legal/institutional barriers arises from the granting of exclusive franchises by government. Instances of the issuance of **government franchises** are few in number in e-commerce, but do appear in one important area, that of cable TV franchises. Over the years, local governments awarded monopoly franchises for the building of local cable TV systems. Originally, cable or community antennae TV (CATV) was intended to bring more and stronger television signals to rural areas that were far from the signal transmission sites of the broadcast television stations. Local communities were told that the limited household density, along with the cost of providing the infrastructure, would require a monopoly grant to encourage firms to enter the market and sign up all of the interested customers. After all, a local cable system is just another form of communications network. It is capable of experiencing the kinds of network externalities discussed in Chapter 5 and creating a market where competitive stability is unlikely. Given the lure of a monopoly franchise, thousands of small, independent, local cable TV firms sprang up across the nation, attracted by the potential for economic profit.

However, with the introduction of original programming such as HBO, ESPN, MTV, and CNN, cable TV connections became attractive to all TV owners regardless of

---

7 The U.S. Copyright Act, 17 U.S.C. sec. 101-810.

8 A detailed survey of copyright law can be found at **http://www.law.cornell.edu/topics/copyright. html**.

9 This clause created a legal tension when author Alice Randall tried to publish a parody of Margaret Mitchell's classic Civil War novel *Gone With the Wind*. In 2001, the 11th U.S. Circuit Court of Appeals granted Randall permission to publish her book, entitled *The Wind Done Gone*. The Court viewed the work as political parody that was protected by the First Amendment, which overrode the intellectual property protection provided by the copyright law. See David D. Kirkpatrick, "Mitchell Estate Settles "Gone With the Wind" Suit," *The New York Times*, May 10, 2002, p. C6, and available at **http://www.hollandsentinel.com/stories/052601/new_0526010024.shtml**.

10 The U.S. Copyright Act, 17 U.S.C, sec. 107.

the strength of the local broadcast signal. Today, approximately two-thirds of U.S. homes are cable TV subscribers. The latest trend in cable TV market structure has been consolidation such that "the top seven cable operators—AT&T, AOL Time Warner, Comcast, Charter, Cox, Adelphia, and Cablevision—now control more than 80 percent of the nation's subscribers."[11] Giant cable distributors now square off against giant content providers such as Walt Disney, Viacom, and AOL Time Warner in a struggle over who carries what programming and on what terms. More detailed discussion of this conflict appears in Chapter 8, which deals with mergers and the convergence of television and computers, with the Internet to form an expanded e-commerce entertainment system. Recall from the discussion in Chapter 3 that one of the major obstacles to expanded e-commerce and the utilization of the imbedded fiber-optic capacity is the last-mile problem. The build-out of the cable system as a collection of local monopolies gives this technology a more than two-to-one head start over DSL in the race to wire end-users with broadband connections. The regional Bell phone companies claim that the broadband playing field is so uneven that they should be relieved of some of their regulatory constraints in order to allow them to catch up.[12] Clearly, government franchise activity has had an effect on competition in at least one area of e-commerce.

ERECTING AN E-COMMERCE LEGAL BARRIER

The preceding discussion brings us to the point of identifying the fundamental tension associated with the creation a legal/institutional property right. Are patents, copyrights and government franchises essential to stimulate, protect, and reward invention, artistic creation, or risky capital investment? Or are these grants basically a means to create a barrier that sustains unnecessary monopoly profits by forestalling entry? The purpose of the following sections is to see how this conflict has played out within the context of e-commerce.

e-Commerce Software and the Copyright Approach[13]

At first, the creators of computer code turned to the copyright laws as a means of protecting their intellectual property. Specific lines of code are now and always have been seen as worthy of copyright protection. However, a conflict soon arose as to whether the intellectual property protection granted by the copyright extended to the entity created by the code as well as to the sequence and content of the lines of code developed to achieve the desired end. If protection did extend to the entity, then the copyright holder would effectively own the result of the code. If it did not, then anyone could legally create the identical result as long as he used a different computer code sequence and instruction content.

In 1988, Apple computer sued Microsoft for copying the Macintosh screen display or *desktop metaphor* created by Apple using a **graphical user interface (GUI)**. GUI employs icons to organize the appearance of the computer screen and to access instructions by mouse click rather than typed instructions.[14] Similarly, in 1990, Lotus Development Corporation sued Borland for copying the series of pull-down menus and discover-command instructions found in their Lotus 1-2-3 spreadsheet. Neither Microsoft nor Borland copied the code written by Apple and Lotus. However, they

---

11 Seth Schiesel, "In Cable TV, Programmers Provide a Power Balance," *The New York Times*, July 16, 2001, p. C6.

12 Andrew Backover, "Cable Consolidation Could Spell Trouble for Phone Companies," *USA Today*, July 16, 2001, p. 4B.

13 The information in this section and the following one have been adapted from James Gleick, "Patently Absurd" *The New York Times*, March 12, 2000, pp. 44–49.

14 For a history of this case, see **http://www.me.utexas.edu/~me179/topics/copyright/case2.html**.

duplicated the "look and feel" of the product created by the code. What the plaintiffs were looking for was a higher level of copyright protection for the "structure, sequence and organization" resulting from the code.

In April and again in August, 1992, Judge Walker dismissed the Apple suit saying the Apple "argument would extend Apple's copyright to any current or future computer system using a highly utilitarian approach to displays and would exempt Apple's individual copyright claims from the usual scrutiny." The Judge wrote "This would afford too much protection and yield too little competition."[15]

The Lotus suit suffered a similar fate, although the firm's complaint reached all the way to the U.S. Supreme Court. The Appellate Court's decision determined that the Lotus 1-2-3 menu structure was a "method of operation" that could not be copyrighted. Judge Michael Boudin, compared the Apple claim to one for the configuration of the QWERTY key arrangement on a standard keyboard. If it were possible to copyright this arrangement of keys, he said, typists "would be the captive of anyone who had a monopoly on the production of such a keyboard."[16] At the Supreme Court level, the appeal was denied and the Appellate Court's decision was upheld in a tie vote 4–4.

The closeness of the Supreme Court vote suggested strong judicial opinions on both sides of the issue. Traditional copyright law protects the *tangible form* of intellectual property, the words of a book or the notes and lyrics of a song, but not the *ideas* embodied within it. How was this rule to be applied in a meaningful way to protect the intellectual property embodied in a new form of expression, namely computer software? The rejection of the Apple and Lotus suits provided strong evidence that e-commerce intellectual property was not likely to receive any greater protection under the copyright laws.

e-Commerce Software and the Patent Approach

Given the preceding results, two additional events, one bureaucratic and one judicial, helped to redirect the efforts to erect entry barriers in e-commerce toward the use of patent system. First, the bureaucratic thinking in the Patent Office evolved to where the it began to interpret and accept the outcome of computer code as a "method of doing business," which is subject to protection through a **business methods patent**. Originally, software patent applications had to be written in such as way as to describe them as an apparatus and link them back to some type of machinery, which was the original focus of the patent-granting process. Even a company as code-dependent and sophisticated as Microsoft did not receive its first software-based patent until 1988. Individual patent examiners began to move in a direction on software and e-commerce code that was different from the court's decisions relative to copyright protection. Code became viewed as a machine that could accomplish through software the kinds of results that were previously achieved through hardware.

Author James Gleick claimed that the change in thinking was affected by the congressional decision in 1991 requiring that the Patent Office support itself entirely on the fee income generated by the patent application process. Applicants became customers and the more customers the greater the fee income. Of course, applications won't be submitted unless they have a reasonable chance of being accepted, but this subtle shift toward patent leniency downplays the responsibility of the Patent Office to protect the interests of all Americans, whose economic welfare is also affected by the decisions of the office.[17] Individual patent examiners may have the final say in granting a patent, but the courts have the final say in determining the validity of a patent. Challengers to a patent may sue the holder in court if they feel that the patent was awarded incorrectly. Keep in mind,

---

15 "Copyright Ruling Against Apple Computer Is Reaffirmed," *The New York Times*, August 8, 1992, p. A38.

16 See "High Court Punts on *Lotus vs. Borland* 01/17/96," **http://www.swiss.ai.mit.edu/6805/articles/ int-prop/lotus/supremes-punt-lotus.html**.

17 Gleick, "Patently Absurd," Ibid, p. 47.

however, that court-based patent challenges usually require a substantial effort involving overwhelming legal fees. Small firms and individuals with limited resources are less likely to mount victorious patent defenses.

The second support for e-commerce patents came from the judicial appellate decision in the 1998 *State Street Bank* **case**, as rendered by the Appellate Court.[18] State Street Bank was charged with violating a 1993 patent governing the computerized accounting procedures used to manage a complex portfolio of mutual funds. At trial on the Federal Court level, Judge Saris found the patent to be a cover for a business method using data-processing technology. As such, it was not subject to patent protection according to the "business method" exception to the patent laws. Judge Saris also noted, "Mental processes, and abstract intellectual concepts, are not patentable, as they are the basic tools of scientific and technological work." Lastly, the judge observed "patenting an accounting system necessary to carry on a certain type of business is tantamount to a patent on the business itself."[19]

The Appellate Court reversed the trial judges' decision, acknowledging that the Supreme Court had earlier identified three categories of subject matter that are not subject to patent protection, namely "laws of nature, natural phenomena, and abstract ideas." The Appellate Court did note that the software covered by the patent embodied a mathematical algorithm that, while standing alone in its abstract form was not subject to a patent, did produce a "useful, concrete, and tangible result." Therefore, "This renders it statutory subject matter, even if the useful result is expressed in numbers such as price, profit, percentage, cost, or loss." Lastly, the Appellate Court stated, "Since the 1952 Patent Act, business methods have been, and should have been, subject to the same legal requirements for patentability as applied to any other process or method."[20] The decision reaffirmed the legality of patenting "business-methods" as they might be applied to computerized business practices. James Gleick noted that this was "powerful conclusion, in a digital age, and it opened the floodgates."[21]

REVISITING THE AMAZON.COM ONE-CLICK PATENT

In September 1999 Amazon.com received patent No. 5,960,411 covering a computer-based one-click ordering method for executing purchase orders over the Internet. Amazon was painfully aware that a large percentage of Internet purchases get selected for potential purchase using the "shopping cart model" and then become abandoned before the final credit card transaction is completed. It was Amazon's assumption that the time and inconvenience associated with typing in credit card and shipping information led a portion of the potential buyers to abandon the carts.[22] Because Amazon always tried to differentiate itself from other Internet retailers on the basis of ease of customer use, the firm set about to find a better way to execute the order command. It solved the problem by using the single click to simultaneously send both the order and an identifier based upon a cookie that was left on the computer the last time it was used to order from Amazon. The cookie triggers the retrieval of credit card and shipping information previously left and stored on Amazon's computers. A screen then appears with the order and shipping information already in place ready to be confirmed by the buyer. Confirmation allows Amazon to charge the registered account and ship the merchandise immediately.

---

18 *State Street Bank & Trust Co. v. Signature Financial Group, Inc.,* U. S. Court of Appeals, 96–1327. See **http://www.ll.georgetown.edu/Fed-Ct/Circuit/fed/opinions/97-1327.html.**

19 Gleick, "Patently Absurd," p. 48.

20 *State Street Bank* case, op. cit.

21 Gleick, "Patently Absurd," p. 48.

22 Conversely, potential buyers may have abandoned the carts after securing and printing all of the desired information, because they wanted to comparison shop other sites or get off-line information before making a final commitment. Amazon's inconvenience assumption may not be the only reason for cart abandonment.

The one-click approach is really a good system and now Amazon had a patent to protect their pioneering intellectual property efforts from potential pirates. The book-selling rival Barnes&Noble.com (BN) was one potential pirate that was easy to spot. They had been using an identical one-step purchasing system as part of their Express Lane feature prior to the granting of the Amazon patent. Amazon filed suit in October 1999 and won a preliminary injunction in December 1999, keeping BN from using version of the one-click ordering model. To comply, BN introduced the intervening step of confirming the order.

How big a competitive advantage the one-click method conveys to Amazon relative to BN is open to conjecture. However, if the Amazon rights had been secured with a *copyright*, then BN could simply have written code around the copyright, generated the same result, and continued using the one-click Express Lane feature. The patent covered a method of doing business and thereby granted broader, if shorter-lived, protection for Amazon.

Early in 2001, however, an appeals court overturned the preliminary injunction against BN noting, "BN has mounted a substantial challenge to the validity of the patent in the suit."[23] All of these issues were to be sorted out at trial in the fall of 2001 as BN legally questioned the validity of the Amazon patent. Perhaps BN could have challenged the "new" part of the patent claim by reviewing prior art and showing the existence of other Internet sites using the one-click ordering command before the submission of the Amazon patent. BN might also have tried to prove that the one-click method was not "unobvious," and that any computer programmer or e-commerce retailer could have come up with the process. Regardless of the possibilities, the court proceedings were halted in March 2002 when Amazon and BN came to an out-of-court settlement, with conditions not disclosed.[24]

PRICELINE.COM'S REVERSE AUCTION PATENT

The firm of Walker Asset Management has been assigned the rights to patent No. 5,794,207 for the application of the **reverse auction** process to the buying of products and services using a computer. In turn, the firm licensed the right to use the patent to a related firm, Priceline.com. Priceline used the patent as the basis for their "name-your-own-price" approach to selling travel arrangements, including airfares, hotel stays, and car rentals over the Internet. The Walker patent will serve a number of purposes for the discussion of patents as they relate to e-commerce. First, it will show how tenuous some of these "new" e-commerce patents may be. Second, it may serve to illustrate how valuable a patent can be as a piece of intellectual property. And third, it helps to demonstrate how strong or how worthless the patent may be as a potential barrier to entry.

The Walker patent doesn't claim that it was the creator of the reverse auction process. After all, the concept of a buyer-originated, conditional offer to purchase has been around for a long time. Rather the patent was granted on the basis of Walker being the first to describe the steps in the process as applied through the use of a computer and using a credit card as the payment identifier. Because it was doubtful that any other firm applied the reverse auction technique in exactly the same way, the patent was granted for the invention of a "new" method of doing business. By extension, this interpretation of the patent process opens up broad possibilities for applying existing business techniques to a wide range of e-commerce transactions using the computer. Of course, Gleick made this exact point in response to the *State Street Bank* decision. Is the application of the reverse auction using a computer and credit card really a "new" invention worthy of a patent, or is it just an extension of an old idea?

---

23 "Courts hand . . . ," available at **http://www.internetnews.com/ec-news/article/0,,4_589701,00. html**.

24 Laura Rohde, "Amazon, Barnes and Noble settle patent dispute," available at **http://www.cnn. com/2002/TECH/industry/03/08/amazon.bn.dispute.idg/**.

The Priceline system is clearly beneficial to the airlines because it helps in the sale of **distressed tickets**. In the first few years, several of the airlines cooperated with Priceline, making their unsold seats available through the reverse auction process. Some, such as Delta, even accepted shares in the firm as an inducement to participate.[25] After all, airlines make thousands of regularly scheduled flights per day, and as many as 3 million seats per week are empty at takeoff time.[26] The marginal cost of filling that empty seat is near zero. As a flight gets closer to takeoff, the airline has the revenue incentive to fly with the seat occupied at half-fare, rather than keeping it empty at full fare. Even well in advance of the departure date, the airline benefits if it "locks in" a few passengers, despite the fact that the revenue may be below full cost. All of this time-sensitive ticket pricing, geared to potential flyer characteristics, involves the science of **yield management**, which is complex stuff. Of course, the airline must be careful not to allow the discounted price of distressed tickets to cut into the sale of full-fare tickets. As part of this approach they use the Priceline system to employ restrictions and introduce the concept of uncertainty.

Patents Create Value for the Holder

How does the patented, name-your-own-price system, create value for Priceline? And how valuable is it? It is valuable both as a system for generating current profits through ticket sales and as an intangible asset. First, the firm must get the concept up and running, and make it known to the public. Then it hopes that enough price-sensitive buyers on the Internet are willing to put up with the restrictions in order to make the service profitable. A buyer using Priceline must make a binding offer to purchase, secured by her credit card, to fly on an unknown airline, on a route and at times chosen by the airline, as long as it gets her from point A to point B within one travel day. The buyer assumes all of this uncertainty solely in exchange for getting the tickets at a price below published airfares. In addition, the potential buyer must wait to see whether any airline accepts the offer. It is not an approach targeted at people who are risk-averse or those who place a high dollar value on their time either in transit or in experiencing fast ticket purchases. To their credit, after three years in operation, Priceline earned its first current profit on the sale of tickets in the second quarter of 2001.

The patent may have a second source of even greater value for the firm as an **intangible asset**. These assets, owned by the firm, may contribute to the profitability of the firm in undefined ways and are therefore difficult to value. For example, Yahoo! is a well-known brand name, which helps to steer users to the portal when they want to conduct an Internet search, but how valuable is the name? How does the firm go about assigning value to the brand name? How do the owners of Yahoo! go about capturing the value of the brand? The Priceline patent, which conveys an exclusive right to a specific application of the reverse auction process, faces the same intangible feature and valuation problems. The name-your-own-price process works well for airline tickets, but suppose that it can be extended to cover the purchase of other big-ticket items, such as cars, appliances, real estate, or consumer electronics. Suppose that **haggling** over price using the Web becomes a preferred method of buying for an ever-growing number of buyers. Now, the reverse auction patent takes on enormous value because the license holder(s) can monopolize an increasing number of expanding market segments, protected from competitors by the patent.[27]

Monopolies show a greater potential for making economic profits above normal returns. These economic profits usually lead to higher equity values for the owners of

---

25 Martha Brannigan, "Delta Ponders Sale of Priceline State, Could Join Hotwire," *The Wall Street Journal*, October 23, 2000, p. B8.

26 Clare Saliba, "Hotwire.com Leaps into Net Travel Fray," **http://www.osopinion.com/perl/story/4637.html**.

27 Thomas E. Weber, "E-World: Intangibles Are Tough to Value, But the Payoff Matters in Dot-Com Era," *The Wall Street Journal*, May 14, 2001, p. B1.

the firm. Therefore, the greatest potential worth for the patent usually lies in the discounted present value of the **expected flow of economic profits** over the lifetime of the patent, not in just the individual quarterly profits as earned. The more that investors see, or think they see, the potential for profitable expanded use of the patent, the more the stock of the firm holding the patent will be worth. Investors become like children at Christmastime, with "visions of sugarplums" dancing in their heads. They see the potential of owners becoming dot-com millionaires and drive up the equity price in response. These aspirations surely help to explain how the market value of Priceline's stock rose above $150 per share without ever having made even $1 of profit.

Patents as an Entry Barrier

How well does the patent work as a barrier to entry? How successfully does its patent protect Priceline's monopoly position as a reverse auction seller of airline tickets? Mostly, the answer is not very well. Although the details are sketchy, the fact is that Microsoft created a Web firm, Expedia.com, which was indistinguishable in purpose and function from Priceline. Priceline challenged Expedia by suing Microsoft in court for patent infringement. As noted earlier, however, patent infringement cases are hard to prove, time consuming, and costly. For whatever reason and for an unspecified royalty payment, the two parties resolved the dispute, and the suit was dropped. Expedia.com exists today as both a successful entrant and full-fledged rival to Priceline.

Furthermore, six of the major airlines, including American, United, and Northwest, banded together to create their own site, Hotwire.com, as a place for marketing discounted flight tickets directly to the public. Their attempt at **disintermediation** cuts the intermediary and its profits out of the system. In many ways, the Hotwire purchase process is more favorable to the buyer, who makes a nonbinding inquiry regarding ticket prices rather than committing to a binding offer price linked to a credit card. A number of the uncertainties are retained by Hotwire, primarily as a way of preventing all but the most price-sensitive air travelers from jumping from the published fare market into the deep-discount, distressed fare market. The substantial consumer response to Hotwire likely diverted business away from Priceline.

Also, many of the same airlines opened up a full service, e-commerce, airline ticket and travel site, Orbitz.com, in June 2001.[28] This site lists the existing low-cost fares for American, Continental, United, Northwest, and Delta, along with sale prices on hotels, car rentals, cruises, vacation packages, and other travel deals. It is another airline attempt at disintermediation by marketing directly to travelers over the Internet, bypassing the need to share profits with travel agents. Although it was examined and approved by the Justice Department, the site is seen as more of an immediate competitive threat to travel agents. However, it offers the potential to develop into collusive behavior on the part of the airlines, limiting the sometimes aggressive, competitive pricing of airfares. The conclusion is that, because online travel bookings amounted to more than $20 billion in 2001, or 10 percent of all travel purchases, the profit generates a considerable incentive for a variety of firms and approaches to overcome strategic entry barriers, enter into the market, and compete with Priceline.[29]

THE FUTURE OF E-COMMERCE PATENTS

Patents appear to be a popular, if dubiously profitable, avenue for firms to protect their intellectual property. The number of business methods patent applications rose

---

28 Tom Spring, "Orbitz Stokes Web Airfare Wars, Critics Say," available at **http://www.thestandard. com/article/0,1902,26907,00.html**.

29 The Orbitz vision has another dimension as the firm filed to issue public stock as a potential IPO. See, Susan Carey "Travel Web Site Orbitz Files for IPO," *The Wall Street Journal*, May 21, 2002, p. D5.

176 percent, from 2,821 in fiscal 1999 to 7,800 in fiscal 2000, with the Patent Office issuing 899 business methods patents that year.[30] Not all of these patents are specifically e-commerce related, but those that are contribute to walling off, as private property, important segments of what was up to now an open, innovative, and highly beneficial Internet. Apart from generating dubious profits and serving as a weak entry barrier, why are e-commerce patents so popular, if they hold potential harm for the Internet? Historically and in cyberspace, firms employed patents as both a **sword and a shield**. Companies use patents aggressively, as a sword to intimidate rivals, by either extracting license fees or keeping competitors at bay. Conversely, as a shield, a portfolio of patents can be raised to deflect the suits of others, or used as a bargaining chip to secure cross-licensing agreements at little or no cash cost.[31] For example, in 1998, CoolSavings.com received a business methods patent for a system of distributing coupons and promotions via the Internet. They promptly sued nine rivals for patent infringement and two other firms that did business with the challenged rivals. In turn, the rivals secured patents of their own and countersued CoolSavings.[32] The results of these patent wars are usually long hours spent in court, a considerable expense for legal counsel, higher product prices for consumers, and, in general, a lot of wasted resources.

The noted legal scholar, Lawrence Lessig, makes this point and more as he examined the tension inherent in the future of the Internet as an open information system versus one that is regulated and walled off by a system of patents. Lessig structured his arguments on the basis of weighing the benefits and costs of granting and applying both software and business methods patents in cyberspace. His conclusion was that, at this time, the risk from potential patent-based harm outweighed the currently identifiable benefits that might be derived from stimulating further cyberspace innovation. Therefore, he called on Congress to "declare a moratorium on the offensive use of software and business-method patents. Only when we are reasonably confident that (patent) regulation will do some good should Congress allow regulation to go forward."[33] Lessig supported his conclusion by noting, "What is most striking about this explosion of regulation in cyberspace is that it is not the product of legislators or policy makers. No agency decision or Congressional act launched patents into cyberspace. The explosion of patents has resulted entirely from court decisions."[34]

This **judicial activism** contrasts with **legislative inaction** in other Internet-related areas, including the Congressional moratorium on the taxation of Internet sales, the FTC's restraint in regulating Internet privacy, and the FCC's refusal to force open-access rules on broadband cable systems. In each case the government body recognized its own information limitations and took a wait-and-see attitude, letting the market evolve its own potential solutions. Introducing regulation into cyberspace will change both competitive behavior and the nature of innovation. Therefore, regulators should move forward only if the market provides an inadequate response and they are sure that the regulations will do no harm, as well as produce some good.

In responding to questions and criticism, the Patent Office has introduced additional steps in its review process for awarding business methods patents.[35] First, it now requires review of the patent application by a "second set of eyes" beyond those of the examiner handling the application. This step is to ensure that the process is not obvious

---

30 "Fewer Patents on Methods Get Clearance," *The Wall Street Journal*, March 21, 2001, p. A3.

31 Gleick, "Patently Absurd," p. 46.

32 Scott Thurm, "The Ultimate Weapon," *The Wall Street Journal*, April 17, 2000, p. R18.

33 Lawrence Lessig, "Online Patents: Leave Them Pending," *The Wall Street Journal*, March 23, 2000, p. A22.

34 Lessig, "Online Patents," p. A22.

35 The laxity of the patent process was highlighted when a five-year-old boy was granted U.S. patent No. 6,368,227 for a method of swinging on a playground swing. Teresa Riordan "Patents: The Patent Office Faces Huge Backlogs, Extremely Technical Inventions, and Absurd Ones," *The New York Times*, May 13, 2002, p. C2

or simply a computerized application of something done in a different way before. Second, the Patent Office is moving to ensure a better understanding of the "prior art." Many computer techniques and processes were developed in the pre-patent era and were never fully written down or were kept as trade secrets. The Software Patent Institute has developed a database to help examiners review older computer science information. Third, examiners are being sent into the field to contact firms and determine which processes are obvious or common practices, so as to avoid awarding ineligible patents. Lastly, the Patent Office has revised the training manuals requiring more study of actual firms and the industry before passing on a patent application.[36] Opponents of these revised procedures say that they are unfair and that the Office is changing the law by its behavior. They claim the Office is erecting roadblocks to business-method patent applications and treating them differently from other types of applications. These changes makes it more difficult for information technology inventors to secure protection for their ideas.[37]

SUMMARY AND PROSPECTS

By researching the history and intricacies of the patent system, the discussion in this chapter explains why BN introduced an extra step into its checkout process. More importantly, it also explains why other e-commerce firms want similar protection for their intellectual property. Keep in mind that a patent is not a guaranteed ticket to profitability or even survival. Mercata held the patent on the technology for an Internet group buying scheme known as a **group aggregation model**. Their process let the final price of the product fall depending upon the number of persons who signed up. The larger the number of subscribers, the lower the price of the product would be. Therefore, committed buyers had the incentive to pass the word to friends and get them to sign up on a specific deal so that all buyers could get the product at the lowest possible price. "A great new idea," said many observers, and one backed by a considerable amount of advertising to bring it to the attention of the public. Even a patent couldn't keep them in business, however; they folded in early 2001.[38] The difference between being "new" and being "better" is evident in the ability to attract a critical mass of customers to make a business model profitable.[39]

Second, what about the evidence offered regarding our primary patent tension characterizing Internet patents as either a stimulus to innovation or a barrier to entry? Strong evidence indicates that the Internet was an extremely innovative sector even before patents were introduced. Motivated by a combination of curiosity and a drive to advance the frontiers of knowledge, the scientists working on the Web and Internet built rapidly upon and borrowed from past accomplishments to make their own contributions. In fact, it was effectively argued that the pace of advance was in no small way enhanced by the openness of the process. Monetary incentives played a minor or nonexistent role. The introduction of profit-based e-commerce to the Web has changed the dynamic. Commercial firms want as big a competitive advantage as possible relative to their rivals and want the advantage to last as long as possible. Patents help in these areas, but they are not insurmountable. They can be circumvented, challenged, or may fail to deliver sufficient levels of profit. They may delay entry by making it more difficult, but

---

36 Anna Wilde Mathews, "U.S. Will Give Web Patents More Scrutiny," *The Wall Street Journal*, March 29, 2000, p. B1: and William M. Bulkeley, "Fewer Patents on Methods Get Clearance," *The Wall Street Journal*, March 21, 2001, p. A3.

37 Bulkeley, "Fewer Patents," p. A3.

38 Keith Regan, "Allen-Backed Mercata Bows Out," available at **http://www.ecommercetimes.com/ perl/story/6492.html**.

39 Thomas Weber, "E-World: Priceline Woes Suggest Novelty Isn't Enough to Succeed on the Web," *The Wall Street Journal*, October 16, 2000, p. B1.

if the profit is there, someone will be clever enough or strong enough to forge a successful entry plan. The best that the patent holder can hope for is to portray the patent as an intangible asset, drive up the value of the firm, and sell either the company or the stock before the market eventually shows how fleeting the patent advantage is. The e-commerce firms that have become successful are earning their profits not because they hold a patent, but because they a provide a more efficient service to their customers.

Third, the subsidiary tension, raised by Lessig, questions the future of the Internet as an open versus a walled-off technology. On the one hand, it is doubtful that the Internet will ever again be the playground of pure science and creativity as it was prior to the introduction of the profit incentive. Too much is at stake to go back to the older pattern of behavior. On the other hand, patents covering key features of e-commerce will most likely be harder to secure, more difficult to defend, and offer at best only limited protection against competition. As in many cases where technological change is rapid, history has shown that the creativity of the market driven by thousands exceeds the ability of one to isolate and monopolize a profitable segment of that market.

Lastly, the discussion looked at e-commerce patents as potentially wasteful of resources, harmful to the consumer by raising prices, and an impediment to the spread of technology on the Web. As such, they are inefficient, unnecessary, and counterproductive.

KEY TERMS AND CONCEPTS

business methods patent	legal life of a patent
cookies	legislative inaction
copyright	methods of doing business
disintermediation	one-click ordering
distressed tickets	patent
expected flow of economic profits	patent criteria: useful, novel, unobvious
fair use doctrine	prior art
Faustian bargain	public good
government franchise	racing behavior
graphical user interface (GUI)	reverse auction
group aggregation model	*State Street Bank* case
haggling	sword and shield
intangible asset	trade secrets
intellectual property	yield management
judicial activism	

DISCUSSION AND REVIEW QUESTIONS

1. What is the difference between a patent and a copyright? What types of creative work does each protect and for how long?

2. Coca-Cola's secret formula, known as X-7, contains the recipe for the syrup used in their soft drink. Why has the firm never sought patent protection for this valuable formula? How does the concept of a patent as a Faustian bargain help to explain their actions?

3. Identify the three key criteria for extending a U.S. patent.

4. Did the creators of computer code receive their desired level of security when they pursued copyright protection for their intellectual property? Why?

5. Identify and discuss the two events that made the patent approach more effective in protecting intellectual property.

6. Does Amazon.com's one-click ordering method convey a competitive advantage? Why?

7. Has the Priceline.com patent kept other firms from competing with Priceline? Why? Has the patent served as an effective entry barrier?

8. How has the patented reverse auction, name-your-own-price system conveyed value to Priceline.com?

9. How can firms employ their store of patents as both a sword and shield?

10. Are patents and copyrights necessary to encourage and reward creative efforts?

11. Are patents economically efficient or do they primarily create monopoly profits by forestalling entry?

12. Is the future of the Internet and its benefit to society better served by keeping the Internet an open system or one protected and controlled by a collection of patents? Why?

13. Distinguish between *judicial activism* and *legislative inaction* as these terms apply to issues relating to the Internet.

WEB EXERCISES

1. Access the money section of USAToday.com at **http://www.usatoday.com/money/front.htm.** Type in the stock symbols for Amazon.com (AMZN) and Priceline.com (PCLN) in the Quick Quote box. How well have these two firms been doing in terms of stock value over the past two years? Does it look like they have been helped a great deal by their patent protection?

2. Go to the legal site containing information on copyrights at **http://www.law.cornell.edu/topics/copyright.html**. Click on Recent Decisions on Copyrights under the Supreme Court heading. Examine the first case listed to identify the issues involved as well as the nature of the decision.

3. Link to the site for the U.S. Patent and Trademark Office at **http://www.uspto.gov/**. Click on About USPTO and examine the range of intellectual property (IP) options that are offered protection by this office.

4. Access the USPTO patent data by geographic region at **http://www.uspto.gov/web/offices/ac/ido/oeip/taf/asgstc/regions.htm**. Click on your home state to see the number of patents granted and the identity of the major patent recipients.

CHAPTER
7

Introductory Case

METALLICA VERSUS THE DIGITAL WORLD OF NAPSTER

Whether a given listener likes their music or not, Metallica is one of the best known and most popular heavy metal bands. They have been around as a musical unit since 1981, sold more than 80 million albums worldwide, and won six Grammy Awards. Their 1991 album "Metallica" received a Diamond Award from the Recording Industry Association of America, indicating U.S. sales of that item alone in excess of 10 million units. They are a leading concert draw, attracting more than 2.2 million paying fans to their most recent worldwide concert tour.[1] Their popularity early in the 1980s grew at least in part as a result of their deliberately free distribution of a demo tape "No Life Til Leather," which they encouraged fans to bootleg or copy and distribute as they saw fit. Moreover, the band permitted fans to make copies of their live tour performances and to distribute them among their friends. How much more fan friendly can you get? It's as if George Steinbrenner gave away free tickets to Yankee home games.

Then, in April of 2000, the band did something that seemed out of character. They sued the Internet file-sharing firm, Napster for

1. Copyright infringement
2. The unlawful use of digital audio interface device
3. Violating the Racketeering Influenced & Corrupt Organizations Act (RICO)[2]

Not only did they charge Napster, but also they initially added the names of a few colleges to the suit, including the University of Southern California, Yale University, and Indiana University. These schools were cited as places where college students had been using the broadband college Internet lines for music file sharing as well as term paper research. What the band objected to was the free exchange of Metallica studio recordings through Napster, which was a profit-oriented firm. In order to reinforce their case, the band collected the "handles" or screen names of some 335,435 Napster users who were offering Metallica songs through the service.[3]

Metallica's actions placed them in a difficult position relative to their fans. On the one hand, the fans wanted access to the band's music. Napster offered that access on a global scale at a zero price for the traded music. Many fans reacted angrily at the suit, as well as having their handles identified and brought to the attention of Napster for "deregistration" action.[4] On the other hand, the band spent a considerable amount of time and creative effort composing their music. Lars Ulrich stated the bands position as follows, "We take our craft—whether it be the music, the lyrics, or the photos and artwork—very seriously, as do most artists. It is therefore sickening to know that our art is being traded like a commodity rather than the art that it is. From a business standpoint, this is about piracy—a/k/a taking something that doesn't

---

1 http://www.encyclopedia-metallica.com/news/2001-07-22c.shtml.

2 RICO is a federal law, with severe penalties, that was originally written to target organized crime.

3 Matt Richtel and Neil Strauss, "Metallica to Try to Prevent Fans from Downloading Recordings," *The New York Times*, May 3, 2000, p. C1. The hip-hop artist Dr. Dre filed a similar suit against Napster.

4 Napster acted swiftly to bar some 300,000 screen names associated with the Metallica information as required by U.S. copyright laws. See Jeri Clausing, "Report Proposes Update of Copyright Act," *The New York Times*, May 22, 2000, p. C6.

Copyrights and e-Commerce:

Protecting Intellectual Property in the Digital Age

belong to you, and that is morally and legally wrong."[5] In simple terms, the band wanted to be paid for the exchange of their copyrighted material rather than having it traded freely online.

In late 1999, the Recording Industry Association of America (RIAA), the umbrella organization for the music companies, also sued Napster for copyright infringement. The industry claims considerable economic harm from Napster and others amounting to upwards of $4.2 billion in lost revenues in 2000 related to illegal music distribution.[6] What the Metallica suit did was to alter the appearance and perhaps the nature of the conflict. As *RIAA v. Napster*, the case looked like the greedy music companies attacking a small, Internet friend of fans and free music. As

Metallica v. Napster, the case became an aggrieved artist challenging the work of Napster, a profit-oriented commercial pirate that was hiding behind a façade of fan friendly free music. This conflict took on much wider implications, though, because any material that can be digitized, or reduce to strings of zeros and ones, can be copied and transmitted over the Internet. Initially, the issue focused on the pirating of music because the digital files are simple and relatively short. Films, books, video games, and almost all other forms of entertainment are also susceptible to the **digital copying problem**. It is only the quality of the transmission as well as the broadband or last-mile problem that has kept these latter areas from being "Napsterized."

These suits form the basic digitized information tension to be examined in this chapter, namely: the copyright protection of intellectual property versus the right of free distribution of digital information (entertainment). At first, the resolution of this tension may look like a "slam-dunk" in favor of copyright protection. However, the issues to be resolved are numerous, economically significant, and involve a clash of legitimate as well as conflicting rights.

U.S. COPYRIGHT LAW AND THE DIGITAL AGE

The discussion in Chapter 6 showed that the copyright laws always protect music, films, and books. Copyrighted material cannot be reproduced without permission or payment, but how are these laws to be applied in the digital age? Does the law cover only the material being copied, or can it be extended to cover the technology that may allow others to copy protected works? And if so, how? In 1998, Congress passed the **Digital Millennium Copyright Act (DMCA)**, which spelled out the boundaries for electronic copyright protection.[7] In doing so, Congress tried to balance the rights of copyright

---

5 Available at **http://www.wired.com/news/politics/0,1283,35670-2,00.html**.

6 Associated Press, "New Stealth CDs Aimed at Piracy," *Connecticut Post*, August 25, 2001, p. B2.

7 See Public Law 105-304, 105th Congress, available at **http://www.educause.edu/issues/dmca. html**.

holders with the rights of individual consumers, along with the right of free speech. Key provisions include the following:

1. The **antidevice provision**: Prohibits the manufacture or distribution of any device designed to circumvent technological copyright protections.
2. The **anticircumvention provision**: Makes it a criminal offense to circumvent antipiracy measures built into commercial software, including music and films.
3. Allows the breaking of copyright protection devices for encryption research and to test security systems.
4. Exempts Internet service providers from copyright infringement liability for simply transmitting information over the Internet. ISPs are expected to remove material from a user's Web sites that appears to constitute copyright infringement.
5. Requires that "Webcasters" pay licensing fees to record companies, and limits their ability to provide music-on-demand services.
6. States explicitly that "[n]othing in this section shall affect rights, remedies, limitations, or defenses to copyright infringement, including fair use."[8]

Almost immediately, the critics of the law pointed out a number of limitations.[9] First, the act had little to do with copying or copyright infringement. Rather, it prohibited ways of gaining access to encrypted material, rendering it susceptible to copying. Therefore, DMCA transfers the protection of the author's rights from the copyright to the technology that guards it. Software tools, which in other circumstances might be legal, become illegal if they can be used to defeat encrypted commercial software. Second, the imposition of criminal penalties substantially exceeded the level of sanctions normally imposed for copyright infringement. Third, although the wording of the act explicitly reaffirmed the validity of the fair use exception, the effect of the act was to revoke the rights that consumers traditionally held to copy portions of a copyrighted work.[10] The **Audio Home Recording Act (AHRA) of 1992** explicitly granted legitimate owners of music the right to make copies for their personal, noncommercial use.[11] If the work is encrypted, however, and both devices and efforts to circumvent the encryption are a criminal offense, then, in reality, consumers are denied their legal right to copy the material. In the same vein and for later reference, the U.S. Supreme Court ruled in the 1984 *Sony Betamax* case that if a new technology had substantial, noninfringing uses, it could not be held accountable for illicit uses.[12] Therefore, it was legal for consumers to make an off-air videotape of a program originally broadcast via television. Such taping was deemed to be a fair use by the Court. Lastly, the Copyright Act protects material for a finite period of time. The technologies protected by DMCA, on the other hand, which guard the copyrighted material, are exposed to no such time limit. Therefore, DMCA offers broader protections than the copyrights it was intended to protect. Lawrence Lessig, the noted Internet legal scholar, branded DMCA as "bad law and bad policy."[13]

European Copyright Laws

In April 2001, the European Parliament passed a set of guidelines for modifying national copyright laws so as to extend protection from the analog world into the

---

8 The UCLA Online Institute for Cyberspace Law and Policy, "The Digital Millennium Copyright Act," available at **http://www.gseis.ucla.edu/iclp/dmca1.htm**.

9 Jeffrey W. Reyna, "How Do You Feel About DCMA," available at **http://www.upside.com/ Upside_Counsel/392073660.html**. Accessed October 2001.

10 Amy Harmon and Jennifer Lee, "Arrest Raises Stakes in Battle Over Copyright," *The New York Times*, July 23, 2001, p. C1.

11 "The Audio Home Recording Act of 1992," available at **http://www.virtualrecordings.com/ ahra.htm**.

12 *Sony Corp. of Am. v. Universal City Studios, Inc.*, 464 U.S. 417, 454 (1984).

13 Lawrence Lessig, "Jail Time in the Digital Age," *The New York Times*, July 30, 2001, p. A17.

digital one.[14] The European Copyright Directive looks similar to the U.S. laws but places less emphasis on outlawing anticircumvention devices and more emphasis on protecting the rights of consumers. The directive allows for encryption as protection against illegal copying and ads legal protection against the use of anticopying devices. Encryption is a new permitted right for holders of copyrights and was not allowed under the application of the copyright laws to analog material.[15] In addition, the directive does not contain an explicit fair use provision. However, a lengthy list offers suggested exemptions from the copyright infringement penalties, including copies made for technical, personal, and archival uses. In effect, European citizens are guaranteed the right to make copies of digital material for private use.

Key Cases Testing the Digital Millennium Copyright Act

Despite the fact that DMCA is only a few years old, it has already spawned a number of significant test cases. The *Napster* case, covering the pirating of music files, was probably the most prominent one and led to the clearest interpretation and application of the act. The second was a successful record industry suit against MP3.com, involving the creation by MP3.com of an Internet storage service holding CD music files that were copied without prior permission. A third case, filed against a magazine publisher and his Web Site 2600, focused upon the distribution of computer code designed to overcome the encryption used to protect copyrighted DVD movie films. The fourth case involved the arrest in the United States of a Russian graduate student who was associated with a Russian-based firm that had a program to crack the encryption protecting a piece of business software. And lastly, a case was brought against a Princeton computer scientist who, with colleagues, was the winner of a legitimate contest to remove a digital watermark used to protect music industry CDs. His attempt to publish a paper detailing their findings and methodology led to a written threat of prosecution under DMCA by the RIAA. Each of these cases will be discussed in turn, taking care to show how they test the boundaries of this chapter's clash-of-rights tension, which pits the rights of copyright holders against the rights of consumers, free speech, and the free flow of information on the Internet.

THE RECORDING INDUSTRY ASSOCIATION OF AMERICA VERSUS NAPSTER

A college student anywhere who has never heard of Napster must either not be much of a pop music fan or spends a great deal of time in the library dealing with course-related assignments. Here's a short summary of the *Napster* case: Napster was a private Internet firm that acted like a music search engine. It allowed users to locate specific songs stored on personal computers spread across the Internet and to download those songs in a file format called MP3. The MP3 format allows "computer users (to) compress music into files that are close to CD quality yet small enough to travel quickly over the Internet."[16] Shawn Fanning, a 19-year-old college dropout from Northeastern University, wrote the Napster software in 1999.

Be aware of two important points at the outset. First, nothing is illegal in the Napster technology per se. It is a legitimate program for the location and transfer of information. It could be used without legal problems for the exchange of noncopyrighted material or

---

14 Lori Enos, "EU Proposes New Digital Copyright Laws," available at **http://www.newsfactor.com/perl/story/8826.html**.

15 Brandon Mitchener, "Down to the Wire: EU Digital Copyright Bill," *The Wall Street Journal*, January 22, 2001, p. B6.

16 Amy Harmon, "Potent Software Escalates Music Industry's Jitters," *The New York Times*, March 7, 2000, p. A1.

for the exchange of copyrighted material for which permission had been secured. Second, nothing is wrong in making **MP3 files** of music that you already own. The AHRA took care of that in 1992. The making of tapes, or the **"ripping" of CDs** to make MP3 files, and then the exchanging of those tapes or files with friends, is illegal **piracy of intellectual property**, however. Prior to Napster, these acts of theft had been tolerated by the RIAA for three reasons. First, the Association could not do much about individual, isolated acts of piracy done in secret. Second, the copying and transfer process was time consuming and difficult. This factor kept it a low-scale operation that had little effect on the profits of the industry. And third, tape-based copying leads to a gradual decline in the quality of the copy.

The creation of the MP3 file technology and Napster led to a change in the scale of the music-copying problem. Digital copying using MP3 files led to copies that were almost identical in quality to the original, so the making of copies no longer led to a degradation in music quality. The Napster software solved the problem of one music fan finding another individual willing to share the desired tunes. Napster computers did not store the traded music. Rather, they centralized the indexing and listing of music files, as well as provided the software that facilitated the exchange process. This capability greatly enhanced the potential scale of music piracy and the efficiency of the operation. Napster also helped to create an **ethical disconnect** in the minds of music fans. Most fans would never steal a CD from their local music store, but they saw no problems in exchanging copyrighted music files, for free, over the Internet.[17] College students were among the first users of Napster because they had broadband Internet access at school. After all, each song would take a long time to transfer using a dial-up modem connection. This linkage of college students with college broadband facilities underscores the logic of Metallica suing the schools as well as Napster. The colleges unwittingly facilitated the exchange process. Actually, the colleges didn't want the students accessing Napster for purposes of file transfer either, because it used up so much of the expensive bandwidth that was supposed to be used for academic purposes.

In some respects, the recording industry itself was also partly responsible for the copying problem. For decades the industry has maintained an **album mentality**, which held that the most profitable way for it to sell music was by **bundling** popular tunes together with other songs and selling them all in a high-priced album or CD. The segment of fans who just wanted to buy one or two songs from the album was ignored by this all-or-nothing approach. Without doubt, it is the absolute right of the recording firms to sell their product as they see fit, but their persistence in bundling disregarded both the desires of the consumers to possess individual songs and the creation of a file-sharing technology that let consumers fulfill their wants. With the appearance of Napster, it became evident to all that the barriers to freedom of music choice were not technological barriers, but instead were commercial and strategic barriers.[18]

Faced with this challenge to its commercial strategy, the recording industry chose to attack the technology rather than devise a legal, fee-based, file-sharing alternative. This reaction is not inconsistent with past attempts to block new technologies and concepts by factions of the entertainment/media industry. For example, book publishers in the nineteenth century wanted to ban the lending of books through libraries. The owners of sheet music sought to ban the use of scrolls in player pianos. Filmmakers wanted to ban the video home recorder (VCR) in the *Sony Betamax* case. The music industry pushed for constraints on the digital audio tape recorder as a way of forestalling efforts to copy music. These shortsighted attempts to hold back new business models based on new technology were not always in the best long-run interests of the challenging industry. For example, the legalized sale of movies in VCR and now DVD formats has proved to be a substantial revenue source for the film distributors.

17 Harmon, "Potent Software," p. C6.
18 Clay Shirky, "Freedom, One Song at a Time," *The New York Times*, July 15, 2000, p. A13.

Napster's Defense and the Court's Verdict

Napster hired David Boies, the prominent antitrust attorney who prosecuted the government's antitrust case against Microsoft, as its chief courtroom lawyer. The firm raised several issues in its defense, including the following:[19]

1. It invoked the *Internet service provider* defense. Napster claimed that it was an ISP and therefore exempt from prosecution under the provision of DMCA.
2. It claimed a *limited knowledge defense*. Napster carried out only a limited function; it did not store MP3 files on its servers, it didn't engage in the trading of copyrighted material, and it had no way of knowing or have reason to know of direct infringement.
3. It claimed a *fair use defense*. The exemptions granted under the Audio Home Recording Act of 1992 should be applied and extended to music copies made over the Internet. If the users of Napster were not guilty of copyright infringement, then Napster had no contributory liability.[20]
4. It claimed the *Sony Betamax defense*. The Supreme Court declined to ban the technology of the VCR in spite of potential illegal use. Therefore, by analogy, the actions of Napster should not be prohibited under DMCA despite the potential for illegal use by some of its members.

At the time of the appellate court's decision in February 2001, Napster had a total of 58 million registered users worldwide and was adding 300,000 new subscribers daily. An estimated 10.5 million different monthly users of the system at home and at work shared tens of millions of copyrighted files.[21] At its peak in February 2001, 1.57 million daily users connected to the Napster servers, sharing an average of 220 MP3 music files each.[22] File sharing via Napster accounted for an estimated 5 percent of all Internet traffic. Illegal free file sharing of a wide range of copyrighted material had the potential to become the "killer app" that would soak up the unused fiber cable capacity. The Napster phenomenon had grown to enormous proportions.

The U.S. Court of Appeals for the Ninth Circuit agreed with the trial court that the actions of Napster constituted a contributory liability and were therefore a direct violation of the Digital Millennium Copyright Act. It instructed the trial judge to structure an injunction that would require Napster to halt the exchange of copyrighted material. However, the Appellate Court stopped short of banning Napster outright, noting that it may be used for "commercially significant noninfringing uses."[23]

Some Consequences of the Napster Decision

The court decisions shut down the old Napster music model based upon the free, direct exchange of music through a centralized server. Napster was forced to file for bankruptcy protection in June 2002.[24] However, the technological genie is out of the bottle. Its popularity among millions of music fans worldwide means that the use of file-sharing technology is unlikely to be restrained in the future. Always remember that Napster didn't copy the songs; music fans did. Napster's actions were similar to those of Al Capone, as he offered an insightful economic response to a question about why he engaged in illegal

19 See Matt Richtel, "Foes Hone Strategy for Web Copyright Clash," *The New York Times*, June 16, 2000, p. C6; and Lee Gomes, "Napster Stakes Out 'Fair Use' Defense of Music Sharing," *The Wall Street Journal*, July 5, 2000, p. B2.

20 Richtel, "Foes Hone Strategy ," p. C6.

21 Matt Richtel, "Appellate Judges Back Limitations on Copying Music," *The New York Times*, February 13, 2001, p. A1.

22 Ron Harris, "Napster Shuts Down to Retool," *USA Today*, July 3, 2001, p. 3D.

23 Richtel, "Appellate Judges ," p. C8.

24 Nick Wingfield, "Napster Files for Chapter 11 Shelter," *The Wall Street Journal*, June 4, 2002, p. B6.

liquor sales. Capone simply stated that, "Prohibition is a business. All I do is supply a public demand."[25] It is exactly what Napster did. The recording firms may have won this battle, but they are at risk of losing the war. The Napster victory reaffirmed the industries' right to enforce copyright protections, but they are fast losing the ability to do so.[26] The growth in the file-sharing technology continues to outpace the ability of the legal system to police it.

The demise of the Napster model led to the birth of a myriad of hopefully legitimate, as well as openly renegade, Web sites created to take advantage of variations on the peer-to-peer **file-sharing technology**. Three of the more prominent Napster rivals include BearShare.com, LimeWire.com, and Madster.com. BearShare and LimeWire use an improved variation of the **Gnutella** open-source, free-to-all software program. It is a file-sharing, pure peer-to-peer software system that allows for the direct exchange of files. Gnutella functions without the aid of a central computer or a single company to coordinate the interactions. It distributes the file-sharing activity across the entire range of participating personal computers connected to the Web, without revealing the location of the computers on the Internet. This capability renders the exchange of files highly fragmented and nearly impossible to trace or stop. Ironically, Gnutella was originally developed by an AOL programmer and mounted briefly as **freeware**, which was available to any and all on an AOL site in early 2000.[27] AOL quickly removed the potentially offensive code, but again the genie was out of the bottle. The Gnutella software is alive and being improved by thousands of independent programmers. The irony is that AOL unwittingly contributed to the development of a software package that facilitates the illegal and uncompensated copying of its own Time-Warner video and music products.

The Madster (formerly Aimster) file-sharing software also has a connection to AOL, although they prominently deny any affiliation with AOL on their homepage. Aimster interacts with AOL's Instant Messenger by allowing people on an AOL buddy list to search and exchange files among themselves using private e-mail messages. As such the firm does not know what is being exchanged or have the capacity to censure that exchange. Therefore, it feels that it is beyond the reach of the Napster court ruling. The firm began in August 2000 and by the end of the year, some 2.5 million AOL users had registered at the Madster site, with more that 1 million users a day exchanging files.[28] In a bold offensive move to protect its interests, Madster sued the major recording companies seeking a court ruling that the firm does not violate recording industry copyrights by allowing music files to be shared over the Internet.[29]

The Record Companies Face Some Important e-Commerce Choices

For the $1.4 billion recording industry, illegal file sharing is a **disruptive technology** that poses a serious economic threat. For all of 2001, album sales fell for the first time in 10 years, down by 2.8 percent. For the first six months of 2002, sales were down by 8.3 percent relative to the same period in 2001.[30] Given the threat, what alternatives are available to the recording companies? Clearly, the firms always have the option of changing

25 Humbert S. Nelli, "Italians and Crime in Chicago: The Formative Years, 1890-1920," *American Journal of Sociology*, 74, 4 (January 1969), p. 391.

26 Clay Shirky, "The Music Industry Will Miss Napster," *The Wall Street Journal*, July 28, 2000, p. A14.

27 Lee Gomes, "Renegade Gnutella May Become a Web Standard," *The Wall Street Journal*, May 29, 2000, p. B6.

28 Matt Richtel, "Aimster Heads Down a Path Already Taken by Napster," *The New York Times*, June 1, 2001, p. C2.

29 "Aimster Up, Napster Down for Now," available at **http://www.wired.com/news/mp3/0,1285,44790,00.html**.

30 Edna Gundersen, "Any Way You Spin It, the Music Biz Is in Trouble," *USA Today*, June 5, 2002, p. 1A.

their current business model and start making songs available over the Internet themselves. The question is: How to implement this change? One of the strengths of the marketplace lies in the fact that it frequently provides more than a single answer to that kind of question. First, Bertelsmann, the giant European publishing, music, and entertainment conglomerate purchased the assets of Napster.[31] They are looking to capitalize on the Napster brand name and its easy-to-use software to create a music sale and exchange service that is both legitimate and revenue generating. Such a system would have to satisfy the copyright laws and generate sufficient funds to make the royalty payments.

Second, the big five recording companies united to form two competing blocks of firms designed to bring fee-based music services directly to consumers via the Internet. Pressplay markets the songs from Sony Music and Universal Music, whereas MusicNet, in alliance with RealNetworks, uses the RealOne file transfer technology to license the music of BMG (Bertelsmann), EMI (British), and AOL-Time Warner on a subscription basis.[32] These joint ventures signal the willingness of the major recording firms to face the reality of the marketplace and unbundle the songs from the CD format, making them available individually. It's an important step in getting the firms to change their business models and embrace the Internet, but it is an entirely different issue to determine how they are going to allow their music content to be distributed as an e-commerce product. In theory, the two alliances permit the record companies to maintain their full control over both the content and distribution system. The firms can dictate the prices and terms of music distribution. They can minimize the adverse impact of the Internet service on CD sales, optimize the profit stream from the dual revenue flows, and give them direct access to their customers. This **direct control model of Internet music distribution** allows the record companies to project their existing economic power over the music industry onto the Internet.

In practice, however, the first version of MusicNet's direct control model was largely unsuccessful in signing up large numbers of subscribers.[33] As opposed to some 40,000 MusicNet subscribers, the file-sharing programs from Morpheus and Kazaa have been downloaded 89.3 million and 64 million times respectively as of June 2002. The attractiveness of the MusicNet service is limited by play restrictions that prohibit the transfer of songs to portable play devices, which rules out the exchange of songs with friends, and that causes downloaded songs to be erased after 30 days on the computer hard drive. In comparison, illegal file-sharing services allow all of these options for a zero fee as opposed to the $9.95 per month rate charged by MusicNet. Next, substantial content gaps exist in the music available on MusicNet, including the absence of all Sony and Universal songs. The service is also limited by antitrust concerns, which restrict the ability of the otherwise independent and competitive recording firms to plan and coordinate their sales via MusicNet. Lastly, the MusicNet alliance with RealNetworks brings the Internet music seller into potential conflict with the music subscription plans and competing music play format offered by Microsoft. Microsoft bundled its own music operating system, Windows Media Player, into its operating system, Windows-XP, and plans to offer music as part of a broader subscription-based service called Hailstorm. Further fragmentation of the e-commerce music market can be a real obstacle to its future acceptance and expansion as a successful commercial venture. Chapter 8 looks further into the nature of the potential conflicts and struggle among media, software, and e-commerce titans.

A third model for making songs available via the Web involves e-commerce start-ups that are securing Internet play and downloading rights. The Rhapsody Digital Music

---

31 John Schwartz, "Bertelsmann, in a Reversal, Agrees to Acquire Napster," *The New York Times*, May 18, 2002, p. C2.

32 Available at **http://www.pressplay.com/** and **http://www.musicnet.com/**.

33 The following information has been adapted from Anna Wilde Mathews, Martin Peers and Mick Wingfield, "Off-Key: The Music Industry Is Finally Online, But Few Listen," *The Wall Street Journal*, May 7, 2002, p. A1.

Service division of Listen.com became the first Internet music firm to license the music catalogs from all five major music labels.[34] For a monthly fee of $9.95, the subscriber can listen to any number of some 150,000 tunes, on what the firm describes as a "celestial jukebox" at **http://www.listen.com/**. However, the service does not allow for either downloads or burning a tune to the subscriber's CD. Licensing is the first step for the record firms in developing an **intermediary control model of Internet music distribution**. Here, third-party intermediaries acquire the music distribution rights from the recording firms. Even though antitrust concerns may have motivated this crack in the direct control model, the reality is that a third-party service, which is able to license music from any firm, will be able to solve many of the content gap problems. The Internet may lead to disintermediation in some areas, but it may stimulate intermediation in others where special skills, brand identity, or legal constraints are key issues. However, the recording firms are trying to avoid surrendering profits to the Internet music distributors as they did with MTV in the early 1980s. There, the recording firms established "a licensing model that many music executives view as the costliest error in the industry's history."[35] Moreover, it isn't a simple task for just any firm to offer a song list over the Internet legally. The firm must secure both the **recording rights** to the sound of the music from the music labels and license the **composition rights** to the melodies and lyrics from the music publishing firms. Acquiring a third set of **performance rights**, covering the public performance of a work, may also be necessary.[36]

The licensing of third party intermediaries will create competition for the recording firms' own Internet efforts, posing an optimal pricing problem for them. What combination of direct and indirect distribution, along with the pricing structure, will maximize the profits of the recording firms? Is it in the best interests of the record firms to encourage entry and broad distribution of their products? Or should they avoid indirect distribution, keep the sales and profits all for themselves, and run the risk of being challenged by either antitrust enforcement or Congress for stifling competition?

Issues and Questions Surrounding the Economics of Pricing Internet Music

Faced with the reality of illegal file sharing, the recording firms are working to find a potential pricing point that is low enough to discourage music piracy but still high enough to leave them with an adequate profit margin to support their business.[37] Part of what the recording firms fear is **cannibalization**, or the substitution of legal music downloads of individual songs in place of the purchase of the entire CD. Warner Music is allowing the digital downloading, in an MP3 format, of songs via an AOL pilot program for a charge of $0.99 each, but industry experts believe that the price per downloaded song must drop to $0.25 before the payment alternative would halt pirating and encourage legal copying. At $0.25 per Internet download, the price would yield a margin, under certain conditions, of perhaps $0.10 per Internet copy. The record companies currently average a $5 profit margin per CD sold. Therefore, for every CD sale that is cannibalized or lost to copying, the firm would have to sell 50 downloads to retain the identical profit margin.

In an ideal world, with a low enough price, the record firms could recapture millions of dollars of today's lost profits by converting the majority of illegal copies into legal ones. Second, the record firms may be able to leverage their profits upwards by promoting a

---

34 Amy Harmon, "Grudgingly, Music Labels Sell Their Songs Online," *The New York Times*, July 1, 2002, p. C1.

35 Harmon "Grudgingly," p. C3.

36 See Don Clark, "Music Sites Hope to State Humming," *The Wall Street Journal*, July 16, 2001, p. B5; and Matt Richtel, "Internet Music Start-up to Obtain Licenses," *The New York Times*, July 16, 2001, p. C2.

37 The material in this section has been adapted from Harmon "Grudgingly," p. C1; and Gundersen, "Any Way You Spin It," p. 1A.

wider range of CDs from artists with more limited appeal, rather than expending the majority of their effort on developing mega hits from a limited number of superstars. Lastly, the ease and ability to preview more music online may encourage fans to buy the CDs, try new music, and even expand the level of their total expenditures on a combination of recorded and downloaded music.

A darker scenario is also possible. Currently, the industry releases some 7,000 new titles per year, with fewer than 10 percent of them being profitable. The 700 high-profit albums cover the losses from the remaining CDs, along with the costs associated with artist development. Some evidence supports the assertion that most of the decline in CD sales for 2001 was among the already heavily price-discounted top 10 albums of the year. Therefore, price cuts at the retail level did not discourage Internet piracy of the most popular CDs. Under this situation, the risks to the industry from legal Internet downloading are considerable. Even with low-priced Internet music sales, fans may continue to illegally copy the biggest hits, while providing insufficient revenue from single song downloads to cover the operating costs of the firm. If this scenario is realized, the industry might be forced into an even more radical change in its business model, such that recorded music becomes primarily a vehicle to promote the artist, as the major labels look elsewhere for the source of their revenues. Where and what will be that new source?

Apart from these concerns, a host of other unresolved questions remain about e-commerce as applied to a for-fee Internet music system. For example, will music fans pay to belong to several subscription services simultaneously to get access to all of their favorite artists and tunes? Or will the competing blocks be forced to allow some form of mutual access for a portion of the subscription fees? As individual songs become available for copying, how will the payment system work? **Online micropayment systems** have not succeeded in the past, and credit card merchant charges are too costly to allow small payments of from $0.10 to $1.[38] What will happen to the songs from independent record labels and access to garage bands? Will Pressplay and MusicNet share their systems with others?

How will music fans raised on the Napster model react to a **pay-for-play system** as opposed to a **copy-and-skip system**? Were the Napster users really looking for freedom of choice rather than freedom from cost? Will they skip the fuss and expense of a subscription or per-play charge system and continue to use free, peer-to-peer, file-sharing technologies? Will Napster-like Internet sites continue to multiply by appearing offshore, in places such as Holland or the West Indies, where they are not easily pursued by U.S. copyright enforcement? Will the interests of music fans, who love their favorite current groups and songs, be greatly expanded by the potential diversity of legitimate tunes accessed via the Internet? As a result, will the exposure to more groups with more songs, lead music fans to spend more money on recorded music? Lastly, will today's enemy of the recording business become its biggest friend and source of profits tomorrow? It happened before with the sales of VHS home versions of Hollywood movies.[39] The outcome is uncertain, and markets sometimes work in strange and unexpected ways.

OTHER MEDIA COPYRIGHT CASES

The Recording Firms Target MY.MP3.com

Prior to the Napster suit, the five major recording companies won a judgment against MP3.com and its **virtual locker service**, MY.MP3.com.[40] MP3.com started out as a legal, rebel music service, listing the songs of unknown bands, and offering them for free listening and downloading. With the introduction of the locker service, MP3 ran afoul

---

38 Don Tapscott, "Napster Decision, A Business Opportunity," *The Wall Street Journal*, February 14, 2001, p. A22.

39 Paul Goldstein, "The Next Napster May Be an Insider," *The New York Times*, July 28, 2001, p. A21.

40 Anna Wilde Mathews and Colleen DeBaise, "Judge Says MP3.com Broke Laws, Owes Damages to Seagram Unit," *The Wall Street Journal*, September 7, 2000, p. B16.

of the copyright laws. Virtual lockers, in general, allow the owners of CD music to store their tunes on the provider's servers, enhancing the potential degree of music portability. The owners would then be able to access a download of the music at times and places that are convenient to the locker holder. This activity can be legal as long as the CD owners "rip" the songs from their own CDs and upload them into the locker, or load licensed music from the servers provided by the service.

What MY.MP3.com did was to make the loading process much easier and thereby attractive to use. All the locker holder had to do was to insert the CD containing the tunes to be stored into the computer drive, allowing MY.MP3.com to confirm the presence of the CD and establishing presumed ownership of the music. MY.MP3.com then would load the desired songs from *its own database* of some 80,000 CDs, and the locker holder would then access the songs by logging into the password-protected account. The MY.MP3.com approach conflicts with the copyright laws in several areas, including the transfer of the songs as well as their storage and retrieval. First, the digital copies of the songs made by MY.MP3.com were done without the permission of or licensing from the record companies. Second, it was impossible to know for sure that the CD inserted into the computer drive was actually owned by the person holding the locker. It was also too easy for the locker holders to share passwords with other music fans, giving them illegal access to the library of songs.[41] The case cost the MP3.com parent in the neighborhood of $170 million in settlement costs, judgment fees, and legal expenses.

However, in an interesting twist to the story, Vivendi Universal SA, whose Universal Music division won the biggest judgment against MP3.com and is the world's largest record firm, agreed to purchase MP3.com for $372 million.[42] They intend to use the MP3.com technology to offer listener-paid Internet music through Pressplay in competition with MusicNet, which employs the technology developed by RealNetworks. This purchase, along with the investment by BMG in Napster, the purchase of Emusic.com by Universal and the MusicNet RealNetworks alliance, can be seen as an attempt to resolve an important, media-related, e-commerce tension. On the one hand, availability of music on the Internet poses a strong challenge to the current market power of the giant entertainment firms, including their recording subsidiaries. Internet music has the potential to alter the recording firms' access to customers, as well as the fans' access to music, artists, and distributors. However, strategic behavior by the media firms may allow them to further consolidate their existing power and to extend it into a new distribution medium.

The actions by the recording firms attempt to shift control of online music and profits away from the upstart dot-com companies and back into the hands of the five major recording firms. The dot-com start-ups set out to challenge the music distribution reach of the recording firms, with the possibility of offering both artists and music fans more choices. As Internet distributors come under the influence of the recording firms, however, they fail to "democratize" the music business or curtail the industry's current level of market power. Rather, the major firms appear to be consolidating their power and position by reaching forward and controlling the online business as well.[43] Keep in mind that this potential strategy, along with others, raise questions that go beyond those listed in the previous section. For example, will the media firms' reactions to the potential shift in the balance of market power be successful? Will it allow them to control online music and rein in the spread of competing technologies? Will antitrust authorities be moved to intervene in this extension of market control?

---

41 Martin Peers, "MP3.com Has Infringed on Copyrights of Five Record Firms, Judge Decides," *The Wall Street Journal*, May 1, 2000, p. A3.

42 John Carreyrou and Anna Wilde Mathews, "Vivendi Universal to Purchase MP3.com for $372 Million in Cash and Stock," *The Wall Street Journal*, May 21, 2001, p. C3.

43 "Online Upstarts of Music Join Major Record Labels," *The New York Times*, May 22, 2001, p. C7.

The Recording Firms Target Webcasters

The recording industry also felt threatened by Webcasters that provided e-commerce music services. **Pure Webcasters** are Internet-only music stations that provide songs on an **almost-on-demand** basis.[44] They include MTV's Radio SonicNet, MusicMatch's MX, and Launch's Launchcast. In varying formats, they all come close to allowing listeners to choose the music they want to hear from a specific artist when they want to hear it. It is similar to traditional radio broadcasting, but with an interactive twist. As such, pure Webcasters come close to mimicking the results of a personally downloaded song library, without the need to deal with a Napster-like firm or to buy the copyrighted music. Some traditional broadcast radio stations also retransmit or **simulcast** their signals via the Web.

The RIAA was so concerned about potential consequences of this form of Internet music that they lobbied to have specific restrictive provisions inserted into the DMCA. First, the restrictions limited the ability of Webcasters to sequentially play multiple selections from a single album or multiple songs from the same artist. Without these provisions, the sales of CDs might suffer or the pay-for-play services of the record firms themselves might be adversely affected. Second, the DMCA also required Webcasters to pay royalties to the recording firms for the use of the sound recordings, in addition to the fees currently paid to the artists and publishers for the right to play their songs. Traditional broadcast radio stations have never paid a royalty to the recording firms for each play of a specific song. The over-the-air play was considered as having sufficient promotional value to compensate the recording firms. If the Webcasters were going to utilize an almost-on-demand format, however, the RIAA felt that they should pay for the right to play the sound recordings. In June 2002, the Librarian of Congress, working for the U.S. Copyright Office, set the royalty rate at $0.007 per song per Web listener for both pure Webcasters and simulcasters.[45] The rate will be a relatively limited burden to the largest Webcasters of popular music, including AOL, Yahoo!, Microsoft, and RealNetworks.[46] Given the low revenues earned by most small pure Webcasters, the royalty rate threatens their continued existence. If Internet music consolidation occurs, a part of the value of the Web will be lost. Music diversity and the tastes of small audiences will be sacrificed in favor of rigid play formats with broader appeal and more formulaic programming.

The legal struggle between the recording firms and the Webcasters demonstrates two points. First, it shows how creative e-commerce sites can be in delivering services tailored to the tastes and convenience of the customer. Second, it shows how persistent the defenders of the old ways and their market power can be in extending their control into new technologies to demand compensation for the use of their creations.

The Film Industry Targets Scour.com and DeCSS

The film industry, like the recording firms, encountered its problems with copyright infringement and violators of the DMCA. Some 24 recording companies and film studios combined to file suit against Scour.com, a Web site whose search technology allowed for the illegal online exchange of both copyrighted films and music.[47] Several college students at UCLA founded Scour in 1999. The suit was resolved fairly quickly when Scour agreed to sell its assets to Listen.com, a music search site backed by the five major record labels.[48]

---

44 Jefferson Graham, "Net Radio Tangos with the Law," *USA Today*, July 3, 2001, p. 3D.

45 Amy Harmon, "Internet Radio Criticizes Rate on Royalties," *The New York Times*, June 21, 2002, p. C2.

46 The Internet and media giant AOL finds itself on both sides of the table on this issue. It is both a Webcaster that must pay the new royalty fee and Warner Music that will receive part of the payments. See Julia Angwin, "Web Radio Showdown," *The Wall Street Journal*, May 15, 2002, p. B1.

47 Anna Wilde Mathews and Bruce Orwall, "Record Firms, Studios Sue Scour Alleging Theft via Its Site on Web," *The Wall Street Journal*, July 21, 2000, p. B6.

48 Matt Richtel, "Web Company Will Sell Assets to Settle Suit on Music Files," *The New York Times*, November 2, 2000, p. C1.

The film industry faced even a greater security challenge. Illegal copying of VCR and DVD films costs the industry an estimated $250 million to $2.5 billion in annual lost revenues.[49] Therefore, it was no surprise that the DVD Copy Control Association and the Motion Picture Association of America (MPAA) filed two lawsuits against the distributors of a video encryption-cracking program called **DeCSS**. DeCSS was written by an anonymous German programmer and distributed by Jon Johansen, a 15-year old Norwegian member of a European "hacker" group.[50] The original intent was to reverse-engineer the **content scrambling system (CSS)**, an encryption technology used by the film industry to protect movies recorded in the DVD format. The decrypting ("De"CSS) was designed as a way to allow the film to be played on a Linux-based system. However, the result was a program that counteracted the encryption for all uses, leading to a violation of DMCA. The suits were designed to stop Eric Corley, a hacker magazine and Web site editor, from both publishing the 60 lines of cracking code in downloadable form and using his Web site to link to other sites that also made the code available.[51]

The two injunctions were granted and have effectively blocked the downloading of the digital code.[52] The futility of the effort was demonstrated by the fact that the code itself is protected by the First Amendment as free speech. Therefore, it has been printed as a protest on T-shirts. It is also available in word form for hand copying at various sites, along with instructions on how to use it.[53] The *DeCSS* case introduces another aspect of the initial "clash of rights" tension described earlier in this chapter. Specifically, what is the proper balance to be struck between protecting copyrights and protecting the right of free speech? The case also raises more questions about the ability to protect copyrighted material in the digital age. Lastly, detractors from the decision ask whether the DMCA goes far beyond what is necessary to protect the rights of copyright holders. Look for the next round of encryption cracking to focus on the Internet-based, video-on-demand services being introduced by the major movie studios.[54] The videos will be encryption protected but as, a computer illiterate yet technologically savvy neighbor once said, "If a human being put it together, a human being can take it apart."[55]

Digital Copyrights for Books and Authors

The problems associated with applying old-media rights in a new-media age are not limited to the music and film industries. The conflict over copyrights on digitized forms of information has also spread to the publishing industry. There, a tension arises between publishers and authors over the distribution of books and other previously printed material in a new electronic form. Author–publisher book contracts have traditionally assigned the copyrights for printed material to the book publishers. If the publisher wishes to distribute that information in a digitized form, such as an e-book, does it require an additional compensation to be paid to the author? This problem is a major one for works published before the mid-1990s—which is the date when publishing contracts began to require authors to waive their electronic reproduction rights because contemporary sales of older works are an important source of profit for many publishing

49 Matt Lake, "Tweaking Technology to Stay Ahead of the Film Pirates," *The New York Times*, August 2, 2001, p. G9.

50 J.S. Kelly, "Interview with Jon Johansen," available at **http://www.linuxworld.com/linuxworld/lw-2000-01/lw-01-dvd-interview.html**.

51 Deborah Durham-Vishr, "DeCSS: Round One to Hollywood, but the fight continues," available at **http://www.cnn.com/2000/TECH/computing/08/23/decss.part2.idg/**.

52 Bloomberg News, "Web Site for Hackers Will Not Appeal," *The New York Times*, July 6,2002, p. C2.

53 "Gallery of CSS Descramblers," available at **http://www.cs.cmu.edu/~dst/DeCSS/Gallery/**.

54 Rick Lyman, "Hollywood, an Eye on Piracy, Moves to Rent Movies Online," *The New York Times*, August 17, 2001, p. A1.

55 Thanks, Cy A., for this practical observation.

houses. In one case, an electronic publishing start-up, RosettaBooks, published pre-1990s works by such prominent authors as William Styron, Agatha Christie, George Orwell, and Kurt Vonnegut.[56] The firm secured the rights to digital editions of these and other key works, even though the original print publisher held the traditional copyright.[57] It will be up to the courts to determine whether the publishing rights to the hard and soft cover print books extends to the distribution of electronic books as well.

In a related issue, the U.S. Supreme Court has already weighed in on the side of freelance authors in their copyright challenge against newspaper and magazine publishers. The publishers had made the archived contributions of freelancers available, under license and for a fee, as part of electronic databases after the original printing of the article. This practice went on without the permission of or additional compensation paid to the authors. As such, it was found to be an infringement of the copyrights retained by the freelancers and therefore a violation of the copyright laws.[58] The Court found that the electronic database versions, allowing the storage and retrieval of the material from a vast range of articles, were new presentations of the material outside of the original publication context and not merely a revision of the original work.

Lastly, the issues of copyrights and fair use by the owners of books are appearing within the context of electronic textbooks.[59] Textbook publishers face several economic problems. First is the task of keeping the information up-to-date. Second is the cost of textbook printing and distribution. A third problem involves competition from the used textbook market. They also face the problem of illegal photocopying. Most, if not all, of these problems can be eliminated through the technology of **digital rights management** if the textbook comes in DVD form. Here, the transaction between publisher and student can be transformed from a *sales* contract to a *license* or rental agreement where the publisher is allowed to add on restrictive conditions. Encryption may keep the work from being copied and periodic payments may be required to keep the disk active or up to date after initial acquisition. In the absence of payment, the DVD will self-destruct beyond some specified license termination date. It may not be long before students download, either directly or through their college bookstore, an entire semester's worth of books from a collection of e-commerce Web sites. It would be a more efficient, less expensive, but potentially far less permanent method of book exchange than the current textbook distribution model.

PROTECTING COPYRIGHTED MATERIAL: DIGITAL WATERMARKING AND ENCRYPTION

The two most technologically sophisticated methods for the protection of copyrighted, digital material involve digital watermarking and encryption. A **digital watermark** is an electronic signal or "flag" imbedded throughout a work signifying copyright protection. Devices that read or copy digitized files could be programmed to detect the digital watermark and deny access to anyone other than a legitimate owner. Marking copyrighted files in this way could put an end to the illegal file sharing of music, films, or books. The digital watermark approach, however, transfers the responsibility and expense of developing and installing copyright protection technology from the holder of the copyright to the makers of playback devices.[60] Therefore, device makers openly oppose accepting the watermark approach because it makes existing computers and

---

56 See **http://www.rosettabooks.com/**.

57 David D. Kirkpatrick, "Old-Media Rights in the Digital Age," *The New York Times*, July 19, 2001, p. C1.

58 Linda Greenhouse, "Freelancers Win in Copyright Case," *The New York Times*, June 26, 2001, p. A1.

59 Thomas E. Weber, "Protecting Copyrights: How E-Books Will Be Like Parking Meters," *The Wall Street Journal*, September 11, 2000, p. B1.

60 Amy Harmon, "Piracy or Innovation? It's Hollywood vs. High Tech," *The New York Times* March 14, 2002, p. C1.

playback equipment obsolete and potentially violates the case-based copying rights of consumers established under the fair use doctrine. Watermark technology might also hurt the profits of device makers. It could stunt the long-term growth of device sales, which are in part fueled by the ability to copy or transfer digital material to a number of playback systems. Given the impasse with the equipment makers, the music industry has not been able to adopt this protection technology. Therefore, it has been forced to pursue the more inefficient and ineffective course of challenging the copyright offenders in court on a case-by-case basis.[61]

This microeconomic impasse based upon cost and profits has a larger macroeconomic implication as well. Some members of Congress feel that the inability to agree on technology safeguards for copyrighted material makes the movie studios unwilling to offer "high-quality programming for digital television and broadband Internet services that would generate consumer interest and, in turn, economic growth."[62] Therefore, the impasse creates an additional tension, on the national level, between the priorities of protecting intellectual property and promoting growth enhancing technological innovation. The potential here is for Congress to step in and mandate a resolution of the impasse.

As a point of fact, the digital watermark may not be a foolproof protection method either. An entertainment industry-backed group, the Secure Digital Music Initiative, offered a $10,000 prize to anyone who could remove a digital watermark from a musical recording. A multi-university academic team headed by a computer science professor, Edward W. Felten, from Princeton University, succeeded in removing the marking. The team declined the prize in the name of academic freedom and went to publish their findings. They were challenged by the RIAA and threatened with prosecution under the provisions of DMCA. This challenge sets up a tension between the freedom of scientific research and the anticircumvention prohibitions contained within DMCA. Although DMCA specifically exempts encryption research from prosecution under the act, the technique employed by the team may not fall under the exemption making them potentially subject to prosecution.[63]

The issue was partly resolved when the RIAA relented and the decryption information was published in a research paper.[64] The research team is still pursuing its court case against DMCA in the name of freedom of scientific research. In his latest declaration to the court, Professor Felten explained, "I understand that Defendants advocate an interpretation of the DMCA that would outlaw analysis of systems that might be used to control the use of copyrighted materials. . . . [S]uch an interpretation would effectively prevent analysis of critical systems, and so would have a disastrous effect on education, research, and practice in computer security."[65] It is another instance where defenders of an open-source system feel that the DMCA goes too far in limiting the rights of others in the name of protecting the rights of copyright holders.

The second technology for protecting copyrighted digital material is encryption. **Encryption** is a software approach that involves scrambling or degrading the copyrighted digital content and unlocking the scramble only to those who have an authorized password. As with watermarking technology, music encryption might render some portion of the existing stock of CD playback equipment obsolete. Also, given that encryption is a software-based solution, the technology is subject to decryption by software code.

---

61 In an alternative approach, the recording firms introduced a copy prevention tactic called "File-spoofing," which places degraded music files on the Internet to snare unwary pirates and discourage illegal copying. See, Nick Wingfield, "Behind the Fake Music," *The Wall Street Journal*, July 11, 2002, p. D1.

62 Harmon "Piracy, or Innovation," p. C6.

63 David P. Hamilton, "Digital-Copyright Law Faces New Fight," *The Wall Street Journal*, June 7, 2001, p. B10.

64 Jennifer Lee, "Delayed Report on Encryption Flaws to Be Presented," *The New York Times*, August 15, 2001, p. C6.

65 Available at **http://www.eff.org/Legal/Cases/Felten_v_RIAA/20010813_eff_felten_pr.html**.

Legitimate device makers say that it would be easy to write code that would allow the transfer of copy-protected material, but that such an act would expose them to prosecution under provisions of the DMCA.[66] Music encryption ultimately leads to many of the same kinds of problems associated with the film industry's attempt to stifle the usage and spread of the DeCSS technology.

A related area reveals another example of potentially criminal violations of the anti-circumvention provisions of DMCA. This case involved the arrest and jailing of a visiting Russian computer science graduate student who presented a paper on decryption. His employer, a Russian firm, pointed out security flaws in the Adobe encryption software and then wrote code to override a portion of the restrictions on making copies of e-books. In his case, the crime was not copying but rather circumventing security measures designed to prohibit copying.[67] The actions by the Russian firm were perfectly legal in Russia. However, the fact that the computer code can be accessed in the United States extended the reach of U.S. copyright law to cover actions taken outside the borders of the United States. Two potential consequences arise from this case. First, as noted previously, the DMCA extends the law well beyond the protection of the copyright and infringes on the rights of legitimate consumers to use their copyrighted material. Second, prosecution in this case acts to intimidate security and encryption researchers who seek to crack and report on deficient code. The very security of encryption depends upon the freedom to undertake such research.[68]

SUMMARY AND PROSPECTS

Reflections on *Metallica v. Napster*

Metallica v. Napster is where the chapter's discussion about copyrights and e-commerce in the digital age began. It started out simply enough as a business tension, with a commercial musical group suing to stop another commercial firm from copying the group's music without compensation. As the story unfolded the issue quickly escalated into a whole new set of tensions, conflicts, and questions. It pointed out tensions between the rights of copyright holders and the rights of free speech. It raised questions about the Internet as an open source, facilitating the free flow of information, and about the right of consumers to make legitimate use of the digital material they purchase. It touched off conflicts over the use of new laws, such as DMCA, to protect the rights conveyed by older laws, such as copyrights, and how the reach of the new laws can extend far beyond the grasp of the old. It created questions about the range and limits of technology. It created social tensions pitting the combined ability of laws and technology against the moral shortcomings of society.

Strategic Reactions to Digital Piracy

What is the outcome of this discussion? In the twentieth century, federal agent Eliot Ness became a folk hero by chasing down violations of the ill-conceived laws prohibiting the production and sale of liquor. In the twenty-first century, will there be a squad of copyright police chasing down violators of the ill-conceived copyright protection laws? In the end, the route to combating digital piracy represents a final tension: Will copyright owners choose to fight piracy through legal challenges or through neutralization via technology?

---

66 Amy Harmon, "CD Technology Stops Copies, But It Starts A Controversy," *The New York Times*, March 1, 2002, p. C1.

67 Amy Harmon and Jennifer 8. Lee, "Arrest Raises Stakes in Battle Over Copyright," *The New York Times*, July 23, 2001, p. C1.

68 Lawrence Lessig, "Jail Time in the Digital Age," *The New York Times*, July 30, 2001, p. A17.

The RIAA wants to control what music consumers hear, and when and how they hear it, as well as how much it will cost them to listen. Much the same thing can be said about the MPAA and films, but these industry organizations should also recognize that an opposing cadre of young, technically sophisticated persons is just as passionately committed to an open-source Internet as a vehicle for the free flow of just about all information. The RIAA and MPAA can't stamp out all copying through legal enforcement. The best short-run hope is a technological fix to make it more difficult for the average citizen to satisfy his or her desire for free entertainment. In the long run, the record labels, film distributors, and print publishers will have to construct new business models that actively embrace the evolving e-commerce technology, making it more open while still profitable for all. Given the amount of money involved and the creative juices unleashed by the profit incentive, does anyone doubt that the new mode will be the ultimate direction for the protection of intellectual property in the digital age?

KEY TERMS AND CONCEPTS

album mentality
almost-on-demand music services
anticircumvention provision
antidevice provision
Audio Home Recording Act (AHRA) of 1992
bundling
cannibalization
composition rights
content scrambling system (CSS)
copy-and-skip system
DeCSS
digital copying problem
Digital Millennium Copyright Act (DMCA) of 1998
digital rights management
digital watermark
direct control model of Internet music distribution
disruptive technology

encryption
ethical disconnect
file-sharing technology
freeware
Gnutella
intermediary control model of Internet music distribution
MP3 files
online micropayment system
pay-for-play system
performance rights
piracy of intellectual property
pure Webcasters
recording rights
RIAA v. Napster
ripping CDs
simulcast
Sony Betamax case of 1984
virtual locker service
Webcasters

DISCUSSION AND REVIEW QUESTIONS

1. Why might Metallica draw the distinction between the free exchange of bootlegged, live performance music, and the exchange of copyrighted studio recordings?

2. Why is the digital copyright problem described as a "clash of rights?" What rights are in conflict here?

3. How does the Digital Millennium Copyright Act (DMCA) extend copyright protection from the copyrighted material to the technology that transmits or portrays the material?

4. How does the wording of the DMCA effectively deny the right to copy material that is legitimately in the hands of lawful owners?

5. Identify and discuss three of the limitations that arise out of the DMCA.

6. Prior to Napster, why did the RIAA grudgingly tolerate acts of intellectual property theft? How did the combination of MP3 technology and Napster software change this tolerance?

7. Explain how "bundling" by the recording firms creates commercial as opposed to technical barriers to the freedom of music choice.

8. How did the *Napster* case reaffirm the right of the recording industry to protect copyrighted material, while at the same time diminishing its ability to do so?

9. How are the results of the suits that are blocking the electronic transfer of DeCSS technology being thwarted by the First Amendment right of free speech?

10. Compare the direct control model of Internet music distribution in terms of its theoretical impact on e-commerce versus its impact in practice. Why do the recording firms introduce such tight play restrictions on Internet service subscribers?

11. How has the economics of intermediation by Listen.com worked to overcome the forces of disintermediation in the distribution of Internet music?

12. Is the concept of an Internet virtual music locker a legal service? What characteristics made the MY.MP3.com run afoul of the copyright laws?

13. What are Webcasters? How have the recording firms used their power to control competition from Webcasters?

14. In what ways does the *DeCSS* case highlight the clash-of-rights tension?

15. What is digital rights management? How can it be employed to affect the availability, quality, and price of college texts?

17. What is the difference between copyright protection secured by a digital watermark as opposed to encryption? Why do device makers oppose the watermark approach?

WEB EXERCISES

1. Link to at least three of the following Web music sites: Pressplay.com, MusicNow.com, Emusic.com, MusicNet.com, and Listen.com. Compare the service offerings in terms of price, the ability to stream (listen to multiple songs without downloading), ability to download, and the ability to copy individual songs or albums to your own CD. Which site yields the best deal for the consumer? Why?

2. Link to one of the pure Webcasters, such as Launchcast.com or MusicMatch.com, and see how they go about matching their library of songs with the tastes of listeners. You don't have to sign up for the pay service; most will allow you sample the site for a limited amount of time.

3. Link to the BRS Web radio directory at **http://www.radio-directory.fm/**. See if your college radio station is simulcasting over the Web, or look for your home town FM favorite to listen while you are at school.

4. Connect to Rosettabooks.com and check out the number and range of titles for e-books that are available at the site. Are any of the names familiar to you?

5. Link to the site **http://www-2.cs.cmu.edu/~dst/DeCSS/Gallery/** at Carnegie Mellon University, which contains a discussion of and links to the DeCSS code. Why would someone make this code available on the Web?

6. If you are not already familiar with the Gnutella based music copy software, link to **http://www.morpheus.com/**, **http://www.kazaa.com** or one of the Napster clones such as **http://www.mp3downloadcenter.com/** and see what they have to offer in the way of music services.

CHAPTER

8

Introductory Case

AOL BUYS SOMETHING BIG, REAL, AND STRATEGIC

One of the great Biblical stories of the Old Testament is that of David and Goliath. Goliath was the champion of the Philistines, big, strong, and battle-hardened. He towered over David, a Hebrew, who was nimble, cunning, and quick-witted. The story goes that David slew Goliath, bringing the giant down with a single stone from a sling. Gaining courage from David's victory, the Hebrew army proceeded to destroy the army of the Philistines.

Suppose for a moment that we revise history. Let's assume that when David and Goliath met on the battlefield, they found a common interest and joined forces. Size and strength were united with quickness and strategic purpose. Together the Hebrews and Philistines came to dominate what is now the Middle East, warding off threats from the Babylonians, Persians, Egyptians, and any others who might challenge their supremacy. If these Biblical rivals had only joined together rather than fighting to the

death, perhaps the course of human history might be different today.

By analogy, the world of e-commerce may have already seen its own, but different, version of David and Goliath. In this case, the huge, 80-year-old entertainment and information empire called Time Warner played the role of Goliath, while the 15-year-old ISP and Internet portal, America Online, assumed the role of David. In January of 2000, the two potential combatants met, thought that they saw the value of uniting rather than competing, and agreed to merge their assets.[1] It took the Federal Communications Commission and Federal Trade Commission nearly a year to approve and shape some of the competitive terms, but the two companies were finally allowed to join forces in January of 2001. The creation of AOL-Time Warner (AOL-TW) had the following potential effects. First, the union extended the reach of the two separate firms into new markets, focusing attention upon the possible benefits of media size and diversity. Second, it raised the possibility that changes in the marketplace were reshaping the entertainment landscape. Third, it showed how changes in technology might be encouraging the convergence of entertainment, information, communications, and online services.

The new firm embraces considerable potential, but it also faces many hurdles. It may survive, profit, and grow, or it may sink into a financial morass of conflicting goals and incompatible products. Just because two firms have a common vision, resulting in a merger, doesn't necessarily mean that the combined firm will be a business success. Given these risks, why would the two firms merge as one rather than remain as independent competitors? In this case, the answer is that the formation of the AOL-TW media giant offers a clear test of the profit prospects resulting from the vertical union of media content with Internet distribution. The merger allows for the identification of two important tensions that underscore the discussions in this chapter. The first tension pits the ability of a merger to create profits through efficiency and innovation versus the ability of the merger to create profits based upon the accumulation and exercise of market

---

1 Richard Siklos, et al., "Welcome to the 21st Century," *BusinessWeek*, January 24, 2000, pp. 36–44.

Structural Change Through Mergers

power. The second tension arises between firms that are vertically integrated suppliers of a product such as media content and distribution versus those firms that remain as independent stages in the e-content supply chain.

THE ECONOMICS OF MERGERS

Merger Types with Some e-Commerce Examples

A **merger** combines two or more separate firms into a single legal entity. The merger may be friendly, involving mutual consent, or it may be hostile, in which one firm seizes control of the other from the hands of the existing management.[2] Mergers can be grouped into three broad types and may include a number of subclassifications. First, a **horizontal merger** occurs between two or more firms that sell either the same product or products that are close substitutes for each other, in the same geographic market. Because the firms were direct competitors prior to the merger, the effect of a horizontal merger is to eliminate a competitor and raise the level of industry concentration. Whether the elimination of a competitor also reduces the intensity of competition is unclear. The merger may raise the scale of output for the surviving firm, creating efficiencies of size and making the combined firm a more vigorous competitor, which provides benefits to consumers. The merger between the online recruiting firms CareerBuilder.com and HeadHunter.net would exemplify a horizontal merger in cyberspace.[3]

A **vertical merger** occurs between two firms that stand in a buyer-supplier relationship to one another. The union takes two previously independent firms and organizes them together into a single, vertically integrated, production system. It creates a decision-making model based upon an hierarchical command and control management system. This new model substitutes for a system of market decisions based upon price signals and enforceable contracts. With a vertical merger, the gamble is that coordination based upon human decisions within a single firm will lead to greater efficiencies, enhanced synergies, and higher profits than would a series of arm's-length, market-based negotiations and transactions among independent firms. The AOL-TW merger, as well as the acquisition of the TV broadcast network ABC by Disney, contains elements of a vertical merger. In each case, a company involved in entertainment content creation merged with a firm that enhanced the means of distributing that content to the desired audience.

The final type of general merger is a **conglomerate merger** between firms that either sell unrelated products, or sell the same product but in different geographic markets. As such they are not direct competitors. However, prior to the merger, they may have served as **potential competitors**, with one or both of the firms contemplating

---

2 An *acquisition* involves one firm buying out or taking over the assets and operation of another. The discussion in this chapter makes no distinction between acquisitions and mergers, referring to both types of unions as a merger.

3 Patricia Callahan, "Venture to Buy HeadHunter, an Online Recruiter," *The Wall Street Journal*, August 27, 2001, p. B4. The two firms survive as one at **http://www.careerbuilder.com**.

their entry into the market of the other. Conglomerate mergers are divided into three subcategories: product extension mergers, market extension mergers, and pure conglomerate mergers. **Product extension mergers** occur between two firms producing items that are complementary to one another. For example, in July 2001, the Dutch supermarket group Ahold, already the owner of retail supermarket chains in the United States, acquired the online grocery firm Peapod.[4] Also in April 2000, the traditional store-based cosmetics firm Estee Lauder acquired the brand name and assets of the cosmetics e-tailer Gloss.com.

Market extension mergers occur between two firms that produce the same product but sell it in different and noncompeting markets. Although these markets have traditionally been thought of as geographically different, for purposes of e-commerce, they may be conceived of a being spatially different. Prior to its own demise, the online home grocery delivery firm Webvan, operating in San Francisco, acquired one of its Internet rivals HomeGrocer, which served markets in Portland, Oregon, and Dallas, Texas.[5] Another example would be the merger of the two Baby Bells, SBC, which serviced the southwestern portion of the United States, and Ameritech, which provided telecom service to the central United States. Lastly, **pure conglomerate mergers** involve a union between two firms that operate in totally separate product markets. The purchase of the broadcast network NBC by the industrial and finance firm General Electric would qualify as a pure conglomerate merger.

Merger Motives I: Increased Scale for Efficiency and Innovation

Two of the economic goals associated with most business unions are to raise the level of profitability and to boost the potential for long-run survival. As the first tension noted, these goals can be achieved by either enhancing the level of economic efficiency within the merged firm, or by increasing the level of market power that the larger merged firm might wield over consumers or suppliers. The discussion in this section outlines the elements of the efficiency justification. The next section looks at the sources of merger-enhanced market power. The most common trigger for efficiency enhancement arises from the appearance of technical economies of scale. The post-merger firm, operating at a larger scale of production, may be able to reduce the cost per unit of the product. Cost-cutting advances, including worker skill specialization, division of labor, and the use of a larger, more technologically sophisticated plant, all come into play here. Scale also allows for the elimination of duplicate effort. Two independent firms require two physical headquarters as well as two management, marketing, legal, human resource, and accounting departments. Headquarters functions typically demonstrate **increasing returns to scale**, which means that the combined firm can achieve the same or possibly greater levels of output in these areas with fewer personnel and at a lower cost per unit of output.

A second source of potential efficiencies involves the concept of **synergy**. A merger-based synergy is similar to an economy of scope, which results when the combined firm can carry out a production activity in a less costly or more effective manner than if it were undertaken separately by the two firms. A synergy also arises when the merged firm is presented with profit opportunities that would have been less available to the two firms if they remained independent. Time Warner, with its rich array

---

4 Sarah Ellison, "Ahold Will Buy Rest of Peapod for $2.15 Per Share, or $25 Million," *The Wall Street Journal*, July 17, 2001, p. B3.

5 Jim Carlton, "Webvan Sets Deal to Buy HomeGrocer," *The Wall Street Journal*, June 27, 2000, p. B6. One of the reasons cited for the merger was to avoid the loss of funds that both firms would have experienced as each targeted the Atlanta market area as their next market area. At that point potential competitors would have become direct competitors.

of entertainment and information content, such as magazines, had been unsuccessful in reaching a Web audience. With AOL's Web expertise and youthful subscriber base, this content could be loaded into cyberspace in ways that were less open to the two firms acting alone. Also, their ability to coordinate the cross-promotion of a single proprietary item or an advertiser message across a range of media audiences is considerably enhanced. The combined firm was thought to exceed either the speed or the ability to accomplish the same result through arm's-length market negotiations. In another example of potential synergies, the acquisition by AT&T of two large cable TV systems, TCI and MediaOne, was thought to offer substantial benefits by bundling telephone, cable, and Internet connections through one hookup. Lastly, synergies can arise in the area of research and development. Here, the combining of research budgets reduces wasteful duplication of effort, while the commingling of scientific talent can enrich research productivity and scientific exchange. This issue was part of the reasoning behind the mergers in the pharmaceutical industry, including Glaxo/Smith Kline and Pfizer/Warner Lambert/Pharmacia.[6]

A third source of potential merger-related efficiency comes from replacing weak or shortsighted management. The threat of replacement through merger serves as a market discipline designed to keep current management focused on the creation of shareholder value. However, on some occasions, the innovator, who was good at bringing a commercial product or process to market, may still run the firm. In reality the innovator may lack the skills for daily management, the experience to meet new challenges, or the vision to lead the firm into new markets. In other instances, an outsider may have a vantage point from which to see more potential value in a firm than is evident to insiders, who are trained in less efficient ways of thinking. In either case, the market sees a gap between actual and potential performance, along with the need to replace the existing leadership with those who have a more appropriate skill set. For example, the conglomerate Tyco International took over and apparently reenergized U.S. Surgical and CIT Financial, along with some 137 other firms from 1997 to 2001.[7] On the other hand, a merger may not be the only answer to the market gap problem. Innovative leadership may be obtained simply by hiring a new CEO to recast the firm. This route for change was taken by the board of directors at IBM when Louis Gerstner was chosen as CEO, and he succeeded in reshaping the focus and profitability of the firm.

Lastly, efficiencies may be achieved through **economies of diversification**, where firms merge to reduce the risks associated with excessive exposure in a single market. A classic example would involve a merger between two airlines; one holding primarily north-south routes that are heavily traveled in winter and a second airline whose routes are concentrated east-west, with heavy summer travel. The merger would allow planes to be diverted to service the routes with the greatest seasonal traffic demand. A second example of economies of diversification would arise from the merger of a snowmobile engine maker with a boat engine firm. The seasonal shift in demand would more efficiently use the production capacity and help to keep the skilled workforce together as well as fully employed. In an e-commerce-related field, Qwest acquired US West. Qwest was a fiber-optic capacity firm that provided long distance phone, data, and Internet access services, while US West was a Baby Bell that provided local telephone service within the states of the Rocky Mountain region. The merger was intended to help Qwest stabilize its earnings and share values as fiber-optic revenues fell at a time of excess capacity.[8]

---

6 Robert Frank and Scott Hensley, "Potent Mix: Pfizer to Buy Pharmacia for $60 Billion," *The Wall Street Journal*, July 15, 2002, p. A1.

7 Tyco purchased 137 firms from 1997 to 2001. See "The Most Aggressive CEO," available at **http://www.businessweek.com/magazine/content/01_22/b3734001.htm**.

8 See "Qwest U.S. West Merger a Done Deal," available at **http://news.cnet.com/news/0-1004-200-2196765.html?tag=rltdnws,** November 2001.

Merger Motives II: Elimination of a Competitor and Increased Market Power

Even though profits may rise as a result of merger-related efficiencies, they can also appear because the merger enhanced the level of market power. Horizontal mergers demonstrate the clearest link to rising market power. First, they result in the elimination of a direct competitor. Potentially, this event reduces both the threat of price competition and the complexities associated with strategic behavior. Fewer rivals means fewer possible combinations of reactions by rivals in response to any strategic initiative undertaken by the surviving firm. Second, the merged firm is of greater absolute size within a specific market. If it is sufficiently larger than its rivals, it may be able to bully and dictate market behavior of smaller firms, who fear retaliation if they fail to go along. The appearance of size disparity may also serve as the initial force in the creation of a **price leadership model** within an industry. Here, the dominant firm sets a higher-than-competitive market price that is followed by the smaller firms. Price leadership is often part of a less-competitive oligopolistic market structure. Third, a successful horizontal merger within an industry may trigger the desire on the part of smaller firms to merge as well in order to stay competitive and to avoid the potential threats posed by a disproportionately larger rival. The waves of mergers in the petroleum, pharmaceutical, and financial industries may have been triggered, at the start, by the potential for efficiency gains. But they may also be the result of this copycat size effect. Further, the acceptance of the first merger by regulatory authorities may make it easier for the second tier of firms to adopt a similar strategy.

Vertical mergers occur along the supply chain between previously independent suppliers and buyers. They are accompanied by their own list of potential market power and competitive constraints. First, by engaging in vertical integration, the larger merged firm may raise the dollar height of the capital barriers required to enter the industry. With a diminished number of independent firms in the supply chain, the potential entrant may have to consider entering at both production stages rather than just one. Consequently, the cost of entry increases, raising the already high risks associated with entry and discouraging potential entrants from becoming actual competitors. The merger of AOL and Time Warner, which united entertainment content with the flow through of Internet distribution, exemplifies this type of vertical merger concern. Second, a vertical merger raises the potential for collusive and noncompetitive behavior. Control over multiple stages of production may give previously competitive firms greater powers to jointly set prices or dictate terms of sale. Lastly, they present the potential for **market foreclosure**. A vertically integrated firm, formed by merger, may limit access to a portion of the market by still-independent suppliers and thereby limit the options for firms that lie above or below the sphere of control. Again, the AOL-TW merger exemplifies this possibility. The firm produces its own programming, such as the entertainment channel HBO, the news channel CNN, and the sports-oriented channel WTBS. Through their control of access to a large segment of the Internet and cable audience, they have the power to freeze out rival cable properties such as Fox, Disney, and NBC, limiting AOL-TW entertainment, news, and sports offerings to their own properties. In the same vein, they might give their own programming preferential treatment, while providing audience access to competitors on terms and conditions that place the rivals at a competitive disadvantage. This issue is addressed in greater detail in a later section of the chapter.

Lastly, conglomerate mergers also contain a set of anticompetitive threats. The first involves the removal of the competitive benefits associated with a **potential entrant**. Potential entrants are thought to exist on the fringes of an industry that is attractive to them. The existence of a potential entrant may restrain the tendency of firms within the industry to collude or otherwise exploit any market power that they might possess. Collusion or exploitation tends to result in higher profits that would attract the attention of the potential entrant, turning the firm into an actual competitor. The **de novo entry** of a vigorous new competitor could disrupt existing pricing and profit relationships, along with causing a redistribution of market shares. This redistribution might, in turn, lead to a period of prolonged losses that more than outweigh the short-term gains generated by initial collusive behavior that attracted the entry. When a conglomerate merger removes this potential entrant, this beneficial market restraint is lost. Second, conglomerate mergers create the potential for **cross-subsidization**. This anticompetitive concern arises when a merger allows the use of revenues and profits earned in one market to be used to subsidize the losses earned in another. Strategically, a subdivision of the firm in the market with losses can use the transferred funds to price its product below cost so as to drive out competitors. After rivals exit, the survivor can raise its price above the competitive level with the intent of generating profits that will more than recoup the dollar losses. A third potential anticompetitive result emanating from conglomerate merger is **reciprocity**. This situation arises when one level of a vertically integrated firm purchases goods or services from an independent firm on the condition that the independent buy a portion of its supplies from another division of the vertical firm. For example, an entertainment firm might buy only the technical services of a production studio if that studio purchased its advertising or Internet interconnection services from a corporate relative of the entertainment firm.

A general source of power-based merger consequences arises from **pecuniary economies of scale**. Technical scale economies result in real cost reductions, but pecuniary economies simply lead to a shifting of revenues and profits among firms based upon merger-created size or power disparities. For example, assume a horizontal merger occurs between two firms, which as independent entities bought 15 percent of their resource inputs from the same supplier. Now, at 30 percent, the merged firm becomes a proportionately larger share of the supplier's total sales. Previously, the supplier had some bargaining power relative to the two smaller buyers, so as to charge a price that included a competitive profit. With the merger, more of the power shifts into the hands of the buyer. If the buyer switches to a different supplier, the seller is left with a larger percentage of its production capacity idle. Realizing this point, the buyer may demand a 5 to 10 percent across-the-board reduction in purchase prices. The seller relents, either accepting a lower profit margin for itself or trying to force the same kind of cost reduction onto its suppliers. For the merged firm, its costs are lower and it appears that the union generated efficiencies. However, from the perspective of society, the efficiencies are illusory. They simply represent a transfer of profits from the supplier to the merged and more powerful buyer.

Finally, some fraction of mergers are motivated by **empire building**. Captains of industry with big egos may want to lead big firms. Executive compensation packages, industry prestige, public respect, and a certain degree of insulation against hostile takeovers are frequently tied to the absolute size of the firm being guided. For example, no matter how attractive General Electric might appear to be as a merger partner, the sheer size of the world's largest firm makes it almost immune as a takeover target. As firms around them grow in size, the "urge to merge" may overcome otherwise sensible corporate leaders, who don't want to be left behind in the size race. The possibility of empire building as a motive for mega-mergers is supported by the number of large mergers that failed to add shareholder value as expected. These disappointments include mergers in manufacturing, financial services, and telecommunications. It is surprising to see the range and extent of poor post-merger results, especially in light of the **due diligence requirements** that call for a full review of the potential conditions and consequences of a proposed mega-merger before it is completed.[9]

As a way to close this efficiency-versus-power discussion of mergers, it is instructive to look at a merger that contains some potential e-commerce overtones. This merger involves the corporate union of the New York Yankees baseball team with the New Jersey Nets basketball team and the New Jersey Devils hockey team. The combined entity, called YankeeNets, was assembled as a means to create a new independent cable

---

9 Steven Lipin and Nikhil Deogun, "Big Mergers of '90s Prove Disappointing to Shareholders," *The Wall Street Journal*, October 30, 2000, p. C1.

television channel called Yankee Entertainment and Sports Network (YESN) that would supply the cable games for each team.[10] Arguably, the Yankees are the number one franchise in professional sports, with a large national and potentially global following. They are leveraging their value into other professional sports markets to form a network that can package and sell games, along with related sports programming, 12 months a year. From there, they are integrating forward into the content distribution end of the entertainment business by ending their current links with individual cable stations, and transferring the profits from the cable carriers back to the sports franchise through the licensing of the YES network. The potential here for enhanced sports marketing and profitability is enormous, ranging from free to pay-for-view cable or Internet broadcasts, to an array of possible interactive e-commerce opportunities. How much of this effort involves real efficiencies versus power versus ego is uncertain. However, it appears that one possible goal of the network's formation is an **initial public offering (IPO)**, which will give the public the opportunity to become part owners of YankeeNets, as well as providing equity liquidity and a potentially large monetary windfall for the current equity owners.

CONTEMPORARY MERGER ACTIVITY: MOTIVATIONS, SUCCESSES, AND FAILURES

In the decade of the 1990s, major combinations were recorded in key industries such as airlines, banking, integrated oil, pharmaceuticals, health care, telecommunications services, and telecom infrastructure. Three infrastructure firms, Cisco Systems, JDS Uniphase, and Lucent Technologies, owed some significant portion of their growth to acquisitions that expanded their product line and added to their revenues and market share. Cisco in particular used its rapidly rising stock value as a means of acquiring **intellectual capital** as well as physical products. The purchase of skilled, creative, and innovative engineering talent that was already organized into a productive unit was a hallmark of their acquisition strategy. This process was so successful that for a brief time in March 2000, Cisco became the nation's most valuable industrial company, with an equity value of $555 billion, exceeding the worth of the previous leader, Microsoft.[11]

Some Internet-related mergers were challenged and eventually disallowed by U.S. or European regulators. The most prominent was the proposed merger of the second and third largest U.S. long-distance phone companies, WorldCom and Sprint, who together would have controlled some 53 percent of the Internet backbone service linking ISPs and Internet users.[12] Despite the blockage of a few high profile mergers, however, the regulatory attitude toward mergers softened somewhat in the 1990s for a number of reasons.[13] First and foremost was the trend toward the globalization of markets. The forces of globalization were interpreted as requiring mega-firms with the resources and reach to operate efficiently anywhere in the world. Also, consolidations were happening outside of the United States in Europe and Asia as well. Large domestic firms were seen as

---

10 Richard Sandomir, "YankeeNets Getting Own Cable Network," *The New York Times*, September 11, 2001, p. D6.

11 The collapse of Internet investment caused Cisco's market capitalization to fall to $118.8 billion as of August 31, 2001, placing it twentieth behind the global leader GE at $407 billion. "The World's 100 Largest Public Companies," *The Wall Street Journal*, October 1, 2001, p. R10. Additional information is available at **http://www.nasdr.com/1420/schapiro_16.htm**.

12 David Ruppe, "Merger on Hold: Worldcom, Sprint Withdraw from EU Review," available at **http://abcnews.go.com/sections/business/DailyNews/worldcomsprint000627.html**, November 2001, for the U.S. DOJ blockage; and Tim McDonald, "EU to Block Worldcom/Sprint Merger," available at **http:// www.ecommercetimes.com/perl/story/3611.html**, November 2001, for the EU reasons for blocking the merger.

13 Louis Uchitelle, "Whose Afraid Now That Big Is No Longer Bad?" *The New York Times*, November 5, 2000, p. 3–1.

necessary to meet the challenges of foreign competitors. A second motive for the softening was the accelerating pace of technological change. If markets are changing rapidly, they erode the forces supporting entrenched market power, which allows new firms to enter and compete with existing market leaders. Mergers that create new leaders will find these leaders being challenged by foreign competitors, additional mergers, or the market pressures resulting from "creative destruction."

The third source of regulatory restraint was the movement toward deregulation, which led to major structural changes in the airline, banking, telecommunications, and railroad industries. Because federal regulators originally feared a rise in market power, firms in these industries were prohibited from engaging in mergers that also increased scale, lowered costs, and improved efficiency. In time, regulators grew to appreciate that higher concentration could be offset by the forces of domestic competition, globalization, and technological change. Consequently, they showed less concern about mergers among firms that may have once held entrenched power, created in markets that were previously regarded as natural monopolies.

Lastly, regulators became more willing to accept the efficiency argument as a basis for offsetting any adverse consequences resulting from mega-mergers. For example, the advantages of cost sharing in oil exploration and drilling formed a persuasive rationale for allowing the mergers among the integrated petroleum firms. Mergers among bookstores and firms in the linerboard, corrugated box, and the food processing industries were justified by the efficiencies resulting from the elimination of the excess capacity that restrained profits. Despite these mergers, prices to consumers did not rise. Moreover, the absorption by Boeing of McDonnell-Douglas left only two airframe manufactures. Yet, competition between Boeing and Airbus remained so ferocious that neither acquired the ability to exercise market power. Behavior in the aircraft market mirrors the vigor of competition between Coke and Pepsi, the dominant **duopoly** in the cola soft drink market. Their competition is so intense that carbonated beverage prices have fallen over the past decade on an inflation-adjusted basis, and sales promotions are ubiquitous.

Market Reactions to Contemporary Mergers

Investor evaluations of the potential outcomes resulting from individual mergers was mixed. A number of merger successes were measured in terms of increased equity values for the stock of the acquiring firm.[14] The purchase of SunAmerica Insurance by AIG, the merger of Travelers Group with Citicorp and the union of the two regional Bell phone companies SBC and Ameritech, each led to a respectable increase in stock values. However, two big banking mergers, one between First Union and CoreStates and a second between Banc One and First Chicago led to 45 percent declines in stock values. One of the largest negative assessments leading to a decline in shareholder value involved the Internet related acquisition of the cable firm Tele-Communications, Inc. (TCI), by AT&T. This merger contributed to a fall by half in the value of AT&T's equity stock and eventually led to the proposal to break up AT&T into four independent units.[15]

Beginning in March 2000, overall stock values began a prolonged decline, which lasted through most of 2002. Initially the bursting of the speculative bubble that had built up, especially in e-commerce and Internet stocks during the 1990s, as well as the reaction to the events of 9/11 drove the decline. However, the period of broadest decline in 2002 was fueled by reports of accounting scandals, corporate malfeasance, insider trading, and a general collapse in investor confidence in the accuracy of the quarterly financial reports being released by corporations. This decline undermined the market value of almost every firm, pulling down the value of the good along with the bad and

---

14 Lipin and Deogun "Big Merges of the '90s," p. C1.

15 Margaret Johnston and Matthew Woollacott, "Armstrong Details AT&T Breakup Plan," available at **http://www.nwfusion.com/news/2000/1025armstrongatt.html**.

the ugly. The fall in the stock value of almost every firm involved in e-commerce or Internet mergers matched or often exceeded the drop in the overall indexes. The decline in the Dow industrial index did not reach the level of a bear market, or a fall of 20 percent below its previous peak, until mid-July 2002.[16]

However, by that date, the value of AOL-TW stock had dropped by 75 percent since achieving its peak in late March 2001, just after the completion of the merger. Similar or even worse results were recorded for Internet hardware or service firms, including Cisco, Lucent, Nortel, JDSU, CMGI, Amazon.com, and Priceline.com. The combination of cost-reducing efficiencies, expected synergies, or the increase in market power, if they occurred at all, were able to insulate AOL-TW from the financial troubles of the day.[17] Specifically, changes in general accounting rules forced the firm to write off as a loss some $54 billion in merger-related goodwill in the first quarter of 2002.[18] Also, allegations of aggressive but legal accounting practices by AOL from July 2000 through March 2002 were reported. The practices deceptively inflated the amount of gross revenues.[19] Lastly, evidence that the anticipated advertising synergies were "stymied by a cumbersome structure and bitter corporate infighting" emerged.[20] In fact, the merger may have made the value situation worse for the original Time Warner equity holders because the stock value of the combined firm was pulled down by a decline in AOL advertising revenues and concerns over its accounting practices.[21] These kinds of adverse economic and financial consequences are not an unusual outcome of the merger process, as shown in the following section.

Historical Evidence on Merger Outcomes

Two economists, David J. Ravenscraft and F. M. Scherer, undertook an extensive study of the post-merger economic effects of some 6,000 mergers between 1950 and 1976.[22] They concluded the following were generally true regarding post-merger performance.

1. Operating efficiency typically fell following the merger.
2. In most mergers, profitability fell or was not substantially increased.
3. Synergies, improved management efficiencies, or a better internal reallocation of capital did not happen as expected.
4. Some evidence indicated that concentration rose as a result of mergers in the banking, airline, pharmaceutical, and telecommunications industries.
5. Almost half of the acquired units were eventually sold off.

In another source covering a broad survey of several domestic and international reviews of post-merger performance, Scherer and Ross noted:

> To sum up, statistical evidence supporting the hypothesis that profitability and efficiency increase following mergers is at best weak. Indeed, the weight of the evidence points in the opposite direction: efficiency is reduced on

---

16 Craig Karmin, "Blue Chips Enter Bear-Market Territory," *The Wall Street Journal*, July 17, 2002, p. C1.

17 Bruce Orwall and Martin Peers, "Rocky Marriages: The Message of Medial Mergers: So Far, They Haven't Been Hits," *The Wall Street Journal*, May 10, 2002, p. A1.

18 Mercury News, "AOL Time Warner taking $54 Bln Goodwill Charge," available at **http://www.siliconvalley.com/mld/siliconvalley/2932648.htm**.

19 Jonathan Weil and Julia Angwin, "Arcane Practices in Accounting Fuel Recent Woes," *The Wall Street Journal*, July 19, 2002, p. C9.

20 Matthew Rose, Julia Angwin and Martin Peers, "Bad Connection: Failed Effort to Coordinate Ads Signals Deeper Woes at AOL," *The Wall Street Journal*, July 18, 2002, p. A1.

21 Gretchen Morgenson, "Broad Skepticism Over Accounting Punishes the Stock Price of AOL," *The New York Times*, July 15, 2002, p. C1.

22 David J. Ravenscraft and F. M. Scherer, *Mergers, Sell-offs, and Economic Efficiency* (Washington: Brookings, 1987).

average following a merger, especially when relatively small firms are absorbed into much larger lines of business.[23]

This news takes on a chilling tone in the face of the number of mergers that take place in the global economy and the amount of effort that apparently goes into the pre-merger due diligence investigation. These facts may help to explain why other firms absorbed so few of the ailing dot-com firms and, when mergers did occur, they frequently resulted in an unfavorable outcome.[24] Even Internet infrastructure mergers were not immune to disastrous results. JDS Uniphase, a maker of products for the fiber-optic communications market, completed its $41 billion acquisition of SDL, a maker of products that speed data, voice, and other Internet traffic over fiber-optic cables, in mid-2000.[25] In late 2001, JDSU announced one of the largest losses ever recorded in modern business history, decreasing the value of its assets by $39.8 billion in the third quarter of 2001 and $6.9 billion in the fourth quarter.[26]

U.S. ANTITRUST LAWS CONTROLLING MERGERS

Section 7 of the Clayton Act, which was passed in 1914 and amended in 1950, is the principle antitrust law that spells out the federal government's position on the potential anticompetitive or monopolizing effects resulting from mergers.[27] The statute prohibits any person engaged in commerce from acquiring the stock, share capital, or assets of any other person "where in any line of commerce or in any activity affecting commerce in any section of the country, the effect of such acquisition may be substantially to lessen competition, or to tend to create a monopoly." Over time, both the courts and those charged with administering the Clayton Act have broadly interpreted this prohibition. Section 7 has already seen some important applications in the area of mergers affecting competition within e-commerce.

The reference to **any line of business** allowed the courts considerable creative latitude in defining the type of economic activity that is adversely affected by the merger. They are not bound by any preconceived notion of the affected market, product, or industry. The reference to **any section of the country** gives the courts leeway in defining the geographical scope of the case. In various situations, courts chose to accept a broad geographic definition including the nation as a whole. In other cases, they elected to define the affected physical area as one as small as a specific city, a collection of contiguous counties, or a general class of areas spread widely across the entire nation. The two phrases, "may be substantially to lessen competition" and "tend to create a monopoly," have been interpreted as yielding power to the courts to halt a merger in its **incipiency**, before it takes hold. First, the merger does not have to reach the level of actually creating a monopoly to be deemed illegal. It only needs to be proven that the merger tends toward the creation of a monopoly. Nor does the law require irrefutable evidence that a monopoly will result. It requires only that proof be advanced regarding the possible creation of a monopoly. Second, even if monopoly is not a potential or definable result, a merger can be halted if it *may* substantially lessen competition. Again, the halting of the merger does not require conclusive proof that it will substantially lessen competition.

---

23 F. M. Scherer and David Ross, *Industrial Market Structure and Economic Performance*, 3rd ed. (Boston: Houghton Mifflin, 1990), p. 174.

24 For example, Webvan absorbed HomeGrocer and Pets.com absorbed Petstore.com. Soon after, both of the acquiring firms disappeared as well. See Jennifer Rewick and Suzanne McGee, "Dot-Com Mergers End in Dashed Hopes," *The Wall Street Journal*, November 15, 2000, p. C1.

25 Laura M. Holson, "JDS Who? Fast Growth, Farflung Fold and Worriers," *The New York Times*, July 17, 2000, p. C1.

26 Scott Morrison, "JDS cuts goodwill value of long-term assets by $5.3 bn," available at **http://news.ft.com/ft/gx.cgi/ftc?pagename=View&c=Article&cid=FT3D3GK6TRC**.

27 Clayton Act, 15 U.S.C. §§12-27, 29 U.S.C. §§52-53

Revisiting the Issues Raised in the AOL Merger with Time Warner

Armed with the language and interpretations of the Clayton Act, the Federal Trade Commission undertook an investigation of the potential competitive consequences of the AOL-TW merger. They were joined in this oversight by the Federal Communications Commission, which had merger approval power granted under the provisions of the 1934 Communications Act. The merger was first proposed in January 2000 and amounted to a $165 billion purchase of Time Warner by America Online.[28] As of 1999, the level of economic activity of 80-year-old Time Warner was nearly four times that of AOL, with $27.3 billion in annual revenue, 69,000 employees, and with a **market capitalization** of $112.6 billion.[29] Conversely, the 15-year-old and smaller AOL had 2000 revenues of $6.89 billion, 15,000 employees, but a nearly 20 percent larger value for its equity shares at $133 billion.[30] Investors, who regarded AOL as a growth company, created the higher market cap for AOL. They held expectations that AOL would experience a rapid rise in future earnings tied to the expansion of the Internet. Therefore, investors assigned a much higher **price-to-earnings (P/E) ratio** for the stock of AOL than for the stock of Time Warner. As the introductory case discussion indicated, what AOL did with its more highly valued stock was to buy a media entertainment and information entity in a big, real, and strategic way.

Time Warner was itself the product of two earlier mergers. The first was the 1989 union of Time, the publishing and cable TV empire, with the movie production company, music, and film assets of Warner Communications. The second merger occurred in 1996 when TW absorbed the assets of the Turner Broadcasting System. These assets included CNN, TBS, and TNT cable networks, as well as additional cable TV franchises. When finally assembled, the Time Warner media content giant had one of the largest subscription bases and most popular collections of entertainment, information, and cable distribution assets. Its properties and 1999 market share of each included the following:[31]

Print: *Time*, *People*, *Sports Illustrated*, *Money*, *Fortune*, and *Entertainment Weekly*, among 33 magazines with 120 million readers, making Time Warner the market leader with 21 percent of all magazine sales

Film: Warner Bros. Studios, New Line Cinema, Turner Classic Movies (MGM film library) with 15 percent of the domestic box office receipts and 18 percent of video sales

Music: Warner Music with 15 percent of the market

Television: CNN Group (75 million subscribers), Turner Classic (36 million) HBO/ Cinemax (35 million), Cartoon Network (59 million), WB Television Network, and 16 television shows in production at the Warner studios

Digital Content: CNNi and various magazine Web sites

Cable: Time Warner cable system with 20 million subscribers, or 22 percent of the cable distribution market

To this array of Time Warner content and cable distribution, AOL brought its own relatively minor Internet content in the form of Moviefone, MapQuest, and the retail services provided through its portal linkages. Most importantly, though, AOL brought its 24-million-household subscriber base. AOL also possessed the skill and experience to spread the Time Warner content over an entirely new distribution medium linked to its AOL and Compuserve ISP franchises. The merger was viewed as the realization of the

---

28 Saul Hansell, "America Online Agrees to Buy Time Warner For $165 Billion; Media Deal Is Richest Merger," *The New York Times*, January 12, 2000, p. A1.

29 "Time Warner: An Entertainment Blue Chip," available at **http://news.bbc.co.uk/hi/english/ business/newsid_597000/597405.stm**.

30 "AOL: The Internet Company That Grew Up," available at **http://news.bbc.co.uk/hi/english/ business/newsid_597000/597479.stm**.

31 Martin Peers, "A Media Behemoth in the Making," *The Wall Street Journal*, January 12, 2000, p. B8.

long-anticipated convergence of information and entertainment content with distribution through cable and online services. The merger connected the **four A's of media contact**, linking *assets* with complementary *audiences* allowing for a wide range of *advertiser* opportunities and providing the *access* to tie these elements together into a coherent, profitable, strategic package. The merger yielded unparalleled opportunities for the **cross-promotion** of products. For example, the selling of Time Warner entertainment products on pre-release or more favorable terms to AOL's subscribers was just one possibility. It also offered the potential for **multimedia listings** for specific advertisements and advertisers across print, film, cable, and Internet outlets.

The union also extended the theory of *merger synergy* to its extreme, with expectations as to the range of new products and selling opportunities that might emerge from the media conglomerate.[32] First, TW music artists might be featured on AOL with sample tracks, easy ordering, or fast downloads of CDs over the Internet. Second, the combined AOL-TW subscriber base exceeded 100 million persons at the time of the merger. The firm knew a great deal of personal information about their subscribers, including what they liked and bought, what they watched and listened to, and what their entertainment or information preferences were. The potential was to use this database to target specific proprietary products and advertising to subscribers most likely to respond. Lastly, they could use their subscriber information to deliver a specific audience, young or old, male or female, or based on some other characteristic across multiple media to an external advertiser. For example, advertising might be coordinated for a rock concert or a new line of cosmetics by placing spots in youth-oriented print and on cable TV slots, as well as the opening screen on AOL, with tickets or products available via a credit card over an AOL connection.

AOL-TW and the Potential Effect on Competition

The AOL-TW merger of content and distribution could have a disruptive impact on the competitive strategies of pure distribution firms such as AT&T Broadband, ComCast, and Charter Communications that shied away from creating and delivering their own content. Conversely, major media content competitors such as Walt Disney/ABC, Viacom/CBS, and News Corp/Fox chose to deliver their content over the airways, through broadcast television, or through a system of "pipes" owned by others to link directly into homes or offices. A third group of Web rivals include Microsoft, Yahoo!, EBay, and Amazon.com, who provide their own unique forms of content, access, and distribution. Each of these may begin to wonder how their future customer base and revenue flows will behave, given that they provide only a portion of the vertically integrated services available from AOL-TW. Just as the merger between BP and Amoco triggered other large combinations in the petroleum industry, a profitable outcome for the merger of AOL and Time Warner may eventually prompt other consolidations.

Again, the apprehension on the part of AOL-TW rivals would appear to be a mixture of the fear of outright foreclosure on the one hand, exacerbated by the fear of competitive disadvantage on the other. Assume that a media content company has a new production asset. If the content firm lacks a guaranteed distribution channel, how will that asset be brought before a profitable audience? Given that all content producers are independent from a number of competitive distribution channels, then competitive markets will work to unite the best entertainment assets with the best means of access. Vertical integration between content and distribution may allow the entertainment programming to be generated by the in-house content division and delivered vertically to the distribution division. Quality differences may be a compelling issue in some cases. Who is to say whether significant differences in quality can be identified among reality programs, talk shows, sit-coms, news hours, soap operas, or drama shows? *Seinfeld*, *ER*, and *Friends* are rare creative successes that audiences demand to see. Conversely, a vertically integrated seller may promote a "buzz" around a hot program character or a star performer. Then it may deliver titillating material, which is so well packaged that it is sufficient to attract a salable audience.

---

32 Richard Siklos, "Welcome to the 21st Century," *BusinessWeek*, January 24, 2000, pp. 36–44.

Even if an independent content producer can achieve access to distribution, it may be granted on unfavorable terms. The producer might be coerced or forced to allow the distributor to become a partner in the profits of the content firm as a condition of carriage. These types of issues have been around for a long time in the movie industry[33] and led to the imposition of **financing and syndication (Fin-Syn) rules** in the television industry.[34] The **vertical Fin-Syn rule** prohibited the networks from taking a financial interest in the programs that they aired. The **horizontal Fin-Syn rule** prohibited the networks from participating in the syndication of those programs in the profitable rerun market. The FCC ended these rules in 1995. These rules limited the relationship between television production firms and the network broadcasters.

The absence of the Fin-Syn rules, along with the potential for disruptive changes resulting from the AOL-TW merger, may alter the competitive balance between content producers and content distributors in a major way. If the merged firm can be made profitable, it may well drive others to copy the union of content and distribution.

Regulatory Approval of the AOL-TW Merger with Conditions and Limitations

The FTC finally approved the merger with conditions in December 2000, followed by FCC approval with additional stipulations in January 2001. Acceptance by the FTC involved a **consent order**, which is a negotiated settlement, between the FTC and the merging firms. The order was designed to remedy any anticipated anticompetitive effects and lay out the conditions under which the merger was allowed to go forward. The focus of the FTC's concern was the impact of the merger on Internet service. The FTC feared that the merger might lead the combined firm to deny competing ISP firms access to its broadband cable technology. Under the proposed order, the FTC's antitrust concerns would be resolved in the following ways:[35]

1. Requiring AOL-Time Warner to make available to subscribers at least one nonaffiliated cable broadband ISP service on Time Warner's cable system before AOL itself began offering service, followed by two other nonaffiliated ISPs within 90 days, and a requirement to negotiate in good faith with others after that.[36]
2. Prohibiting AOL-Time Warner from interfering with content passed along the bandwidth contracted for by nonaffiliated ISPs, or discriminating on the basis of affiliation in the transmission of content that AOL-Time Warner has contracted to deliver to subscribers over their cable system, including the transmission of interactive triggers or other content in conjunction with ITV services.
3. Requiring AOL-Time Warner to market and offer AOL's DSL services to subscribers in Time Warner cable areas where affiliated cable broadband service is available in the same manner and at the same retail pricing as they are in those areas where affiliated cable broadband ISP service is not available. The proposed consent order would be effective for a term of five years.

The FCC was concerned about the effect of the merger on access to and the interoperability of AOL's Instant Messaging service. Therefore, approval by the FCC involved the following conditions:[37]

---

33 See *United States v. Paramount*, 334 U.S. 131, 68 S.Ct. 915, 92 L.Ed. 1260, (1948).

34 James N. Tallbot, "Will Mega-Media Mergers Destroy Hollywood and Democracy?" available at **http://www.legalinterface.com/aba%20media%20concentration%20w-bkg.htm**.

35 "FTC Approves AOL/Time Warner Merger with Conditions," available at **http://www.ftc.gov/opa/2000/12/aol.htm**.

36 Some small ISPs have not been happy with the way they have been treated under the open access condition. See Julia Angwin, "Open Access Isn't So Open at Time Warner," *The Wall Street Journal*, May 6, 2002, p. B1.

37 "Conditional Approval of AOL-Time Warner Merger," available at **http://www.fcc.gov/transaction/aol-tw-decision.html**.

1. The firm must allow access to competing ISPs in a nondiscriminatory manner.
2. With Instant Messaging it must comply with one of the following three procompetitive options before it offers any IM-based high-speed services:
   a. AOL-Time Warner may show that it has implemented an industry-wide standard for server-to-server interoperability.
   b. AOL-Time Warner may show that it has entered into a contract for server-to-server interoperability with at least one significant, unaffiliated provider of names and present directory-based services (IM rival). Within 180 days of executing the first contract, AOL-Time Warner must demonstrate that it has entered into two additional contracts with significant, unaffiliated, actual, or potential competing providers.
   c. AOL-Time Warner may seek relief by showing by clear and convincing evidence this condition no longer serves the public interest, convenience, or necessity because of a material change in circumstances.

Neither regulatory body chose to intervene to control the potential clash between providers of content and providers of distribution networks. Nor was any relief provided for the potential competitive problems arising from the AOL-TW merger, which allowed the vertical integration of content and distribution in a single entity. In the subsequent time period, this conscious regulatory decision not to intervene created multiple clashes among e-commerce titans.

CLASH OF E-COMMERCE TITANS

A combination of forces including horizontal mergers, vertical integration, and technology convergence, along with a rapid expansion in consumer demand altered the pitch of the competitive playing field in the areas of media content design and customer distribution. These forces fashioned a clash of interests among industries, which previously found mutual benefit and avenues for cooperation and interaction. Examples of clashing industries include the traditional businesses in cable and broadcast TV, television programming, telecommunications, and media content creation, along with the newer fields of computer and Internet access, as well as e-commerce. These industries find themselves and their individual firms hurled together in the same, rapidly changing market and technology settings. Once together, they have clashed with each other in terms of their goals, business models, and strategic initiatives. On one level, a number of minor skirmishes includes the following:

1. A conflict between cable operators, with their own broadband access, who refused to sell advertising time on their cable systems to firms providing competitive DSL broadband phone connections[38]
2. A clash between Charter Cable and the ESPNews channel over the latter's free Internet streaming of much of the content carried and paid for by Charter[39]
3. A move by AOL to enhance its business news channel CNNfn by reassigning cable rival CNBC to a much higher numbered and less attractive channel location on the Time Warner cable system in the all-important New York City market.[40]

However, other clashes, such as between Time Warner and Disney/ABC, or AOL and Microsoft, have been much broader in scope and more serious in magnitude, with larger potential repercussions for Internet access and the growth of e-commerce. If this list of

---

38 Seth Schiesel, "Cable Giants Block Rival Ads in Battle for Internet Customers," *The New York Times*, June 8, 2001, p. A1.

39 Sally Beatty and Leslie Cauley, "ESPN Pulls Channel from Cable System in Dispute over Streaming-Video Limits," *The Wall Street Journal*, May 30, 2001, p. B7.

40 Jayson Blair, "AOL Time Warner Reverses Itself on Cable Shift After Pressure by NBC," *The New York Times*, August 3, 2001, p. B6.

forces and clashes wasn't enough to generate significant amounts of turmoil, the U.S judiciary weighed in as it cast aside decades'-old rules that limited the ownership and subscriber reach of cable, broadcast, and content creation companies.

In response, media companies are "bulking up," either by forming alliances with like-minded complementary firms, or through a system of mergers and acquisitions. What is clear from all of this activity is that the creation of size and economic integration in one firm begets the desire for size and economic integration in another. As a result, the financial resources, economic power, and market reach of these firms are expanding rapidly. What is not clear is what all of this growth and integration will mean for efficiency and consumer welfare. Will the titans continue as ferocious rivals, with no firm able to best the others? Or will the titans evolve into a noncompetitive "live and let live" oligopoly model, with each dominating its own sphere of market influence and, in turn, exploiting the consumer? The next few sections will examine this tension by looking at three of the more significant confrontations between titans. Lastly, the chapter will close out the discussion by reviewing the nature and possible consequences of the judicial intervention that may further alter the competitive landscape.

Major Confrontation: Time Warner versus Disney/ABC

On May 1, 2000, Time Warner cable pulled the Disney-owned ABC broadcasting stations off of the TW cable systems in a number of large cities, including New York and Los Angeles.[41] The TW action was done strategically just prior to a critical "sweeps week" with the intent of injuring the network ratings for ABC. (Sweeps week is a time period when network and program audiences are carefully measured to determine network rankings that affect current and future advertising rates.) The loss of the cable audience would have been devastating for ABC. The source of the conflict was over the terms of the negotiations required by the **Cable Television Consumer Protection and Competition Act of 1992**.[42] The act vests certain rights and options in local broadcast TV stations relative to their signal being carried by the local cable TV system.[43] The first option is that the local station may invoke a **must-carry provision**, which requires the cable operator to retransmit the station's signal in the cable basic tier, but without paying compensation to the local station for carrying the signal. The second option is a **retransmission consent provision**. Here the two parties enter into negotiations to determine the terms, including compensation, on which the local station will permit the cable operator to rebroadcast the signal. Compensation can take many forms, including cash payment or the payment of in-kind services.

For the rights to retransmit the local ABC signal, Disney wanted extensive compensations including cash payment, the shifting of the Disney Channel from the premium to the basic tier, and for TW to add two minor Disney channels to their system. It also wanted to retain the ability to exploit the convergence of TV and the Internet by having access to interactive features such as commercials with links to the Internet or digital TV that would allow viewers to purchase goods. Disney feared that the proposed merger of AOL and Time Warner would reserve interactive access in ways that would favor the integrated company. Up to this point, Disney had always assumed that the quality and popularity of its cable programming (ESPN, Disney Channel) would ensure cable carriage. Now they weren't so sure; foreclosure was a looming possibility. Therefore, they were negotiating to leverage the retransmission of the popular ABC broadcast signal as a way to guarantee long-term access for Disney cable channels and

---

41 Terry Pristin, "Blackout of ABC on Cable Affecting Millions of Homes," *The New York Times*, May 2, 2000, p. A1.

42 See "Digital Television and Cable TV," available at **http://www.benton.org/Policy/TV/legislation. html**.

43 *Broadcast TV* refers to a channel signal sent out antenna to antenna over the airwaves. *Cable TV* refers to a narrowcast channel signal that is transmitted to a receiver over a direct wire link.

on favorable terms. Conversely, TW saw itself as being strong-armed by Disney in a way that would pack added channels onto its limited channel space and force it to incur hundreds of millions of dollars of additional costs over the 10-year life of the agreement.

The two parties settled the dispute fairly quickly on terms that were not made public.[44] Disney took the opportunity to appear before the FTC and request that, as a condition of its approval of the AOL-TW merger, competitors be guaranteed access to consumers via cable in ways and on terms equal to those any other AOL or Time Warner company might receive. They feared that a merged AOL-TW would exercise too much control over cable distribution of independent programming and interactive access to the Internet via cable channels. Despite this warning, neither the FTC nor the FCC imposed any such conditions.

Major Confrontation: AOL versus Microsoft

A second major clash is playing out between the titans of AOL and Microsoft. In the early 1990s, the two firms engaged in guarded cooperation because each was pursuing a different goal. Microsoft wanted people to get onto PCs using the Windows operating system and AOL wanted people to get online using the AOL portal. In 1996, the two firms entered into a cooperative, **symbiotic agreement** where each benefited by its association with the other. For its part, Microsoft agreed to host the AOL icon with connecting software as a preloaded item on the opening desktop of Windows. Microsoft did this despite the fact that it had launched its own rival ISP, Microsoft Network (MSN), in 1993. Prime placement on the desktop real estate would help AOL to attract customers and establish it as the number one ISP. In turn, AOL agreed to use Microsoft's Internet Explorer as the default browser for AOL customers, which helped Explorer to become the number-one browser, dethroning rival Netscape Navigator from that position.

All went reasonably well between the two firms until Microsoft began to appreciate the fact that its future survival strategy and link to computers including services, revenues, and profits was evolving. It was moving in the direction of an Internet-based business model rather than having the firm continue as a provider of stand-alone operating systems and software products. At this point, Microsoft adopted the same Internet goal in conflict with AOL, namely to become the dominant firm connecting consumers to the Internet. Microsoft came to realize, just as AOL had done before, that it had two ways to generate future profits. The first was by establishing an ongoing *direct subscription relationship* with Internet users. The second was through the *sale of individual services* to those subscription customers over the Internet. To further its profit goal, Microsoft developed a policy of direct competition, conflict, and confrontation with AOL in the following areas.[45]

1. It accelerated its marketing efforts to secure MSN subscribers.
2. It created a rival and incompatible music player system, Windows Media Player, in competition with the RealPlayer system adopted by AOL.
3. In 1999 it created a rival instant messaging system, Windows Messenger, that to date is incompatible with the AOL system (by AOL's intent).
4. It increased the public's use of its Explorer browser at the expense of Netscape Navigator, which is now part of AOL.
5. It developed its own Internet registration, identification, authorization, and e-commerce payment system, called Passport, which allows one-click shopping over

---

44 Bill Carter, "Time Warner and Disney Agree to End Dispute About Cable," *The New York Times*, May 19, 2000, p. C1.

45 Kara Swisher, "With Enemies Like These, Who Needs Friends?" *The Wall Street Journal*, July 30, 2001, p. B1.

a wide range of e-commerce sites. Passport is in direct competition with AOL's proposed Magic Carpet system.[46]

6. It developed its own digital picture system to rival AOL's.
7. It bundled MSN, Messenger, Media Player, digital pictures, and Passport as part of the Windows XP operating system.
8. It formed strategic alliances with ESPN.com and Yahoo, giving them prime placement on MSN.
9. It announced the introduction of a .NET initiative that will offer a collection of paid Internet services to subscribers.

Most of these actions are aimed at and in direct competition with AOL, which has been aggressive in fighting Microsoft with its own actions:

1. AOL merged with Time Warner, giving it direct access to a level, variety, and quality of content that it will be nearly impossible for Microsoft to match.
2. It made a strategic investment of $100 million in Amazon.com, creating an e-commerce service alliance and potential future partner.[47]
3. It made serious inquiries into the possibility of buying the AT&T cable system.[48]
4. AOL agreed to pay placement and customer bounty fees to computer makers in exchange for locating the AOL icon and software on the opening desktop of Windows XP.
5. It looked into the potential for providing online word-processing software.

In addition, the two firms engaged in a policy of mutual harassment. Microsoft registered complaints about the AOL-TW merger and lack of interoperability of the AOL Instant Message system.[49] For its part, AOL attacked the bundling of Internet access and services features as part of the Windows XP operating system.[50] Curiously, despite the intense competition, conflict, and rancor, a sliver of cooperation still remains between the two firms such that their relationship could be described as a **symbiotic antagonism**.[51] Specifically, Microsoft licensed the rights to produce game products based upon the 2001 Time Warner film *A.I.*[52] Microsoft produced an interactive Internet game that was extremely popular among a global cadre of devoted players. The effort was a precursor for the Microsoft Xbox game console that includes online game-playing capabilities. It seems only natural to link at least some new Xbox games to the initial release of big screen films or TV programs, as a way to cross-promote the two complementary types of entertainment. Because Microsoft lacks original content, it will have to partner with one or more media conglomerates. Will Microsoft and AOL-TW develop additional links in the future? Will those links expand to embrace further forms of cooperation? How might growing cooperation affect the intensity and extent of competition? Lastly, if the vigor of competition is affected, what will be the consequences for the consumer and the direction of e-commerce?

---

46 A third plan, called the Liberty Alliance, is an open architecture system proposed by Sun Microsystems with support from 32 other Internet firms. These firms are worried about Microsoft locking up the Internet payment mechanism with a proprietary system. Don Clark, "Sun, 32 Concerns Join Identification Plan," *The Wall Street Journal*, September 27, 2001, p. B6.

47 Saul Hansell, "AOL Invests $100 Million in Amazon.com," *The New York Times*, July 24, 2001, p. C1.

48 Andrew Ross Sorkin and Geraldine Fabrikant, "AOL Time Warner Said to Be Pursuing AT&T's Cable Unit," *The New York Times*, September 10, 2001, p. C1.

49 John R. Wilke and Julia Angwin, "Microsoft Tries to Lob Monkey Wrench into AOL-Time Warner Deal," *The Wall Street Journal*, December 5, 2000, p. B1.

50 AP, "AOL, Microsoft Locked in Battle," *Connecticut Post*, August 16, 2001, p. C2.

51 "Lords of Net Duel—But Probably Not to the Death," available at **www.usatoday.com/life/cyber/tech /2001-08-16-aol-v-microsoft.htm**.

52 David F. Gallagher, "Online Tie-In Outshines Film It Was Pushing, Some Fans Say," *The* New York Times, July 9, 2001, p. C1.

Major Confrontation: Cable System Operators versus Cable Content Producers

The specific case example of conflict between Time Warner and Disney is just part of a larger generic clash of interests and power between the owners of cable systems and the producers of cable content. The most recent flash point for confrontation involved the sale of AT&T Broadband's cable assets. AT&T assembled the system in the mid-1990s through the acquisition of cable operators TCI and MediaOne. The mergers resulted in AT&T Broadband becoming the largest single cable system, reaching 14 million customers, or 20 percent of the overall number of cable subscribers. The original AT&T strategy was based upon bundling and involved a model of **one-stop telecommunications shopping**. AT&T sought to combine subscriber access to local and long distance telephone service, broadband Internet connection, cable TV entertainment, and interactive services into one service link. With one provider and one bill, AT&T felt that it could offer an irresistibly attractive purchase opportunity for subscribers. Unfortunately for AT&T, subscribers didn't and the firm decided to reorganize into several separate units, including AT&T Broadband (AT&T-B), which contained the cable assets.[53] Comcast, a rival cable operator, made an unsolicited $44.5 billion bid for AT&T-B, which was rejected as being too low.[54] Then the race to purchase the unit was on. Negotiations were held with many potential suitors, including Microsoft, AOL-TW, Disney, Comcast, and another cable rival, Cox Communications.

The motives for the potential suitors varied, but they all reflected differing aspects of the chapter's central tension between mergers motivated by efficiency and mergers motivated by monopoly control. In abbreviated form the suitors and motives were as follows:

1. *Disney/ABC:* Has both cable and broadcast content but fears foreclosure to cable system access. May have liked to buy AT&T-B, outright or with a partner, to guarantee cable access and to use as a bargaining chip to force other cable systems (read AOL-TW) to engage in reciprocal carriage of content on favorable terms.
2. *AOL-TW:* Would become largest cable operator with 22 million subscribers, or one third of market. Would extend cable distribution of its own content and yield considerable leverage to either foreclose access to other content providers or force independents to agree to unfavorable access terms. The merged cable operator would become largest provider of broadband Internet access.
3. *Microsoft:* Wanted leverage through a link with AT&T-B to block AOL-TW plans. Currently Microsoft lacks either cable content or cable system assets. It fears control of cable network by AOL-TW, which could severely limit its plan to become gatekeeper to and e-commerce titan within the Internet.
4. *Comcast and Cox:* Were the third and fifth largest cable operators, but lacked content assets of their own. Their goal is one of bulking up to secure greater leverage in negotiations with the array of economically larger content providers.

In the end, it, was Comcast, with a bid of $47 billion, that eventually secured the right to purchase AT&T-B.[55] Some of these potential mergers might have resulted in increased efficiencies, but it was equally likely that they were motivated by the theory of countervailing power. This theory holds that the creation of the economic power to set prices and conditions of exchange on one side of the market, compels the creation of offsetting or countervailing power on the other side. A brief review of this theory as applied to the cable TV industry reveals that as a first step, mergers increase the power of the cable operators as small local systems are combined into a patchwork

---

53 "AT&T: Breakup III," available at **http://www.businessweek.com/2001/01_06/b3718153.htm**.

54 Corey Grice, "Comcast Makes Bid for AT&T Broadband," available at **http://news.cnet.com/news/0-1004-200-6508377.html?tag=rltdnws**.

55 Seth Schiesel and Andrew Ross Sorkin, "Comcast Wins Bid for AT&T Cable," *The New York Times*, December 20, 2001, p. A1.

of larger, area-wide systems. These mergers benefit the operators in two ways: first it gives them greater revenue needed to update their systems, and second it extends a greater measure of pricing power in negotiations with the individual cable channel content providers. Content providers respond by aligning their interests together into larger media firms including Disney and Time Warner, thereby returning pricing power into the hands of the content providers. Not to be outdone, the cable operators engage in another round of mergers to form regional cable systems covering larger areas. Power growth through mergers was reinforced by a system of cable system swaps in order to achieve a critical geographic mass through audience clustering. In response, the content providers merge again to become media conglomerates covering not just cable content but print, music, film, and Internet access as well. As a final response, the giant cable operators see an additional opportunity to add audience bulk up by linking with AT&T-B.

These shifts in structure result in changes in relative market power. When the content providers have the upper hand they raise the prices that cable operators must pay to carry popular channels, and force the operators to carry minor channels that take up limited and valuable space on the cable systems.[56] They have also been known to ally themselves with DSL phone, ISP, and satellite TV firms in lobbying Washington against various legislative initiatives favorable to the cable operators. When the pendulum swings market power into the hands of the cable operators, they respond by raising subscriber access fees, tightly controlling provider access to new channels, and using audience size to leverage lower per-subscriber charges from the content providers. Whether all of this bulking up creates economic efficiencies and lowers costs is debatable. What it usually means for consumers is a wider range of channel choices, improved service quality through digital connections, access to broadband services, and considerably higher monthly service charges.

JUDICIAL INTERVENTION: REDEFINING CABLE AND BROADCAST TV OWNERSHIP AND PROGRAMMING RIGHTS

Further complicating the issues of cable ownership, programming, Internet access, and market power are two sets of judicial decisions that will most assuredly contribute to an increase in cable-based merger activity. The Cable Television Consumer Protection and Competition Act of 1992 authorized the FCC to impose both cable subscriber and programming limits. The purposes of the limits were first to avoid harmful industry concentration, and second to preserve diversity in programming and ownership, ensuring the existence of multiple voices in the delivery of information. In response to the Congressional mandate, the FCC adopted the following **cable concentration cap rules**:

> *Rule 1:* **Horizontal cable coverage limitation.** No single cable operator was allowed to control more than 30 percent of the total number of U.S. cable subscribers

> *Rule 2:* **Vertical cable content limitation.** No single cable operator was allowed to have more than 40 percent of its channels carry programming produced by an affiliated company.

This move prompted a concern that the cable cap rules created a tension between the public interest of programming diversity and the cable owner's rights of free speech. So, in 1999, the procedure for calculating the percentages was modified a bit in response to a challenge from AT&T relative to its merger with MediaOne.[57]

---

56 Bill Orwall, Deborah Solomon, and Sally Beatty, "Why the Possible Sale of AT&T Broadband Spooks Content Firms," *The Wall Street Journal*, August 27, 2001, p. A1.

57 Mike Paxton, "FCC Cable TV Ruling Helps AT&T, But MediaOne Deal Still Has Some Problems," available at **http://www.instat.com/insights/consumer/1999/fcc_cable.htm**.

Nevertheless, the merger was still found to be in violation of the rules given that the combined firm would own 42 percent of cable viewers and 50 percent of the cable wires. The rules were eventually struck down in March 2001 by a three-judge appellate court panel in Washington, D.C.[58] The rules were vacated and remanded to the FCC for further action on the basis that the percentages cited by the FCC lacked sufficient justification and that the rules themselves were in conflict with the First Amendment. The court determined that Rule 1 violated the cable owner's right to speak to as broad an audience as possible, while Rule 2 violated the cable owner's right to present programming of its own choosing.[59]

Several *immediate consequences* resulted from the decision. First, it became apparent that the FCC decision requiring AT&T to divest some of its cable assets as a condition for approving the merger with MediaOne might not be enforced. Second, the issue was remanded to an FCC whose political philosophy had changed, reflecting a more skeptical view of the public interest value of concentration caps. Depending upon the final action by the FCC,[60] the rules had even more significant long-run implications. First, permanently removing the rules could allow for greater concentration in the cable industry, for example by allowing AOL to acquire AT&T-B. Second, vacating the rules raised a fear that monopoly control over subscribers would allow operators to dictate what was seen and heard, how it was seen, and how much it would cost to see it. The FCC is currently rewriting the horizontal cable control rule.

In a related action, another Appellate Court panel ruled that the government must reconsider its existing FCC rules restricting the ability of broadcast and cable operators to own TV stations in local markets.[61] The goals of these FCC rules were to limit the power of media conglomerates, preserve the diversity of media voices, and limit the power of broadcast networks to enter into local markets.[62] The local television ownership rules were as follows:

Rule 1: **Horizontal TV-ownership limit.** No television network was allowed to own local stations that reached more than 35 percent of the nation's households.

Rule 2: **Cross-ownership rules.** No cable TV system was allowed to own a broadcast television station in the same market where it provided cable services. The rule also set limits on the ownership of TV and radio stations along with TV and newspapers in the same market.

Rule 3: **TV-duopoly rule.** The number of TV stations that a single company can own in a specific market is limited.

Rule 4: **Dual-network rule.** One firm is prohibited from owning more than one of the four major broadcast networks.

The basis for the challenge was similar to ones raised against the cap concentration rules, namely that they violated the First Amendment right to reach the widest possible audience, and second that they stood in the way of the convergence of broadcast, cable and Internet media as well as the ability of media conglomerates to integrate these services efficiently and at lower cost. The potential consequences of abandoning these rules could include the following:

1. It would allow AOL to buy a broadcast network.
2. Absence of the rules would allow Disney/ABC to purchase the assets of a cable system.

---

58 *Time Warner Entertainment Co. v. FCC*, D.C. Cir., No. 94-1035, March 2, 2001.

59 Stephen LaBaton with Geraldine Fabrikant, "U.S. Court Ruling Lets Cable Giants Widen Their Reach," *The New York Times*, March 3, 2001, p. A1.

60 For the FCC notice to review the rules see, "FCC Begins Reviewing Cable Ownership Limits," available at **http://www.fcc.gov/Bureaus/Cable/News_Releases/2001/nrcb0113.html**.

61 Stephen Labaton, "Appellate Court Eases Limitations for Media Ownership," *The New York Times*, February 20, 2002, p. A1.

62 "Court Weighs Easing Limits on Big Media," *The New York Times*, September 8, 2001, p. A1.

3. Both Fox and Viacom are currently over the rule limits in terms of local ownership as a result of previous mergers. These violations would be forgiven and the mergers allowed without remedial action.
4. Any tendency toward increased concentration and integration might threaten the ability of new entrants to innovate, compete, and offer differing views.

The FCC responded to the judicial remand by announcing that it will review all four media-ownership rules simultaneously, with an expected completion date of mid-2003.[63]

SUMMARY AND PROSPECTS

The discussion of structural change through mergers covered a lot of territory in terms of economic theory, current applications, and the identification of some tensions that pull the evolution of exchange over the Internet in different directions. The review suggested that one force behind many of the big media mergers and the resulting conflicts revolves around the ability of the entertainment industry to sell digital e-commerce products. Different entertainment firms develop different strategies as they jockey for size, efficiency, recognition, and a share of the consumer's e-commerce media budget. All media firms recognize the potential for profits from the electronic sale of entertainment properties, but no one is quite sure as to what combination of business structure and strategy is best at tapping into those profits.

The merger of AOL with Time Warner is just one combination of many, and it is too new to conclusively prove that the vertical integration of content and distribution is the superior approach. Media synergy and the centralized coordination of decision making may look good on paper, but they both involve functional limits. Without these limits, society would find much more economic activity organized within a handful of vertically integrated firms, which is clearly not the case. Perhaps maintaining an intensely competitive cadre of independent content producers and content distributors will prove to be the most profitable structure. This method would rely upon markets, negotiations, and competition to unite the best creative talent with the most efficient methods of distribution. The effects of competition from firms with related technologies and e-commerce products, such as Microsoft, Yahoo! Amazon.com, and eBay are still not entirely known. These companies are on the fringes of the e-commerce content/distribution struggle, but each follows its own strategic plan to control overlapping portions of the Internet marketplace. Will they, too, eventually merge, or will they grow internally and remain as independent competitors?

Lastly, if history is a guide, Congress, the courts, and the regulatory agencies will have some say in the future shape of the e-commerce firms and how the various struggles play out. Judicial intervention forces regulators to rethink the existing constraints on ownership and reach of distribution firms. For their part, regulators appear to be backing away from sweeping intervention in the shaping of e-commerce markets. Rather, they are electing to focus on extracting important changes in key but smaller aspects of the industry's evolution. In some respects, Congress is the biggest wild card in the evolutionary process as it steps in to balance forces by passing laws that establish the tilt of the playing field in areas affecting telecommunications, cable, and the protection of digital property rights. The current Congressional preference is to favor competitive market forces where possible, but it would be shortsighted to think that they would be hesitant to weigh in again and wrestle with the issues of access, content, and control. Even Congressional inaction or the threat of action influences the industry.

---

63 Yochi J. Dreazen, "FCC to Review Ownership Rules All at Once in Blow to Media," *The Wall Street Journal*, June 18, 2002, p. A2.

KEY TERMS AND CONCEPTS

any line of business
any section of the country
audience clustering
cable concentration cap rules
Cable Television Consumer Protection
    and Competition Act of 1992
conglomerate merger
consent order
countervailing power
cross-ownership rules
cross-promotion
cross-subsidization
de novo entry
dual-network rule
due diligence requirements
duopoly
economies of diversification
empire building
Financing and Syndication (Fin-Syn)
    Rules
four A's of media contact
horizontal cable coverage limitation
horizontal Fin-Syn rule
horizontal merger
horizontal TV-ownership limit
incipiency
increasing returns to scale
initial public offering (IPO)

intellectual capital
local TV station ownership rules
market capitalization
market extension mergers
market foreclosure
"may substantially lessen competition"
mergers
multimedia listings
must-carry provision
one-stop telecommunications shopping
pecuniary economies of scale
potential competitors
potential entrant
price leadership model
price-to-earnings (P/E) ratio
product extension mergers
pure conglomerate mergers
reciprocity
retransmission consent provision
symbiotic agreement
symbiotic antagonism
synergy
"tend to create a monopoly"
TV-duopoly rule
vertical cable content limitation
vertical Fin-Syn rule
vertical merger

DISCUSSION AND REVIEW QUESTIONS

1. Identify and distinguish between the three general types of mergers. How do vertical mergers alter the nature of the decision-making process?

2. Identify and discuss the economic efficiencies that can result from mergers. Are these expected efficiencies always realized, and how might they enhance competitiveness if they do appear?

3. Identify and discuss the sources of market power enhancement that can result from various types of mergers. How does the AOL-TW merger demonstrate the potential for power enhancement?

4. Does the YankeeNets union appear to be a merger driven by efficiency or the desire to enhance profits through the exercise of post-merger market power? Why?

5. What factors led to the softening of regulatory attitudes toward allowing mergers of all types during the 1990s? Why weren't the regulators worried about merger-based increases in market power?

6. Have the economic and financial consequences of Internet and other mergers typically lived up to the pre-merger expectations? Why?

7. Identify the key merger-controlling provisions in Section 7 of the Clayton Act. How do these provisions work to block anticompetitive mergers in their incipiency?

8. How does the merger of AOL and Time Warner work to create a link between media content and distribution? In what ways does this union pose a threat to other media content or distribution firms?

9. What types of competitive concerns attracted FCC and FTC attention when they approved the AOL-TW merger? How did the two regulatory agencies address these concerns? What kinds of competitive concerns did the two regulatory bodies choose to ignore?

10. Why are media and cable companies "bulking up"? How are they accomplishing this goal? Is it an economic efficiency or market power strategy? Why?

11. What was the nature of the conflict between Time Warner and Disney/ABC? How did the Cable Act of 1992 contribute to this conflict?

12. What was the nature of the conflict between AOL and Microsoft? Why did the two firms at first cooperate and then later find themselves in a goal conflict?

13. Describe the various parts of the conflict between cable system operators and cable content producers. How does the economic concept of countervailing power help to frame an understanding of this conflict?

14. How have recent judicial decisions affected both the cable ownership and programming rights, as well as local broadcast TV ownership rules? What might be the consequences for cable and broadcast efficiency and power resulting from these decisions?

WEB EXERCISES

1. Link to USAToday.com and click on the money section. Get the latest stock quote for AOL and see whether it has moved as much more or less than the general market since July 18, 2002 when the DW closed at 8,409.49, and AOL closed at $12.45. What does this relative movement tell you about the possible success or failure of the AOL-TW merger?

2. Link to Careerbuilder.com. Try entering the word *economist* in the Keywords box and see how many jobs are currently available. What are the skill and degree requirement for these jobs? Next, try typing in the name of the largest city near where you live in your home state. See what kinds of jobs are listed there.

3. Link to Peapod.com and see whether you are able to purchase groceries via the Web.

4. Link to two of the following: Tyco.com, Qwest.com, Nortel.com, or AOLTimeWarner.com. See the firm's story of how it has fared over the recent past, and what they expect to see happen in the next six months or so.

5. If any or all of the preceding exercises result in unfavorable or depressing results, try linking to Dilbert.com to see how bad things might really be in the business world.

6. If you are a sports fan and root for either the Yankees or Nets, or don't hate them too much, link to Yesnetwork.com to see what this cable network has to offer.

7. Link to the following sites, **http://www.ftc.gov/opa/2000/12/aol.htm** and **http://www.fcc.gov/transaction/aol-tw-decision.html**, for a look at the actual approval conditions and limitations associated with the AOL-TW merger as stipulated by the Federal Trade Commission and the Federal Communications Commission.

8. Link to the site **http://www.projectliberty.org/** for the homepage of Liberty Alliance. It is an organization formed to keep the Internet identification and payments structure an open system, rather than one controlled by Microsoft through its Passport program. Who are the members of this alliance and what have they been doing recently?

9. Link to **http://pacer.cadc.uscourts.gov/common/opinions/200103/94-1035a.txt** to see the full text of the Appellate Court's decision in overturning the FCC's cable ownership rules.

10. Link to **http://laws.lp.findlaw.com/dc/001222a.html** to see the full text of the Appellate Court's decision overturning the FCC's local TV ownership rules.

Market Conduct Topics

PART 3

CHAPTER

9

Introductory Case

MICROSOFT BUNDLES UP AGAINST THE COMPETITION

Microsoft and its chairman Bill Gates are known far and wide as the innovators who brought an essential amount of order and connectivity to the world of personal computers. They acquired and improved upon a computer operating system that yielded compatibility between PCs as long as the PC maker followed the IBM open-architecture standards for hardware and software. The establishment of Windows as the operating standard resulted in some important consequences in the marketplace. On the one hand, as of 2000, some 92 percent of all desktop PCs operated with a Windows platform of one version or another.[1] This dominance gave Microsoft an enormous amount of market power. On the other hand, the Windows operating system made the work lives of those who use the system increasingly more efficient and productive, while richly rewarding its innovators for their creative efforts.

What does this PC issue have to do with e-commerce? PCs typically play the role of a "dumb terminal" with just a keyboard, screen, and some memory needed to connect surfers to the Internet, the Web, and the opportunities for e-commerce. In fact, some firms tried to market "net appliances" that connect to the Web without the need for Windows or other complex operating software. Connecting to the Web without Windows is exactly what worries Microsoft, because the firm's franchise and profits are based upon their control over the operating system. What would become of Microsoft if e-commerce didn't need Windows? Could the full range of products in the Microsoft empire be accessed from other suppliers over the Web? Would it mean that consumers could bypass the need to buy anything at all from Microsoft? Obviously, the vision of Microsoft being rendered obsolete by the Web was an act of creative destruction that was more than the company could bear.

How could Microsoft avoid this impending disaster? The answer was fairly simple, have Microsoft become as essential to the functioning of the Web, as they were to the operation of the PC. Efficient Web use requires a browser. Therefore, building a browser, such as Microsoft Explorer, that everyone could use to connect to the Web would be a valuable first step in protecting and extending the Microsoft franchise. Remember, however, the discussion in Chapter 3 indicated that Netscape Navigator was the market leader in the mid-1990s, with a great browser that was being used by just about everyone on the Web. How then might the Microsoft browser compete with the Netscape Navigator browser? One way was to build a better browser and have users choose to convert to the superior product. Another way was for Microsoft to build a browser that does essentially the same thing as Navigator, but to give it away free as part of the Windows operating system. This act of combining the browser with the operating system is an example of the competitive economic strategy of **bundling**, and Microsoft did it with the intent of "cutting off Netscape's air supply."[2] After all why would anyone pay to buy Navigator if they could get Explorer, a suitable substitute, for no extra cost, as part of their Windows operating system? The

---

1 Matt Krantz and Adam Shell, "Let the Negotiations Begin," *USAToday*, June 29, 2001, p. 26.

2 This phrase was used by a Microsoft executive in an e-mail to describe the impact that the free Explorer browser would have on the sales of rival Netscape. Mike France, "Decoding the Trial," available at **http://www.businessweek.com/microsoft/updates/up90129a.htm**.

Creating, Sustaining, and Challenging
Market Dominance in e-Commerce

answer is that they wouldn't, and within three years Explorer became the dominant browser on the Web with an 83 percent market share.[3]

Is this strategic bundling legal or blatantly anticompetitive? Can Microsoft leverage its market power in the operating system area, using it to dominate in the browser market? The Antitrust Division of the U.S. Department of Justice didn't think so. They challenged Microsoft in court for attempting to monopolize the browser market as part of an array of alleged anticompetitive practices. At trial, Judge Thomas Penfield-Jackson ruled, in 2000, that Microsoft was indeed guilty of an illegal predatory act in bundling the browser with the operating system. His remedy was to split Microsoft into two independent units, one controlling only Windows and the other controlling all of the applications software.[4] An Appeals Court in 2001 ordered a new trial on the bundling issues, and set aside the breakup remedy.[5] The Appellate Court indicated that Microsoft had behaved in an illegal manner in some of its dealings with the PC makers and that it did not have an unconstrained right to include any and all features as part of its Windows operating system.[6] The new trail would require the government to show that the tying of the browser to the operating system, if found to be illegal, led to an anticompetitive effect. The test for illegality would be whether consumers were harmed more than they benefited from the bundling.[7]

Even though this case may be interesting, what does it have to do with the broader issues that are part of e-commerce? The answer is that despite the threat of a retrial on the legality of bundling, Microsoft introduced Windows XP, an advanced operating system that bundled even more Internet and e-commerce functions into the operating system.[8] Microsoft's "embrace-and-extend strategy"[9] now included three additional e-commerce software packages. First, Windows XP contained free instant messaging software. Second, it included Passport/Hailstorm software to serve as the basis for a new range of Microsoft-controlled, Web-based subscription services. Lastly, it contained Windows Media Player, a program that delivers business video conferencing, as well as films, music, games, and other forms of Web-based entertainment to the customer. In addition, XP still retains the software to access the Microsoft Network (MSN) ISP. It did, however, delete the software support and access icon for AOL, the leading ISP, and a rival to MSN.

By bundling Internet access features as part of its market-dominating PC operating system, Microsoft becomes a major player in providing and transferring Internet services. Still, the bundling strategy and tactics raise many important questions about competition and efficiency, including the following examples:

Is bundling, which has the ability to create and sustain firm market power, always in the best interests of the consumer, and in

---

3 Kranz and Shell, "Let the Negotiations Begin," p. 2b. In 1998, AOL purchased the Netscape firm for $4.2 billion. See *CNET News*, available at **http://news.com.com/2100-1023-218393.html**.

4 A transcript of Judge Jackson's order splitting Microsoft into two companies is available at **http://www.wired.com/news/antitrust/0,1551,36855,00.html**.

5 For a look at the Appellate decision, link to **http://www.microsoft.com/presspass/trial/appeals/06-28opinion.asp**.

6 Steve Lohr, "Microsoft Sees Clear Victory on Bundling," *The New York Times*, July 9, 2001, p. C1.

7 Jay Green and Dan Carney, "Microsoft: New Rules of the Road," *BusinessWeek*, July 16, 2001, p. 34–35.

8 Mike France, "Get Ready for Windows XP, Trustbusters Are," *BusinessWeek*, July 30, 2001, p. 36–37.

9 Green and Carney, "Microsoft: New Rules," p. 34.

this specific case in the development of the broader Internet and community of Web users?

What effect will the bundling have on e-commerce competitors who provide similar services but aren't fortunate enough to have their software linked to a dominant operating system?

Should society be concerned about the decline of browser competitors such as Netscape? If so, why?

What is the role of government, if any, in stimulating the growth of a competitive e-commerce environment and guarding against the rise of an excessive level of market power?

This introductory discussion of Microsoft's strategic behavior, along with the questions surrounding its consequences, set up the statement of the common tension that underlies the topics to be discussed in this chapter. Undoubtedly, Microsoft's risk taking and technology advances, associated with the development of a broadly accepted operating system, contributed enormous value to general computing and the spread of the Internet. At the same time, some of their tactics, such as bundling, injured competitors and perhaps limited competition. Therefore, within the world of the Internet and e-commerce, how does society balance the tension between defending the use of private property to encourage growth, risk taking, and technological change, while simultaneously ensuring that the use of the property will not inhibit vigorous competition or the ability to compete?

STRATEGIES FOR CREATING AND SUSTAINING MARKET DOMINANCE

The Topic Transition from Market Structure to Firm Behavior

Both the *Microsoft* case and the following sections represent a transition in the discussion of e-commerce and the Internet. Chapters 4 through 8 looked at a few of the *structural issues* affecting these dual topics, including market concentration, entry barriers, patents, copyrights, and mergers. Some of these issues contained a strategic element, such as a merger designed to limit the number of competitors, but the main focus was on the free flow of resources in to and out of an industry. This flow can affect the number of competitors in a market, the intensity of competition, along with the ability to compete. Starting with this chapter and continuing through Chapters 10 and 11, the text looks at specific *behavioral issues* that are primarily under the control of the firm. These strategic initiatives can be used to create as well as sustain market dominance.

This chapter looks at an array of potential individual firm strategies, including the topic of bundling. It also identifies the market forces that work to undermine the strategies as well as the power of government to control behavior through the application of both the antitrust laws and individual judicial decision making. Chapter 10 expands the topic of strategic behavior to examine the various pricing strategies that are open to the firm. Lastly, Chapter 11 investigates the product development policies of various e-commerce firms, in attempt to differentiate their offerings from those of their rivals. The tone of these chapters is not intended to convey the impression that any or all of the strategies are necessarily illegal or in some way anticompetitive. However, each strategy has, as part of its purpose, the goal of setting the products of the firm apart from those of its rivals, thereby making it harder for rivals to steal customers or otherwise increase their market share. As such, they are tools that the individual firm can use to enhance its market power.

First-Mover Advantages

First-mover advantage is a strategy that deliberately sets out to capture the rewards or gains that are seen as a consequence of being among the initial firms to provide a new product or enter into a new market. These rewards are thought to convey a permanent and sustainable advantage, allowing the firm to survive, profit, and grow in ways that subsequent entrants find it difficult or impossible to copy. The e-commerce firms Amazon.com, eBay, and Yahoo! are most often cited as examples of first-mover success stories.[10] However, the strategy is controversial for two reasons. First, at least an equal number of examples show firms succeeding even though they were part of a second or third tier of entrants. How were these later movers able to overcome the alleged inherent advantages associated with being the first mover? And second, numerous examples can be cited of first-mover firms in e-commerce and elsewhere who fell by the wayside.[11] Why weren't these first movers able to take hold of the early entrant advantages and use them to at least achieve survival? These facts beg the question: Are first-mover advantages real and sustaining or are they just part of the general business and e-commerce folklore?

The advocates of being first to market cite a laundry list of advantages including the following:[12]

1. Having the ability to define and exploit a new market, attract market share in the absence of competitors, and gain a product name that is associated with the market itself (xerox for photocopy or coke for cola beverage)
2. Helping to set the rules of the game for competition in the product market, defining the standards through which customers will determine the value added by the product, and positioning the product in attribute space such that it takes favorable advantage of the rules and standards
3. Gaining early experience in the display, sale, and delivery of the product so as to set in motion the efficiencies and reductions in unit cost that are part of the learning curve
4. Gaining a lead time in strategic innovation and preemptive R&D that may result in patents or at least the ability to keep imitators several steps behind the leader
5. Establishing the best collaborative relationships with suppliers to take advantage of their expertise, thereby creating value at multiple points in the supply chain
6. Creating the best, simplest, most user-friendly relationship with customers, thereby raising the psychological barrier associated with buyer switching costs
7. Structuring challenges, opportunities, and rewards to attract and retain the most creative talent that is entrepreneurial, imaginative, and forward-looking

If these advantages are real and desirable, what course of action did the successful e-commerce first movers undertake to capture them?[13] First, they obtained funding as quickly as possible, which allowed them to get their Web site up and operating as they followed a **launch-and-learn strategy**. The first site didn't need to be the best site or the only site. Modifications and additions could be introduced on the basis of customer feedback and incremental innovations. Second, they followed a **get-big-fast strategy**. The goal here was to grow the market so as to take advantage of the economies of scale and scope that helped to lower unit cost. A variety of pricing strategies or free service offers were frequently used to stimulate a rise in customer demand, triggering a positive and reinforcing chain of events. The greater the volume of sales, the larger the scale of the operation, leading to a lower unit cost of production, which in turn justified the low product price, making the entire process potentially profitable. Lastly, the first movers spent large amounts of

---

10 Kevin Maney, "First Mover Advantage No Longer an Advantage," available at **http://www. usatoday.com/life/cyber/ccarch/2001-07-18-maney.htm**.

11 David Needle, "The Myth of the First Mover Advantage," available at **http://siliconvalley.internet. com/views/article/0,2198,3541_333311,00.html**.

12 Adapted from Jim Shepherd, "Is There a First Mover Advantage in Converting to E-Business?" available at **http://www.amrresearch.com/EXV/default.asp?i=19**.

13 Maney, "First Mover Advantage."

money on **advertising strategy** designed to create a brand name and image in the mind of the consumer. Catchy radio spots from Amazon and Yahoo! flooded the airways. Millions of computer disks were distributed by AOL containing the connection software as well as offers of hundreds of hours of free service to new subscribers.

Were these firms really "first movers" in the strictest sense of the term? Does a firm showing identifiable success in an admittedly new e-commerce market convey the aura of a triumphant first mover, regardless of who might have been in that market space before? Certainly AOL wasn't the first ISP. Compuserve, preceded it in the ISP market by five years. Was Yahoo! the first portal/search engine is cyberspace? Again, the answer is not really. Yahoo! Excite, Infoseek, and Lycos all came into existence at approximately the same time in 1993-1994. Yahoo! grew to its place of prominence not by being first, but perhaps by being smarter in terms of running the business, along with the superior ease of navigation for their search engine. The auction site eBay was the first garage sale host and the most successful by far, able to ward off any threats from imitators. That success may have more to do with the unique network externalities among listers and bidders associated with the online auction business. It also may be a function of the growth of related and supporting industries that surround eBay, a topic to be addressed in a following section.

Amazon.com: A Successful First Mover

Amazon appears to be the clearest case of a true Internet first mover that made it exceedingly difficult for imitators to copy or challenge. They accomplished their early position with a minimum of unique features being attached to either their product or their market space. Keep in mind that Barnes & Noble as well as Border's were book distributors with long and profitable histories of sales through the **brick-and-mortar channel**. True, they were late to recognize the importance of book sales via the Web, but once they committed to an e-commerce presence, why weren't they able to match, surpass, or eliminate the upstart Amazon.com?

The answer to Amazon's success may lie in their ability to capitalize on two of the advantages that arise from being the first mover.[14] First, Amazon engaged in continuous innovation, creating new partnerships, as well as finding new ways to satisfy customers and sell products today. In turn, these innovations become tomorrow's basic requirement that imitators must copy if they want to survive as a competitor to Amazon. The Japanese have a word for this approach, it is *kaizen*, a concept that describes part of their competitive philosophy. It means to engage in small and continual product improvement, as well as upgrading. For example, Amazon developed a **collaborative-filtering system** to make additional purchase suggestions to a customer who selected an item. The suggestions are based upon the purchase patterns of other customers who ordered the same item. They were the first to develop a listing for editorial and customer reviews including a rating system. They were the first to include used books from partner dealers, with Amazon acting as an intermediary that allowed customers to link up with others to sell a used title. The economics of this marketplace division, which has been expanded to sell a variety of used and refurbished products, yields a profit margin that is similar to the sales of items from Amazon's new product divisions.[15] It also expands Amazon's market scope, enhancing the return on the Web site and brand name. The marketplace also places Amazon in overlapping competition with eBay, which acts as an intermediary in the sale of new and used items. The list of Amazon "firsts" is both lengthy and significant. They weren't just first to market, they have been first to innovate as well. To date they showed success in overcoming the competitive inertia and the tendency to become "fat, dumb, and lazy," which so frequently infect the market leader. Their success shows how being a first mover

---

14 These advantages are in addition to the value of their strategic patents, which was discussed as part of the material in Chapter 6. See Kamel Mellahi and Michael Johnson, "Does It Pay to Be a First Mover in e-Commerce? The Case of Amazon.com," available at **http://www.managementfirst. com/articles/amazon.htm**.

15 Nick Wingfield, "The Other eBay: Amazon Is Winning Over Small Vendors," *The Wall Street Journal*, July 22, 2002, p. B1.

when combined with drive for creative, continual innovation can enable the firm to stay one step (or more) ahead of the competition.

Second, Amazon built its brand name based upon the highest-quality shopping experience and superior customer service. The Amazon site is customer-centric; it is well-organized, informative, and easy to use. It places an array of buying and information activities within easy reach of the consumer on the home page. The Amazon goal is to get the cyberspace buying experience just right and to continually monitor user feedback so as to adjust and improve upon the process. They diversified into an online superstore featuring a range of products, including software, music, and electronics, that complements both the interests of the Amazon customer base and the efficiencies of Amazon's distribution system.

In achieving this result, the Amazon brand established a reputation for convenience, quality, reliability, and outstanding service. These features raise a **psychological switching barrier** for loyal segments of e-commerce consumers. Consumers are not a homogeneous lot. Some buyers are highly price sensitive and will switch to just about any seller offering a price advantage. However, purchasing from an unfamiliar seller entails the potential for performance risks, unpleasant surprises, and the expenditure of valuable time learning, as well as providing information for, a new Web site's buying and distribution systems. Other consumers value their time and the attributes that are part of the Amazon brand. As such, they stick with Amazon even if the price is slightly higher.[16] They do so not because they are lazy, but because they made either an explicit or implicit rational evaluation of e-commerce costs and benefits that showed Amazon to be the preferred site for purchases.[17] Here, being a first mover and building an attractive, cost-effective brand can combine to create a real barrier against imitators.

What the Amazon story seems to demonstrate is that at least part of the recurring source of first mover, e-commerce advantage may lie in intangible rather than tangible assets. Being first helps the firm hit the ground running, but it is the technical expertise, the focus of management, the base of experiential knowledge, and the innovativeness of the competitive model that help to shield the firm from being crushed by the weight of competition. These **knowledge-based barriers** are not easy for potential imitators to surmount. They are the kind of assets that allow the firm to shape rather than to react to the competitive challenges.

Is the Amazon experience able to serve as a universal first-mover model? The list of dead, e-commerce first movers is long and growing. Garden.com was the first horticultural site, Kozmo.com was the first urban delivery site, eToys.com was the first toy site, and Boo.com was the first high-fashion clothing site. What they all have in common is that they are all gone. Even Netscape, the biggest first mover of them all, as the first to offer easy browser access to the Web, watched its market share diminish dramatically because the firm was unable to counter the bundling strategy of Microsoft. Even Amazon has yet to return sufficient profits to ensure confidence in its long-run survival. The most prominent advantages that being first may offer are the ability to be at the head of the pack in building intangible assets and being able to claim that you were first. Otherwise being a first mover appears to offer few, intrinsic, lasting, insurmountable competitive advantages to e-commerce firms.

The Pursuit of a Fast Second Strategy

Abundant examples in the physical world present imitators who successfully competed with, and sometimes even surpassed, the first mover. For example, General Motors was second to Ford in automaking until it developed a unique auto division and product styling strategy. This new approach captured the imagination of car buyers attracting

---

16 However, strong customer loyalty can tempt firms, such as Amazon, to exploit the consumer. See the discussion in the following section dealing with price discrimination.

17 Jason Fry, "Why Shoppers' Loyalty to Familiar Web Sites Isn't So Crazy After All," *The Wall Street Journal,* August 15, 2001, p. B1.

them away from the low cost, uniform design strategy pursued by Ford.[18] Pepsi Cola proved to be a formidable competitor to Coca-Cola with its initial larger-sized container and its contemporary emphasis on youth and global marketing. Bomar Instruments may have been first to market with a handheld, battery-operated calculator, but the research, production, and marketing muscle of Texas Instruments swamped the Bomar product. Today, MSN may be a distant competitor to AOL, but don't underestimate the power of Microsoft and its desire to dominate the Internet.

What makes an imitator potentially successful? How can a **fast second strategy** of me-too rather than really new yield profits for the imitator? For starters, being first involves a process of trial and error. R&D efforts, the test marketing, and roll out of new products, along with the investment in new production facilities require a considerable expenditure of money and managerial time while simultaneously encompassing risks. The imitator enjoys the luxury of avoiding many of these risks and expenditures. They see what works and what doesn't. Therefore imitators can focus on the most successful products and approaches, providing them at lower cost or higher profit.

Second, as markets develop, they are usually big enough to support more than a single seller. McDonald's was the first, and most successful, of the fast-food franchises. Burger King entered later with basically a carbon copy of the McDonald's menu. It took them a while, but they finally hit upon a successful form of product differentiation. The introduction of a "better-tasting" flame-broiled Whopper allowed them to become a strong competitor to the first mover. The market proved to be big enough to permit a third entrant, Wendy's, with its own profitable variety of burger-related products and salad items. Both Burger King and Wendy's profitably pursued this *creative lemming strategy* of copy, enter, and differentiate.

Lastly, the market does not simply reward the creative new idea or service. Rather, the gains accrue to the firm having the best business model that incorporates the new product. AOL replaced CompuServe not because they were the first ISP but because they saw the potential to combine Web connection with portal services. AOL looks to stay one or more steps ahead of MSN by combining access and distribution along with original content as a result of their merger with Time Warner. Generally, the successful imitator survives in the same way that the successful first mover survives. They see the unmet opportunities or gaps in the market. They fill those gaps with products tailored to consumer demand. They continually innovate, upgrade, reshape, and expand the range of advantages gained by temporary success.

Dominance Bolstered by Related and Supporting Industries

Michael Porter, the Harvard economist, developed an interesting theory detailing the origins and sources of support for creating as well as sustaining **competitive advantage**.[19] One of the key elements is the strength that the leader(s) draw from being surrounded by a high-quality set of related and supporting industries. As the leading firm (or industry) reaches a **critical mass** of business, the volume of its operations allows for the profitable creation of highly specialized services that reinforce the position of the leader. For example, **supporting industries** serve as suppliers to the leader. They enhance the dominant position of a leader by innovations and upgrades that make the actions of the leader more efficient. They help to coordinate the introduction of new products and they yield access to the latest equipment or services. **Related industries** either share activities with the leader or provide complementary products or services. They assist the leader through the flow of both technical and general information. Some services may become so essential to the leader's efficient functioning that they will be absorbed by the leader or tied to the leader through a strategic alliance.

---

18 In a comment allegedly pointed out by Tom Peters, Henry Ford is credited with saying, "I believe that the best strategy is to be the first person to be second." See Maney, "First Mover Advantage."

19 Michael E. Porter, *The Competitive Advantage of Nations* (New York: The Free Press, 1990), pp. 100–107.

The online auction firm eBay is by far the best example of a leading e-commerce firm that spawned the creation of and benefited substantially from the introduction of related and supporting industries. These new eBay service firms are themselves e-commerce entities offering a range of assistance that makes the eBay auction transaction move faster, smoother, and with greater safety. Ebay-related firms provide the following types of Internet auction services:[20]

1. *PayPal*. Facilitates credit card payment between buyers and sellers after the conclusion of an auction.
2. *Ipix*. Allows the easy posting of images of an item being auctioned.
3. *AuctionWatch*. Makes counters available to tell sellers how many potential buyers have looked at the item up for auction.
4. *Andale*. Supplies software to list large amounts of items for auction and billing software to collect on payments.[21]
5. *iSnipeit.com*. Supplies automated bidding services to place a winning bid just before the end of an auction.
6. *SquareTrade*. Offers auction dispute resolution services.
7. *Eppraisals.com*. Sells appraisals of items up for auction on eBay.
8. *Tradenable*. Provides an auction escrow service to hold buyer payments safe while a seller completes a transaction.
9. *United Parcel Service*. Has integrated shipping costs and delivery information into the eBay site.

The PayPal service became so potentially profitable and important to the smooth functioning of eBay that eBay purchased the related firm.[22] This acquisition occurred after eBay began its own competing service, Billpoint, which proved to be less attractive than the then rival PayPal. In other areas, exclusive relationships or preferred alliances formed between eBay and SureTrade, Eppraisals.com, Tradenable, and UPS.

In the final analysis, an important mutual support relationship binds these firms together. On the one hand, the firms frequently owe their existence to eBay and the eBay phenomenon. The e-commerce auction support firms could offer their services to other online auction and nonauction sites, and some do. However, eBay is the biggest site, with the highest volume of transactions. It would be shortsighted of those firms to alienate eBay by working too closely with a smaller competitor. Support for other sites might encourage eBay to either supply the service itself or motivate it to look for an alternate supplier. On the other hand, the services provided by these firms are of significant value to eBay. They expand the eBay market because they make the eBay electronic auction more reliable and attractive to an ever-widening range of U.S. and international participants. They simplify the auction process, building confidence in the eBay brand. As such, they are an important reason, in addition to the existence of network externalities, for the continued dominance of eBay.

Dominance Supported by Mergers

The discussion in Chapter 8 noted the significance of mergers as a way of changing the structure of an industry. They also have a long history in the physical world of serving as a strategy that supports the dominance of a specific firm in a given industry. Two types of merger activity are important for e-commerce. First, **horizontal mergers**, between firms producing the same product and selling in the same market, eliminate a competitor. As such, the result is fewer firms to challenge the actions of the merged firm and fewer scenarios the merged firm must anticipate as it tries to carry out its competitive strategies. Horizontal mergers also increase asset size and output volume. On the one

---

20 Stephen Mihm, "New Tools Are Born to Orbit Around Ebay," *The New York Times*, June 13, 2001, p. H10.

21 Nick Wingfield, "Andale Hitches Its Wagon to eBay's Fortunes," *The Wall Street Journal*, September 27, 2001, p. B11.

22 Matt Richtel, "Ebay to Buy PayPal, a Rival in Online Payments," *The New York Times*, July 9, 2002, p. C1.

hand, greater size can increase efficiency through economies of scale, or lower costs by the elimination of duplicate effort. On the other hand greater size can strike fear in the hearts of smaller rivals, who become more timid in their challenge of the big guy. The few horizontal mergers occurring in e-commerce show only minimal impact on competition. Given the inability of many e-commerce firms to generate profits, the elimination of competitors comes from financial failures rather than mergers. No clear evidence supports gains to the survivors in terms of useable market power.

Vertical mergers between firms at different stages of the supply chain show a less obvious effect on competition than in the physical world. It is often difficult to see how dominance at one level can be transferred to another through merger, or how the merged entity gains any more power than the individual firms wielded prior to the linking. However, vertical integration may make the act of competitive entry more difficult and complex in cyberspace, while lessening the ability of the entrant to secure risk financing.

Dominance Supported by Predatory Pricing

Predatory pricing, or selling a product at a price below cost, is a strategy designed to distort consumer buying patterns, diverting customers away from purchasing the product of a rival. The goal of this behavior is to drive competitors out of the market and then to raise prices above the competitive level. Here the firm expects that it would earn sufficient economic profits to more than compensate for the losses incurred while prices were held below cost. Of course, this strategy of lowering then raising prices assumes that the entry of new competitors is somehow blocked. Blocked entry is necessary because potential entrants will see and try to respond to the incentives provided by the appearance of economic profits.

Despite the fact that the charge of predatory pricing behavior was one of the accusations of illegal behavior levied against Standard Oil at the turn of the twentieth century, economists continue to debate the reality of predatory pricing in the business world.[23] However the topic attracted a considerable amount of academic and legal attention regardless of its importance as an actual strategy.[24] Figure 9-1 displays an analysis of short-run predatory pricing.

The model assumes rising short-run marginal cost (MC), which is consistent with diminishing marginal returns. For ease of interpretation, it employs a constant price (P) that is equal to marginal revenue (MR) and average revenue (AR). A competitive market would yield a long-run equilibrium price of P_1, such that MC = MR, and all costs (ATC) including a normal profit are covered by average revenue (AR). Under what circumstances would a firm's price be considered predatory? Certainly competitive behavior allows for a short-run price, such as P_2, which is below full cost, even though the firm would experience losses. The lowered price and resulting losses represent rational, short-run firm behavior and could be in response to either a drop in market demand or pricing pressure from a competitor.

The P_2 price is not inefficient or necessarily predatory as long as it remains at or above marginal cost because it is covering the alternative value of the resources in their next best use. Only when the price falls below the marginal cost for a given output level would the pricing action be considered predatory. Also, any price such as P_3, below average variable cost (AVC), would serve as potential evidence of predatory behavior. Continuing to produce at this price level would be inefficient and potentially irrational in most circumstances other than one motivated by a desire to drive rivals from the market. As rivals are driven out, the predator can raise price above the competitive level to P_4 and reap supernormal profits. Because marginal cost is difficult to measure in practice, the courts have been willing to accept any evidence of price below AVC as a practical test of predatory behavior. As we will see in Chapters 11 and 12, many e-commerce firms set prices below full cost and probably variable cost as well. However, their

23 Thomas J. DiLorenzo, "The Myth of Predatory Pricing," available at **http://www.cato.org/pubs/ pas/pa-169.html**.

24 P. E. Areeda & D. F. Turner, "Predatory Pricing and Related Practices Under Section 2 of the Sherman Act," *Harvard Law Review*, 88, (1975), pp. 697–733.

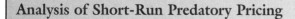

| Analysis of Short-Run Predatory Pricing | **FIGURE 9-1** |

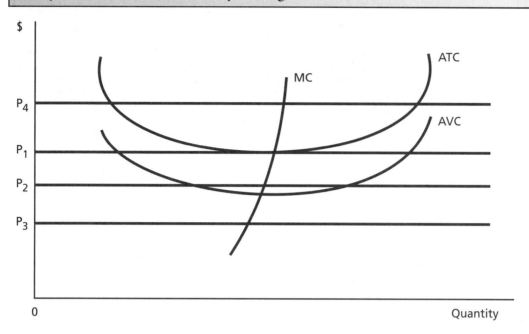

motives were mostly to establish themselves in the mind of the consumer as they conducted a desperate grab for brand recognition and market share. As time repeatedly showed, the only firms they drove from the market were themselves.

Dominance Supported by Price Discrimination

Price discrimination is a second type of diversionary pricing strategy. This tactic starts with a product that has a single unique cost. The discrimination arises when the product is sold to two or more consumers at different prices in the same market. The effectiveness of price discrimination as either a revenue-enhancing or anticompetitive technique rests on the assumption that the consumers have different price elasticities of demand, as shown in Figure 9-2, and cannot cross over into each other's market.

Consumer A shows a more elastic demand for the item then does consumer B.[25] As price rises or falls, the relative quantity response of A will be stronger than that of B. This response may result from B having greater brand loyalty for the product and therefore is less willing to change sellers in response to a change in price. The difference may also appear because A exhibits either a greater range of substitute products from which to choose or more knowledge about the prices of the substitutes that are equally available to A and B. The model assumes a constant marginal cost for product production, regardless of whether it is produced and sold to either A or B. If the firm wishes to maximize profits from its sales to consumer B, it sets $MC = MR_b$. This results in a price of P_b and sales of Q_b to B. If the range of choice or knowledge is greater for A, then it is in the profit-maximizing interests of the firm to lower the sale price to A, thereby drawing A's purchases away from the substitutes. If it offered A the same price of P_b, then MR_a would be greater than MC. It follows that if $MR_a > MC$, then the firm could lower its price to A, sell a greater output level to A, and with the additional revenue being in excess of the added cost, leading to a higher profit level. They would set $MC = MR_a$

---

25 Technically the elasticity value at any point depends upon *slope* and *position*. However, given that both demand curves start from the same intercept on the vertical axis, the slope becomes the determinant of the strength of the consumer's response at any price level that is the same for the two consumers.

FIGURE 9-2   Price Discrimination

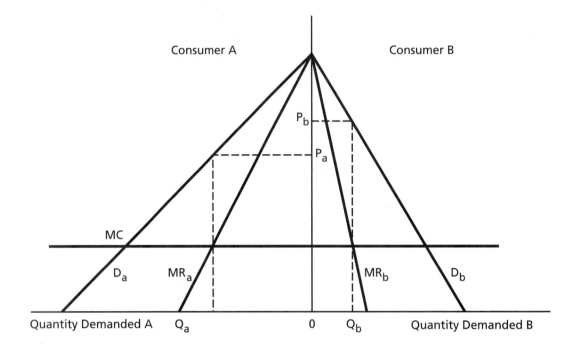

and offer the profit-maximizing price of P_a to A. Notice that while MC is constant, P_a < P_b, which conforms to the definition of price discrimination.

In a real-world example, price discrimination of this type is thought to be rampant in the sale of new cars. Different potential buyers enter the same dealership, at the same time, but with different amounts of knowledge, buying sophistication, and demand intensities. Each car starts out with the same high manufacturer's suggested retail price (MSRP), and customers try to negotiate the price downward with the sales representative. In this circumstance, where every potential buyer negotiates in isolation from every other buyer, it would be highly unlikely that two different buyers would receive the same final sales offer. Again, the separation of the two markets is key to the effectiveness of the discrimination. If one buyer knew that the other was paying a lower price, the potential for discrimination would be far less. In this, and similar situations, e-commerce and the Internet work in favor of the buyer to provide more information about auto prices and to provide contact with potential car dealers.

Despite the availability and value of Internet information, price discrimination finds numerous potential applications as part of sales in e-commerce. Given the ability to remember and track a specific customer based upon previous site visits, it is possible for an e-commerce firm to make an educated guess as to the degree of the consumer's price sensitivity. It doesn't take much in the way of **dynamic pricing**, in the form of price discrimination, to boost profits significantly when the firm is raising or lowering prices across millions of potential customers. Hotels and airlines follow this practice all the time with pricing based upon customer characteristics, day of travel, length of stay, and so on. They extract greater profits by slightly raising prices to less price-sensitive customers and lowering prices just a bit to attract price-sensitive customers away from lower-cost rivals. As long as these markets are separate, such that customers with lower prices can't transfer the product to buyers with higher prices, then the process usually works. Amazon tried this form of preferential pricing in 2000, by selling movies on DVD at different prices to different customers. Key variables determining the price difference seemed to be the type of browser, the ISP, and whether the buyer was a new or repeat customer. It worked for a while, until people caught on and became angry.[26] Amazon apologized for their actions and returned the dollar difference to the higher-priced customers. The combination of computers and the Internet gives sellers a potentially vast array of information to not only better serve customers but to exploit them. Chapter 18, dealing with issues of e-commerce privacy and security, will again take up this issue of Web-based information.

Dominance Supported by Leverage and Foreclosure

The concept of dominance through **leverage** returns the discussion to the earlier topic of Microsoft's bundling of competitive e-commerce products as part of their dominant operating system. Leverage is the potential ability to extend market power from one area into another. By providing the e-commerce software for free as part of Windows, the consequence could be the demise of competitors who must charge for their product. Even if competitors could somehow provide their products for free, the ease of access as part of Windows makes it unlikely that users would want to spend the time and effort to acquire another piece of software. After all, does it really matter to the average consumer whether they access their music through Windows Media Player or through RealPlayer? Leveraging actions such as these open up a wide range of profit-making e-commerce activities to Microsoft as it extends its presence into Web transactions. They also raise the specter of potential harm as competition is restricted or eliminated entirely.

Lastly, the ability to extend and defend dominance comes through the power of **foreclosure**. In this strategy, a dominant firm controls one or more key stages of a market and uses that power to limit competition. The dominant firm may limit the ability of **downstream firms**, such as retailers or product resellers, to secure access to key inputs, or it may limit the ability of **upstream firms** such as manufacturers from securing access to customers. Through these actions, the dominant firm can keep other firms from competing in that market, or it can control the terms of competition in such a way as to place rivals at a competitive disadvantage.

The threat posed by potential foreclosure has a long history in legal cases and significant possible e-commerce consequences as outlined in Chapter 8, which detailed the consequences of vertical mergers. However, charges of foreclosure strategies are being applied in the Internet service industry as well. Covad Communications is an independent seller of DSL Internet access service to businesses and households.[27] The Telecommunications Act of 1996 gave Covad and other DSL sellers the right to rent out telephone lines from the local phone companies in order to provide a service that was in direct competition with the DSL service provided by the local phone company. In effect, Covad was a downstream service seller whose success depended in part upon the terms and access to local phone lines. Covad filed antitrust suits against three of the four regional Bell companies, claiming that the Bells made it difficult and costly to gain competitive access to their local networks. Covad claimed that the Bells denied access for the Covad equipment in their switching hubs. When access to their hubs was finally achieved, the equipment had to be installed in such as way as to make installation costly and difficult to service. Although a lawsuit doesn't necessarily mean that foreclosure has taken place, it does reveal the potential for such actions in the e-commerce arena.[28]

---

26 David Coursey, "Behind Amazon's Preferential Pricing," available at **http://zdnet.com.com/2100-11-523742.html**.

27 Shawn Young, "Covad, One of Last DSL Competitors, Blames Troubles on Bell Tactics," *The Wall Street Journal*, August 9, 2001, p. B1.

28 SBC, one of the Baby Bells sued by Covad, agreed to buy a small equity stake in Covad and to buy $600 million in services from the firm over 10 years as a means of resolving the suit. Shawn Young, "SBC, Covad Set $150 Million Deal Canceling Earlier $600 Million Pact," *The Wall Street Journal*, November 4, 2001, p. B6.

COMPETITIVE FORCES ERODING MARKET DOMINANCE

Of course, nothing lasts forever, not even economic dominance of a market. A variety of competitive forces can arise over time and either gradually erode, or swiftly bypass, the underlying source of support for the dominant position. These forces include the following:

1. *Changes in demand.* Consumer tastes and preferences are notoriously fickle. Loyalty to a particular brand or Web site is often only as strong as the quality of the last purchase experience. In addition, new entrants try to steal existing customers by offering better products or a more satisfying shopping experience in combination with various promotional gimmicks, flashy advertising, or temporary price concessions. For example, in the summer of 2002, Buy.com offered to sell all books at a price 10 percent below that of Amazon.com and to offer free shipping as well.

2. *Changes in technology.* Dominance may be built upon a specific piece of proprietary technology that may be protected by a patent. It might be possible to invent around the proprietary technology, producing a product yielding the same result but without infringing on the protections afforded by the patent. Firms in the pharmaceutical industry do this all the time. They produce similar products with their own unique chemical composition that allows them to compete with the patented original. For example, a range of patented, cholesterol-lowering "statin" drugs are available from the leading prescription drug firms. Conversely, it might be possible to come up with an entirely new technology that outmodes and supplants the current one. For business and popular travel, the railroad replaced the stagecoach, and was in turn replaced by the airplane. High-definition TV (HDTV), with its sharper picture and viewing flexibility based on digital imagery, is in the process of replacing the existing analog TV system. Digital music via the Internet is at least raising a challenge to the dominance of the major record labels.

3. *Diffusion of technology and information.* Knowledge, skills, technique, and imagination are all potentially part of a firm's dominant system. These attributes have the ability to spread like water on a flat surface. They are portable and travel with individual workers as they change jobs and employers. Also, not every employee with a new or better idea will choose to share the concept with the current employer. Silicon Valley is full of firms that gave rise to the development of others, some of which turned out to be direct competitors. For example, William Schockley, who won the Nobel Prize for helping to discover the transistor, left Bell Labs in 1954 to found his own firm Schockley Semiconductor. Gordon Moore and Robert Noyce were among the "traitorous eight" who left Schockley and helped to found Fairchild Semiconductor, the firm that won the patent rights for the construction of the integrated circuit. In 1968 they left Fairchild, along with Andy Grove, to found Intel, the firm that invented the first microprocessor, or computer on a chip. Eventually Intel became the world's largest and most technologically advanced producer of computer memory and logic chips, overwhelming the initial lead held by Fairchild and Texas Instruments.

MARKET DOMINANCE LIMITED BY GOVERNMENT INTERVENTION

Not all dominant positions are challenged solely on the basis of market forces. The market may be too weak or slow in countering a dominant position that has significant detrimental effects on society. In these cases, the federal government, under the powers granted by the **Interstate Commerce Clause** of the U.S. Constitution, can intervene in the market to rebalance the competitive process and to defend the public interest.[29] Government intervention comes in two forms: (1) the enforcement of the **antitrust laws**, and (2) the imposition of regulatory controls. Both of these forms of intervention trace their origin back to the latter half of the nineteenth century, when Congress responded to the public's perception of abusive use of market power by dominant firms and trusts. The **Sherman Antitrust Act** is the oldest of the antitrust laws dating from 1890.[30] In Section 1, the Act prohibits every contract, combination, and conspiracy in restraint of trade. Section 1 was originally aimed at the actions of trusts such as Standard Oil. Today, it is most frequently used to attack conspiratorial price-fixing or market division schemes. In Section 2, the Act prohibits, as a felony, the actions of every person or corporation who either monopolizes or attempts to monopolize or combines or conspires with others to monopolize any part of trade or commerce. Section 2 is generally applied against a firm with a proven dominant position in the market that acted in an unreasonable manner to injure competition.

The Antitrust Division of the U.S. Department of Justice (DOJ) is the primary enforcer of the antitrust laws. However, the Federal Trade Commission (FTC) shares statutory enforcement powers with the DOJ and has acted as the lead complainant in a range of merger, monopolization, and price-fixing cases. The FTC is a **quasi-judicial body**, and as such, it hears cases internally and renders a binding decision that can then be challenged in a court of law. Conversely, the DOJ pursues antitrust cases directly in federal court.

The **federal regulatory approach** to business intervention began in 1887 with the passage of the **Interstate Commerce Act**. The Act controlled the behavior of railroads that transported passengers or property (freight) between two or more states. It listed a series of prohibited actions, most of which involved anticompetitive behavior with respect to the pricing of passenger fares and freight rates or the issuing of rebates on freight. The Act also created a permanent independent body, the Interstate Commerce Commission, whose job was to oversee and administer the provisions of the Act as well as to set and approve rates for the shipment of surface freight and passengers.

The Federal Communications Commission (FCC) is the most important regulatory body governing issues covering intervention in e-commerce. "The FCC was established by the **Communications Act of 1934** and is charged with regulating interstate and international communications by radio, television, wire, satellite and cable."[31] It includes a Cable Services Bureau that serves to carry out FCC authority in the area of regulating cable television. A Common Carrier Bureau is "responsible for rules and policies concerning telephone companies that provide interstate, and under certain circumstances intrastate, telecommunications services to the public through the use of wire-based transmission facilities (i.e., corded/cordless telephones)."[32] Lastly, the U.S. Congress holds the ability to intervene in e-commerce activity by creating new laws or modifying old ones. Congressional action potentially can disturb the existing balance in the playing field that governs the actions of e-commerce sellers, equipment suppliers, and Internet access providers. The judicial system is the final arbiter of the regulatory approach, being the court of last resort for firms claiming a violation of the law or feeling that they have been unfairly treated in the administration or interpretation of the law.

THE ANTITRUST LAWS AS APPLIED TO E-COMMERCE

Revisiting Microsoft's Bundling Issues

Just how far can Microsoft go in implementing its bundling or product integration strategy? What limits the combining of e-commerce activity access along with Internet access

---

[29] The U.S. Constitution, Article I, Section 8, Clause 3, gives Congress the power to regulate interstate commerce. Edmund B. (Peter) Burke, "Why the U.S. Commerce Clause Matters for Internet Law," available at **http://www.gigalaw.com/articles/2001-all/burke-2001-07-all.html**.

[30] Sherman Antitrust Act, 15 U.S.C. §§ 1–7.

[31] Quotation available at **http://www.fcc.gov/aboutus.html**.

[32] Quotation available at **http://www.fcc.gov/aboutus.html**.

software as part of a dominant operating system? This question lies at the heart of the chapter's tension, which pits the ability to use and benefit from the creation of private property, against the public benefit arising from the ability to maintain competition. At what point does the act of bundling become transformed into an act of illegal leveraging? At what point do vigorous acts of competitive behavior become illegal, predatory efforts to "smother" competition? How does the court measure the benefits to consumers from the smooth, easy-to-use, error-free integration of e-commerce software into the operating system? How do courts weigh these benefits against the cost to society from the lessening of competition or the demise of competitors that might be injured by the integration?

These questions are not easy to answer. Microsoft itself is not helping to resolve the tensions as they aggressively insert themselves into the e-commerce marketplace. First, as noted in the opening case, Microsoft seeks to become the dominant software provider yielding entrée to the Internet and electronic transactions. In addition, Microsoft or their partners, also want to become a preferred destination for carrying out certain types of e-commerce dealings including the purchase of music, video, phone service, photography, finance, and travel. Part of this added dominance comes from the control over the access icons that appear on the initially clean opening desktop screen for Windows XP.[33] Computer makers would like the option of loading the access icons for the services of Microsoft rivals such as AOL, RealNetworks, and Kodak onto the XP screen. The screen is valuable "real estate" that the manufacturers can sell for bounty payments or to benefit from revenue-sharing deals. These added funds would either boost the manufacturer's profit margins or lead to lower prices to consumers. Microsoft gave its blessing for the loading of any rival independent icons on the screen.[34] However, the loading can only take place under the contractual condition that the icons for three Microsoft activities be loaded at the same time. Clicking these icons would direct potential customers to Microsoft's Explorer browser, Windows Media Player, and the MSN online access service.[35] In addition, the three spots are reserved on the start menu for the same three services once the start button is clicked.

Second, Windows XP eliminated the software used to run the Java programming language. Java was created by Sun Microsystems, a Microsoft rival, and is used to build Web pages containing animation, sports scores, stock quotes, and so on. This move creates an expense and time burden for the computer manufacturers who must either load their own version of the original Java or a Microsoft variation called Microsoft Java Virtual Machine. The existence of dual versions fractionalizes the Java language and reduces the value of Java as a potential competitor to Microsoft.[36]

Third, Microsoft picked an antitrust fight with Kodak, but relented prior to the shipment of XP.[37] Kodak objected to the structure and photography-related effects of the XP computer code for three reasons. First, XP limited the photo software choices that users saw when they first connected a camera to a computer. Users were encouraged to use Microsoft built-in proprietary photo software with its accompanying links. Second, a lack of cooperation prevented Kodak camera equipment from working easily with XP. Third, XP created preferential links to online photo finishers who were paying partners

---

33 Steve Lohr, "PC Makers and Microsoft Squabble over Desktop Icons," *The New York Times*, August 13, 2001, p. C1.

34 John R. Wilke, Rebecca Buckman, and Gary McWilliams, "Microsoft Yields Ground on Windows XP," *The Wall Street Journal*, July 12, 2001, p. A3.

35 Microsoft claims that this requirement is procompetitive rather than being restrictive. If AOL's access icons appear, then adding the Microsoft icons gives consumers greater choice. Steve Lohr, "The Pendulum Swings to Microsoft, But the Degree Remains Unclear," *The New York Times*, September 7, 2001, p. C1.

36 In 1997, Sun sued Microsoft over the "pollution" issue and won a $20 million court judgment. See Lohr, "PC Makers," p. C1.

37 John R. Wilke, "Microsoft Takes Steps to Ease Kodak Dispute," *The Wall Street Journal*, August 13, 2001, p. A3.

with Microsoft. Kodak wanted other third-party photo-finishing services, including its own, to be treated on an equal footing with the Microsoft partners.[38] Microsoft relented on the first two issues, but still has XP provide preferential contact with photo-finishing partners. Some evidence indicates that the modifications in Microsoft's behavior came as the result of a threat of Congressional inquiry into the its bundling and anticompetitive features contained in XP.[39]

The Microsoft strategy of bundling software with the operating system now clearly extends well beyond the original browser issue. The purpose is clear: to expand the reach and profits of Microsoft well beyond the operating system monopoly. When do the actions of Microsoft cross the line from being an aggressive competitor to being a monopolistic bully? Should the Windows desktop operating system, with its monopoly-creating network externalities, be regarded as a **neutral common carrier**, and be required to treat all users equally with preference toward none? What is the boundary between use of private property and the social benefit from maintaining competition?

Bundling and *U.S. v. Microsoft*: The DOJ Negotiated Settlement

Despite these kinds of competitive questions, attorneys at the DOJ made the strategic decision to negotiate a settlement with Microsoft and not to pursue the bundling issue as part of a 2002 retrial.[40] The agreement failed to impose a **structural remedy** that would involve breaking Microsoft into two or more competing firms. As a result, Microsoft was left free to pursue its bundling strategy. The firm may include any and all Internet and e-commerce access programs as part of their Windows operating system. Most of the major provisions of the agreement involved a **conduct remedy** aimed at correcting for past behavior. Microsoft had engaged in restrictive practices in its dealings with the computer original equipment manufacturers (OEM) and with the producers of middleware software products that competed with programs bundled with Windows. The Appeals Court upheld the trail court's judgment that Microsoft had acted as an illegal monopolist, in violation of the Sherman Antitrust Act.[41] Major provisions of the pact stipulated that Microsoft practices were to be modified to allow better interconnection of competitors' products with Windows and more freedom for OEMs to load non-Microsoft middleware and hide Microsoft software icons.[42] Microsoft acted in the summer of 2002 to modify Windows XP and allow computer makers as well as consumers to hide Microsoft bundled middleware technology and icons. The modified XP also allowed easier linking of non-Microsoft browsers, e-mail, and music play software to the operating system.[43]

These specific conduct remedies might prove to be complex to enforce. For example, Microsoft could write the browser or Internet application code in such a way that it became hard to remove from the operating system without degrading the ability of the system to function. In addition, the set of conduct remedies might prohibit a proscribed set of acts whose restrictive results might still be achieved by an entirely different set of acts not covered in the judgment. In 1994, Microsoft and the DOJ entered into a consent decree, which limited the firm's behavior.[44] The provisions of

---

38 This request was ironic considering that Berkey Photo sued Kodak and lost over a similar "equal footing" issue in 1979. See *Berkey Photo, Inc., v. Eastman Kodak Company,* 603 F.2d 263 (2d Cir. 1979).

39 John R. Wilke and Don Clark, "Senate Panel Plans Hearings over Microsoft," *The Wall Street Journal,* July 24, 2001, p. A3.

40 John R. Wilke, "Microsoft Reaches Tentative Antitrust Pact," *The Wall Street Journal*, November 1, 2001, p. A3.

41 Mary Mosquera, "Microsoft Reaction Mixed," available at **http://www.internetweek.com/story/ INW20010628S0008**.

42 John Wilke, "Hard Drive: Negotiating All Night, Tenacious Microsoft Won Many Loopholes," *The Wall Street Journal*, November 9, 2001, p. A1.

43 Rebecca Buckman and Gary McWilliams, "Microsoft Adjusts Windows' Features," *The Wall Street Journal*, May 24, 2002, p. A3.

44 "Microsoft Agrees to End Unfair Monopolistic Practices," July 16, 1994, available at **http:// www.usdoj.gov/opa/pr/Pre_96/July94/94387.txt.html**.

that decree proved difficult to enforce and led to the later filing of federal antitrust charges against and trial of Microsoft. It demonstrates the problem that can result from any set of conduct remedies. Remedy enforcement requires constant oversight by a quasi-judicial body that is knowledgeable in the business area. Courts cannot exercise this oversight power effectively. Therefore, part of the DOJ-MS agreement was to create a three-member oversight panel to monitor compliance with the various provisions.

Nine state attorneys general, who along with the DOJ were plaintiffs in the original case, objected to the terms of the agreement as being too lenient, and forced a trial in early 2002 on the appropriateness of the penalties. Their goal was to shift the focus of the remedies from controlling past practices, to remedies that would prevent Microsoft from exercising its illegal market power by continuing the same kind of behavior in future markets.[45] They contended that any remedy, which failed to halt the current pattern of conduct, would not be able to restore competition to the software market, including those programs designed to link to and conduct e-commerce via the Internet. To this end, the plaintiffs called for requiring Microsoft to issue a "modular" version of Windows that would allow the OEMs to remove up to 10 Microsoft bundled programs and replace them with competitive software of their choosing. Second, they asked for the court to order Microsoft to auction off licenses for its Office applications software, which would allow it to run on competing operating systems such as Linux. Third, they wanted a court order requiring Microsoft to release the source code for its browser Internet Explorer. Microsoft countered that the remedies requested by the state were unjustly punitive and technically impossible to carry out.

Microsoft's Bundling and European Antitrust Concerns

The issue of Microsoft and bundling is not entirely dead. The European Commission (EC) exercises antitrust authority for most nations in Western Europe. It has begun its own investigation of Microsoft's integration strategy. Their concern focuses on the inclusion of Windows Media Player as part of Windows 98, NT, and 2000.[46] This new investigation was combined with a previous EC inquiry into the charge that Microsoft was leveraging its dominance in the desktop operating system market into the related market for servers that allow the flow of information over the Internet or within business intranets. With these two charges, the EC review went beyond the issues covered in the U.S. case. Mario Monti, the head of the EC's antitrust review, said the commission "wants to see undistorted competition in the market for media players."[47] They recognized the importance of the broad availability of such players, which play a crucial role linking consumers with Internet content as well as e-commerce transactions. Control over the method of contact helps to facilitate control over content and Internet sales. It is unclear how far the EC will pursue its bundling review in light of both the DOJ's decision to drop that aspect of its own antitrust case and the middleware flexibility concessions that have been made by Microsoft. However, don't underestimate the independence and authority of the EC in antitrust matters. General Electric and its CEO Jack Welsh may have, and it cost them the ability to carry out their proposed merger with Honeywell.[48]

---

45 Amy Harmon, "States Seeking Stiffer Penalty for Microsoft," *The New York Times*, March 19, 2002, p. C1.

46 Brandon Mitchner and Ted Bridis, "Microsoft Faces New Allegations from Europe," *The Wall Street Journal*, August 31, 2001, p. A3.

47 Mitchner and Bridis, "Microsoft Faces," p. A3.

48 Chris Frankie, "European Regulators Formally Block Proposed GE-Honeywell Merger," available at **http://www.thestreet.com/stocks/manufacturing/1480452.html.**

Antitrust Issues and the Operation of U.S. B2B Exchanges

Another e-commerce activity where U.S. antitrust officials raise some concern is in the area of **business-to-business (B2B) exchanges**. B2B exchanges bring together, at a single Web location, competing firms within a single industry. The goal of the jointly branded Web site is to boost business efficiency through the cooperative buying and selling of goods. Such a cooperative effort raises the warnings of old from Adam Smith: "people of the same trade seldom meet together, even for merriment and diversion, but the conversation ends in a conspiracy against the public, or in some contrivance to raise prices."[49] With this admonition in mind, the formation of B2B exchanges sets up a tension in the eyes of antitrust enforcers between the opposing forces of encouraging the creative use of the Internet in new, efficiency enhancing ways versus allowing for potentially anticompetitive collusive behavior that injures competition. Three exchanges (all of which have been reviewed and allowed to start up) drew close early scrutiny. The first was Covisint (December 2000), an auto industry consortium including GM, Ford, Daimler-Chrysler, Nissan, and Renault, which started out as an auction and catalog purchase activity, including parts buying from suppliers. The second was MyAircraft (December 2000), which was a joint effort of United Technologies and Honeywell International to "operate a comprehensive open eMarketplace for aerospace after-market products and services in the air transport, business, regional, and military aviation businesses."[50] The last was Orbitz (June 2001), a site created by five airlines—American Airways, Air France, British Airways, United, and Delta—to market flights and other travel services directly to the consumer.

The major areas of antitrust concern include the following potential violations:[51]

1. *Exclusion: Ownership/Membership*. Who will own and be allowed to join a B2B exchange? Will the exchange practice anticompetitive *exclusion* by not allowing other firms to join or participate at a later date?
2. *Leveraging*. Transference of dominance in a physical world industry into dominance in the e-commerce counterpart. For example would the airlines in Orbitz refuse to give travel fare information to competing e-commerce travel sites such as Expedia.com? Will it be legal for the Orbitz.com to market services in such as way as to drive traditional travel agents out of business, thereby eliminating the need to share revenues?
3. *Cartel pricing: Illegal price signaling*. The posting of dated price increases or cuts could be a way of coordinating pricing behavior. Price changes matched by other members of the site would be retained, but collaborators who failed to match the changes would then quickly be withdrawn. This method of arranging cartel-like prices, violates Section 1 of the Sherman Antitrust Act. The site would allow for the exchange of price information without the necessity of direct contact that leaves a trail of evidence. The major airlines were accused of doing something similar using their individual fare sites in the early 1990s. The creation of a single, simple-to-check Web site could make illegal price signaling and coordination easier still.

Antitrust enforcers continue to follow a go-slow approach to applying legal restraints on the formation and operation of more than 700 B2B exchanges.[52] The strategy includes making sure that the exchanges know the authorities are watching, and providing the exchange organizers with some guidance as to how legal collaboration might take place.

---

49 Adam Smith, *The Wealth of Nations* (1775), Book I, chap. X; available at **http://www.adamsmith.org.uk/smith/quotes.htm**.

50 KPMG Consulting, "Honeywell and myaircraft.com Case Study," available at **http://www.kpmgconsulting.com/clients/case_studies/honeywell_myaircraft.html**.

51 Dan Carney, "E-Exchanges May Keep Trustbusters Busy," *BusinessWeek*, May 1, 2000, p. 52.

52 Jill Carroll and Karen Lundegaard, "Antitrust Regulators Aren't in a Rush to Assert Control over Online Market," *The Wall Street Journal*, June 30, 2000, p. B4.

THE COURTS AND THE REGULATORY APPROACH AS APPLIED TO E-COMMERCE

The History of Open Access Case Law

When does private property take on such an importance to the larger community that the government feels compelled to step in and regulate, or at least influence, the use of that private property? This question began challenging both the courts and regulators in earnest at the end of the nineteenth century. The question applies to important issues in the discussion of e-commerce and the Internet. The discussion in this chapter already showed that the question of intervention to foster the public good could include how private property, such as the Windows operating system, is used to gain or limit access to the Internet. Chapter 5 showed that public good considerations encompass the issue of communications access through rival and incompatible instant messaging systems. Lastly, as the next sections will show, the issue of the public good covers the topic of access to the Internet over the phone or cable lines. The key word in answering the question is *access*. When, and under what circumstances, should a firm that controls key access be identified and required to behave as a neutral common carrier? When and how should it be mandated to provide **open access** to any and all competitors, in an unbiased manner?

Two past legal decisions help to clarify the basis for making these kinds of judgments. The first was a railroad case from 1912, *U.S. v. Terminal Railroad Association*.[53] The notorious railroad robber baron Jay Gould helped to organize the Terminal Railroad Association that controlled the bridge and ferry connections across the Mississippi River in St. Louis, Missouri. The Association extracted exorbitant fees from any rivals that wanted to use the connections. The Supreme Court determined that the river spanning linkages were **essential facilities**. Therefore the court required that any competitor either be allowed to join the association or be permitted to use the connections based on **just and reasonable terms**. The wording of this decision, however, placed the court in the position of having to potentially engage in a constant monitoring of what was just and reasonable, which is a regulatory responsibility that a judge and court are not well suited to carry out. Monitoring requires ongoing contact and oversight.

A less intrusive and more judicially appropriate remedy was mandated in the 1945 *Associated Press* (AP) case.[54] The AP was (and still is) a joint news acquisition and distribution group. At the time, it was made up of 65 percent of the nation's newspapers and prohibited the selling of its news to nonmembers. Newspapers that were denied access to the AP suffered a competitive disadvantage. The Supreme Court ruled that "membership may not be withheld through discrimination based on competitive status."[55] Even if a newspaper seeking access to the AP was a competitor of an existing member, the access could not be denied. Thus the court declared in favor of open, nondiscriminatory access. This decision invoked a blanket stipulation of universal open access rather than a subjective condition, such as just and reasonable terms, which would require constant monitoring. A blanket stipulation is enforceable by a court if the evidence demonstrates that it has been violated.

Arguments For and Against Open Internet Access

The advocates for applying the principle of open access to the Web frame their argument in two ways. First, they advance a First Amendment claim that Internet users should

---

53 *United States v. Terminal Railroad Association*, 224 U.S. 383 (1912).

54 *Associated Press v. United States*, 326 U.S. 1 (1945).

55 Robert Pitofsky "Competition Policy in Communications Industries: New Antitrust Approaches," available at **http://www.ftc.gov/speeches/pitofsky/newcomm.htm**.

have the right to speak freely among themselves. They should have the ability to choose their connection without having a third party imposed upon them, regulating the flow of information and ideas. Second, they contend that mandating Internet open access is the best use of private property because it more effectively stimulates innovation and a flow of new ideas. Lawrence Lessig noted that if innovators realize that key parts of the Internet will remain neutral and will not be used against them strategically, they will be more ready to take risks and be creative.[56] Conversely, who in the future would be willing to innovate a new browser technology knowing that Microsoft has the ability to use its operating system to crush any competitor? What upstart ISP would dare to initiate competition in the growing age of broadband technology knowing that they might be denied access to the "pipes" by the cable operators or the DSL providers? Perhaps even more importantly, what source of funding would be willing to risk putting money behind the dreams of the innovator knowing that they faced such obstacles?

Opponents of open access cite the following objections. First, they claim that rather than encouraging innovation and risk taking, open access suppresses it. Who will take on the risks associated with innovation if others can gain access after the fact? Also, if after the fact access is assured, then why not just sit back and free ride on the hard work of others. Both situations lead to an underallocation of resources into the activity. Second, mandating open access may get regulators back into the task of determining the correct prices to be charged for the access. Although the correct price is usually the competitive price, the exact dollar amount is not always obvious in the absence of competition. The correct amount can also change quickly over time with variations in market conditions. Market-sensitive regulatory price changes are not a hallmark of the regulatory process.[57]

Examples of and Attempts at Open Internet Access

The case decisions, mandating open access, establish at least two potential applications in the area of e-commerce. The first involves the ability of private cable operators to dictate the identity of the Internet service provider that will connect broadband cable customers to the Internet. The second involves control over the opening screen and the choice of links to various services or sites provided by wireless Web connections such as through a cell phone.[58]

On the cable access front, a few cities initiated movements toward requiring that local cable franchises open up Internet access to independent ISPs. The City of Portland, Oregon brought the first test case in January 1999. Portland required AT&T to open its cable Internet access to third-party ISPs as a condition for transferring the local cable franchise to AT&T when it acquired the original holder TCI. AT&T challenged this decision in federal court where their position was upheld on appeal.[59] The Appeals Court distinguished between the business of providing cable TV access and the business of providing Internet access. They ruled that TV access is a franchise and subject to local franchise rules and control. However, Internet access is a telecommunications service under the terms of the Cable Act of 1984, therefore subject to regulation by the FCC.[60]

In the wireless Web area, two European actions, both taken in 2000, provide examples of the kinds of open access challenges that U.S. cell phone firms might be facing in the near future. First in England, the British firm BT CellNet Ltd. voluntarily agreed to

---

56 Dan Carney, Mike France, and Spencer E. Ante, "Whose Net Is It, Anyway?" *BusinessWeek*, July 31, 2000, p. 99.

57 Carney, France, and Ante, "Whose Net?" p. 99.

58 Carney, France, and Ante, "Whose Net?" p. 100.

59 Joanna Glasner, "AT&T Prevails in Open Access," available at **http://www.wired.com/news/politics/0,1283,37169,00.html**.

60 For a discussion of the facets and implications of the AT&T position see, "AT&T and Friends File Briefs in Portland Cable Access Case," available at **http://www.techlawjournal.com/internet/19990903a.htm**.

allow wireless customers the right to select their choice of Internet portal provider to appear on the cell phone homepage. This decision reversed the previous policy that directed cell customers to a default homepage belonging to BT CellNet. Second, in France, the court ruled that it was illegal for France Telecom to require its wireless Internet customers to first go to its own Web site as the default homepage. The court required that the wireless Internet users be given a choice of wireless portals.

In the United States, the Sprint PCS wireless Internet service initially did not allow any changes in the homepage provider or configuration. Wireless customers were only given access to a predetermined list of some 30 different Web content or service providers. The reason for this lack of choice is simple but potentially injurious to competition. On the one hand, the homepage on a cell phone is valuable real estate in a manner similar to the opening screen on a desktop or laptop computer. Selling space on the screen generates revenue. The holders of icons on the homepage or those with a preferential slotting as an e-commerce service provider on a predetermined list, secure their positions through **slotting fees** or revenue-sharing agreements with the wireless service provider. Firms that pay the fees recoup their payments though the prices charged to those who access the services. On the other hand, these preferential slotting actions effectively limit the e-commerce options of the cell phone customer and can contribute to the potential stifling of wireless e-commerce competition.[61]

SUMMARY AND PROSPECTS

This chapter showed that, in addition to scale economies, strategic entry barriers, and patents or copyrights, firms use a number of other behavioral tools as a way of potentially dominating a market. Together these strategies create a disturbingly long list of concerns about the competitive consequences resulting from acquiring and maintaining market power. For the most part, e-commerce is so new—and to date generally unprofitable—that few if any firms currently dominate the market. However, one firm with market power is Microsoft, and it is doing its best to generate a growing position in e-commerce. Its behavior is easy to see and its goals are easy to infer. The firm has already drawn a considerable amount of global attention and controversy because its actions clearly embody this chapter's tension between defending the use of private property to encourage innovation and the desire to preserve the ability to compete in cyberspace.

Even though market forces can erode a dominant position, a role remains for government intervention and regulation. However, neither the existing laws nor their creative application may always appear sufficient to deal with the size, potential importance, and speed of change associated with the Internet. The limited number of Internet antitrust and regulatory cases clearly signal to the government to "do no harm" as it works to shape public policy defining the relationship between government and the Internet. The fact that the courts, antitrust officials, and regulators are willing to weigh in from time to time on key issue of access in turn reminds the marketplace that the government recognizes its responsibility "to be ever-vigilant so that harm isn't done in its absence." Perhaps one positive point to be retained from this chapter for future reference is that antitrust officials and regulators in different parts of the globe are carrying on independent reviews of Internet practices. This vigilance may be the best hope to ensure that dominance over the Internet can be avoided or, if it is achieved, that dominance may not be used to stifle the benefits of competition or the ability to compete in e-commerce.

---

61 Carney, France, and Ante, "Whose Net?" p. 100.

KEY TERMS AND CONCEPTS

advertising strategy
antitrust laws
brick-and-mortar channel
bundling
business-to-business
    (B2B) exchanges
cartel pricing
collaborative-filtering system
Communications Act of 1934
competitive advantage
conduct remedy
critical mass
dynamic pricing
downstream firms
essential facilities
exclusion
fast second strategy
federal regulatory approach
first-mover advantage
foreclosure
get-big-fast strategy

horizontal mergers
Interstate Commerce Act
Interstate Commerce Clause
just and reasonable terms
kaizen
knowledge-based barriers
launch-and-learn strategy
leverage
neutral common carrier
open access
predatory pricing
price discrimination
psychological switching barrier
quasi-judicial body
related industries
Sherman Antitrust Act 1890
slotting fees
structural remedy
support industries
upstream firms
vertical mergers

DISCUSSION AND REVIEW QUESTIONS

1. In what ways did the Internet and Web pose a threat to market power and profits of Microsoft? How did Microsoft react strategically to this threat of creative destruction?

2. Describe the nature of the economic tension that exists between defending the use of private property to encourage risk taking and innovation, while ensuring that the use of the property does not inhibit competition or the ability to compete. How is this tension demonstrated with the bundling aspect of the Microsoft antitrust case?

3. Cite evidence in support of both sides of the first-mover advantage strategy, that it is real and sustaining, as opposed to the view that it is simply part of the e-commerce folklore.

4. What are the strategies that e-commerce first movers have used to establish themselves in the marketplace? Are such strategies always successful? Why?

5. What is the difference between tangible and intangible assets that allows a first mover to sustain a competitive advantage? Which asset form creates a potentially more lasting advantage? Why?

6. What is meant by a "fast second strategy"? How can this strategy help a copying firm to be as, or possibly even more, successful than the first mover?

7. Explain the process of how related and supporting firms have grown up around eBay. Why doesn't eBay just buy up all of these firms and supply the services internally as they did with PayPal? Conversely, why doesn't eBay created its own competing division to offer each of these services?

8. How have eBay and Amazon, acting as intermediaries, provided a profitable exception to the e-commerce trend of direct buyer-seller connection and the elimination of the intermediary's function? How does their intermediation improve economic efficiency?

9. Show graphically and explain why a money-losing price below average total cost is still economically efficient in response to competitive pricing pressures. Why is a money-losing price below average variable cost both inefficient and evidence of predatory behavior?

10. What assumptions are necessary for price discrimination to be a profit-enhancing behavioral strategy for an e-commerce firm? How does the Web enhance an e-commerce firm's ability to engage in price discrimination?

11. Why did nine state attorneys general object to the penalty provisions in the proposed agreement between the DOJ and Microsoft? What penalties or conduct remedies did they want to see imposed?

12. Explain how leverage and exclusion can be used to limit competition in e-commerce and the Internet.

13. Identify the nature of the tension that arises as the antitrust authorities try to evaluate the economic consequences of B2B e-commerce exchanges. Have the authorities supported or rejected the establishment of these exchanges to date?

14. What does it mean to identify a firm as a *neutral common carrier*? How does this concept arise as part of the discussion of e-commerce and the Internet?

15. Identify the nature of the enforcement problem that the court created for itself in requiring *just and reasonable terms* as the basis for resolving the *U.S. v. Terminal Railroad Associates* case in 1912. How is enforcement better handled within the *Associated Press* case of 1945? Why?

16. Identify and distinguish between the arguments of advocates and opponents to open Internet access. Considering the importance and characteristics of the Internet, which side of the argument seems more persuasive? Why?

17. How has the Court distinguished between cable TV access and Internet access in resolving the issue of open access to the Internet via cable TV connections?

18. How might the multiple international Internet regulatory reviews and cases work to keep one or more firms from dominating key aspects of the system?

WEB EXERCISES

1. Link to Covad.com to see the kinds of services and prices charged by this independent seller of DSL Internet interconnection services.

2. Link to CNET News at **http://news.com.com/2100-1023-218300.html** to read a variety of stories detailing the purchase of Netscape by AOL.

3. For a transcript of Judge Jackson's order splitting Microsoft into two companies, link to **http://www.wired.com/news/antitrust/0,1551,36855,00.html**.

4. For a look at the Appellate Court's decision on the *Microsoft* case, link to **http://www.microsoft.com/presspass/trial/appeals/06-28opinion.asp**.

5. To see whether predatory pricing makes sense as an economic strategy, link to Thomas J. DiLorenzo, "The Myth of Predatory Pricing," at **http://www.cato.org/pubs/pas/pa-169.html**.

6. For an assessment of the Interstate Commerce Clause as it applies to Internet law, see Edmund B. (Peter) Burke, "Why the U.S. Commerce Clause Matters for Internet Law," available at **http://www.gigalaw.com/articles/2001-all/burke-2001-07-all.html**.

7. To see a summary of the terms of the 1994 DOJ and Microsoft consent decree, link to "Microsoft Agrees to End Unfair Monopolistic Practices," July 16, 1994, available at **http://www.usdoj.gov/opa/pr/Pre_96/July94/94387.txt.html**.

CHAPTER 10

Introductory Case

SALON MAGAZINE: NOT SO FREE AT LAST

Unless a company is a not-for-profit entity by design, or backed by an eager philanthropist with unlimited deep pockets, it must face the economic fact that firms are in business to make a profit. An **accounting profit** involves securing revenues in excess of **expenses**. Expenses cover all production related cash outlays as well as a charge for the depreciation of capital assets. An **economic profit**, as was noted in Chapter 2, involves earning sufficient revenues above and beyond all of the **opportunity costs**. These opportunity costs include the **explicit opportunity costs**, which are comparable to the expenses recorded by the accountant, and **implicit opportunity costs** that reflect the use of economic (scarce) resources that are not associated with any comparable accounting expense. Usually, such resources are already owned outright by the firm and thereby fail to generate an accounting charge against income. Classic examples would include the implicit costs associated with the effort of the entrepreneur or the use of a fully depreciated asset such as piece of machinery, a factory building, or an office complex. How the firm prices its products or services to generate the revenues necessary to cover these costs is a decision left to management. Problems arise if the firm fails to earn a **normal profit**, which is also an implicit cost that equals the dollar profits the resources could earn in their next best alternative use. Without a normal profit, the firm will eventually close its doors, with the resources relocating to better alternatives. This chapter focuses on these pricing strategies for e-commerce firms, which lead to a normal profit and permit them to survive and grow over time.

Salon is a Web-only magazine that is in the forefront of online publishing. It produces a collection of articles ranging from wire service and original hard news stories to feature stories on arts and culture, politics, entertainment, comics, books, sex, life, and so on.[1] It serves as an Internet competitor to the print magazines *Time* or *Newsweek*, with the added advantage that *Salon* is available free on your home or office computer screen, with fresh stories daily and sometimes hourly. As a Web-based content provider, *Salon* offers the reader the valuable option of obtaining more information on a given topic by hosting hot links to other sites containing related stories. The focus of *Salon* is on delivering quality content and reporting, rather than serving as a photojournalism site. It has been in existence since November 1995, winning numerous awards for best Web site of the year, best online magazine, and for excellence in journalism. *Salon* has a problem however; it is a publicly traded company that isn't making a profit, accounting or otherwise. Originally, the magazine provided its content for at a zero price to readers, supported by paid advertising and links to advertisers. The demise of many dot-com advertisers, along with the general decline in all advertising expenditures from mid-2000 onward, erased a good deal of the firm's source of revenues. To boost revenues, *Salon* began a premium content division in April 2001 and attracted more than 15,000 subscribers. Still, the cost of gathering and producing news content increased to the point where *Salon* was forced to announce that it will make its original political and news coverage available only to paid subscribers.[2] Feature articles and

1 It is available at **http://www.salon.com**. A competitor can be found at **http://www.slate.com**, which is backed by Microsoft.

2 Felicity Barringer, "*Salon*, Magazine on the Web, Will Charge Readers of News," *The New York Times*, October 2, 2001, p. C6.

e-Commerce Pricing and

Revenue Strategies

Associated Press stories would continue as available for free, but followers of its original hard news content would now have to pay a positive price equaling $30 per year or $50 for two years. Although *Salon* is not in immediate financial peril, the imposition of a fee-for-content model raises big questions about the pricing of online services. How many current cyber readers will convert to cyber subscriber status and pay for what they previously received free of charge. Will *Salon's* readers switch and become readers of the rival, and still free, *Slate Web* magazine? What is the right price to charge? How does an e-commerce firm go about determining the right price? How should the fee be charged: annually, monthly, per unit? Will cyber subscribers prove to be loyal and renew their subscriptions? Just like most other products, the pricing of Web content is a tricky business. With the abundant source of free Internet alternatives, few online publishers have been successful in getting readers to pay for Web content, at least up to now.[3]

---

3 Josh McHugh, "Will Online Publishing Ever Fly?" available at **http://www.business2.com/articles/mag/print/ 0,1643,6738,00.html.**

THE ECONOMICS OF PRICING: BASIC THEORY AND GENERAL APPROACHES

The discussion in Chapter 2 showed that economic theory teaches that the **profit-maximizing rule** used to determine price is based on the output level where marginal cost is equal to marginal revenue (**MC = MR**). Figure 10-1 indicates that at this point, the extra revenue earned from the production and sale of the last unit of the product just equals the extra cost of producing that final unit. Overall profit or loss is then calculated by comparing average revenue (AR), which is equal to the price of the item, with average total cost (ATC), which includes both variable and fixed costs per unit as well as a per-unit allocation equal to a normal profit. This model may be accurate in the abstract, but both practical and efficiency limitations affect the ability of any firm to calculate the marginal cost and marginal revenue for dozens or hundreds items that it may produce. It is rare, if ever, that a real firm has sufficient knowledge about its costs and revenues at an output level that is widely different from the current level of production. Moreover, alterations in market conditions such as consumer demand or resource costs might require frequent, expensive, and time-consuming alterations in product price to remain consistent with the profit-maximizing rule. Therefore, actual application of the profit-maximizing pricing rule requires some modification of the analysis. The discussion in this chapter looks at the tension that exists for the firm's choice between two general approaches to the pricing of Web, as well as non-Web, products and services. The first approach is cost-of-service pricing, which is a bottom-up method to establish a product price based upon covering the individual costs of production. The second is a value-of-service pricing technique that establishes a price based upon the worth the consumer

| **FIGURE 10-1** | Calculating a Profit-Maximizing Price and Output Level |

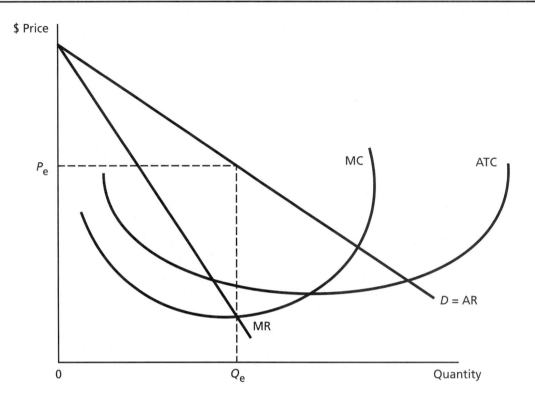

places upon the item being sold. The degree and quality of competition, as well as the elasticity of buyer demand play important roles in both approaches.

Cost-of-Service Pricing

The **cost-of-service pricing** approach involves tallying up all of the explicit costs, both fixed and variable, associated with producing a targeted volume of output and then tacking on a per-unit charge above these costs to represent each item's contribution to the desired level of profit. This economic price will, by definition, allow the firm to survive and grow over time. This pricing technique goes by many names including *cost-plus pricing*, *full-cost pricing*, or **standard-volume pricing**. A prominent example of cost-of-service pricing appears in the automobile industry, where assemblers such as GM or Toyota frequently produce tangible products in anticipation of sale. Therefore, they must determine and attach an initial *sticker price* to each vehicle in September at the start of the model year. Every new car on the dealer's lot comes with a **manufacturer's suggested retail price (MSRP)**, including the car equipped with any accessories. How the process for calculating this price evolves is shown in Table 10-1. First and most importantly, GM must estimate the expected annual output—called the **standard volume (SV)**—for the model being priced. For this example, let's start with the assumption that the expected annual sales level, or standard volume, is set at 100,000 units for the Chevy Blazer SUV.

Next, GM determines that the **fixed costs** (including depreciation charges on buildings and capital equipment, interest charges on company debt, and an overhead allocation for headquarters operations) will amount to $700 million or $7,000 per vehicle at the standard volume. The promotion and advertising budget might be targeted at $150 million, adding another $1,500 per vehicle at the standard volume. The estimate of the **variable cost** per vehicle for labor, parts, and utilities is expected to amount to $12,000 per unit. Shipping costs per vehicle might total $500 and listed separately on the sticker. To this point, we calculate an explicit expense of $21,000. To determine the **profit**

| Cost-of-Service Pricing: Determining Price at the Standard Volume | | | **TABLE 10-1** |

Item	Cost per Vehicle	Cost per Vehicle	Cost per Vehicle
Standard Volume (SV)	100,000 Vehicles	90,000 Vehicles	110,000 Vehicles
Fixed cost overhead and depreciation	$7,000	$7,778	$6,364
Promotion and advertising	1,500	1,667	1,364
Variable cost of labor and material	12,000	12,000	12,000
Vehicle shipping	500	500	500
Profit markup 20% after-tax ROI 30% tax rate	2,300	2,556	2,091
Cost to dealer	23,300	24,501	23,319
Dealer markup at SV 20%	4,660	4,900	4,664
MSRP at SV	$27,960	$29,401	$26,783
Change in SV		–10%	+10%
Change in MSRP		+5.2%	–4.2%

markup, GM might target a 20 percent **return on investment (ROI)** on its capital investment after taxes, as a profit level that is consistent with the opportunity cost of acquiring the capital funds. Assuming that GM has $800 million in capital assets allocated to Blazer production and its average tax rate on profits is 30 percent, then it requires an approximate total markup of $230 million or $2,300 per SUV.[4] We now have a price to the dealer of $23,300 to which we add another 20 percent, or $4,660, for dealer profit and negotiating room. This cost-plus method yields a sticker price of $27,960 for a small Blazer with standard equipment.

Initially, a casual observer might imagine that the MSRP is constant over a relatively wide range of output plus or minus SV = 100,000, which is not the case. Notice how sensitive the MSRP is to changes in the projected standard volume. Assume that the fixed cost, advertising, and the before-tax profit markup totals remain constant, such that they don't vary with changes in the level of output. If the projected standard volume is reduced by 10 percent to 90,000 units and the variable production costs, along with the shipping charges per unit, remain the same, the vehicle cost to the dealer rises by $1,201 to $24,501, or 5.2 percent. Applying the 20 percent dealer markup yields a sticker price of $29,401 at SV_2, which is $1,441 or 5.2 percent higher than the sticker price at SV_1. What happens is that each unit must now carry a larger share of the fixed cost and profit burden. Total manufacturing and delivery costs are lower at the lower volume, but costs per vehicle are higher at $24,501. This proportional relationship yields the traditional, negatively sloped portion of the short-run average total cost curve (ATC) as shown in Figure 10-1. In reality, as the standard volume falls, the assumption of a constant variable production cost per unit may not hold. Average variable cost may

---

4 To earn a total after-tax accounting profit of $160 million or $1,600 per vehicle at the standard volume, requires a before-tax markup of just less than $230 million or $2,300 per vehicle. The amount is a bit more that the sum of $160 million and $48 million because of the need to pay the tax portion ($480) of the sale price of each SUV.

rise as less-efficient combinations of inputs are utilized at lower volumes. Also, per-vehicle shipping charges may also rise as fewer low-cost deals are struck with shippers because the volume being shipped is less.

The Interaction of Consumer Price Elasticity of Demand and Standard-Cost Pricing

The increase in the MSRP creates some serious problems for the dealer at the retail sales stage. Potential buyers exhibit a negatively sloped demand curve based upon two forces. The first is their **ability to pay** for the vehicle, which matches their income (purchasing power) relative to the price of the item. The second reflects their **willingness to pay** for the vehicle, which encompasses both their personal circumstances (preferences + existing auto condition) and the price of the current item versus the prices of substitute vehicles such as a Toyota RAV4 or a Honda CRV. As prices fall, consumers are generally willing and able to buy more of an item resulting in an increase in the quantity demanded. The strength of this consumer reaction is captured within the economic concept called the **price elasticity of demand**. It shows the relative sensitivity of consumer purchases to a change in the price of an item. Mathematically the price elasticity is expressed as the coefficient η such that

$$\eta = (-) \frac{\Delta Q_d \%}{\Delta P\%} \text{ calculated as mid-point formula } \frac{Q_2 - Q_1}{Q_1 - Q_2}$$

$$(-) \frac{P_2 - P_1}{P_1 + P_2}$$

where P_1 and Q_1 are the original Price and Quantity
              P_2 and Q_2 are the new Price and Quantity

If the consumer has a relatively strong response to a price change, then the **elasticity coefficient** has a value greater than 1, and the consumers response is said to be **elastic**. When $\eta > 1$, then the total revenue (TR = $P \times Q$) received from the sale of the vehicles will rise as the price is reduced or fall as the price is increased. Conversely, if $\eta < 1$, then the consumers response to the price change is said to be relatively weak or insensitive and it is referred to as being **inelastic**.[5] With an inelastic consumer response, total revenue rises with a rise in the price of an item or falls with a decline in market price.

Faced with a 5.1 percent increase in the sticker price, Chevy dealers would certainly be hoping that the change in consumer demand was inelastic or less than 5.1 percent, yielding a rise in revenue even as sales volume fell. However, given the high price of a Blazer relative to a typical buyer's purchasing power and the availability of relatively cheaper substitutes, an elastic demand is the more likely outcome. Therefore as prices rise, sales will fall by a relatively greater amount, and if the marginal revenue lost from the unsold vehicles exceeds the marginal cost saved by not producing those vehicles, then profits will drop as well. At this point both the dealer and assembler are faced with the need to layoff employees as well as wrestle with a possible survival threat. This outcome is less threatening if prices are also being raised on substitute products or the income levels of potential buyers are rising, in which case they are better able to afford the price increase.

The example in Table 10-1 can be worked in the other direction as well by assuming an increase in the standard volume to 110,000 units. The same assumptions are made in that the fixed cost, advertising spending, and the profit markup remain fixed in total. Also, shipping and variable production costs are constant per unit. As a result, the per-vehicle cost to the dealer drops to $23,319, with the MSRP falling to $26,783 at SV_3, down by $1,177 or 4.2 percent relative to the MSRP at SV_1. If demand is elastic, not only does the higher SV_3 lead to more vehicles being sold, but total revenue is greater

---

5 The law of demand states that price and quantity demanded are inversely related. Therefore, the sign of this fraction is always going to be negative. To simplify the interpretation of the result, it is common to place a negative sign in front of the equation, allowing the elasticity number to assume a positive value.

as well. As long as the marginal revenue from the sale of the extra vehicles is greater than the marginal costs of producing those vehicles, then profits will rise and the higher estimated standard volume will please customers, dealers, and assemblers alike. Again, the cost reductions might be even larger, if variable production costs and shipping charges per unit decline as the SV rises by 10,000 units.

Sales Deviations from the Standard Volume and the Affect on Profit or Loss

Why don't companies raise the SV to 120,000 or more, thereby lowering the price by even a greater amount and letting the dealers and assemblers retire rich and early? It is one thing to project the standard sales volume, but an entirely different issue to achieve those projected sales targets. The ability to achieve the SV targets depends upon consumer price elasticity, the condition of the marcroeconomy in terms of job and income creation, and the behavior of GM's competitors. Table 10-2 shows that setting the SV too high and therefore the price too low will quickly leave GM with mounting losses if the anticipated sales fail to materialize. Assume that the assembler sets a price determined by a SV of 110,000 units, but that sales fall short by 10,000 or 9.1 percent. Sales of 100,000 units will yield total revenue of $2,231.8 million to the assembler, resulting

Cost-of-Service Pricing: The Effect of Sales Variations from Standard Volume					**TABLE 10-2**

Units	110,000 Standard Volume	100,000 Weak Sales	90,000 Weaker Sales	120,000 Strong Sales	130,000 Stronger Sales
Assembler Costs (in mil.)					
Fixed cost	$ 700	$ 700	$ 700	$ 700	$ 700
Advertising	150	150	150	150	150
Pretax profit markup	230	230	230	230	230
Variable cost	1,320	1,200	1,080	1,440	1,560
Delivery	55	50	45	60	65
Total Cost	$2,455	$2,330	$2,205	$2,580	$2,705
Dealer cost per unit at SV	$22,318	$22,318	$22,318	$22,318	$22,318
Assembler Revenue (in mil.)	$2,455	$2,231.8	$2,008.6	$2,678.2	$2,901.3
Change vs. SV sales $		–9.1%	–18.2%	+9.1%	+18.2%
Accounting Profit/Loss (in mil.)	$161	$91.7	$23.5	$229.7	$426.3
Change SV Profit/Loss		–43%	–85.1%	+42.7%	+165%
Economic Profit/Loss (in mil.)	1	–$69.3	–$137.5	+$68.7	+$265.3

in an after-tax profit of just $91.7 million, down 43 percent relative to the profit at the standard volume. Doubling the sales shortfall to 90,000 vehicles, or 18.2 percent below the SV, yields total revenue of just $2,008.62 million, with after-tax profits falling to $23.534 million, or 85 percent below the profit level at the standard volume. Note that doubling the sales shortfall, doubles the already larger percentage decline in accounting profits. Reducing the unit sales further to 80,000 units would result in an actual accounting loss for the assembler. The dollar magnitude of the profit and loss statement gets out of hand quickly when the firm fails to sell the projected standard volume.

Conversely, accounting profits to the assembler grow faster than sales when sales exceed the standard volume used to set the price to the dealer. At a SV of 110,000 and actual sales are 9.1 percent higher at 120,000 units, the accounting profit after taxes is an additional $68.7 million above the opportunity cost of the invested funds. If sales rise 18.2 percent to 130,000 units, then the accounting profit after taxes reaches $426.34 million. This figure is 165 percent above the profit level at the standard volume and $265.34 million above the opportunity cost of the invested capital. Persistent economic profits of this magnitude might attract industry entrants at some future date. Again with all fixed costs covered by the sales revenue from the first 110,000 units, each unit of remaining sales generates an increasingly higher profit margin. Keep in mind that the per-unit charges for production costs and delivery may also fall as sales rise above the standard volume, which would raise the profit numbers and percentages even higher.

Given the numbers in Table 10-2, it is no wonder that the profits of GM increase faster than sales during a banner sales year, while profits fall faster than sales revenue in an off year. Much of this discussion dealing with standard volume, fixed and variable cost, as well as demand elasticity pertains directly to the pricing of products in e-commerce. For example, how many customers (standard volume) did *Salon* expect to sign up when it set the subscription price at $30 per year? How many regular readers were chased away (elastic response) by the imposition of the fee for feature articles? In the larger sense of the technology and economics of the Internet, the application of standard-cost pricing to Web content begs the question of what is the true cost of service for which customers accessing e-content on Salon.com should be assessed? The incremental cost of an extra surfer reading a *Salon* article approaches zero, while the full cost of hiring reporters to research and write the story, along with the technology expense of mounting and maintaining the article, are substantial. Which of the two costs, incremental or full, should the reader be asked to pay?

Value-of-Service Pricing

Value-of-service pricing involves setting the price for the product based upon the worth of the product to the consumer. Here the seller sets the price to individual customers or classes of customers depending upon the price elasticity of demand. It is a variation of the concept of price discrimination addressed in Chapter 9. Some buyer segments show a strong demand for an item that is not easily discouraged by higher prices. Their demand is price inelastic. Conversely, other buyer segments show a more elastic demand and can be enticed to buy with modest price concessions or discouraged from buying with modest price increases. Their demand is price elastic. The challenge to sellers is to devise a way to tap into these variations in elasticity, improve their revenue yields, and take advantage of the differences in value that consumers assign to their product.

Figure 10-2 represents this dilemma graphically. If a single version of the product is introduced and priced at P_m then the total sales of the item will amount to $0Q_m$ and the total receipts from the sale of the item (TR = $P_m \times 0Q_m$) will amount to the rectangular area bounded by P_m E Q_m0. The relatively low market price, P_m is necessary to attract the buyer of final unit, Q_m. Therefore with uniform pricing, all buyers are able to purchase the item for a price that reflects the value perceived by the last customer for unit Q_m. However, it is apparent that each of the previous customers, who buy the units from 0 to Q_{m1} and pays the P_m, is receiving a some degree of uncompensated value. A

The Price Elasticity of Market Demand   **FIGURE 10-2**

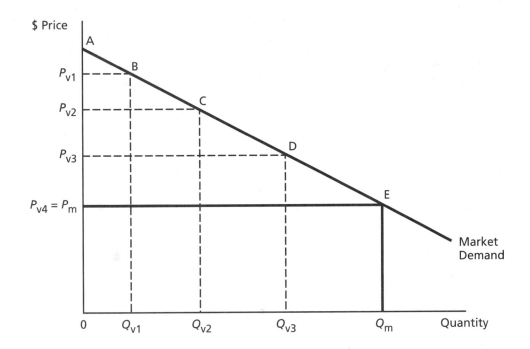

portion of the buyers would then continue to purchase the item even if the price was raised above P_m. Economists refer to this uncompensated value as **consumer surplus**. This uncompensated value lies in the triangular area $P_m EA$, which is located above the price line and below the negatively sloped demand curve.[6] The task for the seller is to find some way to convert this uncompensated value into revenue for the firm. Consumer surplus is a real concept for anyone who has been driving and almost run out of gas. Gliding on fumes into the only gas station for miles, the driver sees the price is fairly high at $2 per gallon. Grumbling and grousing, the driver fills the tank. In reality, the driver might have been willing to pay as much as $3 per gallon in order to avoid running out of gas.

STRATEGIES TO ACHIEVE VALUE-OF-SERVICE PRICING

Versioning to Achieve Value-of-Service Pricing

One approach to value-of-service pricing involves the concept of **versioning**, or developing multiple levels of the same product with different components and different prices.[7] These different versions would then be targeted at different segments of the market, recognizing that not every customer wants or is willing to pay for the most sophisticated version of the product. **Delay** or **versioning over time** is one way to create product variations by releasing the most sophisticated and expensive version of the product first, followed by stripped down and cheaper models at a later date. Polaroid

---

6 Note that firms can only capture consumer surplus in *imperfect competition* where the products are differentiated and the individual as well as the market demand curves are negatively sloped. In *pure competition* the market demand curve is negatively sloped, but each firm faces a horizontal demand curve and lacks the power to raise price or to differentiate its product.

7 Carl Shapiro and Hal R. Varian, *Information Rules* (Cambridge, Harvard Business School Press, 1999), chapt. 3.

practiced this approach when it introduced technological innovations in instant photography. Some buyers just had to have the latest and best equipment. They were willing to pay a premium price, as shown by P_{v1} in Figure 10-2, to be the first to own a new system, leading to the sales volume shown as $0Q_{v1}$. They were the buyers at the top of the demand curve who attached the greatest value to owning the item. Within a short period of time, usually six to nine months, Polaroid released lesser versions that would be priced at successively lower amounts such as P_{v2} and P_{v3}. These would result in added sales of $Q_{v1} Q_{v2}$ and $Q_{v2} Q_{v3}$ respectively. Lastly, a basic model was introduced with its price P_{v4} set equal to the previous P_m and selling the final units of output $Q_{v3} Q_m$. The result was that versioning converted part of the previously uncompensated value into additional revenue for the firm. The firm's total revenue now includes the previous $P_m E Q_m 0$, plus the added revenues within the three vertical rectangles such as $P_{v1} BFP_m$ that lie above the price line. Note that the versioning approach still leaves some uncompensated value to the consumer. However, these triangular areas, such as BGC, are much smaller than before.

Kodak, a rival photography giant, employed a similar versioning strategy but released all of its variations simultaneously rather than sequentially. Kodak camera buyers were able to choose between versions with or without zoom capability, with a succession of better resolution lenses, and with accessories such as a carrying case. Buyers reacted to the range of choices within a process that is referred to as **self-selection**. Here, consumers express their own relative values by selecting from the array of possible offerings and prices rather than having the firm, such as Polaroid, use its market power to strategically restrict the range of choices and accessories. Kodak's **simultaneous multiple version strategy** based upon features and functions offered both risks and benefits. The risk was that some buyers from a higher value segment might talk themselves into buying a lower-priced model when presented with the availability of multiple models. If this happened, Kodak would then lose some revenues on the camera sales. On the benefit side, Kodak also made money from film sales and developing. The faster the new technology penetrated the market, the faster would be the firm's overall rate of profit growth from the sum of the three revenue streams, camera sales, film sales, and developing. Also, Kodak generally offered lower price points for P_{v1} through P_{v4} than did Polaroid in order to hasten the adoption process. Even though Polaroid's instant development process was technologically advanced and popular, it was messy and time consuming. The smaller, lightweight Kodak camera with point-and-shoot technology was simpler to use and found acceptance among a wider consumer audience for the purposes of general picture taking. Hence the logic of the Kodak approach to maximize overall profits rather than focus solely on the profits from camera sales.

Product versioning as an approach to value-of-service pricing can be implemented in a variety of ways other than the Polaroid approach of delay or the Kodak approach of features and functions. Intel offers the same line of computer chips with different operating speeds. Its approach allows game players or professional users to separate themselves from the more casual computer customers who buy PCs for standard word processing or e-mail purposes. PC assemblers offer various computer models with differing levels of technical support. Here sophisticated users with more complex questions and problems are inclined to purchase the versions with the greater level of technical support. Finally, airlines offer tickets with differing levels of convenience including a Saturday night stayover or 14-day advance purchase. This approach allows the carriers to charge higher prices for business customers who place a greater value on short-term, immediate, weekday trips while sill encouraging ticket purchases by more cost-conscious leisure travelers. Regardless of the versioning method, the goal is always the same. The firm wants to encourage customers to explicitly reveal, by their choice of versions, the otherwise hidden full value that they place on the product. It is equivalent to consumers identifying their positions along the market demand curve. Once the true worth of the product for each customer is revealed, including the consumer surplus, the firm can use the information to capture a portion of what would otherwise exist as uncompensated value.

Using Two-Part Tariffs to Achieve Value-of-Service Pricing

Another method for implementing a value-of-service pricing strategy is commonly referred to as a **two-part tariff**. The word *tariff* is used here in the sense of pricing rather than the more common application as a tax or additional charge for imported goods. A two-part tariff is an ingenious scheme in which buyers are charged both a **fixed access fee** and a **price per unit of use**. The per-unit charge is the traditional pricing approach that encourages customers to optimize their usage up to the point where they equate the per-unit price with the additional value received from consuming one more, or the last, unit. It can also lead to the uncompensated value or consumer surplus problem as already noted. The imposition of the fixed access fee is an attempt to capture some of the uncompensated value. To participate in the activity or gain access, the customer would have to pay a lump-sum subscriber charge or a monthly rental fee.

As long as the buyer sees potential value in the product, the fixed access fee does not interfere with the usage decision or per-unit charge. The access fee is a **sunk cost** that was paid in the past and cannot be altered, either raised or lowered, on the basis of usage. Therefore, it has no bearing on either the decision to use or not to use the product or service nor how much to use it. For example, consumers typically lease vehicles with a monthly leasing fee and a charge of $0.10 to $0.15 per mile for every mile driven over a specified maximum. Usually, the maximum is below average annual driving volume of 15,000 miles per year. Do lessees stop driving once they hit the free mileage limit? A few shortsighted ones may, but of if they do, they forgo the benefit of the travel services provided by the vehicle while still having to pay the monthly leasing charge. Most rational lessees will continue to drive for business or pleasure, but make sure the value of the trip is worth the additional mileage charge.

These two-part tariffs offer a wide range of potential application in e-commerce. For example the downloading of either music or movies over the Internet could be priced according to the two-part scheme. Chapter 7 noted that several competing systems for music downloads, including MusicNet and Pressplay, might employ the two-part pricing scheme. For example, to gain access to one or both of the competing song libraries, the potential user might have to pay a fixed monthly subscriber fee of say $2.99 each that is charged automatically to a credit card. Then, in addition, the member might be charged $0.50 to download a specific song to a digital storage locker. The trick is that the music fan can't download the song without first paying the access fee. The music services could introduce a number of variations on this pricing scheme. For example they might allow nonmembers to download the same song but at a higher fee of $1.00. For intense music users it would cheaper to pay to join rather than surrender the higher per-song download fees. Of course, once a person becomes a member they may download even more songs because the download fee per song is cheaper and the access fee is a sunk cost.

A more insidious approach, and hence one that could potentially enhance profits even more for the record companies, might require a small follow-on monthly fee of say $0.05, again to be paid automatically by credit card, for each song that the consumer wanted to retain in their personal music storage locker. In the absence of the follow-on or **retention fee**, the digital file containing the download would be programmed to self-destruct.[8] Of course, all of this pricing to extract money from music lovers depends upon a combination of copyright protection through technology and coordinated, but noncollusive, behavior among nominal competitors. If one music consortium imposes a two-part pricing scheme while the other doesn't, then consumers are more likely to avail themselves of the music library from the firm that charges only a single download fee. However, if they act as cooperating oligopolies, then absent other music options for the consumer, the revenue stream and profits will be higher for

---

8 Each of these two-part pricing schemes requires the existence of an efficient and inexpensive **micropayment service** to handle the revenues from small transactions. No such service currently exists.

all of the Internet music firms, especially if the consortia members own the music and refuse to license it to rival firms.[9]

Using Auction Pricing to Achieve a Value-of-Service Price

Auction pricing offers a third method for enacting a value-of-service pricing strategy. This technique is particularly well suited to the Internet where electronic bids (e-bids) can be submitted frequently from a global, geographically dispersed set of potential buyers.[10] The traditional **English auction** is the type that one might find at the world-famous auction houses of Sotheby's or Christies. It usually involves participants physically congregating together, to hear and see each other as they engage in a **transparent auction process**.[11] The *seller* has some minimum price that he or she is willing to accept in exchange for the item. Each *bidder* has some maximum price that represents the highest amount they are willing to spend on the item. Neither the bidders nor the seller reveal these prices except through the auction process. The last bid is the highest bid, and as a **first-price auction**, it determines both the identity of the winner and the price to be paid. The high-bid winner is the individual who is willing to pay a price equal to the one bid by the runner up plus some incremental amount. As such, the winner surrenders the most value to the seller in the form of both the seller's minimum cash payment plus some additional compensation representing a portion of the bidder's consumer surplus. Figure 10-3 shows this process.

Seller S is auctioning off a decorative silver overlaid glass candy dish and established P_s as the minimum acceptable auction price. It is set as either the opening price without reserve, or as a **reserve price** below which the seller will not complete the transaction with the high bidder. Bidder B begins the auction with an opening bid price of P_{b1}, which happens to match the reserve price of P_s. Bidder C tops this bid price with a slightly higher offer of P_c. Bidder B replies by offering a higher price of P_{b2} topping P_c. Bidder C drops out because P_c was the highest price that she was willing to pay. Bidder B is in control, but not for long. The high bid of P_{b2} is topped in turn by bidder A, who bids an auction price of P_{a1}. Bidder B now drops out because P_{b2} was the maximum value that he attached to the item. In the absence of any further bids the auction closes and the candy dish is handed to bidder A in exchange for the final auction price of P_{a1} plus any sales commissions.

Note two important points. First, by bidding P_{a1}, bidder A revealed and relinquished some but perhaps not all of her consumer surplus. She might have been willing to bid as high as P_{a2} but was kept from doing so by the absence of other bids. Nevertheless, she did relinquish some of her consumer surplus above P_s, which would have been the seller's asking price for the item absent the auction. Second, the process traced out a portion of the demand curve for the item, at least for these bidders at this moment in time. The revealed portion of the demand curve would be $P_a P_b P_c$, formed by the bids of P_{a1}, P_{b2} and P_{c1}. If the seller had more candy dishes available and could contact bidders B and C, affecting a sale to each at their maximum bid prices, then the

---

9 For this reason, the DOJ is looking into the alleged problems that Web music start-ups have had in securing licenses to sell music online. Anna Wilde Mathews and John R. Wilke, "Probe of Competitive Practices, Licensing of Online Music Business Is Expanded," *The Wall Street Journal*, October 15, 2001, p. A3.

10 For an extensive discussion of the various auction processes as applied to e-commerce, see "Auction Deal Engines" in Robert E. Hall, *Digital Dealing: How e-Markets Are Transforming the Economy*, (New York: W.W. Norton, 2002), chapt. 2.

11 *Transparency* means that the participants know the bidders and the bid prices. It may represent a potential benefit for the seller as bidder egos may drive prices above true market value. Some transparency may be lost if absentee participants are allowed to leave a *left bid*, which represents their highest bid price, with bidding done automatically for them by the auctioneer up to the left bid price. Other potential buyers may offer active bids through remote telecom connections.

Auctions and Value-of-Service Pricing   **FIGURE 10-3**

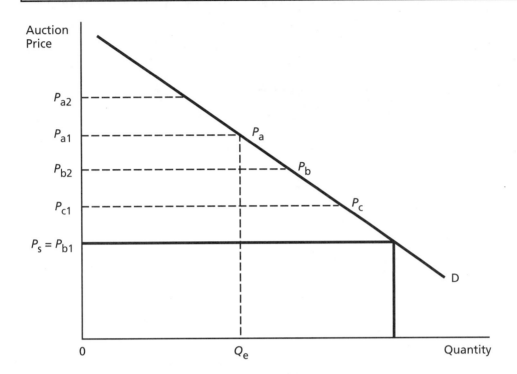

total revenue stream would be further enhanced. Of course, if the seller made these exchanges bidders A and B would likely be irritated, when they learned that the seller sold an identical item to a lower bidder in the same auction. Auction rules normally prevent such behavior. Therefore, for sellers, auctions are best reserved to the selling of one-of-a-kind items or the same item sold one-at-a-time.

The auction process results in a price that may be different from the one that is set as consequence of **haggling**.[12] Haggling involves a negotiation between buyer and seller, where they dicker with each other over the price they are both willing to accept. The haggling process is shown in Figure 10-4.

Initially, the seller (s) asks a high price P_{s1}, while the buyer (b) offers a lower one at P_{b1}. The haggling process involves successive rounds of negotiations and price concessions to determine whether a range of buyer/seller true price overlap will allow a transaction to be completed. If the seller's lowest price is P_{smin} and the buyer's maximum price is P_{bmax}, then a deal is possible at some price within that range. The actual price P_e, will depend upon the skill and relative bargaining power of the two participants. P_e need not always split the difference between P_{smin} and P_{bmax}.

The haggling process recognizes the fact that when a number of units of the product are being sold to the same potential buyer, a producer's surplus can exist. Therefore, the buyer may be able to drive prices down to the level of average cost in order to capture some of that producer's surplus. As a result, haggling offers the buyer the opportunity to turn a value-of-service price into a cost-of-service price. Figure 10-5 shows that for a competitive market, in the short run, with diminishing marginal returns, the sale price for the marginal unit ($P_{profit\ max}$), must normally equal the rising marginal cost ($P = MC$). However, if the price of the marginal unit is also the average price for all units up to the marginal unit, then it may indicate considerable

---

12 Robert D. Hof, Heather Green, and Paul Judge, "Going, Going, Gone: Online Haggling Is the Hottest Thing Happening in e-Commerce," *Business Week*, April 12, 1999, pp. 30–32.

FIGURE 10-4   Haggling to Determine the Exchange Price

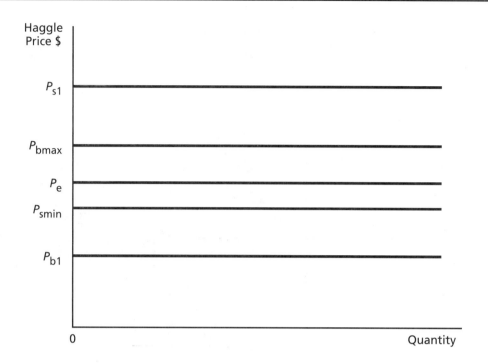

FIGURE 10-5   Producer's Surplus and a Haggle Price

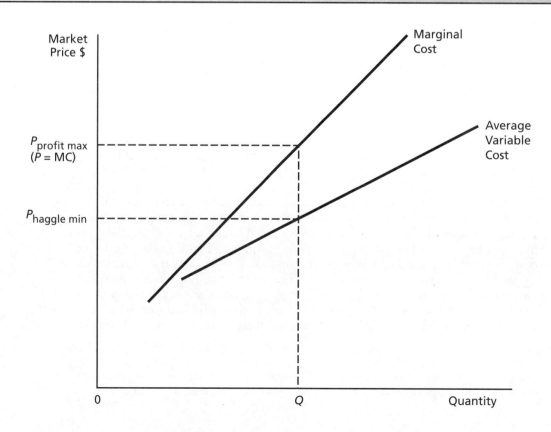

producer's surplus, because the price of the marginal unit exceeds the marginal cost for each of the preceding units. For example, if the marginal cost of the fourth unit is $10, then the profit-maximizing rule says that the consumer should pay a price of $10 for each of the four units or $40 in total. But if the successive marginal costs for each of the incremental units 1–3 were $4, $6, and $8, respectively, then the average cost of all four units taken together would be $28. Consequently, in a short-run, all-or-nothing haggle sale, the haggle price, as low as $P_{haggle\ min}$ would be below the marginal cost of the last unit. Haggle-induced, short-run price concessions can continue as long as the total revenue received from the sale of all units exceeds the total variable cost of production. In the case of e-commerce, one form of implicit, modified e-commerce haggling appears when a Web merchant offers a price concession, such as free shipping or a 10 percent discount, if the dollar total of a single sale exceeds $100, or some other minimum value. The buyer is tempted to accumulate enough items to meet the minimum value, while the seller is acknowledging that the value of the larger sale is worth sacrificing some of the producer surplus in exchange.

PRICING MODELS AS APPLIED TO E-COMMERCE FIRMS

eBay Auction Pricing

The e-commerce firm eBay, was founded in 1995 and once billed itself as the "Great American Garage Sale."[13] It has become one of the most popular Web sites providing the opportunity for the original peer-to-peer (P2P) as well as business-to-consumer (B2C) and lately business-to-business (B2B) sales contacts. It tapped into the human psychology of both the buyer wanting to purchase an item at a price below cost and the seller wanting to dispose of an item at the highest possible price. eBay has been profitable from the first day of its operation owing to some unique strategic characteristics that will be explored in Chapter 11. The focus here is with the ability of eBay's auction process to set a final price that approaches value-of-service pricing. An eBay auction is primarily an English auction with some interesting modifications. First, the items listed by a seller in an eBay auction are usually left up to bid for one to seven days, ending on a specified date and time. This set limit makes it difficult for bidders to participate on an ongoing basis. eBay solved this bidder participation problem by introducing an automated system of **left bids**, as shown in Table 10-3.

The item is a Derek Jeter 1993 Topps rookie baseball card. Every potential bidder sees the existing high bid of $20.00 and knows that it fails to meet the seller's unknown reserve price, which was set at $25.00. Each new bid is treated as a maximum bid, and must be at least equal to the existing high bid plus some predetermined increment, in this case $2.00. Bidder 2, a Yankee fan, enters a $22.00 bid but finds that she has been outbid. Bidder 1's left bid maximum of $24.50 was automatically activated by the eBay software bidding system. In the eBay system, the first bidder to offer the price is established as the new current high bidder.

Bidder 2 now has two choices. First, stop bidding and move on to some other item. Or, second, offer a higher bid. Now she realizes she is bidding against some unseen maximum left bid entered by Bidder 1 as well as some unknown reserve price set by the seller. Her next maximum bid(s) can be entered incrementally until she reaches a price that is just higher than the maximum offered by Bidder 1, or she can enter her own personal maximum bid of $30.00, which represents the highest price that she is willing to pay for the item. At a $30.00 bid, the maximum offer from Bidder 1 is breached and Bidder 2 becomes the new high bidder with a price of $26.50, which is $2 above the current high price and $1.50 above the reserve price. Notice, her maximum price isn't

13 James Poniewozik, "The Great American Garage Sale," available at **http://www.salon.com/media/col/poni/1999/06/01/ebay/**.

Table 10-3	eBay Modified English Auction Bidding System

eBay Bidding Sequence	Derek Jeter 1993 Topps Rookie Card
Seller Reserve Price	$25.00
Current high bid: Bidder 1—Reserve not met	20.00
Next higher bid: Bidder 2	22.00

Current high bid: Bidder 1—Reserve not met
    Automated bidding from B1 unseen left bid
    Maximum = $25.00
	22.00

Next higher bid: Bidder 2 Unseen maximum left bid from Bidder 2	30.00
Current high bid: Bidder 2—Reserve met Exceeds B1 maximum by $2.00	26.50
Automated electronic bidding from B2 up to unseen maximum if and when needed	30.00
Final auction price without more bids	$26.50

seen and doesn't come into play unless another bidder enters an offer at least $2 above the $26.50 price. If the auction ends with Bidder 2 at a $30.00 maximum, but a high bid of just $26.50, the winner pays only the $26.50.

Here is where the eBay system differs from a traditional English auction. The maximum bid determines only the identity of the winner, with the price being equal to the second highest price plus the increment. This **second-price auction process** uses a structure and consequences first identified by the economist William Vickrey, winner of the 1996 Nobel Prize in Economics.[14] For our purposes, the **eBay modified English auction** created an approximate value-of-service price. The seller receives a price equal to the $25.00 reserve, which mirrors a cost-of-service price, plus an additional $1.50, which represents a portion of the buyer's consumer surplus. The eBay process involves considerable transparency with a great deal of information being supplied during the bidding process. Only the maximum and reserve values, along with the true identities of the bidders remain hidden.

Priceline.com Reverse Auction Pricing

Another dynamic pricing strategy was adapted to the Web and patented by Priceline.com. This technique encompasses the Internet application of the reverse auction process. **Dynamic pricing** involves tailoring the price of the product to the demand of the individual customer, accomplished through a seller-initiated value-of-service pricing scheme, such as a system of price discrimination as shown in Chapter 9, or an auction pricing system as described in the case of eBay just discussed. What differs in the **reverse auction pricing process** is that it places the pricing initiative in the hands of the

---

14 William Vickrey, "Counterspeculation and Competitive Sealed Tenders," *Journal of Finance*, 16, no. 1 (March 1961), pp. 8-37. For a discussion of Vickrey Auctions in the stamp market, see David Lucking-Reiley, "Vickrey Auctions Predate Vickrey," available at **http://www.vanderbilt. edu/Econ/workpaper/Vickrey_auction_paper.PDF**.

buyer rather than the seller. The Priceline.com system allows potential customers to "name their own price" for a variety of travel products, including airline tickets. The buyer selects a city-pair combination for origin and destination as well as the travel dates. Then the buyer enters a price that he or she is willing to pay for the flight. It represents a binding offer to purchase, which is accompanied by a credit card number. Priceline.com then shops the offer to purchase around to its participating airlines. The airlines have the right to accept or reject the offer, and they have the right to determine the time of departure and arrival, the number of stops and route, as well as the identity of the airports servicing the city-pair. This bidding process remains **opaque**, or obscure to the bidder, as opposed to the more transparent process on eBay, Hotwire.com, or Orbitz.com. Much of the information is hidden from view until the binding offer is accepted, including the identity of the airline. In exchange, the buyer gets the tickets at a price below list and captures some of the producer surplus or excess airline revenue above marginal cost.

What if the bid is rejected by the airlines as too low. Doesn't this encourage the potential buyer to offer a slightly higher price for the recently rejected trip? Does a resubmission turn the reverse auction process into a haggling model of price setting? Not really, because the rules on Priceline.com prohibit the resubmission of the same trip on the same day. This rule works in favor of the airlines because it encourages the potential buyer to make the most reasonable bid so as to possibly get the fare. The resubmission rule also keeps the airline computers from being overloaded with a multitude of frivolous repeat bids, each of which may be mere pennies higher than the last submission. After all, with a reverse auction process that matches computer with computer, it wouldn't take long for some enterprising software engineer to write a demon bidding program that would automatically react to the initial bid rejection and resubmit the bid, upping it by some small amount. Such is the way of markets and capitalism as part of e-commerce.

A reverse auction process is efficient in an electronic market where individual buyers can express their demand preferences quickly and cheaply. Still, why would an airline, or any type of firm, be willing to participate in a plan where they undercut their preferred pricing scheme?[15] Traditional markets involve a **seller-posted pricing model**, where multiple buyers react to the set price. Competition is assumed to keep the seller from exercising monopoly power and setting a high price to exploit the buyer.

This set-price model works well in markets where demand is relatively stable or known. However, it encounters problems in markets where demand is unknown or continually fluctuating, especially when the item is either perishable or a service. Airlines provide a service in the form of travel seats that can't be stored in inventory as can a durable item such as new cars. When the plane departs, the service is provided regardless of whether a passenger occupies the seat. An empty seat means a loss in revenue forever. Moreover, the marginal cost of filling the potentially empty seat is negligible and approaches zero. Therefore, it is in the best interests of the airline to fill every seat prior to departure. However, if it makes a general reduction in price just prior to takeoff, when the number of empty seats is known, the airline will **spoil the market**. Buyers will catch on to the last-minute discounts and wait until the end to buy tickets. This buyer tactic will aggravate the empty seat problem for the airlines.[16] The airline overcomes the empty seat problem by making **selective and secret price**

---

15 Peter Coy, "The Power of Smart Pricing," *BusinessWeek*, April 10, 2000, pp. 160-64.

16 To overcome this problem, airlines used to sell empty seats to college students on a standby basis at one-half the normal ticket price. The theory was that college students placed a lower value on their time spent waiting around the airport until an empty seat appeared. Smart college students caught on and made fake reservations by phone to be paid for at the ticket counter the day of the flight. When they failed to pay, the seat was empty and they were able to secure it at the reduced price. This story is just another example of human ingenuity in the face of markets and prices.

concessions to buyers who are locked into the offer. The deal price is negotiated directly and hidden from other potential buyers. Also, the opaque conditions limit the price concessions to the market segment most sensitive to the ticket price and less sensitive to the time or route of travel. Business travelers, families with children, or senior citizens are less likely to trust their travel experience to vicissitudes of an opaque information and reservation system.

Is the name-your-own-price, reverse auction model the wave of the future? Will the set-price model go the way of the dinosaur? Despite some early optimism, the future of Internet reverse auctions appears to be limited. Reverse auctions are an inconvenient and inefficient way to buy most items.[17] It works best for big ticket items where the price concessions amount to significant savings. Jay Walker, the founder of Priceline.com, discovered this when he opened Webhouse, a reverse auction Internet bid firm designed to sell gasoline and grocery store items. Bidding on packages of Wrigley's gum or bottles of Clorox bleach turned out to be time consuming and not as profitable as bidding on airline tickets and hotel reservations. Webhouse had its devotees, but nevertheless, the firm failed because of a lack of bidder as well as seller participation, and demonstrated some of the limits to the reverse auction process. It would appear that large volumes of low-value, tangible products are best sold through the set-price model.

Second, the selective sale of cheap airline tickets to bargain hunters tends to destroy brand loyalty. Passengers who might have paid $400 for a seat resent the fact that they are sitting next to someone who may have paid only $100 for the same trip. It leads to a perception of a basic unfairness within this kind of system, regardless of the fact that the two passengers may have purchased the tickets with considerably different restrictions. Many firms may resist having their products sold in this manner. Lastly, the nonauction world is getting smarter in terms of varying its own prices so as not to have to dispose of distressed products through a Priceline type of entity. Firms alter their prices through a process of **yield management**, tailoring prices to the caller time of day, the number of vacancies, or some other variables to better accommodate changing demand conditions. They also engage in finer segmentation of the market to allow them to tap the full range of customer demand.[18] For most firms, it costs less in lost revenue and producer's surplus to selectively vary the prices themselves, than to respond to a Priceline type of bid.

Amazon.com and a Penetration Pricing Strategy

Amazon.com is a **virtual** or **Internet-only e-tailer** without any traditional **brick-and-mortar outlets** or storefront to shop at, such as Wal-Mart. At its inception in 1995, Amazon had zero identity among the buying public and a zero sales base. It began as "Earth's Biggest Bookstore" and today it brags about offering "Earth's Biggest Selection" including toys, tools, electronics, health and beauty products, prescription drugs, cars, baby and kitchen items, and a range of services including film processing. This wide variety of products extends well beyond the books, CDs, and videos that still account for almost 70 percent of its annual sales.[19] For the fiscal year 2000, the firm had sales of $2.8 billion, up by 68 percent, employed 9,000 workers, and boasted a market capitalization, or stock value, of $4.88 billion as of July 2002. Yet it has lost money, even by its own generous definition of pro forma earnings, for almost every quarter of its existence.

---

17 "A Revolution in Pricing? Not Quite," *Business Week*, November 20, 2002, p. 48.

18 To see this process in action, try calling a hotel or airline central reservation 800 number to get a price quote. Then go to the firm's reservation Web site. Chances are that a better price will be available on the Web than on the phone. True, some cost differences are inherent in Internet versus telephone sales, but they are often far less than the differences in the product price quotes.

19 "Amazon.com, Inc.," available at **http://www.hoovers.com/co/capsule/3/0,2163,51493,00.html**.

How has the e-tailer priced its products to allow it to grow so big, so fast, without ever making even a dime of profit? The answer is that Amazon.com has been practicing a modified **penetration pricing strategy**, which is a third method to resolve the tension of product pricing via the cost-of-service versus the value-of-service. Penetration pricing is structured to sell products at an amount below today's full cost in an attempt to build sufficient volume and sales revenue to cover tomorrow's full cost. It is a **fixed-price strategy** as opposed to the dynamic pricing approach followed by eBay and Priceline.com.[20] If it can be made to work, the penetration pricing strategy is ideal for taking advantage of the **increasing returns to scale** offered by the Web. Recall that increasing returns involves a situation with **scalable output**, such that a doubling of the sales volume can be achieved with less than a doubling of inputs. If Wal-Mart or Home Depot wants to double its sales, it must double the number of brick-and-mortar retail outlets and perhaps its advertising budget as well. The economics of Web e-tailing, on the other hand, allows Amazon to accommodate twice the level of sales with less than a doubling of its cost structure.

Amazon.com achieves scaleable output because of the following economic conditions. In the short run, Amazon faces two cost components. **Total variable cost** includes wholesale charges for the goods being sold, labor costs, and shipping, which change directly and reasonably proportionately with the volume of output. The second cost component is the **total fixed cost** or **overhead charges** of administration, Web site creation and maintenance, equipment, buildings, marketing, and a normal profit that are all constant and do not vary with output. The profit goal for Amazon is to reduce the per-unit fixed and variable costs down to the point where they are less than the price Amazon is charging for the items. One way to accomplish this goal is by increasing the sales volume and spreading the overhead charges. The sales volume depends upon a combination of branding, or the public's general awareness of the seller; customer loyalty, or repeat purchases by past satisfied customers; and a penetration pricing strategy that makes the seller's products attractive and relatively competitive to the items offered by rivals. The data in Table 10-4 and the equations that follow show how Amazon's penetration pricing system is designed to work.

Amazon.com Penetration Pricing		TABLE 10-4

Dollars/Case	**Case 1**	**Case 2**
Price	$30	$20
Quantity sold	1,000 units	2,500 units
Average variable cost	$10	$10
Average fixed cost including a normal profit	$25	$10
Average total cost	$35	$20
Economic profit/loss	−$5,000	$0.00
Elasticity value: Case 1 price vs. Case 2 price	= (−)(42%/−20%) = 2.14 > 1 indicating elastic consumer response	

20 Robert D. Hof and Linda Himelstein, "eBay vs. Amazon.com: Fixed Prices or Dynamic Pricing? Whichever Wins Biggest Will Shape the Future," available at **http://www.businessweek.com/1999/99_22/b3631001.htm**.

$$TC = TVC + TFC$$

$$P_1 < ATC_1 = TVC/Q + TFC/Q$$

$$P_2 = ATC_2 \downarrow = TVC\uparrow/Q\uparrow + TFC/Q\uparrow$$

In the first instance, where product price is set at \$30, the combination of fixed and variable costs amounts to \$35, resulting in an economic loss of \$5 per unit. However let's reset the product price to the lower amount of \$20 and assume that this move stimulates an elastic consumer response sufficient to raise the quantity demanded from 1,000 units to 2,500 units.[21] The result is that the lower price yields a unit cost of \$20, equal to the new lower price and the firm now makes a normal profit. What happened was that while variable cost per unit rose proportionately, the fixed cost per unit fell enough to lower the overall cost to a level equal to the product price. In fact, Amazon is betting the future of the firm upon an Internet application of the standard volume pricing model shown earlier in the chapter.

Will the Amazon pricing strategy work? Will they ever be able to get a sufficient volume of customers to drive the full cost per unit down to the level of the price? The answer is that it depends. One weakness in the model is that **shopping bots**, such as MySimon.com or Dealtime.com, tend to drive the price down toward marginal cost, which is generally below ATC.[22] Shopping bots, or robot shopping search engines, are sites that constantly send out **Web spiders** or search programs to survey the offering prices for a specific product at different sites on the Internet. The bots present these different prices on a central page at their site so that potential buyers can quickly identify the e-tailer offering the lowest possible price. This service makes it hard for any firm to compete solely on the basis of price. After all, only one can have the lowest price. Fortunately, for Amazon and other firms, price is not the only variable determining the volume of sales. By combining a low price reputation along with customer service, reliable delivery, and ease of site navigation, Amazon and other lower-priced but not lowest-priced sites may be able to reach their goal.

Potential Long-Run Pricing Results from Online Retailing

The economist Hal Varian identified some potentially conflicting pricing results emanating from the sale of products online.[23] In general, economic theory holds that a tension exists between the competitive forces that work to lower consumer prices and the forces of coordinated behavior that work to raise the prices paid by consumers. When this tension is applied to e-commerce, certain Web characteristics tend to lower e-tailer prices. First, e-tailer entry is cheap and easy. It is within the financial reach of even the smallest firm to secure a domain name, create and mount a Web site, list products, and quote prices as well as delivery terms. Big companies such as IBM, have small business units that provide these services in one-stop fashion to existing or prospective new firms. Once the site is up and running, the firm submits its domain name to the major search engines, or it may have been skilled enough to structure the site so that it is easy for the search engine spiders to find the firm. Now the fledgling firm and the tens of thousands of budding entrepreneurs just like it are ready to engage in cutthroat price competition to attract global customers. Of course, as was noted in Chapter 5 dealing with entry barriers and product differentiation, the firm might benefit from distinguishing itself from the rest of the crowd.

---

21 The elasticity value for this price change is shown as $\eta = 2.14$ in Table 10-4.

22 A list of shopping bots along with their technology and focus is available at **http://www.botspot.com/**.

23 Hal Varian, "Economic Scene: When Commerce Moves Online, Competition Can Work in Strange Ways," *The New York Times*, August 24, 2000, p. C2.

Second, the Web lowers the cost of customer search. Potential buyers can go to a general search engine such as Google, Altavista, or Yahoo!, type in the product or concept name and receive dozens if not thousands of responses. Given the ease of search, it's not too difficult to find the seller with the lowest price. Third, the Web lowers the search costs for rivals as well. Your competitors can use shopping bots to see who has the lowest price, along with the terms of sale. Some bots even provide a seller rating that yields information to buyers about the reliability of a previously unknown seller.

Lastly, Varian notes that price competition, whether it be on the Web or in the brick-and-mortar world, involves the implicit assumption that buyers react faster to a price change than do rival sellers. The firm's purpose in lowering its price is to elicit an elastic response, steal customers away from competitors and boost the level of its profits at the expense of its rivals. It assumes that potential buyers see the price cut first and are tempted to purchase at the low-price site, but the Web makes it difficult to keep secret price cuts from being equally visible to your rivals. If rivals can see your price reductions the moment you put them in place, then it gives them the opportunity to respond with an immediate matching price cut. One result is that the relative distribution of customer sales and market shares will remain the same. However, what has changed is that the firms are now selling the same or a slightly greater amount of the product at a lower price and most likely with lower profits. Rather quickly, it becomes apparent to all that e-tail price cutting is of considerable benefit to the buyer, but is self-canceling and impoverishing for the seller. Vigorous price competition on the Web provides a classic case of **ruinous competition** for sellers.

On the other side of the pricing tension, Varian points out that the ready availability of rival price information makes price coordination and the raising of prices potentially easier in the Web world than it might otherwise be in the brick-and-mortar world. It all depends upon the number of Web sellers and their attitudes toward coordinated behavior. If one firm raises its price and rivals notice it quickly, they have two choices: keep their own price constant or match the initial increase. Even though a constant price strategy may allow the firm to steal customers momentarily, the rival may quickly rescind its cut and return to the previous status quo. Conversely, matching the price increase could raise revenues and profits for all at the expense of the buyer. Given the historical level of e-tailer dollar losses and the failure of hundreds of e-tail firms, a consolidation is taking place in e-commerce. Therefore, the ready availability of price information is making it easier to coordinate prices among the few remaining sellers in a particular product category.[24] In the face of the need to stem further losses and to avoid ruinous competition, is the e-commerce market about to embark on an era when the oligopoly behavior and price leadership models described in Chapter 2 begin to appear?

SALON.COM: THE PROBLEM OF PRICING E-CONTENT REVISITED

How does the preceding discussion help to resolve the Salon.com pricing problem? Should *Salon* base its subscription price on the costs of delivering the magazine's information? Or should it price the information according its perceived customer value? Is there some way of charging for the content so as to incorporate both pricing schemes? How can *Salon* best resolve the pricing tensions? If you have checked out the magazine at **http://www.salon.com**, you will see that it attempts to steer a middle course in their pricing strategy. A typical issue of *Salon* carries two economically distinct types of news stories. The first includes some 30-plus Associated Press wire service articles, available without charge, which tell mostly about various events of the day. The cost of providing these free stories is most likely covered by the banner and popup ads that appear on the Salon screens.

---

[24] David D. Kirkpatrick, "Quietly, Booksellers Are Putting an End to the Discount Era," *The New York Times*, October 9, 2000, p. A1.

Then a second set of articles is written especially for the *Salon* audience, by either *Salon* staff writers or expert contributors. These articles provide the kinds of analysis and commentary that one might find on the newspaper page opposite the editorial page (op-ed), or as part of the feature writer columns found in *The New York Times*, the *Chicago Tribune*, or *Washington Post*. They are stories with an emotional or personal contact dimension, or a writer's edge that create reader interest just by the title. Click on one of these stories, and you find two things. The first is a paragraph or two of introductory descriptive tease that gives the reader an idea of what the message of the article will be. The second is a notice that this *Salon* premium content article is available only to subscribers and it encourages the reader to sign up for the premium service to read this and all other *Salon* signature stories. The premium content subscription is an all-or-nothing approach, allowing the reader access to every signature story for the same fixed, annual subscriber fee. The fee clearly doesn't vary with the value of the article to the reader. So, it is most likely based upon some crude estimate of the cost-of-service pricing model based upon the overall expenses incurred by providing these types of articles to the *Salon* audience.

Now the reader is stuck, and so is *Salon* for that matter, facing the classic pricing tension. The reader might like to finish reading the lead article explaining why Ariel Sharon and Yasser Arafat have been brought to the brink by their confrontation, but can't without making a larger, year-long, $30 financial commitment to *Salon*. The article's introductory tease is interesting, but the whole article isn't worth $30. What *Salon* needs is a value-of-service, casual reader, payment system, where articles might be purchased individually. Readers might be willing to pay $0.25 or $0.50 each, via an account linked monthly or quarterly to a credit card, for the right to read or download intriguing articles. This option sets up the same kinds of micropayment problems encountered earlier with the proposed Internet music subscription services. If *Salon* wanted to create a really sophisticated pricing system, it might introduce a two-part tariff, charging readers a low fixed monthly access fee of say $2.50, and then assessing them $0.25 per article based upon a simple password. Or *Salon* might offer readers one month of free articles, followed by an automatic subscription charge to a credit card, if the agreement isn't canceled in time. These suggestions sound a great deal like the pricing models that buyers find in the brick-and-mortal world, which is exactly the point. The economics of pricing is not a whole lot different for retailers or e-tailers. Individual e-tailers, just like retailers, call on different pricing strategies according to the characteristics of their specific products and the behavior of their customers. For every viable product, with sufficient demand for it, the correct method for pricing the product will emerge. The profit motive provides strong incentives for finding practical solutions to a wide range of market problems.

Salon and the Concept of a Contribution Margin

Astute content pricing is not the only way that *Salon* and other e-commerce content producers can earn a profit. In July 2002, the firm began to sell a Weblog listing service to its readers.[25] Weblogs, or blogs, are an increasingly popular way of posting a personal Web site, including a bio, pictures, links, and commentary. *Salon* blogs are aimed at *Salon* magazine customers, who are a self-selected community of like-minded readers. Its not beyond imagination that some subsegment of these readers might like to identify themselves to others, get to know one another, and express as well as share their own opinions. Using a crafty form of cross-platform promotion, some columns and stories carried on Salon.com will identify interesting or popular blogs, directing other readers to those sites. This approach may give the blog creator a measure or impression of status within the *Salon* community, which reinforces the original desire for notoriety and contact with other readers.

---

25 David F. Gallagher, "Salon Media Introduces Weblog Service," *The New York Times*, July 25, 2002, p. C6.

The point to remember here is that the fee for content model is not the only way to generate revenue out of an e-commerce site. Professional and college sports teams sell logo gear as a way to make additional money from the athletic experience. Hollywood studios license the characters from popular movies, such as Star Wars, to adorn everything from toys, to fast-food giveaways, to computer games and cartoons. *Salon* is a brand just like Michigan State, UCLA, Nascar, or the Dallas Cowboys. It has a community of followers who relate to what the brand has to offer, and enjoy being associated with its performance. If the sale of blogs on Salon.com generates sufficient revenues to cover the variable costs of mounting the material and hosting the site, while returning some revenue above those costs, then the service has created a **contribution margin** to help cover part of the fixed costs and earn a normal profit. A sufficient number of contribution margins from a large enough number of salable products can tally up to the necessary profit level. If the cross-promotion generates a larger number of "hits" on the magazine site by Webloggers looking for site references, so much the better for *Salon* to charge higher advertising rates. Smart pricing to generate a profit involves knowing what the true value of the brand is and fully capitalizing on it. AOL-TW tried to capitalize on the synergies created through cross-platform advertising deals in multiple media settings. Unfortunately, they failed to reach their goal, at least initially. Perhaps Salon.com will have greater success; at least it's worth a try.

SUMMARY AND PROSPECTS

The conclusion that emerges from the discussion in this chapter is that product pricing appears as a challenge for all sellers, whether they are e-tailers or retailers. Every seller must balance the market conditions of customer demand, cost of production, and competition with their own approach to product design, business model, and pricing strategy. Every pricing strategy embodies a tug-of-war reflecting the tension between establishing prices based upon the costs of producing the product and the value of the product to the consumer. Competitive markets in the long run should gravitate to a price that is a harmonious reflection of the two approaches. At the start, most firms must make a choice between the two approaches to setting the initial offering price. The introductory case firm Salon.com has chosen what looks to be a cost-of-service pricing model, supplemented they hope by a contribution margin from ancillary activities. Their ultimate survival rests on the correctness of their choice.

Not all firms successfully navigate these tricky shoals in the brick-and-mortar world. Therefore, it should come as no surprise that some, and perhaps many, firms will fail in the virtual world as well. The majority of e-tailers were born at a moment in time characterized by a naïve optimism regarding the new Web technology and its ability to facilitate the sale of products and services. These fledgling e-commerce firms had business models that were new and untested, but they found outside funding, rushed into operation, and quickly became publicly traded firms. As chinks appeared in the e-tailer's armor and funding dried up with the bursting of the stock market bubble, the firms failed to experience pricing success sufficient to generate the revenue streams that would allow them to survive.

Do these results mean that e-commerce as a way of doing business is a failure? Or do they suggest that the majority of business models and pricing strategies developed to date have been the source of failure? The answers to these questions are not readily available, but several facts are clear. The Web is important. It is here to stay, and it is growing in use. The prospect of untapped profits will lure new entrepreneurs to offer product, content, and services over the Internet. The rules and challenges of pricing these items remain the same. However, they most likely will require new approaches as participants in e-commerce learn from and build upon the past mistakes of the first generation of e-commerce firms.

KEY TERMS AND CONCEPTS

ability to pay
accounting profit
auction pricing
brick-and-mortar outlets
consumer surplus
contribution margin
cost-of-service pricing
delay (versioning) over time
dynamic pricing
eBay modified English auction
economic profit
elastic demand
elasticity coefficient
English auction
expenses
explicit opportunity costs
first-price auction
fixed access fee
fixed costs
fixed-price strategy
haggling
implicit opportunity costs
increasing returns to scale
inelastic
inelastic demand
left bid
manufacturer's suggested retail price
   (MSRP)
MC = MR
micropayment system
normal profit
opaque auction process
opportunity costs

overhead charges
penetration pricing strategy
price elasticity of demand
price per unit of use
profit markup
profit maximizing rule (MC = MR)
reserve price
retention fee
return-on-investment (ROI)
reverse auction pricing process
ruinous competition
scalable output
second-price auction
selective and secret price concessions
self-selection
seller-posted pricing model
shopping bots
simultaneous multiple version strategy
spoiling the market
standard volume (SV)
standard volume pricing
sunk cost
total fixed cost
total variable cost
transparent auction process
two-part tariff
value-of-service pricing
variable costs
versioning
virtual (Internet-only) e-tailer
Web spiders
willingness to pay
yield management

DISCUSSION AND REVIEW QUESTIONS

1. Identify the economic rule for achieving profit maximization. How does the implementation of this rule set up a tension between the value-of-service and cost-of-service pricing strategies?

2. What kinds of firms are usually forced to resort to use standard cost pricing? Why is the manufacturer's suggested retail price so sensitive to the choice of a standard sales volume?

3. What is the price elasticity of demand and how does this information influence the cost-of-service pricing strategy? Does the price elasticity of demand also play a role in the value-of-service strategy? How?

4. Are profits more or less sensitive to changes in sales when the firm relies upon standard cost pricing? Why?

5. What kinds of problems do the unique technology and economic aspects of Web e-content create for e-commerce firms, such as Salon.com, as they try to set an access price based on cost-of-service pricing?

6. Show graphically and explain the concept of consumer surplus. How does the presence of consumer surplus encourage firms to adopt a value-of-service pricing strategy?

7. What is versioning and how does it help firms turn a portion of the buyer's consumer surplus into revenue for the firm? How does versioning lead buyers to reveal the otherwise hidden true value that they place on an item?

8. What is a two-part tariff? How might Internet firms employ this value-of-service strategy to extract a greater flow of revenue from the customer?

9. Describe the distinguishing characteristics of a traditional English auction. In what sense is it a transparent auction process? How does an English auction help to capture some of the bidder's consumer surplus?

10. Explain how eBay's bidding process differs from a traditional English auction. Why does a bidder participation problem resulting from the eBay process, and how do they solve this problem with a system of left bids?

11. How are prices determined in a market involving haggling? How can haggling be made to work in favor of the buyer if the exchange is an all-or-nothing trade involving multiple items?

12. Distinguish between a seller-posted pricing model and the reverse auction pricing model. Why does Priceline.com make so much of the reverse auction travel information opaque? How and why does Priceline.com keep their reverse auction from deteriorating into a haggling model of price setting?

13. Was the reverse auction model successful when it was applied to grocery items and gasoline? Why? What are the economic and psychological limits to the reverse auction model?

14. Explain Amazon.com's penetration pricing strategy. In what sense is it an adaptation of the cost-of-service pricing scheme? Is the Amazon strategy threatened by the existence of shopping bots? Why?

15. How does the Web influence the tension inherent between the forces working to drive prices lower and those that work to drive prices higher? If price competition on the Web is to be successful for an individual firm, what implicit assumption must hold? Does the Web work to reinforce or undermine this assumption? Why?

16. Salon.com has chosen to impose a fixed annual fee as its pricing strategy. How does this fee set up a reader conflict with the value-of-service pricing scheme? In what ways might *Salon* resolve this tension?

17. What is a contribution margin? How has Salon.com used this concept to help it potentially generate a sustaining level of normal profits?

WEB EXERCISES

1. Link to **http://www.salon.com/blogs/index.html**, to see whether any of the sites are of interest to you. You can join and post your own information for $39.95 per year including software and hosting, but a 30-day free trial might be fun and informative.

2. If Weblogs aren't your thing, link to the magazine at **http://www.salon.com/**. The stories and features in the free section are interesting and thought provoking.

3. If the content in Salon.com is not to your liking, try linking to *Slate* Magazine at **http://slate.msn.com/**. It is still a free content provider, but note that it is part of the Microsoft Network.

4. Link to USAToday.com, click on the Money section and check out the market capitalization of Amazon.com using the ticker symbol AMZN. Has the firm increased or decreased in value since July 2002? Why?

5. Link to the two shopping bots, MySimon.com and DealTime.com. Check out the prices for the most recent version of the Microsoft Xbox video console. Are the seller prices the same or different for the console? Have some sellers found a limited way of making a price concession by bundling one or two games with the console and selling the package for a single price?

6. For an introduction to the range of bot technology in general link to **http://www.botspot.com/**. Check out the Newsgroup search bot section to see whether it might provide you with a useful link to contemporary information for your next college research paper.

7. Choose your favorite hotel chain or airline to see whether it charges different prices and segments the market between callers to its 800 number and those that make reservations over the Internet. One quick comparison could be an inquiry for room availability and prices at a specific Sheraton hotel, with a telephone number of 1-800-325-3535 and an Internet reservations link at Sheraton.com.

CHAPTER

11

Introductory Case

ESTYLE.COM IS IN STYLE . . . AT LEAST FOR AWHILE

From content to cosmetics, food to furniture, and drugstores to dog stores, the e-commerce landscape is littered with the virtual bodies of more than 100 failed B2C Web companies. Initially, many B2C firms looked to have a great e-tailing idea, wrapped around a business plan sophisticated enough to attract venture capital funding. Some of the firms actually went public. Then reality set in when the neophyte e-tailers began having problems sustaining their initial momentum. Numerous mundane questions started to appear, which were not unlike those that must be answered by traditional retailers. For example, how were the e-tailers going to attract new customers and hold onto old ones? What would they have to do to boost the **conversion rate**, turning page viewers into e-tail buyers? How would they implement their business plan strategy to capture market share, generate revenues, and make profits? Generally, what would they have to do to slug it out with competitors in the market, being pressed on the one side by rival e-tailers and on the other by brick-and-mortar retailers? It became apparent that most of the B2C e-commerce firms weren't going to find answers to these questions fast enough to survive. Moreover, it

became particularly difficult to sustain any new, Web-only retail concept in a down economy and a depressed financial environment.[1]

This environment makes the story and success to date of estyle.com especially interesting. The concept behind the firm was created in November 1998 and they opened up their initial Web site, babystyle.com, in October 1999. Estyle is a privately held, venture capital-backed, women and children's product firm that focuses on serving new and expectant mothers. Estyle.com started out by selling designer maternity clothes, especially for work and evening wear. Office-bound expectant mothers can order a four-piece, basic long-sleeved, mix-and-match pregnancy survival kit for $152, from the designer Belly Basics.[2] Or they can order a stylish evening dress from designer Diane von Furstenberg. Through their newer KidStyle.com site, estyle also offers high-profit-margin infant, toddler, and kids products, including toys, clothing, and accessories, for children up to the age of 10 years. Customers can order T-shirts and pants for a toddler from Ralph Lauren, or a DKNY infant sleeper. Estyle.com is a Web e-tailer with a sound idea, a well-designed site and is selling into an "underserved" (their term), $12 billion annual market. They estimate that the typical, first-time expectant mother spends upwards of $5,000 to $7,000 on clothes, cribs, car seats, toys, and other baby paraphernalia.[3] The sales of expectant mother clothing and baby products are spread out evenly over the year. They do not display the

---

1 After reaching a high of 11,723 on the DOW Industrial Index in January 2000, the stock market began a deep slide erasing 4,000 points from the DOW by mid-July 2002. The Nasdaq Index, which contained many of the dot-com listings, fell by more than 75 percent over the same time span. In March 2002, the U.S. economy entered into a recession that lasted through November. Together these economic and financial forces helped to doom many of the "irrationally exuberant" investors in dot-com equity stocks. The story of the failure of these firms is chronicled in Chapter 15.

2 See the estyle site, available at **http://www.babystyle.com/default.asp**.

3 Margaret Young, "The New Kid on eStyle's Block," available at **http://www.businessweek.com/technology/content/jun2001/tc20010612_097.htm**.

e-Commerce Strategic Behavior:

Product Differentiation and Promotion

risky and technologically expensive seasonal buying pattern typical at many e-tailers. The firm has Cindy Crawford, the well-known high-fashion model, as a celebrity spokesperson. Crawford offers helpful tips on the site and meets with potential customers, to promote estyle products, at upscale fashion sites such as Bloomingdale's. Ms. Crawford and her visits to brick-and-mortar locations help to give a physical presence to an otherwise virtual e-tailer.

Estyle.com has survived while other Web-based baby product competitors including iBaby.com and Babygear.com have folded.[4] The firm still faces formidable Web competition from Babycenter.com, backed by Johnson & Johnson, the giant pharmaceutical and baby product firm, and Babies "R" Us, backed by the Web powerhouse combination of Amazon.com and Toys "R" Us. The Babycenter site sells products

having a little less pizzazz. It is less focused toward stylish pregnancy apparel and places a much greater emphasis on delivering information and helpful hints about mom and kid care. Babiesrus.com is run as a division of Amazon.com and heavily emphasizes baby products such as car seats, swings, toys, games, furniture, and books. It has minimal new mother or childcare information and doesn't list or link to other sites selling clothes for the expectant mother. Besides these prominent Web sites, additional competition comes from the thousands of brick-and-mortar baby product and expectant mother clothing stores found in almost every community across the nation. Let's not forget the Wal-Marts of the world, who sell these kinds of products and just about everything else imaginable, conveniently and at a low price.

How has estyle.com been able to survive? How has the firm been able to attract some $85 million in three rounds of venture capital funding, including $25 million in November 2000, when venture money had almost dried up? Will estyle.com reach profitability in the future despite competing against the Web forces of Amazon and Johnson & Johnson? Together, these questions set up our discussion of the dual tensions that are central to the topics in this chapter. The first looks at the question and nature of the competitive tension between e-tailers and traditional retailers. How can e-tailers compete against the convenience, accessibility, and immediacy provided by local retailers? If e-tailer efficiency and reach begin to swamp the local brick-and-mortar shops, how can retailers respond and stay alive? The second examines the competitive tension among e-tailers themselves. How will these firms establish their identities and market shares in cyberspace? Will they generate enough sales and profits to reward their backers and survive into the future?

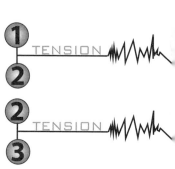

AN ECONOMIC THEORY OF PRODUCT DIFFERENTIATION

Upon first reflection, one might think that the economics of **product differentiation** would begin with a discussion of the firm, research and development, product marketing,

---

4 In fact, typing in either of these two addresses will direct a Web surfer to the estyle site at babystyle.com. Estyle either bought up or licensed the former competitors' names, absorbed their reservoirs of customers and stopped any potential competitor from reactivating the name.

and the production side of the market in general. After all, it's the firm that designs a new product or modifies an existing one to sell to the customer. And it's the firm that puts together the advertising campaign to entice buyers to purchase the item. The popular Harvard economist John Kenneth Galbraith coined the term the **dependence effect** based on this exact concept. In Galbraith's words, the demand for most goods "does not arise in spontaneous consumer need. Rather, the dependence effect means that it grows out of the process of production itself. If production is to increase, the wants must be effectively contrived. In the absence of the contrivance the increase would not occur."[5] Humans are born with the demand for basic necessities such as food, clothing, and shelter. The demand for most other goods, including cars, DVD players, and various forms of entertainment, depends upon the ability of firms to create these products and then market them to an impressionable public, whose tastes and preference can be led and shaped by advertising. Seen in this light, consumers are like children who can be enticed to want the latest fad toy from Thomas the Tank Engine, Bob the Builder, or the Power Puff Girls. Within this **production-based product differentiation model**, consumers are seen as desiring the item itself, for its own sake. Therefore, consumer demand is negatively sloped relative to price and is highly malleable or capable of being shifted by consumer-focused advertising.

A Demand-Based Model of Product Differentiation

Although this production-based model may contain some truth, it is not the only basis for explaining product differentiation. After all, many products are created and brought to the market with huge advertising budgets, only to fail miserably as consumers rejected the item. Have you had a bottle of "New Coke" or driven in an Edsel recently? If you haven't, then creation, production, and marketing can't be the whole product differentiation story. The economist Kelvin Lancaster appreciated this gap in economic theory and developed a **demand-based model of product differentiation** that explained differentiation based upon variations in product attributes.[6] According to Lancaster, consumers show a demand for the individual **product attributes**, or characteristics embodied within a specific product, rather than the product itself. When buyers acquire a product, they are really purchasing the bundle of attributes contained within that product. In this model, buyers are assumed to be as unique as snowflakes, with no two individuals wanting the exact same combination of attributes. Therefore, different consumers are scattered about in an **attribute space** depending on their individual tastes and preferences. For example, consumers have varying preferences for the attributes bundled within different brands of breakfast cereals, including the amount of sugar, nutritional content, color, texture, hot versus cold, or the presence of chemical additives.

The potential location points in the attribute space for cereal may be infinite, but groups of buyers may tend to **cluster** around certain attribute combinations. One cluster may prefer a cold cereal with high sugar content and care little about any possible harm from color additives, leading them to choose brightly colored Fruit Loops. Another cluster may prefer a low-calorie, high-vitamin content, and sugarless cold cereal such as Total. A third cluster may like all of the attributes bundled within Total, but would also prefer some dried fruit to be included in the package such as with Special K Red Berries. Now the task for the firm is to design a product that most closely contains the desired attributes of a cluster, which also includes a sufficiently large number of consumers. Within a demand-driven model of differentiation, tapping a specific market segment correctly could lead to a high volume of sales and potential profitability. Conversely, the failure to bundle the correct or most attractive combination of attributes will result in losses and the possible demise of the product or firm. The key is for firms

---

5 John Kenneth Galbraith, *The Affluent Society*, (New York: The New American Library, 1958), p. 129.

6 Kelvin Lancaster, *Consumer Demand: A New Approach*, (New York: Columbia University Press, 1971).

to recognize that consumers are not a homogeneous lot. Therefore, the seller doesn't have to design a product that appeals to the tastes and preferences of everyone. The firm only has to identify a sufficiently large and profitable market segment to be successful.

This demand-based model applies equally to product differentiation in cyberspace among virtual e-tailers and in physical space among brick-and-mortar retailers. Let's transfer Lancaster's concept into cyberspace and construct a two-attribute consumer demand model for the e-commerce attributes as shown in Figure 11-1. The vertical axis represents an index value (1 to 100) showing a rising consumer preference for Web site convenience including ease of site navigation, checkout and delivery. The horizontal axis shows an index value of consumer preference for customer service including return policy, response time for complaints, and calling numbers for personal contact. The farther out the consumer is along each axis, the higher is their absolute desire for convenience and customer service. One segment of cyber-buyers holds a strong relative preference for the most satisfying purchase experience. They are willing to sacrifice some degree of customer service in exchange for a more satisfactory shopping experience. For the sake of the example, we assume that these buyers want an e-tailer to provide three index units of site convenience for every unit of customer service, a 3:1 ratio. They are clustered along the upper left-hand portion of the graph, extending outward from the origin. Each dot represents a unique customer, each of whom holds a varying potential for current and repeat sales. A second set of consumers prefers to buy from sites that provide a high level of customer service. They will tolerate a great deal of Internet shopping inconvenience to ensure receiving this service. This market segment wants e-tailers to deliver two units of service quality for each unit of site convenience provided, a 1:2 ratio. They are clustered along the lower right-hand portion of the graph, extending outward from the origin. Notice that in each cluster the dots representing some potential buyers lie further out in the attribute space. These buyers have a greater absolute preference for both convenience and service quality than do others in the same grouping. They will be the most difficult and costly customers to attract because a given e-tailer would have to spend even greater amounts of money on site design or customer service to gain their business.

| Cyberspace Customers and Attribute Space | FIGURE 11-1 |

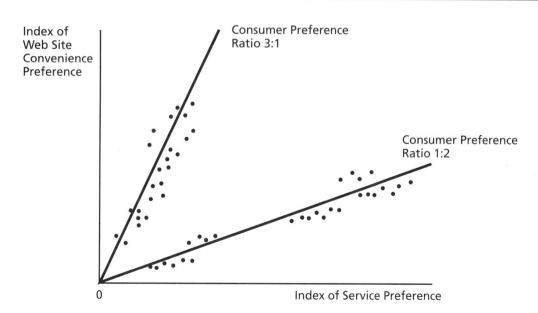

FIGURE 11-2   Firm Attribute Strategy in Cyberspace

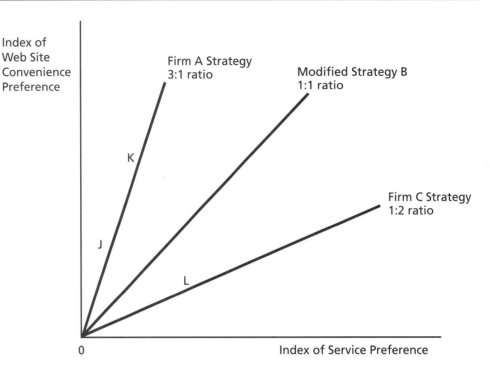

What the discussion shows to this point is a set of revealed consumer preferences and trade-offs for convenience and service. What each firm must do is develop a strategy that will offer the targeted market segment its desired combination of convenience and service quality. It is clear that no single firm, with one strategy, can satisfy all three segments, because the segments have conflicting preferences. The best that they can do is to target one segment and hope that they can attract and hold a profitable number of initial and repeat buyers.[7]

Attribute Variation and Firm Product Differentiation

The details in Figure 11-2 show the rays from the origin representing the *relative* site convenience and customer service strategies for two e-commerce competitors. Firm A follows a strategy that provides convenience and service in a 3:1 ratio. Firm C provides the attributes in a 1:2 ratio, thereby targeting the market segment with the most intense preference for customer service. Next each firm has to determine the absolute amount of convenience and service that it would like to provide. This decision, along with the associated costs, will help to determine the number of consumers to be captured in that market segment, the sales revenue, and the profit potential for the firm. For example,

---

7 Note that an e-tailer might be able to attract and hold more than one segment if they introduce multiple strategies and can put up different *versions* of their product. eBay has an auction-priced market section, but it also sells many of the same products at a fixed price in its Half.com division. The auction division caters to potential buyers with a high low-price preference but a low preference for convenience. Conversely, Half.com caters to buyers with a greater tolerance for higher prices, but who wish to acquire the item right away. As such, Half.com does away with the risk element that Bidder A will loose the item to Bidder B who offers a higher price.

Firm A can spend an amount of money (Total Cost 1), sufficient to allow it to reach point J on strategy ray A. Point J represents the combination of index units of convenience and service that Firm A can provide with a fixed dollar expenditure allocated at the ratio of three units of convenience per unit of service. This will allow it to capture all of the customers with a 3:1 preference ratio along and possibly in the neighborhood of the line segment 0J.[8] This volume of customers may or may not make enough purchases over time to allow the firm to cover its costs and make a profit.

Alternately, Firm A can spend a larger absolute amount of money on site development and customer service reaching the higher point K on strategy ray A. This effort allows the firm to capture an incremental share JK of the targeted market segment. These potential customers show a higher absolute preference for the overall amounts of convenience and service. Recall that e-tailing is potentially characterized by increasing returns to scale. Therefore, a small boost in resource inputs (added cost) may lead to a proportionately greater rise in product sales (added revenue). Consequently, the choice of the absolute cost level resolves itself into a question of whether enough added customers and sales can be found in the JK segment to warrant the extra cost. This issue makes the attribute space model similar to the *MC = MR pricing rule* discussed earlier in Chapter 2.

Competitor C may design its Web site and service mix to attract potential buyers in the market segment with the most intense service preference along strategy ray C at a 1:2 ratio. For starters, Firm C may decide to incur a total cost level sufficient to provide volume L of convenience and service. Again, the profitability of C depends upon the relative costs paid and sales revenue captured by attracting customers to this attribute mix. They too can move out farther in attribute space along the 1:2 ray, depending on the comparison of incremental costs and revenues.

Several equilibrium market possibilities exist. First, both firms may survive side by side, selling similar or slightly differentiated products, at Web sites with different bundles of attributes and at the same or different prices. Second, one firm may survive and prosper while the other firm fails. This result arises when the number of customers or customer demand within its targeted segment is insufficient. Third, both may fail to generate a profit and be forced to modify their strategy by moving to another attribute ratio such as 1:1. One or both of the firms may survive there or near that ratio, if they find a sufficient number of customers and sales volume. Also, in the absence of a firm providing customers with their exact preferred combination of convenience and service such as 3:1, some buyers may be tempted to migrate from other market segments to the next best combination. A customer with a 3:1 preference ration is unlikely to gravitate to the firm providing a 1:2 ratio. They would be more inclined to accept a second-best solution at 1:1, which is closer to their original subjective preferences. Lastly, regardless of the e-tailer's strategy, not enough customers or sales volume may exist to warrant selling the product in cyberspace. Consequently, retailers retain their original market shares and face diminished competition as e-tailers go out of business, vacating the attribute space.

E-TAILER STRATEGIES: PROMOTION AND PRODUCT DIFFERENTIATION

What the discussion has proved so far about product differentiation is that the consuming public is really made up of a set of unique individual buyers. Each potential buyer comes with a personal set of tastes and preferences regarding the attributes of the products he or she would like to purchase. In an ideal world, all consumers would receive a

---

8 The model assumes that some of the potential buyers with preference ratios slightly different from 3:1, such as 3.25:1 or 2.75:1, will gravitate to products with the 3:1 attribute ratio, which is bundled within the product that is closest to their subjective preferences. If they do, then the product or firm has a greater chance of survival. If they don't, then the future of the product or firm looks less certain.

product with attributes tailored to their unique specifications. This concept is similar to going to a new car dealership and ordering a car from the factory. The list of accessories, design, and performance features that the new owner can have on a custom-built car is long, if the buyer is willing to pay the usually higher custom-order price and wait 10 to 12 weeks for delivery. On the other hand, auto firms produce cars for dealer inventories in anticipation of sales. Fortunately, what appears at first to be a set of unique buyers, is often a set of potential customers with relatively small differences in tastes and preferences. Many of these customers tend to cluster around one or more sets of common characteristics in attribute space. Therefore, the auto assemblers produce a limited number of high-volume car versions containing the standard equipment and special features desired by a large market segment. These models might include automatic transmission, power steering, air conditioning, AM/FM/CD players, popular color combinations, and so on. If the potential buy wants a spoiler, sport mirrors, and alloy wheels, the dealer can add them on.

By tailoring production to a market segment the auto assembler can produce more cars, offer them at a lower sale price, and have them available for immediate delivery on the dealer's lot. Some buyers may not get 100 percent of the attributes they originally wanted, but the added convenience of immediate delivery and the lower price usually more than compensate for the few missing items. In this way the auto assemblers are introducing a form of the supply-based product differentiation model into the selling process. The assemblers know the most desirable attributes and build those cars in volume, enticing buyers with slightly different attribute mixes to accept the assembler's choice of characteristics based upon lower price and greater accessibility. As a result, what we see is a market process in which the demand and supply sides interact to determine the eventual outcome.

e-Tailer Advertising: Branding versus Target Marketing

Given an appreciation of the nuances of attribute variation within product markets, how can e-tailers take advantage of this information to differentiate their products to potential customers? One traditional method to create product differentiation is through advertising. Marketing specialists long ago recognized that advertising can be structured to serve either a competitive or informational goal. **Competitive advertising** involves what marketers commonly refer to as **branding**, or advertising designed to place the name of the firm or product in front of the consumer. Branding tells the buyer who the firm is, what it does, and the bundle of attributes that it stands for. At the same time it tries to create a positive attitude toward the brand so that advertising viewers will be converted into customers, who in turn will become loyal, repeat buyers of the product. Advertising to build **brand awareness** is the kind that potential customers might see on television or hear on the radio. Internet and other firms also employed horizontal **banner ads** or **pop-up ads** on Web portal sites to help fix the name of the product or firm in the mind of the consumer.[9] Many of the firms that have become household names on the Web, such as Yahoo!, Priceline, Ameritrade, and eBay, engaged heavily in brand awareness advertising.

9 Jennifer Rewick, "Advertising: Brand Awareness Fuels Strategies for Online Advertisers Next Year," *The Wall Street Journal*, December 28, 2000, p. B2. Some pop-up ads open in a second window and slow down the loading of the site's initial homepage. Viewers can get tired of waiting through the delay and decide to leave, switching to a different Web site before the initial page has fully loaded. Other pop-ups appear unexpectedly, irritating most users. Finally, there are *pop-under ads* that appear when a view tries to close out an existing Web page. Pop-under ads have been employed in high volume and in rapid succession as part of the Internet pornography industry. Their sequential appearance, as one is closed out another one appears, tends to give viewers the impression that they have lost control of their computers. Patrons of *iVillage.com*, a collection of sites for women, expressed such annoyance with pop-up ads that the site has vowed to eliminate most of them despite any loss of advertising revenues. See Jane L. Levere, "Pop Go Those Blasted Pop-Up Ads, iVillage Decrees," *The New York Times*, July 29, 2002, p. C4.

Curiously, other I-sellers, including Pets.com, MotherNature's.com, Prodigy, and Webvan also did a great deal of competitive advertising and nevertheless fell by the wayside.

A study of Internet branding, by David Aaker and Robert Jacobson, set out to identify the characteristics of those e-tailers whose brand awareness efforts led to some measure of later stock market success and those that did not.[10] They determined first that many early efforts at e-tailer branding were mostly a "land grab" in disguise. These branding ads were designed so as to be the first to attract the largest number of visitors to a branded site in a particular product category. Unique "eyeballs" on a brand's Web pages were highly prized and were thought to convey a lasting advantage by serving as the basis for repeat purchases through customer inertia. What the two researchers found was that this expectation wasn't realized unless the firm could convert the brand awareness into **brand equity** or value to the firm. In fact, for some Internet firms such as the original ISP Prodigy, consumers became aware of the brand, but found that it compared unfavorably to that of competitors. The e-mail system was problematic and the log-on sequence was slow with weak customer service. Second, they found that it was a positive consumer attitude toward the brand that drove "both Web Traffic and purchase behavior, especially repeat purchases."[11] These repeat customer purchases were particularly important because of the high cost of attracting first-time customers. Repeat buyers yielded a more profitable return on the initial promotional investment.

Third, Aaker and Jacobson concluded that a relationship existed between brand awareness, attitude toward the brand, and the strength of the business model. For example, they found a significant number of AOL customers who express some form of displeasure with a portion of the firm's services. However, the power of the AOL business model that combines widespread and diversified chat services, along with Instant Messenger and broad access to the Time Warner content, more than compensated for the relatively weak attitude. On the other hand, broad brand awareness and a positive attitude are not enough to keep a weak business model afloat. Pets.com and their backers soon discovered that even a popular sock puppet wasn't enough to overcome the economic inefficiencies of their Web business. Bags and cans of dog food are more efficiently sold and delivered through local retailers for the same reasons that coal moves in high volume by rail or barge, while electronic products move in lower volume by truck. The shipping of individual, large, heavy, and low-value items is usually uneconomic and makes sense only if the item can be shipped in bulk via the lowest-cost carrier. Lastly, they determined that branding works best where the product conveys an element of vitality or energy. The snappy and offbeat branding by Yahoo! and Amazon worked to create a cache and buzz about these firms that attracted new customers and helped the firm to hold onto existing ones. In popular terms it became "cool" to say that you visited these sites. It made you part of an Internet community to talk about your experience and activities there, which in turn potentially created interest in the site among others.

Informational Advertising and Differentiation

Branding and banner ads, along with other methods used to achieve product differentiation, all have their limits. The branding approach is not well suited to taking advantage of the strengths and benefits that are part of the Internet. As a medium for communication, the *Internet* is different from *television*, the great purveyor of brand advertising. The Internet is *interactive* rather than *passive*. Web users are *focused* on a task with a purpose in mind and are not as *receptive* to or *distracted* by what is placed before them. The Internet is good at providing *depth and detail* rather than *broad contact and impressions*.

---

10 David A. Aaker and Robert Jacobson, "What Separates Web Winners from Losers," *The Wall Street Journal*, March 12, 2001, p. A22.

11 For reviews of the Prodigy Internet service, see the Web site epinions.com available at **http://www.epinions.com/cmsw-ISP-All-Prodigy/display_~reviews**. This self-organizing Web site provides unvarnished opinions and user reviews about a wide range of topics.

Consequently, the strength of the Internet is in distributing and reinforcing **informational advertising** rather than brand awareness. For that reason a number of brick-and-mortar retailers are developing their own sites as a vehicle for direct customer contract and product differentiation as opposed to erecting banner ads on portal or general sites.[12]

Proprietary Web sites are a highly efficient way to build customer relationships. The information pitch can be offered in greater detail, with greater depth and aimed at a **target market**. A proprietary site is also highly cost effective. "Television made it possible for there to be 40 different brands of dishwashing liquid, (while) the Internet lets a car maker print fewer brochures."[13] From a *viewer perspective*, visitors typically access a site looking for additional information about a specific product or service, especially where the product is either complex (electronic equipment) or expensive (cars), such that the potential for *gain* from visiting the site exceeds the *cost* of the time spent at the site. From the *firm's perspective*, proprietary site visitors are already interested in the product and are much closer to affecting a purchase than would be the average random viewer of a banner ad. Therefore, the time and effort spent by the firm and directed toward influencing buyer behavior is usually more productive. For example, promotions, including the distribution of free samples that are aimed at proprietary site viewers, are more cost effective and generate higher numbers of buyers and repeat users than products given out randomly in mass mailings or distributed to mall shoppers. E-mails sent to previous proprietary site visitors show a similar high success rate.[14]

Next to proprietary sites, product advertising is seen as most effective in reaching customers and differentiating a product when it is done on a site whose topic is closely related to that of the advertiser. Go to the Kelley Blue Book site at **http://www.kbb.com**, or to **http://www.edmunds.com** to look up the value of a new or used car, and links to the General Motors proprietary Web page, GMBuyPower.com, or to esurance.com, a Web-based seller of auto insurance will also appear. Or go to the foodTV.com site and see links to the home sites for Kraft or Kellogg's. If a viewer is looking for general auto or food information, then the **click-through rate** for ads on a site touting specific food or car-related products or firms should be higher. This news may be encouraging for **narrow topic sites**, allowing them to sell more profitable ads, but it poses a problem for **general information sites** with a high number of visitors, such as news or e-mail. Originally, content sites such as Yahoo!, Salon.com, and TheStreet.com had hoped to pay for the cost of their information through the sale of banner advertising space. Now they must rethink their role on the Web and their revenue sources.[15] Here the business model for AOL may be instructive. The firm "never pinned its hopes on competing with television for advertising that builds brand awareness. Rather it positioned itself to clients as a method of closing sales that can be more efficient than direct mail, point-of-purchase displays and salespeople."[16]

From this discussion, it is apparent that *how* and *where* an e-tailer advertises is as important in the success of the product differentiation process as the *specific content* of the advertising message.

Private-Label Brands: Combining Differentiation with Higher Profit Margins

Advertising may help an e-tailer create an identity or brand-name in the mind of the customer and distinguish e-tailing from retailing, but another level to the *differentiation*

---

12 Saul Hansell, "Advertising: Marketers Find Internet Opens New Avenues to Customers," *The New York Times*, March 26, 2001, p. C1.

13 Hansell, "Advertising," p. C1.

14 Hansell, "Advertising," p. C1.

15 "Paid Online Content Grows 155 percent to $300 Million in Q1 2002, According to Online Publishers Association Report," available at **http://www.comscore.com/news/cs_opa_study_080102.htm**.

16 Hansell, "Advertising," p. C1.

problem faces almost all e-tailers. How does the e-seller distinguish the product line that it carries from the same brand-names offered at all of the other possible shopping outlets? Every merchant can sell Levi's jeans, Hugo Boss cologne, or Nine West shoes in the same sizes, style, fragrance, or colors. What makes the consumer want to visit one site rather than another selling the same product? Economics tells the e-tailer that consumers make their final decision based upon price. On the Web, however, without geographic boundaries, that observation forces e-tailers into successive rounds of price competition, driving revenues down to levels bordering on financial ruin. How can e-tailers, or retailers for that matter, avoid this disastrous result?

The answer is to differentiate the product line by nonprice means that add value to the customers' shopping experience. These nonprice means would include such as things as service, ease of use, reliability, variety, customizing the site to the individual buyer, or just plain being customer friendly. Previously, Chapter 7 showed that Amazon.com is the master of this approach to product differentiation, but another strategy is open to almost any e-tailer: the introduction of **private-label brand** merchandise on the site. The e-tailer orders these products directly from the manufacturer, giving them considerable control over the design and quality of the product. The products are offered side by side with the branded products, but they yield many distinct advantages to the e-tailer. First and foremost, they are not available anywhere else. Buyers can price shop a pair of Wendy Tabb or Michael Dawkins earrings in any number of locations, including the upscale accessory site Ashford.com. But a similar pair of teardrops or hoops from the Ashford Collection is available only on the Ashford site. For a while, the retailer Kmart was fairly adept at resurrecting its financial fortunes based upon the introduction of private-label brands including Martha Steward Everyday for household items and Jaclyn Smith for women's clothing. However, even prominent private brands did not keep Kmart from filing for bankruptcy protection in January 2002. No amount of product differentiation could save the firm when it faced crushing price competition from Wal-Mart.

Besides exclusivity, the private-label strategy offers a number of added benefits.[17] First it allows higher profit margins. The CEO of Ashford notes, "By purchasing directly from manufacturers, we can price 40 to 50 percent cheaper and still make 50 to 70 percent margins."[18] The goal isn't to replace all of Ashford's sales of branded merchandise with private-label product sales. Rather it is to raise the overall profitability of the mix of sales. If 20 percent of sales are Ashford Collection products with a 60 percent margin while the remaining 80 percent of sales are designer-branded items with a 35 percent margin, the private line helped raise the overall profit level. The private-label merchandise also lets the firm reduce customer response time. With a private-label product and direct links to the manufacturer, the e-tailer can react faster to changes in customer tastes and preferences. If a particular item, color, or style becomes an overnight fad, it is generally easier to secure delivery from an independent supplier than from a designer whose supplier may be in Asia and whose work schedule may be planned out for the next six months. Lastly, a private-label product may allow the e-commerce firm to cover gaps in its product line, if a brand-name seller refuses to deal with e-tailers. This advantage was especially valuable during the early days of B2C e-commerce, when sellers of branded products were leery of alienating their existing retail customers by allowing their products to be sold through e-tail competitors.

In general, private-label or house brands allow firms to offer products of superior quality at lower prices, while keeping more of the revenue as profits. However, e-tailers do encounter some risks as they introduce private-label brands with the intent of differentiating their product offerings. First, e-tailers may experience **channel conflict** as they use brand-name products to attract Web buyers and then try to convince them to buy the private-label product instead. Brand-name sellers offer their products in both physical and

---

17 Bob Tedeschi, "E-Commerce Report: Online retailers have set their sights on a lucrative standby of their conventional rivals: Private-Label Merchandise," *The New York Times*, May 8, 2000, p. C16.

18 Tedeschi, "E-Commerce Report," p. C16.

virtual markets. They may refuse to sell their products to e-tailers if they feel that their brand image is being abused, lessened in quality, used inappropriately, or cheapened by comparison with weaker "no name" product lines. Brand sellers may also decline to market through the e-tailer if they feel that their product is placed at a relative disadvantage once the potential customer is attracted to the site. Second, it may be difficult and take time to persuade customers to change their buying habits, move away from a recognized brand, and allocate funds to a private-label product. In the interim, buyer confusion may result in lost sales. Despite these risks, numerous e-tailers have begun to offer private-label products in exchange for the higher profit mix and greater control over quality, marketing, and style.

Differentiation with Lock-In Potential

Another differentiation strategy is available to a few highly visible and popular Web sites. It involves a host firm creating special technologies and programming that allow other sites or programmers to link to the host's site or site information more easily.[19] Microsoft has been the past master in implementing this strategy through their Windows operating system. The Windows software contains hidden software functions called **application-programming interfaces (API)**, which allow easy access into parts of the operating system. Therefore independent programmers can create new applications for the Windows platform without having to recode all of the access steps from the ground up. The existence of APIs improves the efficiency and reduces the cost of the code-writing process. Consequently, programmers are attracted to writing new applications for the Windows platform rather than some other operating system. Once an initial commercial program is tied to Windows, **programmer lock-in** appears as they become more reluctant to write versions for another operating system such as Linux. This multitude of new applications greatly enhances the value of Windows, creating **user lock-in** by making it less attractive to switch computers employing a rival operating system.

eBay is copying this strategy as they produce a variety of software routines that will more easily allow independent sites and sellers of support products to link to the eBay Web site. Subscribers to this eBay service will be able to access and display eBay syndicated listings of material on current eBay auctions on the subscriber's own sites without requiring customers to travel to eBay. This strategy of differentiation through APIs creates numerous advantages. First, it allows subscribers to offer a greater range of material on their own sites without having to go to the expense of encoding their own eBay interconnections. Second, it improves the efficiency of existing interconnection firms, such as Anadale that provides buyer and seller services to eBay users. Anadale found it necessary to change their programming each time that eBay made even minor modifications in its Web pages. The eBay API should limit this reprogramming problem. Third, the adoption of the eBay API technology could greatly enhance the reach of the firm and turn the eBay programming code into an e-commerce operating system. eBay currently controls some 80 percent of the auction market, but less than 20 percent of active Internet users visit the eBay site. With links to and placement on other sites, eBay could reach many more potential bidders or become a broader platform for conducting an even wider range of e-commerce activity. Lastly, the ready availability of eBay-linked APIs could also create a lock-in effect for the subscribers to the service. After all, why would an eBay subscriber link to or list on another auction site once its own internal programming becomes consistent with that of eBay? By extension, the more external locations that carry and display eBay auctions and material for sale, the harder it will become for rival auction sites to compete profitably with eBay.

If the eBay API differentiation strategy results in too much of an increase in market power, the firm may begin to appear on the radar screen of the Antitrust Division of the U.S. Department of Justice (DOJ). By using the strategy of Microsoft as a competitive

---

19 Nick Wingfield, "eBay to Test Technology Linking It to Other Sites," *The Wall Street Journal,* November 20, 2000, p. B1.

model, eBay runs the risk of facing some of the same monopolization charges leveled at Microsoft. Microsoft may be able to argue the broader benefits of the market's adoption of Windows as a universal operating system, but the same argument might not sell as easily for eBay. After all, competing auction sites might prove more beneficial to buyers and sellers than an one huge monopoly auction site. Competitive sites could become more valuable to bidders if one or more **auction aggregation sites** were allowed to collect item listings and current bid prices across the range of rival Web auction enterprises and to centralize them in a single location. These sites would be the functional equivalent of an auction price shopping bot for potential bidders. This approach is exactly what Bidder's Edge used, earning the wrath and a federal court challenge from eBay in December 1999.[20] eBay filed suit based upon charges of copyright infringement and the excess cost and burden that the actions of Bidder's Edge inflicted upon eBay's computer system. The potential threat to eBay from the actions of Bidder's Edge was clear. Who would want to go to the eBay site if all of its auction information along with that of its rivals was located elsewhere at another single location? In turn, the decrease in the number of visitors would cut the volume of advertising on eBay and reduce the firm's ability to sell other services and products to potential bidders. The suit was settled in March 2001 on terms that were favorable to eBay and led to the demise of Bidder's Edge.[21] The Bidder's Edge charge of monopolization may still have some future legs, however. Apparently, eBay likes competition on its site and on its terms, but not between its site and those of other Web auction services.

Differentiation Through the Creation of a Self-Organizing System

One of the most brilliant ideas for Web content differentiation and profitability is site design based on the concept of self-organization.[22] A **self-organizing Web site** is one where site users create the site's content. This active user involvement leads to a highly pluralistic, participatory form for organizing a B2C e-commercial Web site that is built from the bottom up. This approach contrasts with the traditional top-down, site-owner-created content and organization. The classic example of a self-organizing Web site is eBay.[23] Numerous other examples exist, including the open sourcing and volunteer programming effort that led to the creation of the Linux operating system, the structure of the consulting site elance.com, as well as the dozens of other sites that show the prospects for this potentially profitable and popular form of e-commerce. eBay has been profitable from the start, at least in part, because the site users perform the complex work of the site not the site organizers. eBay maintains the automated system including servers and software that allow the users to list and describe their items as well as carry on the bidding process. By involving the efforts of millions of individuals, eBay pushes a considerable amount of the costs for creativity and time associated with the mounting of site listings and trade settlement onto the participants, who willingly accept the not-for-pay assignment. In addition, participants also spend their own time and effort to evaluate the caliber of their auction interaction with other participants through a posted feedback rating system. The result is that eBay sits back, lets its customers do most of the work, and collects a fee from them for their participation at the site. Brilliant!

---

20 Troy Wolverton and Greg Sandoval, "eBay Files Suit Against Auction Site Bidder's Edge," available at **http://news.cnet.com/news/0-1007-200-1497267.html**.

21 May Wong, "Bidder's Edge, eBay Settle Suit," available at **http://www.ocregister.com/science/tech/ebay03cci.shtml**.

22 A great deal of theoretical literature is available on the principle of self-organization as it applies to artificial intelligence, chemistry, physics, and neural networks. For a good starting point, see Chris Lucas, "Self-Organization FAQ," available at **http://psoup.math.wisc.edu/archive/sosfaq.html**.

23 Bernard Wysocki, Jr., "The Outlook: Self-Organization: The Next Big Thing?," *The Wall Street Journal*, July 10, 2000, p. A1.

The Linux computer operating system is another example of a self-organizing effort. All of its code was available on the Web, accessible to any programmer who wanted to try their hand at modifying or improving the operation of the platform.[24] Linus Torvalds wrote the initial lines of code for Linux. He then made the code available to any and all, in the original spirit of the Web. Programmers from around the globe devoted their time and effort to improving the code, each working as an unpaid volunteer. This bottom-up effort was in marked contrast to the top-down way in which the Windows system was developed. For the creation of Windows, an army of paid programmers worked under direct command at Microsoft to assemble the code for the operating system. The two contrasting approaches to operating system design pitted planning, supervision, and collective action against individual effort, intellectual diversity, and personal commitment. Each resulted in a superior computer operating system, with the financial resources and marketing might of Microsoft carrying the day, at least to this point. However, the conclusion is inescapable: self-organization as a means of production is capable of creating something of lasting value that is competitive against systems producing products that are born of supervision and planning.

Our last example of a self-organized e-commerce firm is the entity elance.com.[25] Their site is a **bilateral**, or two-direction, **marketplace** listing both professional services for sale and projects open to bid.[26] Persons providing freelance and consulting services list their specialties, vita, array of services, ratings for past service sales, and asking prices. Conversely, businesses with special project needs can list and describe them in detail asking any or all interested freelance consultants to bid on the project. Project categories include accounting, marketing, legal, software, language translation, and so on. Active bidding occurs on the project side with listings for the lowest price and final date for bidding. Here, elance.com serves as an auction site for professional services in a way that is similar to eBay's auction site for tangible products. Just as with eBay, the users do the "heavy lifting," with the site organizers taking a small listing fee for each transaction. By analogy, the Internet-based, job-listing sites, such as Monster.com, are also self-organizing with the applicants and potential employers doing most of the costly site work. Self-organization is clearly one of the most ingenious and profitable approaches to e-commerce site development. It takes full advantage of the global reach and individual participatory potential of the Web, as well as the Internet's unique technology.

Strategic Partnerships as an e-Commerce Differentiation Strategy

Some savvy Web e-tailers have entered into a **strategic partnership** between retailing and e-tailing as a way to differentiate their product and try to establish themselves as a viable, profitable e-commerce entity. Here the unique assets of each party are blended together to produce a superior shopping experience. The most visible and long-lasting **e-commerce joint venture** has been between Amazon.com and Toys "R" Us.[27] Toys "R" Us discovered that despite its marketing muscle, buying power, and nationwide name recognition, it wasn't all that proficient at selling toys online. Electronic site design and the development of Web-based customer relations required skills that were unique and hard to learn for the giant toy retailer. Conversely, Amazon.com learned that it wasn't as adept at buying toys as cheaply as Toys "R" Us nor as skilled at managing the toy inventory.

---

24 See **http://www.linux.org**.

25 Suein L. Hwang, "Site Seers: For Thriving Dot-Com, One Hot Market Isn't What it Brags About," *The Wall Street Journal*, June 12, 2001, p.A1, or see **http://www.elance.com**.

26 In contrast, eBay is a **unilateral marketplace**, or one-way electronic site, listing only items up for bid. It could conceivably list and describe items that people want to buy and have potential sellers bid to sell them the items at the lowest possible price.

27 Carol King, "Amazon.com, Toys R Us.com Unite," available at **http://www.internetnews.com/ec-news/article/0,,4_434941,00.html**, January 15, 2003.

Putting the two firms together on the Web allowed the union of complementary assets. The strengths of one firm tended to reinforce those of the other, while simultaneously eliminating the greatest weaknesses of the two firms. "Each company will assume responsibility for specific aspects of the toy and video games and baby products stores. Toysrus.com will identify, buy, and manage inventory; Amazon.com will handle site development, order fulfillment, and customer service, housing both Toysrus.com's and its own inventory in Amazon.com's U.S. distribution centers."[28] The partnership currently sells toys and related products through a single **co-branded site** as a division of Amazon.com. The logic and efficiency of the joint venture is witnessed by the staying power of the union as it outlasted its biggest and most widely known online-only rival, etoys.com, which filed for bankruptcy and closed its Web site in 2001.[29] Perhaps the future success of Web e-tailing will involve a healthy dose of clicks partnering with bricks.

I-Publishing: A Web-Direct Method for Increasing Artistic Variety and Content

In Chapters 7 and 8, the discussion of the electronic distribution of print material, movies, and music focused primarily on the problems of copyright protection and mergers. Consider other e-commerce media-related issues, such as how the creators of artistic products avoid the domination and control of publishers and distributors. **I-publishing**, or the direct transfer of artistic material from the creator to the consumer via the Web, offers a vast potential for increased product differentiation, boosting the revenue flow to the artist, and reducing the power of the media giants that have considerable influence over what consumers read, see, and hear. To date, the experience with I-publishing has been centered on the two extremes of the artistic marketplace. Well-established and commercially successful authors such as Stephen King and pop music artists including Prince or Courtney Love tried I-publishing with some measure of success. At the other extreme, unknown *slush pile authors* and *garage bands* made their works available via the Web. In fact, the music site MP3.com began in part as a repository for music produced by unknown bands and singers.

Stephen King received considerable attention in March 2000, when he published the novella *Riding the Bullet* as an **e-book**-only title. It was available as a pay-and-download arrangement through his traditional publisher Simon and Schuster and via a Web agreement with the Web publisher Softlock as well as other Web sites. Some 400,000 avid King fans responded the first day, causing the Softlock servers to crash, and leading to the eventual free distribution of the novella by Amazon.com and B&N.com.[30] The experience proved the point that a well-known author with a dedicated following could sell content over the Internet. His second attempt at Web publishing involved a multi-chapter book, *The Plant*. It was a direct-to-the-reader effort designed to cut out the publisher intermediary along with their part of the purchase price. Just as *The Plant* was a vine that terrorized small publishing houses demanding human sacrifices, the e-book held out the potential for terrorizing large publishing houses demanding financial sacrifices.[31] King's I-publishing methodology for the book was structured as a download-and-pay arrangement. It involved releasing the chapters in electronic installments for free, with the stated requirement that at least 75 percent of the downloaders must send in $1 each per chapter in order to guarantee that the next chapter would be written and made available.

First day downloads through Amazon.com, the firm handling the financial transactions, totaled 41,000, or nearly the same amount as for the earlier novella. Without the

28 King, "Amazon.com."

29 Thor Olavsrud, "Etoys to File for Bankruptcy," available at **http://www.internetnews.com/ ec-news/article/0,,4_599301,00.html**. The site has since reopened as a division of KBkids.com.

30 See **http://members.tripod.com/~charnelhouse/ridingthebullet.html**.

31 David D. Kirkpatrick, "Stephen King Sows Dread in Publishers with His Latest E-Tale," *The New York Times*, July 24, 2000, p. C1.

sales promotion and marketing assistance usually provided by Simon & Schuster, King was forced to make public appearances or pay for his own print advertising.[32] Apart from these aspects, he relied upon his own popularity, the Internet, and word-of-mouth to stimulate sales of the e-book. The publishing of e-books, even by popular authors, can encounter some significant limitations. First, not all Stephen King fans have expensive e-book readers or want to spend time in front of their computer screens reading the book. Second, the downloading of the material may not be compatible beyond the world of IBM clones and the Wintel standard. Third, no protection limits the transfer or sharing of the chapter files once they have been downloaded. Lastly, the efforts at direct I-publishing and exclusive use of Amazon create channel conflict with physical bookstores, who serve as the traditional outlets for Stephen King novels. Perhaps King might receive less favorable treatment for any future retail books. Evidence that all may not be well with the I-publishing effort comes from King's own Web site which notes, "*The Plant* has furled its leaves for the time being." It is unknown whether this suspension of chapter publication is due to other commitments by the author, too many freeloaders who didn't make their chapter payments, or a general lack of success for the I-publishing effort. The fact remains that I-publishing offers considerable potential for extending product differentiation in both artistic content and creativity.[33] It also teases publishers with the potential for considerable production cost reductions and profitable opportunities for versioning.[34]

RETAILER RESPONSES TO THE E-COMMERCE CHALLENGE

If e-tail sales are a wave of the future and destined to capture a significant share of overall consumer purchases, how do traditional retailers respond to the threat? What are the future competitive options available to them? Are small retail establishments destined for the commercial junkyard, squeezed on the one side by the retail giants such as Target and Wal-Mart, while being crushed by the growth of e-commerce on the other? How can retail sellers of a branded product avoid having the owner of the brand "eat their lunch" by circumventing the retailer and selling directly to customers over the Web? How can local sellers of professional services and products protect themselves against the onslaught of distant sellers fueled by the Internet? Answers to some of these e-commerce challenges involve differentiation based upon a niche strategy, or the erection of a shield against e-competitors through local franchising laws and protectionist state regulation.

Niche Strategies for the I-Seller

A **niche strategy** involves selling into a highly specialized segment of the buyer marketplace. Many small retailers carry a unique product line and sell in a limited geographic area

---

32 David D. Kirkpatrick, "King E-Novel Short of Expected Demand," *The New York Times*, July 25, 2000, p. C8.

33 Numerous sites offer self-published e-books including Hardshell.com, Booklocker.com, and Xlibris.com. The latter provides extensive information about self-publishing in both hardcover and e-book formats. It is partly owned and associated with the traditional hardcover publisher Random House. For more information on the growing conflicts between e-book authors, publishers, booksellers, and the technology, see David D. Kirkpatrick, "With Plot Still Sketchy, Characters Vie for Roles," *The New York Times*, November 27, 2000, p. C1.

34 For example, think about going to either the Web or your college bookstore and having all of your 10+ books for the semester downloaded into a single, relatively lightweight, inexpensive, e-book reader. The cost to the student might be one-half or one-third of the hardcover print edition. The publishers would love it too. Hardcover returns and copyright violations via unauthorized duplicating would be eliminated. Different versions could be introduced easily each semester, making earlier downloads obsolete, and a self-destruct mechanism could erase the material one month after the end of the semester unless a renewal fee was paid. It sounds like a win-win situation all around.

defined by travel time and distance. Opening up an interactive sales site on the Web expands the niche into the global marketplace and substantially increases the number of possible buyers. Most product niches are too small to warrant competition or retaliation from high-volume Internet sellers. With this strategy the physical retailer can extend its market from the world of bricks to the world of clicks. Access to these specialty sites is relatively easy as long as the site is structured in such a way as to attract the attention of the Web spiders sent out from the larger search engines. Prominent listing by a search engine is important for attracting new customers. It's not unusual for a firm whose geographic market has been the local community to now be receiving Web orders from Europe, Asia, or Latin America. Initially these orders generate a whole new set of sales and delivery problems, but the marginal revenue derived from Web sales in general may contain a higher profit margin for two reasons. First, the costs of securing the product inventory are already covered by revenue from the physical store. Second, the existing sales staff might meet the fulfillment costs for Web orders without additional labor expense. The result could be that costs, which are normally variable, can be transformed into fixed costs, with a niche-oriented mix of clicks and bricks. Each Web sale would then have a higher contribution margin above variable cost, with the potential for significant profit gains.

For example, a firm in rural Thomasville, Georgia, set up a Web site, Timeforprom.com, to sell prom dresses to regional customers who couldn't get timely access to their local, physical store Unique Boutique.[35] The expectation was for increased sales to customers within a 100-mile radius. When the sales orders arrived they not only came from buyers in rural Georgia, but from other states and places as far away as Hawaii and Japan. The firm enabled these contacts without a great deal of spending on advertising, a costly shopping link to one of the major portals such as Amazon's zShops or Shop@AOL, or a great deal of spending on hardware or software. The key was putting together a site with high visibility to the search engines. Each engine has different rules for finding and listing sites. By the laws of physical space, search engines have to place sites in some sort of priority list. The closer a specific site matches the rules of the engine, the higher will be the placement for that site in the listing order for the engine. The higher the site is on that listing, the more likely it is to be selected and visited by a prospective buyer. For example, typing in the search words *prom dresses* on the Google search engine yields some 39,000 responses. Few Web surfers will go through more than two or three pages looking for a site that is most valuable to them. So a prominent placement on the search response is key to selection.

Franchise Laws and Regulation: Fighting e-Commerce Efficiency with Legal Frictions

One of the realities of e-commerce is that just about any product or service can be secured directly without having to pay for the costs and profits of an intermediary. Of course the risk to the consumer in eliminating the intermediary is that it also eliminates some **value added** to the transaction in exchange for the fees. Insurance brokers and travel agents have expertise and may be better able to tailor a policy or travel package to the characteristics of the buyer. Local bank lenders may introduce subjective elements in approving a loan that might otherwise be rejected by the mechanical scoring system as applied by a remote lender. Intermediaries can and often do perform a useful function in return for their cut of the final sale price. The tension is whether all buyers should be required to use the services of an intermediary in order to purchase a good or service, or whether the intermediary function should be unbundled from the product and the consumer be allowed to purchase the intermediary service and product separately or in combinations of their own choosing.

One way in which retailers can compete against the array of I-sellers and retain their product's uniqueness is to seek out government protection through **state franchise laws**

---

35 Leslie Kaufman, "The Opposite of Amazon.com," *The New York Times*, September 22, 2000, p. C1.

and protectionist legislation designed to block the spread of e-commerce sales. Retailers ranging from local optometrists to radiologists and liquor wholesalers have employed a variety of legal tactics to restrain competition from I-sellers. For example, it can be a felony offense to ship wine directly to customers in seven states including Florida, Indiana, and North Carolina, while it is illegal to do so in 21 others including New York, Massachusetts, and Texas.[36] Local auto franchise dealers have been particularly successful in pursuing this legal strategy.[37] Franchised auto dealers fear direct competition from the auto assemblers as well as from regional pure or hybrid I-sellers including CarsDirect.com and AutoNation.com. Both Ford and GM experimented with owning their own dealerships and either selling or marketing cars as well as car insurance over the Web. The current car sale and delivery system is said to raise customer retail charges and introduce inefficiencies. If the intermediary, (i.e. the local auto dealer) can be eliminated from the transaction, the restructuring of the system offers the potential for retail price savings of up to $1,000 per vehicle.[38] This elimination process is referred to as **disintermediation** and the Web is particularly good at it. Cars can be purchased over the Internet without visiting local dealers, loans can be secured without going through a bank, and various types of insurance can be acquired online without an agent.

Local auto dealers lobbied to establish a series of state franchise laws that prohibit or severely restrict the direct sale of cars to buyers by the auto assemblers. Also, in some states, only franchised dealers can sell new cars or purchase cars at the true wholesale price.[39] The exact wording and protections covered by the franchise laws vary among the 50 states. Also, intense lobbying as well as close personal contact between state legislators and local franchise holders support these laws. State legislators have little incentive to side with the out-of-state assemblers in modifying or overturning the laws, thereby allowing direct car sales over the Internet. This mix of local lobbying and the need to deal individually with the laws in 50 state legislatures makes it difficult for the assemblers to circumvent or alter the prohibitions. In fact, attempts to do so create another example of potential channel conflict for the assemblers. By pushing too hard to restructure the existing retailing system, the assemblers risk alienating the franchises that are the only physical outlet for vehicle sales. Car dealerships frequently hold more than one franchise, for example a domestic brand in combination with a foreign brand. Dealers may be tempted to direct greater internal sales efforts to the marketing of the foreign vehicles at the expense of the domestic brand if they become dissatisfied with the behavior of the domestic assembler.

Other examples of the brick-and-mortar backlash against the spread of e-commerce across state borders or outside of the traditional retail distribution channels generally take the form of **protectionist regulations** that guard against changes in the status quo.[40] In Texas, retail optometrists secured legislation mandating that sellers of prescription contacts first obtain the original hand-signed prescription before shipping contact lenses to in-state customers. This legal barrier makes it more time consuming and costly for external lens providers to sell contact lenses via the Internet to Texas customers. All but six states make it difficult for medical patients to seek an out-of-state second opinion by prohibiting the easy electronic transfer of X-rays and related forms of medical imaging. These legislative barriers help to protect the local radiology industry from external competition. Lastly, since 1935 when the U.S. Congress repealed the federal liquor prohibition laws,[41] the states have strictly controlled the rules, wholesale price

---

36 Katy McLaughlin, "Merlot by Mail: Ordering Wine Online Gets Easier," *The Wall Street Journal*, August 21, 2002, p. D1.

37 Jeffrey Ball, "Auto Dealers, Fearing That Detroit Will Hog the Web, Fight Back," *The Wall Street Journal*, May 10, 2000, p. A1.

38 Ball, "Auto Dealers," p. A1.

39 Ball, "Auto Dealers," p. A1.

40 Amy Borrus, "The Broad Backlash Against E-Tailers," *BusinessWeek*, February 5, 2001, p. 102. Congress holds the power to regulate interstate commerce even in cyberspace.

41 The Volstead Act, allowed the states to set their own individual rules on controlling liquor sales. See **http://caselaw.lp.findlaw.com/data/constitution/amendment18/**.

markups, and retail prices for the sale of alcoholic beverages. These rules tend to support local liquor distributors and yield a protected profit margin for wholesalers and retailers. The laws help to explain why in many states customers tend to see a proliferation of small local liquor stores. Direct-to-customer, interstate sales of wine and liquors would significantly challenge this system of local regulation and undercut the protected profit margins. Therefore in 2000, wholesale liquor distributors successfully lobbied the U.S. Congress to pass a law allowing individual "states to go to federal court to sue out-of-state suppliers that ship alcohol to consumers in states that ban direct shipments across their borders."[42]

These and many other examples of forced differentiation based upon legislative restrictions exist. However, in most if not all cases, the economic impact is the same. The laws create distributional inefficiencies by protecting local firms from external competition. They reduce the level of consumer welfare, trading it off in support of supplier benefits. The laws significantly restrict Internet sales of some products, locking in an anachronistic system that increases the costs for local consumers and reduces the range of consumer choice. Research from the Progressive Policy Institute estimates that "anti-e-commerce efforts cost Americans at least $15 billion a year."[43] Some mitigating benefits are possible from the legislation. For example, barriers to online interstate sales of wine and liquor may help to control easy access to alcohol by underage drinkers. Limiting the remote provision of medical services via the Internet may protect consumers from being exploited by unscrupulous medical practices. The laws may help to preserve small, locally owned businesses, but these laws typically exceed the level of prohibition that would be necessary to achieve the ancillary gains. Overall, the franchise laws and protectionist regulation introduce **legalistic frictions** that slow the spread of e-commerce in the protected markets. Generally, these regulatory obstructions result in the consumer paying a steep price for the continued existence of multiple sources of different products.

THE ESTYLE CASE REVISITED

To this point, the discussion provided some background information on the theory and role that strategic product differentiation and promotion can play in generating profitability. How then does this knowledge help us to understand the potential for the e-commerce introductory case firm estyle.com? How do they continue to attract funding, survive, and grow over time? Estyle has already been a successful practitioner of many of the concepts discussed in this chapter. For example, they identified a niche market for high-end (designer) apparel and baby accessories. This market segment contains upper-income, computer-sophisticated, professional women, with attributes or tastes favoring style, convenience, quality, service, and brand-name products. In the mind of Laurie McCartney, the founder of estyle, the $12 billion pregnancy clothing and baby accessory retail business is highly **fragmented market**. No single firm or group of well-established firms dominates the marketplace. Therefore, entry by a niche firm, focused on the high-end segment, with the potential for buying high-profit-margin products is possible, given that these high-end customers are seen as underserved.

Estyle was an I-seller at birth, but it has grown to serve its target market with multiple channels of distribution including both online and off-line sales avenues. Estyle has introduced its own private-label brand for clothing and baby products. The goal for the firm is to combine the listing and sales of the private-label items with the branded ones, to grow the quality and value of the private-label name in the mind of the consumer. Eventually, the firm would like to see one-half of its sales volume come from the

42 Stephanie B. Goldberg, "Fermenting a Wine-Sales Revolution," available at **http://www. businessweek.com/smallbiz/content/mar2001/sb20010321_758.htm.**

43 Borrus, "The Broad Backlash," p. 102; and Mathew Frankel and Katharine Lister, "How the Middleman Is Fighting e-Commerce and Hurting Consumers to the Tune of $15 Billion Annually," available at **http://www.ppionline.org/ppi_ci.cfm?contentid=2959&knlgAreaID=85&subsecid=108.**

higher-margin private-label items. To achieve this goal, estyle is selling its private-label line through several of the upscale Bloomingdale's retail stores and also makes available a hard copy catalog of its key products. The combination of association with and sales through high-end stores, along with the use of a Cindy Crawford as a product line spokesperson, helps to enhance the estyle brand image. Estyle also uses its advertising budget to inform consumers, connecting with them through messages placed in closely related outlets including parenting magazines and targeted e-mailings to past and prospective customers.

This quick review of the estyle strategy helps us to appreciate why the firm is looked upon so favorably by the venture capital funding firms. Estyle appears to be doing everything right. Yet, even for a firm as strategically sophisticated as estyle, future success is not guaranteed. The firm must continually attract a profitable volume of new customers while holding onto existing ones. Estyle has yet to prove that it can stay in style long term. Longevity is no easy feat in the pregnancy apparel and baby clothes market, where the passage of time leads to a high level of customer turnover.

SUMMARY AND PROSPECTS

How will the competitive tension between e-tailers and retailers be resolved? How will e-tailers establish themselves in the virtual and possibly the physical market places? Just about any conversation concerning e-tailers selling products to Web consumers typically turns to the fact that entry into e-markets is easy, and ferocious price competition will drive profit margins toward zero. As a result, no profitable opportunity can be sustained for Web-only e-commerce. This scenario envisions that in the future, just two types of electronic firms will populate the B2C e-commerce marketplace. Web extensions of the discounters, such as Wal-Mart and Target, whose overall buying power will allow them to define the low price on the Internet will be joined by the Internet versions of the already established **catalog retailers**, including Fingerhut, Lands' End, and J. Crew, who are the recognized experts in direct selling and remote order fulfillment.

The discussion in this chapter showed that this conclusion may not be true for several reasons. First, online e-tailers can survive by employing a *niche strategy*, focusing on *product attributes*, with some sales extensions into the off-line world. A mix of *clicks and bricks* makes a great deal of sense and would appear to be a profitable combination. Second, just because a firm is a **category killer** in the physical world doesn't mean that it can always come up with a compelling Web counterpart. Web site design, electronic customer service, and large-scale order fulfillment involve a unique expertise and can prove tricky for a physical world retailer to master. Potential e-customers wouldn't see Toys "R" Us, Target, and Circuit City *partnering* with Amazon.com unless these category killer retailers felt that a **go-it-alone e-tail site** was a less viable option. Third, being smart about how the firm differentiates its product and where it places its promotional message are just as important as the content of the advertising.[44] Good associations along with branding and information are as important to differentiation as the volume of ad repetition. Lastly, the Web possesses some unique characteristics that, if properly exploited, can lead to survival and profit. Self-organizing systems play to the strengths of the Web. If an I-seller can design an e-commerce site and product to take advantage of this characteristic, an e-tailer can be competitive against both other e-tailers and physical retailers. Elance.com, Monster.com, and eBay along with many others have shown this to be true. As the discussion in Chapter 12 shows, profitability is not a distant illusion for all e-commerce firms.

---

[44] Some 40 years ago, Marshall Mcluhan coined the phrase "the medium is the message." It was his view that the way we acquire information has a greater affect than the information itself. This view may be as true today as it was then. For more information on Marshall Mcluhan, link to **http://www.regent.edu/acad/schcom/rojc/mdic/mcluhan.html**.

KEY TERMS AND CONCEPTS

application-programming interfaces (API)
attribute space
auction aggregation sites
banner ads
bilateral marketplace
brand awareness
brand equity
branding
catalog retailers
category killers
channel conflict
click-through rate
cluster
co-branded site
competitive advertising
conversion rate
demand-based product differentiation model
dependence effect
disintermediation
e-books
e-Commerce joint-venture
fragmented market

general information sites
go-it-alone e-tail site
i-publishing
informational advertising
legalistic frictions
narrow topic sites
niche strategy
pop-up ads
private-label brand
product attributes
product differentiation
production-based product differentiation model
programmer lock-in
proprietary Web sites
protectionist regulation
self-organizing Web site
strategic partnership
state franchise laws
target market
unilateral marketplace
user lock-in
value added

DISCUSSION AND REVIEW QUESTIONS

1. Identify and discuss the common challenges that face all merchants whether they be retailers or e-tailers.

2. What are the two special tensions that e-tailers face as they try to resolve the common challenges? What forces work to pull the e-tailers, such as estyle, into the physical retailing world? Conversely, what forces work to push retailers into the world of Web-based selling?

3. Where do the tensions arise among e-tailers? What can the individual e-tailer do to survive in its rivalry with other Web-based firms?

4. Distinguish between a production-based and a demand-based model of product differentiation. Identify a product in the physical retail world and in the electronic e-tail world that fits each model.

5. Explain Lancaster's theory of attribute space. Are consumers a homogeneous lot in terms of their tastes and preferences? How does the theory of attribute space help e-tailers as they try to position their firms and product lines within a specific market segment?

6. The example in Figure 11-1 showed that some consumers prefer that a Web site offer convenience and customer service in a 3:1 ratio, while others prefer a 1:2 ratio. If e-tailers A and C already exist, would a firm be successful in providing the two attributes in a 1:1 ratio, squarely in the middle of the attribute space, and offer a compromise that would attract customers from both market segments? Why?

7. Distinguish between competitive advertising and informational advertising. How have each been used by e-tailers? Cite an example for each of the two advertising forms.

8. Distinguish between television and the Internet as passive versus interactive mediums. In what ways does this distinction help e-tailers to structure their advertising and product differentiation pitches? How does distinction help to build e-tailer efficiency and the ability to sell to site visitors?

9. In what sense are the how and where of e-tailer advertising as important as the specific content of an ad message in helping to differentiate B2C Web-based products?

10. What are private-label brands? How do they offer a differentiation and profit advantage to e-tailers? What might the e-tailer do to keep its private-label brand from becoming regarded as just another inferior "no-name" product?

11. Identify the general concept of differentiation with lock-in potential. How have eBay and Microsoft used this strategy successfully to retain their hold on the market? What competitive problems can be associated with this approach?

12. What was BiddersEdge.com and how did it pose a threat to eBay? How was the threat resolved?

13. What is a self-organizing Web site? Provide two examples of this type of site. How does the self-organizing characteristic lead to greater efficiency and real profit potential?

14. What is an e-commerce joint venture? Cite an example and explain the nature of the efficiency consequences resulting from the effort.

15. Explain why niche strategies are often successful for small e-tailers, especially those with retail stores that carry the same product.

16. How have franchise laws and regulations been used by retailers to fight the competitive pressures created by Web e-tailers? Should all buyers be required to use an intermediary when purchasing a product or service? Why?

17. How does estyle employ many of the differentiation strategies mentioned in this chapter?

WEB EXERCISES

1. Link to **http://www.babystyle.com/default.asp**, look at the technical structure of the Web site and homepage and, its merchandise array, and make a judgment about the target market for the site. Do the same for **http://Babycenter.com**, the site for Johnson & Johnson's baby products division. How do the sites compare in terms of page style, information content, and products offered? Is there any discernable difference in the target markets for the two competitors?

2. Link to the Kelley Bluebook Web site at **http://kbb.com**. Observe the number of ads listed for auto-related services, including insurance and auto Web sites. Why do these ads appear at what is basically a pricing site for used cars? Check out a competitor at **http://edmunds.com** to see whether the same is true for that site.

3. Link to upscale jewelry site **http://ashford.com** and compare the display and prices of the branded and private-label products. Which is cheaper and why? Why might some buyers still pay the price for the branded product?

4. Link to bid search engine BidXS, at **http://www.biddersedge.com**, which appears to be the successor to the original Bidders Edge. They will allow you to search for items up for bid using their search engine, but be careful, they require your e-mail address first. It is always useful to have a junk e-mail address at Yahoo! or Hotmail to give in these cases.

5. Link to **http://www.elance.com** and examine the bilateral nature of this self-organizing marketplace. How does this type of marketplace take advantage of the

unique technology of the Internet? Check out the self-organizing Web site at **http:// www.epinions.com** and see whether your favorite movie or textbook has been rated by others. Perhaps you would like to rate them yourself.

6. If you are interested in a writers' publishing site that is self-organizing, link to **http://www.suite101.com** to see whether any topics or opportunities there interest you.

7. Link to **http://psoup.math.wisc.edu/archive/sosfaq.html**, to examine the broad applications of the self-organizing concept.

8. Link to h**ttp://www.toysrus.com** and see the interesting result that appears on your screen. Why does it happen, and what are the economic advantages?

9. Link to **http://www.stephenking.com** and see whether *The Plant* has sprouted new roots.

10. Link to **http://www.timeforprom.com** if you want to see a successful niche strategy in action.

PART 4

Market Performance Topics

CHAPTER 12

Introductory Case

PRICELINE VERSUS AMAZON: REACHING AND MEASURING PROFITABILITY

What does the role of profits in different economic systems have to do with e-commerce? E-commerce firms operate in a capitalistic marketplace and must eventually achieve and sustain profitability over time, if they are going to survive. The financial backers of e-firms, be they stockholders, venture capitalists, or family and friends, must obtain a monetary reward or they will withdraw their support. Therefore, it is important to identify the e-commerce firms that are making a profit, and see how much of a profit they are making. It is also essential to see how they define their profitability, what they did to attain it, and to determine their future profit outlook. Of the two most prominent B2C e-firms, Priceline.com and Amazon.com, one achieved sustained profitability while the other is thought to be on the verge of reaching that goal. However, the term profitability means substantially different things to each of the two firms, and therein lies the tale.

Priceline.com is the name-your-own-price supplier of airline and travel services. It first achieved profitability, defined as positive net income, in the second calendar quarter of 2001.[1]

To be sure, the dollar volume of the profit wasn't that much, amounting to net revenues of $2.8 million, or a penny per share, on total sales of $364.8 million. But they were profits nonetheless and notable for two reasons. First, the ability to generate profits was a substantial turnaround for Priceline. Just six months earlier, the firm was beset by a rash of customer complaints regarding tickets sales, service, and the operation of the reverse auction process, which lies at the heart of the Priceline business model. In addition, Webhouse, a related firm, using the same reverse auction strategy to sell retail grocery items and gasoline, had failed. Second, the reported profits were in the form of **net income**, which is a measure of revenue minus all expenses including interest payments, taxes, and depreciation. The definition of net income is based upon generally accepted accounting principles, or **GAAP rules**.[2] Whether this amount of profit will be sufficient to reward the investors is open to debate. However, the dollars are real, they are validated financially, and if they continue to grow, these profits could support the survival of the firm.

On the other hand, Amazon.com is perhaps the largest B2C retailer, with gross sales in excess of $2.8 billion per year. However, it has barely earned any net income according to GAAP rules. In fact, its net loss using GAAP standards grew from around $150 million in 1998 to $1.4 billion in 2000, before falling in 2001 to $567 million, or -$1.56 per share. Yet Amazon claimed that it will show a profit for all of 2002.[3] How can it effect this miraculous

---

1 "Priceline.com Posts a Profit on Sharp Increase in Sales," *The New York Times*, August 1, 2001, p. C8.

2 In 1973, the federal Securities and Exchange Commission (SEC) designated the Financial Accounting Standards Board (FASB) as the private-sector organization responsible for shaping and sanctioning the rules that comprise GAAP accounting. GAAP allows for uniform financial reporting and the comparison of accounting reports across the entire spectrum of ongoing firms, regardless of their line of business. All firms must follow GAAP in/filing financial reports with the SEC. "This **transparency** is what allows investors to compare businesses as different as McDonald's, IBM and Tupperware, and it makes U.S. markets the envy of the world." See "How Priceline Became a Real Business," *The Wall Street Journal*, August 13, 2001, p. A12.

3 Saul Hansell, "Amazon Defies the Naysayers As Losses Drop and Sales Grow," *The Wall Street Journal*, April 24, 2002, p. C1.

e-Commerce and Profitability

turnaround? Are the economies of scale and scope becoming so large that Amazon will be able to further magnify the leverage from its huge capital investment? Does it expect to grow sales or cut costs at such a rate as to propel the firm into the thin ranks of the profitable e-commerce firms?

The answers to both of these questions are probably yes, but they are not the main reasons for Amazon's conviction that it will soon achieve profitability.[4] That confidence is based on the fact that Amazon, like many other e-firms, defines its financial results in terms of **pro forma profits** rather than profits based upon GAAP rules. (In case your skills in translating the Latin language are a bit rusty, the literal meaning of *pro forma* is "according to the form," or, in this case, a better interpretation is the phrase "as if.") Pro forma profits are derived using a name-your-own-accounting-rules system of financial record keeping. Pro forma profits start out by adding up gross sales revenues, minus the cost of goods sold and minus the costs of receiving, servicing, and fulfilling the sales orders. However, *at the discretion of the firm*, the pro forma profit figure excludes the costs of a number of items that might be associated with the initial start-up, one-time expenditures or interest charges on outstanding debt. Economists might identify some of these excluded costs as fixed costs, which must be covered eventually. However, they are not variable costs resulting from the day-to-day operation of the firm. Future revenues could theoretically dwarf these one-time costs, if the firm continues to grow its sales, especially at double-digit rates.

For a start-up business, characterized by increasing returns to scale, and fast-growing sales, the calculation of pro forma profits, which exclude numerous fixed costs, may make some short run sense. By including these fixed costs in its quarterly financial reports, any start-up firm might be supplying an overly pessimistic picture of its current health and survival potential. The firm might be losing lots of GAAP dollars in the beginning, but it might be simultaneously growing its contribution margin above variable cost at such a rapid rate that it would eventually become profitable. If only it can get its sales volume up high enough, the contribution margin will eventually generate sufficient revenues to cover the fixed costs and earn a profit as measured in terms of net income. It is a variation of the standard volume pricing model discussed in Chapter 10.

A TRANSITION TO MEASURES OF ECONOMIC PERFORMANCE

This chapter moves into a discussion that focuses on economic performance. This third area of analysis for e-commerce examines key results-oriented criteria to determine how well individual e-firms are doing and how efficient e-sellers are in their use of society's scarce resources. The subject matter for this chapter is profitability, the first and foremost of the economic performance measures. Profits serve two functions within **capitalism**:

---

4 Michael Mahoney, "Amazon Beats Street for Q2, Gets $100 Million Investment from AOL," available from **http://www.newsfactor.com/perl/story/12221.html**.

(1) they are the compelling force behind the vitality of competitive markets and the reward that makes the competitive struggle worthwhile; and (2) profits can serve as a market signal indicating that resources are being directed to their most valuable ends. The expectation of profits motivates the entrepreneur to take risks, while the presence of economic profit attracts resources to an activity. Conversely, in a market system, the persistent inability of a profit-oriented firm to earn a profit means that resources are being used inefficiently. As a result, the product may be discontinued, resources will be directed to a better use, the business may fail, and the size of an industry will shrink. It is the relentless search for profits that defines capitalism.

Other economic systems, such as **socialism** or **communism**, either downplay the importance of profits as a guiding force, or eliminate the concept of profits altogether. In a socialistic state, private firms still exist, but their profits may be limited by regulation or taxation as a way to avoid consumer exploitation and safeguard the perceived greater good of society. Conversely, the government may subsidize or otherwise protect the profits of national firms, in the name of guaranteeing the survival of competitors and the jobs that they might provide. Both the limitation of profits and the subsidization of losses tend to distort the efficient use of resources. In a communistic state, private property and private firms don't exist. Therefore, profits as a guide to resource use and as a motivation for risk taking are done away with almost entirely. Resources are allocated and goods produced on the basis of a state plan. Here, subjective human decision making takes center stage in determining the type and volume of products to be produced, while profits and price signals play a minimal role. Worker rewards are based upon compliance with the plan, and doled out in proportion to the profits generated by the effort. Centralized human planning can, at times, substitute for individual market decisions. However, the limits of human knowledge as well as the inability to quickly and correctly process large volumes of information render the impersonal and decentralized market as a superior, if still imperfect, vehicle for allocating resources.[5]

Does net income or pro forma income provide the correct view of accounting profits? Which one provides the best information about the current financial health of the firm and where it is going? Which one, if either, corresponds to the opening discussion of the profits that are necessary to guide resource use decisions and reward entrepreneurial risk taking? The answers to these questions are related to the dual tensions that are at the core of this chapter's discussion of e-commerce. The first tension looks at the stresses introduced by the emphasis on accounting profits versus economic profits as a test of the efficacy of any business model. The second tension looks at the prevalence, significance, and problems associated with the reporting of GAAP profits versus pro forma profits in e-commerce financial statements.

LOOKING AT PROFITS: ECONOMIC VERSUS ACCOUNTING CONCEPTS

Almost everyone appears to agree on the definition of **profits** as the residual of total revenue minus total costs. Beyond that point, confusion reigns as honest differences arise over what dollars belong in the revenue component and what items are appropriate for inclusion as part of the cost side. **Accounting profits** generally measure cash received by, or owed to the firm in exchange for the sale of its product minus the costs of doing business. Most of these costs are cash outlays, or **accounting expenses**, for labor, materials, advertising, and any product acquisition costs paid to a previous stage of production. A few costs are allowed that do not require an outlay of cash, such as **depreciation**

---

5 The profit motive is not always the central feature of a market economy. Remember that a market system allows for the existence of various types of deliberately not-for-profit firms as well, such as colleges, hospitals, charities and religious organizations.

of equipment and the **amortization** or writing off of **goodwill**.[6] Part of the confusion arises because both the definition of the cost terms and the way that they are to be applied to the determination of profits are heavily influenced by the business tax code written by Congress and interpreted by the Internal Revenue Service. The federal government wants its share of the profits from each business. In the case of depreciation charges, strict rules in the tax code define the time span over which specific pieces of capital equipment must be depreciated. Also, a limited set of depreciation rate options determines how fast the firm is allowed to depreciate the equipment. The simplest is **straight-line depreciation**, or depreciating a fixed percentage of the asset's value each year over its projected useful life. This option writes off the entire value of the asset. For example, a $1,000 piece of machinery would be depreciated at 10 percent, or $100 per year for 10 years. **Accelerated depreciation** options include sum of the year's digits and double-declining balance, which assign a greater proportion of the depreciation charges to the earlier years of the asset's life. Consequently, they better reflect the way firms actually use new capital equipment. They also raise the depreciation charge and help the firm to shelter more of its profits from immediate taxation. Because the accelerated options fail to depreciate the full value of the asset, they are best applied if the firm intends to dispose of the equipment before its useful life is up.

For the sake of comparison to the concept of economic profits, the actions of accountants as they determine profits according to GAAP rules can be thought of as a scorekeeper in a game or sporting contest. When one side in a contest makes a score, the record keeper adds a number to the total for that team. By analogy, when a *firm* receives money from the sale of its product, the accountant adds those funds to the total revenue count. Conversely, when the firm pays out money to produce or sell the product or to conduct the business, the accountant adds that expenditure to total cost side. When the game is over, the scorekeeper compares points for and against the team to determine whether it won or lost the game. The same is true for the firm. Both quarterly and annually, the accountant looks at the total revenue and total cost to see whether the firm made a profit or loss. Keeping the financial record of money coming into and going out of a business is the primary function of an accountant. The function of an **auditor** is to certify that the accountant keeps the score according to the rules of the game. The accountant is a highly skilled, well-paid scorekeeper, whose mission it is to use GAAP tools and keep track of the financial game.

An Economic View of Cost: Opportunity Cost

In contrast, an economist has a different mission and set of tools available to carry out that mission. An economist is concerned with how well society is using its scarce resources. Are they being used with maximum **economic efficiency**? Are goods and services being produced in the right volume, at the lowest possible cost, using the best technology? If so, then the production process achieves **productive efficiency**. Has society allocated the correct relative amount of resources to each product? Is society producing the right relative mix of goods that is most desired by consumers? If the answers here are yes, then society achieves **allocative efficiency**. The tool for keeping score on the cost side of the economist's ledger is **opportunity cost**. It is a measure of resource value in the next best alternative use for that resource unit. For example, raw crude oil can be refined into either gasoline or home heating oil. The economic cost of using the crude to produce gasoline is the value of the home heating oil that has been given up by transferring the crude from the production of heating oil into the production of gasoline. The way to tell whether this

---

6 Depreciation is a the value of a firm's capital equipment that has been used up in the production process. *Goodwill* is an accounting term that represents the difference between the amount of money that an acquiring firm pays for an acquired firm in a merger and how much accountants actually think the firm is worth. Until an accounting modification in 2002, all firms had to amortize a portion of goodwill annually as an expense against income, thereby lowering the stated value of GAAP net income.

transfer is economically valid or efficient is if the value to the consumer of the gasoline is greater than the value of the home heating oil. This assessment normally shows up in the prices paid for the two products and the profits that they generate.

Opportunity cost is the umbrella concept that encompasses two types of economic charges for using resources. The first is **explicit opportunity cost**, which consists of a tangible cash outlay or financial commitment. If resources, including labor and materials, are purchased in competitive markets, then the explicit charges for wages, salaries, and cost of goods sold are reasonably identical to the accountant's concept of expenses. The second type of opportunity cost, an **implicit opportunity cost**, includes charges for the use of economic or scarce resources for which either no cash outlay is made or where the corresponding accounting charge differs from the true opportunity cost. Two common instances of an implicit opportunity cost include the accountant's calculations for the correct valuation of the entrepreneur's time and an adjustment for failing to correctly account for the value of capital or land used in the production process.

The unique and valuable skills of the entrepreneur provide a major **category of scarce resources**, along with labor, capital, and natural resources. The owner of the business may put in countless hours of work in the hope of striking it rich. Even though the entrepreneur may draw a nominal salary, it may represent a payment far below the value of the entrepreneurial skill if used in the next best activity. If the firm is to survive and stay in business in the long run, then the compensation of the entrepreneur must be sufficient to cover both the physical labor and the creative inputs. An economist would introduce an implicit charge for the creative component, adding it to the explicit charge, to reflect the true cost of using the entrepreneurial resource in the current activity.

The need for an implicit charge for capital usage arises because of the tax code quirks noted previously. The accounting charge for using a piece of machinery reflects some externally imposed, arbitrary depreciation rate, as applied against the historical or original **acquisition cost** of the equipment. The economic cost for the use of the equipment should reflect the actual amount of the useful life that is surrendered as a result of present production. Then a percentage can be applied to the current or **replacement cost** of the equipment. This approach mirrors what some might call the **rental rate** for the equipment, or what it would cost in today's dollars to lease the equipment from an independent owner.[7] Another source of implicit equipment cost distortion involves the use of fully depreciated equipment, for which an annual accounting charge is no longer accruing. To the extent that the equipment contributes productive value here and elsewhere, or even **salvage value** as scrap, the firm should enter a charge reflecting an implicit opportunity cost. Lastly, some firms may own the land upon which a factory is constructed. Even though the factory can be depreciated, leading to an accounting charge, the land upon which it stands can't be depreciated. Unless certain accounting provisions are made, the charge representing the opportunity cost of the land can go unrecorded, and the firm would be underestimating the true economic cost of producing the item.

An Economic View of Profit: Normal Profits and Economic Profits

In economics, two types of profits are normal profits and economic profits. **Normal profits** are the revenues, above the charges for labor, capital, and natural resources, that could be earned if the inputs were directed away from their current use and into their next best use. These profits show up as the necessary reward to the entrepreneur,

---

7 An actual leasing arrangement would involve contract, delivery and entrepreneurial profit charges for the rental agent that would tend to overestimate the true implicit value of the equipment.

who innovates, takes the risks, organizes the production process, and makes the key decisions. As such, normal profits are regarded as an opportunity cost of doing business. They are a necessary cost (of the resources taken away from their next best alternative use) that must be covered by revenues from the current activity. Any firm that wishes to attract these resources away from their next best use must earn sufficient revenues to at least match the forgone profits that could have been earned there. If the firm is earning a dollar amount just equal to a normal profit, then this firm achieves the **economic breakeven** volume of output. At this point total revenue equals total cost, measured in terms of opportunity cost, including a normal profit. The firm can persist at this point and survive in the long run, because there is no better place where the resources might be otherwise used. This economic concept is significantly different from the notion of **accounting breakeven**. The accountant's term involves an output volume that demonstrates equality between total revenue and total cost measured in terms of expenses. Here the firm fails to make any dollar profit and will eventually go out of business if financial circumstances don't change. For example, if total revenue is $1 million, but the cost of goods sold, taxes, depreciation and charges for labor also equal $1 million, no revenue is left over to reward the effort of the owner/entrepreneur. If this situation persists the owner/entrepreneur will turn her efforts to some other activity where a profit can be made.

Economic profits are revenues earned in excess of all opportunity costs, including a normal profit. Although they are great to receive and may involve a sizable dollar amount, the fact that they are above and beyond all opportunity costs means that economic profits are not necessary to keep the resources in their current use. The economic profits could be eliminated and the current distribution of resources as well as market structure would remain the same. However, this statement doesn't imply that economic profits are necessarily frivolous, exploitative, or unimportant for the efficient functioning of the economy. Economic profits act as a magnet, attracting new resources into an industry because the resources can do better there than in their next best alternative activity. Assuming that entry into the industry is easy, the added resources increase the number of competitors, which in turn motivates firms to erect entry barriers against new competitors. The economic profits may also boost the size of the existing firms, as long as **diseconomies of scale**, or the disadvantages resulting from larger firm size, are absent. As such, economic profits serve side-by-side with market prices as a means of signaling the efficient use of scarce resources within a capitalistic economy. Eventually the entry of new firms or the expansion of existing ones leads to an increase in production that will result in a lowering of the market price for the product. Economic profits, which start out as an excess payment that exploits the consumer, ultimately benefit the consumer in the form of lower prices and greater competition.

Although the generation of an economic or normal profit is the goal of every firm, these results do not represent all of the possible market outcomes. It is also possible for a firm to experience an **economic loss**. Here the firm receives revenues that are less than all of its opportunity costs including a normal profit. In an economic sense the firm is losing money. It is earning less revenue than it otherwise could if the resources were directed toward their next best alternative use. Usually a firm will tolerate an economic loss in the short run because it has some fixed resources that can't be reallocated immediately. As long as the firm's current revenues exceed its total variable costs, which are the costs that are experienced solely as a result of the decision to produce some positive volume of output, then it will continue to operate in the short run. The revenue above variable costs will serve as a contribution margin, reducing the size of the firm's losses to an amount that is less than its total fixed costs. In this **loss minimizing case**, the firm will stay open in the short run because it will lose less by producing than the total fixed cost loss it would experience if it shut down. Even though a firm will not be happy with the situation, it will tolerate the loss for now, because no better short-run alternative exists. When the resources that are fixed in the short run become variable in the long run, then the firm will exit the business and direct its resources elsewhere if economic losses continue to persist.[8]

Amazon.com. faces this situation. Even though it is losing money in the short run, it continues to produce because it is making a pro forma profit, such that its losses are less than its fixed costs. With an increasing sales volume and a rising contribution margin, Amazon.com expects to see a profit in the form of net income in the near future.

A second short-run alternative involves economic losses. When the losses from continued operation are so great that they exceed the size of the firm's fixed costs, the firm is losing more money by producing than it would if it ceased operations. The total revenues are insufficient to cover all of its variable costs resulting from the decision to produce. The firm then experiences the **shutdown case**, and it makes sense to stop production, reduce the variable costs to zero, and suffer only the dollar losses associated with the fixed costs. The firm still exists in the short run, but it ceases to operate. A few firms may regularly experience **seasonal shutdowns** at times of slow demand, model changeover, or company-wide vacations. The closing of a firm for lack of revenue, however, is usually a step just prior to filing for bankruptcy. It commonly leads to asset liquidation and the firm's exit from the industry in the long run. It is not a pleasant series of events, but one experienced by more than 600 dot-com firms from January 2000 until now.[9]

What the Difference in Profit Concepts Means for e-Commerce Firms

The preceding discussion can be summarized in Table 12-1 describing the various short-run economic combinations for revenue, cost, and profit, along with their accounting counterpart and the resulting long-run resource allocation response. It is apparent that economists and accountants think of and record profits in distinctly different ways. It is also true that they see firms as playing somewhat different roles in the economy. Which set of views is correct, and how does this discussion relate to the survival of e-commerce firms? First, accounting profits according to GAAP rules are generally greater than estimates of economic profit. The figure for economic profits embraces the explicit expenses and the implicit opportunity costs, including a normal profit.

Pro forma profits > GAAP accounting profits > Economic profit estimate

Therefore, the estimate for pro forma profits is higher still, as firms elect to exclude certain fixed expenditures and unusual, nonrecurring charges from the GAAP cost estimates. Each profit concept has its defenders and may convey a different piece of information about the current financial condition of the firm. However, only the economic concept of profit takes a forward-looking perspective, because it is based upon opportunity cost. Only the economic concept takes into consideration the relative efficiency with which the resources are currently being used and how they might be best used in the future. If a firm fails to earn a normal profit, it will eventually go out of business.

Looking at one or both of the other profit concepts may mislead individuals, but the collective marketplace is never deceived for long. All firms must earn a competitive

---

8 See "Not-Com," *The Wall Street Journal*, May 14, 2001, p. R13, for an interesting story of how the owner/managers of the e-drugstore MotherNature.com decided to close up shop because the expected accounting profits, although positive, would not be enough to adequately compensate the investors.

9 "Latest Dot-Com Fad Is a Bit Old-Fashioned: It's Called 'Profitability'," *The Wall Street Journal*, August 14, 2001, p. A1. Also see **http://www.webmergers.com.** for a current count and discussion of e-commerce failures.

Economics vs. Accounting: Revenue, Cost, and Profit in the Short Run with Long-Run Consequences			**TABLE 12-1**
Economic Situation Short Run	**Total Revenue vs. Total Opportunity Cost**	**Accounting Profit: GAAP**	**Economic Result Long Run**
Economic profit	Total revenue exceeds all opportunity cost	Positive net income	Entry and/or firm expansion
Normal profit	Total revenue equals all opportunity costs allocation	Positive net income	Equilibrium: No change in resource
Loss minimization: Continue to produce in short run	Total revenue less than all opportunity costs but greater than all variable costs	Small net income or net loss	Exit the industry if economic losses persist
Shutdown: Cease production in short run	Total revenue less than all opportunity costs and less than variable costs	Net income negative	Exit the industry if economics losses persist

return, or new resources will cease to flow into its activity, investors will disappear, and the resources already held by the firm will slip away, drawn by better opportunities elsewhere. This unalterable **profit rule of competitive markets** holds regardless of whether the firm is a butcher, baker, candlestick maker, or an e-commerce firm selling its wares over the Web. Even the existence of GAAP profits may not guarantee long-run firm survival, unless they are equal to a competitive return.

Second, a tension arises between the economic and the social view of the firm and its functions. **Economic firms** are mainly thought of as impersonal, intellectual abstractions. They are potentially ephemeral or fleeting in nature, achieving permanency only if they do their job well. That job is to use scarce resources as efficiently as possible by producing the correct volume of output at the lowest production cost, and producing the most desired mix of products. Firms appear because internal organization and supervision are thought to be superior methods for carrying out the production process.[10] Firms are created because budding entrepreneurs see gaps in the market where consumer demands are not being met, or where new technologies as well as novel applications of existing techniques can insert potentially profitable products. These entrepreneurs infuse the market with their personal vision and optimism, attracting others to join them in the risks and rewards. If the physical firm meets its economic challenge, it will survive, profit, and grow. If a particular firm is not a superior production system, it will wither away. Firms may also disappear if they are successfully challenged by better ideas or techniques. Joseph Schumpeter characterized this turmoil in the marketplace as creative destruction, which was discussed in Chapter 2. In summary, economics values firms for the greater good that they bring to society in terms of resource efficiency.

From a societal perspective, **social firms** are analogous to living, breathing organisms that are to be looked at and possibly valued for their own sake. They possess physical assets

---

10 Rather than producing a product from start to finish in-house, the entrepreneur can achieve the same result through **contracting out**, or negotiating in the market to have a collection of individual firms contribute different parts of the product that might, but not necessarily, receive final assembly by the entrepreneur. The comparative efficiency of each technique helps to define the role of and the boundary for the firm and the market as alternative methods for organizing the production process. See Ronald H. Coase, "The Nature of the Firm," *Economica* 4 (November 1937), pp. 386–405.

and develop a corporate culture. They involve **stockholders** who invest some or all of their wealth in exchange for part ownership of the firm. Firms hire real people, who, along with their dependents, often make tangible commitments to their employers. Employees build company morale, or a spirit toward the firm, that affects productivity. Workers are capable of supplying spontaneous creative input as well as physical effort, both of which enhance the firm's profitability. In return the employees receive training, support service and a feeling of belonging, along with their wages and benefits. Workers, investors, entrepreneurs, managers, customers, and suppliers are all stakeholders in the firm. They have an interest in seeing the firm succeed, and each constituency benefits to some degree when the firm makes a profit. The **stakeholders** can be hurt financially, professionally, and emotionally when a firm begins to shrink or fails entirely. More than simple economic resource transformation goes into the life and workings of the firm. In e-commerce, firms can't survive without covering their opportunity costs, but they also can't survive if they fail to recognize that economic efficiency is just one among many important goals. Survival and success in the competitive marketplace is the result of human effort and ingenuity, and not just the rote application of mechanical decision rules.

WHO IS MAKING HOW MUCH MONEY ONLINE AND WHY

The information and data detailing the profitability of e-commerce firms are divided into two categories. The first involves *aggregate profit data* and trends for all I-sellers regardless of product. The figures may also include *industry-specific profit data* tabulated across competing firms. This information is typically collected by a few key consulting organizations, based upon proprietary surveys of public and private I-sellers, and offered for sale in client documents. The second involves anecdotal information about the profit condition of individual, publicly held firms, based upon an examination of their quarterly financial reports. Somewhere in the middle are bits and pieces of information and *inferential profit data* indicating the financial health of privately held e-firms in generally nonpublic industries.

Aggregate and Industry-Level Profit Data in e-Commerce

The annual study, "The State of Online Retailing 5.0," conducted by Shop.org, looked at the financial results covering more than 100 North American e-tailers for the year 2001.[11] Some of the key findings from this study are summarized in Table 12-2.

The survey estimated that the total value of online spending doubled from $25.5 billion in 1999 to $51.3 billion in 2001. Given the rise in dollars spent, it found that 56 percent of the respondents reported profitable operations in 2001, up from 43 percent in 2000. Overall operating margins for the all respondents improved from –15 percent in 2002 to –6 percent in 2001. However, multichannel e-tailers proved to be the most profitable online sellers, with catalog-based firms registering online profit margins, as measured in terms of earnings before interest and taxes (EBIT), of +6 percent. Both store-based firms and Web-based firms each reported negative margins of –5 percent and –13 percent respectively as a group. However, more than one-half of the number of respondents in each of the three categories reported positive EBIT margins, led by a 73 percent figure for the catalog-based firms. The improvements in e-tailer profitability for

---

11 Shop.org is an association of online retailers and a division of the National Retail Federation. It conducts an annual survey of e-tailers in conjunction with the Boston Consulting Group and Forrester Research. Press release results for the 2001 study are summarized at **http://www.bcg. com/media_center/media_press_release_subpage69.asp** or **http://www.shop.org/press/01/ 050201.html**. The Internet research firm ActivMedia Research also conducts a broad annual survey of the e-commerce industry including profitability of B2C and B2B firms. For a summary of recent results, see **http://www.activmediaresearch.com/rn01netprofit.html**.

| Shop.org E-Tail Survey Results 2001 | | | TABLE 12-2 |

e-Tail Indicator	1999	2000	2001
Total Online Spending (bil.)	$25.5	$42.4	$51.3
Respondents reporting profitable online operations		43%	56 %
EBIT margin of online operations	n.a.	–15%	–6 %
Catalog-based companies	n.a.	n.a.	+6 %
Store-based companies	n.a.	n.a.	–5 %
Web-based companies	n.a.	n.a.	–13 %
Percentage of online retailers with positive EBIT			
Catalog-based companies	n.a.	n.a.	73 %
Store-based companies	n.a.	n.a.	51 %
Web-based companies	n.a.	n.a.	55 %
Marketing cost per order	$26	$20	$12
Acquisition costs per new customer	$38	$29	$14
Order conversion rate: (Orders/# site visitors)	1.8%	2.2 %	3.1 %
Percentage of revenue from repeat buyers	31%	40 %	53 %
Fulfillment costs per order	$12	$11	$14

Source: *The State of Online Retailing 5.0*, as reported in "Online Sales in 2001 Generated Profits for More Than Half of All U.S. Retailers Selling Online," available at **http://www.bcg.com/media_center/media_press_release_subpage69. asp**.

2001 were attributed to the overall rise in consumer online spending and improvements in operating efficiency, including tighter expense control, lower marketing costs, and greater sales to repeat online buyers.

The Shop.org industry survey results are important for a number of reasons. First, the data showed that a significant fraction of the sampled firms were experiencing positive revenues on either a net earnings or pro forma basis. Despite the large number of failures among e-commerce firms, not all of the B2C e-tailers were sinking into financial oblivion. Second, they demonstrated that multichannel sellers, who reach the same customers through e-tail and retail links, are increasing their share of online revenues, accounting for 67 percent of online sales in 2001 versus 54 percent in 2000. Third, it is not surprising to see so many of the catalog firms receiving positive revenues as a result of Web sales. To begin, their basic business is **direct marketing**, that includes already-established long distance contacts with their customer base via mail order and telephone connections. Extensive warehousing and fulfillment capabilities currently in place allow catalog e-tailers to treat Web sales as just another delivery channel, but one with low added customer selling costs that lead to high incremental net revenues. For the premier catalog sellers J.C. Penney, L.L. Bean and Lands' End, part of their success comes from their high **conversion rates**, turning 13 to 16 percent of site browsers into product buyers. Their conversion rates are far greater than the overall rate of 3.1 percent percent for all e-tailers.[12]

---

12 Bob Tedeschi, "E-Commerce Report: Catalog Companies Show the Upstarts That They Know a Thing or Two About Internet Selling," *The New York Times*, May 15, 2000, p. C16.

For multichannel catalog sellers, an added benefit arises from the lingering presence of direct mail catalogs in the home, giving them ongoing contact with their target customers. Low customer acquisition costs, high conversion rates, and sales to repeat buyers via numerous channels are keys to an efficient e-tailer operation.

The respectable success rate for store-based e-tailers is a bit more surprising. The larger retailers usually must develop their own Web sites, fulfillment staff, and warehousing capabilities from scratch, which can be an expensive proposition. Alternately, they can partner with an existing Web seller, such as Amazon.com, thereby sharing the cost burden as well as the profits. Small niche retailers with an I-seller presence could be selling from existing storefront stock and fulfilling orders, using existing sales staff, during slow periods. These latter strategies substantially reduce the marginal costs of e-sales, helping some of the niche sellers to report operating profits. Lastly, the fact that only 55 percent of the Web-based sellers are earning positive operating income is not surprising. These firms spend heavily on advertising to generate name recognition in the marketplace and acquire customers. **Customer acquisition costs** for Web-based e-tailers were $85 per buyer in 1999, falling to $55 per buyer in 2000. These numbers were substantially higher in comparison to an average acquisition cost for all new e-tailer customers of $38 in 1999 and $29 in 2000. However, the new customer acquisition costs appear to be moving in the right direction for both Web-based and as well as all forms of e-tailers, dropping to just $14 in 2001. In 2000, the top 50 percent of Web-based I-sellers had acquisition costs of just $14 per customer and in line with the costs experienced by catalog I-sellers.

These high acquisition charges underscore the importance of additional e-sales to repeat customers. The percentage of revenue earned from sales to repeat customers equaled 31 percent in 1999, but rose substantially to 53 percent in 2001, which helps to explain why e-tailers are so intent upon sending inexpensive e-mail messages to their list of past customers, detailing new products, and enticing them with special pricing offers. With the preceding cost numbers it is no wonder that the sum total of e-tailers reported collective operating losses of $5.6 billion in 2000, or 13 percent of revenue received. Despite the fact that this figure was better than the 19 percent loss registered in 1999, it was still indicative of the unprofitable nature of e-tailing in general. Individually, the set of catalog e-tail respondents had an operating profit equal to 12 percent of online sales in 2000, while brick-and-mortar stores had losses totaling 36 percent of revenues from I-sales, and Web-only e-tailers had aggregate losses equaling 94 percent of total revenues.[13]

Individual Firm Profit Results

Profit and loss information is more readily available for publicly held e-commerce firms that must make quarterly financial reports. These firms are divided into three camps: (1) those that have and are continuing to make money on a net income basis, (2) those that are reporting pro forma profits, and (3) those that are still struggling to get their heads above water. Priceline.com, eBay, AOL, Hotels.com, and Yahoo! among a few others, are or were in the positive net income camp. EBay, with its self-organizing structure and elements of natural monopoly, is the unchallenged king of success stories among the publicly held, Web-only, e-commerce firms. It earned positive, GAAP-based, *net income* on more than $1 billion in revenues in 2002, with both sales volume and profits growing quarterly.[14] It diversified its product line and sales venues beyond domestic auctions into foreign auction sites, direct product sales at its Web sites, the ownership of the traditional auction house Butterfield's, and support software designed to reinforce its dominant position. It continues to grow the volume of advertising revenue located on the eBay Web site, even in the face of a precipitous decline in the amount of advertising funds directed toward

---

13 As Web Sales Grow, Mail-Order Sellers Are Benefiting Most," *The Wall Street Journal*, May 2, 2001, p. B8.
14 Nick Wingfield, "Ebay Posts Higher Net, Revenue, Elevates 2002 Earnings Forecast," *The Wall Street Journal*, July 19, 2002, p. B2.

Web banner ads. Even eBay likes to report its financial results in a pro forma statement, however, focusing on operating profit that allows it discretionary powers to exclude charges against revenues such as amortization of goodwill from acquisitions, investment losses, and taxes paid on employee stock options.

Earlier in the e-commerce struggle for profitability, the Internet portal Yahoo! was one of the first Web-only firms to earn positive net income according to GAAP rules.[15] Yahoo! is a heavily advertised, branded site that served more than 210 million individual visitors per month, with more than 700 million page views per day in 2001. However, its business model relied extensively on the shear volume of these eyeballs and their ability to attract advertisers to the site. Some 80 percent of the revenue Yahoo! received was in exchange for client advertising, including banner ads. As online firms began to fail and ad revenues plummeted, Yahoo! slipped into the grasp of negative net income in mid-2001.[16] Consequently, it rejoined the cadre of e-commerce firms that emphasized pro forma profits in their financial press releases. It elected to exclude from the reported numbers the costs associated with payments for employee separation agreements (layoffs), the costs for cancelled contracts, including ones for office space, payroll taxes on employee stock options, and investment losses. As of mid-2002, Yahoo! had again begun to post small amounts of positive quarterly net income.[17] Yahoo!'s return to profitability depends on its ability to cut costs by eliminating money-losing parts of the firm and diversifying away from its reliance on ad revenues. Their new revenue model is based upon sales of premium services, Web music, corporate services, and revenue enhancing entertainment partnerships.[18] Yahoo! also purchased the Web-based employment listing service, HotJobs.com, as a means of generating more fee income. In addition, Yahoo! signed an agreement with SBC, the giant Midwest and Southwestern telecom provider, to supply subscription-based value added services to its DSL customers.[19] This linkup gives Yahoo! a billing relationship with its customers who may have previously accessed Yahoo! services for free. The relationship will allow Yahoo! to identify a portion of its customer base and attempt to sell them additional Web services.

AOL-Time Warner represents a third variation of the tension between financial reporting based upon net income versus pro forma results. As a separate company AOL had positive GAAP net income.[20] It was probably earning an economic profit as well, given the rise in its equity value and ability to attract new subscribers and revenues sources.[21] However, the merged firm now makes a net loss according to GAAP rules.[22] Because it is a "media and entertainment" company with many alleged unique charges, the firm would like investors to look at **cash flow** as measured by **earnings before interest, depreciation,**

---

15 Matt Richtel, "Yahoo! Reports That Earnings Beat Estimates by a Penny," *The New York Times*, July 12, 2000, p. C10.

16 Saul Hansell, "Yahoo! Reports $48 Million Loss in Its First Quarter," *The New York Times*, July 12, 2001, p. C2.

17 Mylene Mangalindan, "Yahoo! Posts Profit and Revenue Rises Despite Ad Slump," *The Wall Street Journal*, July 11, 2002, p. A3.

18 Mylene Mangalindan, "Yahoo! Reports Period Loss, Revenue Drop," *The Wall Street Journal*, October 11, 2001, p. A3.

19 Saul Hansell, "Mr. Semel's Internet Search," *The New York Times*, January 7, 2001, p. C1.

20 Nick Wingfield, "AOL's Net Rose 7% in Third Quarter Due to Strong Ad, E-Commerce Growth," *The Wall Street Journal*, April 10, 2000, p .A3.

21 Prior to the merger, AOL's equity shares were valued at nearly $74 each with a jump to $86 per share on first release of the merger news. See Declan McCullagh, "AOL, Time Warner to Merge," available at **http://www.wired.com/news/business/0,1367,33531,00.html**. AOL was the first Internet firm to make $1 billion in annual revenues, in 1996, and the first to post $1 billion in profit, in 2000. Saul Hansell, "American Online Registers Strong Profit for Quarter," *The New York Times*, July 21, 2000, p. C4.

22 Seth Schiesel, "Online Downturn Means Drop for AOL Time Warner," *The New York Times*, October 18, 2001, p. C2.

taxes, and amortization (**EBIDTA**). This AOL version of pro forma profits is solidly in the positive range, with nearly $2.5 billion in EBIDTA earnings in the second quarter of 2002.[23] The merged firm has a diversified income base, with 45 percent of its revenues coming from ongoing subscriptions, 21 percent from advertising, and the remaining 34 percent primarily from the sales of film and music properties. It also has a failing business plan for the **cross-media selling** of ad space to customers for its various entertainment and information products.[24] In addition, the plan allows for one part of the firm to advertise on another AOL media property, spreading the message of AOL and taking up unused ad space in the time of slow external ad sales.[25] Even though the merger was most likely an act of strategic brilliance by AOL, as argued in Chapter 8, it confused investors who once valued AOL as a rapidly growing Internet company that was earning economic profits. With the retreat to pro forma profitability, AOL is now seen as a more slowly growing media and entertainment firm. Consequently, the stock price of the combined firm initially languished in the $30 to $45 range before falling into the low teens. The later decline reflected not only an overall drop in the equity market, but a loss of perceived economic profitability at AOL and questions regarding an SEC probe of accounting irregularities, as well as confusion in leadership and firm mission.

Revisiting the Amazon.com Case and the Pro Forma Statement Problem

The opening case laid out the financial challenges faced by Amazon.com, which is arguably the best known of the pure-Internet e-tailers. Their get-big-fast strategy, regardless of profitability, allowed them to serve 20 million customers in 2000. Even though consumers bought $2.8 billion in products, however, Amazon still lost $1.4 billion that year. Amazon's strategy of being a broad-based product seller, with items ranging from books and CDs to garden supplies and consumer electronics, runs counter to the successful mail-order strategies as applied by direct sellers who expand into e-sales. These firms focus on a limited selection of specialty items, with a heavy emphasis on private-label products, which boost profit margins and pay for the marketing, warehousing, and fulfillment costs.[26]

Amazon is working intensely to get its costs under control, but it is doing so in the face of a declining rate of growth for its online sales. It developed an 800,000-equation computer model of the firm, designed to help manage every facet of the business from scheduling to product mix. Amazon eliminated products with low profit margins or bulky items that are costly to ship or subject to excessive breakage. It continues to press suppliers for steeper wholesale discounts, while quietly raising prices on the products it sells at retail. It is working with some suppliers to ship products directly to customers, cutting out the expense to Amazon of warehousing and handling. It ships a portion of its telephone customer service to low-cost sites in India, and forms partnerships with retailers to provide the electronic front-end and fulfillment activities for jointly listed products. Despite all of this effort, the achievement of persistent net income profits remains elusive. The pro forma profit numbers also exclude quite a few sizable charges, including $33 million per quarter in interest payments on $2.1 billion in debt, restructuring charges, as well as costs relating to investment losses, stock options, and acquisitions.[27] Outside observers believe that, given the financial success of the firm to date, it is in the best interests of Amazon to stop

---

23 Julia Angwin, "AOL Swung to 2nd-Period Profit, Due to Accounting-Rule Change," *The Wall Street Journal*, July 25, 2002, p. A3.

24 Martin Peers and Julia Angwin, "AOL's Grand Strategy for Ads Proves Hard to Boot Up," *The Wall Street Journal*, October 23, 2001, p. B4.

25 Martin Peers, "AOL Time Warner Floods Several Units With Ads for Other Parts of the Company," *The Wall Street Journal*, November 15, 2001, p. B11.

26 "Listen Up! Its Time for a Profit,," *The New York Times*, May 20, 2001, p. 3–1.

27 "Profitable or Not? It Depends on Who's Measuring," *The New York Times*, May 2, 2001, p. 3–14.

reporting its financial condition in terms of pro forma income and to begin reporting in terms of net income according to GAAP rules.[28] Lastly, in the wake of accounting scandals and questions at other firms, Amazon announced plans to expense its widely distributed stock options starting in 2003. Doing so in 2001 would have widened their net loss by some $396 billion and moved them further from reaching consistent GAAP net income profitability in the near term.[29]

Critics of the Amazon business model point out that its revenue and cost numbers fail to measure up to the standards established by comparable catalog merchants. For successful catalog firms, **fulfillment costs** are 11 percent of revenues and **gross margins** (gross revenue minus cost of goods sold) are in excess of 50 percent.[30] For Amazon the comparable numbers involve higher fulfillment costs at 14 percent, and lower gross margins at 26 percent. The response from Amazon is that its goal is to make up through sales volume, the absolute amount of dollar profits not being generated on a per-unit basis. In order to appreciate the nature of the challenge facing Amazon, consider the following profit equation.

$$\frac{\text{Profit}}{\text{Investment}} = \frac{\text{Profit}}{\text{Sales}} \times \frac{\text{Sales}}{\text{Investment}}$$

One measure of business success is the firm's rate of return on investment, or the absolute amount of dollar profits divided by the value of the invested capital. The targeted return on investment can be achieved one of two ways. Either the firm can target a high profit margin per unit of sales (Profit/Sales) or accelerate its rate of turnover, yielding a higher volume of sales per dollar of investment (Sales/Investment). Even though the catalog sellers emphasize the dollar profits per unit of sales, a lower profit rate at Amazon can still be consistent with a targeted rate of return on investment, if the volume of sales and rate of inventory turnover are sufficiently high. Wal-Mart is the master of this approach, with over half of its inventory stocked and sold before it has to pay the vendor. As a result, Wal-Mart earns a profit on the item and recaptures the cost of goods sold using none of its own funds to finance the inventory.

The Amazon approach is just another variant of the standard volume pricing model. The firm must get its sales volume up to a sufficiently high level to allow its relatively low profit per unit to generate an adequate level of total dollar profit. In a market where the growth in the overall dollar volume of B2C sales is slowing, Amazon must capture either a disproportionately large share of the increased sales or steal existing I-customers away from other sellers. This latter option would appear to be the most likely, given the demise of some 600 e-commerce firms over the past few years.

Can Amazon hang on long enough financially to put all of the pieces together? Will the economics of the marketplace continue to supply resources to Amazon without the firm earning a normal profit, or positive net income, or even pro forma positive operating profits? Some stock analysts who look at rise in gross sales and the expansion in the customer base say yes, but others who evaluate the firm on the basis of its financial results say no.[31] Amazon's **working capital**, or the cash available to pay its bills, continues to dwindle over time. With a diminished cash reserve, the suppliers of products to the firm will demand faster payment or even payment prior to shipment. In the absence of a new infusion of cash, the supplier behavior could create a credit squeeze for Amazon, and place the survival of the firm in jeopardy. The bottom line to this discussion is that firms eventually have to make a normal profit or they will go out of business.

---

28 Timothy J. Mullaney, "Amazon Is All Grown Up, Except for Its Accounting," *BusinessWeek*, August 5, 2002, p. 74.

29 Jonathan Weil and Theo Francis, "The Options-Value Brain Teaser," *The Wall Street Journal*, August 6, 2002, p. C1.

30 "Profitable or Not?" p. 3–14.

31 Gretchen Morgenson, "A Lehman Bond Analyst Paints a No-Nonsense Portrait of Amazon," *The New York Times*, February 7, 2001, p. C1.

Reactions to the Problems Created by Pro Forma Financial Statements

The information problems created by the name-your-own-accounting-rules approach to financial reporting are not limited to the e-commerce sector.[32] Firms as diverse in their lines of business as American Airlines (AMR), Eastman Chemical, Qwest Communications, and Sears Roebuck have all published pro forma financial statements, where usually positive operating earnings are substantially different from usually negative net income.[33] In general, the quality of corporate earnings reports has been deteriorating, leaving individual investors unsure about the true value of the firm.[34] What is potentially worse, the nature of the financial reporting problem isn't uniform across the range of firms that are issuing pro forma results. Some firms report operating earnings while others refer to EBITDA, core earnings, ongoing earnings, or economic earnings. However labeled, these numbers always exclude expenses that the individual firms, at their discretion, choose to consider as special, one-time, exceptional, or noncash. These expenses rarely meet the GAAP test for **extraordinary items** that can be excluded legitimately from net income and reported as a footnote to the financial statement.[35] One of the most egregious pro forma accounting distortions was introduced by WorldCom, which allegedly acknowledged that it incorrectly listed some $3.8 billion in operating expenses as capital expenditures, thereby raising its net income and drastically inflating its EBITDA numbers. Such deception may spell the end to the reporting of and reliance upon EBITDA numbers.[36]

The abuses of the pro forma financial approach have become so egregious that Standard & Poor's, the independent credit reporting agency, called for the establishment of a uniform accounting definition for the pro forma term *operating earnings*.[37] The firm also maintains the S&P 500 stock index, along with publishing the quarterly income valuations for this collection of firms. The price/earnings ratio for the S&P 500 is a closely watched indicator of overall stock market value. Given the abuse of pro forma reporting, investors complain about the lack of earnings transparency and the resulting inability to compare financial performance of firms in the same industry and across industries. Although the S&P proposals are not binding on any firm, they do represent the way in which S&P can judge operating earnings for purposes of credit evaluation and reporting. They propose to recognize as normal expenses, "restructuring charges, write-downs of assets from continuing operations, stock-option expenses and write-offs of research and development purchased from other companies."[38] Conversely, S&P would continue to recognize the following charges as capable of being excluded from the operating income number including, "write-downs of goodwill . . . ; charges from litigation settlements; gains and losses on asset sales; and acquisition/merger related expenses."[39]

---

32 Another variation of pro forma abuse involves hyping the income numbers, or using various accounting tricks to make the gross revenue flow look bigger than it is. For more information on this approach and hyping techniques, see David Henry, "The Numbers Game," *BusinessWeek*, May 14, 2001, pp. 100-110.

33 Jonathan Weil, "Moving Target: What's the P/E Ratio? Well, Depends on What Is Meant by Earnings," *The Wall Street Journal*, August 21, 2001, p. A1.

34 The accounting scandal and financial collapse of Enron in 2001, the world's largest energy trading company, demonstrated the size and seriousness of the pro forma information problem. Enron was forced to revise its pro forma income statements from 1997 to 2000, showing $591 million less in GAAP net income than the pro forma or "recurring net income" as originally reported. See Richard Oppel Jr, and Andrew Ross Sorkin, "Enron Admits to Overstating Profits by About $600 Million," *The New York Times*, November 9, 2001, p. C1.

35 Weil, "Moving Target," p. A1.

36 Martin Peers and Robin Sidel, "Days May Be Numbered for Ebitda Numbers," *The Wall Street Journal*, July 5a, 2002, p. C1.

37 Steve Liesman and Jonathan Weil, "S&P to Wade into Pro Forma Earnings Mess," *The Wall Street Journal*, November 7, 2001, p. C1.

38 Liesman and Weil, "S&P to Wade into Pro Forma Earnings Mess," p. C1.

39 Liesman and Weil, "S&P to Wade into Pro Forma Earnings Mess," p. C1.

As all of these problems surrounding financial statements alert investors to the uncertainties of reported profits, the unalterable fact remains: All firms, e-commerce or otherwise, must eventually make a normal profit, or they face the threat of liquidation.

Inferential Profit Results

Many years ago, it was common in the field of public finance to refer to the **excise taxes** that were levied per unit sold of alcohol and tobacco as **sin taxes**. Well, sin has come a long and potentially profitable way on the Internet. Two industries that are most likely making substantial profits with the potential for even further expansion are e-porn and e-gambling. Both of these industries involve primarily privately held firms, producing little objective data regarding customer volume, revenues, and profits. However, by almost all survey accounts, e-porn is an enormous and economically profitable business.[40] Existence of more than 60,000 e-porn sites on the World Wide Web intuitively tells anyone that cybersex is a moneymaker. If **e-porn** wasn't profitable, the sites would shrink in number and eventually disappear. Reliable data are difficult to secure, but the admittedly anecdotal sources indicate that at least one in four of U.S Web users, roughly 21 million persons, visits an e-porn site at least once a month. Some of the most popular sites experience more than 50 million hits or visits per month.[41] The top 1,385 sites attracted an aggregate of 7.5 million hits per day in 1997.[42] Overall, the adult entertainment business is estimated to generate $10 billion in annual sales, with e-porn accounting for approximately $1 billion, or 10 percent of the total.[43] A few of the larger firms with multiple sites are taking in upwards of $100 million per year, making them by far the most profitable of all Internet ventures.[44]

The combination of competitive pressures, customer demand, and the availability of revenues motivate the e-porn sites to be on the leading edge of Web content delivery technology, with subscription payment systems tied to the credit card industry. Women operate almost one-half of the e-porn sites. Danni Ashe, a former exotic dancer and the owner of one of the more popular destinations, is said to have earned $8 million in 2000. Claims for profit margins are high with some firms bragging about margins of 50 percent-plus. Other reports place the margins in the still respectable 33 percent range.[45] However, entry into the industry is easy and the proliferation of sites increases competition, cutting into the profit stream for the smaller sites. The "smut glut" means that individual site owners must act more like any other businessperson, spending increasing amounts of time controlling costs, differentiating their product, and securing new customers.[46] The Web is still a global communication system, which may lead to competition from cybersex sites located around the world along with the potential to tap the full range of global customers as well.[47]

---

40 See the data and discussion of the structure, marketing and consequences of the e-porn industry at "Pornography: Business Aspects," available from **http://www.sfu.ca/~rcweal/porn/noflash/business.html**.

41 Timothy Egan, "Technology Sent Wall Street into Market for Pornography," *The New York Times*, October 23, 2000, p. A1.

42 Randy Barrett, "Adult Web Sites: Virtual Sex, Real Profits," available at **http://www.danni.com/press/interactive_week_030397.html**.

43 See Frontline "American Porn," available at **http://www.pbs.org/whatson/press/oct01/frontline_porn.html**.

44 "Porn 500," available at **http://www.google.com/search?q=cache:qKdLfAE7-h4:www.insightmag.com/archive/200101088.shtml+web+porn+profits&hl=en,** December 2001.

45 "Profits Push Spread of Web Porn," available at **http://stacks.msnbc.com/news/179152.asp,** December 2001.

46 "Smut Glut Has Porn Sites Hurting," available at **http://www.wired.com/news/business/0,1367,42061,00.html**.

47 "No Slump for Sex Online," available at **http://slashdot.org/article.pl?sid=01/04/04/1515221&mode=thread**.

E-gambling is also a large and rapidly growing e-commerce business area on the Web. A study by the Wall Street investment firm of Bear Stearns estimated that the number of e-gambling Web sites doubled from 2000 to 2001. The total rose from 600 to 700 sites in 2000 to 1,300 to 1,400 sites as of 2001, and were operated by some 250 separate companies.[48] The study estimated that the e-gambling **betting handle**, or dollar total for all forms of Internet wagering, including sporting events, horse racing, virtual casino games, and lotteries, amounted to $1.4 billion in 2000 and projected it to rise to $5 billion by 2003.[49] A Pew Internet survey estimated that approximately 5 percent of U.S. Internet users, or 4.5 million persons, placed a **cyberwager** in 2000 and that 1 million Americans placed a cyber bet daily.[50] The Pew study also found that cyber bettors tended to be older, less educated, have lower incomes, and be equally divided between males and females, with females being the majority visitors to **virtual casinos**.[51] E-gambling sites can be profitable, but profit numbers are elusive given that the industry is heavily concentrated in various Caribbean Islands or Latin American nations.[52] These offshore locations are the result of U.S. laws limiting domestic e-gambling facilities. The remote and unregulated nature of the sites creates a special problem with added risks for the e-gambler, in addition to the risks inherent in the games themselves. A Bear Stearns industry analyst estimated that upwards of "35 percent of Internet casinos might not pay what they owe or might fiddle with the odds in an underhanded way."[53]

The expectation is that legal e-gambling will be expanding within the United States in the near future. The **Federal Wire Act of 1960** may prohibit sports wagering by use of wire communications, but it is unclear as to whether it precludes the casino-type games found on the Internet.[54] Legislation designed to extend the ban to cover Internet gambling failed to achieve a majority vote in Congress.[55] Overall, the U.S. casino industry is a $40 billion per year business, whose revenue flow is being restricted by the availability of offshore casino operations. Internet bettors lose approximately $960 per year versus $511 per year for bettors on lotteries and at traditional casinos.[56] Therefore, rather than continuing to support a ban on Internet gambling, the Las Vegas casino interests have become resigned to the inevitability of e-gambling. The biggest spurs to legislative approval will probably be the arguments that legalization will allow government regulation and taxation, with some of the revenues flowing into federal and state coffers. One firm, Virtgame.com, already has a license to offer Internet sports wagering within Nevada, and the Nevada legislature voted to allow state regulators to license gambling over the Internet.[57] Firms wishing to secure a Nevada license must prove that they have controls that will keep minors from betting and that void bets from adult bettors who are placing wagers from states that prohibit gambling.

---

48 "Online Casino Risk—Collect $$ or Go to Jail?" available at **http://www.newsfactor.com/perl/story/8221.html.**

49 Matt Richtel, "Companies in U.S. Profiting from Surge in Internet Gambling," *The New York Times*, July 6, 2001, p. A1.

50 Matt Richtel, "The Casino on the Desktop," *The New York Times*, March 29, 2001, p. G1.

51 Pew Internet and American Life Project, "What People Do Online: 2000," available at **http://www.pewinternet.org/search.asp**, December 2001.

52 Alex Wong, "Perfectas by Personal Computer," *The Wall Street Journal*, August 27, 2001, p. B1.

53 Richtel, "The Casino on the Desktop," computer hackers scam virtual casinos for large sums as well. Reuters, "Gamblers Get $1.9 Million in Winnings in One Case As Hackers Scam Net Casinos," *The Wall Street Journal*, September 11, 2001, p. B7.

54 Richtel "Companies in U.S." p. A1.

55 Christopher Marquis, "Ban on Internet Gambling Falls Short in House Vote," *The New York Times*, July 18, 2000, p. A18.

56 "Internet Gambling Draws Big Bettors As Vegas Suffers in Air-Travel Slump," available at **http://newsletter.casinocity.com/Issue57/.**

57 Matt Richtel, "Gambling on the Internet Wins a Vote," *The New York Times*, June 5, 2001, p. C4.

As with the expansion of e-porn, the rapid rise in the number of e-gambling sites serves as evidence of its actual or potential ability to generate economic profits. Although entry may diminish the amount of these economic profits generated by e-porn and e-gambling over time, human nature plus the addictive characteristics of both activities will most likely ensure the near-term growth of these forms of e-commerce. The adverse consequences from e-gambling and e-porn may eventually appear as new forms of old social problems that society will have to deal with in the future.

SUMMARY AND PROSPECTS

The discussion in this chapter wove its way through the murky world of e-commerce profitability. The trip revealed tension between the economic and accounting approaches to the definition of profit. The resolution of this tension showed that the economic definition based on the concept of opportunity cost was the one that is ultimately to decide the fate of all firms, including those involved in e-commerce. GAAP profitability may help the firm to achieve economic breakeven, but the rules for determining net income are influenced by the tax code and leave out some common forms of implicit opportunity costs. GAAP net income is nice, but economic breakeven is necessary for long-term survival.

The e-commerce firms and those in other lines of business are not always aggressive in reporting and emphasizing net income in their financial statements. Many firms choose to report pro forma revenues that allow them to exclude certain cost elements at their discretion. The second tension looked at the stresses being introduced in the evaluation of e-commerce firms by issuing financial statements based on pro forma rather than GAAP standards. Pro forma statements may have some value in a limited number of circumstances, but the costs that they exclude are not consistent across firms, lack transparency, and make it difficult to judge the true profit position of the firm. An emerging consensus in the financial profession views the publishing of pro forma data to be increasingly abused. Therefore, impartial financial arbiters, such as Standard & Poor's, are attempting to introduce a uniform definition of operating income, the most common form of pro forma income statement.

This tension among profit concepts was the focus of the introductory case pitting the GAAP profits of Priceline.com against the absence of even pro forma profitability on the part of Amazon.com. Neither firm has achieved economic breakeven, but the absence of GAAP profits at Amazon has called into question the future viability of that firm. Size—in the form of the number of customers and the dollar volume of transactions—is important to the economic efficiency of Web-only I-sellers, but size without economic breakeven spells the eventual demise of any and all firms.

Both the data and identities of firms and industries generating a profit on the Web are limited. The ones that can be identified appear to have something in common, however. One of the biggest assets of the Web is its ability to enhance the flow of information and reduce the cost of providing it. Firms like eBay aid the flow of goods, but their primary function is to provide cheap, fast, and reliable information that is tied to the physical transactions. Benjamin Franklin once said that as a rule for achieving success, "Neither a lender nor a borrower be." In the same vein, eBay is an unquestioned success, but it doesn't buy goods, store goods, or ship goods. It creates a Web community that provides and processes information as efficiently as possible, making money from all who pass through the process. Residing in the eBay story is a lesson to be learned.

Other examples of profitable activities involve e-commerce sites that pander to human weaknesses and addictions. Both e-porn and e-gambling sell a form of information or information experience and do very well at it. They offer a form of **value added involvement** and entertainment, which may hold out a second lesson for e-commerce profitability. Web surfers need to be "hooked" on an activity to generate repeat sales. Even eBay has a certain addictive character to it. The pure sale of information or Web content is more difficult, especially if that information is readily available in a number of places. Some vital, unique, or value-added aspect must be a part of the information to make it saleable and profitable. What almost all newspapers find is that they must give away today's news but can charge for archived information. If it is current, then is common and readily available on the Web, but if it is history and proprietary, such as a previously written article, then customers will pay for it if they need the information and can't get it elsewhere. To make the sale of content profitable, it must be both vital and value added. Only *The Wall Street Journal*, with its current information subscription service and reputation for important business stories, appears to have achieved a critical mass of vitality and value-added content.

The sale of tangible B2C products produces yet another layer of profitability problems. Amazon.com is the largest pure Web seller. It has a great Web site full of a wide range of products and is very user friendly. Yet it still has a profitability problem. Catalog e-tailers such as Lands' End or L.L. Bean have a far narrower product range but make money by treating the Web as just one channel of customer contact. Within their personal attribute space, some customers are more comfortable with telephone ordering, some with ordering by mail, and others with the Web ordering experience. Perhaps the lesson here is that it is difficult for the Web to stand on its own as a unique sales channel. The effectiveness of the Web as an e-commerce tool to sell tangible products may lie in combining it with other selling channels, such as brick-and-mortar or catalog retailing. It may not be a viable standalone e-tailing channel.

Lastly, the chapter said nothing about the profitability of B2B Web transactions. Who are the firms providing these services? How are they making money? Have they survived any better than the B2C sellers? What do they have to tell us about the economics of e-commerce? The information for B2B firms is even less readily available than for B2C firms and industries. Some of the B2B operations are run internally, others are private consortiums of publicly held firms, and still others are independent for-profit entities linking business buyers and sellers. All exist and survive because of their ability to generate efficiencies as well as profits. Therefore, the efficiency aspect of the Web is the next topic to be addressed in our discussion of the economics of global e-commerce.

KEY TERMS AND CONCEPTS

accelerated depreciation	economic firms
accounting breakeven	economic loss
accounting expenses	economic profit
accounting firms	e-gambling
accounting profits	entry barriers
acquisitions cost	e-porn
allocative efficiency	excise taxes
amortization	explicit opportunity cost
auditor	extraordinary items
betting handle	Federal Wire Act of 1960
capitalism	fulfillment costs
cash flow	GAAP (Generally accepted accounting
categories of scarce resources	practice) rules
communism	goodwill
conversion rates	gross margins
cross-media selling	hits
customer acquisition costs	hyping the income numbers
cyber wager	implicit opportunity costs
depreciation	loss minimizing case
direct marketing	net income
diseconomies of scale	normal profit
earnings before interest, depreciation,	opportunity cost
taxes, and amortization (EBIDTA)	pro forma profits
economic breakeven	productive efficiency
economic efficiency	profits

KEY TERMS AND CONCEPTS

profit rule of competitive markets
rental rate
replacement cost
salvage value
seasonal shutdowns
shutdown case
sin taxes
social firms

socialism
stakeholders
stockholders
straight-line depreciation
transparency
value added involvement
virtual casino
working capital

DISCUSSION AND REVIEW QUESTIONS

1. Identify the role of profits as a resource allocation force within capitalism, social-ism, and communism. Which system appears to be more equitable, or fair, versus being more efficient? Why? Which system would you prefer to live and work under? Why?

2. How do profits serve as a performance measure of resource use? How might socialism or communism determine the extent of efficient economic performance?

3. Identify what the term *GAAP* means in determining the level of profit or net income within a firm. Who is responsible for setting the GAAP accounting rules?

4. Identify what the term *pro forma* means in determining the level of profit within a firm. Who is responsible for setting the pro forma accounting rules?

5. Identify and explain the nature of the tension that exists between financial report-ing based upon GAAP rules versus pro forma earnings statements. Which state-ment yields the truest picture of the financial condition of an e-commerce firm? Why?

6. Under what economic circumstances might a pro forma statement of earnings help an investor to understand the current financial viability of a young firm?

7. What is financial transparency? How do GAAP rules help to make the U.S. finan-cial markets "the envy of the world"?

8. Explain the nature of the tension that exists between the concepts of accounting profit and economic profit. Which one is contained within accounting statements that conform to GAAP rules? Which one is better suited to decision making? Why?

9. Identify and compare the recordkeeping responsibilities of an accountant versus an economist. What is the difference between an accounting expense and an eco-nomic opportunity cost? Which concept is correct in determining the actual amount of profit earned by a firm? Why?

10. What are the two most common sets of implicit opportunity costs that must be added to the accountant's list of expenses to reconcile the two different definitions of profits? Are these costs real and necessary? Why?

11. Explain how economic profits and losses work to motivate the allocation of scarce resources. Is the existence of an accounting profit or loss sufficient to generate the same type and volume of resource flow? Why?

12. What is the difference between accounting breakeven and economic breakeven? Which of the two, if either, will guarantee the long run existence of the firm? Why?

13. Under what circumstances will a firm continue to produce in the short run even though it is failing to cover all of its costs? Under what circumstances will a firm

decide to shut down in the short run? Why? Will a firm that is losing money in the short run continue to produce in the long run? Why?

14. Distinguish between the economic view and function of firms and social view and function of firms. Which view has a greater basis in reality? Why?

15. What are the operational characteristics generally associated with efficient and profitable e-tail firms? What types of e-firms are most likely to possess these types of characteristics? Why?

16. Explain how a firm's rate of return on investment can be affected by either its profit margin per unit of sales or by the size of its sales volume. Which approach is most closely associated with the strategy of Amazon.com? Does this explanation indicate why it diversified away from selling just books, videos, and CDs, and into the sale of consumer electronics as well as garden supplies? Why?

17. How profitable are the firms in the e-porn and e-gambling industries? Why are reliable data so scarce for these firms?

WEB EXERCISES

1. Link to the home page for the Financial Accounting Standards Board at **http://www.fasb.org/**. Click on and examine one of its new proposed changes in accounting rules.

2. Link to the homepage for the Boston Consulting Group at **http://www.bcg.com/**. Click on its media center and check the releases to see a summary of its e-tail research findings for the most recent year.

3. Link to the most recent profit survey data for the Internet research firm ActivMediaResearch at **http://www.activmediaresearch.com/**. How does its e-tail profit and revenue numbers compare to those tabulated by the Boston Consulting Group?

4. Link to the homepage for *USATODAY* at **http://www.usatoday.com/**. Click on the Money page and use the quick quote box to get the most recent estimate of earnings per share for Ebay (ebay), Priceline.com (pcln), Amazon.com (amzn), and Yahoo.com (yhoo). Are these firms doing as well, better, or worse profit-wise compared to one year ago?

5. Link to the homepage for *BusinessWeek* at **http://www.businessweek.com/**. Use their search function to type in the keyword *e-commerce*, and find any recent news stories dealing with e-tail revenues, costs, or profitability.

6. Link to the Google search engine at **http://www.google.com/**. Type in the keywords *e-gambling revenues* or *e-gambling profits* to see a list of sites detailing the extent, dollars, and problems associated with this form of e-commerce.

7. Link to the Google search engine at **http://www.google.com/**. Type in the keywords *e-porn revenues*. Check out the list of sites dealing with the extent, dollars, and problems associated with this form of e-commerce.

CHAPTER

13 •————————————

Introductory Case

COVISINT AND SUPPLY-CHAIN MANAGEMENT

Without a doubt, the lion's share of the public's e-commerce attention has been directed toward the growth in B2C transactions along with the birth and demise of B2C firms. The fact is that the dollar volume of B2B Web-based transactions is many times the size of the dollar value of B2C e-commerce. The U.S. Department of Commerce (DOC) has begun to publish sample-based quarterly estimates of retail e-commerce sales. The numbers were made available beginning with the first quarter of 2000.[1] The sum total of e-commerce transactions for 2000 was estimated to be $27.8 billion, or 0.89 percent of all retail sales. When the DOC looked at the dollar volume of B2B sales for 1999, however, it determined that B2B activity covered 90 percent of all online sales. The leading sector in B2B sales was manufacturing with $485 billion in electronic sales, or 12 percent of the B2B total. Unofficial estimates vary, but a consensus places the total for B2B sales in the range of $2 trillion for 2003.

The reason for the high volume of B2B transactions is the efficiency and productivity of the Web as a vehicle for linking business activity. B2B sales reduce the transactions costs of the exchange process. They are conducted person-to-computer or even computer-to-computer, eliminating the need for person-to-person contact or the use of phone and fax technology, the methods that preceded the Web. When people are eliminated from the transactions process, costs are lower, orders move faster, and the potential for error is reduced. B2B e-commerce allows firms to take advantage of two important **strengths of a Web-based exchange system**. The first is the ability to gather, process, and transmit large amounts of information cheaply, while the second is the ability to provide ready access to that information on a 24/7 basis. Firms can mount the most current data on product design and availability, prices, and purchase needs, posting it at a central site with the specifications being instantaneously available globally. Others can access this information at their convenience without delay or endless rounds of telephone tag.

Given these advantages, it is not surprising to see firms in many industries either starting up their own proprietary Web ordering systems or joining together into Web-based **B2B exchange systems**. Covisint is potentially one of the largest of the B2B exchanges that brings together major assemblers and parts firms in the global automobile industry. It was originally announced in early 2000 as a joint venture among General Motors, Ford, and DaimlerChrysler, each of which gave up their individual Web initiatives to form a combined company.[2] Nissan Motors and Renault SA of France quickly joined the three original firms. Although the five firms are fierce competitors in terms of retail sales, they saw the value of a central supply chain site, with a single computer connection and a uniform operating standard for online purchasing.[3] The potential dollar amounts for trade via Covisint are enormous. The auto firms expect to purchase between $240 and $300 billion in car parts, at auction, for their own use. However, for antitrust reasons, the assemblers do not anticipate engaging in collaborative buying, or combining orders for a specific car part or office

---

1 For the most recent data on retail and e-tail sales, see **http://www.census.gov/mrts/www/current.html.**

2 Robert L. Simison, Fara Warner, and Gregory L. White, "Big Three Car Makers Plan Net Exchange," *The Wall Street Journal,* February 28, 2000, p. A3.

3 Information on the firm is available at **http://www.covisint.com/.**

e-Commerce Efficiency

and Productivity

supply item into a single giant offer to purchase. In addition, the founders are encouraging auto parts suppliers, such as Dana Corp, to affiliate with the site. Suppliers would use Covisint to buy a significant portion of the $500 billion of materials that the aggregate of parts suppliers must acquire in order to build components for the auto assemblers. The auto assemblers envisioned that the site could also be used for **supply-chain management** and **collaborative product development** within each firm.

Covisint, incorporated as a stand-alone firm, is independent of the individual auto partners. It is expected to earn upwards of $3 billion in annual revenues from a combination of subscription charges, transactions fees, advertising, and the provision of services. Despite the potential efficiencies and cost reductions resulting from the formation of a centralized buying unit, the auto firms were also motivated to create Covisint by the vision of a future **initial public offering (IPO)**. An IPO would allow assemblers to sell stock in Covisint, earning even greater profits for their efforts. Keep in mind that this entire joint venture is motivated by profits. By creating Covisint, the assemblers created and voluntarily accepted the burdens imposed by an **intermediary**. Covisint will forever charge them for the privilege of participating in the B2B exchange. It is the reverse of **disintermediation** trend, which was cited in Chapter 11 as strength of the Web and a means of effecting cost cutting. The subscription and transactions fees will raise the cost of parts buying. This apparent **efficiency paradox** of accepting intermediation while rejecting disintermediation can be explained by two factors. First, the assemblers assume that the efficiencies introduced by exchange-based online procurement and auction bidding will be sufficient to cover the fees of the intermediary and still leave enough cost savings to boost profits for the auto assemblers. Second, it is also partly explained by the fact that the revenues from the IPO will serve as added insurance that the business model will be profitable as planned.

Assuming that Covisint becomes fully operational by overcoming the problems of meshing buyer-seller interactive computer systems and developing uniform descriptions for remote parts purchases, the changes introduced by the B2B exchange system raise a number of important efficiency questions, including the following:

1. Who will be the ultimate beneficiaries of this novel form of e-commerce?
2. How will the efficiencies be shared among the potential gainers?
3. Is online buying through a competitive *reverse auction bidding process* simply a way of raising assembler profits at the expense of suppliers, who will be under added pressure to offer lower bid prices?
4. Will suppliers be able to boost their profit margins by cutting their sales staffs, reducing errors, and accelerating the pace of order taking?
5. Will any of the efficiencies and cost savings be passed along to customers in the form of lower retail prices for new cars?
6. Will Covisint blossom as a major force in the auto industry, emerging as a true neutral party in the parts transfer process?
7. Will it always be a competitive weapon wielded by the assemblers pushing for lower prices?

These questions outline the distributional tension that surrounds the creation of Covisint and the other forms of B2B exchanges. The efficiencies promised by the formation of B2B e-commerce links are real, but how will the gains and losses be distributed among the interested parties?

ECONOMIC THEORY: EFFICIENCY AND PRODUCTIVITY

The concepts of efficiency and productivity have some important consequences in both micro- and macroeconomic settings. In *microeconomics* efficiency can occur within both the firm and the marketplace. **Efficiency within the firm** begins with the assumption that the owners of the firm want to use the available resources to their maximum benefit. Benefit maximization can be achieved in one of two ways. First, the firm can pursue **output maximization**, by getting the highest volume of production with a targeted amount of dollar cost expended on resource inputs at fixed prices. Alternately, the firm can pursue **cost minimization** by targeting a fixed output level and employing the least costly combination of fixed price inputs that will allow it to achieve the output target. These approaches to firm efficiency can be shown within the context of a set of isocost and isoquant lines as demonstrated by Figure 13-1. Each of the **isoquant curves** are convex to the origin and represent a constant level of output that can be produced with varying combinations of resource inputs, in this case capital and labor. They embody the short-run and long-run technology of the production process. The location of each isoquant curve indicates the relative output volume, with curves lying up and to the right representing greater levels of production. The curves are drawn with a convex slope because, even though it is assumed that capital and labor can be substituted for one another in the production process, they are not perfect substitutes. Moving back and to the left along a given isoquant curve means that capital is being substituted for labor, and the marginal product of capital $(\Delta Q/\Delta K)$ falls as it is added to work with a shrinking amount of labor. To keep the output level constant, the firm must add increasingly

FIGURE 13-1   Output Maximization and Cost Minimization

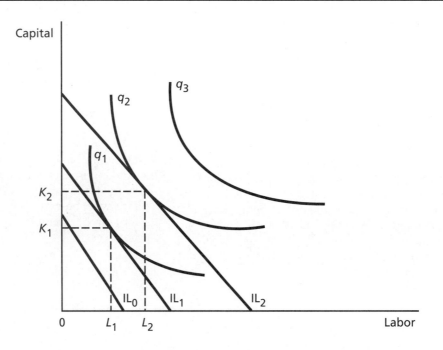

larger amounts of lower productivity capital to compensate for the removal of the labor units. Therefore, the slope of the isocost curve becomes steeper as the substitution process moves up and to the left. Conversely, moving down and to the right along the same isoquant curve, the marginal product of labor ($\Delta Q/\Delta L$) falls with increasing rapidity as more labor is added in place of capital, which makes the slope of each isoquant flatter as the substitution process moves toward the right on the curve.

Each of the **isocost lines** represents the combinations of capital and labor that can be purchased given the fixed price of each resource and a targeted amount of money (TC) to be expended on the purchase of resources. The lines are straight, or have a constant slope, because it is assumed that resources are purchased in competitive markets. Therefore, the market prices for the resources, the interest rate (i) for capital and the wage rate (w) for labor are unaffected by a single firm's hiring more or less of each. The intercepts, or maximum purchases of capital (TC/i) and labor (TC/w), are determined by assuming that all of the total cost is expended on one input. The location of the isocost lines indicates the total amount of money spent on the acquisition of both resources. For example, lines lying back and to the left represent lower levels of total cost.

The goal of output maximization can be shown as follows. Given the prices of the resource inputs, the firm targets some fixed amount of money to be spent on production such as isocost line 2 (IL_2). IL_2 will allow the firm to buy enough resources to produce output level q_1. But producing q_1 would be inefficient because IL_2 is capable of supporting resource combinations that would permit an even higher level of output. The maximum level of output would be a q_2, where IL_2 is just tangent to the highest attainable isoquant curve. The input combination of K_2 and L_2 will yield the maximum level of output attainable with an IL_2 total outlay of funds for resources. Output level q_3 would be greater still, but it is unobtainable given a total expenditure on resources of IL_2.

Targeting the production level shown by isoquant q_1, and finding the combination of capital and labor that would produce q_1 at the lowest possible cost demonstrates the goal of cost minimization. The isocost line or IL_2 intersects q_1 and allows the production of that output level, but it does so at an excessively high cost level. Output q_1 can also be produced at lower cost where IL_1 is tangent to the q_1 isoquant curve. The resulting input combination of K_1 and L_1 will yield the minimum level of cost necessary to achieve the targeted level of output. A lower total cost of IL_0 would be nice, but it will not allow the purchase of sufficient resources to produce the q_1 level of output.[4]

The use of the Web for B2B procurement is a potentially more efficient, less expensive and more capital-intensive interactive system that effectively lowers the cost of capital for the assemblers. As a result the isocost lines pivot in a clockwise fashion, for example, increasing their slope from ILA to ILB_1 as shown in Figure 13-2. The same total dollar amount is being spent on resources, but more output can be produced at an input ratio that favors the substitution of the now relatively inexpensive capital in place of the relatively more expensive labor. If the assemblers produce the higher output at q_2, then some of the benefits of the B2B exchange will most likely be passed along to the consumers in the form of lower car prices for the increased output. Conversely, if the assemblers experience the efficiency gain but decide to produce the same q_1 level of output as before, then they potentially capture all of the benefit from the B2B exchange in the form of a lower overall cost of production. This relationship is shown as their relevant isocost line shifts backwards in a parallel fashion to ILB_2. With this last result, the assemblers use more capital and fewer workers (K_3 and L_3) relative to the initial amounts employed (K_1 and L_1) to produce q_1. However, the workers that remain have a higher marginal product and are potentially capable of claiming an increased wage in return for their greater productivity. Fewer workers with the same amount of capital in

---

4 Note that firms cannot pursue output maximization and cost minimization independently at the same time. Output maximization involves moving up and to the right on the graph, while cost minimization involves moving back and to the left within the quadrant. They are diametrically opposed to one another as independent goals.

FIGURE 13-2   Lowering the Relative Price of Capital

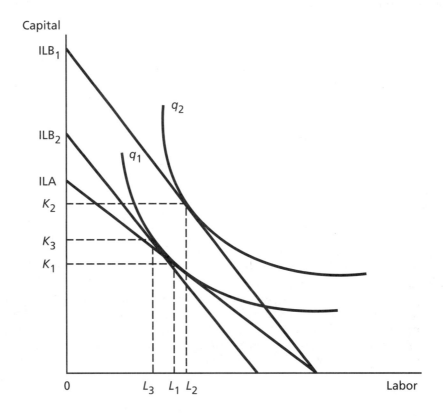

the short run would mean that the remaining workers would move back up the marginal product curve, yielding a higher marginal product. Fewer workers with an improved technology and a larger amount of more efficient capital in the long run would add even more to the productivity of the remaining workers.

Microeconomic Efficiency Within the Marketplace

The use of a B2B exchange also potentially improves microeconomic **efficiency within the marketplace**. The discussions in Chapters 2 and 12 involved enhancing the **static efficiency** notions of productive and allocative efficiency at a moment in time so that society gets the most value out of a given technology set and fixed amount of resources. The introduction of the B2B electronic trading alters the technology set and opens up the potential for society to experience **dynamic efficiency**, which involves the enhanced use of resources over time. With technological change it is cheaper for a given amount of output to be produced regardless of whether the change alters the relative prices of the inputs. In Figure 13-3, output level q_1 is produced with input volumes K_1 and L_1, at a total cost of IL_1, but a technological advance produces the graphic effect of compressing the isoquant lines toward the origin, allowing lower input volumes and cost outlays to produce higher levels of output. For example, discovery of a new technology causes the output volume represented by q_1 to move back and to the left to position q_{1A}.[5] The quantity q_{1A} can now be produced with a lower level of inputs as shown by

---

5 Don't be confused by the use of the terms *down* or *back*. If the introduction of the new technology allows the q_1 output level to be produced at q_{1A}, the firm is more efficient even though the isoquant moves down or back toward the origin.

| Dynamic Efficiency Consequences from the Introduction of B2B Exchanges | **FIGURE 13-3** |

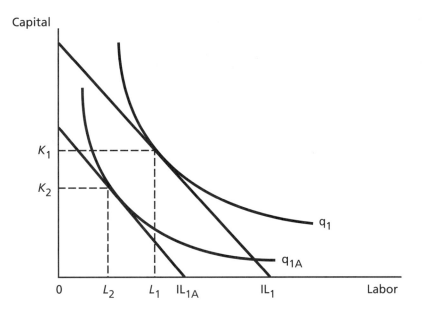

K_2 and L_2 as well as a lower level of total cost as shown by IL_{1A}. Again, some or all of the efficiency gains could be passed along to consumers in the form of a greater output volume and lower retail price. The combination of competition among auto assemblers and the degree of pricing power possessed by each firm relative to the consumer will determine the mix of higher profits or lower product prices.

The introduction of this new technology that compresses the isoquant curves also has the potential effect of altering what is considered to be best practice at each output level for the firm. The long-run average total cost curve (LRATC), displayed in Figure 13-4, shows the lowest unit cost to be experienced by applying the most efficient known technology at each scale of output. When a new technology is discovered, such as the use of B2B exchanges, it changes the knowledge set. The effect is to shift the LRATC downward, allowing the production of each output level at a lower long-run unit cost. Each firm then reacts to the competitive pressures in the market, adjusting its own behavior to what has now become the enhanced level of best practice. These firm and market adjustments reintroduce the drive to achieve the static concepts of productive and allocative efficiency. How these cost curves shift in response to the new technology, along with the extent of competition and the degree of firm pricing power again determine the distribution of the gains between higher firm profits and lower product prices. The example in Figure 13-4 has both the firm and consumers sharing in the gains, with greater firm profits and lower product prices ($P_2 < P_1$).

Macroeconomic Productivity

Depending upon the importance and pervasiveness of any changes in best practice, a change in technology can have macroeconomic as well as microeconomic consequences. **Macroeconomic productivity** is a measure of overall output per worker. It is based on the level of efficiency found among the individual production units and serves as an indicator of the efficiency of the economy as a whole. Most technological changes are too limited in size or narrow in scope to be detectable within the aggregate productivity data, but changes in technology that alter the essential nature of production

FIGURE 13-4   Technological Change Affects Best Practice and LRATC

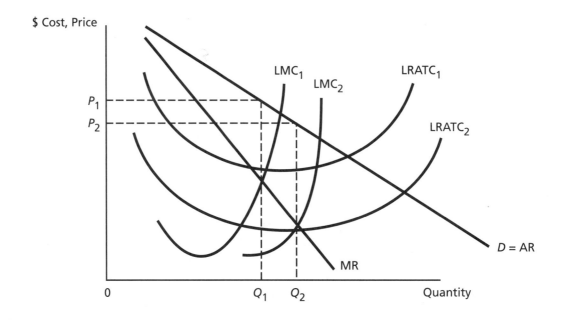

might affect the level of aggregate productivity over time. These sweeping changes would include the discovery of the steam engine, the harnessing of electricity, the creation of the gasoline-powered internal combustion engine and the birth of telecommunications. The question then is whether the introduction of Web-based B2B exchanges in the context of e-commerce has both the importance and the provides the power and scope to influence the aggregate productivity numbers. The question can't be definitively answered here, but an examination of the U.S macro data in Figure 13-5 provides some

FIGURE 13-5   U.S. Macro Data

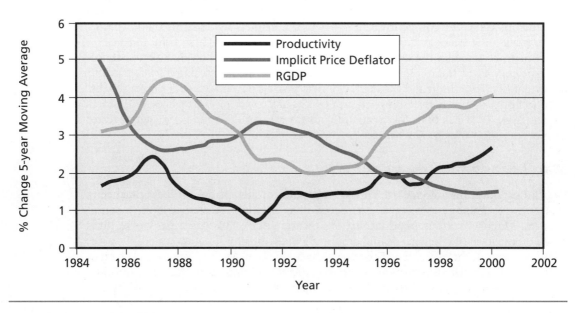

Source: http://www.FreeLunch.com.

tantalizing hints. The productivity trend is calculated as a five-year moving average. Here, the productivity number for each year is calculated as the average of the productivity figure for the latest year and the four previous years. The use of a five-year average rather than displaying the annual data is designed to smooth out variations, including spikes and drops, that might be the result of short-term business cycle fluctuations rather than longer-term secular trends.[6] The graph shows that the productivity curve reached a low value in 1991 registering a gain of just 0.8 percent. Subsequently, the curve displays a steady increase to reach 2.5 percent in 2000. This period of expansion is at least coincidental with the growth of the Web and its use as an efficiency-enhancing medium for business trade. Many other productivity-boosting forces were also at work in this time period, including an expansionary monetary policy that fueled lower interest rates, a more restrained fiscal policy that moved the federal budget from a deficit to a surplus position, lower charges for health care and energy as well as the strengthening of the exchange value of the dollar. Although not conclusively causal, the growth in B2B exchanges was coincidental with these events and consistent with the rise in overall productivity.

By experiencing a gain in aggregate productivity, a given workforce is able to produce more goods and services today than it did yesterday. Consequently, it helps to drive the rise in overall output, as measured by changes in **real gross domestic product (RGDP)**. On the microeconomic level, the gains allow workers to increase their compensation without necessarily reducing firm profits or requiring an increase in product price. Therefore, productivity gains work to keep RGDP growing without necessitating an increase in the overall inflation rate. In summary, productivity gains contribute to an increase in the overall standard of living. Figure 13-5 shows the U.S. macro productivity curve along with one for RGDP and another for the **implicit price deflator (IPD)**. The IPD measures the price changes for all of the items that are part of GDP, including those bought by government, business, households, and through foreign exchange. As such, the IPD incorporates, but is a broader measure than, the consumer price index, which measures the costs of goods bought by households. The local peak for the inflation rate was 1991, when the productivity gain number was at its local low. Subsequently, the inflation measure showed a steady decline in tandem with the rise in the rate of annual productivity. The RGDP curve reached a low in 1993 and rose thereafter coincident with the rise in productivity and fall in the inflation rate. As with the productivity numbers, many forces reinforced this positive trend. However, the appearance and growth of B2B e-commerce exchanges is at least consistent with, if not conclusively causal for, the positive macroeconomic data.

DIFFERENT B2B ORGANIZATIONAL FORMS

Efficiency enhancing B2B exchanges, or net markets, can be arranged into one of four different organizational forms: a bilateral exchange, a horizontal exchange, an independent trading exchange, or a trading hub.[7] A **bilateral exchange** is a one-to-one business model, in which a single seller sets up a Web site listing products and prices in a form similar to a traditional catalog. Potential buyers key in the site's URL and place electronic orders rather than working through a human manufacturer's representative using a process that combines more costly plant visits, along with phone and fax technology. The advantages here are that items are updated faster and cheaper than through a printed catalog listing. Prices can be changed quickly and broadcast to all potential buyers. Industries where bilateral exchanges work best include those with a limited number of suppliers and buyers, so that the identity and reliability of the parties are well known. Products tend to be of standard

---

6 Using five as the number of years is a bit arbitrary and judgmental. Trends can be established using 3- or 10-year moving averages as well.

7 The following discussion is adapted from Stephen Mihm, "1,000 Crates of Sprinkles With That?" *The New York Times*, March 29, 2000, p. G28.

design and quality. Comparison price shopping is possible, but the format provides little ability to set one seller against another to secure a price concession. The exchanges at Dell.com or Gateway.com are good examples of bilateral exchanges, especially their focus on the sale of computers to business buyers. They offer a narrow range of products, such as servers and computers, to a targeted range of technologically savvy buyers.

Horizontal or **functional exchanges** offer a wide range of industrial products, used by most business firms regardless of the buyer's product line. Some are tangible, general supply items, such as office and janitorial supplies, computer software and industrial solvents, rather than the industrial inputs that are part of any specific finished product. These exchanges also serve as an **applications service provider**, hosting catalog services for widely used industrial products, including electronic components, fasteners, hydraulic systems, and other items sold by a variety of different firms. The exchanges may also offer proprietary software services to schedule and track plant or building repair maintenance and spare parts. This field of e-commerce is commonly referred to as maintenance, repair, and operation (MRO) supplies. iMark.com and MRO.com are examples of these kinds of horizontal exchanges.

Independent trading exchanges (ITE) are a third form of B2B trading vehicle. These vertical exchanges link buyers and sellers within a specific industry or product market, including agriculture, steel, paper, chemicals, and construction. They list and trade all of the raw materials and industrial inputs that go into the fabrication of a finished product, with the finished product itself frequently being offered for sale on the site. Independent exchanges work best in fragmented markets with many buyers and sellers of a standardized product. Here the exchange serves the function of an intermediary, pulling together the disparate business units into a central trading location. Historically, the New York Stock Exchange (NYSE), located on Wall Street in New York City, performed a similar centralization function for trading in the equities market. The supermarket chains, including Stop & Shop, Kroger's, or Safeway, with their local stores, do the same for the exchange of grocery items between food processors and consumers. A Web-based ITE further improves upon the efficiency of physical centralization by the use of a single electronic trading standard that eliminates the need for face-to-face contact. In essence, it is the same as the difference between the NYSE, which is a central physical exchange, and the Nasdaq, which is a central electronic exchange. The ITE earns its revenues by charging for each transaction. It has also grown to provide materials management software services to firms in the industry. Examples of an ITE would include NewView.com, which offers supply-chain management and procurement in the steel industry; ChemConnect.com, a neutral trader of raw chemicals, resins, and plastics; XSAg.com, an auction exchange for agricultural supplies; and PaperSpace.com, which offers management services and trades resources, as well as products that are part of the pulp and paper industry.

The final organizational form for a B2B exchange is a **trading hub**. Hubs generally appear in an industry that is dominated by one or a few firms. The industry leader(s) decide to bypass the intermediary and set up their own trading exchange to buy and sell parts, raw materials, and finished goods. Hubs typically involve the trading of a sizeable number of complex parts in high volume that are produced by a relatively large number of suppliers. So, when the dominant firm places its purchasing operations online, the network of suppliers has little choice other than to follow its principal customer onto the Web. Covisint is a prominent example of a vertical trading hub, with a potential IPO kicker thrown in.

EXPERIENCING AND DISTRIBUTING THE B2B EFFICIENCY GAINS

Given the multiple potential organizational forms for e-commerce B2B transactions, how will the efficiencies resulting from the exchanges be divided among the parties? The answer depends upon the play of tensions among some familiar economic concepts, including concentration versus competition and fragmentation versus market power. Market transactions are divided into two sides—buyers and sellers—with the B2B exchanges standing between the two parties and facilitating the transactions. The efficiency gains from e-commerce exchange must be divided among the three parties, buyers, sellers and exchange owners. How will this arrangement evolve? Let's start with a **Case 1 market** that contains one or a few highly concentrated sellers of a product and a large number of smaller disorganized and fragmented buyers.[8] This traditional economic market is dominated by monopoly or oligopoly. Here the dominant firms are likely to choose to operate as either a bilateral exchange or as a trading hub. The disparity in market power will direct the efficiency gains to the dominant firm in the bilateral model, and the exchange will become just another means for the firms with market power to wring cost concessions from their smaller and intensely competitive suppliers. As a trading hub, the market power still resides with the seller and they control the gains. If the hub is managed as an independent exchange it has only a small chance of capturing anything other than normal returns for its exchange services. Its most significant revenue potential is to develop supply-chain management systems that offer value added services to the client base. However, the dominant firms remain as the primary beneficiaries of the hub. If the hub generates a critical mass of customers and is seen as a neutral party, then the hub can potentially evolve into an independent entity, capable of establishing its own equity value based upon its revenue flows.

A **Case 2 market** situation involves the opposite market structure of one or a few dominant buyers and a large number of smaller, disorganized, intensely competitive, and fragmented sellers. This situation generates **monopsony**, single-buyer market power, or **oligopsony**, market power in the hands of a few buyers. In both situations, the sellers lack leverage and are at the economic mercy of the buyers. As in case 1, the holders of the market power can demand a larger share of the transaction value generated by the site. Also, essential buyers can "persuade" captive sellers to undertake some or all of their own materials purchases or product sales on the dominant firm's site. For example, steel firms may be swayed to sell all of their uncommitted, auto-destined steel on the Covisint site rather than on their own exchanges, such as e-Steel.[9] Such persuasion would boost the profit margins for the dominant firm's site. The owners of an independent exchange are unlikely to gain other than normal profits unless the dominant buyers transfer some of their market power to the exchange. They would do so in the hope of recasting their power in the form of equity gains in the ownership of the exchange, rather than exercising their power into the future on a purchase-by-purchase basis. Cashing in on that power today in the form of a current IPO would allow the dominant buyers to immediately receive, as a lump-sum dollar payment, the discounted present value of their market power based revenues to be earned in the future.

Lastly, a **Case 3 market** situation is one where both buyers and sellers are fragmented, small, numerous, and disorganized. Here, there is intense competition on both sides of the market and the owners of a B2B exchange hold the greatest potential for dominating the exchange process. As such, the B2B companies can extract a higher toll from each transaction, capturing more of the efficiency gains. The profits for the exchange owners can be substantial. For example, if the value of B2B e-commerce in 2003 is $3 trillion and exchange owners are able to charge 0.33 percent, or one-third of 1 percent, of the total volume of sales, then exchange revenues would amount to $9.9 billion from trading sources alone. Tack on potential revenues from subscriber fees, advertising, and the provision of supply chain software services, along with the profits from the ownership of exchange, and in certain markets source of cash is potentially endless.

---

8 Richard A. Oppel, Jr., "The Higher Stakes of Business-to-Business Trade," *The New York Times*, March 5, 2000, p. 3–3.

9 Robert Guy Mathews, Karen Jacobs, Susan Warren, and Dean Starkman, "Industries, from Steel to Chemicals, Say One Internet Site May Not Meet Needs," *The Wall Street Journal*, February 28, 2000, p. A16.

Tensions in and Limits to Web-Based B2B Efficiency Gains

For some products and markets, Web-based e-commerce is clearly the superior method of exchange. However, all may not go as planned in the vast expanse of real world B2B net markets. A tension based upon product and market characteristics works to draw some firms into the e-commerce experience, while other firms are kept from realizing the efficiencies resulting from e-exchanges. In these industries, the existing **fax and phone technology model** generates comparable efficiencies, or works even better than the electronic exchanges.[10] Net markets work best in impersonal business environments characterized by a broad scope of traders, making a large number of high-value, predictable trades, involving a durable, standardized product, where prices are uniform and where conditions of sale and shipment are routine. Products such as steel, chemicals, and coded electronic components all fit this description to a greater or lesser degree. Conversely, in **specialized markets**, products may be either perishable or otherwise time sensitive, or perhaps seasonal in nature. A lack of product uniformity may occur as merchandise characteristics vary among shipments. Supply instability may be present, with available quantities fluctuating frequently and widely. Confidentiality in pricing may be important if supply swings lead to the need to make price concessions to some customers, but not all.

Markets with low-margin businesses may not be able to afford the 1 to 2 percent transactions fees that an exchange typically imposes on trades. Transactions that are based on or involve considerable trust among the trading partners may not thrive in a setting where exchanges are impersonal. Here, narrow customer scope may be preferable to a broader client base that is counterproductive when it allows the entry of small, marginal, or financially weak traders into the exchange process. The creation of a series of dominant firm bilateral exchanges may lead to a costly learning curve problem, as each unique procurement system created by an essential and dominant client must be studied, mastered, and integrated into the trader's existing computer system. Lastly, efficient operation of the specialized market may depend upon a personal and confidential exchange of information regarding current conditions and emerging industry trends that would be absent in an impersonal net market. Each of these specialized characteristics applies, as in the produce (fruits and vegetables) distribution business, for example. However, the problems thwarting the spread of B2B exchanges are not unique to this industry. The electronic exchanges will encounter efficiency problems in service delivery whenever an industry tension arises between product variety and human contact versus product conformity and impersonal dealing.

CASE EXAMPLES OF B2B EXCHANGE EFFICIENCY

Employment Exchanges and Economic Efficiency

Employment exchanges are a prime example of how net markets are introducing efficiencies into the job search and employee hiring process.[11] In a global sense **Internet job boards** deal with fragmented markets on both sides of the employment transaction, working to focus the search process onto a single, centralized electronic site. The economics of search, initially discussed in Chapter 1, helps to understand and explain how electronic job markets introduce these efficiencies. Monster.com is the largest electronic job board, with a claim of more than 7 million unique visitors per month. But other market leaders, such as Careerbuilder.com, HotJobs.com (owned by Yahoo!!), and JobsOnline.com, each receive more than 3 million visitors per month. Most sites host a combined list of company job openings and résumés of job seekers organized by job

---

10 The following discussion is adapted from Lee Gomes, "How Lower-Tech Gear Beat Web 'Exchanges' at Their Own Game," *The Wall Street Journal*, March 16, 2001, p. A1.

11 The following discussion is adapted from Alan B. Kruger, "The Internet Is Lowering the Cost of Advertising and Searching for Jobs," *The New York Times*, July 20, 2000, p. C2.

type and geographic area. Looking for jobs and employees, the **matching function**, is made easier, faster, and cheaper by the use of net markets. Arranging and profiting from initial contact is superior via the Web when compared to the previous system of print advertising in help-wanted sections of newspapers and professional publications. These traditional print sources are still being used, but they too have become electronic, with job openings being posted on either individual newspaper Web sites, or on Careerbuilder.com, which is affiliated with the newspaper industry.

The efficiency gains experienced through the use of an Internet job board include the following. First, it is considerably less expensive for a firm to post an electronic job notice than to take out an ad in a local or regional newspaper. The cost for posting an electronic job opening ranges from $0 at JobsOnline.com, to $295 for a 60-day listing at Monster.com. Generally, Internet job listing charges average about 5 percent of the cost of placing an 30-day ad in a major national newspaper such as *The New York Times* or *The Wall Street Journal*. Second, the geographic reach of an electronic job notice or résumé is global, yielding a wider selection of jobs and potential employees. Most job seekers are looking for employment opportunities within their immediate home area. However, some persons, including perhaps recent college graduates, may want to relocate to a job in a specific geographic region, or may be willing to relocate to any region that has attractive jobs available. Conversely, an employer is looking for the best or right person to fill a position. The greater the number of applicants, the more likely it is that the right person will be hired. In general, greater reach makes placing the ad on an Internet job board more cost effective for the firm and search efficient for the job seeker.

Third, an electronic ad is more flexible than a typeset print ad. It is easier for an employer to change and update an ad on the Web as hiring conditions alter. Fourth, the application process for an advertised position is faster and cheaper for the job seeker. The major job boards allow the potential employee to send an electronic copy of his résumé to the employer and even fill out an employment application form via the Web. Fifth, job boards can automatically match the electronic résumés of job seekers with the ads placed by potential employers using computer-matching algorithms. This matching allows an immediate electronic notice to be sent when appropriate new job openings or résumés are posted on the site. Lastly, it's possible for employers to screen applicants electronically by applying Web-based employee entry tests. The tests help to cut down on the costs of interviewing inappropriate candidates and speed up the matching process.

A key point of this discussion regarding the efficiency of job boards is that efficiency breeds usage. Increased usage can lead to rising revenues from a variety of sources, with the potential for profits accruing to the exchange owners. Job boards, as an efficiency enhancing form of e-commerce, make excellent use of the Web's greatest assets, which is to relentlessly drive down the cost of gathering, processing, and distributing information.

Construction Industry Exchanges and Economic Efficiency

With $3.9 trillion in global annual sales, of which $1.2 trillion is in the United States, the building industry is another case where B2B exchanges significantly improve production efficiencies.[12] Construction is a highly fragmented, localized industry, with thousands of small firms involved in architectural, engineering, and construction (ACE) activities, often operating on low profit margins. The firms may be technologically sophisticated in terms of building practices, but they are decidedly low-tech in terms of project management and the coordination of subcontractors. According to a Gartner Group study covering 1999, construction firms spent far less on information technology (IT) per employee ($835) than did firms in manufacturing ($3,500) or financial services ($27,000).[13] For commercial construction projects the IT deficiency causes

---

12 Bob Tedeschi, "E-Commerce Report: Construction Heads into the Internet Age," *The New York Times*, February 21, 2000, p.C1.

13 Mark Roberti, "Cutting Construction Chaos," available at **http://www.thestandard.com/article/0,1902,26800,00.html?body_page=2.**

costly problems because historically, the industry is highly paper-intensive, relying on printed drawings of building design as the basic vehicle for coordinating the efforts of different firms. Still, these blueprints change frequently, sometimes daily on large and complex projects.

Prior to the birth of construction industry Web exchanges, new copies of the physical blueprints had to be drawn up and sent by overnight carrier to the affected subcontractors. Phone and fax technology was used to alert them of an impending arrival of revised prints. With upwards of 50 subcontractors on large projects, it was difficult to remain on the construction schedule with so many changes creating added delays. Physical visits to the construction site were also a common way of communicating changes and determining how well the project was progressing. These delays cost project developers real money in terms of months of lost rental income from apartments or office complexes that weren't completed on time. Developers of retail sites experience losses in rental income and retail sales when malls or retail shopping complexes miss their projected opening dates. Construction was an industry badly in need of the information distribution, coordination, and scheduling efficiencies that could be provided through Web contacts.

More than 400 construction industry dot-coms were launched from 1997 through 2000 in response to this opportunity for efficiency and entrepreneurial profits. Only a handful of large domestic construction exchanges such as Citadon.com, Viecon.com, and BuildPoint.com were among those that were able to survive the ensuing consolidation, however.[14] Most of the firms started out as **project extranets**, offering a central Web site providing password-protected hosting of construction blueprints. As extranets, the information that they held was available via the Web to any authorized source outside of the host firm. Just by itself, this centralized communication function introduced real efficiencies into the construction industry. Changes in blueprint design became electronically available immediately to all subcontractors, with the notification of the change transmitted via e-mail. Construction schedules were also available on the Web site, including start and completion dates, with any changes in material delivery time or subcontractor installations duly noted. Project managers needed fewer trips to the physical site to gather information, check on work schedules, and estimate time to completion. Most of these facts were now available on the electronic site. The benefits derived from these B2B sites were distributed among the parties, including the developers, architects, engineers, construction firms, and subcontractors. Exchange owners made their money by charging fees for hosting the information, for client training, and for customer support.[15]

As the acceptance and popularity of the construction industry exchanges grew, they evolved into the hosting of marketplaces where suppliers of construction materials could post catalogs showing the availability and prices for their products or services.[16] Later, they developed bid management software that would allow the project manager to post specifications for materials or subcontracted activities on the Web site and allow potential suppliers to bid on specific portions of the plan. The ultimate goal is to have the entire construction project procurement process hosted online. At that point, electronic bidding, scheduling, and supply-chain management would drive the realization of additional

---

14 Roberti, "Cutting Construction Chaos."

15 InfrastructureWorld.com is a global construction exchange backed by the engineering and building giant Bechtel, and designed to link participants and expedite the development, financing, and construction of large building projects, such as airports, dams, and highways, especially in Third World nations. The exchange facilitates an examination of project documents online, contains information about the sociopolitical structure of developing nations, and allows for the advertising of as well as bidding on parts of these projects. InfrastructureWorld.com is scheduled to evolve into a "neutral site" not dominated by any single construction entity. See Jim Carlton, "New Web Site Helps Speed Up Building Plans," *The Wall Street Journal*, September 14, 2000, p. B14.

16 Although the dollar numbers for the volume of exchange-linked commercial construction are large at more than $6 billion annually, they still account for less than 1 percent of the domestic construction total. Forrester Research projects that this number will rise to just over 10 percent in 2004. See Tedeschi, "Construction Heads into the Internet Age," p. C1.

construction efficiencies. As with the previously noted job market boards the key to the success of the construction exchanges is their ability to take advantage of the Web's main asset, which is to efficiently assemble, manage, and coordinate the flow of information. In construction, as with many industries, time is money. **Electronic construction portals** help to bring projects to completion on time and under budget, providing cost saving and revenue enhancements greater than the fees allocated to the exchanges. As one project manager noted, "It's the new math of the Internet."[17]

The Covisint Case Revisited: Supply-Chain Management

As was noted in the introductory case, Covisint is the B2B exchange created by some of the key multinational players within the global auto industry. It is designed to bring Web-based efficiencies to the process of supply-chain management, the procurement of parts, and eventually the ordering of new vehicles. Where will these efficiencies come from, and how will they be distributed among the participants? Starting with the procurement process the potential efficiencies are fairly clear.[18] Under the existing parts ordering system, when an auto assembler develops the need for a new part, it begins the contract process by contacting the existing list of suppliers who previously bid on that type of part. Sales representatives for the suppliers meet physically with the assembler to discuss the contract terms and receive the preliminary engineering designs. Competing suppliers must, in turn, submit paper bids and blueprints to the assembler for a preliminary judgment on the contract. Final physical meetings are held to work out the details of the contract and complete the award. The process is time consuming and costly, being paper-intensive and with numerous negotiations conducted face to face.

A Web-based parts ordering system would facilitate the electronic posting and exchange of both preliminary design and blueprint response information. The public posting of an intent to purchase notice on the Covisint site could elicit multiple bids from global as well as local suppliers, including some who may have never dealt with the assembler before. Of course, the notice and bidding process would have to be conducted on separate sections of the Covisint site for each assembler to ensure the confidentiality and security of the individual specifications, bids, and transactions. The separation would also act as an **electronic firewall** to prevent the leakage of information to rivals and maintain the competitive vigor among the assemblers.[19] Some physical meetings might still be needed, but the electronic transfer of information should cut some costs and speed up the process. Originally, the assemblers estimated that the Covisint site might cut as much as 10 percent from the procurement cost for auto parts. With the cost of parts amounting to approximately one-half of the retail price of a $20,000 vehicle, the savings could be as much as $1,000.[20]

The goal of transferring the customer ordering process from the phone and fax approach to a direct electronic ordering approach is a more challenging one, but it offers efficiencies as well as other benefits that are closely tied into improvements in the supply-chain management process. Currently, few vehicles are built custom-order because of the 30 to 60-day time delay from the point that order is placed to the day when the vehicle arrives on the dealer's lot. Most buyers with "new car fever" or an "old clunker" that's ready to die want the vehicle now or within a few days. This immediacy component of consumer demand results in the auto assemblers relying on a **prebuild business model** with vehicles being produced in anticipation of sales, leading to a 50 to 60-day inventory supply on dealer lots. The carrying costs for these prebuilt but unsold units adds to the final sales price for all vehicles.

---

17 Tedeschi, "Construction Heads," p. C1.

18 This discussion has been adapted from the information in Keith Bradsher, "Carmakers to Buy Parts on Internet," *The New York Times*, February 26, 2000, p. A1.

19 Maintaining the vigor of competition was a major factor in the government's concern with and approval of the joint venture. See Karen Lundegaard, "FTC Clears Covisint, Big Three's Auto-Parts Site," *The Wall Street Journal*, September 12, 2000, p. A16.

20 Bradsher, "Carmakers to Buy," p. A1.

What if the customer could place a custom order today and have the vehicle delivered to the lot within 10 to 20 days? Would that entice some significant segment of buyers to switch from a prebuilt to a **build-to-order business model**? A model where customers could design a vehicle with options and color combinations (product attributes) that better fit their tastes, and for which they might pay a small price premium? The assemblers might be able to achieve faster delivery if the retail orders were placed electronically, with the parts requirements totaled electronically and daily (or hourly if needed), and then transmitted to the suppliers for immediate production as well as delivery.[21] This example of a **just-in-time inventory delivery system** is developed to the nth degree, from customer order all the way down to suppler parts. Under this electronic ordering system the inventory carrying costs could be reduced to the bare minimum, with the vehicles being made cheaper and faster, along with yielding greater satisfaction for the buyer. Here the benefits to the customer might not come in the form of a lower price, but in the guise of a product that yields greater value given the tailored attributes. Conversely, the benefits to the assembler and parts suppliers show up in the form of lower costs through more efficient supply-chain management.

With a bit of imagination and a little restructuring of the car-buying process, some of the gains from electronic ordering might be redistributed in favor of the buyer. As of 2001, 62 percent of new car buyers used the Internet to assist them in part or all of the car purchase process. These e-buyers saved an estimated average of $300 to $400 per vehicle relative to buyers who did not use the Internet.[22] As a way of increasing these gains, assume for a moment that instead of auto dealerships being dedicated to a particular vehicle brand, some became drop-off points for car orders and service centers for any car brand. Customers could come into this new age dealer's electronic store, configure their vehicle with the desired attributes and submit the specifications via the Web to any and all assemblers, asking for them to bid on the sale. Here, under this reverse auction scheme, consumers could gain some degree of market power, rather than being mostly at the mercy of the sales staff at the new car dealership. It's just a thought, but the concept demonstrates how the power of e-commerce, when harnessed to the Web, can potentially revolutionize the way in which business gets done, and how the distribution of the efficiency gains might be altered in favor of the consumer.

Efficiency Differences: B2B versus B2C

The preceding examples detailing the origin and types of B2B efficiencies appear to be in sharp contrast to the earlier discussions of the nature of B2C efficiencies that are experienced by pure Web e-tailers. Throughout most B2B net markets, the exchange serves only as an intermediary connecting buyers and sellers. The exchange never assumes ownership of the item being traded. Without either purchasing or holding the product, the exchange does not tie up its own funds. It avoids the labor-intensive process of shipping and receiving, and it does not experience the inventory charges associated with holding, shrinkage, or obsolescence. The chief products of a B2B portal are trade centralization and information exchange. Therefore, the financial resources of the exchange are directed toward assembling the IT hardware, creating the operational software along with the electronic the Web site, and information management that includes gathering and processing as well as distribution. Assembling the hardware, software, and site creation are one-time activities with periodic review, where the exchange may have little or no unique expertise or cost advantage. These tasks can be farmed out to third parties,

---

21 Currently, the best the assemblers can do is to allow potential buyers to build their car on the Web and determine the manufacturer's suggested retail price including all of the desired options. See Bernard Stamler, "The Web Doesn't Sell Cars But Lets Buyers Build Their Own," *The New York Times*, September, 26, 2001, p. G10.

22 Bob Tedeschi, "E-Commerce Report: The World Wide Web is emerging As a Powerful Force in Car Sales," *The New York Times*, September 16, 2002, p. C5.

who are cost-efficient experts in each field. The exchange then spends most of its time on the product, where it has an efficiency-enhancing expertise. It concentrates on doing what it knows best. Firms sign up and remain as loyal repeat users of the exchange for a variety of reasons. They may be dependent upon and must be linked to a few dominant customers. If firms are tempted to leave an exchange they would experience switching costs that inhibit the exit activity. Also, they would sacrifice any efficiency that results from trading at the current exchange. Electronic markets don't change the business model, they just improve the flow. The exchange takes procurement, which is an essential business task, and makes it faster, cheaper, and easier to do.

In contrast, B2C e-commerce firms are discovering that the origins of their cost efficiency are much narrower than for B2B firms. Moreover, they find themselves being faced with unexpected added costs that force e-sellers to surrender some or all of the efficiency gains that originally were thought to make e-tailing superior to retailing. The e-tailers have a big efficiency advantage over retailers in customer contact. Potential buyers reach them electronically. Therefore, e-tailers avoid the fixed costs of physical stores, with their expensive sales staffs, space for parking, and monthly utility fees. Without stores, the e-sellers stay away from the costs of maintaining distribution centers, and handling, and shipping products to the stores that must, in turn, hire the labor for self-stocking. The e-tailers also steer clear of the need for store security costs, including electronic surveillance and guards to deter theft. Lastly, e-tailers have an advantage in the mechanics of customer ordering and processing, which are accomplished electronically without cahiers, scanners, and floor space devoted to customer checkout.

What looked at first like a no-brainer triumph for the e-tailers has evolved into a more expensive operation that has eaten into their efficiency advantage over retailers.[23] Most e-tailers are trading a physical product rather than an intangible product such as information.[24] Therefore, they buy it from manufacturers and hold the item in a way that mimics retailers, tying up part of their capital in inventory carrying costs along with warehousing and handling expenses. In turn, these variable warehousing charges mean that e-tailers must invest in the construction of physical warehouses, just like retailers. A cost advantage for retailers over e-tailers is that retail customers do the labor-intensive acts of picking goods off the self and carrying them out of the store. Conversely, e-tailers pay order pickers to assemble the order and pack it for home shipment. Merchandise returns are a high-cost item for both retailers and e-tailers, but e-tailers are particularly vulnerable to this problem, especially those selling clothing items that can't be examined or tried on before purchase.

E-tailers discovered that, in addition to electronic contact, potential customers want voice contact or at least e-mail exchange with customer service representatives (CSR). E-commerce is not the pure self-service medium that it was originally thought to be. In response, some e-tailers set up live customer service chat lines, working with buyers in real time, to help them through the purchase process. CSRs are labor intensive and expensive, however, which further erodes any lingering cost advantages for pure e-tailers. E-tailers found it expensive to build brand awareness, spending hundreds of millions of dollars in a high-pitched flood of expensive national advertising campaigns.[25] Some e-tailers are opening physical stores or sending catalogs as a way of advancing brand identity and product awareness.[26] Such steps raise their costs in line

---

23 William M. Bulkeley and Jim Carlton, "E-Tail Gets Derailed: How Web Upstarts Misjudged the Game," *The Wall Street Journal*, April 5, 2000, p. A1.

24 E-tailers are in the information business, but instead of selling it to customers, the e-commerce divisions of major retailers are gathering data on customer buying patterns and sending the data back to the retail headquarters to help shape in-store merchandizing policies. See Bob Tedesci, "E-Commerce Report: Online Retail Profits Have Not Materialized," *The New York Times*, July 9, 2001, p. C7.

25 Bulkeley and Carlton, "E-Tail Gets Derailed," p. A1.

26 Rebecca Quick, "New Page in E-Retailing: Catalogs," *The Wall Street Journal*, November 30, 2000, p. B1; and Bob Tedeschi, "E-Commerce Report: Web and Catalog Businesses Are Crossing into Storefront Territory," *The New York Times*, November 20, 2000, p. C12.

with competing retailers, and work to downgrade the significance of the e-commerce revolution to where it is just the equivalent of adding another customer contact channel to those already available to traditional retailing. Lastly, the B2C customer is highly fragmented and potentially disloyal, being swayed by the lowest combined price for both product and shipping. As e-tailer offers of free shipping proliferated, it's little wonder that the Amazon.coms of the e-commerce world, with all of their network economies of scale and scope, found it extremely difficult to earn a profit, while their Wal-Mart competitors of the retailing world continued to expand and make money. In comparison, one key reason that eBay has been a shining star of profitability among a cadre of B2C failures is that the its characteristics and business model make eBay look and act more like a B2B firm than a B2C firm.

The Case of Orbitz.com: An Efficiency and Distributional Puzzle

In Chapters 2 and 9, this text raised questions concerning the unique consequences resulting from the creation of the travel site Orbitz.com. It was viewed both as a potential vehicle for vertical integration that would extend market dominance in the physical world into the world of e-commerce, and as a way to limit the profits as well as threaten the survival of travel agents. In the current context, Orbitz.com also serves as a good example of the range of efficiencies that can result from e-commerce trading, while at the same time demonstrating the distributional tension that surrounds the allocation of those efficiency gains.[27] Orbitz.com was created as a joint venture by five major airlines, including American, Delta, Northwest, Continental, and United. It sells flight tickets directly to buyers, cutting out the $12 to $14 per ticket fee collected by travel agents, the existing non-Web computerized airline ticket distribution systems such as Saber, and other Web-based ticket exchanges including Travelocity.com and Expedia.com. Without the fees charged by the intermediary, Orbitz.com can theoretically offer cheaper fares to both business and leisure travelers. As an added incentive to attract Web customers to the site, the five airlines have pledged to list all of their least expensive fares on Orbitz.com, thereby making it a preferred one-stop-shopping location for ticket purchases. Some of these inexpensive fares may not be available either to travel agents or other Web ticket sellers, which places them at a competitive disadvantage.

Currently, the Orbitz.com site is a clear benefit to consumers. It offers centralized shopping, with the lowest fares listed first, and the potential to force fares downward in the face of open competition among the participating airlines. Because it currently sells only 2 percent of the total number of airline tickets, it doesn't pose a threat to consumers or the travel industry as of yet. However, the possibility that Orbitz.com could expand its market share and that major airline firms could control the prime ticket distribution channel in the future, poses some serious challenges for the continued efficiency and consumer benefit resulting from the airline ticket market. Historically, the oligopolistic (dominant) firms within the airline industry reacted to competitive threats by temporarily lowering ticket prices, driving out or otherwise neutralizing the competitive threat, and then raising ticket prices back to or above their pre-rivalry level. This tactic would be particularly effective if it drove both travel agents and independent Web ticket exchanges out of the market. Clearly the issues of Web exchange efficiency and the distribution of those efficiency benefits among sellers, exchange owners, and buyers is a function of the degree of competitive vigor in the market. Absent the existence of persistent market power in the e-sale of airline tickets, the marketplace should work to the betterment of all parties.

---

27 The following discussion is based upon information adapted from David Wessel, "Airlines' Orbitz: Consumers' Friend or Foe?" *The Wall Street Journal*, August 29, 2002, p. A2.

EFFICIENCIES THROUGH WEB-BASED COLLABORATION

The preceding cases established that where information is the product, the Web, along with the use of B2B exchanges, can dramatically improve efficiency by speeding up the flow, while lowering the processing and transmission costs. Making products and services Web-based removes from the site owner the burden of creating and maintaining a proprietary interconnection system. The Internet technology that supports the Web, along with the interface hardware and browser software are "in the ether," to be used without cost and available to anyone or any firm that wishes to hook up to it. With proper security, firms don't hesitate to put large chunks of their internal businesses on the Web, especially their personnel transactions, from expense reports, to benefits records, to retirement plans. Companies see little need for a large and expensive staff in the office of human resources or elaborate intranets, internal communications systems set up and maintained by the firm, when employees can do these and other functions by going directly online with a browser and Internet connection. It's all an exchange of information, and employees feel more in control when they can access and review their records or make changes at their convenience. Of course those key strengths of the Web were noted in the introduction to this chapter. The Web offers the opportunity to expedite the flow of information and the ability to access that information anytime from anywhere.

Another efficiency-enhancing e-commerce use of the Web, whose benefits may eventually surpass the gains provided by B2B exchanges, or the buying of books at Amazon.com, involves **Web-based collaboration**. One of the goals for Covisint is that of collaborative product design where individual engineers or teams of individual specialists can engage in remote collaboration. Each member of the electronic team would be working on the same project from his or her own geographic location, to create a product that is greater in scope than could be accomplished by any one of them operating independently. The essence of **Internet synergy** is the collaborative intelligence of the Internet whole, which makes it greater than the sum of its individual parts. It is the Web information application of and counterpart to the economic concept of **increasing returns to scale**.

Even though Web-based collaboration may be a goal for Covisint, it is a reality for many other parts of the Web community.[28] For years, computer programmers from around the globe have worked together on the same project. Each would write his or her own share of code during working hours in a particular time zone. Then, as the sun set locally, programmers passed the work off to a collaborating programmer in another part of the world, where the workday was just beginning. For the firm, it was a 24/7 operation; like having three shifts of workers a day, but without having to pay extra for overtime or shift differentials, or having to appease a tired, overworked labor force. This remote collaboration is done over the Internet with the tools of e-mail, attachments, and shared Web pages. What the introduction of the Web did was to include a multimedia dimension to the straightforward system of Internet communication. With the Web came the ability to add sound, images, and motion to the words of the Internet. These tools allowed computers to interact in new and creative ways, challenging the humans behind the machines to alter their **electronic social interaction** as well. Paraphrasing Michael Schrage of the Media Laboratory at M.I.T., these tools helped to move the process of knowledge creation from sharing a design to creating a design together.[29]

With Web-based collaboration, scientists from around the globe will be able to use the Grid Physics Network (GriPhyN) to work together, link computers, and access the data from the operation of the new particle accelerator at the CERN Laboratory near Geneva, Switzerland. These tasks will be accomplished without requiring the scientists to leave their home laboratories. Remote collaborative science changes both the way in which research is conducted and way that individual scientists see their role in the discovery process. The open sharing of data and computing power encourages the open

---

28 The information in this section has been adapted from Katie Hafner, "Machine-Made Links Change the Way Minds Can Work Together," *The New York Times*, November 5, 2001, p. G3.

29 Hafner, "Machine-Made Links," p. G3.

sharing of ongoing results. Openness and sharing raise the possibility of a synergistic outcome where the collective findings from the collaborative effort are potentially greater than what could have been accomplished individually. In fact, without Web-based collaboration, which conveys universal accessibility, some scientists, with the potential to make substantial contributions, may not have been able to participate in the research at all. Therein lies the biggest potential benefit of any form of Web-based collaboration: its openness to new voices and new ideas. The biggest asset of the Web is not just the ability to handle information efficiently, but its ability to function as a vehicle for **universal connectivity**.

SUMMARY AND PROSPECTS

The discussion in this chapter pointed to the conclusion that from a transactions perspective, the Web is big, growing, and above all leads to the creation of economic efficiencies, particularly when the focus of the Web activity is the collection, processing, and transmission of various forms of information. The success of numerous B2B exchanges comes from their attention to this information function, linking buyers and sellers. Exchanges speed up the flow of the information exchange, creating a variety of potential efficiency points in the process of supply-chain management.

Exchanges are intermediaries that levy a toll as payment for their services. The tolls may be small relative to the gains that exchanges generate, but most participants in a business exchange show a profit-based reluctance to sacrifice even a small piece of their market power or gains. These opposing forces create a tension in the B2B marketplace as to how the market will be organized and how the efficiency benefits will be divided among the participants. Normally, disintermediation boosts profits; therefore look for bilateral exchanges or exchange hubs to become the norm, especially if the economically powerful firms are unable to benefit from their participation in an independent B2B exchange through the creation of an IPO. As with other economic markets, the distribution of the efficiency gains will be a function of the degree of interfirm competition, the extent of pricing power held by some of the participants, and the nature of the technology change. Remember, however, that consumers too have the potential to be winners in this efficiency distribution struggle if some coincidental changes take place in the marketing of retail products. The resolution of the distribution tension may not always go to those who are initially rich and powerful, an important lesson to be learned from the Web as it is applied to e-commerce.

The Web may not be the answer to the entire range of business inefficiencies. In certain industries, product characteristics, time sensitivity, or the nature of the exchange process may not lend itself to easy adaptation to the electronic exchange model. The existing phone, fax, and direct contact model may work just as well. Also, there appear to be important structural, behavioral, and characteristic differences between B2B and B2C applications of the exchange process. In particular, the information emphasis of B2B exchange is a much smaller part of B2C markets. Therefore, the opportunities for efficiency enhancement in B2C are less pronounced. In fact, they are so much less that some or all of the efficiency advantages possessed by e-tail firms over their retail rivals may be lost in the reality of the B2C world. Pure B2C e-tailing may not be a viable e-commerce life form in the long run.

What is viable and potentially of great benefit is the ability for all types of entities, commercial and noncommercial, to use the Web as a collaborative research, design, and information vehicle. Collaborative efforts offer the potential for synergies, where the results are greater than the contributions made by the sum of the parts. Economics refers to this process as increasing returns to scale. The global scope of the Web, with its ability to connect diverse people and ideas quickly, cheaply, and at any time, may lead to collaboration as being the greatest potential efficiency of them all. The ultimate asset of the Web may well be its connectivity.

KEY TERMS AND CONCEPTS

applications service provider
B2B exchange system
bilateral exchange
build-to-order business model
case 1 market
case 2 market
case 3 market
collaborative product development
cost minimization
direct electronic ordering approach
disintermediation
dynamic efficiency
efficiency paradox
efficiency within the firm
efficiency within the marketplace
electronic construction portal
electronic firewall
electronic ordering technology model
electronic social interaction
fax and phone technology model
functional exchange
horizontal exchange
implicit price deflator (IPD)
increasing returns to scale
independent trading exchange (ITE)

initial public offering (IPO)
intermediary
internet job boards
internet synergy
isocost lines
isoquant curves
just-in-time inventory delivery system
macroeconomic productivity
matching function
monopsony
net markets
oligopsony
output maximization
prebuild business model
project extranet
real gross domestic product (RGDP)
specialized markets
static efficiency
strengths of a Web-based exchange
    system
supply-chain management
trading hub
universal connectivity
web-based collaboration

DISCUSSION AND REVIEW QUESTIONS

1. Identify and discuss the strengths of a Web-based B2B exchanges system. Are these strengths for B2B exchanges similar to the strengths identified for B2C exchanges noted in Chapter 1? How so?

2. Identify and explain the nature of the distribution tension created by the efficiencies resulting from B2B e-commerce.

3. Distinguish between an isocost and an isoquant line. What determines the slope and location for each type of line? What determines the intercept of the isocost line? Does the isoquant line have an intercept? Why?

4. Use isoquant and isocost curves to demonstrate efficiency in the firm by comparing the consequences of output maximization with cost minimization. Can the firm pursue both goals simultaneously? Why?

5. Show graphically and explain how the introduction of B2B exchanges create dynamic efficiencies and alter the best practice choice of the firm. What factors influence the identity of the beneficiaries of this technological change?

6. Cite the rationale for the argument that the appearance of Web-based B2B exchanges led to a rise in overall productivity. Is this relationship conclusively causal? Why?

7. Identify the influence asserted by the tension between product variety and the value of human contact versus product conformity and impersonal dealing in determining the effectiveness of B2B exchanges. Under what circumstances are net markets, or B2B exchanges, most likely to generate efficiencies and become a dominant exchange force? Why are B2B exchanges unlikely to thrive in specialty markets?

8. What are electronic job boards? How do they improve the efficiency of the job search process?

9. What characteristics make the construction industry a potentially profitable target for Web-based B2B efficiency enhancement? How can firms in this industry benefit from e-commerce interaction?

10. Discuss how the Web-based build-to-customer-order business model might be structured to direct more of the efficiencies of the system to the buyer in the form of lower product prices.

11. Explain why efficiencies and cost savings are more difficult to capture within electronic B2C markets as opposed to B2B markets. How do these obstacles facing e-tailers give retailers a fighting chance to attract customers?

12. Explain how Orbitz.com is both a potential benefit and threat to the airline ticket buyer. What forces can work to keep the harmful consequences in check? Why?

13. Identify the concept of Internet synergy. Explain how this synergy is created by Web-based collaboration.

WEB EXERCISES

1. Link to the Web site for the U.S. Department of Commerce at **http://www. census.gov/mrts/www/current.html** to examine the most recent data for retail and e-tail sales.

2. Link to the Covisint Web site at **http://www.covisint.com/**. Click on the most recent press releases to see the progress and efficiencies being introduced by the centralized buying power of the major auto assemblers.

3. Link to the following sites as a way of seeing the different focus for each type of B2B exchange: **http://www.imark.com/**, **http://www.chemconnect.com/**, **http://www.dell.com/us/en/gen/default.htm**, and **http://www.covisint.com/**

4. Four of the largest electronic job boards are located at **http://www.monster.com/**, **http://www.jobsonline.com/**, **http://www.careerbuilder.com/**, and **http://www.hotjobs.com/**. Link to at least two of the sites and compare the information format and cost of participation. Search for the same job on both sites and compare the results.

5. Some of the largest construction exchanges are located at **http://www.citadon. com/**, **http://www.buildpoint.com/home.html**, and **http://www.viecon.com/en/ default.asp**. Link to each of these sites and compare the quality of the information on their homepage as well as their range of building services.

6. Link to the Web-based airline ticket exchanges **http://www.orbitz.com/** and **http://www.travelocity.com/**. Search for the ticket prices on a one-week round trip ticket from Los Angles to Dallas, or from Miami to New York. Do the in ticket prices differ? If so, which site has the lowest fares?

CHAPTER

14

Introductory Case

LOUDCLOUD GOES PUBLIC

In Chapter 3, the text noted that the technology of the Web and the advent of the browser had transformed the Internet from its origins as a vehicle designed to support national defense and scientific communications, into a system designed to organize and retrieve information. In turn, this simplicity of Web access and information flow opened up an entirely new set of opportunities for commercialization of the Internet through e-commerce. This latter transformation is just one example of the potentially unpredictable and disruptive nature of technological change. Technological change is one of the forces that generate product or service gaps in the market that lead to what the economist Joseph Schumpeter referred to as the process of **creative destruction**. Entrepreneurs see these gaps and envision the birth of profitable new business models, new products, new markets, and new ideas as well as more efficient ways to conduct current transactions. Often the entrepreneur will be motivated to create a new firm as a way to capture some of these opportunities. The topics examined in this and the next chapters detail how, as part of the Internet age, entrepreneurial e-commerce firms were encouraged, financed, and either grew and survived or floundered and failed as they sought to fill market gaps.

The tale begins with Loudcloud, just one of hundreds of e-firms that reached the stage of public investment during the heyday of the Internet investment craze. Loudcloud (now known as Opsware Inc. and listed with the

stock ticker symbol OPSW) is a global outsourcing services firm that uses proprietary software to manage and automate a wide range of Internet-site infrastructure and activities for enterprise firms.[1] It has specialized expertise to host and automatically monitor client Internet activity to keep Web sites from crashing when thousands of customers try to access the site simultaneously. The firm has an impressive client list including EDS, MetLife, Adidas, Blockbuster, Cablevision, Fannie Mae, Ford Motor Company, and USAToday.com among others. Loudcloud was founded in 1999 by a core of well-known Internet professionals including Marc Andreessen, who was one of the founders of the highly successful browser firm Netscape. It quickly secured first-round private financing, including money from Benchmark Capital, a leading private venture capital (VC) firm.[2] Quarter by quarter, the firm increased its client base, boosted its revenues, and reduced the size of both its pro forma and net income losses.[3] It is a growing firm, with a valuable product, a dominant market position, and experienced leadership that should guide it to GAAP profitability some time in the future. All it needed was more money to sustain the losses until it achieved sufficient scale to become profitable.

Private investors in general become leery about being the major risk takers in a mature, start-up firm. They become concerned about having to constantly put more dollars into a promising, but as yet, money-losing enterprise. Also VC investors want to be able to withdraw their money, hopefully with a profit, to be reinvested in today's most promising new start-ups. Consequently, Loudcloud executives decided to take the firm public, with an **initial public offering (IPO)**. An IPO allows the firm to sell

---

1 For more information, link to the firm at **http://www.loudcloud.com/**.

2 Suzanne McGee, Mylene Mangalindan, and Lisa Bransten, "Doing an Internet IPO in This Climate Takes Grit, Loudcloud Learns," *The Wall Street Journal*, April 6, 2001, p. A1.

3 See Web Host News, available at **http://thewhir.com/marketwatch/ops082302.cfm**.

Venture Capitalists and IPOs

some of the ownership shares in the broader equity market. For many start-ups, the IPO will raise the final round of working capital that should tide the firm over until it becomes profitable. Undertaking an IPO would also create an actual market-determined dollar value for Loudcloud, and provide the market **liquidity** to allow some or all of the early-stage private VC investors to sell their shares at a possible profit. Exactly why then is the firm being taken public? Is it because the firm has reached a level of business maturity where survival and actual profitability are reasonably at hand? Or is it because the original investors want out after breathing some life into a promising concept that turned out empty.

An IPO is legal activity that is highly regulated by the Securities and Exchange Commission (SEC). It is accompanied by a **prospectus** that spells out in some detail the risks and uncertainties associated with the company and its future. The prospectus serves as a **caveat emptor**, or a buyer-beware warning to potential stock market investors. The fact is that many investors from among the general public, even those who are attracted to IPOs, are less informed and sophisticated than the relatively more savvy venture capitalists. With an IPO, some of the ownership of the firm is passing from a limited number of experienced investors to a much larger number of smaller, less knowledgeable investors. Herein lies the functional tension that is part of the **VC-IPO model of firm creation**: on the one hand it is an efficient vehicle for the creation of new companies, while on the other, it is a way to create and sell stocks at a profit for the early investors. This tension raises a number of questions. For example, is the model designed to enhance the creation of long-run wealth and value, or is it simply a way for VC inside investors to make a fast buck? Do VC-IPO activities primarily serve the interest of society or the interests of VC investors? Are the two outcomes necessarily in conflict with one another? What has been the recent history of VC-IPO activity as it related to e-commerce firms? What market forces work to determine the economic benefits or losses resulting from the VC-IPO model of firm creation?

THE LOGIC AND EFFICIENCY OF THE VC-IPO INVESTMENT MODEL

Market gaps and entrepreneurial vision may be a driving force behind capitalistic progress, but a potential problem comes with the birth of e-commerce firms or any other gap-filling business activity. The entrepreneurs who see the gaps and conceive of ways to fill them profitably may not be the individuals who have the resources to carry out those plans. After all, the concept of **entrepreneurship** covers many functions. Perhaps the most visible one is where the individual serves as an innovator, or person who develops a commercial application of an invention and brings it to the marketplace.[4] Other key entrepreneurial functions including serving as a risk-taker, a decision maker, or acting as a catalyst to bring the other resources together along with organizing the production process. A lot of people come up with commercial ideas but lack the managerial ability or money to carry them out. Conversely, more than a few people with a lot of money possess little insight as to how to put that money to work profitably in a commercial enterprise. Occasionally, the innovator and risk taker may meet at a business seminar or through a social contact. They may discuss common business interests, reach a meeting of the minds, and form a **partnership**, with each specializing in what he or she does best. This type of partnership is one of the purposes and potential outcomes of human networking with business and personal colleagues.

Partnerships that are fashioned in this way can be risky, however, and are certainly an inefficient way of constructing a business marriage. Allocating funds in this manner is akin to participating in a form of **investor roulette**. What entrepreneurship needs is a marketplace where innovators and potential financial investors can be brought together quickly, cheaply, and at reduced risk. As with any **Schumpeterian market gap**, someone will fill the gap if it includes a potential for profit. Hence, the emergence of the venture capitalist and the creation of the venture capital firm. The **venture capitalist** is an intermediary who unites risk takers and innovators. A **venture capital firm** is typically structured as a **limited partnership** in that partners are responsible for losses only to the extent of their financial participation in the firm. In this way the partnership acts like a corporation where personal fortunes of the VC partners are shielded from being taken by creditors. It is registered with the Securities and Exchange Commission and composed of investing partners as well as managing partners. The **managing partners** organize the VC firm and use their business experience as well as investment expertise to actively run the enterprise. They typically put up 1 to 3 percent of the firm's assets and solicit the remainder of the funds from the **investing partners**, who are passive participants, entrusting their money to the skills and experience of the managing partners. For their efforts, the managing partners charge annual fees amounting to an average of 2 percent of the invested funds.[5] They also retain the **carry**, which is anywhere from 20 to 35 percent of the profits of the VC firm, as compensation for their expertise in investing the money of the funding partners. If the managing partners do well in selecting investment targets, then everyone receives a high rate of return on the invested funds.

(Some definitional distinctions are important here between the ways in which some concepts are used in economics and finance. In economics, the term *capital* refers to the tangible, human-made resources, such as buildings, machinery, tools, or equipment, that go into the production process. The term *investment* describes the act of acquiring these tangible, productive capital resources. In the financial field, *capital* refers to money used to start or run a business. The term *investment* describes the flow of these capital funds into the firm by the owners or investors. Even though this text presents e-commerce economics principles, the financial definitions for these terms apply in this chapter.)

Venture capital investing is a high-risk, exceedingly speculative activity. The VC firm is often placing bets on unproven start-ups that may exist on the cutting edge of technology and commercial ideas, with little or no revenues, lots of potential early losses, and only the hope of future profits. As shown in Figure 14-1, the VC firm assumes a level of risk much higher than other funding sources might be willing to accept. After

---

4 Note the difference between *invention* and *innovation*. An **inventor** comes up with a new product or method of doing business. The **innovator** turns the product or process into a commercial application. Inventors and innovators can be one and the same, but are not always the same person. The McDonald brothers invented the contemporary fast-food concept, but Ray Kroc was the entrepreneur who franchised the idea of a simple, inexpensive menu of hamburgers, fries, and a milkshake, turning it into a global commercial enterprise. See Eric Schlosser, *Fast Food Nation: The Dark Side of the All-American Meal* (New York: Penguin Books, 2001).

5 Amy Cortese, "Venture Capital, Withering and Dying," *The New York Times*, October 21, 2001, p. 3–1.

Risk Reward Continuum for Sources of Firm Funding	**FIGURE 14-1**

Highest Risk   Lowest Risk
Highest Expected Return   Lowest Expected Return

HH   LL

| VC Firms | Stock Market Investors | Bank Lenders | Commercial Paper Lenders | Bond Holders |

all, if the entrepreneurial start-up could get money from a bank, the bond market, the commercial paper market, or the stock market, they would be well advised to do so. Often, in exchange for the high-risk funding, the VC firm takes over a portion of the ownership of the start-up. Why then would the entrepreneur give up an ownership share of a cherished idea or product? The answer is simple, without the VC funding no firm exists to support and promote the entrepreneurial idea. The entrepreneur gains by retaining a fraction of something operational, which is usually preferable to holding 100 percent of an idea that is nonfunctional. Therefore, the VC firm performs an important efficiency function on the continuum of firms that supply funds to various businesses. VC firms provide high-risk dollars to the most fragile of firms. However, VC investors subscribe to the expectation that, even though many of these firms will fail with the loss of all funds, enough will be big winners and provide spectacular returns to compensate for the assumption of the added degree of risk. At the other end of the risk-return continuum, **bondholders** lend money to the firm in exchange for a predictable interest payment and the eventual return of the loaned funds. They are creditors whose standing is superior to that of firm owners or **stockholders** in the event that the firm fails. However, unlike a stockholder, they do not usually participate in the profits of the firm. Therefore, bondholders are a low-risk, low-return source of funding.

VC investors purchase a share of the start-up entity, wait for it to become profitable, and then enjoy a stream of economic profits over the expected life of the firm. Right? Well not exactly, which is where the IPO concept and the firms such as Loudcloud come into play.

VENTURE CAPITAL AND IPO ANNUAL DATA

Both the number and dollar volume of total venture capital activity rose dramatically during the second half of the 1990s. Much of this rapid rise involved the funding of nascent Internet firms. The expansion was so rapid that it led to a fear that the birth of the Internet as an e-commerce entity created an unsustainable speculative financial bubble. This fear was borne out starting in March of 2000 as both the Dow and Nasdaq stock indexes began their steep and prolonged declines.

At the end of 2000, more than 1,000 venture capital firms were in operation, which was twice the number in existence as of 1995.[6] Together, they managed some $200 billion in investor funds. Data on VC activity is collected quarterly by PriceWaterhouseCoopers as part of their MoneyTree survey of the largest 1,000 venture capital firms.[7] The data in Figure 14-2 show that the number of overall **rounds of VC financing** rose by more than 425 percent, from a low of 1,313 in 1995 to a peak of

---

6 Cortese, "Venture Capital, Withering," p. 3–1.

7 The most recent data is available at **http://www.pwcmoneytree.com**. The quarterly data is tabulated in conjunction with the National Venture Capital Association, available at **http://www.nvca.com**.

FIGURE 14-2   Venture Capital Funding Rounds

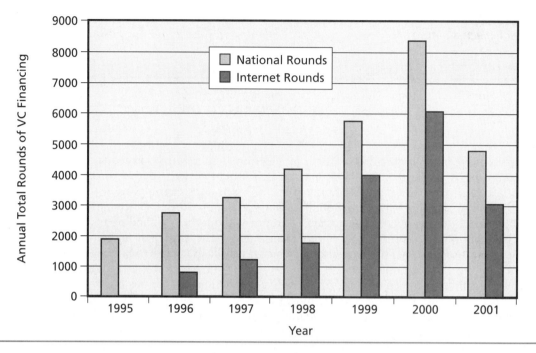

Source: PriceWaterhouseCoopers, available at **http://www.pwcmoneytree.com**.

5,630 in 2000. Financing rounds include **seed financing** at the earliest stage before the management team has come together; first, second, third, and later financing rounds as the firm grows to produce and sell their product; and, lastly, **mezzanine financing**, which raises the last round of venture money just prior to embarking upon an IPO.

The decline in the stock market combined with the onset of a recession in March 2001, helped to cut the number of financing rounds in 2001. During the expansion period, the number of **Internet-related financing rounds** grew even faster at almost 650 percent, going from 689 in 1996 to 4,470 in 2000.[8] Given the frenzied interest in Internet-related business opportunities, it was not surprising to see that Internet-related financing rounds grew significantly as a share of all VC financing activity, rising from 37 percent of all financing rounds in 1996 to 79 percent in 2000.

As both the number and relative share of Internet-related financing rounds rose, the amount of money directed into Internet and e-commerce start-ups rose as well. Figure 14-3 shows that in 1995, the total dollar volume of all VC financing amounted to almost $6.85 billion. This dollar figure grew by 1,320 percent to $90.5 billion in 2000. The growth in the volume of dollars allocated to high-risk venture activity was heavily driven by the attractiveness of funding for Internet-related start-up firms. Dollar funding for Internet start-ups rose from $3.2 billion in 1996 to $74.8 billion in 2000, or by 2,338 percent. Lastly, Internet start-up funding, as a share of all VC dollar investments, rose from 32 percent in 1996 to 83 percent in 2000. Financial speculation in Internet and e-commerce firms appeared to be rampant.

---

8 Funds directed to firms in the Internet-related subcategory include those providing business service for online sales, e-tailers and online auctioneers, content providers, ISPs, Internet infrastructure firms, software, and database maintenance firms. The MoneyTree survey results did not provide Internet subcategory data for 1995.

Venture Capital Funding Totals   **FIGURE 14-3**

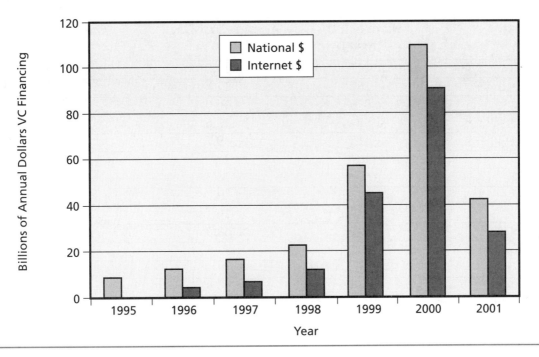

Source: PriceWaterhouseCoopers, available at **http://www.pwcmoneytree.com/PDFS/GPEreport%202001.pdf,** February 2002.

The Level of IPO Activity

The numbers representing the level of IPO activity are almost as stunning. Prof. Jay R. Ritter, at the University of Florida, maintains a Web site that tracks the annual number of IPOs with an offer price of $5 or more.[9] Professor Ritter also calculated the average percentage first-day return to initial investors, as well as the gross proceeds from the sale of the stock at the offer price. A portion of this information is reproduced in Table 14-1. What the data show is that from 1990 to 2000, the number of new IPOs rose from 111 in 1990 to a peak of 664 in 1996. The number of IPOs subsequently slackened a bit from that peak, but the gross proceeds derived from those offerings continued to rise, going from $4.45 billion in 1990 to a peak of $66.1 billion in 2000, or an increase of 1,485 percent.[10] Lastly, the average first-day return for an IPO went from a respectable 10.5 percent gain in 1990 to a whopping 68.6 percent average return in 1999, a more than sixfold increase.

To be sure, periods of intense IPO activity occurred prior to the 1990s. For example, in 1983, 523 IPOs raised a bit more than $12 billion, with an average first-day return of 8.8 percent. Still, the 10-year stretch from 1990 to 1999 saw a 76 percent rise in the number of IPOs, a threefold gain in the average first-day return and a nearly fivefold rise in the amount of money raised relative to the previous decade of the 1980s. In the year 2000 alone, more money was gathered in by IPOs than was raised in all of the IPOs for the period of 1980 to 1989. Granted the numbers are not subdivided to show the data for just Internet- or e-commerce-related IPOs. It might be

---

9 See the summary statistics collected and tabulated by Prof. Jay R. Ritter at **http://bear.cba.ufl. edu/ritter/killian.pdf**.

10 The dollar amounts are in **current dollar terms**. The 2000 figure would be lower by about 40 percent if it were expressed in **constant dollar terms**, minus inflation, using the CPI.

TABLE 14-1			IPO Activity, 1990–2000
Year	**Number IPO Offerings**	**Average First-Day Return %**	**Gross Proceeds ($ mil.)**
1990	111	10.5	4,453
1991	287	11.7	15,765
1992	396	10.0	22,198
1993	503	12.6	29,232
1994	412	9.7	18,103
1995	464	21.1	28,866
1996	664	16.5	41,916
1997	483	13.7	33,216
1998	318	20.1	34,850
1999	491	68.6	65,471
2000	385	55.5	66,100
1980–89	2,348	6.9	62,596
1990–99	4,129	20.9	294,070

Source: Prof. Jay R. Ritter, University of Florida, available at **http://bear.cba.ufl.edu/ritter/killian.pdf**.

inferred, however, given the amount of VC dollars directed toward Internet start-ups, that many of these were likely to have been Internet-related IPOs. VC dollars generate considerable pressures directed toward getting the start-ups to the stage of a public marketing of the stock as quickly as possible. The age of the firm from founding to an IPO averaged 6.2 years in 1990. The average lead time dropped to 4.0 years in 2000, and an increasing number were going public only a year or two subsequent to their founding.[11] Consequently, knowingly or not, purchasers of IPO stock in the late 1990s were acting more like **late-stage venture capitalists** than traditional investors in an ongoing concern. In 1999, only 25 percent of the firms were profitable at the time of the IPO.[12] As late-stage VC they were assuming more risk than their IPO investor counterparts of 10 years ago.

The Origin of Funds for Venture Capital Investments

Where do VC firms get their high-risk funds? Who puts money into high-risk investments and why? Table 14-2 contains data indicating that these firms get their dollars from a wide range of investment sources. Individuals and families have been supplying an increasing share and ever-rising amount of total VC dollars. This source provided almost 19 percent of total VC dollars as of 1999, up from 4.2 percent in the 1985-1990 period. Conversely, less of the money is coming from institutional investors such as pension funds, down from 59.2 percent in 1985–1990 to just 20 percent in 1999. This decline is somewhat unexpected considering the large, growing pools of long-term retirement funds, and the potential interest of pension funds in diversifying a small portion of their investments into high-risk, but potentially high-return VC activities. Again, the direction of movement was away from larger

---

11 Steve Lipin, "Venture Capitalists 'R' Us," *The Wall Street Journal*, February 22, 2000, p. C1.
12 Lipin, "Venture Capitalists 'R' Us," p. C1.

					Banks Insurance Co.	**Non-financial Corp.**	
Year	**Persons Families**	**Pension Funds**	**Endowments Foundations**	**Intermediaries**			**Government**
1985-90	4.2	59.2	0	0	13.7	11.3	11.6
1990-95	14.5	41.9	15.6	1.8	10.4	10.8	0.6
1999	18.9	20.0	18.2	10.9	10.5	12.7	0

Sources of Venture Capital Funding by Percent   **TABLE 14-2**

Source: "Venture Capitalists 'R' Us," *The Wall Street Journal*, February 22, 2000, p. C1.

professional funding sources, which are better able to diversify their risks and bear up under any losses, and into numerous smaller funding entities, who were less sophisticated, perhaps less diversified and less able to withstand investment losses. Perhaps the glitter of potential IPO rewards worked to blind individual investors as to the risks that they were taking.

With almost 13 percent of the VC dollars, some of the nation's largest nonfinancial firms, both traditional and high-tech, have become significant sources of venture capital funds.[13] Intel, the leading maker of computer chips, created a venture capital arm, Intel Capital, in 1990. At first, they took on strategic investments in related companies such as chip-making equipment firms. The investments were seen as an adjunct to Intel's own R&D budget, with the products from the equipment firms helping Intel to better design and manufacture its own chips. However, they soon expanded their investment objectives from chip-related activities into Internet-related firms. It is important for Intel, which makes most of the chips that power the computers and servers that access the Internet, that the Internet continues to grow globally. Intel holds investment stakes in more than 425 companies including 70 in Asia, where it placed $400 million in VC funds into a variety of Internet and telecommunications firms.[14] Intel is not the only giant firm with VC investments. The ranks of traditional corporations with VC capital investments include General Electric, Microsoft, IBM, and Comcast. Some are looking for strategic links, others are hoping to sell products to the fledgling firms as they grow, while a few are looking for a higher return on their funds than they might be able to earn through internal expansion. On some occasions the investments were just a form of **crony capitalism**. Here, investment by a high-profile, large firm in a small start-up would help raise the credibility of the start-up, which might make it easier to take the start-up public at a high IPO price, yielding big profits for the helpful investing firm. Regardless of motive, existing corporations were an important source of VC capital funds.[15]

---

13 Knight Ridder, "Corporations Use Start-ups as Strategy," *Connecticut Post*, June 9, 2000, p. B5.

14 Karen Richardson, "Venture Firms in Asian Markets Watch and Wait," *The Wall Street Journal*, October 30, 2001, p. B11L.

15 One of the more interesting venture capital funds is In-Q-Tel, which is funded entirely by the U.S Central Intelligence Agency. It invests in private firms developing products involving internal security including Web-based security and information flow. Some $2 billion per year in research money is also available from the U.S. Department of Defense through its funding arm the Defense Advanced Research Projects Agency, or DARPA. Money from this agency helped to fund the creation of the Internet as well as the stealth bomber. See Amy Crotese, "Suddenly, Uncle Sam Wants to Bankroll You," *The New York Times*, December 30, 2001, p. 3-1.

The Importance of VC Activity to the U.S. Economy

Venture capital investment may create wealth for individuals, but it also leads to the birth of jobs and income for members of the workforce, as well as contributing to the overall level of U.S. gross domestic product. In 2001, the National Venture Capital Association commissioned an independent assessment from the economic research firm DRI-WEFA, of the current overall impact that VC investments from 1970-2000 have had.[16] The results of the study showed that some $273.3 billion in VC invested funds created 7.6 million jobs and more than $1.3 trillion in revenue in the year 2000. These figures amounted to 5.9 percent of total U.S. employment and 13.1 percent of U.S. GDP. The investments were in a wide range of industries including computers, consumer goods, medical health communications, energy, electronics, and biotech. Most of these industries experienced considerable technological change, which helped to erode the market power of the existing dominant firms, allowing entrepreneurial start-ups to emerge with new strategies and products. The job and revenue numbers portray an admirable track record considering that that invested VC funds amounted to less than 1 percent of the value of all investment over the 30-year time period.

The NVCA study broke down impact figures for 2000 by state, with California leading the way in both job creation, at 1.4 million, and in revenues generated, with $270.6 billion. The states of Texas, New York, Georgia, Massachusetts, Washington, Pennsylvania, and New Jersey were also in the top 10 for both categories. Not surprisingly, these same eight states made the list of the top 10 locations hosting firms within their borders that received the most in venture dollar investments. Each of the top 18 states had more than 100,000 jobs attributable to VC investing, with Michigan the lowest at 103.6 thousand. The top 15 states each had revenues generated by firms created through VC activity in excess of $20 billion, with the lowest state being Connecticut at $22.9 billion. The list of the fastest-growing 15 states for VC investment for the period 1996-2001 was topped by Maryland (58.9 %), Minnesota (35.7 %), and Massachusetts (35.3 %). Even lower-ranking states such as Florida (13), Virginia (14) and Illinois (15) had five-year compound annual VC investment growth rates of 14 percent or higher. Although these numbers are impressive, they clearly represent investments in a multitude of industries and not just in e-commerce-related activity. However, the data show the potential positive affects that VC investing can have on the recipients, their regional locations, and the nation as a whole.

The Extent of Global Venture Capital Activity

Venture capital activity is not limited to the United States. Almost every region worldwide experienced an upsurge in VC investment over the past few years. As with their domestic data, the PriceWaterhouseCoopers MoneyTree survey led in tracking the level of global VC activity.[17] The United States was by far the number one source of investment funds raised ($153.9 billion) and with the most invested ($122.1 billion) in 2000. The United Kingdom was a distant second with $16.3 billion raised and $12.2 billion invested. Other key nations included Germany (4) at $5.7 and $4.4 billion, Israel (6) at $3.3 and $3.2 billion, Hong Kong/China (8) at $5.8 and 2.2 billion, and Japan (10) at $4.5 and $2.0 respectively.

In North America, the level of private equity and venture capital investment in 2000 rose by 27 percent relative to 1999, an amount equal to 1.19 percent of the region's GDP. For Western Europe, investment rose by 20 percent, but equaled a much smaller 0.39 percent of the region's GDP. One of the largest gains in VC investing occurred in

---

16 See NVCA, "Three Decades of Venture Capital Investment Yields 7.6 Million Jobs and $1.3 Trillion in Revenue," available at **http://www.nvca.com**, Industry Research, Venture Capital Statistics (release date October 22, 2001).

17 PriceWaterhousesCoopers, "Global Private Equity 2001," available at **http://www.pwcmoneytree. com/PDFS/GPEreport%202001.pdf**, February 2002.

the Middle Eastern African area, up by 172 percent to $3.7 billion in 2000, equal to 1.6 percent of the area's GDP. Finally, the largest advance was registered in the Central and South American area with a gain of 429 percent. Investment in this region also totaled $3.7 billion.

These national and regional comparisons are informative for the following reasons. First they show that most areas of the globe are supporting new ideas and strategies. Even regions with less-developed public capital markets and IPO prospects are recognizing the economic value of financing new firms. Human ingenuity, creativity, entrepreneurship, and risk taking are not limited to the United States alone. People are willing to marry money with new ideas, even in parts of the world where incomes are relatively low and investments in high-risk projects might not be expected. The success of these investments holds out the prospect of faster future rates of economic growth in these regions. Second, the data show how extensive the U.S. VC effort really is. Not every funded idea is a good idea, capable of surviving and prospering on its own. Also, the United States with a great expanse of wealth will surely squander funds on poorly conceived projects, but part of the suspense of VC investing is in not knowing which projects will turn out to be commercial hits and which will fail. By funding a larger number of activities, U.S. VC firms are at least raising the potential absolute number of successes. More importantly, the relatively ready availability of VC funds encourages more dreamers to hone their ideas into entrepreneurial initiatives and to present them for funding review. VC dollars and funding activity encourage and reinforce the **economic pluralism** of the marketplace, which in turn raises the potential for increased future U.S growth in GDP.

Lastly, U.S. VC activity is impressive not just because of its absolute size, but also because of its relative lead over the rest of the world. Outside the United States, the sum total of global VC activity was just a bit more than one-third that of America. The U.S. lead over some of its global competitors such as Germany and Japan is impressive. Other regions may be growing rapidly in percentage terms, but their absolute numbers are still small. When dreamers want to see their ideas turned into entrepreneurial reality, the place to go is clearly the United States. This **brain drain**, where the United States attracts some of the best and brightest entrepreneurs from foreign nations, is likely to continue into the future. VC funding has helped to keep the United States as the preeminent land of economic opportunity. Despite all of this national and global VC activity, a practical warning is called for: the quality and results of the spending are far more important measures of VC effectiveness than the absolute amount being invested.

THE ROLE OF VENTURE CAPITAL FIRMS IN THE E-COMMERCE IPO FRENZY

The existence and activities of venture capital firms make a positive contribution to the functioning of financial markets. First, the role of venture capital firms as an expert intermediary, bringing together entrepreneurs who need money and money sources that need profitable outlets for their funds, serves a valuable and efficient economic function. Second, the VC firm as an investment vehicle engages in both a pooling of funds and a **diversification of portfolio risk**. Even though all of the start-ups that the firm invests in are high risk, not all are anticipated to fail. The traditional view anticipated three to four out of every 10 start-up investments would be expected to fail with the loss of all funds. Three to four would be expected to generate some returns to the investors, while two to three would reap huge profits and more than compensate for the losses.[18] The few home runs would justify the numerous strikeouts. With a **pooling of funds**, no single VC investor would have all of its money tied up in a failing start-up. All investing partners in a given VC fund would loose a fraction of their money with the failures, and

---

18 Peter Elstrom, "The Great Internet Money Game," *BusinessWeek*, April 16, 2001, pp. EB16-24.

gain a fraction of the profits with the successes.[19] The risks would be spread across a large number of start-ups so as to increase the probability of a positive net return. Relying on managing experts to do the investing further raised the likelihood of a successful outcome. With both pooling and diversification the VC firm performs the valuable financial function of reducing the risks for the investing partners.

Most entrepreneurs begin their business adventure with money obtained from **angels**, or friends and family, who put up the initial **seed money**. But they quickly run out of rich or willing friends and begin to put together a formal business plan that can be presented to the executive committee of a VC firm. The turndown rate for funding appeals is high.[20] If the entrepreneur has a good idea and makes an effective presentation, however, the VC firm may make a funding offer. Keep in mind that the VC firm is offering high-risk ownership money, and before the investment can be made, the parties must agree on a value for the firm as well as how much is to be surrendered in exchange for the funding.[21]

A tension arises within the **start-up valuation problem**. The entrepreneur wants to set as high a value for the firm, with as small a share of ownership being given to the investor, as possible in return for a fixed amount of money. Conversely, the VC firm wants to place a low value on the start-up at the time of funding commitment, and thereby receive a high fraction of the firm's equity value in trade for the given dollar investment. This desire for a low valuation creates a contradiction for the VC firm. The VC managing partners are now persuaded to put their own money into the start-up because it has great potential. However, to get the most equity ownership in return for their investment, the VC firm must now argue to the entrepreneur that the idea is not worth as much as the entrepreneur thinks it is. At first, the VC firm might appear to hold the upper hand in these negotiations. After all, they control the cash. However, for the most promising start-ups with a list of prominent founders or the best promise of quick profitability, a bidding war may ensue among VC firms to provide sizable financial support in return for minimal equity participation. After reaching an agreement, the start-up becomes a closely held corporation with shares held by the founders, angels, and the VC firm.

With the money in hand, a professional VC firm does not just let the entrepreneur go away and do his or her own thing. The VC firm will meet frequently with the entrepreneur, perhaps have managing partners sit on the board of directors and in general provide advice, experience, support, and discipline in the early stages. The managing partners have been through the birth of many businesses in the past and offer valuable insight. After all, it's partly their money and a strong possibility remains that the firm will come back for more rounds of funding before it reaches the point of profitability or an IPO. In the 1990s, some of the VC firms went to the extreme of setting up **business incubators**, or locations offering both physical and managerial support of their most fragile investments.[22] Firms such as Internet Capital Group, CMGI and Idealab! supplied physical office space, administrative support, and legal services along with the funding. This arrangement allowed the VC firm to keep close tabs on the start-up and to cross-fertilize their development with that of other start-ups in the VC firm's stable.

---

19 The returns can be staggering. Juniper Networks earned more than 5,000 times the invested capital for its VC investors. See Cortese, "Venture Capital, Withering," p. 3–1. The IPO for a firm called CacheFlow netted a gain of 525 percent in one day for buyers of the IPO stock, a 14,342 percent gain for round one or Series A investors, a 5,491 percent gain for round two or Series B investors, and a 2,662 percent return for the less risky round three or Series C investors. Suzanne McGee, "CacheFlow: The Life Cycle of a Venture-Capital Deal," *The Wall Street Journal*, February 22, 2000, p. C1.

20 One prominent VC firm, Garage Technology Ventures, is reported to have received 10,000 business plans for potential funding in 1999. See Max Boot, "The New Economy Learns the Old Rules," *The Wall Street Journal*, June 12, 2000, p. A30.

21 McGee et al., "Doing an Internet IPO," p. A1.

22 Elstrom, "The Great Internet," p. 22.

Investment Bankers Underwrite the IPO

If the start-up is fortunate, it gets the business up and running, produces a product, finds some buyers, and begins to generate gross revenues. Chapter 12 showed that gross revenues are different from profits. However, a firm with a product and a growing number of satisfied customers will create an excitement about the prospects for the firm. If this buzz of excitement is loud enough, or can be made to appear so, it may attract the attention of one or more investment bankers. An **investment banker (IB)** is a firm, such as Goldman Sachs, Merrill Lynch, Morgan Stanley, or Credit Suisse First Boston among many others, that **underwrites** the IPO. In this process, the IB lines up the legal and financial aspects of an IPO as well as finds buyers for the stock. These firms make money from their underwriting fees. The aggregate of IPO underwriters earned more than $2.1 billion in fees from 1997 through 2001.[23] An IPO underwriting offer from an IB also can entice the start-up's management team and VC investors with the potential of stock market liquidity and the ability to earn high profits from the equity sale of their original investments. Therefore the profit sources for both the VC and IB firms are different from that of the IPO investors. The investors look to make money out of the increases in equity value after the IPO, while the IB reap fee income from the IPO itself, and the VC reaps capital gains from the sale of their relatively lower cost, pre-IPO investments. For the most promising Internet start-ups aggressive competitive bidding among the IBs took place to see who would bring the IPO to market.[24]

The IBs play a crucial role in the financial process. They perform the **due diligence review** to determine the quality of the business plan and the soundness of the financial footing of the start-up before bringing it public. They are motivated to be cautious in their review because the first purchasers of the stock in an IPO are often the existing institutional and individual clients of the IB. The clients rely upon the underwriting standards of the IB to ensure the reasonableness of the investment. No rational IB would want to mislead or alienate their best clients, who generate revenues for the IB in other areas. Although not a guarantee of firm survival and profit, the underwriting review provides a professional financial filter to ensure that only those firms that are ripe for public offering get to the IPO stage. In the years prior to 1995, one rule of thumb of underwriting was not to take a company public until it had amassed three profitable quarters.[25] As the heavy investor demand for IPO stocks and the desire for IB profits rose they overcame the rules restraining past behavior and firms were brought to market quicker and at a shakier stage in their development. In light of the subsequent demise of many of the IPO firms, the investment banking firm of Solomon Smith Barney revised its underwriting standards so that, as a minimum, IPO candidates need to have reached the level of $10 million in quarterly revenues and expect to be profitable in no more than two quarters.[26] In effect, these higher standards will make it more difficult for start-ups to secure public funding in the future.

During the IPO boom, one more link in the VC-IB-IPO stock market chain was the role played by the financial analyst. A **financial analyst** is a technical specialist who undertakes an independent, ongoing review of the financial health of firms or industries in their area of expertise. They write reports for clients detailing their findings, offering assessments of future earnings, and making stock purchase recommendations. As such, the financial analysts are on the stock-selling side of the market, and many are the employees of the IB that is, or has brought, an IPO to the market. Ideally, the analyst works in the best interests of the potential stock investor or current holder, such that the

---

23 Elstrom, "The Great Internet," p. 21.

24 Calico Commerce, a B2B e-commerce software firm, had 15 investment bankers contacting the firm with offers to underwrite its IPO. Greg Ip, Susan Pulliam, Scott Thurm, and Ruth Simon, "The Internet Bubble Broke Records, Rules, and Bank Accounts," *The Wall Street Journal*, July 14, 2000, p. A1.

25 Elstrom, "The Great Internet," p. 18.

26 Elstrom, "The Great Internet," p. 20.

information in the reports and the recommendations from the analyst reflect the true value of the firm. Lastly, **financial planners** (formerly known as stockbrokers), who actually market these IPOs to their clients, use the reports prepared by the financial analyst to persuade prospective buyers that the IPO is a sound investment.

THE LOUDCLOUD CASE REVISITED

Loudcloud, with its history of VC funding and an IPO, has been tracked through all of the preceding steps. Loudcloud emerged at the tail end of the Internet investing bubble, such that *BusinessWeek* used the Loudcloud IPO to mark the end of the Net mania.[27] The firm started out in 1999 with $2 million in seed money from Marc Andreessen, of Netscape fame, and $15 million from Benchmark Capital, a VC firm.[28] A second round of financing encountered the firm valuation problem with some potential VC investors wanting to assess the worth of Loudcloud at only $100 million, or one-tenth of the $1 billion that the founders thought was a fair value. The final compromise was a value of $700 million and sufficient stock was placed in a third round of financing in June 2000 to raise $120 million in funds and ensure the continuation of short-term operations. The firm wanted to go public with an IPO in December 2000, selling 9.5 percent of its equity that would value the firm at $1.25 billion. The IB firm of Morgan Stanley was chosen as the lead underwriter, joined by Goldman Sachs, but the overall decline in the stock market, starting in April 2000, rendered the December IPO plan impractical. Therefore the IPO was adjusted and rescheduled for March 2001, with 27 percent of the firm to be sold at a firm value of $732 million.[29] Prior to the IPO, Loudcloud approved a reverse stock split, where the firm effectively reduced the number of shares outstanding, in a move that would help to support the IPO price. However, this new valuation would mean that the IPO offering price would also assign a lower per-share price for the firm than was paid by the investors in the last round of VC financing.

In February 2001, the executive team headed out on a cross-country set of meetings to explain the firm and sell the IPO to potential institutional and private investors. One problem was that the Loudcloud was only 18 months old. It had orders for more than $100 million, but the firm's nine-month revenues totaled just $6.5 million with losses of $107.6 million.[30] The package was a difficult sell in a down market, with a sliding economy, where investors in previous e-commerce IPOs were registering heavy losses. The offer price was lowered to $6 per share, with 34 percent of the company being sold to raise $150 million on a firm valued at $440 million.[31] The firm survived the process, but it is a much humbler operation today. It is conserving cash, cutting expenses, and focusing on profitability rather than growth.

BURSTING THE IPO SPECULATIVE BUBBLE AND THE AFTERMATH

The Magnitude of the Decline

As of early 2002, Loudcloud is still alive and providing an important service to Internet firms. However, many of its potential dot-com clients have gone out of business. From January 2000 through the end of October 2001, 716 dot-com firms failed, with 491 of

---

27 Ben Elgin, "The Last Days of Net Mania," *BusinessWeek*, April 16, 2001, pp. 110-118.

28 The following account is a compilation of information obtained from McGee et al., "Doing an Internet IPO," *The Wall Street Journal*, p. A1; and Elgin, "The Last Days," *BusinessWeek*, pp. 110–118.

29 McGee et al., "Doing an Internet IPO," p. A1.

30 McGee et al., "Doing an Internet IPO," p. A1.

31 Elgin, "The Last Days," pp. 112–113.

those terminations happening in 2001.[32] At the peak of the speculative bubble in late March 2000, Internet stocks as a group were valued at $1.4 trillion. At that point, the *USA Today* index of 100 Internet stocks reached a peak value of 210. Since then, it has fallen to a low of 47 with a value of 53 in December 2001.[33] A comparable decline in asset value would place the worth of the Internet stock group at around $353 million or a drop of almost 75 percent. The decline in equity valuations may actually be greater than 75 percent given the replacement within the *USA Today* index of Internet firms that have failed or been absorbed in mergers. The bursting of the Internet speculative bubble caused substantial losses for many people.

IPO Deals Gone Sour: Questions of Accountability and Conflicts of Interest

How did the IPO bubble get so big, so fast, and why did it burst so quickly? Was it the result of the interplay of market forces, or of more sinister forces led by people who helped guide the speculative excesses for their own personal gains? Certainly there were plenty of warnings about speculative equity fever. The most famous public reflection came from Alan Greenspan, the chairman of the Federal Reserve Board, who in December 1996 raised the question of possible "**irrational exuberance**" that might be arising in the stock market.[34] One part of the collapse might be attributed to human nature with a combination of "mob psychology, the human capacity for denial and a get-rich-quick mentality" contributing to the speculative frenzy.[35] This explanation places the responsibility for the bubble and its collapse on the shoulders of the buyers, including stock purchasers and the **online stockbrokers** who helped make the term **day trader** part of the popular vocabulary in the late 1990s. Certainly mutual funds were big buyers of Internet IPO stock, with some funds being created solely to trade in that narrow segment of the equity market. The actions of the mutual funds were driven by customer demand, and the public wanted to buy Internet stocks both individually and as parts of more diversified investment pools. The profits were there from Internet investing, at least in the beginning, and the lure of easy money helped to fuel the greed of buyers that propelled the stock values beyond reasonable bounds.

However, actions on the seller's side of many of the IPOs enriched the sellers beyond their normal compensations. These actions were not generally visible to buyers and helped to hype the buyer demand for the stock. One of these actions involved the integration of both VC and IB functions within the same firm. In their traditional role, the IB was a neutral party, examining the worthiness of a start-up to be brought forth as an IPO. But there was intense competition among IBs for the underwriting business and its lucrative fees. Moreover, a potentially greater dollar payoff came with being a late-stage VC investor. As a **pre-IPO investor**, the IB would be putting money into a less risky stage of the start-up's development, when it was on its feet, producing revenue if not profits, and approaching the point of seeking an underwriter for its IPO. At this point, the firm usually presented less **business risk** of failure prior to reaching the IPO stage. Some IB firms began to create their own venture financing arms that would place VC funds from the IB in the start-up just before the IPO event.[36] A portion of these VC investment dollars would often be drawn from an employee venture pool. This pool allowed regular, albeit high-salaried IB employees, to participate in two levels of IPO

---

32 Richard Williamson, "Dot-Com Failures Pass 700," available at **http://www.interactiveweek.com/ print_article/0,3668,a%253D17477,00.asp,** February 2002.

33 See *USA Today* Internet 50, available at **http://www.usatoday.com/life/cyber/invest/inindex.htm,** February 2002.

34 See **http://www.finpipe.com/secret.htm**.

35 Ip et al.,"The Internet Bubble Broke," p. A1.

36 Mark Maremoun, "As Wall Street Seeks Pre-IPO Investment, Conflicts May Arise," *The Wall Street Journal,* July 24, 2000, p. A1.

profits, one from the venture investing and the other from the IPO fees. These additional VC revenues would help the IB to attract and retain highly valued employees by allowing them to receive a greater level of compensation than through the normal channels of salary and bonus income. This type of arrangement was so common that it was referred to as a "new investment-banking model."[37]

Another possible reason for this VC investment action by an IB, apart from the normal invest-for-profit motive, might have been to create an inside link with the start-up. Having the VC arm of the IB as an investing partner might entice the start-up to use the underwriting arm of the same IB to take the firm public. The VC investment would yield a competitive edge for the IB in its underwriting rivalry with other IBs. On the other hand, the VC investment by the IB might have been an attempt to "strong-arm" the start-up into letting the IB put short-term funds into a potentially profitable venture.[38] In this scenario, the IB would advise the start-up that financial reports from its research department were among the most respected and visible in the start-up's business area. Credible reporting would be seen by the start-up as an important ingredient in any successful IPO, as well as a factor to retain investor attention after the IPO was completed. Reports indicating even higher prices for the shares in the near future might keep the holders of the new stock from selling today thereby experiencing a quick but smaller profit. Such selling pressure would in turn drive down the stock price, diminishing the incentive for others to hold on to their stock. Therefore, if the start-up wanted to be taken public by a top IB with sufficient credibility in the technical area to help bolster investor interest, it should allow the venture-funding arm of the IB to invest in the less risky late stage of VC funding.

Regardless of the motivation, the investment of VC funds in the start-up that they were bringing forth as an IPO created at least the perception, if not the reality, of a potential conflict of interest. This conflict lies at the heart of the tension, identified at the start of the chapter. Was the investment banker underwriting the IPO because it is ready for the public equity market, or was the IB sponsoring the IPO as a way of getting its own VC money as well as the underwriting fees out of the project? Of course all of this information was not available to the potential IPO investors, who knew nothing of the existence and amount of VC funding involvement by the IB. Even if IPO investors knew of these IB venture funds, how would they interpret the use of this money? Would it be seen as a conflict of interest causing them to avoid the IPO, or would it be seen as the IB having so much confidence in the start-up that it put its own dollars into the firm?

A second set of seller-side sources for the Internet bubble and its demise involved the role of the financial analyst. Just as the IB firms were not prohibited by SEC regulations from holding VC interests in the firms that they brought to an IPO, financial analysts were not prohibited from owning stock, either directly or through investment pools, in the firms that they reviewed or recommended. They too could be pre-IPO investors. Moreover, they were not prohibited from selling their personal stock in a company that they were actively recommending others to buy.[39] Documented stories tell of financial analysts and executives from their IB firm selling part or all of their stock holdings in a recent IPO, while at the same time recommending that others should purchase the stock.[40] Part of the reason for the need to have glowing reports on the firm by financial analysts has to do with the fact that stock issued prior to the IPO is regarded as restricted stock and is subject to a **lock-up period**. Because the stock can't be sold for at least six months from the date of the IPO, the IB firm holding such stock would want the equity value for the new firm to retain as much of its opening run up in price as possible. In part this value retention can be achieved by the analyst

---

37 Maremoun, "As Wall Street Seeks," p. A1.

38 Maremoun, "As Wall Street Seeks," p. A1.

39 For SEC stockholder guidance on the potential conflicts of financial analysts, consult the investor alert available at **http://www.sec.gov/investor/pubs/analysts.htm**.

40 Gretchen Morgenson, "Buy, They Say. But What Do They Do?" *The New York Times*, May 27, 2001, p. 3–1.

repeatedly casting a favorable light on the stock with a series of buy recommendations and increases in future share price projections.

Any action by executives from the IB that ordered or coerced the analyst to make such recommendations would constitute illegal **stock manipulation**. However, if an analyst saw his or her own profits as being linked to the successful sale of either direct or pooled stock, nothing prevented the analyst from issuing biased financial assessments and projections.[41] As a corrective deterrent, either the IB or the SEC could have banned stock ownership by the analyst in the firms that they covered, or they could require even more detailed disclosure of the linkages as part of the analyst's report. However, they chose not to follow either of these routes. An SEC study, reported in July 2001, revealed that pre-IPO investments by financial analysts were a frequent but not universal behavior pattern. The SEC found that 16 of 57, or 28 percent of analysts surveyed had made pre-IPO investments in firms that they later covered.[42]

A third set of seller-side stimulants for the IPO bubble involved the beneficial results from an overstatement of the order book.[43] The **order book** contains the names of potential institutional and individual buyers, along with the amounts of their share purchase requests for a given IPO. A number of mutual funds, each putting in a commitment to buy a 10 percent share allocation, would usually oversubscribe the order book, making the IPO look like an even hotter transaction. The combination of a limited amount of shares being offered, along with the excess offers to buy, would almost guarantee that no mutual fund would have to live up to its full commitment. Independent rating agencies used the order book and level of institutional buying interest as one means of evaluating the potential for a successful IPO. The artificially inflated demand would attract the interest of other potential buyers who could not get an IPO allocation. The apparent manic atmosphere of professional buyers surrounding the IPO would entice others into buying the shares in the aftermarket on the first and subsequent days of issue, helping to ensure a sizable run up in market price.

The SEC's Investigation of IPO Activity

Two additional sell-side practices proved to be so egregious that they drew enforcement attention from the Securities and Exchange Commission as well as U.S. Attorney's Office in Manhattan.[44] They both involved the cooperative behavior of the IB and potential mutual fund buyers of the IPO stock. Investment fund managers are partially compensated on the basis of their fund's performance. Having a large position in a hot IPO with a rapidly escalating price would boost fund performance and manager rewards. The shares of the hottest IPOs were often oversubscribed at the offering price prior to issue. Therefore, IBs had to find some way of allocating the limited number of shares among those wishing to buy. One way of attracting a larger allocation is alleged to have been for a fund manager to pledge a certain level of additional aftermarket purchases of the stock.[45] This practice is called **laddering**, and a pledge of this form of buying support in the aftermarket, or a requirement to do so in exchange for an allocation

---

41 In May 2002, the investment banking firm of Merrill Lynch agreed to pay a $100 million fine and to make internal structural changes, without admitting guilt, in settlement of charges by the New York State Attorney General. The investigation charged that the firm's financial analysts gave out "tainted advice," misleading investors with favorable stock ratings designed to win substantial investment banking fees. See Patrick McGeehan, "Merrill Lynch Under Attack As Giving Out Tainted Advice," *The New York Times*, April 8, 2002, p. C1; and Associated Press, "Merrill Lynch to Pay $100m for Conflicts," *Connecticut Post*, May 22, 2002, p. C3.

42 Scott Thurm, "When Do Analysts Cover Their Own Interests?" *The Wall Street Journal*, December 10, 2001, p. C1.

43 Ip et al., "The Internet Bubble Broke," p. A1.

44 Susan Pulliam and Randall Smith, "SEC's IPO Inquiries Advance on Two Fronts," *The New York Times*, November 28, 2001, p. C1.

45 Ip et al., "The Internet Bubble Broke," p. A1.

of stock, could raise regulatory concerns regarding market manipulation depending upon how explicit the agreement was.[46] The actions could violate the antifraud or anti-manipulation provisions of the SEC's rules.

The second set of questionable seller-side stimulants for the IPO bubble is alleged to have involved the payment of excessive commissions on the trading of other stock in exchange for an extra allocation of shares in a hot IPO. Here the recipient of the extra allocation would agree to bring a targeted level of additional business and fees back to the IB as a payment for receiving the shares. An exchange of outsized fees on transactions related to the allocation of IPO shares would amount to an **illegal kickback**, with both the firms and individuals involved being subject to SEC sanctions as well as criminal charges.[47] Such abusive allocation practices would help to support a demand frenzy in the aftermarket for the IPO stock among firms that were denied participation in the initial offering. In late 2001, the investment banking firm of Credit Suisse First Boston (CSFB) "agreed to pay $100 million to resolve a federal investigation into alleged abuses in its distribution of shares of initial public offerings of stock."[48] The SEC and the regulatory arm of the National Association of Securities conducted the investigation.[49] From 1999 to 2000, CSFB earned $717.5 million in fees from underwriting start-up IPOs, the largest amount of any IB. The firm did not admit or deny its guilt in settling the case.[50] This case, along with others that are still pending, may lead to new SEC rules governing the issuance of IPO shares.[51]

Given the final disposition of the SEC investigation and the potential for civil litigation, it would appear that the Internet portion of the IPO mania was not just an unsound, crazed buyer reaction to an opportunity to participate in new technology. To be sure, investment manias have been around for a long time, starting in the mid-seventeenth century with the Tulip Mania in Holland. Observers frequently draw parallels between the Tulip Mania and the frenzied investment in Internet IPOs.[52] The excessive market reaction to Internet IPOs, with the resulting loss of large amounts of investor funds, also felt a serious push from the sell side. The accuracy of some e-commerce assumptions as well as the viability of some forms of e-commerce firms undoubtedly deserve to be reevaluated in the light of the failure of so many. However, the demise of such a large number of dot-coms cannot be fully attributed to the unworkable nature or dismal future of e-commerce. The age-old motivation of **"infectious greed"** along with the manipulation of markets for personal gain certainly had a hand in and contributed to the

---

46 Pulliam and Smith, "SEC's IPO Inquiries," p. C1.

47 Pulliam and Smith, "SEC's IPO Inquiries," p. C1.

48 Susan Pulliam, Randall Smith, Anita Raghavan and Gregory Zuckerman, "CSFB Agrees to Pay $100 Million to Settle Twin IPO Investigations," *The Wall Street Journal*, December 11, 2001, p. A1.

49 The investigation by the Manhattan U.S. attorney's office into alleged illegal kickbacks was closed in November 2001, without bringing criminal charges. See Randall Smith and Susan Pulliam, "CSFB Won't Be Prosecuted in IPO Probe," *The* Wall Street Journal, November 29, 2001, p. C1.

50 "Report: CSFB to Pay $100m in IPO-Related Case," available at **http://www.usatoday.com/money/stocks/2001-12-11-csfb.htm**, December 2001. Leaving the issue of guilt unresolved is a standard strategy in cases that could later involve civil class-action lawsuits, where an admission of guilt could be used as evidence. As of the end of 2001, "Wall Street firms, including CSFB, face(d) more than 1,000 lawsuits seeking class-action status, brought on behalf of investors in 263 companies that went public during the boom. The lawsuits typically allege that the firms manipulated IPO share in deals benefiting preferred investors." See Pulliam et al., "CSFB Agrees," p. A1. Accessed in December 2001.

51 A third set of questionable IPO share allocation practices is called *spinning*. Here the IB issues some shares to the personal brokerage accounts of financial executives who work at firms that the IB currently does business with or would like to do business with in the future. The IB would then repurchase the shares soon after the IPO, creating a quick profit for the short-term holder. See Pulliam et al., "CSFB Agrees," p. A1.

52 See Tulipmania.com available at **http://www.sunwayco.com/news10.html**.

final outcome.[53] E-commerce, or the application of the Web to commercial activities, has been tarnished by the IPO episode, but as the earlier chapters showed, it is a sound channel for many forms of business activity. Fear not, e-commerce is here to stay.

Venture Capitalists: Doing Things Differently After the Bubble Burst

The venture capitalists who survived the demise of some of their e-commerce firms and the setbacks in the IPO market apparently learned two lessons: one is to change their ways of doing business and run a tighter operation,[54] and the other is to get more security for the funds they invest. As one VC partner put it the industry needs "to get back to building companies as opposed to building stocks."[55] To achieve this end, the VC firms put more resources into nurturing existing start-ups already in their portfolios. They also practiced portfolio triage, or demanding big changes in, as well as cutting off the flow of funds to, firms with serious management, revenue, or financing problems. At the peak of the IPO mania, VC managing partners spent 75 percent of their time exploring new deals and just 25 percent of their time working with the existing firms in their portfolios. The goal is to reverse that time allocation model, returning it to the 25/75 split that was more common in the pre-Internet mania days. Some VC firms are bringing in more management expertise in the form of a management partner or a human resources partner to provide advice for their start-ups. Others are tightening up the due diligence review, eliminating the shortcuts, and performing deeper research on the industries surrounding the potential start-up as well as the validity of the technology. Each of these actions involves an attempt to avoid the mistakes of the recent past.

VC firms are also finding that, following the end of the VC-IPO frenzy, the balance of power in the market for start-ups has moved from the hands of the previously aggressively sought-after entrepreneurs, and into the hands of the VCs who are providing the funding. The VCs are exercising that added market power by attaching more onerous and restrictive conditions to the extension of late-stage funding, which occurs just prior to the IPO.[56] They remember what happened to the late-stage investors in Loudcloud, who watched the value of their investment fall as the IPO was continually repriced at lower levels, and they want to avoid the same fate. The business risk may be lower with late-stage financings, but the **market risk** during the IPO is still present and may have grown as the IPO market cooled. Therefore, to protect themselves against the added market risk, VCs are adding new provisions to their offers of late-stage financing. First some are requiring a **liquidation preference** that binds the start-up to pay a fixed amount of funds to the VC before other investors receive any funding, in the event of the termination of the firm. This preference gives the late-state VC investors senior status relative to earlier investors, allowing them to recoup their funds before earlier investors get any money if the firm is liquidated or sold to another enterprise at a loss.

Second, some late-stage VC financing agreements may contain a **retroactive repricing provision**, which "allows the number of shares a venture investor receives to fluctuate with the value of the IPO. So if a company has to cut its expected IPO price in half, for example, the late-stage investor might get twice as many shares, effectively adjusting the price it paid for the original stake to reflect the decline in the valuation."[57] At the time

53 Federal Reserve Chairman Alan Greenspan emphasized the phrase in his July 2002 Congressional testimony as a way to sum up the array of stock and accounting scandals and improprieties that adversely affected U.S. financial markets. See "Greenspan Blasts Infectious Greed," available at **http://www.smartpros.com/x34743.xml**.

54 Linda Himelstein, "Crunch Time for VCs," *BusinessWeek*, February 19, 2001, pp. EB 23-32.

55 Himelstein, "Crunch Time for VCs," p. EB27.

56 Suzanne McGee, "Late-Stage Venture Firms Play Hardball," *The Wall Street Journal*, May 17, 2001, p. C1.

57 McGee, "Late-Stage Venture Firms," p. C1.

of the late-stage financing this provision may protect both the entrepreneur and the investor given that it avoids potential conflicts over the start-up pricing problem prior to the IPO. Finally, some agreements contain a **ratchet provision**. Here, in the event of the start-up needing another round of financing before going to an IPO, the present late-stage investors would maintain their current ownership share in the firm, even if they were not participants in the later financing round. Each of these provisions is designed to protect the interests of the late-stage VC investors at the expense of the entrepreneur. However, if the restrictions reduce the risk of late stage investing, then they also improve the likelihood that more start-ups actually get to the IPO stage.

SUMMARY AND PROSPECTS

A review of the VC-IPO model of firm creation turns up mixed results, at least as applied to the birth of Internet and e-commerce firms. The model is a story of both heroes and villains. It reflects a tension between the building of firms and the building of stocks. **Market heroes** often introduce substantial efficiencies in directing the flow of risk capital and the advancement of technology in this story; however, **market villains** sometimes succeed in twisting the process of firm creation to favor their own personal gain at the expense of others. As heroes, VC firms both reduce the risks associated with early-stage funding and give support to the ideas of start-up entrepreneurs.[58] It is unlikely that firms such as Loudcloud would be either in existence today or have achieved their rapid rate of expansion without the infusion of substantial amounts of external, investments. It is not enough to have a great idea or product. Every firm needs a viable business plan and the expertise to carry it out. Venture capitalists provide management assistance and strategic guidance to the heads of start-up firms along with the financial backing. In return they can earn huge returns if their risky bets turn out to be big market hits.

The public focuses on the enormous returns from a few highly visible successes, and nothing sinister is inherent in this process. The market structure for venture capital firms is neither a monopoly nor even an oligopoly. Venture investing is generally a small-scale enterprise, with a large number of firms and reasonably low entry barriers. If an investor has the money to put up and the ability to weather the losses as well as enjoy the gains, then just about anyone can play.

Just like venture capitalists, the investment bankers play a role. They take the start-up public, acting as a professional financial filter to apply underwriting standards that ensure that the start-up is ready for a public stock offering. A considerable amount of trust is required in the IB relationship: trust by the start-up that the IB will get the highest possible price for the shares through an IPO, and trust by the investors in the IB that it performed the due diligence investigation in support of the appropriateness of the offering. Taking a firm public allows smaller, less risk-tolerant investors to participate in the future of the firm, and it permits the firm to tap a broader funding pool than supplied by VC investors. An IPO also provides access to liquidity that allows both entrepreneurs and VC investors the potential to experience capital gains on their investment, by selling off some or all of their ownership claims. Together the VC and IB arms of the model help the macro economy by giving birth to start-ups and the public firms that create substantial numbers of new jobs and add significantly to the level of GDP. On the hero side of the story everyone is a winner.

The VC-IPO model can and often does create opportunities and wealth, but it also may attract greed and suspect operations. The potential to make a lot of money as part of the normal flow of the VC-IPO firm creation model draws various investors. Here, the benefits to society and the benefits to the participants are in reasonable harmony with one another. If demand at the IPO end can be whipped into a frenzy, however, the

---

58 Randall E. Stross, "Venture Capitalists Aren't Villains," *The Wall Street Journal*, July 25, 2000, p. A22.

opportunity is even greater to make more money, faster, and with a larger number of deals. If the rules can be stretched a bit, then more profits can be created. This scenario played out for at least some of the participants and firms that were part of the 1990s IPO mania. The villains were pursuing actions where historic behavior and rules-of-thumb should have warned them that a portion of their dealings were unsound. At one extreme, some of these actions were suspect or lacked a moral compass, while at the other extreme actions became criminal in nature or perhaps subject to civil penalties. In hindsight, the rules governing the financial game were not always clear, nor could they always fully anticipate the twists and turns that might be devised based upon personal avarice. Looking forward, the SEC and other bodies may well alter the playing field to eliminate or restrain some of the more egregious behavior. The VC-IPO model works well to raise efficiency under normal circumstances. It is too important and valuable a structure to allow it to be tainted by the actions of a few.

KEY TERMS AND CONCEPTS

angels	late-stage venture capitalists
bondholders	limited partnership
brain drain	liquidation preference
business incubators	liquidity
business risk	lock-up period
carry	managing partners
caveat emptor	market heroes
constant dollar terms	market risk
creative destruction	market villains
crony capitalism	mezzanine financing
current dollar terms	online stockbrokers
day trader	order book
diversification of portfolio risk	partnership
due diligence review	pooling of funds
economic pluralism	pre-IPO investors
entrepreneurship	prospectus
financial analyst	ratchet provision
financial planners	retroactive repricing provision
illegal kickback	rounds of VC financing
infectious greed	schumpeterian market gap
initial public offering (IPO)	seed financing
innovator	seed money
internet-related financing rounds	start-up valuation problem
inventor	stock manipulation
investing partners	stockholders
investment banker (IB)	underwrite
investor roulette	VC-IPO model of firm creation
irrational exuberance	venture capital firm
laddering	venture capitalist

DISCUSSION AND REVIEW QUESTIONS

1. Identify and discuss the nature of the VC-IPO start-up financing model. How do venture capitalists fill a gap in the market? What efficiencies do they bring to the process of creative destruction?

2. What is a venture capital firm? How is it structured? Where do they get their money? What kinds of expertise do the managing partners have and how are they rewarded?

3. What is the nature of the tension that exists within the VC-IPO model? Doesn't everyone always want the start-up firm to succeed in the marketplace? Why?

4. Why would a venture capital firm want to eventually sell off some or all of its shares subsequent to the IPO of a start-up firm? If the firm and the IPO are successful, why wouldn't a VC firm want to hold on to the shares?

5. Examine the figure for the risk-reward continuum of different financing vehicles. Which instrument offers the lender or investor the lowest level of risk, and the highest level of risk? How is reward correlated with the risk taken? Why?

6. How did the level and composition of U.S. venture capital activity change in the 1990s? Why? How does the level of activity in the United States compare to the rest of the world? Why is this difference important?

7. Identify and explain the nature of the start-up valuation tension that exists between the entrepreneur and the venture capital firm. Why would the VC want to invest in a firm that it claims has a low current value?

8. What are investment bankers? What functional role do they play in the IPO process? How did investment bankers go wrong in their manipulation of the IPO process?

9. What is a financial analyst? What functional role does the analyst play in the IPO process? Where did some analysts go wrong in their manipulation of the IPO process?

10. Identify and discuss some of the major causes of the bubble in the IPO market. Were the majority of these problems on the buyers' or sellers' side of the market? Explain.

11. Identify and explain some of the consequences resulting from the SEC and New York State Attorney General's investigations into IPO conflicts of interest.

12. In the aftermath of the IPO bubble burst, how have venture capital firms and investment bankers changed their behavior? Which parties are hurt and helped by these changes? Why?

WEB EXERCISES

1. Link to the homepage of *USA Today* at **http://www.usatoday.com/**. In their Money section, type in the stock symbol OPSW for Opsware Inc. (the new name for Loudcloud), and see how well (or poorly) they are currently doing. Check out the most recent press releases to find their current quarterly financial status.

2. Link to the PriceWaterhouseCoopers Web site at **http://www.pwcmoneytree.com**. Look for information dealing with the most recent quarterly survey of venture capital activity. How much was invested in total? Which industries received the most dollars of investment funds? What stage of firm activity attracted the most money?

3. Link to the NVCA site at **http://www.nvca.com**. Access their research article "Three Decades of Venture Capital Investment Yields 7.6 Million Jobs and $1.3 Trillion in Revenue," to be found by clicking on Industry Research and then Venture Capital Statistics. The study can be accessed by its release date, which was October 22, 2001. See where your home state ranked in terms of jobs and revenues created by venture-backed companies in 2000.

4. Link again to the National Venture Capital Association homepage at **http://www.nvca.com**. Look for their study entitled "DRI-WEFA Study Identifies Venture Capital As a Key Factor Powering U.S. Economic Growth" in their Research section. It had a release date of June 26, 2002. How important is venture capital financing to U.S economic growth?

5. Link to the TulipMania.com site of Mark Tarses at **http://www.sunwayco.com/ news10.html**, and read his brief analogy linking the IPO bubble with Tulip Mania that gripped Holland in the 1630s. History does repeat itself.

6. Link to the warning published by the Securities and Exchange Commission at **http://www.sec.gov/investor/pubs/analysts.htm**. Read the investor warning about the potential conflicts of interest that can affect a stock rating by a financial analyst.

7. If all of this discussion caused you to be overcome by a near fatal bout of MEGO, link to **http://www.bored.com/**, and check out the list of crazythoughts.com, which outlines some of life's unanswered questions.

8. Link to the *USA Today* Internet 50 Index and see the list of survivors and how they are doing, available at **http://www.usatoday.com/tech/techinvestor/ internet50.htm**.

CHAPTER

15

Introductory Case

WEBVAN AND WEBHOUSE: GROCERY SALES VIA THE WEB

The logic seemed to be inescapable! People have to eat. Many people dislike grocery shopping, or are so pressed for time that they feel they can't spare any for trips to the food store. Therefore, the Web, with its ability to remove the distance and time barriers from the shopping experience, was an ideal medium for consumers to buy groceries. This logic wasn't lost on Internet entrepreneurs and investors, who poured a great deal of money and talent into developing the prospects for online grocery sales. Two rival firms, with vastly different approaches to selling groceries over the Internet, were Webvan and WebHouse. Each firm had its own unique vision of the **trade-off between time and money** held by different segments of the grocery-buying public. However, both firms failed within months of each other, at the time of the 2000-2001 general dot-com collapse.

The grocery industry seemed to be a natural target for entry by Web entrepreneurs. In 2000, grocery sales for the year totaled $457 billion, with an annual growth rate of 5.1 percent, or $22 billion per year.[1] First, it was apparent that with these sales numbers and growth rates, online grocers needed to capture only a small fraction of the huge trade volume to be successful. In June of 2000, *BusinessWeek Online* reported a projection that by 2004, online grocers would sell some $8.8 billion in products. Even at that high absolute dollar sales figure,

the number would amount to only 1.65 percent of the $535 billion in projected total sales.[2] Second, the grocery business is a highly fragmented industry with some 128,000 individual stores selling grocery products in 2000.[3] Almost 32,000 chain and independent supermarket stores report $2 million or more each in annual sales. Smaller grocery stores, with less than $2 million in annual sales, totaled 37,000 units, while some 58,000 convenience stores also sold grocery products. Third, it is a business with relatively easy entry and where coordinated retaliatory action is unlikely. Product suppliers would be willing to sell their branded and unbranded products to the Web grocers, without fear of alienating their retail customers.

Almost everyone must participate in the grocery-buying process at some point and usually on a repetitive basis. Given the volume of consumers, it would be fairly easy to target the attributes of one or more segments of the buying public that might be attracted to shopping online for grocery items. Webvan and WebHouse set out to target consumers at different ends of the buying spectrum. For some consumers, grocery shopping is a positive experience. It can serve as a pleasant diversion, getting the person out of the home or office, while allowing them to think about something other than the pressures of the day. It facilitates interaction with other people, requires minimal planning, and encourages the sampling of new products. Lastly, it can be combined with other activities to allow for an efficient use of shopping or travel time.

Despite these potentially positive results, many shoppers see the process of buying groceries is tedious and time consuming. Grocery shopping serves as a distraction taking precious

---

1 These figures are drawn from U.S. Department of Commerce, U.S. Census Bureau data available at **http://www. c-store.com/00national.html**, February 2002.

2 Information available at **http://www.businessweek.com/ebiz/0006/dm0613.htm**.

3 Information available at **http://www.fmi.org/facts_figs/keyfacts/stores.htm**.

Learning from Dot-Com Failures

time away from alternative activities such as family interaction or work obligations. It involves long checkout lines, lugging heavy bags, and additional driving to and from the supermarket. Within family units some men may grocery shop regularly, however the bulk of the grocery shopping responsibilities traditionally falls on women, and women have much less time than in the past to spend on this activity.[4] The 2000 census data showed that 60 percent of the U.S. women of working age were in the labor force.[5] Of the mothers with children under three years of age, 61 percent were in the workforce, while those with children from age 3-5, 71 percent were in the workforce.[6] Also, 49 percent of all U.S. women 50 years of age and older were working full time.[7] For these women, their schedules don't leave a lot of time for grocery shopping. Lastly the median income for U.S. families where both the husband and wife worked full time, year-round equaled $74,018, with an average income of $88,672 in 2000.[8]

The evidence indicates that many people with little or no time to devote to grocery shopping, may have sufficient income to be attracted to a premium, online grocery shopping opportunity. Hence, the creation of the **virtual supermarkets** including Webvan and its sister Web grocery services Peapod, Streamline.com, Shoplink Netgrocer, and HomeGrocer, among others. The business model for each was built on the assumption that a sufficient number of affluent, time-pressed buyers would shop for their groceries

via the Web and make the virtual supermarket a profitable venture. It allowed the buyer to substitute a slightly higher cost of purchase for the savings in time. Each firm developed its own variation on the virtual supermarket theme. Webvan adopted a **high-tech central distribution model**, with deliveries made from automated warehouses. They used a fleet of their own trucks, powered by computerized delivery routines, to provide products to their customers in a timely fashion. Peapod initially adopted a local **store-based delivery model**, where the pick-pack-deliver tasks were undertaken from the shelvers of local supermarkets. Lastly, Netgrocer adopted a **limited-menu third-party delivery model** by selling only nonperishable items online and scheduling delivery via FedEx.

The Webvan operation looked to be so compelling that it attracted $1.2 billion from a combination of venture capitalists and IPO equity investments.[9] At its peak, Webvan offered its services to 750,000 active customers, in seven mostly West Coast metropolitan markets, with plans to expand to a total of 26 geographic areas. The service was convenient, given that the customers could place an order 24/7, at their convenience. It was trustworthy, with orders packed properly with quality items. It was reliable as a result of delivery times scheduled within a narrow window. It was also cost competitive, with delivery charges set on a decreasing cost scale depending upon the number of minimum value orders delivered per month. It was a can't-miss business, with a service that was ideally suited for access over

---

4 Men purchase 25 percent of all grocery items and 82 percent report that they undertake grocery shopping regularly. See Brenda S. Sonner, Gail Ayala, and Richard Mizerski, "A Comparison of the Responsiveness of Male Shoppers Versus Female Shoppers to Sales Promotions," available at **http://www.sbaer.uca.edu/Research/1995/SMA/95swa076.htm**.

5 For Census labor market results, see **http://www.prb.org/Content/NavigationMenu/Other_reports/2000-2002/2000_United_States_Population_Data_Sheet.htm#section4**, February 2002.

6 "Work Related Child-Care Statistics," available at **http://www.dol.gov/dol/wb/public/wb_pubs/child2001.htm**.

7 "More Older Women Working Full Time," available at **http://www.ctnow.com/business/hc-shorttakes1217.artdec17.story?coll=hc%2Dheadlines%2Dbusiness**, February 2002.

8 "Historical Income Tables—Families," available at **http://www.census.gov/hhes/income/histinc/f13.html**.

9 Saul Hansell, "An Ambitious Internet Grocer Is Out of Both Cash and Ideas," *The New York Times*, July 10, 2001, p. A1.

the Web, to a targeted market segment. Despite the logic and financial support, the firm failed in mid-2001.

The buying service WebHouse targeted customers at the other end of the grocery-buying spectrum, away from the affluent, time-pressed consumer. WebHouse was the creation of Walker Digital Corp., headed by Jay Walker, which owns the patent rights to the reverse auction buying process that was licensed to the sister firm Priceline.com. The WebHouse business model was based upon the assumption that a segment of the grocery market exhibited attributes that included a low value placed on their own time and a high value placed on getting the lowest possible price for a purchased item. The model also assumed that these buyers would be willing to spend some of their time haggling over the purchase price of each grocery item. The potential buyer would go online with a grocery shopping list, enter the name of each item (not the brand) individually and be given a choice of making a binding credit card bid to buy it at different price points. A grocery chain, working in conjunction with the manufacturer of the product, would respond electronically as to whether they accepted the offer to buy at that price. At the end of the shopping session, the buyer would print out a list of items along with their accepted prices, and take that to a participating local store. There the buyer would pick the items off of the shelf, along with any other non-WebHouse items and receive the WebHouse items at the prepaid, reverse auction price. The WebHouse model added another step into the already tedious grocery shopping process, but it did so in exchange for the opportunity to buy at least some items at a guaranteed lower price. The model offered the buyer the opportunity to sacrifice time in exchange for a dollar saving. The model also had the efficiency advantage that WebHouse itself would never own or handle the grocery items being traded. They were just an e-commerce intermediary, linking bidders and sellers through the reverse auction process. Like many of the B2B exchanges, all of the variations of the Priceline model are **asset-light companies** that set up markets and earn their profits by facilitating the trades in those markets. Despite the logic of the WebHouse business model, the firm, which began its operations in January 2000, failed in October 2000.[10]

3
4

Why did these two "can't-miss" B2C firms fail, and what can be learned from the failure by other e-commerce firms? What are the market forces that supply the tension between e-commerce success and failure?

THE ECONOMICS OF FIRM FAILURE

Business Failure Is More Common Than Success

A baseball fan once asked Ted Williams, the late great Boston Red Sox Hall of Famer, what it took to hit .400 for an entire season. In his typically curt manner, Williams replied that all the batter had to do was to get two hits in five at-bats for every game. Even the man who was arguably the best hitter the game has ever known had to admit that, as a batter, you fail more often that you succeed. It is one lesson that e-commerce or any industry can take from sports. Whether firms are manufacturing cars, steel, television sets, or something else, the history of these industries is rampant with stories of individual failures. In small service and retailing industries, such as restaurants, gasoline stations, and clothing stores, the failure rate is even greater. In every year from 1991 to 1998, in excess of 70,000 U.S. firms failed, with a peak of more than

10 Julia Angwin and Nick Wingfield, "How Jay Walker Built WebHouse on a Theory That He Couldn't Prove," *The Wall Street Journal*, October, 16, 2000, p. A1.

97,000 in the post-recession year of 1992.[11] The number of annual failures averaged 10 percent of the annual number of new incorporations. Despite the high absolute number of failures, the annual failure rate of 80 or more per 10,000 listed enterprises was a low 0.8 percent. Failures among small firms with liabilities of under $100,000 were more than twice as numerous as failures among firms with more than $100,000 in liabilities. Failure is clearly a common result of risk taking.

A second lesson that e-commerce firms can take from baseball is that it's important to learn something from each failure. A good batter makes an out seven out of every ten times at bat. The three hits often come because the hitter has learned something valuable about the pitcher during the previous at-bats. For example, what different pitches does he throw? What do they look like on their way? What is his favorite pitch sequence and location? Successful hitting involves timing and anticipation. If the batter can anticipate the next pitch, almost any major league player can get a hit. This intense study of pitchers by hitters and hitters by pitchers is called the "game within the game." If you ask a batter why he made an out, he might respond that the pitch was too fast or broke unexpectedly, too hard to see, or was in a location that was too hard to handle. By analogy, if you ask the former owner of a failed firm why it failed, you get a variety of answers including lack of sufficient investment funds, cash flow problems, disappointing sales, poor planning, or a lack of business experience. What separates the good major league hitter from the journeyman minor leaguer, as well as the eventually successful entrepreneur from those who eventually give up and go to work for someone else, is an ability to identify and learn from past fatal errors.

Firm Failure and Microeconomic Theory

Microeconomic theory allows for two possibilities in the short run, when the firm experiences money-losing revenue and cost combinations. In the **loss minimization case**, the firm loses money but continues to produce because doing so will limit its loses to a level that is below its fixed costs. In the second or **shutdown case**, the firm responds to its losses by ceasing operations in the short run, because to do so limits the loss to the amount of their fixed costs. Both of these cases are shown in Figure 15-1. For the sake of visual simplicity, the examples are framed within the perfectly competitive market structure model, by employing horizontal demand and revenue curves. However, the results can be easily generalized to the three imperfectly competitive market structures of monopoly, monopolistic competition, and oligopoly, where demand and revenue curves are negatively sloped.

The firm demonstrates the typical U-shaped marginal and per-unit cost curves based on the law of diminishing marginal returns. The average total cost (ATC) curve, lies above the average variable cost (AVC) curve, separated by the amount of average fixed cost (AFC). At price P_1, the firm equates P_1 with the marginal cost (MC) to find the profit maximizing output level, which is Q_1. However, at Q_1, the firm's revenue per unit (AR) is slightly less than its ATC, therefore the firm is making an economic loss. The choices available to the firm are either to produce Q_1 and accept the short-run loss or shutdown and experience a loss equal to the size of the firm's fixed costs. In this case the firm will elect to produce because the price of P_1 is earning sufficient revenue to cover all of the firm's variable costs with a contribution margin (AB) that helps to reduce the size of the losses below the amount of the fixed cost. Note that the proper short-run comparison is between AR and AVC, not AFC. Fixed costs are either sunk costs, already paid and can't be recouped, or they are mandated current payments that can't be avoided short of financial default. Therefore, they play no role in the short-run decision to produce or not to produce.

---

11 These figures are taken from the *Economic Report of the President*, Council of Economic Advisors, January 2001, Table B-96, available at **http://w3.access.gpo.gov/usbudget/fy2002/ erp.html**. The data cover **business failures**, where the value of the firm's financial liabilities exceeds the value of its financial or physical assets. An additional number of **business closures** occur for reasons unrelated to financial failure.

FIGURE 15-1   Firm Short-Run Losses and Production Reactions

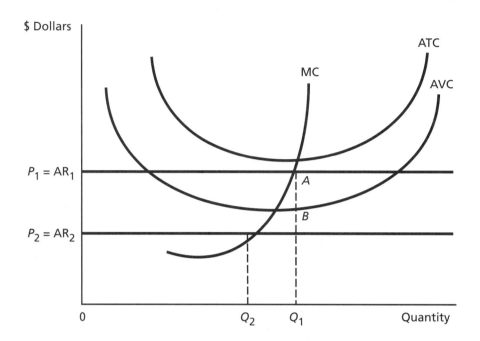

Given that economic cost is based on the concept of opportunity cost, the firm will not be satisfied with these economic losses in the long run. The concept of opportunity cost tells the owners of the firm that another activity will earn a higher return using the same resources. The owners will be motivated to move their resource to the next best activity (i.e., exit the current business) if these losses persist in the long run. This drive for the most efficient use of resources, as directed by opportunity costs, becomes the explanatory factor behind economic failure in the long run.

Now let's assume that the price of the product is lower at P_2 rather than P_1. Here the profit maximizing output level falls to Q_2. It is readily apparent that the line representing revenue per unit (AR$_2$) lies below both the ATC and the AVC. The AVC represents the opportunity costs associated with the decision to employ variable resources for the production of the item in the short run. With $AR_2 <$ AVC, these costs can't be covered in full. The firm is not only losing an amount equal to its fixed costs, but it is losing an additional dollar volume equal to the distance that the AR_2 curve lies below the AVC curve times the number of units produced. Therefore, it is in the best interests of the firm to cease production by shutting down and limiting its losses to the size of its fixed cost. An important difference distinguishes between shutting down and **going out of business**. If the firm has some fixed resources that account for its fixed costs, then the firm does not have the option of going out of business in the short run. If market conditions don't change as those resources become variable in the long run, however, then the firm will redirect its efforts away from the current activity and into the next best use.

The Discounted Cash Flow Model: When to Pull the Plug

The preceding microeconomic firm analysis is correct for decisions based on a comparison of current revenue versus current cost. Most firms have a decision-making time horizon that extends beyond today, especially for e-commerce start-up firms such as Webvan. They invest funds today with a reasonable expectation that the first few years of operation may bring losses. These losses may continue until the business reaches sufficient scale in the future to allow for a profitable level of operation. Therefore, even though the firm may currently face either a shutdown or loss minimization case, it may continue to produce over an extended period of time based on the expectation that profitability will improve in the future. The **discounted cash flow model** of expected future income helps the firm to make the correct production decision today. Both conceptually and mathematically, discounting is simply the reverse of compounding, which involves earning interest on interest, and is a process that is more familiar to the general public. In **compounding**, an individual puts a given amount of money in a banking account, such as a certificate of deposit (CD), for a fixed period of time and receives a guaranteed annual interest payment in return. At the end of the life of the CD, the person gets back the original funds along with the accrued interest. For example, if an individual puts $1,000 into a CD for two years at the compounded interest rate of 10 percent per year, the amount that the person would receive back at the end of two years would be $1,210. The interest payment on the original $1,000 would yield $100 per year, or $200 in total. The extra $10 comes from the interest earned on the first $100 during the second year. The formula for this process is shown in Figure 15-2. The principle (P), or the original amount deposited, earns interest during the first year at interest rate (i). This formula yields a new dollar total of R_1, which is reinvested at (i) for the second year. After two years of compounding the total dollar value equals R_2, which is returned to the saver. In the compounding formula, the principle and the interest rate are known, while the resulting value is unknown and must be calculated.

The **discounting** process switches the identities of some of the known and unknown variables in the compounding equation. Here the annual cash flows (Rs) minus the operating costs are estimated and the rate of discount is known. The task is to calculate the unknown discounted present value (DPV) of this future cash flow. The present value or current worth of the flow will be less than the simple sum of the cash flows, because money has a time value or opportunity cost over time. Therefore, funds received in the future are worth less than an equal amount of money received today. If a person was to receive an amount of money R_2 two years from now, then the discounted present value (DPV) of that amount would be determined by dividing R_2 by $(1 + r)^2$, with r equaling the time value or **discount rate** of the funds and the squared value representing the two-year waiting period for the money. If, as in a business, the owners expect a net cash

---

Formulas for Compounding and Discounting	**FIGURE 15-2**

Compounding Formula:

$P(1 + i) = R_1, \ R_1(1 + i) = R_2$

Substituting for R_1: $P(1 + i)(1 + i) = R_2 = P(1 + i)^2$

where P = Principle
$\quad\quad i$ = Interest rate
$\quad\quad R$ = Revenue earned in some future period

Discounting Formula:

$DPV = R_2/(1 + r)^2$

where r = Discount rate
$\quad DPV$ = Value today of a future sum R

Expanded Discounting Formula:

$DPV = R_1/(1 + r) + R_2/(1 + r)^2 + R_3/(1 + r)^3 + R_4/(1 + r)^4 + \ldots + R_n/(1 + r)^n$

where n = Total number of time periods

		Case A	Case B		Case C	Total U.S.
Year	**Scenario 1** Net Cash Flow ($ mil.)	DPV Cash Flow r = 0.10 ($ mil.)	DPV Cash Flow r = 0.05 ($ mil.)	**Scenario 2** Net Cash Flow ($ mil.)	DPV Cash Flow r = 0.10 ($ mil.)	Grocery Sales ($ bil.)
2000	–$600	–$600	–$600	–$600	–$600	$457
2001	–500	–455	–476	–450	–409	468
2002	–400	–331	–363	–300	–248	492
2003	–300	–225	–259	–150	–113	516
2004	–200	–137	–165	0	0	542
2005	–100	–62	–78	150	93	569
2006	0	0	0	300	169	598
2007	100	51	71	450	231	628
2008	200	93	135	600	280	659
2009	300	127	193	750	318	692
2010	400	154	246	900	347	727
2011	500	175	292	1,050	368	763
2012	600	191	334	1,200	382	801
2013	700	203	371	1,350	391	841
2014	800	211	404	1,500	395	883
2015	900	215	433	1,650	395	927
2016	1,000	218	458	1,800	392	974
2017	1,100	218	480	1,950	386	1,023
2018	1,200	216	499	2,100	378	1,074
2019	1,300	213	514	2,250	368	1,127
2020	1,400	208	528	2,400	357	1,184
Total	$8,400	$684	$9,084	$18,900	$3,880	$15,945

TABLE 15-1   Webvan's Projected DPV Under Differing Assumptions

flow for each year into the foreseeable future, then the DPV formula would be expanded to cover the sum of the years up to the final or nth year.

Discounting Applied to the Webvan Case

Using some heroic assumptions, it is possible to calculate what the profit outlook was for Webvan and why investors might have chosen to close the firm, rather than allowing it survive to the point of potential profitability. Let's assume that the $1.2 billion was all that the firm would have needed in the form of investment in warehouse space, delivery trucks, and capital equipment to eventually reach a profitable scale of operation. As a going concern, Webvan lost almost $600 million in 2000, its last full year of operation.[12] Let's construct a future net cash flow scenario for the firm based on the following assumptions. The firm's time horizon is 20 years, in which Webvan reduces its losses by $100 million per year. In the year 2007, Webvan begins to make a profit above operating costs, with the profit increasing by $100 million a year thereafter. In the year 2020, Webvan would earn $1.4 billion in revenue net of operating expenses (calculated in constant dollars), which is a respectable sum of money in the grocery industry. If the annual discount rate r equals 10 percent, then Table 15-1 shows the present value of this sum of combined profits and losses in the column labeled Case A. The simple sum of the net

---

12 "Webvan's Loss Widens to $173.1 Million; Plan is Set to Cut Costs," *The Wall Street Journal*, January 26, 2001, p. B6.

cash flows would total $8.4 billion, which would more than cover the original investment of $1.2 billion, making Webvan appear to be a highly profitable investment. However, that calculation comes before taking the time value of the money flows into consideration through discounting. When the flows are discounted at 10 percent, the DPV is only $684 million or just about one-half of the original investment. Even if the $1.2 billion is regarded as a sunk cost and not subject to recovery, the $684 million in discounted cash flow is unlikely to be sufficient to motivate continued operation given the uncertainty surrounding the figure and the potential need for a further cash infusion before the revenue stream turns positive. This result renders Webvan as unprofitable considering both the short-run microtheory cases and discounted future earnings models. Even though the firm is expected to earn $1.4 billion in 2020, the cash has only a discounted present value of $208 million today.

Webvan would become profitable if either the discount rate was reduced to 0.05 percent as in Case B, or if the rate of net revenue gains was accelerated to $150 million per year as opposed to $100 million as in Scenario 2, Case C. However, a 0.05 percent discount rate is unrealistically low for an uncertain business investment. Many mature manufacturing firms target a 15 to 20 percent annual rate of return after taxes, which might serve as a competitive discount rate for estimating the potential profitability of Webvan. Alternately, the faster rate of revenue gain, shown in Case C, would require Webvan to earn $2.4 billion net in 2020. Profit margins in the retail grocery industry typically average between 0.8 and 1.2 percent of gross sales. At a 1 percent margin, an absolute dollar profit of $2.4 billion for Webvan would mean that it was selling approximately one-half of the value of all of today's U.S. grocery sales. Assuming that U.S. grocery sales were to grow at a compound annual real rate of 2.5 percent per year, then Webvan would be selling one-fifth of the total of $1.184 trillion in all U.S. grocery sales in 2020. Although it is not an impossible sales figure for Webvan, it would be highly unlikely.

These numbers, inexact though they may be, make it easier to understand why the investors pulled the plug, but they don't tell the full story. First, if Webvan was losing $600 million per year in the near term, it would have required an added investment of perhaps $1 billion to cover those losses. After all, investors can wait for their money in the future, but workers and suppliers want to be paid today. The insertion of the added funds would have raised the level of risk for the shareholders. Second, the projected spreadsheet numbers did not account for future risks or uncertainty. How might one or more recessions over the 20-year span reduce the annual cash flows? Would Webvan's growing profits attract additional competitors? Would increased scale lead to inefficiencies or diseconomies that might lower the margin on sales? A 20-year time horizon is a long span in any industry, even a reasonably mature and stable one. To account for uncertainty, cash flow projections normally perform a **sensitivity analysis** to see what happens to the results under different assumptions. For example, raising the discount rate above the competitive level to say 20 percent might protect against the affects of uncertainty. Alternately, lowering the rate of revenue growth or cutting the number of years in the projection might be tried. Each of these alternative scenarios worsens an already unfavorable outcome, and makes the decision to close Webvan even more understandable.

DOT-COM FAILURES AND INTERNET JOB LOSSES

Aggregate Data

Monthly data collected by Webmergers.com reveal the extent of the rapid rise in the number of dot-com shutdowns subsequent to the stock market reaching its peak in March 2000.[13] The ensuing decline in equity values closed off much of the start-up access to IPO funds, contributing to the demise of 762 dot-com firms through the end of 2001. The data in Table 15-2 indicates that with just five shutdowns in the first quarter of 2000, no

---

13 Information available at **http://www.webmergers.com/editorial/article.php?id=46**, February 2002.

TABLE 15-2		Dot-Com Shutdowns and Internet Jobs Lost*	
Month	**Dot-Com Shutdowns 2000**	**Internet Jobs Lost 2000**	**Dot-Com Shutdowns 2001**	**Internet Jobs Lost 2001**
January	1	303	56	12,828
February	2	101	59	11,649
March	2	25	47	9,533
April	1	327	56	17,554
May	13	2,660	62	13,419
June	17	1,652	61	9,216
July	20	2,194	40	8,697
August	10	4,193	46	4,899
September	22	4,805	32	2,986
October	36	5,677	36	4,840
November	50	8,789	21	2,901
December	49	10,459	21	2,403
Unknown	2			
Total	**225**	**41,515** at 496 firms	**537**	**100,925**

Sources: Based on information available at **www.webmergers.com** and **www.ChallengerGray.com**.
* The data on Internet jobs lost covers more industries and firms than just the dot-coms shutdown. Internet firms covered include online retailers, technology support and customer services, firms that build and maintain Internet infrastructure online consumer services, Internet service firms including financial consulting and information services companies.

dot-com failure was evident at that point. The number rose steadily throughout the remainder of the year, however, such that 225 dot-coms in total closed their doors in 2000, with 99 ceasing operations in the final two months. The failure rate continued to rise during the first six months of 2001, when an additional 341 firms closed. However, the shutdown pace slackened in the second half of the year, leaving the failure total at 537 firms for 2001, or more than twice the rate of 2000. Webmergers.com points out that the two-year failure number is equal to just 10 percent of an estimated 7,000-10,000 Internet companies that received some degree of formal funding. Some unknown subset of the remaining firms may have been mortally wounded and exposed to additional near-term failure or absorption by other dot-coms. However, the failure rate still left a respectable number of dot-coms alive and operating as of early 2002, hoping that the equity markets would recover and the pressures contributing to the rate of dot-com failures would subside.

Looking at the dot-com shutdowns grouped by area of business, the largest absolute number and percentage of closures was among e-commerce firms in both 2000 (121 = 54%) and 2001 (204 = 38%) as shown in Table 15-3. These would be firms selling B2C or B2B products such as eToys, Furniture.com, Value America, PlanetRx.com and Petopia.com. In 2001 the scales tipped toward the failure of B2B firms. Content providers were the second largest group of e-commerce closures in 2000, with 61 firms and 27 percent of the total, with the numbers rising to 129 firms and 24 percent of the total in 2001, including such well-known entities as DrKoop.com, TheStandard.com, and Bigfatradio.com. Even access firms were not immune from the shutdown plague with 19 = 8% in 2000, and 52 = 10% in 2001. These numbers would include the demise of firms such as Excite@home and Northpoint Communications.

Internet Shutdowns by Sector				**TABLE 15-4**

Sector	Year 2000		Year 2001	
	Number	**Percent**	**Number**	**Percent**
Access	19	8%	52	10%
Content	61	27%	129	27%
e-Commerce	121	54%	204	54%
Infrastructure	17	8%	113	8%
Professional services	7	3%	39	3%
Total	**225**	**100%**	**537**	**100%**

Source: Based on information available at **http://www.webmergers.com/editorial/article.php?id=46**, February 2002.

When dot-com firms fail, the investors and the entrepreneurs are not the only individuals who suffer as a result. At one time the labor market for workers, who were skilled in various aspects of the Internet, defined the concept of a "hot" job market. College and even high school students who were knowledgeable in Web languages, such as html or Java, found part-time, summer, or full-time jobs that paid them more than their parents earned. These payments included the allure of achieving immense potential wealth though stock options, if and when the firm went public with an IPO. Some of the best and the brightest of students cut short their undergraduate or graduate schooling to start their own firms or to work 16-hour days for a start-up. Mature, experienced workers with Internet applicable skills were commanding six-figure incomes with tens of thousands of options for future stock in the firm.[14] The lucky ones became overnight multi-millionaires when their firms went public. Layoffs were practically unknown in the industry, where the norm was to hire new workers, build the business, and hire additional new workers. The expansion was so furious that in Silicon Valley, California, the home of many of the dot-com firms, residential real estate values were driven to average $480,000 per home sold in 2000.[15] The area's boom also led to a ratio of eligible males to females, of three-to-one in some communities, said to be second only to that of Alaska.[16]

At the peak of the boom in March 2000, the number of publicly announced Internet-related layoffs totaled a mere 25 persons nationwide (see Table 15-2). As the bubble burst, those numbers changed quickly. September job cuts numbered 4,805 with the monthly number reaching 10,459 in December. For all of 2000, a reported 41,515 jobs were lost at some 496 Internet firms. The job losses gained momentum into 2001 reaching a peak in the month of April 2001 at 17,554. From December 1999 through October 2001, dot-com retail, software, hardware, and service firms surrendered a total of 137,136 positions. Many of these displaced workers found it increasingly difficult to secure new positions in the remaining dot-com firms as the industry continued to implode.[17]

---

14 Catherine Bergart, "Around the Web World in 44 Days," *The New York Times*, September 10, 2000, p. 3–1.

15 Information available at **http://sanjoseproperty.com/**.

16 For the combination of a whimsical and scientific male-female availability survey to test the 3:1 ratio, see Peter Berg, "The Silicon Valley Dating Game," available at **http://semisober.com/bars/bar-part1.pdf**.

17 Matt Richtel, "Promised Land No Longer," *The New York Times*, November 10, 2001, p. C1, which documents the exodus of workers from the Greater San Francisco, Silicon Valley area.

General Business Forces Causing Firms to Fail

Each failed e-commerce firm—all 762 of them in 2000 and 2001—has a unique story to tell.[18] Regardless of whether a failed firm is Web-based, it still remains a business entity, exposed to the forces that can kill any commercial undertaking. These forces can be loosely grouped into two camps: internally based failure forces and externally based failure forces. The **internal failure forces** are generally the result of actions either taken or not taken by the owners of the firm. They are frequently related to some aspect of the business plan. They may start with a faulty business plan that is either being based upon incorrect assumptions or laced with overly optimistic projections of sales and revenues. Perhaps the entrepreneurs failed to develop a real comprehensive plan at all, in which case the firm is almost universally doomed from the outset.

Given that a comprehensive plan with reasonable parameters exists, the second set of internal failure threats comes from failing to execute the plan properly. For example, the entrepreneurs may have little business management experience. They may not know much about hiring, managing, and compensating workers to enhance teamwork and productivity. They may be weak in decision-making skills, conflict resolution, or employee dismissal if workers fail to perform or if business conditions change. Neophyte entrepreneurs typically have limited or no experience in handling business finances, including attracting and utilizing investor funds, control over costs, bill payment, and the management of revenues, if any.

Lastly, a reluctance or lack of awareness about the need to rethink the business plan as market and business conditions change often becomes a factor. New managers who are learning-by-doing may be too focused on carrying out the strategies and achieving the objectives of the current plan to see changes in the circumstances surrounding the plan. The key is to recognize and admit that the plan, which was so brilliantly conceived by management yesterday, needs to be reworked, modified, or scrapped entirely today. Managing and incorporating creative change in an organization is a difficult challenge for any leadership team. It is doubly difficult if that team brings only limited business experience to the situation.

External failure forces originate from outside of the firm and threaten its continued existence, profitability, or competitive position. Business consultants are constantly reminding existing firms to perform a **SWOT analysis** that looks at the combination of the business's strengths, weaknesses, opportunities, and threats. External threats can include changes in consumer tastes and preferences. Buyers are fickle, especially in e-commerce markets where it is so easy to type in a different URL. Rapidly changing tastes and preferences for fashion items, entertainment, and numerous design features can cause today's paying customer to vanish almost overnight. With only electronic contact, it is difficult to determine why that customer disappeared. A second threat comes from a changing competitive environment. Not only may a new or existing competitor come up with an innovative or better product, the product may be offered to the customer through a better electronic experience or even just at a lower price. Avoiding failure requires keeping a close eye on what all forms of competition are doing, including electronic, catalog and retail competitors.

Lastly, firms may fail because the general economic climate has altered. Business cycles happen, albeit with less frequency today than in the past.[19] The recession in 2001 was triggered by a combination of forces including the higher interest rate policy initiated by the Federal Reserve and the vicious attack on the World Trade Center by foreign extremists. Together the two events helped to sink a number of e-commerce firms that were already suffocating under the weight of their own internal deficiencies. In a

---

18 Michelle Kessler, "More Mergers, Acquisitions of Dot-Coms Likely," available at **http://www. usatoday.com/money/tech/2001-12-28-dotdeads.htm**.

19 Recessions averaged two per decade in the 1950s, 1970s and 1980s. But the 1990s saw just one, early in the 10-year span. See "Recession, Then a Boom? Maybe Not This Time," *The New York Times*, December 30, 2001, p. 3–1.

recession, the overall level of consumer demand falls, and what was a purchase necessity yesterday becomes a postponable luxury today. Financing becomes more expensive or dries up entirely as venture capital-investing partners fail to live to their financial commitments to supply new funds, or as banks call in existing loans and tighten their lending criteria for making new loans.

These forces are not the only ones causing business to fail. Nevertheless, the list of internal and external factors provides a starting point for an analysis of prominent e-commerce failures.

e-Commerce-Specific Causes of Firm Failure

Tim Miller, writing for Webmergers.com developed a list of "Top Ten Lessons from the Internet Shakeout" to help explain why so many e-commerce firms failed to survive and grow.[20] His list includes the following e-commerce-specific failure observations:

1. *Nothing changes overnight.* The rate at which customers were willing to switch to B2C sellers and adopt dot-com innovations was well below the optimistic estimates, which led to an oversized and unsustainable scale of e-commerce investments.
2. *New stuff doesn't replace old stuff.* E-tailing did not replace large chunks of retailing as was originally expected. Therefore, large and costly investments missed their sales targets and lacked the revenue to support their scale.
3. *Too early? Too bad.* Products and firms came online before the broadband technology was in place to support them.
4. *Many Internet start-ups were "un-Internet."* Firms popped up to simply transfer non-Web sales activity to the Web channel. They did so without the creative application of Web-specific assets and tools.
5. *Speculative frenzies led investors astray.* Many smart investors became convinced that the traditional investment rules didn't apply to the Internet and dot-coms. Consequently, they fell victim to the herd mentality and learned or relearned a painful principle about investment rules
6. *Free is folly.* Giving way free content or products can't be made up with revenue generated by some other activity. The value proposition within the business deserved more attention.
7. *Narrowcast was used to broadcast.* The Web is a narrowcast medium that e-firms tried to employ to reach wide and undifferentiated consumer markets. The Web is best at reaching limited markets not broader markets where low margins, massive marketing, and high infrastructure costs doom the venture.
8. *The $50 million rule can kill.* Venture investors needed big projects to absorb large amounts of funding. Scaling e-commerce firms to generate $50 million in revenue killed off firms that might have survived at a lesser scale on revenues of $10 to $20 million.
9. *It is hugely difficult to build the chicken and the egg simultaneously.* Creating both ends of the market concurrently is expensive and time consuming. Potential e-commerce intermediaries (B2B exchanges, etc.) had to build both a critical mass of buyers and sellers quickly and at the same time.
10. *Prediction tools must improve.* Many dot-com failures involved a mistake in timing. The industry needed better tools to estimate the speed at which new technologies could spread.

The value of this top 10 list is that, together with the external and internal failure forces, it helps to paint a picture of where some of the dot-com firms, to be examined in the next section, went wrong.

---

20 Information available at **www.webmergers.com**.

CASE STUDIES OF E-COMMERCE FIRM FAILURE

The Rise and Fall of Boo.com: Crushed by Lavish Excess and Failed Technology

Boo.com, born in 1998, was a pure Web e-tailer of trendy clothing and accessories. The goal of the firm was to marry the scope of and frenzy surrounding the Internet with the mystique of the fashion business, through the artistry of graphic design and Web-based display. Its business plan was to create "a fashion e-tailer, selling urban chic clothing from the likes of DKNY, Vans, and Fubu that was so cool it wasn't even cool yet."[21] Boo would buy products from the luxury sportswear brands and sell them at full price in the global Internet marketplace. They would be European-based, with headquarters in London, and satellite offices in Paris, New York, Munich, and Stockholm. The firm would project a global reach offering clothing on the site in seven different languages, while accepting payment in 18 different currencies. The centerpiece of the Boo buying experience was the virtual changing room. Here a virtual mannequin, tailored to the dimensions of the buyer, would "try on" the clothing and accessory items using highly detailed, three-dimensional graphics. The technology would give the buyer the ability to zoom in and out from any angle, to view the product in all of its fashion glory. The hook to buying fashion items through Boo, rather than through a traditional retailer, was to be part of the Boo Web fashion experience. The Web, the graphics, and the fashions were presented as a package that would sell the site. It was to be the ultimate Web site for branded fashion. Unfortunately, instead, Boo.com became the poster child for how not to run a high-priced Web start-up.

Boo was managed by two individuals who together had some past experience in the fashion industry and who had previously created and sold an Internet bookstore for a sizable profit. Their timing was impeccable, their reputation was good, their contacts were extensive, and their ideas were appealing, grandiose, and sexy. Boo attracted $135 million in funding with the investment banking firm of J.P. Morgan taking the lead and looking to an eventual IPO. Additional investors included a variety of VC firms, along with Luciano Benetton, the head of the clothing chain, Bernard Arnalult, head of the luxury-goods empire LVMH (Louis Vuitton Moet-Hennessy), and the Hariri family, with wealth from construction and utilities in Lebanon. The buzz around Boo landed the two founders on the cover of *Esquire* as the lead in its story on the "Cool Companies of 1999."

Transferring Boo from a conceptual business plan into a functioning reality proved to be a leap that was beyond the skills of the entrepreneurs. The entrepreneurial managers quickly lost control of both the financial and technology ends of the business. All of the software driving the Boo Web site was to be built in-house from the ground up.[22] The interactive programming features along with the rich graphics proved to be difficult or impossible to deliver, or deliver on time. The important and tricky tasks of customer service and order fulfillment were also to be created and staffed totally in-house. A considerable amount of time, effort, and money was directed toward the development of Miss Boo, a computer-animated **avatar**, who would serve as the site's hostess, fashion symbol, and shopping helper. Miss Boo was the electronic face for the firm and her "look" was considered to be vital to the business. Hair stylists, serving as consultants, designed her hair color, length, and shape. Copywriters were hired to construct how the human-like character would look and act, as well as determine what she would say and how she would say it. A $42 million advertising campaign proclaimed the launch of the Web site. Much of that budget was wasted however, because the campaign went on even though the debut of the site was delayed for six months. Satellite offices opened and the payroll climbed to 420 workers with little to do given the debut delay.

---

21 Andrew Ross Sorkin, "From Big Idea to Big Bust: The Wild Ride of Boo.com," *The New York Times*, December 13, 2000, p. G3.

22 Christopher Cooper and Erik Portanger, "Money Men Liked Boo and Boo Liked Money: Then It All Went Poof," *The Wall Street Journal*, June 27, 2000, p. A1.

The Boo.com site finally opened in early November 1999 to horrible reviews.[23] It was slow to operate on dial-up services without a high-speed connection. The flashy graphics took too long to load and the site was too complex to navigate easily. The site's operating system was built to interact with computers using the Wintel technology. Therefore, it was not compatible with Apple's MacIntosh computers. Lastly, only one out of every four attempts to buy an item actually went through. Despite attempts to rein in costs and redesign the site, Boo.com failed in April 2000. The bad site experience along with the collapse of IPO opportunities made it impossible to secure additional public financing. Various reports placed the loss at upwards of $185 million to investors, who under other circumstances were careful and knowledgeable about where they place their money. Today, only the name of Boo.com lives on as part of a larger clothing enterprise called Fashionmall.com.

What can be learned from the failure of Boo? First, raise as much money as possible because the firm can never be sure as to what the future funding climate will be the next time it needs money. Boo did well in this regard. Second, be careful how the money, is spent. Remember, image is nice, but cash is king. Hoards of extra workers with high salaries, lavish expense accounts, and multiple paid consultants eat up lots of cash, fast. Third, don't overreach especially in areas that involve the image of the start-up and time-sensitive technology. Launch and learn. It's better to do a small task well and expand from there, rather than to start big and fail miserably. Lastly, be sure that the sophistication of the site is compatible with the prospective customers' level of technology and their ability to use it. Many e-customers would have to spend a lot of full-price dollars on fashion merchandise at Boo to make it profitable. The complexity of the technology made that scenario unlikely.

Adcritic.com: Flattened by the Failure to Capitalize on Its Own Success

AdCritic.com was a B2C hobby/business, which became so popular that its client service costs outstripped its ability to generate revenue.[24] The firm archived and supplied steaming videos of television commercials, free of charge, to what quickly grew to be a huge consumer audience. The site was started for a cost of $7,000 in early 1999. It eventually amassed a library of more than 3,000 goofy, risqué, offbeat, and rarely seen commercials, along with the more common ads seen on broadcast television. The NFL championship football game is typically a time when advertisers display new, creative, and entertaining ads. In the days immediately after the end of the January 2001 Super Bowl game, the site was inundated with 1.8 million users. In one single 24-hour period, the viewers downloaded more than 12 terabytes of streaming video ad data. That data volume was equal to more than one-half of the total amount of information stored on the computers at the Web site for the Library of Congress. AdCritic was by far the most popular streaming video site on the Web.[25]

The problem was that the site's popularity got far ahead of its ability to generate sufficient revenue to cover its hosting and bandwidth usage charges. Normally the host would charge about $120,000 for supplying that much bandwidth. However, despite the fact that the host only charged AdCritic one-fifth as much, the firm had no revenue model in place that would bring in the cash flow to cover the charges. It operated under the vague assumption that if you supplied compelling content, enough traffic would appear to draw in the money. They had the traffic, with 500,000 visitors per month on average. Also, the site offered value added to the advertising industry by providing an ongoing tally of an ads popularity and effectiveness. The operators of the site still couldn't think of a way to make it pay for itself. Some thought was given to developing a research

---

23 Cooper and Portanger, "Money Men Liked Boo," p. A1.

24 The Adcritic story is adapted from Andrew Zipren, "Adcritic.com's Creators Say It Is a Victim of Its Own Success," *The New York Times*, December 20, 2001, p. C5.

25 Zipren, "Adcritic's Creators Say," p. C5.

business relating to the ads that would cover the costs. Also, an attempt was made toward the end to charge advertising firms to post their content and to register the names of some 40,000 viewers who worked in the advertising field. Similar firms with a B2B focus, with little viewing by a consumer audience, were able to operate profitably by charging the ad agencies to post their material and making the content available to other clients in the advertising profession.

What are the lessons to learned from the demise of AdCritic? First and foremost every firm needs a business plan that at least thinks about generating revenues to cover costs. Compelling content isn't enough to ensure e-commerce survival, especially when the content is given away free of charge. Second, banner ads provide an ineffective way to generate site traffic for the advertiser and ad spending in general has fallen in a down economic climate.[26] For a content site to succeed, it must be able to tap directly the dollar worth of the value added either to the visitor or the supplier of the material, or both. Relying solely upon cashing in on the indirect value of visitors to third-party advertisers just doesn't seem to pass muster. Lastly, if the present owner can't see how to turn a profit from a potentially successful dot-com business, then sell the firm or merge it with someone else who can. Changing the business plan as conditions alter is an important part of any commercial activity.

Kozmo.com and Urbanfetch.com: Urban Delivery Services that Failed to Deliver

What is the answer to those late-night hunger pangs or when there is no time to fix dinner? Domino's delivers! The restaurant chain has become a profitable landmark on the American scene, with the quick home delivery of hot pizza and assorted fixings. If Domino's can succeed with the home delivery of just one item, why can't another firm be profitable with the urban delivery of a number of convenience items including snacks, rental videos, drinks, toilet paper, aspirin, and cigarettes? The list could include anything that enough customers would want in a hurry, but didn't have either the time or energy to get for themselves. Better still, let the customer order the items and pay for them via the Internet. It sounds like an e-commerce business model in the making, and it was for Urbanfetch.com, Kozmo.com, PDQuick.com, and a few other B2C urban delivery services. Whether in hindsight these entities were really **new economy Internet firms**, which also employed bicycle messengers, or just **old economy firms** that received orders via the computer is open to question. However, Kozmo.com, which began in 1998 and operated in 11 cities, attracted $280 million in venture funding before failing in April 2001. Their motto was "Urban delivery in an hour" and they provided "e-mmediate gratification" for eager customers, who were on the last mile of the retail product chain.[27]

B2C urban delivery was truly a learning-by-doing experience. The firms started out as a free service with no minimum order size. They had certain economic advantages such as immediate payment, limited inventory, inexpensive labor, and a sufficient number of convenience-minded customers. However, the logistical problems in scheduling orders, traffic congestion that slowed delivery, and the predominance of low-margin items made profits elusive.[28] The firms turned to strategies that would raise revenues and lower the cost of the service. Kozmo.com instituted a $5 minimum order size that raised the average value of a delivery from $10 to $17. They computerized the order screen to identify geographic delivery clusters that raised the number of deliveries per messenger from one to three per hour. The firm assigned numbers to each item to build greater efficiency into the order picking and packing operation. They altered their delivery menu to include a

26 Vanessa O'Connell, "Serenity, Liquor—but Little Recovery—in 2002," *The Wall Street Journal*, December 20, 2001, p. B1.

27 Clay Shirky, "Why Kozom and Urbanfetch Couldn't Deliver the Goods," *The Wall Street Journal*, October 16, 2000, p. A36.

28 "Urbanfetch Closing Web Site and Becoming an Office Courier," *The New York Times*, October 13, 2000, p. B7.

larger number of high-margin products including DVD players, office supplies, and gift items. In December 2000, Kozmo.com became profitable in its New York City market with a positive cash flow, but the profit wasn't large or broad enough to satisfy the investors, who pulled the plug on the firm within months.

What are the economic and e-commerce lessons that might be learned from the operation and failure of these urban delivery systems? First, they needed to figure out how to get 24-hour use out of a 24-hour asset. By building a companion daytime delivery business to go with the evening delivery service, Kozmo.com would have better used the fixed assets and perhaps brought the operation to greater profitability faster. After all, the McDonald's restaurants began serving breakfast 20 years ago, not because breakfast sales were necessarily profitable in their own right, but because they at least covered their variable costs and made a contribution to covering a portion of the fixed charges. Second, with a delivery service already in place, Kozmo.com easily parcel delivery from local retailers or food delivery from neighborhood restaurants. A larger breadth of operations would allow for the introduction of added efficiencies through economies of scope. The parcel delivery giant, known today as UPS, began in Seattle, Washington, as a local delivery service in 1907. It delivered a mix of items and spread geographically to a number of West Coast cities as well as New York City, where it became the main delivery service for Macy's.[29] Adding the delivery of items from different sites increases the traffic volume, boosts customer awareness, raises the potential for repeat customers, and offers a greater opportunity for profitability. Lastly, the 11-city scale of operation was probably too big an area with which to start. Operating in fewer cities with time to perfect the business model would have helped to hold down the cash burn rate and perhaps allowed the e-commerce entity to prove its lasting value.[30]

THE FAILURE OF WEBVAN REVISITED

If online grocery ordering and home delivery is such a "can't miss" e-tail service, then why did Webvan fail? Was it because of its own internal deficiencies, because of external failure forces, or some combination of both? The **pick-pack-deliver (PPD) strategy** is really an old approach to grocery sales, having been a way of business for dairy and bakery firms, among others, from the 1920s through the 1950s.[31] In the post–World War II period, the birth and rapid spread of supermarket chain stores made it cheaper, easier, and a better all-around experience to shop centrally for groceries. It provided social interaction and allowed buyers to examine the products for quality as well as make price comparisons. Moving the grocery-buying experience online had to overcome the general level of satisfaction that some 75 to 80 percent of the buying public had with the current system. That left just 20 to 25 percent who were dissatisfied and could be the initial target segment for the online grocery firms. However, nothing guaranteed that the online experience was the right approach to overcome their problems with the retail grocery model, such that enough buyers would switch to make the Webvan approach profitable.

Webvan applied a high-tech central distribution model to the online grocery business. They constructed numerous 100,000 square foot distribution centers costing in excess of $25 million each.[32] Their backend operations that funneled the orders into the warehouses required 1,000 servers and 16 employees to manage. The focus of the Webvan model was scale, such that each warehouse had to fill and deliver 4,000 orders per day just to break even. With the delivery of bulky items and the traffic congestion found in most metropolitan service areas, the trucks were lucky to make 22–30 deliveries each per day. Conversely, suburban grocery delivery led to the absence of customer density, such that the distance between stops worked to slow down the delivery process.

---

29 Information available at **http://www.historylink.org/output.CFM?file_ID=2089**.
30 Associated Press, "E-mmediate Gratification," *Connecticut Post*, August 30, 2000, p. D2.
31 Roger Blackwell, "Why Webvan Went Bust," *The Wall Street Journal,* July 16, 2001, p. A22.
32 Linda Himelstein, "Webvan Left the Basics on the Shelf," *BusinessWeek*, July 23, 2001, p. 43

The technology and service ends of Webvan's business model functioned well, as most customers were satisfied with the service. However, attracting repeat customers did turn out to be a problem when more than one-half of its first time users failed to place a second order. It seems buyers discovered that online ordering took up more time in planning and sitting at the computer than they had first anticipated. The repeat order problem revealed a few flaws in Webvan's operating assumption that people, who were pressed for time, were too busy to go grocery shopping. First, if buyers were busy and so time pressed, how were they to find the time to go online at night to order and where would they get the time to stay home and accept the delivery? Second, a typical customer turned out to be a homemaker, with several young children, who found it difficult to get out and shop. The original high-income target market had fewer children, dined out more, and therefore bought fewer groceries. What Webvan's retail grocery competitors discovered is that the high-income, time-pressed buyer desired greater access to higher-profit-margin prepared foods. What they wanted to eliminate was cooking not shopping.[33] Lastly, those who did enjoy the Webvan experience would have been unlikely to pay the $30 to $35 full cost for the pick-pack-delivery of complex, heterogeneous grocery orders.[34]

Possibly the greatest blow to the survival of Webvan model was the realization by its investors that there was another and possibly better approach to the delivery of online grocery services. Tesco is England's largest grocery chain, and it runs a locally based, technologically simple, cost-efficient online grocery service.[35] Their system employs a store-based distribution model, which offers a technology and efficiency tension in opposition to the central distribution model backed by Webvan. The Tesco model treats online sales as an evolutionary event in the sales of grocery items rather than a revolutionary change in the way that the grocery business is conducted. Tesco invested some $56 million to set up a program, which delivered $422 million in annual sales for 2000, with a $7 million in profit. Their preliminary market studies focused on determining the size of the geographic area, which was large enough to serve a profitable number of potential customers from a central warehouse. Tesco found that the area was too large to be covered efficiently, given the metropolitan traffic congestion and the limited number of stops that each truck could make per day.

Their solution was to fill the online orders from their local stores, where delivery times could be cut to a maximum of 25 minutes. Order pickers at local stores can fill up to six orders simultaneously using a computer-directed routing system that scans the items into a virtual cash register. This lower-tech system cuts picking time by one-third. The Tesco store-based system also cuts the PPD cost because it treats online orders as just another sales channel. Prior to the introduction of its online division, the retail customers were already covering the overhead costs for each Tesco store. If the online sales yield a contribution margin above variable costs without cannibalizing some of the existing retail sales, then they contribute to the overall profitability of the Tesco operation. Arguments favoring the allocation of some of the fixed overhead and depreciation charges to the online sales become inappropriate and irrelevant.[36] The Tesco decentralized model has

---

33 Devon Spurgeon, "Traditional Grocers Feel Vindicated by Webvan's Failure," *The Wall Street Journal*, July 11, 2001, p. B4.

34 Blackwell, "Why Webvan Went Bust," p. A22.

35 Suzanne Kapner, "Early Winner in Online Food," *The New York Times*, July 20, 2001, p. C1.

36 Because overhead and depreciation charges are fixed and fail to vary with the type or volume of output, their allocation among the different products or functions that they cover is arbitrary and without basis in economic reasoning. For example, the cost of checkout personnel at the cash register could not be logically apportioned among the meat, dairy, fresh produce, and frozen food departments. For that reason, products are priced sufficiently above their variable costs, based upon demand elasticity and competition, to yield a collective contribution margin that would cover the fixed costs, while earning a normal profit. One might argue that the retail customers are paying too much for their products, because the physical stores also service e-tail customers. Still, it would take competitive pressures from other retail grocers, including those with and without online customers, to drive the retail prices lower.

been adopted by the GroceryWorks.com division of Safeway stores and is being tested in the United States.

At a loss of $1.2 billion, the demise of Webvan might be regarded as the most expensive **beta test** failure in history.[37] What lessons can other e-tailers draw from this event?[38] First, *know your product*. E-commerce involves two parts, and it is easy to be mesmerized and become overconfident in the technology end of the business. "If you can't master inventory management, sourcing, transportation and distribution, customer attraction and retention, warehousing and logistics, it doesn't matter how great your Web site is."[39] Second, *know your customer*. Make sure that the e-commerce product offers buyers a solution to their problems that is better than the one they already have. If 75 to 80 percent of grocery shoppers are satisfied with the current system, then it will be difficult to get them to change their buying patterns in the absence of a quantum improvement in the process. Making the shopping remote, electronic, and delivery-based may not be sufficient. Third, *know how your customer and product interact*. The original targeted market segments may not respond to the product in the way that the business model's assumptions initially led the entrepreneur to believe. Other market segments may see the e-tail product as better fitted to their lifestyle. Most B2C products and services are scalable. Therefore, launch and learn by researching and market testing widely at a smaller scale before risking $1.2 billion in capital investment.[40] Lastly, *know your market*. The best markets for successful e-commerce entry are those with high profit margins and inefficient operations. These characteristics do not describe the retail grocery industry. Although it is fragmented, the grocery industry is a low-margin, highly efficient operation, which is being pressured to become even more efficient by the entry and growth of Wal-Mart superstores. Intense competition combined with large scale usually means added buying power that will reduce wholesale costs and yield lower prices for the consumer. A market with relentless downward pressures on costs and margins is not an inviting target for entry by a higher-cost e-tail competitor, regardless of how large and diversified the market might be.

THE FAILURE OF WEBHOUSE REVISITED

The application of the reverse auction pricing model to the sale of groceries and gasoline proved to be hugely popular with the buying public. More than 15,000 customers tried the service in the first week of operation and the traffic volume became so high that the computer system crashed on average of once a day.[41] The network of 7,200 participating grocery stores and 6,000 gasoline stations ranged from New York to California. Consumer acceptance should have been no surprise, given the average savings of 25 percent or more on grocery items and $0.10 to $0.20 cents per gallon on gasoline. Although the savings were real to the customers, they were a financial illusion created

---

37 The concept of a beta test comes from the software industry, where new software products are distributed to a limited number of test users prior to commercial sale. The idea is for the testers to use the software and to discover any glitches or bugs in the programming before the product gets into the hands of the general public.

38 The lessons presented here are adapted from Roger Blackwell, "Why Webvan Went Bust," p. A22.

39 Blackwell, "Why Webvan Went Bust," p. A22.

40 Taking the time and patience to perfect the Webvan model in a single test city placed the firm in a Catch-22 situation. As an early venture capital investor noted, Webvan "had a unique opportunity to raise a lot of capital and build a business faster than Sam Walton rolled out Wal-Mart. But in order to raise the money, (they) had to promise investors rapid growth." The vision of profits in the VC-IPO model overcame the logic of the commercial activity. Saul Hansell, "An Ambitious Internet Grocer Is Out of Both Cash and Ideas," *The New York Times*, July 10, 2001, p. A1.

41 Julia Angwin and Nick Wingfield, "How Jay Walker Built WebHouse on a Theory That He Couldn't Prove," *The Wall Street Journal*, October, 16, 2000, p. A1.

by WebHouse subsidies. WebHouse's sister company, Priceline.com, often subsidized the match between airline ticket bids and the airlines lowest price during the start-up stage of the business. The logic of filling in the gap with its own money was to allow Priceline to build up sufficient volume so that it couldn't be ignored as a force in airline ticket sales. The volume would attract participation from almost all of the airlines. Priceline achieved this goal, but only with the help of warrants that offered an equity share in the business to the airlines who joined the service. This subsidy approach was applied at WebHouse, with a loss in excess of $5 million per week at its peak and a total loss of $363 million at the time of failure in the fall of 2000.

The participating stores and gasoline stations provided a portion of the subsidy under the assumption that profitable non-WebHouse items would be purchased in addition to auction items. Also, it was hoped that the event would attract new customers to the stores. However, encouraging manufacturers to participate in funding the subsidies proved to be more difficult for WebHouse. The efficiency logic tempting the manufacturers was that the WebHouse model would be a partial substitute for expensive coupons, which manufacturers traditionally used to encourage customers to try new products. Also the WebHouse model would allow the manufacturers to engage in a limited form of price discrimination. They would give selective discounts only to the customers who had the most elastic or price sensitive demand, without having to cut the general price to all customers.[42] Despite these appeals, manufacturers saw participation in the reverse auction process differently. In their mind, it was really a permanent price concession that would contribute to an erosion of the brand's image and one that would have a low probability of attracting and holding new customers.[43] In addition, the firms were not happy with the ability of the bidder to see the actual value of the price concessions on an item-by-item basis. WebHouse had plans to eventually deal with this objection by requiring consumers to bid on bundles of items, so that the price concession per item would be less transparent. Lastly, by using credit cards to lock in the bids, WebHouse was exposed to the 2.5 percent processing fee charged by the credit card companies, which added extra costs to each transaction and further boosted the size of the losses.

What are the lessons to be taken away from the failure of WebHouse? First, Jay Walker, the creator of WebHouse, was right: a large segment of the buying population will spend considerable time haggling over prices if the savings are big enough. The haggling process created a degree of snob appeal and became a personal contest, driven by egos of the buyers, to see who could extract the lowest possible price.[44] Not only does the name-your-own-price model work well in the travel industry, under the right conditions it may be transferable to other markets as well. Second, the investment community abandoned WebHouse when it saw the **burn rate** for weekly losses and when the stock market turned sour on the potential for Internet IPOs. WebHouse could have become profitable at some scale of operation, but that scale was not visible in the immediate future. Therefore, the venture capital investors rose up "to shoot the lame pon(y) in (the) stable."[45] Lastly the geographic scope of the operation was probably too large an area with which to start. It was born as a national system before the technology bugs were worked out. The national scope meant a larger burn rate with bigger losses. A region-by-region phase-in might have allowed the technology to be perfected, cut the interim losses, and allowed word-of-mouth advertising among enthusiastic buyers to encourage more vendor participation.

In the final analysis both Webvan and WebHouse were correct in that they saw a real and substantial market for their services. Neither firm was able to answer two important questions positively. First, would a subset of target market customers be willing to pay the full cost of providing the service? Second, was that subset of participants large

42 The price-sensitive customers would have the greatest price elasticity of demand and therefore be the least loyal to a particular brand. Saul Hansell, "Priceline's WebHouse Club Abandoned as Investors Balk," *The New York Times*, October 6, 2000, p. C1.

43 Hansell, "How Jay Walker," p. C1.

44 Hansell, "Priceline's WebHouse Club," p. C1.

45 Hansell, "Priceline's WebHouse Club," p. C1

enough to make the e-commerce venture profitable enough to compensate for the risks and earn a competitive return that would cover the value of the invested funds?

SUMMARY AND PROSPECTS

The evidence supports the view that business failure is common. Moreover, the mortality rate for high-risk start-ups based on new business models employing new technologies that target new markets is even higher than among the general population of firms. Economic markets support this process of business risk taking as they direct valuable resources into new efforts and take those resources away for other uses if and when the start-ups fail to live up to the original entrepreneurial optimism. The cycle of firm birth and death is a learning process as well, with tomorrow's investors and entrepreneurs gaining insights from the successes and mistakes of today's participants in the struggle for survival and profit. Even though large absolute numbers of firms fail, they generally represent only a small fraction of the total number of businesses. Many firms do survive past the birth stage, growing over time, learning how to adapt to the multitude of market challenges, and solving the tension between the forces of business success versus failure.

The examination of dot-com birth and failure reinforced the view originally offered in Chapter 14 that markets demonstrate economic pluralism. A variety of often-opposing business models are created to deal with the same perceived market gap. For example, Webvan and Tesco created a technology tension by adopting centralized versus localized distribution systems. Webvan and WebHouse created a target market tension by seeing the Internet as a way to focus on customer segments with different views on the trade-off between time and money. Webvan saw Internet grocery sales as a vehicle to tap the customer segment that attached a high value to its time and a lower value to paying more for convenience and simplicity. WebHouse saw the Internet as a means of creating a business model to serve the buyer segment that likes to spend time haggling over price if it will save them some extra money. Although none of these business models is right or wrong in the abstract, their practical application usually shows the superior efficiency of one approach or neither of the approaches.

It is unusual for an entire class of start-ups to fail, but it is not unexpected if the failures are the result of errors in planning or in timing. Some of the examples of dot-com failure discussed in this chapter had plans that fell short of understanding the customer market and how to leverage Web technology to provide a superior, value added alternative to the customer relative to the current set of choices. Others reflected failures of timing or scale where the expectations of the entrepreneur and the demands for size from investors grew faster than the market or current technology could accommodate. Failure on an excessively large scale can be expensive. Some of today's failed e-commerce ideas may reemerge and prosper in the future, either in the guise of smaller firms or as extensions of physical firms,[46] perhaps as universal access to broadband technology takes hold. Despite the rash of recent failures, the Web as a hub of commercial activity is here to stay. This fact is demonstrated strongly in Chapter 16, which looks at some of the B2C services, as opposed to products, that can be delivered over the Web.

---

46 For example, in early 2002, two large West Coast supermarket chains, Albertson's and Safeway, entered into Web-based grocery sales in limited markets. See Michael Singer, "Bay Area Web Grocers Set to Compete," available at **http://ecommerce.internet.com/news/news/article/ 0,3371,10375_989861,00.html**.

KEY TERMS AND CONCEPTS

asset-light companies
avatar
beta test
burn rate
business closures
business failures
compounding
discount rate
discounted cash flow model
discounting
external failure forces
going out of business
high-tech central distribution model

internal failure forces
limited-menu third-party delivery
    model
loss minimization case
new economy Internet firms
old economy firms
pick-pack-deliver (PPD) strategy
sensitivity analysis
shutdown case
store-based delivery model
SWOT analysis
trade-off between time and money
virtual supermarket

DISCUSSION AND REVIEW QUESTIONS

1. Identify and discuss some of the key aspects of grocery retailing that made the product a natural target for Web sellers. Is physical grocery shopping a pleasurable and value added experience or a bothersome experience lacking in any redeeming features?

2. Explain how rival Internet grocery sellers Webvan and WebHouse targeted different segments of Internet food buyers. How did each grocery-buying segment relate to the trade-off between time and money?

3. Distinguish graphically and explain the difference in microeconomic theory between the loss minimization and shutdown cases in the short run. If fixed costs must be paid, why don't they play a role in the decision to produce or not to produce in the short run?

4. Can a firm go out of business in the short run? Why?

5. Use the concept of discounting to explain why the investors and entrepreneurs at Webvan may have decided to closed the firm for good even though the number of customers served was growing, and the firm looked to be profitable within the next seven years. Would the application of a sensitivity analysis have changed their decision? Why?

6. Pick a topic from Tim Miller's list of specific failure observations and match it up with an e-commerce firm known to you or some firm already mentioned in this book. Where did this failed dot-com go wrong? Why?

7. Look at Miller's failure list along with the set of internal and external forces causing business failure and identify which of these applied to Boo.com. Were any other failure forces unique to this firm? Explain.

8. Perform the same analytical postmortem for Adcritic.com and Kozmo.com. What might these firms have done in order to become profitable and survive?

9. How did the physical characteristic of urban/suburban customer density contribute to the problems faced by Webvan?

10. Identify and discuss some of the flaws inherent in the Webvan model of customer behavior for those who are pressed for time. Who was the typical Webvan customer? Why did the original target buyers often fail to return as repeat customers?

11. What was the nature of Tesco's store-based distribution model for online grocery sales? How did it offer a strong organizational and technology challenge to Webvan's high-tech central distribution model? Which proved to be more efficient and why?

12. In general, how did consumers react to the Internet sales of groceries by Webvan and WebHouse? How and why was the issue of scale so important to each firm? Explain.

13. Identify the forces that led to the failure of WebHouse. Were these forces present in the case of Webvan? Why?

14. Identify and discuss the lessons that e-tailers in general can draw from examining the results of the Webvan and WebHouse experiences. What two essential questions were never answered by the experience of either Webvan or WebHouse? Why are these important questions for all e-tailers to answer?

15. As a general summary for the material in this chapter, identify and discuss a number of the forces that support the tension between the success and failure of e-commerce firms. Which of these forces are unique to the world of e-commerce and which affect all businesses, virtual and physical? Can these forces be generalized from the world of online grocery shopping to any type of B2C e-commerce activity? Why?

WEB EXERCISES

1. Link to the site for the convenience store industry at **http://www.c-store.com/retailtrend.htm** for the latest update on retail grocery sales. See also the data for population and c-store numbers by state at **http://www.c-store.com/trendsreports.html**.

2. Link to the Web site for the Food Marketing Institute at **http://www.fmi.org/facts_figs/** to secure general data and information on the food retailing industry. See how the number of stores in various food categories are changing over time.

3. To see the offerings of one of the surviving Web grocers, link to Peapod at **http://www.peapod.com/** or to Netgrocer at **http://www.netgrocer.com/**.

4. Type in the URL of **http://www.Boo.com** to see how recognizable Web names continue to live in cyberspace even if the firms disappear.

5. Anyone who finds the concept Adcritic intriguing may visit the resuscitated Web site at **http://www.adcritic.com/**.

6. An urban delivery service at **http://www.pdquick.com/** is still alive and functioning in a modified format. Other localized services can be found, with some interesting product differentiation characteristics, at **http://www.urbanorganic.net/UO1/** in metropolitan New York City, and **http://www.spud.ca/** for those who live in the Vancouver area of British Columbia.

CHAPTER 16

Introductory Case

INDUSTRIES MAKING USE OF E-COMMERCE LINKAGES

The discussions in the previous chapters built the case that the firms and industries experiencing the greatest success through the introduction of e-commerce demonstrate some combination of the following characteristics. First, they serve a market showing considerable fragmentation among buyers and sellers. Here, one-on-one contact involves a high incidence of task repetition. Second, they operate in markets containing a substantial amount of static information and where the product is fairly standardized. Third, they function where the volume of information can be readily transformed into a digital format and displayed at a secure Web site. As such, users can obtain quick, easy, and convenient access, along with being able to manipulate or respond to questions at the site. Fourth, they represent a market in which interested parties eagerly bear an increased amount of the search costs because of the expected return to be gained from the search process. Lastly, e-commerce appears in markets where electronic interaction in the form of computer-to-computer contact can automate the workflow, removing the need for human intervention and error and resulting in faster and more accurate completion of a given task.

Each of the e-commerce case applications to be discussed in this chapter, including health care, education, finance, and real estate, demonstrate one or more of the previously noted characteristics. They are all service activities traditionally requiring and delivered via considerable individual provider-customer contact. Several Internet sites emerged in each of the areas, offering Web-based commercial links as a better solution to the market needs of customers or suppliers. The specific firms identified as providing the e-commerce contact may or may not succeed, but they at least have the potential to do so, given the inherent efficiencies that they offer to the marketplace.

THE HEALTH CARE INDUSTRY AND E-COMMERCE

Health care as an industry is increasingly dependent on the scale of its operation to allow a flow of revenue sufficient to cover its full costs. The Norman Rockwell image of the individual doctor providing one-on-one, home-delivered care to a patient that he or she has known for 20 years or more has been replaced by doctors banding together in group practices. These practices help to both spread the growing costs of office overhead, and give the doctors a nonmedical life as opposed to being on call 24 hours a day. In addition to the need for scale, other factors, such as the complexity of today's health care delivery system, the introduction of regulatory controls, and the increased sophistication of the services being delivered, offer numerous points of entry for the provision of Web-based health care services. These factors include the following:

1. The hosting, accessing, and delivery of medical information via the Internet
2. The handling of medical office tasks, including scheduling, recordkeeping, and patient billing
3. The linkage with third-party medical service providers, including hospitals, laboratory testing firms, pharmacies, and insurance carriers
4. The automation of ordering for supply-chain management of medical supplies
5. Compliance with federal regulations regarding the portability of patient medical information

e-Commerce Applications:

Health Care, Education, Financial Services, and Real Estate

e-Health Information

The Internet is at its best in hosting, organizing, and delivering information. Therefore it should come as no surprise that a survey conducted by the Pew Internet and American Life Project revealed that the most common activity among the 52 million **health seekers** who searched the Internet on a monthly basis was to look for information on diseases and treatment, clinical trials, and healthy diet programs.[1] On the demand side of the health care market, many people facing medical challenges want to have more control over the events affecting them. They want to participate actively in their own health care programs. Therefore, they are willing to bear a great deal of the information search costs. The self-help motivated acquisition of **e-health information** is one way to gain some of that control. Internet information helped individuals to improve how they cared for themselves, and aided them in making important decisions about whether to seek a doctor's care. The information told them how to treat an illness and how to question a physician about a specific medical problem.[2] On the supply side, health professionals also acknowledge an important and efficient role for the Internet in the treatment of chronic illnesses, including allergies and thyroid problems. In these cases patients must attend to and manage their condition on a daily basis. Therefore the introduction of online interactive contact between clinicians and patients raises the quality of the care delivered.[3]

Doctors can also access Internet information as an efficient means of generating quick answers to the medical questions raised by patients.[4] Rather than spending time consulting a colleague or reading a possibly outdated medical text, the doctor can use the Internet to get information on drug efficacy or prescription dosage with the patient still in the office. This capability saves time for the doctor, while reducing the need for and expense of a return visit. Readily available e-health information may also limit some unnecessary and costly referrals to specialists. Online physician information also helps to improve the quality of medical care offered to rural residents, where local doctors can learn about new treatments and drugs almost as quickly as their counterparts in the urban research hospitals. Physicians can receive regular e-mail notices giving specialists updates on the latest information in their fields. One long-range Internet health care goal is the automatic integration of online patient medical records with the latest

---

1 Pew Internet and American Life Project, "Fervent and Engaged Health Seekers," available at **http://www.pewinternet.org/reports/reports.asp?Report=26&Section=ReportLevel2Field =Level2ID&ID=134**.

2 Reuters, "Web Users Search for Medical Advice Most Often," *The Wall Street Journal*, November 27, 2000, p. B14.

3 Mary M. Cain, Jane Sarason-Kahn, and Jennifer C. Wayne, The Institute for the Future, "Health e-People: The Online Consumer Experience," available at **http://www.informatics-review.com/ thoughts/chf.html**.

4 Milton Freudenheim, "Medical Web Sites Transforming Visits to Doctors," *The New York Times*, May 30, 2000, p. C1.

information on treatment protocols. Here the newest information would be continuously scanned to determine whether specific patients with chronic medical problems could benefit from the latest scientific advances. The bottom line is that for parts of the costly and complex health system, the Internet provides a faster and more efficient way to deliver higher-quality medical care at a lower cost.

Despite the value of the information obtained, two sets of problems arise from direct access to Internet health care by consumers. First, a Harris Interactive poll revealed that the major complaints among a sample of the estimated 100 million health seekers who looked for e-health information in 2000 were:

1. The need for better data
2. The general absence of the ability to interact with health care clinicians online
3. The concern over the site's ability to protect the privacy of those who contact it looking for health care information.[5]

Respondents wanted to do more health-related transactions via the Internet including the online scheduling of office visits and the receipt of laboratory test results. Having an Internet relationship with the physician improved the perceived quality of the health care delivered. This result is particularly important at a time when pressures for cost containment reduce the amount of time that doctors are able to spend one-on-one with individual patients.[6]

The second set of problems was uncovered in a survey undertaken by a nonprofit group of health care professionals.[7] The survey reviewed information on 18 English and 7 Spanish language health sites. The site URLs were obtained through search engines, using keywords involving specific medical conditions. The survey found the following:[8]

1. Internet search engines are not an efficient tool for locating specific health care information. Many of the referenced sites were promotional in nature, selling services or products.
2. Consumers generally find accurate medical information on Web sites, but it can be incomplete or contradictory at times.
3. Web information can be difficult for average users to read or understand.

These findings represent a typical **market failure problem**. The textbook model of competitive markets assumes that information about the product and the transaction is reasonably available to all of the participants. However, the e-health marketplace, along with other markets, are subject to **information asymmetries**. Here, the parties on one side of a transaction have considerably less knowledge about a subject than do the parties on the other side. For the layperson, it is difficult to separate clinical trials and alternative medicine from pure quackery.[9] As a result, buyers can be misled into making the wrong choice based upon outright deception, myth, and ambiguous or incomplete information. For example, consumers hire lawyers, or plumbers and other members of the building trades, send their children to a variety of colleges, or patronize hairdressers,

---

5   Concerns over Internet privacy and security are strong recurring themes in almost all user surveys, regardless of the initial topic. See "Consumers Demand Combination of 'High Tech' and 'High Touch' Personalized Services to Manage Healthcare Needs," available at **http://www.harrisinteractive.com/news/index.asp?NewsID=166&HI**.

6   Laura Landro, "Health Journal: More People Are Using Internet Health Sites, But Fewer Are Satisfied," *The Wall Street Journal*, December 29, 2000, p. A9.

7   California Health Care Foundation, "Proceed With Caution: A Report on the Quality of Health Information on the Internet," available at **http://ehealth.chcf.org/view.cfm?section=Industry&itemID=3973**, January 2002.

8   See the executive summary "Evaluation of English and Spanish Health Information on the Internet," available at **http://www.rand.org/publications/documents/interneteval/execsum.html**.

9   For example, some sites advocate urine therapy for fighting problems from cancer to baldness. See Joseph Weber, "When Web Sites Play Doctor," *BusinessWeek*, August 18, 2000, p. 80.

without having full information about the quality of the service being rendered by the professionals. Reputation, or word-of-mouth recommendations can go only so far in overcoming the problem of buyer ignorance.

One way to help rebalance the information scales is through a neutral, **professional certification process**. The nonprofit American Accreditation Health Care Commission (AAHCC) developed standards and accredited 13 online health care sites, measured by the quality of their information, their disclosure about funding and advertising sources, their linkage to related sites, and other issues covering site privacy and security.[10] The certification helps to build trust in the information received just as the licensing of lawyers and plumbers, along with the accreditation of colleges by professional bodies, helps to ensure at least a minimal competence in the technical area. Accreditation and licensing are not foolproof, but they offer added information to the buyer in much the same way that *Consumer Reports* magazine provides information to the purchaser of manufactured products.

e-Health Management Centralized Online

WebMD was one of the sites certified by the AAHCC. It provides health care information to the general public as well as to members of the medical profession.[11] The firm's goal is to become more than just a trusted Internet information source. WebMD wants to serve as the **gatekeeper**, or general access point, for the multitude of daily medical transactions. It is a commercial, for-profit firm that is selling an online service. The firm offers to connect the various parts of the fragmented health care system from patients and doctors to labs, pharmacies, hospitals, and insurance providers. WebMD is striving to be the central administrative vehicle providing the Web sites and software to facilitate a wide range of medical services, including patient scheduling, record keeping, patient treatment authorization, and billing, as well as claim filing. In general, WebMD wants to be the efficiency-enhancing intermediary in the health care industry.

The firm was formed in the spring of 1999 with the merger of WebMD, an online e-health information site, with Healtheon Corporation, which focused on the processing of Web-based medical transactions. Those transactions currently total some 30 billion units per year. They have an average cost of $8 to $10 each, when done using the traditional paper-based systems, along with fax-and-phone technology. Currently only 10 percent of the transactions are being done in digital form, mostly over private electronic networks such as Envoy, which was bought by WebMD. By connecting the parties via the Web, the goal is to reduce the transactions costs to the neighborhood of $0.25 each, saving approximately $280 billion in annual health care charges.[12] To achieve this end, it entered into more than 80 deals, including the acquisition of more than 17 medical service companies. One of the largest and most strategic was the acquisition of Medical Manager, which builds and markets the practice-management software utilized in 185,000 medical offices throughout the nation.[13]

The WebMD business model is a laudable and potentially profitable one, but it faces several challenges. First, the firm needs to get more doctors to use the system. A survey of physician behavior revealed "only 17 percent of doctors said they use the Web for obtaining or transferring medical records, and only 8 percent use it for health insurance claims processing."[14] However as the security level of the Web improves and the federal

---

10 URAC, "URAC Directory of Accredited Organizations and Resource Guide: 2002 Edition," available at **https://webapps.urac.org/bookstore/bookdetail.asp?id=15**.

11 For more information, see **http://my.webmd.com**.

12 Ann Carrns, "Creating an Internet Health Colossus," *The Wall Street Journal*, February 15, 2000, p. B1.

13 Carrns, "Creating an Internet Health Colossus," p. B1.

14 Ann Carrns, "Internet Use by Physicians Is Increasing, But Numbers Continue to Come Up Short," *The Wall Street Journal*, May 10, 2001, p. B9.

privacy regulations are clarified, more doctors are expected to use the Web for transaction purposes. In 1996, Congress passed the **Health Insurance Portability and Accountability Act (HIPAA)**. This legislation is expected to drive physicians toward the use of a WebMD type of electronic transactions model for two reasons. First, the Act requires that "all external transactions between hospitals, doctors and insurers must be in standardized electronic language."[15] Second, the electronic system must contain "safeguards to protect patients' privacy and prevent unauthorized access."[16] The WebMD product package creates the degree of electronic recordkeeping required by the Act's first phase, which was initiated in 2002. However, until the level of usage rises to generate a profitable scale of activity, the firm will continue to lose money. WebMD's operating losses, which are calculated on a net income basis, have averaged around $20 million per quarter, with a full loss of $4.62 billion, including restructuring charges and a write down in asset values, in the third quarter of 2001.[17]

A second challenge for the firm is to create more value added to the medical professionals from the use of the integrated Web system. The firm brought the various administrative and informational parts of the e-health system under one roof, but it failed to convince the administrative heads of group medical practices that the integrated application of the online system provides efficiency gains that exceed those achieved by operating the parts as individual units. Simply finding a way to streamline the back office operation is not enough. Doctors want tangible, patient-related medical results that improve the quality of care or speed its delivery. For example, they would like the ability to integrate patient treatment with clinical data to enhance the care for chronic medical problems, or a system that would allow them to write point-of-care prescriptions via the Internet using wireless handheld devices.[18]

Pfizer Health Solutions, a competitor to WebMD with a more limited scope, developed a combined online and software response to the patient care need.[19] It offers a cost effective online disease management program for patients with chronic ailments. These medical problems last for more than one year and generally can't be cured, including heart disease, hypertension, arthritis, diabetes, or asthma, and account for more than 75 percent of the U.S. direct medical costs.[20] Individuals enter daily data into a diagnostic software program over a secure Web connection that monitors even minor changes in the health of the patient. If the data show some abnormal movement, then timely medical interventions may forestall the growth of more serious medical complications and limit the number of costly hospital stays. The potential market for this kind of online medical care is substantial given the fact that 80 percent of those 65 years of age or older suffer from at least one chronic ailment.

WebMD also lags in its ability to convert visits to its consumer Web site into scheduled appointments and revenue flow for the participating medical practices. Just as WebMD needs scale to be profitable, the participating medical practices need increases in the number of patients to raise their operating scale, and be motivated to participate in the integrated WebMD system.

The final challenge for WebMD comes from the entry of new rivals. The activities of WebMD, its possibilities for profit, and its potential for dominance as a central linking force within the health care industry have not gone unnoticed. Competitors appear to confront the growth of WebMD. McKesson HBOC, the nation's leading distributor of

---

15 Milt Freudenheim, "Confronting the Reality of a Health Care Vision," *The New York Times*, February 28, 2000, p. C1.

16 Freudenheim, "Confronting the Reality," p. C1.

17 WebMD financial data can be reviewed at **http://biz.yahoo.com/fin/l/h/hlth.html**.

18 Tyler Chin, "Physician Apathy Led to WebMD's Downturn," available at **http://www.ama-assn.org/sci-pubs/amnews/pick_00/tesb1113.htm**.

19 Information available at **http://biz.yahoo.com/prnews/011011/nyth028_1.html**, January 2002.

20 Laura Landro, "Health Journal: Computer Programs Help Physicians Track Chronically Ill Patients," *The Wall Street Journal*, January 4, 2002, p. A7.

pharmaceutical products opened its own e-health unit, iMcKesson.[21] The firm provides Web-based health care services to some 20 percent of the more than 5,000 large-group practices employing more than 50 doctors.[22] iMcKesson's parent already uses a large sales force to regularly visit group practices and hospitals, so the firm can efficiently inform potential clients about the new medical management services system. The iMckesson Web network allows the processing of lab tests and the transmittal of pharmacy scripts, as well as providing contact with triage nurses or mental health professionals by Internet or phone on a 24/7 basis.[23] Competition also arises from the managed-care companies that created MedUnite as an interactive network to conduct eligibility checks, claims filing, and patient referrals.[24] Major managed care insurers such as Aetna, Anthem, Cigna, Oxford, and WellPoint, which already cover some 61 million persons, see a range of opportunities and challenges from the WebMD business model.[25] These firms would prefer to be their own gatekeeper rather than having to surrender some operational control and pay an intermediary, such as WebMD, to perform the function.

Skeptics point out that the insurers may not truly want to speed up the payment flow to doctors, because the managed care firms invest the premiums paid by their clients and earn interest on the **float**. The longer the insurers delay from the time of billing to the time of payment, the more money they can earn in the form of interest. The insurers counter that efficiencies and cost savings introduced by reducing submission errors based upon the transfer of electronic versus paper claims will more than offset any interest losses that they might suffer from initiating a faster payments process.[26] The lesson here is that the potential for profits and market power will generate a great deal of competitive interest, if the model looks to be successful. This situation provides another instance of the tension created by the Web between the forces of intermediation versus the forces of disintermediation. The Web is ideal for creating disintermediation by empowering individuals and firms to do things for themselves. With direct interaction, they are able to bypass the involvement and costs associated with a intermediary. Conversely, the Web also allows for the creation of new forms of intermediation in otherwise fragmented industries, where innovative, efficient, and centralized marketplaces can be created to link buyers and sellers. At times, some of the current participants who gained from the old system don't want to deal with and pay for the creation of a gatekeeper standing between themselves and the parties on the other side of the market. Consequently, a competitive struggle emerges between the Web-minded gatekeeper with efficient new ideas, and the representatives of the existing structure. The latter would like to impose a similar Web-based system on the market, but retain their existing power while earning the gatekeeper revenues as well.[27]

e-Health and Hospital Supply-Chain Management

Hospitals, which spend an estimated $83 billion per year on medical supplies and equipment, are a natural target for the introduction of B2B Web efficiencies in the supply chain. Currently, hospital materials management is based on a mostly manual paper-phone-fax

---

21 Rachael Zimmerman, "McKesson Plans to Launch Internet Health-Care Unit," *The Wall Street Journal*, June 12, 2000, p. B14.

22 Solution-Soft, "Case Study: iMcKesson," available at **http://www.solution-soft.com/casestudies/iMcKesson.pdf**.

23 Information available at **http://www.access-health.com/about/news/prel-comp-health.asp**, January 2002.

24 Ann Carrns, "Health Plans Create a Rival for WebMD," *The Wall Street Journal*, November, 15, 2000, p. B8.

25 Information available at **http://www.medunite.com**.

26 Carrns, "Health Plans ," p. B8.

27 Patients can sometimes engage in their own form of disintermediation by going online to buy cheaper prescription drugs from online pharmacies. In what is acknowledged to be a "murky" legal area, U.S. consumers can buy drugs from Canadian online pharmacies at prices considerably below those charged in the United States. See Sana Siwolop, "Buying Your Pills Online May Save You Money, But Who's Selling Them?" *The New York Times*, September 29, 2002, p. 3–10.

technology working through independent links among hospitals, distributors, and product manufacturers.[28] Paper orders for supplies are sent from operating areas within the hospital to supervisors for approval. The paper orders are then passed to the materials management department where paper catalogs are searched to find distributors who carry the desired item. Calls are made to the distributor to get a current cost quote. Then a purchase order is cut and faxed to the distributor to initiate the purchase process. In turn the distributor, who is basically a storage and delivery intermediary, may have to reorder from the manufacturer. Some hospitals banded together, forming **group purchasing organizations (GPO)**, to aggregate the buying power of several hospitals and negotiate volume discounts. An industry study estimated that upwards of $11 billion in supply-chain management charges could be eliminated by better practices, including a Web-based ordering system.[29]

Centralized online market makers such as medibuy.com offer a streamlined alternative where orders are placed and moved electronically over the Web. An e-mail order would be generated within the hospital to be approved electronically and passed along to the materials manager. There it would be matched with either a manufacturer or distributors through an electronic catalog search, with the software highlighting the vendor offering the item at the lowest current price. The response would be turned into an electronic purchase order to be passed along in digital form for accurate fulfillment and quick delivery. Besides cutting costs, an online ordering system could generate other benefits, such as introducing price consistency into the process by eliminating pricing errors and guaranteeing that the correct price was charged for the item. Also, electronic records of orders placed would allow the hospitals to eliminate unnecessary purchases and better identify repeat buying patterns. Repeated patterns might encourage doctors to use lower-cost products and devise alternatives if they were aware that peers were using the less expensive but equally effective items.[30] Simpler and more efficient ordering, better prices, and the enhanced use of lower-cost materials are just some of the benefits from moving **health supply-chain management** online.

DISTANCE LEARNING: EDUCATION ONLINE

A second service area where the Web may hold some distinct advantages is in the delivery of education online, or distance learning. Much of the public discussion of distance learning focuses on Web as an alternative channel for the delivery of college-level courses for both undergraduate and graduate students. However, the use of the Web for education has many other applications, including the delivery of high quality education to disadvantaged students,[31] making advanced placement classes available to rural high school students,[32] providing corporate training via the Internet, and **eduCommerce**, which mixes the delivery of noncredit courses with the sale of products and services.[33] At the college level, nearly 70 percent of all higher education institutions offer some form of distance learning, with approximately 1.5 million students enrolled in Web classes.[34]

---

28 "E-Commerce Coming to Health-Care Industry," *The Wall Street Journal*, February 28, 2000, p. B4.

29 American Hospital Association, "Efficient Healthcare Consumer Response: Improving the Efficiency of the Healthcare Supply Chain," (released November 1996) available at **http://www.ahaonlinestore.com/default.asp?PCatID=21**, January 2002.

30 "E-Commerce Coming," p. B4.

31 Leslie Cauley, "On Desolated Indian Land, A Catholic School Helps Introduce the Digital Age," *The Wall Street Journal*, July 7, 2000, p. B1.

32 Jacques Steinberg, "As Teacher in the Classroom, Internet Needs Fine-Tuning," *The New York Times*, July 7, 2000, p. A1.

33 Lisa Guernsey, "Education: Web's New Come-On," *The New York Times*, 3/16/2000, p. G1. For a sample list of eduCommerce courses, link to Barnes and Noble at **http://www.bn.com/**, and click on online courses.

34 Daniel Golden, "U.S. Is Inclined to Lift Aid Ban for Web Studies," *The Wall Street Journal*, January 31, 2001, p. B1.

The schools offering distance learning courses vary widely in their backgrounds and involvement in the process. They include Ivy League colleges, such as Harvard, Yale, and Columbia, which list specialized or limited course offerings, the commercial for-profit schools including the accredited University of Phoenix, and the pure online or **virtual colleges**, including the accredited Jones International University. The University of Phoenix has one of the largest all online programs, enrolling more than 29,000 students, offering bachelor's and master's degrees in business, education, nursing, and technology among others, and a doctoral degree in management.[35]

Higher education is a $225 billion per year enterprise. However, it has been characterized by Dr. Arthur Levine, the president of Teacher's College at Columbia University, as being low productivity and high cost, with a minimal use of technology and bad management.[36] For students who want convenience, service, quality, and affordability, the online educational alternative opens up a new learning channel. Distance learning is education stripped of its physical costs of campus construction and overhead expenditures. It offers the potential for assembling an all-star cast of global professors with a wealth of knowledge, practical experience, and teaching skill. The online faculty would present courses of the highest quality at the lowest cost to any student anywhere, who has the desire and determination to learn online. The best education would no longer be the property of the social and financial elite.

As Dr. Levine notes, online colleges focus their efforts on the *business of education* and aren't distracted by the need for and costs of surrounding it with the *business of campus life*. Distance learning eliminates the *explicit costs* of campus buildings, sports programs, physical libraries, dormitories, and cafeteria facilities, along with their support staff. Gone are the expenses of providing various forms of diversion and entertainment to hold student interests during nonacademic hours. Absent too, at least potentially, are the *implicit opportunity costs* of obtaining a college education. E-students can take online classes from home while continuing to work full-time. Distance learning can take advantage of the cost savings resulting from the technology convergence that is affecting a wide range of organizations, including publishing (textbooks), information storage and retrieval (libraries and museums), telecommunications, and institutions of higher learning.[37]

Some Limits to the Value of Distance Learning

Before students rush to abandon the current campus-based educational system and enroll in the new electronic one, however, it is important to acknowledge the academic tension that exists between defining education as an **interactive process** as opposed to seeing **education as an interpersonal process**.[38] Is value added to the learning process if a real-time teacher, as opposed to a virtual instructor, is available for questions inside and outside of the classroom? Or is education simply the act of being exposed to and mastering a body of knowledge and facts that a degree recipient is expected to know? Distance learning is a potentially more isolating learning experience. It is easier for the student to fall into the routine of being a passive information recipient, rather than being an actively engaged partner in the learning effort. Distance learning is less adept at providing student-teacher interaction. In some instances, by design, the all-star professor delivering the lecture is not accessible at all. Graduate students or others who freelance in a variety of courses handle questions via e-mail, testing, or chat activities. Distance

35 Information available at **http://www.university-phoenix-online.info/**.

36 Dr. Arthur Levine, "The Soul of a New University," *The New York Times*, March 13, 2000, p. A21.

37 For example, imagine taking an online, for-credit class at your convenience from your living room. The course would use inexpensive and up-to-date electronic textbooks (**http://www.course.com**), take the students on a virtual tour of the Louvre museum in Paris (**http://www.louvre.fr**), employ data from the U.S. census (**http://www.census.gov**), keep them up to date with daily events (**http://www.usatoday.com**), and integrate all of the material with the latest information on scientific research and discovery (**http://www.nsf.gov**).

38 Joshua Green, "No Lectures or Teachers, Just Software," *The New York Times*, August 10, 2000, p. G6.

learning offers chat study rooms as an alternative to traditional student interaction in the form of in-person study groups, team activities, or the stimulation resulting from socialization with like-minded peers. The dynamics of the classroom, where interesting discussions evolve spontaneously, or students rise to challenge each other and their professors on the finer points or broader themes of the course material are, by necessity missing. Learning as reasoning, critical thinking, and creativity are harder, albeit not impossible, to generate as part of a virtual classroom.

The assembling of the online, all-star teaching faculty is not always guaranteed as part of a distance learning program and doesn't happen without controversy. Prof. Arthur Miller is one of the most widely recognized members of the Harvard Law School faculty. He is a renowned teacher and capable of stimulating student interest in even the most esoteric or mundane legal topics. In 1999, Professor Miller agreed to participate in the development of and to appear on videotape via the Web, as part of the Concord University School of Law online degree program.[39] Harvard Law School saw this arrangement as a conflict of interest, where Concord was trying to raise the image of its own program as being on par with Harvard by hiring Harvard faculty as Concord professors. It was Harvard's position that the only place to earn a Harvard degree was by taking courses at Harvard. This situation begs the intellectual property rights tension as to who holds the proprietary control over the content of a course, the professor whose intellectual effort assembles and delivers the material, or the institution that provides the structural support and compensation for the creation of the course. In his defense, Professor Miller denied that he was "teaching" at Concord. "He never meets, interacts, or exchanges e-mail with any of the Concord students. They are tested and graded by other faculty at the school. When they have questions, about the material in the tapes, it is those teachers, not Mr. Miller, who respond to them."[40] Therefore Professor Miller did not see his distance learning activities as being in violation of the Harvard rule that bars faculty from "teaching" at another academic institution during the school year. Two questions arise from this examination of Web-based distance learning: First, how are professors of quality to become involved in an online program as part of an all-star faculty if their home institutions forbid their participation? Second, if those who give the lectures don't feel that they "teach" in the traditional sense of the term, how does distance learning fulfill the interpersonal portion of the learning process?

Lastly, the federal government instituted two rules that affect the extension of federal financial aid to distance learning students.[41] First, the 50 percent rule prohibits colleges that offer more than 50 percent of their courses through some form of distance learning from participating in federal financial aid programs, such as Pell grants and student loans. The second is the 12 hours of instruction rule, which says that students must be enrolled in a total of 12 hours of instruction, including exams and exam preparations, in order to be considered as full-time students eligible for financial aid. The U.S. Department of Education (DOE) may grant up to 50 waivers of the 50 percent rule, and has done so for a number of online-only schools, including the Concord program. The University of Phoenix, on the other hand, agreed to pay a $6.4 million settlement to the DOE in March 2000 for allegedly counting student learning time activity, including unsupervised chat room time, as part of the 12 hours, and thereby granting federal financial aid to ineligible students.[42] These incidents indicate the potential need for a governing body experienced in distance learning to certify and accredit the online education effort as well as to monitor the quality of these electronic education programs.

39 Amy Dockser Marcus, "Why Harvard Law Wants to Rein in One of Its Star Professors," *The Wall Street Journal*, November 22, 1999, p. A1. Concord is a division of Kaplan Educational Centers, owned by the Washington Post Co.

40 Marcus, "Why Harvard Law," p. A1.

41 Golden, "U.S. Is Inclined," p. B1.

42 Golden, "U.S. Is Inclined," p. B1.

Web Research as a Learning Supplement

If distance learning should come with a limited interpersonal warning label, what about the potential for students to use the Web as a learning supplement, as a convenient way to acquire large amounts of information quickly and easily? Here too the Web introduces a second academic tension between serendipitous learning gained by roaming the library stacks and acquiring information by randomly browsing through the attached hyperlinks.[43] To an important extent, libraries and professional librarians act as filtering entities and validation points to attest to the worth of the works they house or recommend. Conversely, anyone can put information on a Web page and link it to other sites. The content of the page may be fact, opinion, deliberate deception, or prejudice. This matter cannot be judged in isolation. The Web is great at revealing the diversity of information, but the accuracy or value the information conveyed must be checked against other independent sites. It is not enough to validate the reported facts by just connecting to the listed hyperlinks, for they may also contain the same inaccuracies or biases.

The efficient searching of complex databases is a skill that librarians demonstrate through the use of **Boolean search tools**.[44] Most Web surfers lack knowledge of these Boolean skills and conduct more limited keyword searches. Also, different search engines respond differently, if at all, to standard Boolean commands such as NOT, OR, NEAR, AND or ( ). Perhaps the Web should come with a search at your own risk warning label as well. All is not lost with a Web-based search, however. The Web is less imposing for the novice scholar and provides an instant response, which can sustain and reinforce the search process.[45] Web searches can reveal more views and, with some digging, place them in their proper context. The Web can deepen a search faster and easier than a card catalog, with the potential of producing a research product as good or even better.[46] Just as the word processor helped to create better writing, the Web can be a tool to help generate better research results.[47]

E-FINANCE: MANAGING MONEY AND CONDUCTING FINANCIAL TRANSACTIONS ONLINE

The financial services industry is a third area where e-commerce applications of Internet and Web technologies have appeared extensively. Broadly defined, **e-finance** includes the Web activities of traditional banks along with pure Internet or **virtual banks**, firms supplying various forms of **digital cash** for bill payment or transactions purposes, electronic investment services ranging from electronic stock and bond-buying firms to investment advisory services, and, lastly, insurance brokerage activities. Each of these financial services involves a significant element of information listing and transfer, with the electronic cost savings accruing to the e-finance firm. Consumers are willing to bear the transactions costs in terms of time spent carrying on the activity in exchange for the convenience of Web access, the relatively high value added obtained from the service by

---

43 Lori Leibovich, "Choosing Quick Hits Over the Card Catalog," *The New York Times*, August 10, 2000, p. G1.

44 Danny Sullivan, "Boolean Searching," available at **http://searchenginewatch.com/facts/boolean.html**.

45 Leibovich, "Choosing Quick Hits," p. G1.

46 Proprietary or archived information may be available online only by paying a fee. Search engines do not generally list responses to keyword searches in these kinds of databases. No free use is available for microfiche copies of back issues of *The New York Times*, and *The Wall Street Journal*, as one might find in a standard library.

47 Unfortunately commercial sites such as digital term paper mills and college admissions essay services can pollute the leaning process. See Paul Glader, "Admissions Essays Made Easy—But at a Price," *The Wall Street Journal*, January 10, 2002, p. B1, and Laurie J. Flynn, "The Wonder Years: Homework Is Free Online," *The New York Times*, September 10, 2001, p. C4.

performing it online, and the wider range of competitive options that lead to either lower charges or a higher quality of bundled services. With these advantages in mind, e-finance looks like the classic win-win situation, with all parties better off as a result of having engaged in the activity. In fact, one source places the total number of financial service Web pages as being second only to those devoted to pornography.[48] Even though substantial potential efficiencies are present, profits often proved elusive for e-finance firms. Moreover, other obstacles or characteristics render some services as less inviting to the bulk of potential customers. What follows is a brief summary of how well the electronic delivery of financial services is working in a number of key areas.

Virtual Banking: The Rise of Internet-Only Banks

Internet-only banks, such as Wingspan.com, Telebank.com, and Netbank.com, sprang up quickly as a way of taking advantage of the potential for Web-based efficiencies. They exist only in cyberspace, without branches, tellers, and the other overhead costs normally associated with traditional banking operations. Consequently, they could, and frequently did, pass along some of their cost saving in the form of higher deposit interest rates and lower loan rates, compared to their brick-and-mortar competitors. According to a study conducted by the Gartner Group, Inc., approximately 9.5 million account holders manage their accounts using electronic banking. However, pure e-banks have captured only 2 percent, or approximately 225,000, of those individuals.[49] As a result, the low scale of operation resulting from the minimal consumer acceptance of e-banks keeps e-banks from reaching their most efficient cost level.[50]

A number of possible reasons explain why consumers are reluctant to deal with virtual banks.[51] First, the absence of a physical branch network makes it difficult to make deposits and carry on other normal banking transactions. The e-banks are usually hooked into one or more automatic teller machine (ATM) systems, thereby eliminating some of the physical inconveniences. Consumers, however, have been slow to adopt electronic banking in general and banking at virtual banks in particular. Second, most of the e-banks were set up as independent operations without any connections to the physical banking system, including a traditional parent if they had one. For example, Wingspan.com was created as its own entity, totally separate from its parent, Bank One, a large midwestern traditional bank with branches. This separation was thought to impress customers with the entirely new banking experience offered by Wingspan.com. However, the plan backfired to the extent that it cut the firm off from access to the Bank One branch system and the trusted brand name of the parent. Therefore, Wingspan.com spent a considerable amount of advertising funds to both inform the public of its existence and to create an image of trust as well as reliability.

Lastly, the virtual banks did not offer any compelling reason for customers to bank exclusively through an e-bank, as opposed to banking at a local brick-and-mortar institution that opened up an electronic banking channel. Electronic banking lacks a **killer application** to either uniquely meet an unfulfilled customer need, or to provide an existing set of traditional banking services in a clearly superior fashion. **Electronic bill presentation** combined with easy online payment presents one such killer app, but it failed to capture the imagination of either creditors or bill payers. Given these obstacles, a number of e-banks faded into the sunset or became divisions of other institutions. Within just a few years of their birth, Wingspan.com was reabsorbed by its corporate parent Bank One,

48 "'Fool' Followers Suffer, Not Gladly," *The Wall Street Journal* July 2, 2001, p. C1.

49 Plunkett Research, "Overview of the Online Trading, Banking and Investment Industry," available at **http://www.plunkettresearch.com/finance/financial_websites_overview.htm#3**.

50 Robert DeYoung, "Learning-by-Doing, Scale Efficiencies, and Financial Performance at Internet-Only Banks," available at **http://www.chicagofed.org/publications/workingpapers/papers/Wp2001-06.pdf**.

51 Brian Nottage, "E-banks Are E-busts," available at **http://www.dismal.com/todays_econ/te_032800.stm**, May 2002.

and Telebank.com became an extension of the electronic brokerage service E*Trade. Netbank.com is still independent and offering free bill paying services and above-market interest rates on deposit accounts. Others adopted an electronic banking focus to serve B2B customers. To date, virtual banking has not proved to be a major success.

Bricks-and-Clicks: Traditional Banks with an Electronic Delivery Channel

Most traditional brick-and-mortar banks responded to the advent of e-finance by treating the Web as a supplementary channel for the delivery of standard banking services.[52] Banks started out with **informational Web sites** telling viewers about the institution and its products, but requiring them to contact the physical branches to obtain services. From there, banks evolved **brick-and-click operations** by creating **transactional Web sites** that allowed retail customers to check their balances and move funds between accounts, as well as apply for car loans, home mortgages, and credit cards. Business customers can also apply for loans, and, in addition, wire transfer funds, and access cash management along with payroll services, all via the Web.

The key difference between virtual banks and brick-and-click sites is that traditional banks did not need a killer app or compelling reason for customers to use the channel. Customers retained the option of using the physical branch system for the delivery of services if they were satisfied with that form of contact. In fact, even the most avid electronic customers still occasionally visit a branch to deposit checks or undertake some function best handled in physical space as opposed to cyberspace. Traditional banks still retain the option of taking their services to a higher electronic plane by offering more unique e-commerce products, such as electronic billing and issuing electronic money or electronic checks. But they don't need to go forward any farther or faster than their customer base is willing to travel. Unique e-Commerce banking products can emerge gradually based upon customer demand rather than upon technological availability, which requires the institution to prove to the customer why she might need the new service. For example, the popularization of **electronic funds transfer (EFT)**, or electronic checks, has been a goal of a number of private firms in the United States for many years. The financial recordkeeping software Quicken.com and MS-Money possess electronic bill-paying capabilities. However, these features are little used despite the fact that the programs themselves are popular.[53] It is difficult to change consumer behavior on the basis of technological capability alone.

Traditional banks, be they brick-and-mortar or brick-and-click, are facing a strong challenge in the key e-finance area of mortgage lending and refinancing. Mortgage loans have been a staple of the banking industry, especially savings banks, for more than 100 years. They are a fairly homogeneous product, with low **default risk** and a steady profit flow from origination fees and interest payments. In addition, mortgages provide a liquid asset for the issuing bank. Part or all of the bank's mortgage portfolio can be packaged together into a **mortgage-backed security** and sold in the secondary market to raise funds that will allow the bank to originate new loans. These product characteristics, along with their high information content, make the mortgage-lending business an attractive target for e-finance institutions.[54] Numerous mortgage-lending tasks can be easily automated and delivered via the Web, including the borrower's search for the best loan terms, the filing of the loan application, and a number of tasks associated with the loan approval process.

Literally dozens of dot-com mortgage lenders offer highly competitive products to Internet-savvy customers. Heavily advertised e-lenders such as LendingTree.com, E-Loan. com, LoansDirect.com, Countrywide.com, DiTech.com, and HomeAdvisor.com are

---

52 John Wenninger, "The Emerging Role of Banks in E-Commerce," *Current Issues,* 6, no.3, Federal Reserve Bank of New York, March 2000.

53 Plunkett, "Overview of the Online Trading."

54 Larry Armstrong, "Click Your Way to a Mortgage," *BusinessWeek*, March 6, 2000, pp. 174–176.

among those offering more than $20 billion in online financing.[55] Each firm has its own variation on the e-mortgage lending theme. For example, LendingTree works through real estate brokers, who submit loans to the sites put out to be bid on by the actual lenders. E-Loan skips the brokers and solicits loan applications directly from individuals, while IndyMac Bancorp finances its own loans directly with customers. Regardless of the operational structure, a number of the e-mortgage firms are earning profits, including E-Loan and IndyMac Bank. Even Priceline.com has its name-your-own-mortgage division, which began to turn a profit early in 2001.[56] In general, the e-mortgage lenders have been successful in skimming part of a profitable product off of the top of the traditional bank portfolio.[57] Consequently, the Web creates more intense competition for traditional lenders, as well as providing greater choice and better products for the consumer.

Digital Cash: An Internet Unique, e-Finance Innovation

The use of electronic checks may not have stirred much public interest, but the same cannot be said for the use of digital cash. Digital cash involves the electronic transfer of money from one party to another without the direct exchange of credit card numbers, checks, or account information. PayPal.com is by far the most popular supplier of digital cash, which is currently used primarily to settle transactions conducted over electronic auction sites such as eBay and Yahoo. PayPal.com, launched in October 1999, has some 10.5 million registered accounts and averages $125 million per quarter in money transfers, serving as the intermediary between transacting parties.[58] Digital cash payments through PayPal.com cover 65 percent of electronic payments on Web auction sites. This amount is more than twice the 25 percent market share of its major competitor Billpoint.com, which is majority owned by eBay in cooperation with Wells Fargo. PayPal.com earns its revenue through a two-part pricing strategy, with a fixed fee of $0.30 per exchange and a variable charge amounting to 2 to 4 percent of the value of each transaction.

An American Express survey showed that some 85 percent of Americans and 79 percent of respondents worldwide cited concerns over privacy and security as the dominant issues influencing Internet usage, especially as these concerns relate to transactions and the transfer of funds.[59] In the PayPal system, the money to be transferred is obtained from the party making the payment by tapping a prearranged credit card number or the funds in a deposit account. In this way the party receiving the funds via e-mail need not have a merchant account with the credit card company, nor does the payer need to reveal his or her credit card number to a range of unknown recipients. This layer of security, on top of the convenience and ease of use, make PayPal.com an attractive substitute for other forms of Internet banking. Admittedly, PayPal.com holds a number of key advantages, including its demand-driven existence, a large number of users engaging in a sizable dollar volume of transactions, and its reputation as safe and secure. Nevertheless, the firm still has not turned a profit to date. PayPal.com and the e-financial service of digital cash is another case where the scale of the activity is crucial to the future financial health of the firm.

Electronic Investment Services: The Democratization of Stock Trading

The only e-finance activity that may have grown faster than e-mortgage lending is the e-stock brokerage business. As of early 2001, approximately 140 online e-stock brokerage

---

55 Bob Tedeschi, "E-Commerce Report: In a Shaky Economic Climate, Mortgage Refinancings Have Helped One Segment of Business: Online Lenders," *The New York Times*, October 22, 2001, p. C8.

56 "Priceline Expands Stake in Online Mortgages," available at **http://www.newsfactor.com/perl/story/14055.html**.

57 June Fletcher, "The Great E-Mortgage Bake-Off," *The Wall Street Journal*, June 2, 2000, p. W12.

58 "Can PayPal Pull This Off?" *BusinessWeek*, October 29, 2001, pp. EB30–31.

59 Epaynews.com, available at **http://www.epaynews.com/statistics/bankstats.html#17**.

firms were operating.[60] Web-only and brick-and-click hybrids rushed into the market to effectively revolutionize some important steps in the investing process.[61] First, they changed the way that people gather information about investing opportunities. Previously, account customers at physical brokerage houses, such as Merrill Lynch, Paine Webber, Smith Barney Harris Upham, or Dean Witter, had direct access to professional research, performance data, and advice from account executives within the firm. Potential investors without a brokerage account were left to seek general information in the local newspaper or *The Wall Street Journal*. As a result, independent research services such as *Value Line* were created to give every subscriber the opportunity to gain access to the best, most recent information about firms, industry trends, and stock performance. The Web changed the semiexclusive nature of the investors club. Data, charts, real time (or slightly delayed) stock quotes, and copies of legal findings are available at multiple sites on the Web, from Money.cnn.com to USAToday.com or MotleyFool.com, as well as the homepages of traditional stockbrokers.

Second, the Web changed the way in which investors placed their trades. Previously, investors called or faxed their account executives and placed an order to buy or sell a specific stock at a given price. With the advent of the Web, investors still need a previously established account in order to trade. Such an account can be set up by filling out a Web application and combining it with an electronic transfer of funds. One big difference between stock trades at traditional brokers 10–15 years ago and trading with e-brokers today is the cost of executing an e-order. In the earlier period, an executed trade would cost anywhere from $39 to $89 per standard round lot 100-share order. This transaction cost limited both the number of people who engaged in stock trading and the volume of trades that they made. It also gave rise to the birth of the **discount brokerage firms** such as Charles Schwab and Quick & Reilly. Their fee schedules were a more reasonable $19 to $29 per round lot trade, although the discount services were originally stripped of the investment advice activities.

Even these fee schedules look high in comparison to the execution rates charged by the **deep discount e-brokers** spawned by the Web. As in other industries, Web efficiencies relentlessly drove down the cost of doing business electronically. Some services began to provide fee-free trading for certain classes of customers.[62] Others offered low fees of $5 to $13 dollars per trade for general accounts. The ease and speed of entering orders online, combined with the minimal execution charges, worked to greatly reduce the entry barriers to stock trading for most interested investors. As in most markets, when points of friction are reduced, the level of market activity rises accordingly.[63] The changes were so revolutionary that they gave rise to a new breed of stock market participant known as the **day trader**. These people experienced almost mythical successes during the bull market of 1994–2000, which motivated some people to give up their day jobs and become full-time Web stock traders, while others created an intellectual support industry around them.[64]

The advent of e-trading prompted some important adverse impacts on stock trading and stock markets in general.[65] First, it generated more of a short-term mentality, changing the character of the stock market from one dominated by investors to one more heavily influence by the actions of traders. Firms listed on the exchanges want their stock to be held by **investors**, who buy the shares and hold them for the dividends and capital gains to be earned over an extended period of time. Stability in ownership allows firm managers to make longer-term investment decisions that might not have an immediate

---

60 Emily Thornton, "Why E-Brokers Are Broker and Broker," *BusinessWeek*, January 22, 2001, p. 94.

61 Gaston F. Ceron, "Invest in Stocks," *The New York Times*, November 13, 2000, p. R32.

62 Patrick McGeehan, "Ameritrade Offering Free Electronic Trading," *The New York Times*, April 22, 2000, p. C2.

63 Ceron, "Invest In Stocks," p. R32.

64 David S. Nassar, *How to Get Started in Electronic Day Trading*, (New York: McGraw-Hill, 1999).

65 Ceron, "Invest In Stocks," p. R32.

payout, but hold the promise of substantial future gains. **Traders** show little interest in the long-run activities of the firm. Rather, they purchase a stock with the intent of **flipping** it within a matter of days or weeks in response to favorable price movements. Day traders shorten the time perspective even more, holding a stock for just hours or minutes, with the hope of experiencing a quick capital gain.[66] The introduction of real-time, 24/7 financial news on CNBC and CNNFN also helped to reinforce the day trading mentality. The actions of traders tend to make the price of the stock more volatile, with a greater number of shares traded each day. The extremely short-term actions of day traders are similar to but have a significantly different impact upon markets than the actions of arbitragers. The **arbitrage activity** takes advantage of small price spreads for a given stock among different markets or within different time spans. The goal of the arbitrager is to make a profit on the spread. Their actions also work to introduce stability into the market by moving the price of the stock toward a single value. The volatility and instability created by day traders can scare away investors, who shun uncertainty, prefer price stability, and fear the short-term loss of part of their invested funds.

Second, the ease of e-trading can lead some participants to take on more risk than they can handle. Equity markets can move quickly, both up and down. Even with the speed of electronic trading, it can be difficult to unwind complex positions quickly enough to avoid being crushed by an adverse trading tide. The opportunity for rapid unwinding assumes that the trader is experienced and informed enough, along with being sufficiently disciplined to admit a mistake and abandon a trading position before conditions deteriorate even farther. Given human nature, this sort of experience and discipline remain elusive for most traders, either traditional or electronic, and serious losses can result.

Lastly, an equity market that allows easy and low-cost access for all, including the unwary and novice investor, is the perfect target for scam artists, who prey on the combined forces of human innocence and greed. Prior to e-trading, investment scams were more likely to be perpetrated by sophisticated con artists skilled in the ways of markets and humans. Today's scam artists frequently know little about the markets that they target, but are computer skilled and intuitively knowledgeable about the human weaknesses of their online targets. Two examples will demonstrate this point. The first involved a 15-year-old, whom the Securities and Exchange Commission alleged engaged in a **pump-and-dump stock scam** using Internet chat rooms.[67] He would acquire shares of inexpensive stocks with low trading volumes and then talk them up with false messages left on stock trading boards. As others responded to the hype and bought the stocks, he was a seller in deals that "earned him almost $273,000 in illegal gains."[68] Without admitting or denying the SEC accusations, the 15-year-old agreed to turn over $285,000 in profits and interest as a settlement of the case. The second stock fraud case involved a 17-year-old, whom the SEC alleged bilked some 1,000 investors out of more than $1 million through his site called "Invest Better 2001."[69] The site promised investors risk-free returns of 250 percent to 2,000 percent on their funds through a pooling of money to make sports bets at online sports books. In this case, the SEC was able to retrieve some $900,000 of investor funds.

Online Insurance

A final e-finance area that attracted a bevy of electronic entrants is **e-insurance**. Again, the traditional industry contains many of the characteristics that make electronic contact

---

66 One common rule of day trading was stated in the following terms, "I'm an electronic day trader. I seek opportunities wherever I can find them. I'll hold trades as long as I have to in order to reach my objective, *but not overnight*" (emphasis added). Nassar, *How to Get Started in Day Trading*, p. 172.

67 Gretchen Morgenson, "S.E.C. Says Teenager Had After School Hobby: Online Stock Fraud," *The New York Times*, September 21, 2000, p. A1.

68 Morgenson, "Online Stock Fraud," p. A1.

69 Michael Schroeder, "Another Teen Is Cited by SEC for Stock Fraud," *The Wall Street Journal*, January 8, 2002, p. C1.

fast, efficient, easy, and cheap. It is a paper-intensive industry, selling a standardized product, with little brand loyalty and where simple comparison shopping via the Web will lead to policy sales based upon the lowest cost.[70] The intermediation–disintermediation tension is present in e-insurance. On the one hand, *proprietary e-insurance firms*, such as esurance.com and Conseco.com, sell their own brand of insurance directly to the public on their own Web sites. However, sites for *insurance supermarkets*, including Quotesmith.com and InsWeb.com, act as insurance intermediaries, and offer quotes from a stable of hundreds of insurance firms in response to a customer inquiry.

The appearance of electronic insurance supermarkets tends to pose a serious economic problem for other firms in the insurance industry. First-time customers tend to be unprofitable for insurance carriers, especially those providing auto insurance. Unknown drivers are more difficult to underwrite in terms of their accident risks and may switch from insurer to insurer. Only when the customers renew their policies in subsequent years do the carriers begin to make a profit. If at renewal time, the Web makes it easier for customers to hop electronically from seller to seller, searching for the best deal, then the profits in the industry will be driven toward zero. Profits will be diminished or erased by the intense price competition on the one hand, and the tendency to have loose underwriting standards to attract new policyholders on the other.[71]

The new auto e-carriers may also have unique problems in passing along any of their cost savings generated by their Web efficiencies. First, auto insurance rates are regulated by individual state agencies that may slow down the pace at which e-insurance firms can pass along their savings. Second, e-insurance firms providing auto coverage may be able to hold down their costs on the *acquisition side* of the business but may be inexperienced in *managing the claims side*. Some 80 percent of auto policy revenues are paid out in the form of claims for accident injuries and vehicle damage. Experienced claims adjusters help to hold down the cost of claims and guard against the filing of false claims. E-carriers such as Esurance have experimented with contracting out their claims adjustment activities as an added way of saving on insurance costs. This outsourcing could prove to be an expensive experiment.

ONLINE REAL ESTATE BROKERS

The final example of an area in which the Web is changing the way in which traditional firms do business is in the real estate market, both residential and commercial. Traditional residential real estate firms enter into an exclusive sales contract with the homeowner in exchange for providing a number of free selling services. They spend time showing the home to prospective customers, they incur the costs of displaying the property in newspaper and other advertising, and they list the property in the area-wide Mutual Listing Service (MLS) real estate book that goes out to all area member real estate agents. They provide these services in exchange for a commission that is approximately 6 percent of the sale price in the event of the sale of the property. Six percent amounts to $12,000 on a home selling for $200,000. With those kinds of dollars, it isn't surprising to see a number of residential **e-real estate firms**, such as erealty.com or ziprealty.com, emerging. The greater New York realty firm Your Home Direct or yhd.com will list and sell your home over the Internet for as little as a 2 percent commission. Other e-real estate firms will list the property on a real estate Web site for a fixed fee, usually in the range of $500, and allow the seller to entertain offers directly from buyers or from brokers with buyer contacts, without a further payment to the listing service. Some of the discount Internet brokers save money by shifting a portion of the selling tasks to the homeowner who, for example, may be responsible for showing the home.

---

70 Deborah Lohse, "Major Auto Insurers Are Warming Up to Internet Sales," *The Wall Street Journal,* February 15, 2000, p. B4.
71 Lohse, "Major Auto Insurers," p. B4.

As in most of the other industry examples chronicled previously, the residential real estate business has a number of characteristics that make it attractive to conduct at least part of the process online. The real estate brokerage service involves a fairly standardized product with a considerable amount of information. Prospective buyers can search the listings of available homes at their convenience and even conduct video home tours without leaving the seat in front of their computer. Physical visits still need to be arranged, but some of the initial paperwork such as filing a mortgage application can be done via the Web. One obstacle for the discount Internet realtor is getting traditional brokers to show the Internet listing to their potential customers. It is common practice for agents of the buyer and seller to split the sales commission, with each receiving 3 percent. If traditional brokers continue to demand their full share of a transaction, then the source of savings in commissions for the e-seller is limited to the discount offered by the listing agent.

Recognizing their vulnerability to Internet competitors, local real estate boards establish their own Web sites, many of which are linked to Homestore.com. This firm operates a family of realtor Web sites including Realtor.com, which is the official site of the National Association of Realtors. Homestore.com "has created the only truly national property-listing service because of its exclusive contracts with many of the local Multiple List Service that Realtors and brokers use to post homes for sale."[72] The Antitrust Division of the U.S. Department of Justice initiated an investigation covering the potential purchase of Move.com, a competing e-listing service, by Homestore. The merger would give Homestore access to the 200,000 sales agents and listings of three major nationwide real estate chains including Century 21, Coldwell Banker, and ERA. The Justice Department expressed concern about "exclusionary conduct and monopolization of Internet realty sites in the United States."[73]

Brokers in the commercial real estate market are also feeling the pressures from Internet competitors. This market is even more fragmented than the residential one. Therefore commercial Internet listing services perform a real service to the entire industry by collecting raw data on available space and centralizing it on the Web.[74] With prospective tenants and buyers able to do more of the electronic searching and document exchange themselves, the tendency is to look for concessions on the commissions being charged. The challenge is for the brokers to provide more value as part of their participation including "juggling tricky office requirements in crowded markets, haggling for better deals and analyzing the financial consequences of a real-estate purchase."[75] As one broker stated, with their sophisticated consulting services, brokers are protected, at least in part, from Internet competition because, "The Net does not think."

SUMMARY AND PROSPECTS

This chapter outlined a number of e-commerce industries in which linking the delivery of a portion of the product to the Web produces a good fit. The four industries of health care, education, financial service, and real estate are all service oriented, with secondary links to the sale and delivery of a tangible product. About two-thirds of the examples covered B2C activities, while the remainder, such as supply-chain management, commercial real estate, and the back office operations of group medical practices, took a B2B focus. The industries also typically involve activities that most

---

72 Jerry Guidera, "U.S Widens Inquiry of Homestore.com, Reviewing Bid for Cendant's Move.com," *The Wall Street Journal*, November 7, 2001, p. A4.

73 The financial actions of executives at Homestore.com also attracted the attention of the SEC in terms of securities fraud. See David D. Kirkpatrick, "Guilty Pleas Are Expected at Homestore," *The New York Times*, September 25, 2002, p. C1.

74 Motoko Rich, "For Brokers, the Internet Looms Ever Larger," *The Wall Street Journal*, August 25, 2000, p. B12.

75 Rich, "For Brokers," p. B12.

individuals come in contact with at some point in their lives. It may be easier to see and relate to the kinds of subtle changes in the delivery and quality of the business products being introduced by the Internet and its multimedia cousin, the World Wide Web.

Lastly, these industries demonstrate many of the key structural and content characteristics that make service delivery online a potentially successful activity. First, each industry delivers a fairly standardized product. Although some doctors may be more skilled than others and some schools may deliver higher-quality courses then others, the process of professional certification, bank examination, or external regulation offers the Web customer a minimally acceptable level of competence. Second, each industry contains a strong information component, where buyers may receive greater value by bearing some of the search costs and conducting a part of the information gathering on their own time, at their own pace. The search doesn't have to be perfect, 100 percent accurate, or complete. What the results of the search can do are to reduce some of the information asymmetries, leaving the consumer better informed and better able to deal with the industry professionals as the buying process moves off-line and into direct contact.

Third, the industries are highly fragmented, with many buyers and sellers. Bringing them together in a central electronic location helps to boost the efficiency and lower the cost of delivering the service. Fourth, Web technology allows for an electronic flow of information among the humans in the service chain. This flow is accomplished with minimal need for the competing paper-fax-phone technology that often slows down the information exchange process. Finally, the Web offers the potential for a truly automated electronic flow of information from computer to computer, eliminating most of the human intervention. Humans experience conflicting demands, live on a time schedule, make mistakes, and inject emotion into the flow. These elements can reduce the processing speed and introduce errors into the information flow.

Nevertheless, intervention by human professionals can also improve the quality of service, by introducing judgment, concern, and guidance, by weighting the pieces of information and suggesting alternative courses of action, and by challenging the human customers to behave or think differently. When consumers perceive the Web as being electronic and remote, the question of trust arises in their minds. As the technology begins to limit the human interaction in the delivery of the service, the question of quality begins to appear. It is not just the field of education that asks the question as to whether the delivery of quality service is more interpersonal than it is interactive. Medical professionals want to be able to deliver a better quality of care to their patients. Educators want to leave students with the ability to think and reason on their own, rather than graduating automatons that can spit back verbatim, undigested facts. Bankers and brokers want to serve their communities, making them better places to live.

What, then, is the future of the Web in these service industries? Is it in existence just to drive down costs, reduce profits, and eliminate inefficient humans? Hardly! The concept that "The Net does not think" is one of the most important observations to date. The Web is a supplemental tool to achieve efficiency and service, but it is not the service itself. The discovery of the wheel was one of the most important events in human development. It reduced the level of human drudgery, raised the volume of tasks accomplished, and eliminated some of the need for human brawn. Rather than putting people out of work, the wheel may be the discovery responsible for creating more jobs than any other innovation. With less need for manual labor, people were given the chance to develop more intellectual skills and services. So it is and will be with the Web. It will be the humans who will find ways to add value to Web-based, e-commerce services, rather than the other way around.

KEY TERMS AND CONCEPTS

arbitrage activity
boolean search tools
brick-and-click operations
day trader
deep discount e-brokers
default risk
digital cash
discount brokerage firms
disease management
distance learning
e-Finance
e-Health information
e-Insurance
e-Real estate firms
electronic bill presentation
electronic funds transfer (EFT)
50 percent rule
flipping
float

gatekeeper
group purchasing organizations
Health Insurance Portability and
    Accountability Act (HIPAA)
health seekers
health supply-chain management
information asymmetries
informational Web site
investors
killer application
market failure problem
mortgage-backed security
professional certification process
pump-and-dump stock scam
pure e-banks
traders
transactional Web site
virtual banks
virtual colleges

DISCUSSION AND REVIEW QUESTIONS

1. Identify the four industry or product characteristics that accompany the products or services most likely to be profitable when provided via the Web. What makes the Web a superior vehicle for the delivery of these items?

2. Explain how the Web can better satisfy the patient demand for medical information while also improving the quality of health care supplied.

3. Identify and discuss some of the problems and limitations associated with the delivery of health care information by the Web.

4. Identify and discuss some of the problems that limited the success of WebMD.

5. What are some of the advantages and disadvantages of distance learning? What is the nature of the academic tension between education as an interactive versus an interpersonal process?

6. Is Professor Miller from Harvard creating a conflict of interest by offering his course as part of the Concord University School of Law online degree program? Why?

7. Have the virtual banks been successful as competitors to physical banks? Why?

8. What is PayPal.com? How is it able to create a special niche in the e-finance marketplace?

9. What are some of the problems associated with the electronic trading of stock? Distinguish between the actions and motivations of day traders versus investors. Do both have a place in the stock market? Why?

10. How does the existence of online insurance companies affect the profitability of all insurance firms? Why?

11. What is meant by the phrase "The Net does not think"? How does this concept provide a bit of comfort to traditional real estate and other service providers who face competition online?

WEB EXERCISES

1. To see a sample of the range and quality of health information available on the Web, link to WebMD at **http://my.webmd.com**. If the quality of the food in the school cafeteria is promoting weight gain, read up on WebMD's latest diet information.

2. If you would like to know more about your rights as a consumer under the Health Insurance Portability and Accountability Act of 1996, link to HIPAA online at **http://cms.hhs.gov/hipaa/hipaa1/default.asp**.

3. To see how WebMD is doing financially as a business link to the latest data at **http://biz.yahoo.com/fin/l/h/hlth.html**. Type in the WebMD name at google.com to see whether any recent articles detail its current professional status.

4. If you are tired of all this academic work and hate the amount of "spam" or unsolicited e-mail that you receive on an almost daily basis, link to a diversionary game at **http://torturegame.emailsherpa.com/** and take electronic revenge on spammers.

5. If a B2C or B2B eduCommerce course may be of interest, link to either **http://www.bn.com/** and click on online courses, or go to **http://home.click2learn.com/**.

6. To learn about eduCommerce in general link to **http://www.e-learningxp.nl/hyperlink/artikelen/educommerce.pdf**.

7. For a look at a full array of online courses leading to a certified degree link to the University of Phoenix online at **http://www.university-phoenix-online.info/**. Check out their headings for programs, accreditation, and cost.

8. Link to the Concord University School of Law online degree program at **http://www.concord.kaplan.edu/info/custom/concord/index.asp?source=600019**. Click on the link Faculty and Lecturers. Is Professor Miller still associated with the school? Click on Admissions and find their current tuition schedule. How does the tuition amount compare to a traditional physical law school?

9. To brush up on your Boolean search tool commands in order to undertake more efficient Web searches link to **http://searchenginewatch.com/facts/boolean.html**. The site also links to numerous articles that evaluate the relative merits of the different search engines.

10. For a closer look at a virtual bank link to **http://www.netbank.com/**. See how their loan and deposit rates compare to your physical bank.

11. Link to **http://www.esurance.com/** to see the range of products and price offered online.

12. Link to **http://www.homestore.com/** to see the range of real estate services available from this site.

13. For a look at a legitimate Canadian seller of prescription pharmaceuticals to U.S. residents link to **http://www.canadameds.com/**.

Issues in e-Commerce and the Internet

CHAPTER

17

Introductory Case

TAXING FINAL SALES: E-TAILERS VERSUS RETAILERS

Ever heard the old saying, "Nothing is as certain as death and taxes?" Living and dying are part of the human condition. They are also part of the business life cycle, especially as witnessed by the rapid appearance and demise of so many e-commerce firms. Taxes, too, generally come with an aura of inevitability surrounding them. If you doubt it, try going for a few years without paying taxes to the IRS on earned income. The revenuers may be slow to respond, but except in rare cases, they are like the Texas Rangers: they always get their man or woman. Despite a broad base for items to be taxed, an interesting and important anomaly is associated with some e-tail sales using the Internet. If consumers buy the latest CD from Bruce Springsteen or Barenaked Ladies at the local music store, they pay a sales tax on the item. Conversely, if the purchase is made over the Internet from Amazon.com, the buyer escapes paying a sales tax on the same item. Is this distinction just an oversight by the tax collector, or is some deliberate reason behind this unequal treatment of the same purchase, depending on the seller?

The government taxes a wide variety of items in the United States. Items subject to taxes include the income of individuals and businesses, the value of tangible property, asset transfers at the time of death, goods entering the country that are produced elsewhere, and the sale of products for final use. The taxes levied on the sale of final goods come in two forms: excise taxes and sales taxes. An **excise tax** is a fixed amount of money levied per unit sold. For example, federal, state, and sometimes local excise taxes are levied on each gallon of gasoline sold. It doesn't matter whether the price of the

gasoline without the tax is $0.60 or $1.10 per gallon, the federal excise tax of $0.185 per gallon remains the same. Federal excise taxes, sometimes called **sin taxes**, are also levied per pack of rolled cigarettes and per gallon of alcohol. As an act of public policy, Congress and some states raised the cigarette tax over the past few years as a way of improving public health—using the higher price to discourage smoking.

A **sales tax** is levied *ad valoreum*, or according to the value of the item being purchased. No sales tax is levied at the national level in the United States. However, some tax experts advocate the introduction of a **value added tax**, similar the ones that exist in Europe, which have the same revenue-raising capacity as a national sales tax. Most states and sometimes localities levy sales taxes. Both the **sales tax rate** and the **sales tax base**, or list of items subject to the sales tax, vary widely among the states. However, almost all would tax the sale of a music CD, DVD movie, or a child's toy. If the buyer shifts the purchase from a local retailer to an Internet e-tailer, the situation may change, however, because a portion of the online sale of consumer goods is currently sheltered from taxes by federal law. This anomaly reflects the key tension that is the focus of this chapter, which pits the desire of Congress to *foster the growth of the Internet* against the public policy goal of *maintaining tax neutrality* by creating a simple, level playing field for the levying of state sales taxes. The federal exemption creates an uneven playing field, which places the retailer at a competitive disadvantage, making it relatively more attractive to shop online. The difference can be small or large depending on the percentage of the state and local sales tax levy. In some cases it can be enough to change consumer behavior, tilting the purchase in favor of the e-tailer and against the retailer, especially if the e-tailer also provides free shipping. Although the e-tailer sale may help promote the expansion of e-commerce, it hurts the state that loses the ability to collect the sales tax and support local

The Taxation of e-Commerce

spending. Why would Congress decide to legislate this hole in the tax law? Will this temporary moratorium be made permanent? How does it affect seller and buyer behavior? Are tangible sales conducted online the only items with a sales tax exemption? What might be the consequences for online sales if the exemption is repealed? These taxation and e-commerce questions will be examined within the following sections.

THE ECONOMICS OF SALES TAXES AND E-COMMERCE COMPLEXITIES

The data in Figure 17-1 list the sales tax rate as of January 1, 2002, and the percentage of state revenue collected from general sales tax receipts as of 2001. The figure shows the wide variation in rates among the states and the heavy extent to which most states depend on sales tax revenues to finance services and transfers to local governments. For all 50 states, the sales tax rate averaged 4.63 percent. Five states, including Alaska, Delaware, Montana, New Hampshire, and Oregon, did not levy a general tax on final sales. Two states, Virginia and Colorado, had a sales tax rate below 4 percent. On the upper end, Rhode Island and Mississippi levied the highest sales tax rate of 7 percent. From 1999 to 2002, the trend was to lower the state sales tax rate as the strength of the national economy brought surplus revenues into most state treasuries. In 1999, the 50-state average was 5.36 percent with New York, California, Alabama, and Washington, all registering rates at or above 8 percent. In 2001, the 50 states relied on the sales tax to raise 32.1 percent of their total state-based revenues, on average. This figure was down slightly from 32.3 percent in 2000. However, six states depended on the general sales tax to raise more than 50 percent of their state-generated funding: Florida, Nevada, South Dakota, Tennessee, and Texas, with Washington relying on the tax to raise a whopping 63.6 percent of its state-based revenues. Apart from those states that don't levy a general sales tax, only three states, New York, Virginia, and Vermont, raised 20 percent or less of their revenues from the sales tax. The conclusion is that state revenue generated by the tax on retail sales is a vital part of the income flow for most states. Any disruption in a state's capacity to collect sales tax revenues seriously affects its ability to balance the state budget.

One problem resulting from the states relying so much on the sales tax for their revenue involves the fact that the sales tax is a **regressive tax**. Persons with lower income levels generally pay a higher percentage of their income in the form of the tax, because low- and middle-income individuals tend to spend a larger percentage of their income on tangible, taxable items than do wealthier persons, who may save more of their income. Therefore, poorer individuals bear a greater relative **tax burden** for the financing of state government via the sales tax than do higher-income residents. A second concern arises from the fact that the data in Table 17-1 display only the state sales tax numbers. Approximately 7,800 sales tax jurisdictions include numerous county and local governments that levy their own

TABLE 17-1			State General Sales/Use Tax Rates and Percentage of Revenue Raised		
State	**Tax Rate % (1/1/2002)**	**% Revenue 2001**	**State**	**Tax Rate % (1/1/2002)**	**% Revenue 2001**
Alabama	4.00	26.7	Montana	0.00	00.0
Alaska	0.00	00.0	Nebraska	5.00	33.8
Arizona	5.60	46.4	Nevada	4.25	53.5
Arkansas	5.13	36.1	New Hampshire	0.00	00.0
California	6.00	26.9	New Jersey	6.00	29.9
Colorado	2.90	26.0	New Mexico	5.00	40.5
Connecticut	6.00	32.8	New York	4.00	19.6
Delaware	0.00	00.0	North Carolina	4.50	22.1
Florida	6.00	59.0	North Dakota	5.00	27.6
Georgia	4.00	34.1	Ohio	5.00	32.1
Hawaii	4.00	46.8	Oklahoma	4.50	24.2
Idaho	5.00	30.6	Oregon	0.00	00.0
Illinois	6.25	27.3	Pennsylvania	6.00	32.1
Indiana	5.00	35.3	Rhode Island	7.00	31.0
Iowa	5.00	34.0	South Carolina	5.00	40.5
Kansas	4.90	34.9	South Dakota	4.00	52.7
Kentucky	6.00	28.8	Tennessee	6.00	57.3
Louisiana	4.00	33.4	Texas	6.25	50.0
Maine	5.00	30.6	Utah	4.75	36.4
Maryland	5.00	24.5	Vermont	5.00	13.8
Massachusetts	5.00	21.8	Virginia	3.50	20.2
Michigan	6.00	34.7	Washington	6.50	63.6
Minnesota	6.50	27.9	West Virginia	6.00	27.1
Mississippi	7.00	49.0	Wisconsin	5.50	30.7
Missouri	4.23	31.7	Wyoming	4.00	36.1
State Average				4.63	32.1

Sources: Tax collections information available from: **http://www.taxadmin.org/fta/rate/00taxdis.html**; sales tax rate information available from **http://www.salestaxinstitute.com/sales_tax_rates.html**.

sales tax in addition to the state percentage.[1] These tax rates, where applicable, averaged 1.6 percent in 2001. Therefore, in some regions, the importance of the sales tax extends beyond the state treasury.

The origin of the sales tax levy for most states in the United States dates back to the time of the Great Depression in the 1930s.[2] States and localities were concerned about maintaining the stable flow of tax revenue to support the delivery of vital community services, including courts, police, fire, education, and public works. Revenues from property

1 "Sales Tax Rate Analysis 2001," available at **http://www.vertexinc.com/cybrary/sales_tax/ 2001_tax_facts.asp**.

2 Much of the information in this and the following paragraphs has been adapted from David Clay Johnson, "Coming Soon to a Web Site Near You: A Simpler Sales Tax," *The New York Times*, September 22, 1999, p. R20.

taxes, fees, and licenses all declined with the depression, but consumers still had to buy basic items. On that basis a tax on the general sale of merchandise was instituted in many states. **Sales tax administration in the industrial age** was a fairly simple proposition. The merchant collected the tax at the *time* and *place* of sale, when ownership of the item transferred physically from the merchant to the buyer. Both the buyer and the seller easily knew the tax rate, the list of taxable items, and the jurisdictions levying the tax. The seller made the physical payment by transferring the revenues to the appropriate jurisdiction, acting in the capacity as an unpaid agent of the state. Figure 17-1 demonstrates that in most cases, the **tax incidence** or *financial burden* was borne by the buyer, when the seller pushed all or most of the tax forward as an addition to the final purchase price. S_1 is the supply curve representing the availability of the item without the sales tax, while S_2 shows the higher sales price to the buyer with the sales tax, equal to the distance AB. If the market demand for the product is relatively elastic, such as D_1, then the tax could motivate a drop in sales to Q_2, as some consumers forgo the purchase rather than pay the tax. Consequently, the seller is forced to bear some of the burden in the form of a lower product price. The height of the price increase from P_1 to P_2 is less than the height of the sales tax AB. However, for many taxed items, the market demand is relatively inelastic, as in D_2, given the limited number of good substitutes. Consumers are left with no way to purchase the product and avoid the tax without going across the border to another jurisdiction with a lower tax, or buying the item tax-free through a catalog seller. Exercising either of these options involves extra cost and a time delay. Therefore, the seller is generally able to shift most or all of the tax forward onto the consumer.

Sales Tax Administration in the Information Age

Sales tax administration in the information age becomes a more intricate and uncertain activity. The sale of e-commerce items introduced a double layer of complexity.

The Incidence of a Sales Tax   **FIGURE 17-1**

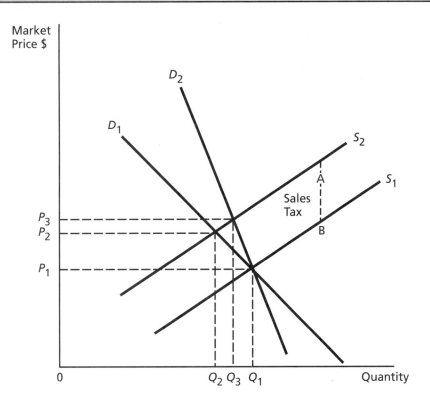

First, are **jurisdictional issues**. If an online sale takes place across the borders of different taxing districts, which jurisdiction's sales tax rate would apply, that of the seller or the buyer? This confusion over *where* a sale occurs, begs the question of *when* a sale takes place for purposes of taxation. For example, is it when the item is paid for and shipped, or only when the final consumer receives it? Internet sales are highly fluid and open to a variety of where and when interpretations. Is the sale location the home office of the seller, the location of the servers that record the electronic transaction, the shipping location of the warehouse, the location of the buyer at the time of purchase, the billing address for payment, or the shipping address for delivery? Suppose a buyer who lives in Connecticut goes on a business trip to New York City. There, he or she uses a hotel computer to buy a book from Amazon.com, using a credit card. The book is to be sent to a grandchild with a different last name, who lives in Massachusetts. Amazon's computers are located on a server farm in Oregon, while its headquarters are located in Seattle, Washington. The book is shipped from a warehouse in Kentucky, with the credit card company sending the bill to the buyer's work address in Rhode Island.

Where and when did the actual transaction take place, and who gets to collect the sales tax? If the answer is Rhode Island then the buyer pays an additional 7 percent in sales tax. If Oregon is the correct answer, the buyer pays no extra charge. If the answer is New York, the buyer could rightly claim that he didn't pay for it in New York, purchase it from a New York vendor, or take possession of it in that jurisdiction. If the server or warehouse location is the right answer, it isn't too difficult for the seller to practice **tax avoidance** and locate in a zero sales tax state or even just physically offshore, outside of the boundaries of any U.S. state. Of course, if the firm says that it is operating offshore, but really isn't, this may be **tax evasion**, which is an illegal scheme to keep from paying the tax, and some or all of the executives can go to jail for that kind of deception. A final jurisdictional quandary arises if the residential or billing address of the buyer is selected as the correct taxing jurisdiction. The collection of the state sales tax is easy, because everyone lives in a unique state. A **problem of multiple tax jurisdictions** arises, however, if the county and/or city of residence also levy their own sales taxes in addition to the state. In excess of 4,800 cities, 1,500 counties, and 139 special purpose school districts impose a sales tax.[3] Moreover, these taxing entities alter their tax rates frequently; a total of 771 jurisdictions altered their state and local sales tax rates in 2001, while 530 changes were recorded in 2000.[4] At present, no perfect mapping instrument can locate every buyer within the proper set of tax jurisdictions. Even postal ZIP codes spread across city and county lines on some occasions. Taxing complexity seems to grow almost exponentially as final sales take place in cyberspace.

The complexities aren't limited to just jurisdictional issues. A second set concerns the problems of **identification of taxable items**. Different jurisdictions apply different rules that vary widely in their tax treatment of such items as food, clothing, and health-related products. Exemptions abound and some of them are temporary; for example, exemptions instituted to stimulate holiday sales. It becomes an almost Herculean task for online sellers to know and comply with all of the varying sales tax complexities, especially for small niche sellers. It would require them to record and send out quarterly checks to each taxing jurisdiction where sales were made. The effect would be to discourage small businesses from selling on the Web and thereby limit the extent of competition and buyer choice. Both buyers and sellers can realize benefits from the simplification of identifying tax jurisdictions and taxable items.

---

3 Johnson, "Coming Soon," p. R20.

4 Vertex Inc., "Sales Tax Rate Changes in 2001," available at **http://www.vertexinc.com/cybrary/ sales_tax/2001_tax_facts.asp**.

TAXES ON REMOTE SALES TRANSACTIONS AND THE LAW

Historically, both the U.S. Constitution and the U.S. Supreme Court have taken clear stands on the issue of applying taxes on trade across jurisdictional borders.[5] The commerce clause of the Constitution, Article 2, Section 8, clearly assigns to Congress the power to regulate trade among the states. The intent of the commerce clause was to allow for the development of national markets that would speed the rise of trade and hasten the economic integration of the diverse regions. As a result, the power to tax trade has generally been interpreted as stopping at the state border. Most states adopt a use tax as a complement to the in-state sales tax. A use tax shifts the *physical payment burden* to an in-state consumer, who buys a product from an out-of-state seller for use in the state of residence. The buyer is required to report the sale, and pay any positive difference in the amount of the sales tax on the item in the state of residence minus the sales tax paid in the state where the item was purchased. If a resident of New Jersey, with a sales tax of 6 percent, goes to Delaware, a state without a sales tax, and purchases a wide screen TV for $1,500 and brings it back home for viewing, then the New Jersey resident is required by law to report the purchase and pay a use tax of $90.

It should come as no surprise that the dollar amount of the use tax collected in most states is minimal. The use tax is difficult to enforce and collect, given its focus on the individual buyer and the fact that most residents are unaware of their tax liability. However, states with use taxes have tried to redirect the collection and payment burden onto the shoulders of the out-of-state seller. In a number of cases, the U.S. Supreme Court crafted decisions that allow the states to exercise a limited ability to collect taxes on **remote sales transactions**. These cases all involved out-of-state, mail-order firms that sold products to in-state residents. The crucial element in all the cases is the identification of a **nexus**, or "a connection between the state and the merchant."[6] Prior to World War II, the department store chains of Montgomery Ward and Sears & Roebuck had retail outlets in the state of Iowa, as well as out-of-state catalog operations that sold tangible items to Iowa residents. The state saw no difference between the retailers selling their products to Iowans through their retail stores or their catalog divisions. Therefore, the state tax commissioner required the two firms to collect and pay the use tax on items sold and shipped to state residents. In both cases, the U.S. Supreme Court agreed that the state could require the firms to collect and pay the use tax on the firms' catalog sales, because companies formed a nexus with the state through the physical presence of their retail outlets.[7]

In a number of subsequent cases, the Supreme Court sharpened its definition of a nexus. For the purposes of requiring the collection of a sales tax, it defined two ways of identifying whether a seller maintains a physical presence within a state: "(1) through the ownership of a place of business (retail operation, warehouse, or office), or (2) through an agency relationship that constitutes a de facto in-state physical presence."[8] With an agency relationship, some identifiable third party represents the seller within the tax jurisdiction. The states of Arkansas and Minnesota are using the agency relationship to levy sales taxes on Internet sales where a physical store within the state takes returns or makes exchanges.[9] In the absence of this nexus, the state must resort to collecting the use tax from its residents directly.

---

5 Much of the information in this section has been adapted from Daniel G. Swaine and Robert Tannenwald, "Should Interstate Sales Be Taxed?" *Fiscal Facts*, 25 (Winter 2000/2001), Federal Reserve Bank of Boston, pp. 1–4.

6 Swaine and Tannenwald, "Should Interstate Sales Be Taxed?" p. 2.

7 *Nelson v. Sears and Roebuck & Co.* (1941); and *Nelson v. Montgomery Ward & Co.* (1941).

8 Swaine and Tannenwald, "Should Interstate Sales" p. 3.

9 Andrew Caffery, "Rules and Regs: E-Commerce Sales Tax Makes Inroads," *The Wall Street Journal*, September 16, 2002, p. R13.

Congress and the Internet Tax-Freedom Act

In 1998, Congress asserted its authority over the regulation of interstate commerce by passing the **Internet Tax-Freedom Act (ITFA)**, which created a three-year moratorium on the application of a variety of new Internet related taxes.[10] In particular the language of the Act established the following points:

1. A three-year moratorium on new special taxation of the Internet
2. A three-year moratorium on multiple and discriminatory taxes on electronic commerce
3. A commission to study questions of remote sales
4. The principle of no new federal Internet taxes as the sense of Congress
5. The Internet as a tariff-free zone

The first provision limited the states from levying new Internet access taxes on the services sold by Internet service providers, such as AOL, MSN, or Earthlink.[11] The second provision protected against the levying of new taxes on consumers or vendors involved in e-commerce transactions, through strained interpretations of nexus. The third provision gave the commission 18 months to study the problems associated with Internet taxation and return action recommendations to Congress. The fifth provision extended the no tax concept to global e-commerce transactions, including forestalling the imposition of tariffs. The framers of the legislation cited two reasons for its passage: first, to give the Internet and e-commerce time to grow, and second, to keep multiple taxing jurisdictions from each taxing an Internet transaction that relied on a decentralized, packet-switching technology.[12] An electronic order to buy could be taxed in new and creative ways by multiple taxing jurisdictions as it passed in pieces through different routes of the fiber network.

The Internet growth concern is a contemporary application of the eighteenth-century **infant industry argument**, created by Alexander Hamilton.[13] The argument postulates that a young and developing industry deserves protection from competition until it matures and is able to compete on an equal footing. Without the protection, its existing competitors could overcome the infant firm before it had an opportunity to experience the full range of its competitive advantages. Supporters of the online tax exemption argue that the Internet is characterized by **network externalities**, where the cost of e-commerce transactions are reduced and the value of the flow of information to all users is increased with the number of members in the network. The imposition of a tax would constrain the growth of the network, limiting the number of participants, and thereby impose an unnecessary cost burden on the remaining users. Therefore, the Internet qualifies as an infant industry worthy of subsidy, through the absence of a tax. The tax prohibition will help to encourage the participation of additional users, who will generate incremental benefits for all other existing members. Conversely, the imposition of a tax would work to crush the infant firm, which might otherwise be capable of competitive survival in its mature state, and would be an example of **market failure**.

Opponents of the Congressional Online Tax Moratorium

Conversely, opponents of the moratorium point out a number of problems with the Congressional exemption. First, it creates an **uneven playing field** between tax-exempt e-tailers and retailers, who must charge their customers a higher price in the form of the sales tax. Consequently, by altering the relative prices for the same good and discriminating

---

10 P.L. 105-277, 105th Congress, H.R. 4328, Title XI. See The UCLA Online Institute for Cyberspace Law and Policy, available at **http://www.gseis.ucla.edu/iclp/itfa.htm** to see the provisions of the Act.

11 The 10 states with existing ISP taxes were allowed to keep them under a grandfather clause.

12 P.L. 105-277.

13 Alexander Hamilton, Report on Manufactures, 1791, available at **http://www.oberlin.edu/~gkornbl/Hist258/ReportMfres.html**.

by type of seller, the **tax asymmetry** may potentially alter consumer buying patterns. Such a change would be to the detriment of both the retailers and the jurisdictions that rely on the taxing of transactions to raise a significant portion of their operating revenues. To demonstrate these assertions, let's reexamine the information in Figure 17-2. With a greater inelasticity of market demand for a product, the seller can push a larger portion of the tax forward onto the buyer. One of the characteristics determining the degree of inelasticity is the number of good substitutes. Online sales are a substitute, sometimes good and sometimes imperfect, for retail sales. Therefore, a moratorium on the taxation of e-tail sales, creates a lower-priced substitute for retail sales and renders the retail market demand more elastic. Fewer retail purchases will be made, less revenue will be collected, and sellers will necessarily absorb more of the tax in the form of lower product prices. A study by professors Donald Bruce and William F. Fox, at the University of Tennessee Center for Business and Economic Research, estimated the collective revenue lost to the states from untaxed e-commerce transactions at $13.3 billion in 2001, with loss projections rising to $45.2 billion in 2006 and $54.8 billion in 2011.[14] California, Texas, and New York were hardest hit, with revenue losses above $1 billion each in 2001.

Second, the moratorium motivates e-tailers to undertake **tax-induced behavioral gymnastics** to avoid the creation of a nexus for purposes of taxation. For example, Wal-Mart operates retail stores in almost every state and also ran an e-tail sales operation.[15] Initially, it had to collect taxes on Web sales in any state where it had this physical presence. The collection of taxes irritated its online customers and reduced the potential volume of Wal-Mart's e-tail sales. To solve the problem, Wal-Mart established the e-tail unit as a separate Web firm. This broke the nexus in most states, leaving Wal-Mart to collect taxes in just four states where the Web company still had a nexus. Also, Goodguys.com, the e-tail cousin of the electronics retailer Goodguys, located their online unit in the Oregon because of that state's zero sales tax levy. Lastly, the e-tailer 800.com located its East Coast distribution center in Delaware for the same reason.[16] These tactics render the payment of the sales/use tax the equivalent of a **tax avoidance shell game**, where retailers as e-tailers hide the sales transactions from the taxing jurisdictions. In response, some states tried to claim that the computer chips and wires connecting customers and e-tailers form the core of a nexus or physical presence, which would allow the levying of sales/use taxes on final e-commerce transactions. These *tax tensions and market distortions* will only worsen as more products, including music sales, software subscriptions, and video downloads, along with other forms of entertainment, grow with the use of broadband connections.[17]

Lastly, it is the history of infant industry exemptions that they frequently fail to achieve their desired end and become difficult to eliminate when the justified time span passes. More often than not, protected industries become fat and lazy, hiding behind the wall of protection rather than sharpening their competitive skills. They also tend to seek out additional political support, which makes it difficult to terminate the protective legislation. The review commission, whose work was intended to resolve the tension between the supporters and opponents of an Internet tax exemption, reached its termination date on April 21, 2000, without the required two-thirds majority agreeing on a set of action recommendations to place before Congress.[18] In late November 2001, Congress extended the provisions of the Act until November 1, 2003.[19] The extension

---

14 Donald Bruce and William F. Fox, "State and Local Sales Tax Revenue Losses from E-Commerce: Updated Estimates," available at **http://www.statestudies.org/ecomreport.pdf**.

15 Kara Swisher, "Boom Town: E-Tailers Faced Death; Now Can They Handle Taxes?" *The Wall Street Journal*, April 9, 2001, p. B1.

16 Robert Gavin, "Look, No Sales Tax," *The Wall Street Journal*, May 1, 2001, p. B11.

17 Swisher, "E-Tailers Faced ," p. B1.

18 David Clay Johnston, "Agreement on Internet Taxes Eludes Deeply Divided Commission," *The New York Times*, March 21, 2000, p. C1.

19 David Hardesty, "Internet Tax-freedom Act Extended," available at **http://www.ecommercetax.com/doc/120201.htm**.

was offered in the hope that the states could agree on a simplified Internet transactions taxing system. An effort called the **Streamlined Sales Tax Project**, which involves a group of 30 states, is meeting regularly to achieve that end by no later than 2003.[20]

Potential Resolutions of the e-Commerce Taxation Tension

Potential solutions to the taxing tension are met by some combination of political and technical resistance.[21] The first potential solution involves state agreement on a **uniform tax solution** by adopting a common sales tax rate and list of taxable items. This direction is unlikely given the history of the sales tax in each state and the importance that it plays as a revenue source. The second possibility would be the creation of a **third-party collection solution** with the adoption of a national sales tax rate and base for online sales. The same amount would be collected on the same set of online items regardless of jurisdiction. The funds could then be rebated to the states on the basis of ZIP codes. Both the tax rate and base would be set at compromise levels, but the plan would limit the e-tail versus retail distortion, and stem some of the loss of tax revenues. Although the **national sales tax plan** may be a reasonable approach, a lack of political will to impose new national taxes make this approach unlikely. The tax would somewhat impede the development of the Internet as a vehicle for e-commerce. Finally, it might encourage tax avoidance through the growth of offshore e-commerce Web sites, where the tax wouldn't apply.

Another possibility might be to model the solution to the e-commerce tax tension after the federal approach to levying taxes on cell phone usage.[22] Cell phones are portable, and a geographically complex tracking system had been used to levy taxes on usage in different states and cities depending on the call. In 2000, Congress simplified the taxing process by declaring that each cell phone would have a primary service area for the purposes of collecting state and local taxes. For most phones, it would be the billing address. For centrally billed corporate phones assigned to geographically dispersed employees, the service area would be tied to the telephone area code. The legislation resolved the cell phone problem of identifying user location for tax purposes, which is a problem similar to the e-commerce customer location dilemma. The federal legislation shows that the e-commerce tension can be resolved. For example, Congress could mandate the adoption of an **origin-based transaction tax system** for online sales, with the tax paid at the location of the principal place of business rather than at the *destination end of the transaction*.

Taxes on Internet Access

Besides effectively declaring a moratorium on the collection of use taxes on Internet transactions, the Internet Tax-Freedom Act also limited the imposition of *new* **Internet access taxes** on the providers of Internet connection services or ISPs. At first glance, this looks like a traditional infant industry exemption to foster the growth of connections to the Internet. However, many ISPs are no longer just portals to the Internet. They now provide products and services on their sites, including news, photos, music access, and links to long distance phone service. Seeing these added services, the states would like to be able to raise revenue by taxing them. In 2001, a short-term window of opportunity opened for states to levy some access taxes when the original ITFA expired in the middle of October and before it was renewed and extended at the end of November. However, states were

20 Russell Gold, "States Hold Off on Taxing Web Access," *The Wall Street Journal*, October 31, 2001, p. B8B.

21 For an outline of some of the resolution options, see Adam D. Thierer, "After the Net Tax Commission: The Gregg-Kohl Nexus Solution," available at **http://www.heritage.org/Research/InternetandTechnology/BG1363.cfm**.

22 David Clay Johnston, "Passage of Cellular Phone Tax May Solve E-Commerce Riddle," *The New York Times*, July 18, 2000, p. C6.

reluctant to rush in with new Internet access taxes. They feared that they would confirm the worse apprehensions among moratorium proponents about states introducing burdensome taxes that would throttle the growth of the Internet.[23] Also, the states set as their goal the taxation of the much larger pie of Internet transactions, not just Internet access. Texas was one of the states that were grandfathered by the ITFA and allowed to collect Internet access taxes. These revenues amounted to $45 million in 2001, but the taxation of Internet transactions would yield more than $1.2 billion. A nearly 30:1 revenue ratio stands as sufficient motivation to go slow in applying the new access taxes.

The *cable operators* that provide broadband Internet access would also like to claim a tax-free status for their service. The Ninth U.S. Circuit Court of Appeals in San Francisco ruled in June of 2000 as part of its decision in the case of open access, declared that the "Internet services delivered over cable TV lines are telecommunications services, not cable TV services."[24] As such, the local franchise fees, averaging 3 to 5 percent per month, that are charged to cable operators on the basis of delivering a cable TV service would not apply to the portion of the bill charged for the delivery of a broadband or telecommunications service. The affect would be to lessen the cost to cable broadband customers and possibly hasten the penetration of broadband usage. Paradoxically, the cable operators historically and aggressively argued that they aren't providing telecommunications services. This argument provided a way for them to avoid the same type of stringent federal and state controls under which telephone companies operate.

TAXING E-COMMERCE AND THE ISSUE OF OFFSHORE WEB MERCHANTS

One of the key points emphasized in this book is that e-commerce is truly a global phenomenon. Sellers can tap a worldwide consumer market, while buyers can price and purchase products from any e-tailer located anywhere on the globe. If online markets are global, then it is reasonable for e-tailers to locate their cyberspace operations in the geographic space that provides them the most advantageous mixture of profitable sales along with the lowest tax liability. On the one hand, some e-commerce firms may be content with shuffling the location of various online transactions, among states within the borders of the United States, with the narrow purpose of getting the most favorable sales/use tax treatment. Other e-tailers, however, may adopt a broader tax avoidance perspective and include the minimization of corporate income tax, worker payroll taxes, and property tax payments in their location calculations. As a result, the physical location of Web transactions for purposes of taxation can be heavily influenced by low tax rates, tax exemptions, or even the absence of tax laws. These deliberately legislated tax policies convey a competitive advantage to Web sellers who choose to locate within these tax jurisdictions.

E-tailers can domicile anywhere, and a number of them are choosing to locate in friendly **offshore tax havens**, such as Bermuda, "which has a rich history of helping foreigners shave taxes," as well as other Caribbean tax havens.[25] The e-tailer Playcentric.com offers music and video products via the Web from servers located within the confines of Bermuda. Its operating units are in Barbados and it ships products from an entertainment store chain in Toronto, Canada. By locating the various parts of the business in the most tax-friendly nations, Playcentric.com can potentially undercut the lowest price for products offered by similar e-tail firms operating in full tax jurisdictions.

Not surprisingly, with advances in telecommunications technology and installation, more entrepreneurs recognize the advantages of an offshore e-commerce location. They

---

23 Gold, "States Hold Off," p. B8B.

24 Leslie Cauley, "Firms Offering Web via Cable Seek to Avoid Fees," *The Wall Street Journal*, January 8, 2001, p. B10.

25 The material in the following discussion has been adapted from Michael Allen, "As Dot-Coms Go Bust in U.S., Bermuda Hosts Odd Little Boomlet," *The Wall Street Journal*, January 8, 2001, p. A1.

are relocating to enhance as well as shield their profits. Initially, casino and gaming sites that were trying to evade U.S. gambling laws triggered the movement, but the number of sites and the diversity of their products have grown. For example, Ships-for-sale.com operates a vessel exchange market, crew location service, and ship insurance Web site from the island of Cyprus. Booksonbiz.com sells business books from a site in Bermuda, while Furs.com sells mink, lynx, and chinchilla coats, among other items, from a site located on the same island. At least for now, the offshore tax laws of most nations still trail the technical possibilities for the location of online selling. High-tech hotels hosting more than a million Web sites have appeared in nations such as Panama. The "Principality of Sealand" has a Web site called datahaven.com, with servers selling subscriptions for secure e-mail and other services. It operates from an abandoned antiaircraft platform located in the North Sea, and claims to be immune from any subpoena of its e-mail records by other nations. Businesses can be set up and run from an offshore Web site for a minimal amount of money by contacting and filling out an electronic application at Bahamas.net. The earlier discussion in Chapter 7 pointed out the financial and copyright problems created by Napster and its file-sharing cousins. The illegal electronic transfer of music and video files prove hard enough to stop when the servers are located in the United States. They may be impossible to control when the servers are located offshore in Asia, Africa, Russia, or on a barren island in the South Pacific.

Despite the lure of untaxed or low taxed profits, the prospective offshore e-tailer should heed a word of warning. Although e-commerce firms can reach everywhere but live nowhere, the human owners of the firm have to live somewhere. Consequently, laws governing the taxation of offshore profits in the nation where the owners of the firm actually live may be in effect. Some countries may not tax the offshore income of their citizens, but the Internal Revenue Service goes beyond its name and places a tax on the external income of U.S citizens earned worldwide.

SUMMARY AND PROSPECTS

The chapter began by highlighting the competitive tension arising between the taxation of retail sales transactions and the current federal moratorium on the collection of similar taxes on e-tail transactions conducted over the Internet. This tension produced two important e-commerce problems. First, the tax asymmetry creates an uneven playing field that conveys a small competitive price advantage to online sellers. Depending on the dollar volume of each sale and the jurisdictional tax rates, the savings could offset the cost of shipping the final goods sold online. This difference might tilt some sales to e-tailers and away from retailers. Second, all but a few states rely quite heavily on the revenues generated by their sales tax to pay for the costs of goods, services, and transfers provided to state residents. A substantial migration of customers from taxable retail to tax-free e-tail and subsequent decline in tax revenues could undermine an important portion of a given state's tax structure. Individual states historically tried to surmount the problem of taxing the in-state sales via out-of-state firms by requiring the seller to collect a use tax from the buyer at the time of sale. The U.S. Supreme Court allowed this form of taxation as long as the seller had a nexus, or physical presence, in the state that required the collection of the use tax. The states would like to extend this nexus concept for the purposes of collecting taxes on the sale of online goods.

The subsequent discussion pointed out some valid reasons for imposing the moratorium on the taxation of e-tail sales. The first involved the problem of e-tailers collecting and transmitting payment for sales in multiple taxing jurisdictions with varying tax rates. The problem is compounded by the fact that there is no simple way of determining the geographic location of the buyer at the time of purchase, or which jurisdiction's tax rate should apply and at what stage of the transaction. Confusion is also created by the nesting of tax jurisdictions one inside the other, with some sales potentially being taxed multiple times by states, localities, and even special taxing districts. Lastly, the problem of a multiplicity of tax bases comes from different jurisdictions taxing different items and sometimes altering the items taxed and the tax rates at different times of the year. Depending on how these problems are eventually resolved, the collection and payment of sales/use taxes could prove to be beyond the capacity of small e-tailers, leaving the online market to the mercy of just the largest and most technically sophisticated e-commerce firms.

The Internet Tax-Freedom Act also created a moratorium on the application of new taxes on ISPs. This provision might be justified by applying the infant industry argument based on the fact that Internet connections generate network externalities. Here, the addition of one more user increases the value of the network to all of the existing users. The imposition of an access tax might slow the growth of the network, reducing the number of network participants and keeping the network from reaching its optimal scale, leading to an inefficient market result.

Regardless of how these issues are finally resolved, the result is most likely to lead to a considerable amount of geographic and legal gymnastics, as firms jockey to avoid paying the transactions tax. First, some e-firms will locate their taxable activities in domestic jurisdictions with the lowest sales/use tax burden. States may race to reduce the level of e-tailer taxation trading tax revenue in exchange for experiencing the job gains and added property tax revenues. Second, e-firms will construct legal separations between their retail stores and e-tail sites as a way to limit the application of nexus rules that allow the taxation of transactions. Third, some firms will turn to offshore Web sites and physical location in tax-friendly countries, which may aid in the avoidance of multiple forms of tax payments, including sales/use taxes. If anyone doubts that prices and taxes have an impact on economic behavior, all she needs to do is examine the consequences of e-tail taxation resolution to see that relative markets matter.

KEY TERMS AND CONCEPTS

excise tax
identification of taxable items
infant industry argument
Internet access taxes
Internet Tax-Freedom Act (ITFA)
jurisdictional issues
market failure
national sales tax plan
network externalities
nexus
offshore tax havens
origin-based transaction tax system
problem of identification of taxable items
problem of multiple tax jurisdictions
regressive tax
remote sales transactions
sales tax
sales tax administration in the industrial age

sales tax administration in the information age
sales tax base
sales tax rate
sin taxes
Streamlined Sales Tax Project
tax asymmetry
tax avoidance
tax avoidance shell game
tax burden
tax evasion
tax incidence
tax-induced behavioral gymnastics
third-party collection solution
uneven playing field
uniform tax solution
use tax
value added tax

DISCUSSION AND REVIEW QUESTIONS

1. Distinguish between the concepts of an excise tax and a sales tax. How is each levied? Which governmental entity levies the sales tax? Are all consumer purchases treated the same by the sales tax? Why?

2. What is the nature of the public policy tension that surrounds the final sales of e-commerce items? Which entities are helped and hurt by this tension?

3. Based on the data in Figure 17-1, which states are the most and least dependent on sales tax revenues for the receipt of funds? How does your home state compare in terms of its sales tax rate relative to the state with the highest rate?

4. What does it mean to say that a tax is regressive? Why is the sales tax regressive? Explain how Figure 17-2 shows the regressive nature of a sales tax.

5. Identify and distinguish between sales tax administration in the industrial versus the information age. Why is Internet sales taxation so much more difficult? How do questions of multiple tax jurisdictions and the identification of taxable items contribute to the confusion surrounding Internet sales taxation?

6. What is a use tax and how is it similar to and yet different from a sales tax?

7. What is a nexus? How has this legal concept been used to determine whether a state can legally levy a sales tax on a remote transaction?

8. What is the Internet Tax-freedom Act of 1998? How did this federal law affect the taxation of Internet transactions? Explain how Congress relied on the implicit use of the infant industry argument and the existence of network externalities to justify the adoption of this posture on the taxation of Internet sales.

9. Identify and discuss the arguments used by the opponents of the Internet Tax-Freedom Act. Why has the resolution of this tension between the proponents and opponents of Internet sales taxation been delayed?

10. Identify and discuss the range of solutions to the Internet sales tax problem. How might the compromise used for cell phone taxation be applied to Internet sales?

11. What are "offshore tax havens"? Why might a particular nation create these kinds of tax structures? How does their existence complicate the issue of taxing Internet sales?

WEB EXERCISES

1. Link to the sales and use tax data page maintained by the Sales Tax Institute at **http://www.salestaxinstitute.com/sales_tax_rates.html**. Which states have the highest and lowest current sales tax rates? How does your own state's sales tax rate compare to that of neighboring states?

2. Link to the tax revenue by source data for 2001 maintained by the U.S. Census Bureau Tax Administration at **http://www.taxadmin.org/fta/rate/01taxdis.html**. What percentage of your home state's revenue is obtained through the sales tax? How do these data compare to that for 2000, which is available at **http://www. taxadmin.org/fta/rate/00taxdis.html**? You may be able to get these data for 2002 as well by replacing the 01 numbers in the URL with the designation 02.

3. To see the annual survey of sales tax rates for counties and cities, link to Vertex Inc. at **http://www.vertexinc.com/cybrary/sales_tax/2001_tax_facts.asp**. To see whether the data for 2002 or beyond are available, change the date in the URL to 2002. How have average sales tax rates changed during 1981–2002?

4. See the UCLA Online Institute for Cyberspace Law and Policy at **http://www.gseis.ucla.edu/iclp/itfa.htm** to view the provisions of the Internet Tax-Freedom Act of 1998.

5. Type in the URL for the Streamlined Sales Tax Project at **http://www. ecommercetax.com/SSTP.htm** to see the latest events designed to resolve the Internet sales tax problem.

6. Link to **http://www.playcentric.com/**, the offshore e-entertainment e-tailer, to see whether its advantageous tax status encouraged it to sell CDs or DVDs cheaper than U.S. competitors.

7. Link to **http://www.datahaven.com/** and see the kinds of services offered by the offshore server site.

8. Type in the URL for **http://www.bahamas.net/bahamas/** to enjoy the calypso music and see how little information is necessary to set up a Web or e-commerce site in that tax-friendly nation.

CHAPTER

18

Introductory Case

BIG BROTHER IN THE DIGITAL AGE

In 1949 the writer and social visionary George Orwell published the book *1984*. The story was set in a time when the central authority known as "Big Brother" had the ability to watch every action and hear every sound uttered by average citizens.[1] People never knew exactly when the Thought Police were actually plugged into their movements, nor did they know how the information, obtained through this surveillance, was being used at any point in time. All they knew was that their privacy had been compromised.

Mentally time shift forward to the present, and either attempt to purchase an item online, or respond to one of those ubiquitous e-mails offering to send a free gift if only the individual provides some personal information. By filling in those boxes at a number of apparently unconnected Web sites, a single individual might provide a wide variety of personal information. This digital data could include both physical and e-mail addresses, age, income, marital status, number of children along with their names and ages, educational level, a credit card number, product likes and dislikes, vehicles owned, and perhaps some medical information or even a social security number.

After multiple encounters, and without becoming too paranoid, a frequent online respondent might become curious as to where this information is being kept and for how long, who has access to it, how is it being used, and whether it is being shared with unidentified third parties. After all, once the information is digitized, it can be stored, sorted, and transported electronically with great ease. Even personal criminal and civil court records along with property records are increasingly finding their way onto the Internet.[2] Also, with some effort, the digital data could be combined with offline information obtained at grocery or retail stores, issuers of credit cards, public records on criminal or civil cases, land records, magazine subscription services, employment histories, medical histories, and so on. In the end, today's digital Big Brother could have an electronic profile of each of us, to be used for whatever purpose the unseen holder of information deemed appropriate. Even George Orwell might be amazed at this electronic turn of events.

PUBLIC CONCERN REGARDING INTERNET PRIVACY AND SECURITY

Perhaps no other Internet-related issue generates more intense and persistent user concerns than the topics of Internet privacy and security. In November 2001, the Internet Technology Association of America (ITAA), conducted a random telephone survey of 800 households. The results showed that 71 percent of the respondents expressed the opinion that they were either very concerned (35%) or somewhat concerned (36%) about the issue of the Internet and computer security.[3] In a separate question relating to Internet privacy,

---

1 For an online version of Orwell's *1984* novel, see **http://www.spy.org.uk/1984.htm**.

2 Jennifer 8. Lee, "Dirty Laundry, Online for All to See," *The New York Times*, September 5, 2002, p. G1.

3 See "ITAA Poll Finds Almost Three of Four Americans Concerned About Cyber Security," available at **http://www.itaa.org/news/pr/PressRelease.cfm?ReleaseID=1008095083**.

Internet Privacy and Security

33 percent of the respondents indicated that they were very worried that their personal information, which was stored on the Internet, would either be stolen or otherwise misused. An additional 41 percent indicated that they were somewhat worried about the privacy of their personal Internet information. In response to a third question, fully 78 percent of the survey participants said that they were either very concerned or somewhat concerned that their personal information, held by the government, could be misused.

These concerns about Internet privacy and security can hold significant consequences for the conduct of e-commerce. For example, research from CyberDialogue indicted that 27 percent of potential e-tail buyers abandoned their purchase because of concerns regarding the abuse or misuse of personal data associated with the transaction. These abandoned purchases were estimated to cost e-tailers some $3.7 billion in lost sales.[4] Another study by Forrester Research indicated that 37 percent of existing e-tail customers would purchase more goods online if they weren't so worried about privacy issues. Another 34 percent of respondents, who did not purchase online, would begin to do so if they did not have to worry about privacy.[5] The estimate of lost sales from respondents with these kinds of concerns totaled $15 billion. Lastly, a survey by Statistical Research indicated that 67 percent of respondents typically abandoned a Web site when asked for personal information.[6] One in five of the respondents admitted to giving false personal information as a means of gaining access to a Web site. Respondents in this study expressed concerns over the use of cookies to track Internet activity, the potential abuse of credit card information given to complete Web purchases, and the possible sale or sharing of personal information with third parties, including other commercial Web sites.

The Tension Between the Issues of Internet Privacy and Internet Security

From an electronic perspective, topics of Internet privacy and security describe two distinctly different types of Web concerns. **Internet privacy** involves making sure that no unauthorized entity gains access to and/or uses personal information that has been transmitted over and stored on the Web. **Internet security** involves protecting the technical integrity of the Internet against unauthorized and/or illegal intervention. The privacy concern is directed toward the individual, while the security topic looks at issues relating to the reliability, integrity, and safety of the entire Internet system. The security concern encompasses both an internal and external dimension. The **internal security dimension** looks to protect the Internet against a variety of criminal dangers including intrusions by hackers, the planting of viruses or worms, and attempts to shut down parts of the network through the introduction of denial-of-service attacks. The **external security dimension** looks to protect the Internet from being used as a vehicle for terrorist attacks designed to cripple key parts of the U.S. economy such as financial services, energy delivery, and the operation of public infrastructure.

---

4 NUA, "Privacy Issues Costing Online Retailers," available at **http://www.nua.ie/surveys/index. cgi?f=VS&art_id=905357388&rel=true**.

5 NUA, "Privacy Issues Inhibit Online Spending," available at **http://www.nua.ie/surveys/index. cgi?f=VS&art_id=905357259&rel=true**.

6 Statistical Research Inc., "Even Veteran Web Users Remain Skittish about Sites that Get Personal," available at **http://www.statisticalresearch.com/press/pr060701.htm**.

The problems of privacy and security may be technically distinct, but their resolution involves a degree of overlap and interaction. This overlap is especially relevant where the government tries to introduce electronic means to gain intelligence that will improve national security or protect Internet integrity. Clearly, the desire on the part of most Internet users is for greater Internet privacy *and* security. However, recent U.S. federal action shows that these two goals may not be fully compatible. Some government security efforts create a tension between enhancing Internet security versus maintaining personal privacy. The government has or proposes to initiate a number of measures to monitor general Internet traffic, including private e-mails, looking for signs of illicit activity. Casting a wide and indiscriminate net for catching and interpreting illicit activity, however, also results in the capture and review of a considerable amount of perfectly legal transmissions that Internet users would like to feel are their private business.

The broad approach would be analogous to having government agents opening and reading all forms of private mail, as they looked for a few letters that might convey threats, harmful bacteria, or some other form of illegal activity. As a result, some federal security actions, designed to bolster Internet security, diminished the perceived level of personal confidentiality. In turn, they intensified the public's skepticism and concern over the extent of their Internet privacy. The purpose of this chapter is to identify and discuss the range of privacy and security concerns, while evaluating the different approaches that might be introduced to resolve this tension in a reasonable manner.

INTERNET PRIVACY: THE NATURE AND EXTENT OF THE PROBLEM

Just as it is the nature of a cat to chase a mouse, it is the nature of the Internet to facilitate the collection and dissemination of information. No matter where you surf, what you see or do, who you converse with, or the personal information that you convey to others, your clicks and key strokes leave a potentially permanent electronic record of who you are and a tell-tale trail of where you have been. As one observer put it, "The nature of information technology is to create information."[7] Just in case you remain unconvinced of this premise, the next time you are in your Internet browser, click on the little down arrow that lies at the far right of the address window. A window will drop down listing the URLs of the last 25 or so sites that you visited. Worse yet, a number of these and other sites have left a coded message in the form of a **cookie** on your computer. The next time you visit the site, the cookie tells the server that you have been here before. It lets the server identify who you are, if you gave them that information before, and it allows the accessing of information about what you did at the site each of the last times you visited. The fact is that many Internet users realize that they have most likely already gone beyond the point of digital no return. The Internet has acquired and has control over the information in the surfer's **digital soul**. The online world has the potential to know all, see all, and most importantly remember all, with the ability to efficiently aggregate the information into one easy-to-read **online profile**.

Wherever an Internet user goes they can't help but leave a little bit of themselves behind. For example, your ISP has a record of e-mails sent, received, and what was said. Also, the typical surfer gives a variety of sites a wealth of personal information. Perhaps not all of this information was given to the same site, but if the e-firms can trade digital information collected across different sites, then they can assemble some or all of these separate personal facts into an online profile. Lastly, if they can link this online information to your off-line activities, then they probably know as much about you as you do yourself. Some people are so concerned about having an electronic presence on the Internet that they go to great lengths to avoid being found there.[8]

---

7   Holman W. Jenkins, "On Web Privacy, What Are We Afraid Of?" *The Wall Street Journal*, August 2, 2000, p. A23.

8   Jennifer 8. Lee, "Trying to Elude the Google Grasp," *The New York Times*, July 25, 2002, p. G1.

One scary result of being able to assemble this electronic mass of personal information is that many firms are intensely interested in securing this combination of online/off-line behavioral information. For some it has economic value as a marketing tool to target you with ads tailored to your tastes and preferences. For others it has value as a potential weapon to be used in marital divorce cases, to deny you a home loan or a medical insurance policy, or to be used by your employer as evidence for immediate dismissal. Lastly, some firms just collect the data, treating it as a commodity to be sold at a profit to other firms. The buyer's intent is to use the information as the basis for either sending junk snail mail, or spamming you with unwanted e-mail, pitching any variety of products, services, or ideas. At the very least, the history of your Internet travels, your likes and dislikes, as well as a record of your purchases opens up the user to a future barrage of advertising tailored to entice the surfer to buy, subscribe, visit, or in some other way contribute to the revenue flow and profitability of an e-seller. Some Web users may be flattered and respond positively to the level of quality and individual nature of this approach, but others find the level of personal knowledge held by others to be a potential threat and invasion of privacy.

Cookies: Benign versus Threatening

It has happened to just about every Web surfer at some point in time. You visit a site to conduct a transaction, find information, view general content, or ask a question. Then, some time in the future, you revisit the same site and it greets you by name, or at least seems to display some information about who you are and your previous visits. It's a bit weird when you experience it for the first time. It can also be a bit comforting, much like stopping by the neighborhood tavern, where everyone knows your name. After this phenomenon of cyberspace recognition happens a few times, most surfers take it for granted and come to assume that it's just the way the Web is.

Well not quite. What the surfer has experienced, for better or for worse, is the product of a cookie, which is a small file placed on your browser's software by a server during an earlier visit to the Web site. Each time a computer links to a Web site server, the server looks for and links to the cookie. If it fails to find a previously placed cookie, then it will attach one for the first time as it sends the Web page back to your browser. The information in the cookie helps the server to see who you are and what you have done at the site before. The link can also trigger the server to search its own files to summon any additional information they might contain about the surfer. The cookie can't tell the server who you are by name, unless you gave it that information on some previous visit. It can't even be sure that the person who visited last time is the same person at the keyboard this time. All the server knows for sure is that this computer visited the site some point in the past and a cookie was deposited at that time.

The first file containing a cookie was written in 1994, by Lou Montulli, a 24-year-old Netscape programmer, who was attempting to solve a troublesome problem facing e-commerce.[9] Every time Web users returned to a Web site to conduct transactions, she had to reenter the same information including name, shipping, and billing instructions. Depending upon the circumstances, this task could involve a considerable number of keystrokes. Besides being annoying and time consuming, the need to constantly reenter the same information raised the potential of introducing errors into the results. The Web lacked a memory, and travel on the Internet was just a discontinuous series of unrelated site visits. The absence of a memory raised a hassle factor, or barrier to e-commerce, that discouraged some users from undertaking potential transactions. Hence, the cookie file was created both as a way to stimulate more e-commerce sales for the firm, but also as a way to make the Web more convenient for the users. Anyone who has been greeted by cookie-based completed forms containing the correct shipping and billing information

---

9 The following information has been adapted from, John Schwartz, "Giving the Web a Memory Cost Its Users Privacy," *The New York Times*, September 4, 2001, p. A1.

can attest to the added speed, simplicity, and accuracy that existence of cookies bring to any transaction.

The existence of the cookie also brings a coincidental side effect. It transforms browsing from an anonymous activity into one that holds the possibility of identifying the surfer, along with creating a record of where the surfer goes and what the surfer does. The information reduces the amount of the surfer's personal privacy and gives others a degree of access and the ability to monitor behavior. As such the creation of the cookie led to the birth of a Web-based tension between functional convenience and personal privacy. For those who are aware of the tension, cookies set up an almost classic conflict in that you can't live with them if you value your privacy, but you can't live without them either, if you want to conduct a large number of convenient transactions on the Web. One of the more subtle problems created by cookies is the way in which they are installed on the browser. Most browsers are programmed to accept cookies as the default setting unless the user manually changes the instructions. The rule is to accept the cookie unless they are explicitly blocked. Surfers with privacy concerns might wish to have the controls read the other way, blocking the attachment of cookies unless they are explicitly accepted. Also, cookies are placed without first notifying the surfer that a server is attempting to install a cookie. Such notification could give the surfer the option of either accepting or rejecting the cookie and thereby exercising some control over the loss of privacy.

Individual site cookies are generally benign in that they have certain privacy protections built into their structure. For example, each site uses its own individual ID number to identify its cookies, which in turn can only convey information back to the site that place the cookie originally. Different sites cannot read the cookies placed by others or the information that they contain. Also, the Web browser itself does not have a unique ID number that it surrenders to the Web site in response to a cookie placement. If such a unique browser number existed it could allow the aggregation of data across the totality of sites visited by that single computer.[10]

The Saga of DoubleClick and the Potentially Sinister Cookies

The benign nature of most **single-site cookies** changed dramatically with the introduction of **third-party cookies**. Internet advertising firms, such as DoubleClick, Engage, and 24/7 Real Media, were formed to centralize the Web advertising effort. They would buy banner ad space on client sites and add the sites to the advertising network. The advertising firm would then manage the display and vary the content of the banner ad from a central location, determining which surfer saw what ad. By centralizing the content they could feed personalized ads to that space, depending upon the recent past surfing behavior of the visitor. This capability would allow "marketers to deliver the right message, to the right person, at the right time."[11]

The technology they developed to achieve this goal involved offering ads at thousands of Web sites, based upon a common cookie, which was placed on the browser whenever the surfer visited a site in the client network. The common cookie served as a tracking device that allowed the third-party advertising firm to engage in **online profiling** as the surfer visited a multiple of sites in the network. The information was fed back to the central third-party, who then would create a **target marketing campaign** that was beamed to the surfer as they traveled to related sites. By engaging in the target marketing of personalized ads, the firm increased the likelihood that the surfer would click through to the advertising site and purchase the product. For example, if a surfer looked at a site containing information about new cars, it might mean that the viewer was in the market for a new vehicle. Therefore, as the surfer traveled to different sites in the

---

10 To see the cookies (and delete them if desired) on the Internet Explorer browser, open the browser from the Start button and click on the Tools menu. Click on the Internet Options button and then on the General tab. Click on settings and lastly click on View Files to reveal the list of cookies attached to the browser.

11 A DoublClick advertising theme quoted in Schwartz, "Giving the Web a Memory," p. C10.

client network, the common cookie would alert the new site that the surfer had previously looked at new car information. In turn, the site would call up banner ads from the third-party advertiser, showing links to specific brands of new vehicles, insurance providers, or perhaps sites to get competitive price information about new vehicles.

If the surfer registered at one of the sites giving a name and e-mail address, the central marketing firm not only knew what content the person was looking at, but their personal identity and how to contact them. This powerful and valuable information is only a step or two away from potential serious abuse. For example, suppose a surfer visited several sites providing health information about cancer or AIDS. Insurance firms might buy this information and use it as the basis for refusing to sell health or life insurance to the individual. If the surfer visited various sites revealing a sexual preference or orientation, a potential employer might refuse to offer a job to the surfer. Lastly, in the guise of security, an employer might use the information to spy on existing employees to see where they went or what they looked at while off-duty. The results might then be used as grounds for dismissal. In fairness to the central advertisers, DoubleClick pledged that they would not collect data on medical, financial, or sexual behavior, or on the surfing habits of children. However critics of this pledge pointed out that it was not legally binding and could be changed any time at the discretion of DoubleClick.[12]

The potential for privacy abuse multiplied almost exponentially when DoubleClick purchased the firm Abacus Direct in 1999. Abacus tracked the purchase behavior of off-line customers as they bought products at retail outlets and from mail-order catalog firms and publishers. The goal was to link the online and off-line purchase profiles into a new saleable database called *Abacus Alliance,* setting up the potential for even greater target marketing based upon consumer profiling. This union of information on e-tail, retail, and surfing behavior would give the firm an enormous and valuable personal profile of almost every consumer in the nation. The move to link Web behavior with names, addresses, and other forms of personal information created a storm of protest from privacy advocates and prompted a probe from the Federal Trade Commission. Seeing the downside, executives from DoubleClick changed direction and stated that they would not create and sell the links for now. The firm, however, "didn't rule out connecting such data in the future, once privacy standards are set."[13]

Examples of Other Potential Internet Privacy Threats

The DoubleClick **online/off-line privacy threat** may be eliminated for now, but other firms are loading up Web browsers with various forms of tracking software or engaging in **electronic eavesdropping**. The numerous reports of electronic eavesdropping incidents support the conclusion that it is not an isolated, random, or declining activity. For example, surfers who installed popular software for file sharing also unknowingly accepted a Web tracking program.[14] Also, **Web bugs** are invisibly added to Web pages to gather information about the visitors to a particular Web site. Both AOL and Geocities used this technology in the past.[15] Other firms found gender-based differences in keyboard and mouse usage that allow the firm to distinguish among the users of a computer in the same family. The **biometric data** results in the creation of user silhouettes that can provide important information for advertisers.[16] Lastly, Comcast, the

---

12 Bob Tedeschi, "E-Commerce Report: Critics Press Legal Assault on Tracking of Web Users," *The New York Times*, February 7, 2000, p. C1.

13 Andrea Peterson, "DoubleClick Reverses Course After Privacy Outcry," *The Wall Street Journal*, March 3, 2000, p. B1.

14 Associated Press, "Music Software Users Installed Tracking Program Unknowingly," *The New York Times*, January 5, 2002, p. C2.

15 John Schwartz, "Web Bugs Are Tracking Use of Internet," *The New York Times*, August 14, 2001, p. C1

16 William M. Bulkeley, "Software Uses Clicking Patters to Customize Ads," *The Wall Street Journal*, May 25, 2001, p. B1.

nation's third-largest cable company, for a brief time stored data that would allow them to track the individual Web browsing behavior of its 1 million high-speed Internet subscribers without first notifying them.[17] Privacy advocates feared that, regardless of whether Comcast ever used individual information, law enforcement agencies or the courts could subpoena the records and use them in ways beyond the control of Comcast.

Perhaps the largest potential future threat to privacy may come from a Microsoft project called **Passport**.[18] This centralized program of consumer identification is designed to store personal information, including credit card data, in exchange for greater security and simplification of Web shopping, communication, and collaboration. It is part of a larger Microsoft project dubbed Hailstorm, which is intended to be a fee-based super secretary. It would keep track of personal appointments, be an electronic repository for personal medical, financial, and insurance information, send reminders and messages about weather or travel conditions, and have knowledge about personal computer usage that would permit the transfer of information at the most convenient time. The operation of the entire system would require a considerable amount of individual trust in Microsoft and its ability to keep the information private and secure.

A related issue involves the degree of Internet privacy afforded to employees as part of the workplace. The topic received substantial public attention when it was learned that federal court administrators had installed a program to monitor the site visits of the 30,000 members of the federal judicial system, including clerks as well as 1,800 federal judges. Although the monitoring focused on visits to Web sites hosting gambling, pornography, streaming video, and music, individual judges and the Judicial Conference viewed the unauthorized monitoring of communications as a violation of judicial privacy.[19] The monitoring of judicial computers was terminated after strong public objection by numerous federal judges.[20] Just because the judges and their clerks were able to free themselves from workplace monitoring does not mean that the electronic movements of other workers escape the watchful eye of their employers. Firms have a legal right to monitor the use of company-provided equipment and computer systems. A 2001 survey taken by the American Management Association revealed "more than three-quarters of U.S. firms now monitor their employees' phone calls, e-mails, Internet activities, and computer files."[21] This number was twice what it was in 1997, with more than 27 percent of the firms reporting that they monitored employee e-mail. Firms undertake this monitoring for productivity reasons, fearing that up to 25 percent of workers spend 10–30 minutes per work day surfing sites unrelated to work activity and for the protection of trade secrets and to discourage harassment.[22]

Lastly, the introduction of **presence technology** will allow others to monitor the usage or location of desktop, laptop, and handheld computers, cell phones, wireless Web pads, auto communications systems, and virtually any other device connected to the Web.[23] Currently, the instant messaging version of presence technology allows anyone to see whether a person on his buddy list is connected to the Web and whether he is actively working at the machine. The existence of presence awareness has benefits in that any Web-connected person is within instant reach, always in touch. The downside is that

---

17 Matt Richtel, "Comcast Says It Will Stop Storing Data on Customers," *The New York Times*, February 14, 2002, p. C5.

18 Associated Press, "Big Bill Is Watching You," *Connecticut Post*, May 16, 2001, p. B1.

19 Neil A. Lewis, "Rebels in Black Robes Recoil at Surveillance of Computers," *The New York Times*, August 8, 2001, p. A1.

20 Neil A. Lewis, "Plan for Web Monitoring in Courts Dropped," *The New York Times*, September 9, 2001, p. A34.

21 American Management Association, "AMA Survey on Electronic Monitoring and Surveillance," available at **http://www.amanet.org/research/emssurvey.htm**.

22 Bonny L. Georgia, "Invasions of Privacy," *Access Magazine*, April 1, 2001, p. 10.

23 Lisa Guernsey, "Sure, You Can Surf, But You Can't Hide," *The New York Times*, February 7, 2002, p. G1.

others, sometimes unknown to the person being monitored, can "watch" what surfers are doing and eventually, in conjunction with global positioning technology (GPS), know where they are physically. This capability may lead to erosion in the level of personal privacy that at least some Web users may not want to experience.

PROTECTING INTERNET PRIVACY: LAWS VERSUS TECHNOLOGY

Some Internet users may have a low level of privacy concern and be willing to accept less anonymity in exchange for greater Web convenience or even lower-cost services. From an economic perspective, these individuals are making a benefit-cost calculation. Are the gains from convenience and cost worth the sacrifice in terms of privacy?[24] Others might like to be assured that the information made available at one site will not be transferred to operators of other sites without their knowledge, permission, and perhaps payment. Web users may feel violated as cookies and bugs collect and aggregate information across a network of sites, to yield a composite personal profile that contains more information than the individual would feel comfortable revealing to any single site.

What can be done to protect Web surfers who want to participate in e-commerce but also wish to avoid the sacrifice of personal privacy? Two suggested approaches may increase the level of Web privacy. The first is a **legal approach to enhanced Internet privacy**, which involves the introduction of governmental action through new laws requiring a site to obtain the informed consent of a visitor before collecting, exchanging, or aggregating information. One aspect of the legal solution involves rebalancing the tension that lies between the opt-in versus opt-out policies toward Web user participation in the exchange of site information. A 2000 Federal Trade Commission study revealed that 75 percent of sites on the Web follow an **opt-out policy** as their default setting, or standard position on privacy. This policy allowed them to collect and exchange information with other sites, as well as to track surfer movements, in the absence of a specific directive from the individual denying the sites the right to undertake these actions.[25] Conversely, the default position of the sites following an **opt-in policy** denies them the right to exchange or collect personal information unless they were specifically permitted to do so by the Web user. Just this simple change in the default position regarding Web privacy policy would go a long way to protect personal privacy.

Before 2000, the FTC pursued a policy of industry self-regulation as the most efficient method to protect Internet privacy. An FTC study found, however, that only 41 percent of the sampled sites informed visitors of their privacy policy and provided them with some ability to participate in how their personal information would be used.[26] Moreover, only 20 percent fulfilled the set of voluntary fair information practices that the FTC was urging Internet firms to adopt. The FTC looked at the sites in terms of their performance relative to four privacy standards: "notification of privacy policies, access to data collected and a chance to correct errors, choice on how data is used; and security of the information."[27] As a result of the study, the FTC asked Congress to pass new legislation to protect consumer privacy on the Internet. A few federal laws protecting online privacy include the limits on collecting data relating to children under the **Children's Online Privacy Act of 1998** and the **Gramm–Leach–Bliley Act of 1999**, which require financial institutions to notify their customers regarding the privacy policies of the institution. Opponents of the

---

24 Virgin Entertainment went so far as to offer Web users a free Internet appliance in exchange for their willingness to part with personal data and allow tracking of their moves on the Internet. See Julia Angwin, "Virgin to Trade Web Use for Personal Data," *The Wall Street Journal*, April 10, 2000, p. B16.

25 Thomas E. Weber, "E-World: To Opt In or Opt Out: That Is the Question When Mulling Privacy," *The Wall Street Journal*, October 23, 2000, p. B1.

26 Glenn R. Simpson, "FTC Seeks Measure to Protect Privacy on Web," *The Wall Street Journal*, May 23, 2000, p. A4.

27 Simpson, "FTC Seeks Measure," p. A4.

new laws, including the Online Privacy Alliance, released studies showing that the laws would limit the ability of e-commerce firms to share or sell consumer information and cost some $17 billion per year in added expenses.[28] One of the points that the opponents made was that the e-commerce privacy was better protected by applications of new technology rather than the passage of new laws.

The Web and legal scholar Lawrence Lessig, among others, championed the **technology approach to enhanced Internet privacy**, which involves the use of a code-based solution to achieving privacy in cyberspace.[29] The ability of the Internet to limit personal privacy arises because computer code makes it so easy to collect and profile visitor data, while making the actions difficult to detect by that visitor. Lessig supports raising the level of detection through a code-based privacy system such as the one built into the **Platform for Privacy Preferences (P3P)**, developed by the World Wide Web Consortium. The system would work as follows.[30] On the firm side, an e-commerce or other Web site would translate its privacy policy into a standard P3P code format, listing characteristics such as the degree to which it shares data with partners, the existence and extent of cookie placement, along with its intended use. This P3P information would become part of the code attached to the site's Web pages. On the visitor side, either the browser or a separate P3P sensitive program is used to predetermine the level of desired privacy. It would require the visitor to preapprove settings indicating the amount of privacy erosion to be tolerated. The settings would include the type of information that can be collected and the usage of that information. When the visitor arrived at a site, the user's software would read the P3P encoded privacy policy, comparing the site policy with the predetermined tolerances for privacy set by the visitor. If the site's privacy policy fell short of the visitor's preferences, the browser would automatically block the transmission of certain information and alert the visitor to the conflict.

The technology approach sounds promising in that it appears to be efficient and simple in its application. However, it has some potential flaws. First, the complexity of the initial settings, which might require users to make decisions covering dozens of privacy values, may be more than the average surfer is willing to understand or tolerate. In addition, the consequence of the settings, while yielding enhanced privacy, may well impede the rapid surfing of the Web and lead to the program being turned off by many Web users.[31] Lastly, the coverage and effectiveness of the technology approach requires the majority of high-visit Web sites to voluntarily participate in the P3P solution.[32] This participation may force the sites to make some important information choices. Many sites would like to see the privacy code distinguish between safeguarding personal information, while at the same time allowing the site to continue to collect anonymous consumer data, such as the number of site visits and unique visitors, as well as visitor demographics, which might still be shared internally and externally.

INTERNET SECURITY: THE NATURE AND EXTENT OF THE PROBLEM

The vulnerabilities of the Web and individual Web sites to **cybercrime**, unauthorized intrusions and other breaches of security are growing at an alarming rate. The **computer emergency response team**, now known as CERT, is a federally funded coordination center located at the Software Engineering Institute on the campus of Carnegie

---

28 Ted Bridis, "Industry Studies Attack Web-Privacy Laws," *The Wall Street Journal*, March 13, 2001, p. B6.
29 Lawrence Lessig, "Technology Will Solve Web Privacy Problems," *The Wall Street Journal*, May 31, 2000, p. A26.
30 Glenn R. Simpson, "The Battle Over Web Privacy," *The Wall Street Journal*, March 21, 2001, p. B1.
31 Simpson, "The Battle," p. B1.
32 Jason Sykes and Glenn R. Simpson, "Some Big Sites Back the P3P Plan; Others Wait," *The Wall Street Journal*, March 21, 2001, p. B1.

CERT/CC Statistics, 1988–2001				TABLE 18-1

Year	Incidents Reported	% Change	Vulnerabilities Reported	% Change
1988	6			
1989	132	2,100.00	n.a.	
1990	252	90.91	n.a.	
1991	406	61.11	n.a.	
1992	773	90.39	n.a.	
1993	1,334	72.57	n.a.	
1994	2,340	75.41	n.a.	
1995	2,412	3.08	171	
1996	2,573	6.67	345	101.75
1997	2,134	–17.06	311	–9.86
1998	3,734	74.98	262	–15.76
1999	9,859	164.03	417	59.16
2000	21,756	120.67	1,090	161.39
2001	52,658	142.04	2,437	123.58
Total	100,369		5,033	

Source: Information available at **http://www.cert.org/stats/cert_stats.html**.

Mellon University near Pittsburgh. The CERT Coordination Center is responsible for tabulating the number of **computer intrusion incidents** and reported **system vulnerabilities** involving security weaknesses in specific technology or products each year. It also provides technical assistance and training in response to compromises in computer security. CERT annual data for reports of incidents and vulnerabilities is presented in Table 18-1. The figures show the dramatic increase in the volume of incidents that took place from 1998 to 2001. CERT defines an incident as a term "that groups together any related set of activities; for example, activities in which the same tool or exploit is used by an intruder." If the same virus tool is used to intrude upon more than one computer or appears over an extended period of time, the event is reported as a single incident. Also, CERT tabulates only incidents where it receives a report through its information gathering system. Therefore, as CERT acknowledges, the data on incidents may well understate the magnitude or expanse of the intrusion problem.[33] In 1998, there were 3,734 reported incidents. By 2001, that number grew to 52,658. In the same period, the number of reported vulnerabilities grew from 262 to 2,437, or a more than ninefold increase. Some of the reasons for the growth in numbers results from a greater awareness and reporting of individual incidents by system operators. Still, the tools and level of sophistication of hackers also increased, allowing them to automate their attacks and create more numerous incidents.

The economic cost of these attacks has been and can be substantial. The Internet security firm, Computer Economics, estimated the global costs associated with some of the more prominent virus attacks that have occurred in recent years.[34] Their data, shown in Table 18-2, indicate that the most damaging virus was the Love Bug in 2000, with an estimated global cost of $8.75 billion. It has become the standard by which to measure the severity of other attacks, registering the maximum amount of adverse economic

---

[33] CERT, "CERT/CC Statistics 1988–2002," available at **http://www.cert.org/stats/cert_stats.html**.

[34] CEI, "Malicious Code Attacks Had $13.2 Billion Impact in 2001," available at **http://www.computereconomics.com/**, March 2002.

TABLE 18-2		Estimated Costs of Malicious Web Security Attacks

Estimated Global Cost of Specific Computer Virus Attacks Analysis by Incident				Estimated Global Cost of Security Lapses Analysis by Year	
Year	Code Name	Worldwide Economic Impact ($U.S.)	Cyber Attack Index	Year	Worldwide Economic Impact ($U.S. bil.)
2001	Nimda	$635 million	0.73	2001	13.2
2001	Code Red(s)	$2.62 billion	2.99	2000	17.1
2001	SirCam	$1.15 billion	1.31	1999	12.1
2000	Love Bug	$8.75 billion	10.00	1998	6.1
1999	Melissa	$1.10 billion	1.26	1997	3.3
1999	Explorer	$1.02 billion	1.17	1996	1.8
				1995	0.5

Source: Computer Economics, available at **http://www.computereconomics.com/**.

impact to date on a subjective scale of 1–10. The attacks by the two **computer worms** Nimda and the various versions of Code Red in 2001 exploited vulnerabilities in various Microsoft products, and cost the operators of computer systems more than $3.25 billion in cleanup expenses and lost productivity. Worms differ from viruses in that they do not require human intervention to spread to other computers. They are self-propagating and spread rapidly across the Internet, locking up computers and blocking other forms of Web traffic.[35] Computer Economics further estimated the global costs for all malicious code attacks in 2001 was $13.2 billion, or more than 26 times the estimated cost inflicted just six years earlier. The same report listed the vulnerability of computer systems in various industries to potential privacy management problems. The banking and finance industry was thought to have the highest vulnerability, followed closely by the transportation industry. The federal government was assessed as having the lowest level of vulnerability with the insurance industry being rated just slightly higher.[36]

The opportunities for malicious attacks appear to be growing faster than the ability to suppress them. For example, the expanding use of wireless networks as a form of communication and Internet connection will allow hackers to intercept private messages and break into systems. Also, the introduction of residential high-speed networks make it more attractive for external hackers to gain control of individual computers enabling them to launch **denial-of-service attacks** that paralyze a Web site by overloading it with bogus traffic and requests for information.[37] In late October 2002, a denial-of-service attack crippled nine of the 13 root computers that manage the entire global flow of Internet traffic. These computers, run by the U.S. government and various private groups, are spread out geographically around the world as a way to avoid physical disasters

---

35 One variation of the Code Red worm was designed to assault the computers serving the White House Web page in July 2001 by flooding them with a denial-of-service attack. See Robert Lemos, "Web Worm Targets White House," available at **http://news.com.com/2100-1001-270272.html? legacy=cnet.**

36 Lemos, "Web Worm."

37 Associated Press, "Despite More Security, Net a Dangerous Place," *Connecticut Post*, January 23, 2002, p. D14. For a description of the mechanics of a denial-of-service attack, see CNet News, "How a Denial-of-Service Attack Works," available at **http://news.com.com/2100-1017-236728. html.**

or attack. It was "the most sophisticated and large-scale assault against these crucial computers in the history of the Internet."[38]

The terrorist attack on the World Trade Center intensified the public's fear of being exposed to **cyberterrorism**. The perpetrators used the Internet in a criminal way to engage in attack planning and communication. More sophisticated fanatics could launch terrorist attacks on the domestic electronic infrastructure. "Of greatest concern are cyberattacks that could bring down electric power grids, automated teller machines and public transportation systems, disrupting the economy and posing safety risks to the public."[39] The probability is growing that the fears created by cybercrime and cyberterrorism involving incidents, vulnerabilities, as well as acts of external aggression, will lead to some restraint on the current level of freedom, privacy, and openness enjoyed by Web users.

Why the Internet Is Not Secure

You may recall from Chapter 3 that the predecessor of today's Internet was Arpanet, which was a Department of Defense project to provide a secure internal communication system in the time of national attack. All of the focus of the network was directed toward protecting national or external security. During the construction phase, little or no attention was paid to guarding the internal security of the Arpanet. It was an open system. After all, everyone who gained access and became an internal member of Arpanet was a known entity and considered to be trustworthy. Because the security risks to the network were thought to be external, the system was also designed to be as decentralized as possible. The network would deliver information over any one of dozens of equally efficient electronic routes in the event of nuclear or other external attack. This arrangement would allow the network to resist failure based upon the loss of specific links or nodes.[40] When Arpanet made the transition from being a system of defense communications to an Internet system of global communications and e-commerce, these characteristics of openness and decentralization were carried over as well and became central features of the expanded network. Together, they still serve as the greatest source of the Internet's strength as well as the greatest source of its security weakness.

The Internet is a **decentralized network** in that no one owns it. Also it has no central boss or controlling authority. No one runs the Internet or even manages it. It exists as a cooperative effort among government, business, telecommunications carriers, and academic entities, along with a "loose confederation of self-governing standard setters and rule makers."[41] The closest that anyone comes to managing the physical operation of the Internet are the backbone telecom firms including Worldcom, Sprint, Cable, and Wireless USA, along with Verizon. These firms agree to **peering arrangements** that allow for the exchange of communications traffic among each other at no charge.[42] Today's Internet is also a fully **open network**; anyone can join who will abide by a few membership rules. In 1991, the year that the World Wide Web was first conceived, 727,000 computers, mostly in the United States, linked to the Internet with an Internet protocol or numerical IP address. By the end of 2001, this number grew to more than 175 million connections

---

38 Associated Press, "Powerful Attack Cripples 9 Key Internet Computers," *Connecticut Post*, October 23, 2002, p. D2.

39 Associated Press, "Powerful Attack," p. D2.

40 Mike McConnell, "Security and the Internet: Get Serious About Cyber-Crime," *The Wall Street Journal*, February 17, 2000, p. A16.

41 David P. Hamilton, "Redesigning the Internet: Can It Be Made Less Vulnerable?" *The Wall Street Journal*, February 11, 2000, p. B1. Three of the more prominent standard setters are the Internet Engineering Task Force (IETF) that sets the technical standards for the Internet, the World Wide Web Consortium (W3C) that deals with Web interoperability protocols, and the Internet Corporation for Assigned Names and Number (Icann) that assigns Internet addresses and top domain names, such as .com, .edu and .org.

42 Katie Hafner, "The Internet's Invisible Hand," *The New York Times*, January 10, 2002, p. G1.

globally.[43] Because of its core strength of openness, new computers and new networks are connecting to the Internet on a daily basis, increasing the value of the system to all users. The increasing number of links also magnifies the problems associated with maintaining network security. By analogy, an Internet security expert noted that the problem of malaria was solved when the U.S. capital was constructed in Washington, D.C., not because the bug was licked, but because they drained the swampland. With the magnification of the number of Internet links, the electronic swampland is being enlarged at an alarming rate.[44]

Internet and e-Commerce Security Measures

The process of achieving **online security** resides at three levels. The first level is security for firms and computer systems connected to the Internet; second is the higher level of maintaining the security of the Internet itself; and the third is guarding against the Internet being used as a weapon in criminal activity or with the intent of undermining national security. Site security is a fairly straightforward but potentially expensive operation. It includes a series of **online hygiene habits**, such as regular use of antivirus software, establishing and changing passwords, and disconnecting from the Internet when not in use. Networks connected to the Internet need to create firewalls to keep their systems from being attacked or used in attacks on other sites. Firms need to train employees in the secure operation of the system and to hire Internet security personnel to monitor the system, guarding against intrusion. Software firms producing operating systems and applications programs need to guard against technical flaws in their products' codes that allow external attacks. In the past, various Microsoft products demonstrated security lapses that facilitated a particular type of hacker activity called a buffer-overflow attack.[45]

It is when the pursuit of security reaches the level of protecting the integrity of the Internet itself or enhancing national security that the safety countermeasures potentially raise conflicts with the goal of personal privacy involving individual Internet travel. First, the major participants on the Internet, including ISPs, e-commerce firms, government, and software and hardware developers, need to introduce better filters to identify and quickly terminate malicious Internet traffic such as denial-of-service attacks. This effort requires a monitoring of traffic type and volume that is not currently done.[46] Second, hacker attacks could be diminished and security improved if it were possible to authenticate and track the origin of each piece of Internet traffic. Currently, hackers can use fake IP addresses on attack packets, making it extremely difficult for authorities to identify the actual source of an attack. The use of an encryption key to mark each packet would facilitate tracing it back to its origins. Also, introducing an Internet authentication service to ensure that both senders and servers are who they say they are would further limit attacks. However, both of these systems would also eliminate the current level of anonymity among Internet users, thereby greatly reducing the amount of Internet personal privacy.

Lastly, the FBI created a piece of investigative software called Carnivore that intercepts and reviews information on e-mails sent from an ISP.[47] The program is a form of packet sniffer, and can only be installed under court order in a manner similar to a traditional telephone wiretap. Carnivore can be used in criminal investigations to identify illicit e-mail traffic involving child pornography, fraud, or identity theft. It can also be used in intelligence investigations to identify and track e-mail traffic involving terrorism and threats to national security. However, once installed, it must browse the headers of all the ISP e-mail traffic to find the communications being sent by or to the criminal target. As such, the data intercept program potentially compromises the privacy of all e-mail communication. The

---

43 Hafner, "The Internet's Invisible Hand," p. G1

44 Hamilton, "Redesigning the Internet," p. B1.

45 Don Clark, "Cigital Says Microsoft Program Isn't Secure," *The Wall Street Journal*, February 14, 2002, p. B6.

46 McConnell, "Security and the Internet," p. A16.

47 John Schwartz, "Fighting Crime Online: Who Is in Harm's Way?" *The New York Times*, February 8, 2001, p. G1.

Carnivore investigative program has the power and potential to do more than just monitor e-mail traffic headers. It can also be set to identify the use of certain words or phrases contained within the universe of e-mail traffic. If Carnivore were to be used in this way, it could raise considerable questions regarding the violation of the Fourth Amendment's Constitutional protection against unwarranted search and seizure.

Despite the investigative power of the Carnivore software, **encryption programs** that send e-mails in scrambled code can block the ability of the software to read the intercepts, without access to the keys that unlock the code. Contemporary commercial browsers can enable strong encryption that would require a prohibitively costly amount of computing power to decipher without the encryption key.[48] The encryption capability is located in the browser to make e-commerce users feel comfortable giving credit card information over the Internet, or leave Web users secure as they carry out online banking transactions or stock purchases. Mathematicians also developed private e-mail programs, such as Pretty Good Privacy, which encrypt messages using the latest technology and are exceedingly difficult to decrypt.

The Clinton administration argued for the creation of key escrows or encryption backdoors to allow law enforcement agencies to read encrypted files. These proposals to **regulate encryption** were shown to be unworkable for several reasons. First, strong encryption was already out in the commercial world and would be impossible to recall. Second, the repositories for the code keys would themselves become the target of hackers. Third, foreign Internet users beyond U.S. law would simply refuse to use U.S.-made software if it contained an encryption backdoor accessible to U.S. agencies. Lastly, code writers in other countries had the skill to develop their own encryption technology without decipher keys or backdoors, and would sell their products in competition with U.S. software firms. In the face of these realities, the federal government abandoned its attempt to regulate encryption in 1999.[49] Federal agencies do have software that will allow them to read computer keystrokes before the information is placed in encrypted form, offering limited ability to defeat encryption if the reader software can be attached to the computer.

SUMMARY AND PROSPECTS

The topical survey in this chapter established the fact that Internet users are concerned about the levels of privacy and security provided by the system. The Internet is growing rapidly as an essential part of daily activity, with domestic and global e-commerce becoming increasingly dependent upon the speed, efficiency, and low cost provided by the communication links. However, the people and firms that use the Internet for e-tailing, financial transactions, B2B exchanges, information storage and access, as well as general communications are also becoming increasingly aware of its vulnerabilities. Acts of unauthorized snooping, information gathering, personal profiling, cybercrime, and cyberterrorism are becoming a more threatening part of the network, with the potential to reduce the levels of trust and usage that the Internet currently enjoys.

Internet users want to protect their individual privacy while at the same time guaranteeing the security of the system. Unfortunately, the two goals require a trade-off rather than being enhanced and achievable simultaneously. It need not always be the case, however, that the goals are antagonistic rather than mutually reinforcing. Limiting commercial threats to privacy from third-party sources would appear to be possible without reducing the level of system security. The existence of benign cookies is a fact of digital life, because they convey so much functional convenience to the e-commerce buyer and are of considerable informational value to the individual seller. Still, third-party purveyors of cookies and information aggregators do not hold an unauthorized right to that information.

---

48 Lee Gomes, "Experts Say Encryption Can't Be Limited, a Setback for Lawmakers Seeking Change," *The Wall Street Journal*, September 26, 2001, p. B5.

49 John Schwartz, "Disputes on Electronic Message Encryption Take on New Urgency," *The New York Times*, September 25, 2001, p. C1.

Personal data are still the property of the individual. Such data are not in the public domain, to be traded like a commodity, even if part of Internet travel and contact.

The solution here isn't a choice between laws versus code, but a combination of both. Requiring a change in the default settings on browsers and site privacy policies from an opt-out to opt-in standard would return information control to the individual. Putting a simple version of the P3P standard, or similar software, onto each browser would help surfers to make informed choices regarding the ability of sites to gather personal information and exchange it with others. These straightforward acts would help tip the balance of Internet information power into the hands of the individual and return to them the ability to decide for themselves their level of cooperation.

Enhancing security without sacrificing privacy poses its own set of challenges. The Internet began as a U.S. military and scientific communications system encompassing technical openness and technical decentralization. It was a community of scholars and like-minded participants that embodied the ideals of freedom of speech and freedom of assembly. These characteristics allowed the Internet to be transformed into a global network for communications and commerce. Technical decentralization does not necessarily require that, for security purposes, there also be administrative decentralization.

Already governing bodies are emerging to set up some rules of Internet behavior. They include Icann, which oversees the creation and organization of higher-order domain names. No reasons would preclude a similar group from being created to oversee uniform network security standards, such as technical controls and monitoring against cyberterrorism, as well as the introduction of domestic standards for thwarting cybercrime. Perhaps the network can be partitioned into secure systems and more open areas, with firewalls built to halt unauthorized travel between them. Individual system sites could then decide for themselves the portion of the network and the level of security where they would choose to locate. As with the privacy issue, the answer to the network security problem may lie in informed user choice.

A global network requires international cooperation to maintain system security. Creating minimum network security standards, as well as knowing which nations and network members are and are not abiding by them is an important step in guarding system integrity and ultimately guaranteeing a level of personal privacy for its users.

KEY TERMS AND CONCEPTS

biometric data
Children's Online Privacy Act of 1998
computer emergency response team
  (CERT)
computer intrusion incidents
computer system vulnerabilities
computer worms
cookies
cybercrime
cyberterrorism
decentralized network
denial-of-service attacks
digital soul
electronic eavesdropping
encryption programs
external security dimension
Gramm–Leach–Bliley Act of 1999
Internal security dimensions
Internet internal dimension
Internet privacy
Internet security
legal approach to enhanced Internet
  privacy

online hygiene habits
online/off-line privacy threat
online profile
online profiling
online security
open network
opt-in policy
opt-out policy
passport
peering arrangements
Platform for Privacy Preference (P3P)
presence technology
regulation of encryption
single-site cookies
system vulnerablities
target marketing campaign
technology approach to enhanced
  internet privacy
third-party cookies
web bugs

DISCUSSION AND REVIEW QUESTIONS

1. Identify and discuss the ways that the Internet can compromise the privacy of individual users. How have Internet users reacted to this fear of being identified digitally? How has it affected e-commerce?

2. Distinguish between the concepts of Internet security and Internet privacy. Why does a potential tension arise between achieving these two Internet goals?

3. What are electronic cookies? How do they help to simplify the process of e-commerce?

4. What is the nature of the tension between personal privacy and functional convenience that is created by the placing of electronic cookies?

5. Identify and distinguish between single-site cookies and third-party cookies. How did the e-commerce firm DoubleClick try to turn benign single-site cookies into more sinister third-party cookies?

6. What is a target marketing campaign? How do third-party cookies help to make these types of advertising pitches more profitable to e-commerce firms?

7. How did DoubleClick try to unite online and off-line sources of personal data? Were they successful? Why?

8. Distinguish between the legal approach and the technology approach to enhanced Internet privacy. What is the nature of the tension that exists between the opt-in versus opt-out policies toward the exchange of personal information over the Internet?

9. Examine the data in Tables 18-1 and 18-2. How big is the Internet security problem? Does it appear to be growing over time? Why?

10. Why isn't the Internet secure? What actions can be undertaken to make it more secure?

11. What is Carnivore? How does it exemplify and aggravate the tension between Internet security and Internet privacy?

12. Discuss the distinction between technical and administrative decentralization as these concepts relate to the Internet and the issue of Internet security.

WEB EXERCISES

1. Log on to the search engine **http://www.google.com** and type in your own name or that of an adult family member or close friend. See how much information is available about this private citizen on the Web. The results should convince you that an individual doesn't have to be a prominent member of the community to have an Internet presence.

2. Link to the homepage for the Internet advertising and marketing firm DoubleClick at **http://www.doubleclick.com/us/**. Click on its privacy link and review its privacy policy. Are you comfortable with its pledges regarding the use of personal Internet information for advertising purposes?

3. Link to the CERT Web site at **http://www.cert.org/stats/cert_stats.html** to view the most recent data on the number of computer intrusion incidents and system vulnerabilities.

4. Link to the homepage of the information technology security firm Computer Economics at **http://www.computereconomics.com/**. Click on the Press Release link and see whether they have updated the information on the global cost for malicious code attacks during the most recent year.

5. Link to the McAfee virus and Trojan horse information page at **http://vil.nai.com/VIL/newly-discovered-viruses.asp** to get the names of the new computer threats identified in the last 30 days or so. Click on the name of one of the recent discoveries to see what it is and how it works.

CHAPTER

19

Introductory Case

THE INTERNET AS A PARADOX: IRAN AND CHINA

The nations of Iran and China are similar in some important ways.[1] They both maintain a relatively restricted physical world. Iran is a theocracy, with restrictions based on the principles of Islam and the Qaran, with certain practices and topics forbidden. Men and women may not socialize or interact freely. Popular music and other forms of contemporary entertainment are banned. The conduct, dress, and role of women are severely limited. Feminist ideas and speech are forbidden. China is a totalitarian system, with restrictions based on Communistic ideology and the teachings of Chairman Mao. Political dissent and criticism of government policy are not tolerated. Pornography and access to Western ideas are strictly controlled, and the flow of printed news is tightly restricted. After all, it was Chairman Mao who preached "control of information and control of the gun were the two pillars of Communist Party power."[2]

Despite the restrictions of the physical world, both nations tolerate, at least to some extent, the openness of the virtual world. In each county, average citizens have access to the Internet, with some 2 million users in Iran, and, since 1995, perhaps 50 million in China. Internet contact is achieved mostly through cybercafés, where inexpensive access is readily available. Within Iran the Internet is uncensored today, despite past government attempts to restrict access and the flow of information. Iranians can assemble freely in online communities to speak, criticize, interact, and otherwise engage in many of the activities forbidden within physical communities. In China, the cyber police still use filters on government-controlled Internet servers in an attempt to block links with thousands of sites identified as antisocial or subversive. These sites include URLs dealing with pornography, government criticism or political dissent, and those exposing liberal points of view or delivering uncensored news. However, the efforts to create official firewalls that block offending sites set off a technology cat-and-mouse game that involves frequently changing URLs and the use of proxy servers to avoid detection as Chinese surfers link with forbidden sites.

If these two nations exercise so much authoritarian control over their physical worlds, why do they tolerate the openness of the virtual world? Why has each nation spent the money to wire the countryside with fiber optic technology and advanced Internet infrastructure? The answer is apparently the same in both cases: Those in control recognize that the openness of the Internet offers the promise of a faster rate of national economic growth and technological progress. Scientists and engineers, business and financial firms, students, artists, and general citizens must have contact with the rest of the world to be a productive part of today's global marketplace involving the exchange of goods, information, and ideas. Allowing citizens to gain electronic linkage with the outside world sets up a potential tension between the openness of the virtual world and the restrictions imposed in the physical world. Internet access creates a paradox, or conflict between its use as a way to achieve the economic goal of a faster pace of growth, and its use as a tool of internal social and political change. How this paradox will be resolved is not clear. When and how will the freedoms experienced in the virtual world migrate to and bring about change within the physical world? Conversely, can any nation, ruled by a central authority, prevail against the inconsistency of control as revealed by the Internet?

---

1 The information in this case is adapted from two separate but cojoined articles by Nazila Fathi and Erik Eckholm, "Taboo Surfing: Click Here for Iran. And Click Here for China," *The New York Times*, August 4, 2002, p. Wk-5.

2 Fathi and Eckholm, "Taboo Surfing," p. Wk-5.

e-Commerce and Society

With this case and its revealed tension in mind, the question to be examined in this chapter is: Does the introduction of the Internet and e-commerce have the ability to introduce some elements of change in the social, political, and cultural structure of that society? If so, how powerful is the Internet as a force for change?

JUDGING THE GAINS FROM EMPOWERMENT: WHO BENEFITS AND HOW MUCH

Chapter 1 introduced the idea that, if knowledge is power, then the Internet and e-commerce tend to empower the user. What, then, do these forces of change offer to society as a whole? Is the Internet a "win-win" technology, where everyone has the opportunity to gain, or will it bring a mix of Internet winners and losers? If both gains and losses occur, who will be the winners and losers, and how much is at stake in the contest? Will the Internet serve as a democratizing, decentralizing force that empowers the individual and levels the commercial as well as the social playing field? Or is it a vehicle facilitating the growth of scale, the centralization of economic activity such that it works to reinforce the social divide?[3] These questions are but a few of some important economic and social issues that surround the creation and use of the Internet. Alan Murray, the Washington Bureau Chief of *The Wall Street Journal*, examined these and related questions in his book *The Wealth of Choices*.[4] He grouped the social issues of Internet-related power and gain into what can be characterized as a tension between interpreting the Internet from the perspective of the populist myth versus the monopolist myth.

Understanding the Populist Myth

The **populist myth** identifies the Internet as a force that liberates and empowers the individual. The Internet reduces the cost of acquiring and distributing information, and renders that information readily available to almost everyone, anywhere in the world. It takes management hierarchies, based on the upward flow of proprietary information, and flattens them. One of the traditional functions of middle management was to gather, process, and interpret information, which was then passed up the chain of command. Today, the decision makers at the top of the hierarchy can access the information faster and directly themselves, while using their own skill and experience to interpret the results. The existence of a more perfect information process is consistent with fostering the growth of more competitive markets. Economic power arises in part because of imbalances in market information, where one party to a transaction knows more about the nature of the agreement than does another. If a consumer lacks information on the full range of available products, their location, price, terms of sale, or quality, then those who are aware of the limitations of the buyer can take advantage of the gaps. Eliminating the imperfections in the market places more power in the hands of the consumer.

---

3 The discussion in this section is inspired by and adapted from Alan Murray, "Who Wins in the New Economy?" *The Wall Street Journal*, June 27, 2000, p. B1.

4 Alan Murray, *The Wealth of Choices*, (New York: Crown Business, 2000).

The Internet allows for **disintermediation**, which can work to the economic advantage of both buyer and seller. The informed consumer can eliminate the need to deal with intermediaries, who control information and charge a fee for access and service. The Internet allows the knowledgeable consumer to deal directly with the seller. The seller too can reach out directly and at lower cost to the individual customer, bypassing the control of the wholesaler or customer aggregator. A ready example of individual empowerment and the squeeze that it places on the intermediary is seen in the travel agency business. Twenty years ago, even the simplest commercial travel required the assistance of a travel agent, who was the repository for information on carrier schedules, ticket fares, and ticketing. Agents commanded up to a 10 percent service commission from the carriers in exchange for connecting the carriers with their own customers. Today, almost anyone can plan an entire trip via the Web, either by choosing among package deals, or by selecting the individual components of the trip a la carte. Electronic travel aggregators such as Travelocity.com or individual travel service providers such as Southwest.com maintain automated sites that dispense e-tickets and trip confirmation notices at the drop of a credit card. With a buyer e-mail address, service providers can notify potential customers of travel bargains or changes in scheduling. The linkage is direct, seller to customer, without the services of a physical intermediary. Travel agents still wrote about 80 percent of all airline tickets issues in 2001 and can save search time as well as help travelers to avoid ticketing mistakes. However, the Internet option has emboldened carriers such as American Airlines to reduce the commissions paid to travel agents and place caps on the absolute dollar amount paid regardless of the cost of the ticket.[5] Travel agent services and commissions are being reduced, placing the future of the industry at potential risk. The survival of the travel agent industry rests on the ability of individual agents to provide value-added services in addition to the mechanical issuance of tickets. Activities such as the packaging of travel and accommodations, travel tips, and specific destination information not available at a Web site, may make it worthwhile for some segment of buyers to continue paying higher prices for physical as opposed to electronic service.

Understanding the Monopolist Myth

In the **monopolist myth**, Murray sees the Internet as a vehicle to concentrate economic power and social dominance in the hands of a few large firms. Companies such as Microsoft, Cisco, and AOL are newborns in the time span of business history. However, their pace of growth and their concentration of assets have been so rapid that they are (or were) among the leading firms in business size and power. Economies of scale and network externalities combine to propel an ever-increasing share of the market into fewer and fewer hands. The added costs of expansion are so low, while the gains are so great, that the dynamics of the market push the structure in the direction of control by two or three large firms. In this circumstance, the advantages to the firm of being the first mover are substantial. It gets to establish the best customer links, brand name, best location, and contacts with suppliers. Being first leads to size and network externalities that further reinforce those advantages of being first.

By extension, these same first-mover benefits can spill over to affect both the individuals and nations associated with the first-mover firms. The dynamic of Internet markets could create a winner-take-all outcome, where the benefits of personal empowerment become overwhelmed, and the individual turns out to be marginalized by the sheer scale and power of the e-commerce firm. The economic interests of the consumer are generally protected by competition, but the compelling force of Internet markets may create a level of industry concentration that robs the consumer of competitive protections. On a larger scale, Murray questions, "What does that leave for the latecomers?"[6] The aggregation of

---

5 Shannon Stewart, "The Changing Role of the Travel Agent," available at **http://www.womenof. com/Articles/et021297.asp**: and Kathy Fieweger, "RPT-Travel agencies Hit as American Cuts Commissions," available at **http://www.thestandard.com/wire/0,2231,26416,00.html**.
6 Murray, "Who Wins?" p. B1.

| The Digital Divide in the United States: Internet User Characteristics | | | **TABLE 19-1** |

Internet User Characteristic	Internet Usage 1997	Internet Usage 2001	Percent Growth, 1997–2001
Income			
Less than $25,000	10%	25%	150%
Greater than $75,000	45%	75%	67%
Gap: High vs. Low	35%	50%	
Race/Ethnicity			
Whites	25%	59.9%	140%
African Americans	13%	39.8%	206%
Gap: W vs. AA	12%	20.1%	
Hispanics	11%	31.6%	187%
Gap: W vs. H	14%	28.3%	
Residential Location			
Urban	35%	57.4%	64%
Rural	29%	52.9%	82%
Gap: U vs R	6%	4.5%	

Source: "White House Spurns Efforts to Close 'Digital Divide'," *The Wall Street Journal*, February 27, 2002, p. A22.

scale and power may lead to the creation of a **digital divide** between the holders of information and those who are data deprived. The potential then is for the divide to reflect the current gap between rich and poor individuals and between rich and poor nations, as well as between the wired and unwired worlds. In addition to the digital divide, the possession of knowledge and information, without the power to act on it, can lead to disappointment and frustration. How will the Web users in China and Iran react as the central authority continues to impose restrictions on their physical world?

Just how real is the extent of the digital divide in the United States? Table 19-1 contains data on this issue from the U.S. Commerce Department for two time periods, 1997 and 2001. The interpretations of the data are ambiguous and contradictory, with some interpretations of the indicators showing that the divide is narrowing, while others imply that it is increasing.[7] In 1997 the gap in Internet usage between wealthy and low-income individuals amounted to 35 percent. That gap widened to 50 percent by 2001. A look at the *growth* in the rates of Internet usage for the two groups over the five year span, however, shows that usage by low-income individuals grew at a rate more than twice as fast as the higher income group.

Data on usage for individuals by race and ethnicity showed a similar dichotomous result. The Internet usage gap between Whites and African Americans grew from 12 percent to 20.1 percent. The growth in Internet usage by African Americans, however, was almost one and one-half times that of Whites. For Hispanics the gap doubled from 14 percent to 28.3 percent, and the growth in the rate of Hispanic Internet use was one-third greater than that of Whites. The gap numbers show the current condition while the growth numbers indicate the future trends and potential for the gaps. Statistically, the gains in the growth rates reflect in part the lower starting points for the disadvantaged groups. Continued expansion at those rates will surely narrow the Internet usage

7 Yochi Dreazen, "White House Spurns Efforts to Close 'Digital Divide'," *The Wall Street Journal*, February 27, 2002, p. A22.

gaps over the next three to seven years. The power of a faster rate of usage growth is shown in the final comparison of the divide based on residential location. Here, the Internet usage gap narrowed from 6 percent to 4.5 percent between urban and rural users. In rural areas, the usage base was relatively large to begin with, therefore the higher rate of growth in rural usage allowed the residents of these areas to narrow the usage gap with their urban cousins by 28 percent.

The U.S. government attempted to bridge at least a part of the digital divide by way of the universal service charge levied on telephone services that are provided interstate or internationally. Money from the Universal Service Fund (USF) money is used to support the development of telephone and Internet service along with the installation of computers in low-income, rural, or otherwise underserved areas. The fund, administered under guidelines established by the Federal Communications Commission, was allocated approximately $4.7 billion in 2001 and $5.5 billion in 2002. The money paid for the installation of computers and Internet services in schools, libraries, senior citizen centers, for rural health care providers, and other places allowing communal usage, providing or enhancing Internet access in locations where it might not otherwise have been made available.[8]

Which of Murray's models, if either, will prevail is not currently obvious. Perhaps the description of the force and evolution of the Internet in terms of collective myths exaggerates the potential social impacts resulting from the network. After all, other seminal changes in communications technology, such as the telephone and telegraph, were thought to shrink distance and hold the potential to change the social structure. Instead, even though they altered the efficiency and methods of business operation, and perhaps our social behavior, they proved to be too limited in their ability to alter the balance of economic power. This chapter presents a few examples of where the Internet has been a force for change, and then lets other social scientists and humanists interpret the meaning of the size, frequency, and importance of the consequences.

THE POWER TO CHANGE THE PATH OF ECONOMIC DEVELOPMENT

Nicholas Negroponte is the cofounder of the M.I.T. Media Laboratory, and is regarded as a foremost visionary regarding the future of the digital world.[9] In his opinion, the Internet affords developing nations the electronic equivalent of physical leverage. In physics, the principle of the lever allows the user to multiply the usable force resulting from the application of a lesser amount of pressure. By the same token, the Internet will allow persons in the developing world to leapfrog the traditional pace of development, using Internet leverage to speed progress.[10] This leverage appears because the model of usage and access in the developing world is and will be different from that of the developed world.[11] Each computer hooked up to the Internet in a developing country has many different users accessing the Web. Therefore, the more limited telecom infrastructure in the developing world exerts a greater potential impact through multiple users and usages. For example, one wired computer in a school classroom displayed global events and allowed dozens of students to access the outside world. Also in the developing world, the potential is relatively greater for infrastructure innovation, including wireless telecom connections and satellite links to the developed world. Already China boasts more mobile phone users than the United States.[12] These links will speed the pace of

8 Link to **http://www.shore.net/support/usf.html** for a brief summary of the USF, along with answers to some frequently asked questions about the charges.

9 Nicholas Negroponte, *Being Digital* (New York, Alfred. A. Knopf, 1995).

10 Nicholas Negroponte, "The Next Billion Users," available at **http://archives.obs-us.com/obs/english/books/nn/bd40696.htm**.

11 See the transcript of a speech by Professor Negroponte at **http://www.ciionline.org/speeches/Speech3.html**.

12 "China," *BusinessWeek*, October 29, 2001, p. 50.

technology diffusion, making the Web accessible to more users, even in areas with unreliable wire-based telephone connections.

Internet-Led Economic Development in Guyana, Cambodia, and the Philippines

Numerous anecdotal stories support **Negroponte's developmental leverage hypothesis**. These stories include using the Internet in developing nations to connect to markets, train labor, educate children, teach governance skills, and generally to expand horizons while raising living standards. For example, some links are indirect between rural villages and the Internet. Internet firms such as eZiba.com and oneNest.com display the products from global artisans to be sold to both wholesale and retail buyers. Villagers in Nepal work traditional copper products, including pots and vases, to be sold on the sites at wage rates that are twice the rate of compensation found in local blue-collar jobs.[13] The local result is to create jobs in rural villages and boost living standards.

In rural Guyana, female tribal weavers banded together to create and sell native handwoven hammocks.[14] At first, they tried to sell the hammocks to museums and individual customers though mailed advertisements, with minimal success. Then a satellite phone service brought to their village allowed them to set up a Web site to sell their product to the world. Rather quickly, the weavers sold some 20 hammocks at prices ranging up to $1,000 each.

Not all positive economic benefits of the Web are accepted enthusiastically, even in developing countries. The influx of money disturbed the local power hierarchy, turning previously powerless and impoverished female weavers into some of the most potentially powerful people in the village. Those who would be adversely affected by the role reversal rose up to take control of the weaving organization and to protect the "culture" of the local village. As a result, the Web site has gone dark.

In Cambodia, the Net expanded the horizons of the inhabitants of the rural village of Robib. The village connected to the Internet through the combined efforts of a satellite dish link, solar power, and the helpful assistance of a number of benefactors.[15] The Web contact provides educational instruction to some 400 village children, a commercial outlet for the village products made using local silk weaving skills, and access to telemedicine assistance from Massachusetts General Hospital in Boston. Others on the Internet can link to the village at their Web site **http://www.villageleap.com**. Once there, visitors can see photos of the village, appreciate part of its culture, buy village products, contact villagers through e-mail, and begin to understand how such a Web link can potentially change the lives of rural Southeast Asian villagers. For surfers from the developed world to travel electronically to the village of Robib is a learning experience. For residents of Robib to be participants, even remotely, in part of the rest of the world is nothing short of an electronic miracle. As Negroponte notes, the "The past 150 years of development have been one of urbanization. To be rural has meant to be poor. The Net could bring some of the same opportunities to the rural world and maybe even turn being rural into being rich."[16]

The Internet allows for further **globalization of the work effort**. On the one hand, firms in the developed world can use the Internet to outsource labor-intensive activity to other parts of the world, thereby lowering their labor costs. On the other hand, the electronic workers in the remote developing nations experience job opportunities and increases in their living standards that the local economy could never offer. For example, the Internet service provider AOL handles upwards of 90 percent of its 600,000

---

13 Miriam Jordan, "Web Sites Revive Fading Handicrafts," *The Wall Street Journal*, June 12, 2000, p. B1.

14 Simon Romero, "Weavers Go Dot-Com, and Elders Move In," *The New York Times*, March 28, 2000, p. A1.

15 John Markoff, "It Takes a World Wide Web to Raise a Village," *The New York Times*, August 7, 2000, p. C1.

16 Markoff, "It Takes a World," p. C1.

monthly subscriber online billing and technical support questions form a service center located in the Philippines capital of Manila.[17] **Internet telephony** combined with a fiber optic undersea cable connects the Philippine call center with AOL customers anywhere in the world. These jobs are good for Manila workers, paying three times the local minimum wage, including health care, daily meals, along with free phone and Internet access for after hours use. Elsewhere, former fishermen in remote Icelandic villages use Internet telephony to set up calling centers to conduct telephone interviews.[18] The Internet connections are considerably cheaper than using the regular telephone lines for placing interview calls. The Internet links let people work where they live, rejuvenating rural villages and stemming the costly migration to urban centers in search of work. The Web lets computer programmers in India work on the same project with colleagues in England and the United States. The digital Internet allows insurance companies to outsource claims processing to workers in Ireland and the Caribbean. Each of these individual Internet cases helps to raise local living standards and reduce the level of poverty in rural or Third World nations.

THE POWER TO CHANGE CULTURE

Few surfers living in the United States recognize and appreciate the significance of the fact that English is the underlying language of the Internet. The United States was the birthplace for the technology of the Internet and remains its decentralized home. The technology of the Internet is described using English words and ideas. The vast majority of global Web sites, if not written in English, offer an English language option.[19] This English language dominance of the Internet serves as an important first mover advantage for U.S. firms as well as being an important usage benefit for U.S. residents. English-speaking surfers have functional access to many domestic and global Web sites that wisely cater to the large number of English-speaking users. Non-English speakers must adopt English as a second language to gain full access to the Web community, as well as its treasure trove of information and contact. U.S. firms almost exclusively face e-commerce competition from other U.S. firms, unless the international competitors design their site with an English text component.[20] Although some U.S. firms such as the clothing retailer Land's End maintain foreign language Web sites, the vast majority of U.S. firms require that their customers master English in order to do business with them.

The dominance of U.S. Web design, sights, and sounds, along with English as the de facto Web language prompts a charge of **electronic colonialism**. Here the digital invasion of U.S. ideas and culture substitute for physical intervention. Different nations react in varying ways to this perceived **cultural infiltration**. For example, in

---

17 Tom Friedman, "Under the Volcano," *The New York Times*, September 29, 2000, p. A27.

18 Almar LaTour and Edward Harris, "Who Needs Fish? Villagers in Iceland Cast Bets on the Net," *The Wall Street Journal*, August 1, 2000, p. A18.

19 To appreciate this point, visit the URL for three of the world's great art museums: the Louvre at **http://www.louvre.fr**, Madrid's Museo Del Prado at **http://muesoprado.mcu.es**, and the American Museum of Modern Art at **http://www.moma.org**. Notice that the first two provide information and tours in their national language of French or Spanish, along with an English option. The United States museum provides only an English option. Lest you think that it is just a indication of the relative numbers of persons who speak each language as their native tongue, reflect upon the fact that 330 million people in the world speak Spanish, a number comparable to the 377 million who speak English.

20 One of the more interesting multilingual Web sites is maintained by Fiat, the Italian-based, global auto firm. Its homepage at **http://www.fiat.com**, starts out in English, but has information in more than a dozen languages including Chinese, Japanese, Spanish, and even Hungarian. To its credit, General Motors too has a multilingual Web homepage at **http://www.gm.com/flash_homepage**. However, the access page is in English and must be understood by international users to get to the foreign language material.

Japan, the electronics giant Matsushita, which produces the Panasonic brand of products, requires that all managers seeking promotion must be able to pass an English language competency test.[21] Firm leaders feel that Japan is not global in its thinking because of the language barrier, despite the fact that most Japanese school children have had up to six years of training in English by the end of secondary school. For Matsushita to be competitive in global markets, older managers must increase their international awareness by being able to deal directly with international suppliers and customers. Being competitive globally requires the ability to think with a global mind-set, and the first step is being conversant in English, the global language of the Internet and business in general.

The Cultural Impact of the Internet in Europe

This degree of active capitulation is not so prominent in other parts of the world. The technical language of the Internet has seeped into the traditional Spanish language. The **linguistic intrusion** has created a form of Spanglish, with hybrid words that combine Spanish and English together.[22] For example, Spanish Internet users *imailiar*, or send an e-mail, rather than use the Castilian equivalent of *enviar un correo electronico*. They *resetear*, or restart the computer, rather than *volver a prender*. Lastly, they *brainstormear* to dream up ideas, rather than *intercambiar ideas en forms intense*. Defenders of the Spanish language and culture have come together in groups to protect Castilian Spanish from the Internet form of linguistic pollution. They look to encourage and promote the usage of the correct Spanish version of computer-related terms.

Defenders of a uniquely European society note that the U.S. media giants tend to dominate Web content, from music and videos to imagery and entertainment.[23] Off-line, Europe has been and remains a diversity of cultures starting with language and continuing on through art, architecture, cuisine, politics, religion, attitudes toward work, business, and government, as well as contemporary mores. Online, however, the pressure of the melting pot drives Web users toward cultural homogeneity led by American style, tastes, and values. What the Europeans would like to do is to identify and define the characteristics of a European online culture to distinguish the European Web from its American counterpart.

To achieve this end, different European online tastes are being defined through creative exchanges among Web content designers in the major European stylistic centers of London, Paris, Berlin, Barcelona, and Amsterdam. Some think that one common denominator delineating the different European online cultures is music. Distinctly European Web sites might be created on the basis of the musical score that accompanies the information content or advertising pitch. Others note that humor is culturally based and a distinguishing characteristic. Jokes, visual effects, and tales of adventure and romance have links in context to current or past national events and family traditions that render them most meaningful within a unique cultural setting. The online world is acting to tear down many of the old European cultural barriers based on prejudices and stereotypes. Europe online is changing the region just as the introduction of the euro reduced the barriers to inter-European trade created by the inefficiencies of multiple currencies. By retaining and playing to what is unique among the differing European cultures, the European Web looks to create a form of content and style of presentation that offers an attractive, constructive, and competitive alternative to the structure and style of the American Web.

---

21 Kevin Voigt, "Japanese Firms Want English Competency," *The Wall Street Journal*, June 11, 2001, p. B7A.

22 Sam Dillon, "On the Language of Cervantes, the Imprint of the Internet," *The New York Times*, August 6, 2000, p. 4–3.

23 Ben Vickers, "In Internet Age, Europe Looks to Define Its Many Cultures Against U.S. Online," *The Wall Street Journal*, April 2, 2001, p. B9F.

The Cultural Impact of the Internet in Asia

Refocusing on Japan, a combination of cultural and national characteristics creates a uniquely Japanese Internet usage structure.[24] Japanese homes are limited in square footage, and residents find it difficult to devote space to the traditional U.S. Internet lineup of desktop computer, workstation, printer, and peripherals. Also, the small space means that in the Japanese society, citizens spend more time engaging in activities away from the home than Americans typically do. Lastly, the fixed cost of wired telephone service and the variable usage fees are often greater than the comparable cost for service in the United States. Consequently, access to the Internet through broadband cable or DSL connections is a more expensive choice, making the wired world a less attractive option.

Japanese Internet users are increasingly choosing to secure their Internet connections using a wireless telephone connection. Young Japanese Internet users have in particular worked to create their own Web environment through their use of NTT DoCoMo's i-mode wireless Internet service. The service was introduced in February 1999, and grew to 30 million subscribers by February 2002. That number covered 24 percent of the nation's population. For more than two-thirds of the Japanese subscribers, the cell phone i-mode connection was their only access to the Internet. A comparable figure for the United States would require nearly 70 million mobile phone Internet subscribers. In fact, as of early 2002, the United States accounted for fewer than 1 million mobile Internet users, just 1 percent of the world's wireless Internet customers.[25]

Killer apps for i-mode users include access to electronic finance, information retrieval, electronic game playing, and the transmittal of short e-mail messages. All of these applications are accessed in Japan at usage prices close to the rates being charged by wired phone services. The aggressive acceptance of the i-mode connection blurs the distinction somewhat between the cell phone and the computer as a means of communication. Moreover, the Japanese lead in customer acceptance of cell phone-based Internet technology gives that nation the potential of global leadership in the push to provide a broader range of third generation (3G) mobile Internet services.[26]

In China, the concern over the potential for cultural change brought by the Internet extends to who has the right to accept applications for and issue domain names in Chinese.[27] Currently a single protocol exists for registering domain names based on the use of English. VeriSign is the dominant firm in the Internet address registration business. When it wanted to begin to accept domain names in Chinese, Korean, and Japanese characters as a way of making the Internet more multicultural, the Chinese government in Beijing declared that the right to issue Chinese character domain names was theirs alone. They asserted this right as a means of protecting the nation's interests, its national culture, and to secure access to the fees from the registration process. The Chinese viewed VeriSign actions as an attempt to recolonize China through control over that nation in cyberspace.

The Chinese government proposed the introduction of a rival domain assignment system incompatible with the one currently in use. As a result, internal Chinese users would be unable to access sites whose names were not approved by the government. The government approval process would prohibit names that were inappropriate or offensive, while reserving certain names for assignment to the most appropriate user. This approval process could also be used to limit dissent and to control the flow of information within China. However, some of the government's fears regarding the infringement of Chinese sovereignty may be justified. When VeriSign opened up the registration process in November 2000, **cybersquatters** purchased a considerable volume of common government, personal, and business names they had no intention of using themselves, but hoped

---

24 John Markoff, "New Economy: The Internet in Japan is Riding a Wireless Wave," *The New York Times*, August 14, 2000, p. C4.

25 "Eurotechnology Japan," available at **http://www.eurotechnology.com/imode/faq-wap.html.**

26 Markoff, "The Internet in Japan," p. C4.

27 Gren Mannuel and Leslie Chang, "Will Language Wars Balkanize the Web?" *The Wall Street Journal*, November 30, 2000, p. A17.

to be able to sell later at huge profits. Regardless of the merits of the Chinese position, the outgrowth of the trade and cultural war over domain name assignment has the potential to "splinter the Internet into mutually inaccessible realms that destroy the universality that is the heart of its appeal."[28]

Cultural Preservation and the Digital Divide

Viewed from afar and outside the perspective of the United States, the Internet holds the potential to introduce a considerable amount of **cultural turbulence**. Similar to the introduction of television 50 years ago, the appearance of the Internet today threatens to turn a global mix of distinct and diverse cultures into a single bowl of homogenized soup.

Is the existence of a digital divide across national boundaries necessarily a bad thing? Tom Friedman, author of the best-selling book *The Lexus and the Olive Tree*, and a feature columnist for *The New York Times*, frequently writes about trends in the Internet and globalization. He raises the issue of cultural consequences from the digital divide when he poses the question, "Isn't it better for indigenous people like the Eskimos in Alaska not to be connected, in order to preserve their own unique traditions and not have them washed away by a flood of pop culture and smut that comes through the Internet?"[29]

Friedman's answer is that the loss of cultural identity all depends on how the Internet is managed. Firms such as Viatru, the successor to World2market.com, the marketer of Third World handicraft products, see the Internet as a vehicle for two-way exchange. It has the power to bring the good and the bad of the twenty-first century to remote settlements. The Internet also has the ability to show the rest of the modern world the social structure, customs, religion, art, language, and native craft skills that belong to the diversity of native cultures. We can see and learn from them as much as they can see and learn from us. The Internet has the reach to display native cultures, making them interesting and attractive to us, as well as working to preserve them, by providing a global market for their products and practices.

THE POWER TO CHANGE SOCIAL BEHAVIOR

Historically, while the introduction of the entertainment portion of television may have blurred cultural distinctions, it also helped to bring the people of the world closer together in terms of their knowledge of current events. The major news of the day can be seen live as it happens, or almost so, by way of the satellite transmission of digital images. Events and information aren't just local or regional any more, but have the ability to become worldwide in scope. A global audience can see in real time the horrors of war and famine, religious conflict, and terrorist attacks no matter where they occur. News, opinions, and emotions are sent from their sources simultaneously into the homes of viewers in North America, Asia, and Europe. For better or worse, television as a news medium has enhanced human connectivity.

However, beyond television, the Internet is a more complex medium and may create varying results for different users. The technology may create a social tension between enhanced connectivity for some versus greater personal social isolation for others. Initially, one might assume that a similar kind of **enhanced connectivity** would result from the spread of the Internet. In fact, the Internet might be an even greater source of connectivity than television, given that it is an interactive medium that allows a two-way tension of conversation and ideas. The Internet is multidimensional in that it combines attractive communications features from writing, radio, television, printed news sources, and telephone contact. The connectedness of the Internet allows more options for human contact compared to television, where the information flow is one-way and the viewer is a passive recipient. The Internet allows for people who hold a common

---

28 Mannuel and Chang, "Will Language Wars?" p. A17.
29 Thomas L. Friedman, "Digital Divide or Dividend?" *The New York Times*, March 16, 2001, p. A19.

interest to assemble quickly and efficiently, regardless of their physical location. Together, they create a virtual community to share their views.

Contrary to the connectivity model, some social research raises the possibility that the Internet may be an **isolating technology** for some users. Political science professor Norman Nie of Stamford University conducted a study in 1999 showing that for some 13 percent of the respondents, the hours spent on the Internet take away from the time spent interacting with real human beings, including friends, family members, and coworkers.[30] Another 8 percent of those surveyed reported attending fewer social events. He also found that work brought home to be completed during evening hours over the Internet cut into the time available for other activities. Frequently, time was allocated to the Internet at the expense of accessing and viewing other media offerings including interaction with television, books, magazines, and newspapers.[31] Still, some young Internet surfers use television and the computer simultaneously in a form of **electronic multitasking**. In Nie's opinion, "Today's patterns of Internet usage foretell a loss of interpersonal contact that will result in the kind of isolation seen among many elderly Americans."[32] Critics of the Nie study quickly pointed out that his analysis of the survey results fails to draw attention to or conclusions regarding 85 percent of the 2,600 respondents who reported no change in time spent with others as a result of Internet usage.[33] A later Pew Project study reported "more than 60 percent of (their) respondents said the Internet had a positive impact on their connection to friends and family."[34]

Even if Internet users do spend less time interacting with real persons, is there any harm in that? In 1998, Professor Robert Kraut and colleagues of Carnegie Mellon University published the results of a study of 169 subjects showing that heavy Internet users were more likely to express feelings of **social isolation**, loneliness, and depression than less intense users.[35] Moreover, for those who were on the computer alone and anonymously "the size of their social networks declined over time."[36] However, given the results of a later three-year follow-up study, Dr. Kraut tended to modify these conclusions. His later study led him to conclude that the negative social effects experienced by Internet users declined over time and may be transitory. Symptoms of depression dropped and the subjects no longer reported feelings of loneliness in conjunction with Internet usage. Using the standard terminology of social psychology, he concluded, "When Introverts are using the Internet, it seems to hurt their social well-being, their social connectedness."[37]

The Internet as a Polarizing Force

In addition to the personal social consequences of the Internet, further speculation surrounds the potential adverse impacts of the Internet on democratic behavior and the well-being of the broader society as well. Some see a tension between the Internet as a source of shared culture and values versus as a source of group polarization. Nicholas Negroponte identified the potential for what he calls "The Daily Me," which is the ability for Internet users to apply filtering software that will develop an individualized flow of news and information, reflecting the individual's personal tastes, interests, and biases.[38] Law professor Cass R. Sunstein interprets this personalization as a potential

---

30 John Markoff, "A Newer, Lonelier Crowd Emerges in Internet Study," *The New York Times*, February 16, 2000, p. A1.

31 Dennis K. Berman, "Survey Suggests Access to Internet Reduces Time Spent Watching TV," *The Wall Street Journal*, November 29, 2001, p. B11.

32 Markoff, "A Newer, Lonelier Crowd," p. A1.

33 Lisa Guernsey, "Cyberspace Isn't So Lonely After All," *The New York Times*, July 26, 2001, p. G1.

34 Guernsey, "Cyberspace," p. G1.

35 Robert Kraut, "Internet Paradox: A Social Technology That Reduces Social Involvement and Psychological Well-Being," available at **http://www.apa.org/journals/amp/amp5391017.html**.

36 Guernsey, "Cyberspace," p. G1.

37 Guernsey, "Cyberspace," p. G1.

38 Cass R. Sunstein "The Daily We: Is the Internet Really a Blessing for Democracy?" available at **http://bostonreview.mit.edu/BR26.3/sunstein.html**.

threat to the functioning of our democracy, because it contains a **polarizing tendency**.[39] First, the filtering limits the individual to seeing only like-minded viewpoints.[40] By filtering out unwanted information and opinions before the fact, the reader sees only what agrees with his perspective and reinforces his original biases. Second, the Internet offers extremists and fringe groups the ability to form their own communities and use the technology as a weapon to spread hate, including racial, antireligious, and antigovernmental material. Granted, free speech is protected by the Constitution, but reinforcement of prejudices and stereotypes, even within a virtual community, makes them appear more socially acceptable and may encourage some to act on those hatreds.

Lastly, the screening of information based on predetermined filters limits learning by chance; the opportunity to see something new and different based on a random encounter. To Sunstein, social value and strength for democracy can be found in maintaining a common experience, including exposure to various opinions and information on the Internet. His position reflects the lawyer's concept of the **public forum doctrine**, where individuals "have access to an audience and (where) listeners ought to be exposed to a diversity of views."[41] Originally, the Internet was intended as a vehicle to enhance democracy, where everyone was able to speak. Information filtering, however, leads to a situation of **political fragmentation**, where few of the speakers are being heard. This filtering distorts the ideal embodied within the U.S. motto *E Pluribus Unum*, "From many, one."

THE POWER TO CHALLENGE ACROSS NATIONAL BORDERS

The Internet was created as a borderless technology, allowing communications anywhere in the globe at anytime. On the Web, information, ideas, links, data, pictures, sound, commentary, and entertainment flow from source to receiver without interruption. They flow without the imposition of **Internet censorship standards** that block the passage of what is deemed to be evil and offensive. The absence of explicit, flow-controlling standards has itself become a standard, however, creating an Internet that some see as a free-wheeling and lawless frontier. A few standards are implicit and based on U.S. laws, customs, and moral traditions, mostly because the United States was the original home of the Internet, as well as the location for many of the Web sites and the technology that supports them. Also, a narrow set of international behavioral standards has evolved, keeping the Internet from existing in legal limbo. For example, a nearly unanimous global voice condemns use of the Internet to transmit child pornography.[42] Also, the Council of Europe developed a document that defines child pornography, along with electronic vandalism and online fraud, as cybercrimes. Moreover, it sets up rules as to how nations should police the Internet.[43] When an act occurs in cyberspace that violates the laws of some nations but not others, whose laws should prevail? Apart from cybercrimes on which global agreement has been reached, which nation(s), if any, has legal jurisdiction in cyberspace?

Content Conflict in Cyberspace: France and Yahoo!

The question of law enforcement in cyberspace lies at the heart of the legal problems faced by Yahoo! in its confrontation with the French judicial system. Yahoo! is a U.S.-based firm, whose auctions are accessible from any Internet-linked computer worldwide. Until late in the year 2000, the Yahoo! auction site allowed the listing of Nazi

---

39 Cass R. Sunstein, *Republic.com* (Princeton: Princeton University Press, 2001).

40 Stephen Labaton, "Click Here for Democracy," *NYT Book Review*, May 13, 2001, p. 20.

41 Labaton, "Click Here," p. 20.

42 Warren Hode, "19 Countries Join in Raids on Internet Pornography," *The New York Times*, November 29, 2001, p. A11.

43 Paul Meller, "Europe Moving Toward Ban on Internet Hate Speech," *The New York Times*, November 10, 2001, p. C3.

memorabilia and other hate-related material. Many persons might find this material to be offensive. However, holders of these items have a free speech right to exchange them, which is protected under Section 1 of the U.S. Constitution. Despite the U.S. bias toward free speech, in France and other parts of Europe hate-speech laws forbid the sale or distribution of these items. Such national laws limiting this form of speech can be fully explained and justified on the basis of the death and devastation that these nations and their citizens suffered at the hands of the Nazis in World War II. Besides, it is their country, and the citizens can decide to pass and abide by just about any law as long as it doesn't infringe on the sovereignty of another nation.

A cross-border conflict has arisen over these items because the Yahoo! Web pages can be accessed from within France. In response, the French courts declared their national right to electronic sovereignty within their own borders. They ordered Yahoo! to apply technology that would block Internet access to the offending items from computers within France, and fined the firm when it failed to comply.[44] On the one hand, Yahoo!'s refusal to activate the blocking technology involves effectiveness and coverage issues. On the other hand, other sites, including eBay, have introduced technology fixes that at least make it more difficult for foreigners to gain access to material banned within their country. On a broader level, the Yahoo! conflict is over the more important issue of whose laws will prevail in cyberspace. A U.S. federal court ruled that the Constitutional right of free speech took precedence over French law and therefore Yahoo!, located in the United States, was not bound by the French court's decision.

Yahoo! has little in the way of assets in France that can be seized in lieu of the firm's refusal to pay the fines levied. Also, the offending material was removed from the Yahoo! site. However, the tension between free speech versus national sovereignty as the default enforcement standard for Internet content isn't likely to go away soon. For example, a French hate group could avoid French legal prohibitions by setting up a Web site in the United States. They would then be able to beam their illegal message back to a French audience, while hiding behind the protection of the First Amendment.[45] In a related case, Google voluntarily, but under foreign government pressure, blocked some 100 Nazi and hate Web sites from being shown in response to search requests by French and German citizens.[46] Such **silent blocking** leaves Google customers without any indication that their requests are being only partially filled. Also, no consistent standard guides how Google or any other censor might go about determining which sites to place on the blocked list and for whom.

France is not the only nation wanting to exercise its digital authority within its borders. Others have taken it on themselves to apply technology fixes that will limit the ability of its citizens to access objectionable external Web sites. In Saudi Arabia, Internet users are banned from linking to sites that contain pornographic material, information that is critical of the royal family or Islam, gay sites, and chat rooms. In a move designed to financially favor the state-run telephone monopoly, the Saudi government also banned access to Internet telephone services.[47] In China, "the prohibition includes the sites of Western publications, human rights organizations and Falun Gong, the banned spiritual movement."[48] The Chinese Internet police have gone so far as to block internal Internet access to Google, redirecting attempts to link to the search engine toward sites more consistent with governmental policy.[49] Media rights advocates estimate that some 20 nations place substantial limitations on Internet access.

44 Mylene Mangalindan and Kevin DeLaney, "Yahoo! Ordered to Bar the French from Nazi Items," *The Wall Street Journal*, November 21, 2000, p. B1.

45 Meller, "Europe Moving," p. C3.

46 John Schwartz, "Study Tallies Sites Blocked by Google," *The New York Times*, October 25, 2002, p. C8. The study conducted by Jonathan Zittran and Ben Edelman entitled "Documentation of Internet Filtering Worldwide," and can be seen in full at **http://cyber.law.harvard.edu/filtering/**.

47 Jennifer 8. Lee, "Punching Holes in Internet Walls," *The New York Times*, April 26, 2001, p. G1.

48 Lee, "Punching Holes," p. G1.

49 Joseph Kahn, "China Toughens Obstacles to Internet Searches," *The New York Times*, September 12, 2002, p. A3.

Not every government in every country feels that in accepting the Internet, it must be bound by the U.S. free speech standard. Governments may wish to control contact as well as the flow of information and images for a variety of religious, political, economic, or authoritarian reasons. Conversely, if individual, enforceable national standards prevail as soon as an electronic signal crosses the border, then the Internet risks becoming balkanized. It will see its Web pages reduced to the acceptability level of the narrowest set of behavioral constraints. Internet content could become the intellectual equivalent of electronic pablum as sites are required by law to avoid any material that would offend even the most outrageous sensibilities of any nation anywhere. This possibility poses a serious challenge to the Internet. A conflict of this sort between free speech and national sovereignty is not easy to resolve within a decentralized organizational structure.

SUMMARY AND PROSPECTS

From a review of the material in this chapter, two points become apparent. First, the topic of social change is not one usually found in an economics text. However, it is important for economists, students, and Web users to recognize that the Internet is not just a vehicle for e-commerce efficiency. The Internet also brings with it the potential to introduce change in economic status quo, social structure, the source and balance of political power, and human relationships, as well as personal behavior.

Some of the anecdotal evidence tilts the question of who benefits from the Internet in favor of the populist myth, as people in even some of the most remote parts of the world appear to gain from access to the Internet. Perhaps, in an absolute sense, the largest corporate users in the developed world gain the most. In a relative sense, however, even small absolute gains in economic well-being can double the rate of advance in the developing world. Also, even though the digital divide is real, it appears to be diminishing as the poor of both industrialized and developing countries gain more knowledge of and contact with Internet technology.

Second, once the discussion leaves the relatively factual world of economics, the number of unresolved issues and tensions grows significantly. Areas within the social sciences and humanities have a more fluid analytical structure than the discipline of economics because human behavior and values interact in complex ways. What first appears to be the consequence of a new communications medium, such as the Internet, may not demonstrate those expected lasting effects in the long run. The Internet and e-commerce, with their values and American bias, challenge existing cultures. With the challenge also comes the opportunity to recognize and appreciate what is different and valuable about each society. Efforts to protect these cultural differences may lead to a review of what is worth defending and what can be made better by blending and adaptation.

The Internet's impact on personal behavior may be the result of individual predisposition. The group challenge to society is more troublesome. Just about anyone or any group can build and support a sophisticated Web site. Just because a site must be allowed, however, doesn't mean that its message must be endured, especially when the information on that site may be false, bigoted, or otherwise harmful to broader social values. Turning the spotlight on and speaking out against harmful sites can ensure that their destructive message is not spread unnoticed and without larger condemnation.

Lastly, the tension of free speech versus national sovereignty may be the most vexing of the Internet social issues. Openness, along with the absence of censorship and control, have been among the defining characteristics of the Internet to date. But just as these characteristics caused problems for Internet safety and security, they pose challenges to societies that hold legitimately different values. There is no easy resolution to this tension. Perhaps the best hope is to realize that Internet and Web are still young and evolving. Tomorrow's Web may not look or function in the same way as today's technology. Therefore, as the technology and the computer code evolve, they may be more flexible in allowing individual entities to choose the parts of the Internet that they wish to join.

In the larger context, the Internet as a force for social change may prove to be equally or even more important than the gains from heightened efficiency, especially outside of the United States.

KEY TERMS AND CONCEPTS

cultural infiltration

cultural turbulence

cybersquatters

digital divide

disintermediation

electronic colonialism

electronic multitasking

enhanced connectivity

globalization of the work effort

internet censorship standards

internet telephony

isolating technology

linguistic intrusion

monopolist myth

Negroponte's developmental leverage
hypothesis

polarizing tendency

political fragmentation

populist myth

public forum doctrine

silent blocking

social isolation

virtual community

DISCUSSION AND REVIEW QUESTIONS

1. Identify and distinguish between the openness of the virtual world and the restrictions within the physical world that are part of both the Chinese and Iranian societies. If these societies are so constrained in certain ways, why do they allow citizens to have access to the Internet?

2. Identify and discuss the tension that open Internet access creates in both China and Iran. What will it take for the ideas and openness of the Internet to migrate into and work to change the restrictions found in the physical world?

3. Identify and discuss the populist myth as it relates to the gains resulting from the Internet. How does disintermediation lend support to this interpretation?

4. Identify and discuss the monopolist myth as it relates to the gains resulting from the Internet. How does this interpretation see the Internet affecting individuals and nations?

5. Examine the data in Table 19-1, which shows the extent and trend of the digital divide in the United States. What has happened to the usage gap between rich and poor U.S. citizens, and among Whites, African Americans, and Hispanics? Conversely, where has the growth in usage been the greatest within these comparison groups? Does the size of the digital divide appear to be growing or shrinking?

6. How can the Internet serve as a tool of economic development in the Third World? How is this view supported by Negroponte's developmental leverage hypothesis? Cite a Third World example where this leverage may have appeared.

7. Why has English come to dominate the distribution of information on the Web? How has adoption of English as the de facto Web language created problems and unfavorable reactions in non-English-speaking nations? Cite an example.

8. How do people and governments in Asia attempt to impose their own cultural presence and rules for Internet usage? Cite an example.

9. In what ways is the Internet a more complex electronic medium? How can it lead to a tension by serving as a vehicle to enhance connectivity for some users while generating social isolation for others?

10. Identify and discuss the nature of the tension that exists between the Internet as a source of shared culture and values versus its ability to create group polarization. Is the Internet a vehicle to enhance democracy or a means to create political fragmentation? Explain.

11. Is the Internet an unrestrained, freewheeling, and lawless frontier? Why?

12. Whose laws should apply in cyberspace? Why? Cite an example of the problems that arise when the laws of one nation are to be applied in cyberspace.

13. How does the Internet potentially set up a tension between the principles of free speech and the imposition of national sovereignty?

WEB EXERCISES

1. Link to the feminist Iranian Web site at **http://www.badjens.com/** to see the kinds of issues that affect and interest Iranian women.

2. To access some early data and research on the extent of the digital divide in the United States, link to the Falling Through the Net research series located on the National Telecommunications and Information Administration Web site at **http://www.ntia.doc.gov/ntiahome/digitaldivide/**.

3. To see the current status of and topics dealing with the digital divide globally, link to the research and news page of the Digital Divide Network at **http://www.digitaldividenetwork.org/content/sections/index.cfm**. Or, link to the information site for the Public Broadcasting System's 2002 two-part television series detailing the extent of the digital divide in the United States at **http://www.pbs.org/digitaldivide/**.

4. Link to **http://www.shore.net/support/usf.html** for a brief summary of the Universal Service Fund, along with answers to some frequently asked questions about the charges.

5. Link to the global handicraft wholesale marketing site OneNest at **http://www.onenest.com/**, or the retail site of eziba.com at **http://www.eziba.com/StoreFront** to see the range of items available for sale.

6. If woven silk items are of interest to you and you would like to deal with the artisans directly in the village of Robib, Cambodia, link to their Web site at **http://www.villageleap.com/**.

7. To appreciate the importance of English as the language of the Internet, visit the URL for three of the world's great art museums, the Louvre at **http://www.louvre.fr**, Madrid's Museo Del Prado at **http://museoprado.mcu.es**, and the American Museum of Modern Art at **http://www.moma.org**. Notice that the first two provide their information and tours in national language of French or Spanish, along with an English option. But the American museum provides only an English option.

8. Link to the study detailing the extent of global Internet filtering at **http://cyber.law.harvard.edu/filtering/**. Link to one of the listed sites to see the nature of and problems resulting from the act of filtering in different situations.

CHAPTER 20

Introductory Case

A LAND OF PROMISE RINGED BY MOUNTAINS OF CONCERNS

In the 1990s, the advent of public access to the Internet, along with the birth of the World Wide Web, raised vast expectations. These technologies offered the possibility of an advance so powerful it would radically alter the way in which people obtained information, conducted business, and communicated. The public Net held out the promise of changing the operation of markets, improving efficiency, and altering social as well as political relationships. It would challenge the powerful, empower the little guy, excite the imagination, stimulate innovation, and enhance cultural diversity. At one time or another, cyberspace visionaries promised that the Net would cure what ails us, bring the world together, and allow a giant intellectual leap forward. It would accomplish all these things, while letting us have fun using it and making us rich in the process.

That initial irrational exuberance was quickly tempered by the demise of more than 800 Internet start-ups, the loss of trillions of dollars of invested funds, and the spectacular travails of key firms such as Enron, Global Crossing, Lucent Technologies, and Worldcom all linked to the set of unrealistic Internet expectations. The Internet, Web, and e-commerce continue to expand, but their image changed from a land of boundless promise to one ringed by a mountain of concerns. Throughout the technology, one finds numerous problems, obstacles, limitations, and questions. To date, the technology failed to deliver on its perhaps exaggerated economic promise, or live up to its social, cultural, or democratic potential. A number of reasons account for these failures.[1]

1. Companies developed an enormous over-capacity of transmission capability relative to current use. The rapid supply of Internet capacity overwhelmed the growing demand for Internet connections, such that much of the excess capacity remains dark today. This overzealous expansion led to the demise of many firms that built the fiber optic network, as well as the loss of funds by investors.

2. The industry must overcome the problem of broadband interconnection, the last-mile problem of linking the broadband pipes to the end user. Even when the cable or DSL connections are available, potential users frequently decline to sign up for the service. As of 2002, fewer than 10 million U.S. Internet connections were achieved using broadband links. What will be the role for wireless broadband connections? To what extent will they challenge or complement the heavy investment made by both phone and cable companies in hardwired links?

3. New technology raises a great number of intellectual property issues, ranging from the illegal duplication and transmission of copyrighted material, to the patenting of key parts of the system. The former leaves the owners of copyrighted entertainment less willing to offer it for sale in digital form and thereby limiting a potential use of the Internet and its excess capacity. Patents, in turn, create barriers that impede Internet growth by making the technology less accessible and free flowing.

4. If the demands for Internet access and e-commerce services are to grow, then the technology must be made easier to use. Employing the hyper-linked Web still involves wasted effort and false starts. The technology does not anticipate user needs or carry out user instructions. It does not do all that users want, where they want,

---

1 The following of concerns have been adapted from the discussion in Judith H. Dobrzynski, "So, Technology Pros, What Comes After the Fall?" *The New York Times*, July 29, 2001, p. 3–1.

The Future of e-Commerce

and the Internet

when they want, as fast as they want with the expected results.

5. The technology is still looking for a killer application(s) that will compel usage, leading to a quantum leap in demand. E-mail, with 3.5 trillion messages sent in 2001, is a high-volume application, but it bypasses the Web. Napster and its functional cousins created a killer app, but one that was illegal and ran afoul of the intellectual property laws. What new or transplanted endeavor will generate regular and repeat activity, drawing millions of global users to the Internet?

6. The medium has yet to devise a generally applicable business model or set of models that encourage the profitable payment for Web content and services. The virtual world started with the promise of free access and free content, based on advertiser support. It trumped the promise of free services with the pledge of product prices that would be below those of the physical world, based on lower transactions costs. However, the virtual world of free services and low product prices turned out to be the digital equivalent of a Paul Bunyan tall

tale. The economics of the industry will not generally support free content and unrealistically low prices. Therefore, absent the price lure, how will e-commerce firms structure a business model with sufficient value added to sustain a competitive profit rate and allow the firm to survive?

7. How will the Internet deal with the charge of cultural imperialism? It is currently a U.S.-centric system in language, values, technology, and usage. The greatest growth potential lies outside of the United States, however, in places such as China, Brazil, and India. How will the Internet adapt and change in order to make itself as accessible as possible to non-English-speaking users?

8. The Web currently exists as a decentralized, ungoverned technology. The altruistic cooperation of voluntary citizen soldiers may soon reach the limits of its ability to smooth out territorial, content, security, or other forms of national conflicts. The Web has considerable current commercial value along with exceptional future potential. Will it be able to realize this potential in an ungoverned cyberworld?

The task of this chapter is to look at the how some of these obstacles and problems might be dealt with in the near future.

OVERCAPACITY: THE TRENDS TOWARD CONSOLIDATION AND CONCENTRATION

Three trends are bringing resolution to the problem of network overcapacity: (1) increased global usage, (2) consolidation on the demand side, and (3) increased concentration on the supply side. Sample usage data from comScore Networks showed that as of February 2002, the worldwide Internet population was at an all-time high of 308.7 million unique users.[2]

---

2 comScore Networks, "Online Activity Paints a Rich Picture of the Minds, Hearts and Interests of World Citizens in February," available at **http://www.comscore.com/news/feb_online_picture031102.htm**.

| **TABLE 20-1** | | | Market Share Data in Sample e-Commerce Categories | |

e-Commerce Category	Rank	Web Sites	Visitors (mil.)	Percentage of Category Users Attracted
Search and Navigation	1	Google.com	15.2	30.3
	5	Looksmart.com	6.7	13.3
General Health	1	WebMD.com	5.9	22.6
	5	DietSmart.com	1.1	4.0
Weather	1	Weather.com	9.1	64.0
	5	Intellicast.com	1.3	8.9
Maps	1	Mapquest.com	13.1	82.4
	5	Randmcnally.com	0.5	3.3
General News	1	MSNBC.com	11.5	32.1
	5	Washingtonpost.com	3.3	9.3
Flowers/Gifts	1	Americangreetings.com	7.1	41.5
	5	WeddingChannel.com	0.7	4.3

Source: Amy Harmon, "Exploration of World Wide Web Tilts from Eclectic to Mundane," *The New York Times*, August 26, 2001, p. A1. The data were originally supplied by Jupiter Media Metrix.

Non-U.S. Internet users were estimated to be in the majority, with 177.5 million individuals, or 57.5 percent of the total. On the one hand, the minority share for U.S. users is surprising given the head start of the Internet in the U.S. and the prevalence of wired computers at home, work, and in universities. On the other hand, the United States population at 286 million is only 4.5 percent of the global number of 6.5 billion persons. It should not come as any shock to see that the greatest growth in future usage will come from individuals living outside of the United States. What is surprising is that the number of minutes spent per visitor and the number of Web pages viewed per visitor are greater by 10 percent or more for non-U.S. visitors than for those from the United States. Clearly, as the number of Internet users grows worldwide, the intensity of usage may be expected to rise as well. Eventually, these gains should help to eliminate some of the excess capacity.[3]

Demand Consolidation: Evidence and Possible Causes

Evidence also shows **visitor demand consolidation** in that the growing number of users is being attracted to an ever-decreasing number of sites. Viewer demand is focusing in on the top one or two sites in each category, increasing the market share of the leaders as well as the spread between the volumes of visitors at the most popular site in each category versus the fifth most popular site.[4] The data in Table 20-1 from both Jupiter Media Metrix and comScore Networks reinforces this point. The top search or navigation site was Google.com, with 15.2 million visitors, or 30.3 percent of the total number of individuals

---

3 A word of caution here: Recent evidence shows that in the United States, the rate of growth of new visitors and type of usage among existing Web surfers is falling. The length of the average online session declined from 90 minutes in 2000 to 83 minutes in 2001. Also, fewer users see the Web as a place to learn new things. Because it lacks compelling content, the Web is viewed more as a practical place for conducting business quickly, rather than as a vehicle to explore new areas. The Web may have evolved from a toy box into a toolbox. See Lisa Guernsey, "As the Web Matures, Fun Is Hard to Find," *The New York Times*, March 28, 2002, p. G1.

4 Amy Harmon, "Exploration of World Wide Web Tilts From Eclectic to Mundane," *The New York Times*, August 26, 2001, p. A1.

who visited that type of site. The fifth most popular site in the search category was LookSmart.com, with 5.9 million visitors and just 13.3 percent of the market share. For Internet users seeking general news, the most popular site was MSNBC.com with 11.5 million visitors and 32.1 percent of the market. The newspaper site Washingtonpost.com was the fifth most visited site with 3.3 million visitors and 9.3 percent of the market. The widest spread was between sites yielding map information, with Mapquest.com at 82.4 percent of the visitors versus just 3.3 percent for number five, Randmcnally.com. Similar findings were reported by comScore Networks. Within the travel category, the leader was Expedia.com, which attracted 16.1 million visitors, while number five, Priceline.com, attracted some 5.5 million viewers. In the diet category, ediets.com led the number of viewers at 7.8 million, while dietdivas.com was listed at number five with 159,000 visitors.[5]

The reasons why this trend toward demand consolidation is taking place remain open to speculation. However, a number of possibilities are likely.

1. *A flight to quality.* The leading sites may do a good job of arranging and displaying information. They may be the most user friendly, with the best content and the greatest degree of functionality.
2. *Readily recognized brand names.* These sites have differentiated themselves from the pack and used that uniqueness to attract and hold a loyal customer audience.
3. *User trust.* This element may be especially important when users need to reveal personal information or act on the content at the site.
4. *Lack of public interest in competitive diversity on the Web.* Users who engage in content searches as well as experiment with different e-commerce sites experience a cost measured in time spent. Therefore, they may be more willing to accept satisfactory site performance rather than spend the extra effort with the uncertain hope of securing better performance. As such, the site selection activity becomes a benefit-cost calculation process. This user tendency favors the first mover or at least the lone survivors out of what was the originally much larger class of vigorous Internet competitors.

Increased Concentration on the Supply Side

Overcapacity is certainly affected by the trend toward Internet concentration and consolidation on the supply side. The failure of some 800 plus Internet firms reduced the number of current actual competitors in the product delivery portion of the e-commerce marketplace. Also, replacement competitors are unlikely to emerge, at least in significant numbers, once the e-commerce climate rebounds, primarily because many of the original dot-com firms achieved their prominence and operating scale on the basis of excessive investments as part of the venture capitalist-IPO financing model. The losses suffered by the past stockholders in these failed e-commerce IPOs should make new investors less gullible in the purchase of IPO stock. Also, the heightened risk that would attend any venture capital-led attempt at revival of this method of Internet start-up financing would work strongly against their large-scale support of new e-commerce start-ups. The trend toward concentration at the product delivery level is evidenced by the fact that as of 2002, three e-commerce firms, Monster.com, CareerBuilder.com, and HotJobs.com, control approximately 66 percent of the digital job recruitment market.[6] Just two years earlier, some 10 firms of relatively equal size were aggressively competing in this market. Despite their profitability among e-commerce sites, it would appear unlikely that a major start-up firm would find the financing to challenge the current electronic job boards leaders.[7]

---

5 comScore Networks, "Worldwide Internet Population and Online Travel Set Altitude Records in January," available at **http://www.comscore.com/news/jan_altitude_020702.htm**.

6 "Why the Sudden Rise in the Urge to Merge and Form Oligopolies?" *The Wall Street Journal*, February 25, 2002, p. A1.

7 Monster.com is the most profitable e-commerce site on the Web, with pretax operating income of $150 million in 2001, edging out eBay which had $140 million in operating profit. See "The Monster That's Feasting on Newspapers," *The New York Times*, March 24, 2002, p. 3–1.

Long-term survival in cyberspace, along with changes in venture capital attitudes, appear to convey some lasting benefits by combining to protect profitable firms from competitive threats by new entrants.

Consolidation affects the technology delivery as well as the product delivery end of the Internet. The principal supplier of home-linked, Internet broadband service is the cable-TV industry. Consolidation here continues at a rapid pace. If the proposed acquisition by Comcast of AT&T Broadband is allowed, then just three firms, AOL-Time Warner, Comcast, and Charter Communications, will control 65 percent of the U.S. cable market.[8] More mergers are possible given the court decisions that struck down limits on cable ownership and scale of operation. Financial scale, geographic customer scope, and regulatory permissiveness should lead to even larger cable firms. This advantage may make it easier, less costly, and more profitable for cable firms to extend broadband service to a wider number of subscribers.

Supplier consolidation trends are not limited to the cable field. Four wireless telephone companies, including Verizon Wireless, AT&T Wireless, Sprint, and Cingular, control 64 percent of the market.[9] Again, regulatory ease contributed to the consolidation as the Federal Communications Commission (FCC) allowed individual wireless firms to control larger amounts of the electromagnetic spectrum. Further consolidations are possible with the three users of the GSM, (global system for mobile communications) wireless system, AT&T Wireless, Cingular, and VoiceStream, being the most likely first candidates.[10] A union of the two CDMA, (code division multiple access, which is a form of cellular technology) technology firms, Sprint PCS and Verizon Wireless, could follow this initial merger. Such mergers would introduce cost savings based on scale economies and the elimination of duplicate capital structures. However, it might also cause a degree of harm for subscribers if it eliminated some current price competition. The profitable offering of telephony-based access to the Internet and mobile commerce requires a large volume of potential customers and high scale of usage. The consolidation of the wireless market points the surviving firms in that direction.

Supplier concentration, demand consolidation, and increase usage should eventually overcome the excess capacity problem. Economic theory cautions, however, that high concentration, approaching the level of oligopoly control, brings its own set of potential problems. Oligopolistic firms tend to become less price competitive as they try to find ways to coordinate behavior and become less concerned about technological innovation as well as product quality. In the face of oligopoly, the Schumpeterian view of the market as a source of creative destruction becomes less valid. The countervailing forces to these tendencies may lie in the rapid rate of change afforded by the technology of these industries, along with the existence of interindustry competition. Online e-tailers face strong competition from physical retailers, oligopolistic cable operators face intense competition from satellite providers and DSL-based broadband, while cell phone services face competition from other forms of wireless services. These related competitors might work to constrain the ability of the oligopolies to exploit their pricing power and delay or tilt the introduction of technology to favor their interests over that of their customers.

PROFITABILITY: MAKING THE WEB PAY OFF COMMERCIALLY

Given the trend toward Internet concentration in both product delivery and technology delivery, will the enhanced market power lead to the development of a general model of business profitability? Here the discussion of future prospects is best divided into two subtopics: the potential profitability of e-commerce firms, and the potential for a positive return on investment in B2B Web activities. The latter topic is clearly the easier of the two, because business use of the Web is already in place, profitable, and growing. B2B

---

8 "The Monster," p. 3–1.

9 "The Monster," p. 3–1.

10 Andrea Petersen, "Wireless, Yet Aiming to Link Up?" *The Wall Street Journal*, March 25, 2002, p. C1.

profitability comes in the form of cost savings and increased efficiency, which contribute to a healthier bottom line. Business use of the Internet takes advantage of the technology's greatest assets in its ability to allow individuals to communicate effectively at low cost and to facilitate the easy access to and transfer of information. The Web also helps to overcome a significant real-world business problem. Firms that stand in a customer-supplier relationship often employ different computer systems and software, which are either functionally incompatible or would at best be difficult to synchronize. However, on the Web, these firms can meet and do business in a medium that is both universal in its accessibility, and technologically neutral in its interaction with company-specific hardware and programming. The Web makes B2B e-commerce interconnections easier.

A cautionary but optimistic note about these current B2B efficiency gains is provided by Frances Cairncross, a senior editor at the European business magazine *The Economist*. She argues that despite the cost savings to date, the business innovations that will fully exploit the efficiency potential of the Internet are yet to come.[11] To realize these gains, Cairncross feels that firms must make significant changes in management practices and corporate culture.[12] For example, the lowly world of corporate purchasing management will require an infusion of resources and respect, which acknowledge purchasing as the site where the next wave of Internet efficiencies will arise. Also, making Web links with subcontractors more efficient will require greater levels of trust and mutual cooperation, especially if information on changes in customer order levels is to be redistributed electronically and automatically through the parts supply chain, using either private extranets or independent B2B exchanges. In the end, Cairncross sees the efficiencies being realized not just because of the adoption of the technology. Rather, they are captured because management makes the conscious changes in its business practices that are necessary to reap the potential productivity gains offered by the Web.

e-Tailing and Profitability: Lessons Learned About Scale and Diversity

For e-tail sites, the opportunities for profit exist. Capturing them may require a rethinking of the **interaction of scale and diversity in Web sales**. The original view of e-commerce was one of infinitesimally low marginal order cost, which would compel and justify a profitable, large-scale operation. The scale of the e-tail firm combined with the universal accessibility of the Web would create and sustain a revolutionary, stand-alone business. Hindsight revealed at least two problems with this view. First, the fixed costs of site development, branding, and order fulfillment overwhelmed the actual scale of sales that could be achieved and sustained via the Web. Whether the product was books and videos, grocery items, or clothing, the reality of consumer buying patterns never lived up to the aggressively optimistic model of large scale and low cost. The number of buyers almost never led to a sales volume sufficient to generate enough revenue to cover all of the costs while earning a normal profit. Even the cost reductions based on moving down the fulfillment learning curve, or increasing the scope of products offered under one e-tail roof, were not sufficient to counter the diminished number of buyers and lower amount of dollars per sales order.

The second problem with the e-tail scale and cost model was that the vision of a stand-alone, e-tail empire obscured the reality of the role that e-commerce could play as part of the broader retailing picture. The Web is not an e-tailing island. Rather, it is a way that firms can leverage their expertise and physical assets into providing another vehicle for reaching customers conveniently, with quality products and service. Although the outcome remains to be seen, it is possible that Amazon.com may survive and prosper. However, it is unlikely that any new Amazons will appear for a long time, if ever.

---

11 Frances Cairncross, *The Company of the Future*, (Cambridge, MA: Harvard Business School Press, 2002).

12 "A Management Revolution Still in the Making," *The New York Times*, March 17, 2002, p. 3–5.

Moreover, even Amazon recognized the value of partnering with other firms that possess retail assets, as well as other product delivery forms.

The Value of Smaller Scale and Diversity of Contact Scope

Considered in a different light, the issues of scale and scope may still be keys to developing a business model of general e-tail profitability.[13] The lessons from the Web's immediate past appear to imply that smaller scale is better scale, while diversity in the scope of contact surpasses diversity in product scope. First, niche e-tailers are generally alive and well, because their small and specialized market makes them easier to manage and less vulnerable to profit-eroding competition. By staking out a corner of the Web, the niche e-tailer can tap a broader audience and overcome the physical limitations of having access to too few customers within a specific geographic area. Also, moving upscale in terms of a combined value-added product line, along with a quality service level tends to boost the profit margins for niche e-tailers. These moves also help to make them more impervious to retail forms of competition. Therefore, one route to a profitable, Web-based business model is through smaller scale and specialty content.

A second lesson learned is that a multichannel approach to reaching the consumer base is superior to a Web-only sales system. Catalog sellers have been successful in moving onto the Web, because they see e-commerce as just one of a number of sales avenues. The consumer market is segmented by convenience in how individuals want to buy, in the same way that they are segmented by taste and preferences into what they want to buy. Not all consumers have the time or like to shop in a physical store, feel comfortable buying via mail and phone, or have the trust and technical savvy to shop online. Some buying segment prefers one sales vehicle relative to the others. One buying segment even spends time watching HSN or QVC on television, treating the event as a buying experience combined with entertainment. Catalog retailers recognize and capitalize on these differences.[14]

Just as physical retailers and catalog operations moved forward into e-commerce, some previously stand-alone e-tailers have begun to move backward into other channels of customer contact. For example, the e-travel firm Expedia.com combined with Classic Custom Vacations to cross-produce both Expedia's more affordable online travel packages, along with the decidedly upscale Classic vacation accommodations marketed off-line to customers through travel agents.[15] Here, Expedia leveraged its key assets of travel buying and packaging expertise. Expedia has come to redefine itself as a travel packager, not just a travel e-tailer. Expedia's scale allows it to buy bulk hotel reservations and airline seats cheaply, while its skill in packaging allows it to combine the vacation parts into attractive value-added travel packages, which sell at profitable markups. The combination of online and off-line sales venues permit it to market travel packages of different quality and price to different market segments.

Upscale travel marketing is not the only potential new distribution channel for Expedia.com. The cable TV conglomerate USA Networks, which owns the cable TV channel Home Shopping Network (HSN), also owns Expedia.com. Expedia is expected to begin leveraging its buying and packaging expertise through the marketing of travel packages via HSN. It also expects to market similar packages over a new cable travel channel that USA anticipates creating in the future. The lesson for future e-tailers isn't that e-commerce is king over all, but rather that a profitable set of business skills can be

---

13 The ideas in this section were inspired by Heather Green, Rochelle Sharpe, and Arlene Weintraub, "How to Reach John Q. Public," *BusinessWeek*, March 26, 2001, pp. 132–133.

14 In February 2002, the upscale clothing firm, which began life as a catalog entity, had greater sales revenues via the Web than they did through their catalog operations. See Bob Tedeschi, "E-Commerce Report: The catalog Business J. Crew Reaches a Milestone As Its Sales over the Web Exceed Sales from the Catalog," *The New York Times*, March 25, 2002, p. C6.

15 Bob Tedeschi, "E-Commerce Report: Online Travel Businesses Are Finding That There Is Money to Be Made Offline," *The New York Times*, March 18, 2002, p. C5.

fungible. Whether retailers in another venue develop the skills, or they are created as part of an e-commerce start-up, the skills can be transferred and profitably leveraged within related marketing channels.

The Profitable Sale of e-Commerce Content

The profitable sale of Internet content poses its own set of unique problems. First, a large portion of the information on the Web is displayed as an undifferentiated, commodity-like content, including stock quotations, sports scores, breaking news, and weather reporting. These services will survive, but most likely remain free and advertiser supported. At best, they may serve as a free link to additional value-added services, such as proprietary content analysis, specialty reconfiguration, and packaging with other content, or the sale of yesterday's content through an archived information service. Each of these revenue connections to otherwise undifferentiated content have been tried, with some success, through either a term subscription service or a point-of-delivery a la carte fee schedule.

The fee schedule approach offers the widest potential audience and profit opportunity, but runs up against the second problem, which is the absence of an efficient and broad micropayment system. The micropayment technology is complex and expensive, involving billions of potential transactions, many involving charges in a range somewhere between $0.10 and $1. At some point a viable micropayment system will emerge. Perhaps it will be vendor financed through charges of 2 to 3 percent of sales and linked to a credit card billing system much like the Paypal system today. Or it could be buyer financed through prepaid lumps of cash like a telephone card, or a pre-usage withdrawal of $10 to $20 from a credit card with charges billed against the funds on deposit. The micropayment intermediary could then earn its profits from some combination of the short-term investment of funds waiting to be used and vendor subscription fees. Digital automated billing via the Web makes the service possible, demand in the form of high-volume usage will make it a reality.

MAKING THE WEB EASIER TO USE

Commercial use of the Internet technology and its multimedia application, the World Wide Web, are barely a dozen years old. However, new versions of both are already on the drawing boards. They won't appear all at once, but like a new version of the Windows operating system, the parts will be ready for delivery individually over the next few years. The new systems will be more powerful and allow users to accomplish more tasks with less effort. They will combine **smart technology** with **smart code** to deliver more services in a more timely fashion. The services will be accessible with greater ease and without the human drudgery that is part of today's search-and-find information system. Using smart technology, the **Internet version 2.0** will be fully broadband, wireless, and employ the IP V.6 addresses system that will link just about every electronic appliance or product with a transmitter to the Web. Imagine refrigerators that can reorder food on their own, water heaters that seek out the cheapest electric rates from an array of suppliers, or cars where service problems can be diagnosed from the convenience of the owner's garage.

Broadband, with always-on access, provides direct Web connection through the ISP to an information site, eliminating the need for dial-ups and disconnects. Universal broadband can carry more data over wider pipes, creating the demand for more digital bytes carrying streaming video including real-time sports, entertainment events, movies on demand, live news reporting via Web cams, real-time gaming, and so on. Also, the networking of television, computers, and Web delivery of this streaming video will allow the transfer of images to the big screen digital TVs, many of which are gathering dust in today's electronics stores. This networking will permit consumers to enjoy the digital entertainment in the comfort of their own homes, with a clarity level that exceeds today's television signal. The fact is that much of this technology is already here if the viewer has the ability to cable together the connections on the typical computer, DVD player, and TV.[16] Most likely, in the not-too-distant future, this networking will be done through a TV set-top box, like Microsoft's Xbox, perhaps using a variant of the Windows operating system. It doesn't take much to see this streaming video as the answer to the killer app question.

Ease of Use Stimulates Demand and Potential Profit

Why go to all the effort to access video from the Web via the computer and television link-up when the same types of choices are available through the current multichannel cable, satellite TV, and pay-per-view systems? "One reason is the difference between a lot of choices and a staggering number of choices."[17] Imagine every television show being transmitted from a unique Web site that hosts both current and past episodes. Here, Web users would be able to link to the site for individual viewing at a time and date that was convenient for the viewer rather than for the program scheduler. The Web would serve a function similar to that of a universal TiVo personal video recorder, allowing any viewer to order up any show at a time when it was the best for her to watch. Already HBO conducts a modified version of this **time shifting** by immediately repeating the showing of its popular original programming, such as *The Sopranos* or *Sex in the City*, within a week of the original cablecast. They take care to *day shift* and *hour shift* the program to capture viewers unable to see the original showing or those who wanted to see a repeat.

Imagine a unique Web site for every movie ever made, for every sporting event ever played, for every episode of every TV series ever produced. Each of these would be downloadable for free with advertising included, or for a modest micropayment of say $0.50 without advertising. One can envision a profitable future consumer segment for perpetual Web reruns of *Friends*, *ER*, and *Seinfeld*, just as there seems to be an inexhaustible cable market for *The Honeymooners*, *I Love Lucy* and the movie *Casablanca* today. The economics of this arrangement are mind-boggling. On the demand side, the range of consumer choices is truly staggering. On the supply side, the vision of a perpetual stream of revenues derived from existing properties, provided to customers at nearly zero marginal cost, is the digital equivalent of finding the leprechaun's pot of gold for the owners of the broadcast rights.[18]

What about protecting intellectual property rights? Won't viewers download 20 episodes of *The Honeymooners* once, pirate the digital signal, file-share the films with other fans, and deprive the artists and copyright holders of compensation? The answer is that some persons will steal intellectual property, but the majority most likely won't, because the micropayment system trivializes the cost of viewing, tilting the choice in favor of pay-per-view rather than pirate-and-swap. Downloading and storing 20 hours of *The Honeymooners* takes time and space on a CD or computer hard drive. Why would the majority of fans illegally pirate the material when the same result can be obtained for $0.50 any time a viewer would like to see the episode? The minimal download cost makes pirating an inferior choice for all but the stingiest and most wanton of the potential pirates. Conversely, $0.50 per episode, times 10,000 global views per week, times 52 weeks generates $260,000 in revenue per year. It is not an insignificant sum of money. In many cases it should be sufficient for most programs to cover the cost of the site, pay some royalties, and still earn a tidy profit.

---

16 Neil McManus, "For Couch Potatoes, the Web Delivers," *The New York Times*, January 3, 2002, p. G5.

17 McManus, "For Couch Potatoes," p. G5.

18 Movie distributors are currently pushing theater chains to accept and exhibit digital films beamed by satellite, sent via fiber cable, or delivered on digital disks rather than mailing roles of movie film from theater to theater. The digital system improves the quality of the showing and lets the audience see the movie as it was actually created in digital form. See Anna Wilde Mathews, "Cinema's Digital Divide," *The Wall Street Journal*, March 28, 2002, p. B1.

Web Version 2.0, a Code-Smart User Servant

The discussion in Chapter 3 noted that Tim Berners-Lee is the universally acknowledged creator of the Web. Rather than resting on his great accomplishment, Berners-Lee has spent the past 12 years protecting the open nature of the Web and working to improve its functionality.[19] His current vision is for a **Web version 2.0** that is a **semantic Web**, where the smart code controlling the Web is able to understand human language. This would render the Web much easier to use and potentially far more productive. The semantic Web would not be based on artificial intelligence, where programs strive to understand the spoken word. Rather, it will make use of a new generation of more sophisticated computer code called **extensible markup language**, or **XML**.

The original code of the Web was **hypertext markup language (HTML)**. It was limited in function to specifying the appearance of the Web page including page color, type size, location, and imagery. The XML code includes information tags containing keywords or terms that would be set off within brackets and trigger actions by a smart software program functioning as an intelligent messenger or digital agent. The tags point the agent to a digital library containing a common resource description framework (RDF), which functions as a digital dictionary or thesaurus to convey the meaning of the words and terms. To gain full functional semantic understanding of the interrelationships among XML terms and RDF concepts, the agent next links to an ontology that acts like a digital encyclopedia. The ontology details the logical relationships among the XML terms and RDF concepts. The combination of terms, concepts, and interrelationships forms a comprehensible instruction for the digital agent, which can then perform a variety of functions related to the meaning of the XML tag.

Using Smart Code and Digital Agents

One application of the XML smart code might be in the field of e-health. For example, a physician might issue a new drug prescription <drug name>, for a specific patient <patient ID>, to treat a perceived medical problem <diagnosis>. The patient might also be receiving drug treatment for other illnesses <drug name>. The new prescription might be coded with the additional tag <known interaction>, which "would point to other drugs that interfere with the (new) medication. Then, when a doctor bats out a prescription on the computer, a software agent could verify that the drug is appropriate for the diagnosis, check the patient's records to see what other medicines the person is taking and determine whether any of them are likely to interfere with the new prescription."[20] The outcome of the smart code would be potentially safer and more effective patient care.

In addition to e-health applications, many other types of advanced functions are embodied within the semantic Web, which can potentially improve the Web's ease of use while increasing its level of productivity. For instance, digital agents will be able to engage in searches and interact with other agents as they conduct online commerce. Do-it-yourself travel arrangements are one of the most successful e-commerce applications, but for anyone who has tried to coordinate low-cost or complex travel arrangements involving air travel, car rental, multiple hotel stays, and ground transportation, the task can be daunting and highly inefficient. Consulting multiple Web pages, at multiple travel sites, with multiple combinations of flight times and dates, is time consuming, tedious, and frustrating in the extreme. For many potential business and leisure e-travelers, it is easy to understand why they still rely primarily on experienced travel agents to arrange the itinerary.

Suppose the potential e-traveler could fill out a simple information form listing the desired day and time of air departure and return, a description of acceptable accommodations, the characteristics of a preferred car rental contract, the extent of intercity travel,

---

19 The information in this section is adapted from Otis Port, "The Next Web," *BusinessWeek*, March 4, 2002, pp. 96–102.

20 Port, "The Next Web," p. 98–99.

along with a specified price or quality range for each service.[21] With the proper XML tags, the traveler could hand this wish list off to a digital agent, who would use the smart software program to educate itself as to what all of these travel terms meant. Armed with this semantic information, the agent could then conduct Web searches to find travel packages or individual travel arrangements that fit or closely matched the desired itinerary. It would conduct negotiations with the digital agents from the travel vendors, getting prices along with conditions, and report the findings back to the e-traveler for a final decision. A human may still have to modify the original plan to seal the deal, but the digital agent does all of the tedious and time-consuming electronic work.

Another potential use for digital agents might involve the ability of the XML tags to aid cross-discipline research by distilling ideas and integrating information at different Web sites. The world is full of bright scientists and humanists who continually discover and publish small pieces of truth and ideas that potentially enhance the range of human knowledge. One problem is making that information known and accessible to the rest of the research community, both in one's own discipline and across multiple disciplines. Publishing the information on a Web site helps, but the transfer process is further limited by differences in language and culture, along with the fact that there may be hundreds of thousands of Web pages on which the information can reside. Imagine giving a digital agent instructions to search out Web pages in a certain topic area, read and interpret the content, condense it, and report back the findings. It could hasten the spread of knowledge, while encouraging collaboration among geographically dispersed and culturally different scholars.

In summary, making the Internet and Web versions 2.0 smarter with technology and code should render them easier to use and more productive.

BROADBAND: WIRED VERSUS WIRELESS CONNECTIONS TO THE INTERNET

Today, the ability to capture the power of the Web is limited by the last-mile problem, which leaves most users linked to the Internet via dial-up service over existing telephone connections at a relatively slow speed of 56 kilobits per second. Both ease of use and the demand for profitability necessitate that the future of the technology must be broadband in its interconnections. Currently, the cable TV giants with their broadband modems and the telecommunications carriers with their DSL service are slugging it out for wired supremacy in technology delivery. The telecom carriers invested billions of dollars in buying spectrum rights. The new spectrum rights allow them to set up the 3G (third generation) infrastructures and deliver high-speed Internet connections via the cell phone network. Universal broadband is coming, but it may not arrive via a hardwired package. Wireless technology provides a competitive challenge to cable and DSL, as an alternative way to link to the Internet.

For the proponents of **m-commerce**, (*m* for mobile), or the buying of products or services over the wireless Internet, the introduction of 3G networks can't come fast enough. Global consumer enthusiasm for m-commerce has fallen rapidly. In June 2000, 32 percent of cell phone subscribers with Internet connections said that they intended to use the phone for an e-commerce transaction. By January 2002, this number declined to 1 percent of the subscriber base.[22] Some tried the mobile Internet connection and found it wanting, because the **wireless applications protocol (WAP)** that dominates today's 2G wireless Internet is slow and lists few applications. Also, in the United States, the **short message service (SMS)**, which is so popular in Europe and Japan, was limited by problems of **SMS interoperability**. Cell phone subscribers using one Internet

---

21 The basics of this search process are outlined in Port, "The Next Web," pp. 98–99.

22 Kevin J. Delaney, "Consumers Lose Interest in Buying Online with Mobile Telephones," *The Wall Street Journal*, March 20, 2002, p. B5.

connection standard couldn't easily send text messages to subscribers who use a different system.[23] Only in the spring of 2002 did the major U.S. cell phone firms finally agree to allow interoperability among their different proprietary instant message systems.[24] A faster, higher-quality 3G wireless Internet service connection for phones, handheld computers and laptops offers the promise of a way to overcome some of these problems, especially if the computer connections can be made direct, bypassing the need for either a cable or infrared connection to a cell handset.[25]

Japan is the current leader in the introduction of 3G cell phone systems, whereas U.S. wireless firms have yet to put a full 3G system into place. Japan faces a **competitive struggle** for dominance in the transmission standard between two incompatible rival systems, W-CDMA (wideband) versus CDMA 2000 (broadband). They compete in a marketplace to determine which system will become the preferred 3G Internet mobile-phone connection technology.[26] W-CDMA, championed by NTT DoCoMo, provides fast transfer speeds at 384 kilobits per second. The infrastructure has been expensive to install ($10 billion), however, and is incompatible with the existing Japanese cell phone technology. Also, W-CDMA subscribers will need to purchase new handsets that currently cost upwards of $400 each. CDMA 2000, supported by rival phone firm KDDI, is slower at 144 kilobits per second, but it is cheaper to install and compatible with the existing handsets. It is unclear whether the eventual dominant 3G cell phone standard will come from one of these systems or some other technology such as TD-SCDMA. China, which is already the world's largest cell phone market with 180 million accounts and rising, championed this domestically developed standard as a way to generate business for Chinese equipment vendors rather than importing phones from Europe or the United States.[27] It may be unsuitable for large-scale networks and is incompatible with phone standards in other parts of the world. The goal of global interoperability would be set back by Chinese adoption of this standard.

Wi-Fi Mesh Network Internet Connection

Making a wireless connection doesn't always mean using cell phone technology. **Wi-Fi**, or **wired fidelity**, offers a wireless Internet alternative to the cell phone. Wi-Fi is also known as **IEEE 802.11b**, the designation for interconnection standards developed by the technicians at the Institute for Electrical and Electronics Engineers.[28] This wireless linkage utilizes a low-power radio transmitter/receiver plugged into a DSL or cable Internet line. The transmitter sends out a radio or infrared Internet connection signal that can be received by any properly configured laptop or desktop computer, within a range of 300 to 500 feet from the transmitter.

The keys to the potential expansion for Wi-Fi wireless are its extremely low cost for installation and operation, and its super fast transmission speed. First, the infrared signal operates in the light spectrum, while some other 802.11b technologies operate in the industrial, scientific, and medical (ISM) frequency of the radio spectrum. None of these frequencies requires the acquisition of potentially expensive airwave space and licenses from the FCC. Therefore, no need for royalty payments can drastically reduce the charges for connection to the system. Therefore, Wi-Fi offers a significantly lower-cost,

23 Peter Loftus, "Text Messaging in Mobile Phones Is Getting Upgraded," *The Wall Street Journal*, March 12, 2002, p. B13D.

24 Peter J. Howe, "Verizon Wireless to Allow Intercarrier Short Messaging," *Boston Globe*, April 1, 2002, p. C2.

25 Stephen H. Wildestrom, "The Wireless Laptop Made Simple," *BusinessWeek*, March 25, 2002, p. 20.

26 Robert A. Guth, "Wireless Standards Fight It Out in Japan," *The Wall Street Journal*, March 21, 2002, p. A15.

27 Matt Pottinger, David Pringle, Pui-Wing Tam, and Andrew Batson, "China's Schism on Cellphones Rocks Industry," *The Wall Street Journal*, November 21, 2002, p. B1.

28 Information available at **http://standards.ieee.org/wireless/index.html**.

competitive challenge to the wireless cell phone services. Second, the technology and equipment necessary to establish a Wi-Fi base are inexpensive and falling in price. Wireless network cards for computers, Wi-Fi transmitters, and range-boosting antennas can together cost well under $400 to purchase and install. Lastly, Wi-Fi is super fast, with connection speeds at up to 11 megabits per second, compared to the 50 to 300 kilobit-per-second speeds offered by cell-based Internet connection systems.

Currently, individual **Wi-Fi hotspots** can be found in some airports, hotels, college campuses, office complexes, Starbucks coffee shops, and other enclosed spaces.[29] These individual **WLANs** or **wireless local area networks** can potentially be tied together into a **wireless mesh network**.[30] Just as the Internet involves the interconnection of individual computer networks, mesh routing would involve the seamless interconnection of Wi-Fi sites, creating a blanket of wireless networks. Individual base stations could be chained together in a series of interconnected Wi-Fi links that would build a **wireless cloud** within a geographic area. This "cloud" would allow wireless, mobile Internet computing in the same way that interconnected cell phone sites allow wireless, mobile telephony.

At present, the tendency is toward wireless **Wi-Fi free riders** that result from bandwidth bleeding from unsecured Wi-Fi hotspots, where proximate external users can access the unsecured private WLANs created by others.[31] The suppliers of the Internet services linked to the base station regard this uncompensated use of their wired connections as a form of theft.[32] The evidence does show that Internet users would be willing to pay for a commercial Wi-Fi link to the wireless Internet. Two of the early commercial Wi-Fi mesh services firms were Ricochet, which had wired parts of cities using pole-top radio transmitters, and MobileStar, which was "attempting to build a broadband wireless ISP with nodes across the country."[33] Unfortunately, both firms were forced into bankruptcy. New companies springing up to take their place include Boingo Wireless, led by Sky Dayton, the founder of the ISP service Earthlink, and Sputnik, which sell "software and services that make it possible for wireless users to roam among networks."[34]

The Internet 2.0, if it is not totally wireless, will offer a significant wireless component. For now, the discussion demonstrates an apparent competitive tension between 3G cell-based wireless technology versus Wi-Fi wireless technology, within the technical structure of the wireless connection and the source of wireless delivery. Despite the current tension, a few industry leaders see the potential for combining the two systems in a cooperative wireless technology rather than persisting as competitive systems.[35] Seamless meshed networks of 3G and Wi-Fi interconnections are technically possible, with each system independently allowing the user to enjoy its unique benefits. Genuine mobile computing is the strength of the 3G system, while a super fast connection speed is the strength of the Wi-Fi system. A subscriber could connect his phone, handheld, or laptop to the 3G system while on the go, switching the same equipment over to the Wi-Fi connection when he becomes anchored within range of a Wi-Fi hotspot, such as an airway terminal or coffee shop.

The technology is here today to provide the service, but three sets of obstacles impede its implementation. The first is the need to develop the software that will mesh the billing between the two systems. Second is the need to develop a system to allocate the revenues between the wireless giants, such as Verizon and VoiceStream, and the current multitude of small Wi-Fi providers, each with a few limited service areas. Lastly is the

---

29 Jesse Drucker, "Airport Lounges, Unplugged: New Wireless Options Debut," *The Wall Street Journal*, October 30, 2002, p. D1.

30 John Markoff, "The Corner Internet Network vs. the Cellular Giants," *The New York Times*, March 4, 2002, p. C1.

31 Amy Harmon, "Good (or Unwitting) Neighbors Make for Good Internet Access," *The New York Times*, March 4, 2002, p. C1.

32 Harmon, "Good Neighbors," p. C1.

33 Bob Liu, "The Fallout from MobileStar," available at **http://www.internetnews.com/isp-news/article/0,,8_902841,00.html**.

34 Markoff, "The Corner," p. C1.

35 Peter J. Howe, "Wireless Connection," *The Boston Globe*, March 22, 2002, p. E1.

customer service issue that emanates from the fragmented nature of the Wi-Fi technology. With potentially so many providers operating in small geographic areas, who will guarantee the quality and integrity of the Wi-Fi network? The first firm to solve these problems may come to dominate the delivery end of wireless e-commerce within the Internet 2.0.

WHO WILL GOVERN THE INTERNET?

Recall from the technology discussion in Chapter 3 that the Internet was originally an idea created and supported by the U.S. Department of Defense. Starting with the mid-1960s through 1990, the technology evolved from a secure method of military communications into a vehicle in support of scientific research and interpersonal contact. In the 1990s the Internet became a public multimedia platform, capable of supporting commercial activity, including e-tailing as well as B2B transactions. In the early 1990s, the National Science Foundation (NSF) accepted responsibility for managing the nondefense portion of the Internet.[36] This task included the assignment of domain names, such as *www.thomsonlearning.com*, and the numerical Internet Protocol or IP address, used to steer a request for linkage or an e-mail communication to a specific site within the network. The NSF contracted out the domain name registration activity to a single private firm, Network Solutions, which is now part of VeriSign. For a fee, this firm accepted applications and assigned individual site domain names, within the top-level domain names such as .com, .org, .gov, and .edu.

Numerous problems arose as part of the Internet management system.[37]

1. Network Solutions was a monopoly registrar, and concerns grew over the lack of competition in the name registration process.
2. Conflicts arose between trademark holders and domain name holders as cybersquatters saw the potential for being the first to register business names and then reselling the domain name to the firm at a handsome profit.
3. Commercial interests desired a management structure that was less informal and better able to protect their investment.
4. Internet users outside of the United States wanted a greater say in how Internet decisions were being made and how the Internet was being run.
5. The need to create additional top-level domain names continued to grow. Internet professionals felt that a body, free from government and responsible to the Internet community, should manage the domain creation process.
6. Given the increasing commercial use of the Internet, it became less appropriate for the U.S. government to manage the decision making and funding of these management efforts.

These concerns created an obstacle to global Internet expansion in the form of an Internet governance tension between Internet control as a purely government function versus control as a purely private function. Recognizing this tension and in response to the preceding issues, the Clinton administration, through the Department of Commerce, acted in 1998 to create more competition in the domain registration process and to move the management of the Internet into private hands. The IP address assignment function was given to a private, not-for-profit firm, the **Internet Corporation for Assigned Names and Numbers (Icann)**, while additional firms were allowed to register domain names. Icann would remove the U.S. government from control over the Internet, privatize Internet decisions, and give Internet stakeholders a voice in the Internet decision process. It was felt that the removal of all governmental control would

---

36 For an early history of Internet governance, see U.S. Department of Commerce, "Management of Internet Names and Addresses," available at **http://www.ntia.doc.gov/ntiahome/domain-name/6_5_98dns.htm**.

37 The following discussion is an adaptation of the points developed in "Management of Internet Names and Addresses."

further stimulate global acceptance and growth of the Internet. Privatization would foster free speech, while keeping cyberspace open and available to all parties in an unbiased manner. Icann also became the central body responsible for forging a global consensus on other technical Internet issues. Currently, the Internet user community at large elects five of the 19 members of the Icann board, while Icann is funded through dues paid by the managers of country-specific domain names.

Icann and Governance

Icann was able to agree on the introduction of seven new top-level domain names including, .biz for business names, .museum for museums, .name for individuals, and .pro for professional sites covering lawyers, doctors, accountants, and so on.[38] However, as a purely private, self-governing body, Icann's functional history is one of prolonged debate, and an inability to reach enforceable consensus on key issues. It also a short of funds needed to carry on its work, when dues payments were withheld by dissatisfied members. In response, Stuart Lynn, the president of Icann, proposed a **hybrid government-private governance model**. Here, the number of board members would be reduced to 15, with five being chosen by governments, and eliminating the five publicly elected posts.[39] His position was that the real-world support and involvement of governments are essential if the work of Internet management was to go forward. The proposal was soundly defeated by the proponents of private and minimal control, at the Accara, Ghana, meeting of the board in March 2002.

The issue of Internet governance is unlikely to go away. The simple fact is that the market demands rules.[40] The Internet has become too important a part of commerce and society to let it drift as an ungoverned and unrestrained body. Even though the Internet evolved as a decentralized and ungoverned medium, the truth is that "the attraction of (any) rules-free market diminishes as a technology is commercialized."[41] Professor Debora Spar of Harvard, in her book *Ruling the Waves*, traced the history of market-driven rule making as applied to different new technologies, including those involving ocean travel, the use of the airwaves, and lastly the Internet.[42] Initially, laws and rules are chaotic at the start of any disruptive technology, but eventually the demands of commerce overcome the forces of anarchy. Professor Spar's analysis focuses on rules made to combat the illegal acts of pirates, who plundered the property rights of legitimate commercial pioneers. However, her point that markets demand rules can be extended to cover the plight of Icann. Here, the economic costs of an Internet without rules are greater market inefficiency and diminished market growth, both of which are unacceptable outcomes. Eventually, "the demand for rules and standards grows, and is satisfied by private cartels or monopolies or, more frequently, by governments, either singularly or internationally."[43] The struggles of Icann "illustrate the difficulties of setting rules without the clout of government."[44] Therefore, look for additional attempts to reintroduce more government involvement in the control of the Internet rule-making procedures and an eventual evolution toward that end.

---

38 Susan Stellin, "Web Addresses Sprout New Suffixes, Needed or Not," *The New York Times*, November 1, 2001, p. G9.

39 Julia Angwin, "Icann Leader Seeks Big Changes in How Internet Is Governed," *The Wall Street Journal*, February 26, 2002.

40 The following discussion is adapted from David Wessel, "The Market Demands Rules," *The Wall Street Journal*, November 29, 2001, p. A1.

41 Wessel, "The Market Demands Rules," p. A1.

42 Debora Spar, *Ruling the Waves*, (New York: Harcourt Brace, 2001).

43 Wessel, "The Market Demands Rules," p. A1.

44 Wessel, "The Market Demands Rules," p. A1

INTELLECTUAL PROPERTY STRUGGLES IN THE DIGITAL AGE

Developing standards that effectively protect intellectual property may prove to be the most difficult to resolve of all the problems. The conflict stands between two key parties to the protection solution, and no obvious technology fix is available for the problem. The discussion in Chapter 7 described the nature of the piracy challenges in both the music and video portions of the entertainment content industry. Everyone wants to be fairly compensated for the use of his or her intellectual property, but that goal is becoming more elusive in the digital age. On the microeconomic level, electronic piracy poses a threat to the flow of funding that supports the creation of new digital content. However, the piracy also creates macroeconomic consequences because it discourages content owners from providing existing entertainment in full digital form. The paucity of digital entertainment content in turn contributes to the slow adoption of digital high-definition television, or HDTV, and the unwillingness of most Internet users to pay for broadband connections. Why should consumers pay for fatter pipes when the range of things they can do once they have the capacity remains limited? This condition can contribute to a lower rate of macroeconomic growth and innovation. This situation alarmed some members of Congress, who proposed legislation to mandate the installation of the embedded antipiracy technology.[45]

The problems surrounding the development of an **antipiracy standard** creates a strategic tension between content owners versus equipment manufacturers.[46] Content owners would like to see the computer and electronic playback equipment manufacturers adopt a **technology approach to standard setting** by creating and installing imbedded copyright protection technology. The technology fix could be based on a digital watermark, where each piece of legitimate copyrighted video and music material would carry an identifying flag that cannot be duplicated even if the material is copied electronically. Computers and playback systems would have embedded technology that would refuse to display any digital film or song where the equipment could not detect the presence of the watermark.

For their part, the equipment manufacturers would like to see the content owners adopt a **strategic market-based approach** to thwarting piracy. They see the technology approach as placing an unfair burden on the manufacturers who must incur the expense and take on the responsibility of protecting the intellectual property of others. Also, the introduction of nonreproducible watermarks could narrow the existing rights of legitimate content owners, keeping them from space shifting material by copying it to other playback units. Some content owners have already introduced copy-protected CDs that will not play via the CD-ROM drive of a PC or Mac computer.[47] When the equipment manufacturers restate their differences with the content owners in this light, the effect is to redefine the standards creation tension in terms of protecting the rights of content owners versus the rights of consumers. The content owners reply that the reason the manufacturers don't want to install the embedded technology fix is that they actually profit by selling equipment that will allow illegal copying. The owners contend that for the manufacturers, piracy is the "killer app" that drives equipment sales and profits.[48] Given that the two sides have difficulty in agreeing on what is at stake in the conflict, the likelihood of a quick resolution of the standards creation problem is diminished.

---

45 Yochi J. Dreazen, "Media, Tech Officials Battle on Web Piracy," *The Wall Street Journal*, March 1, 2002, p. B2.

46 Amy Harmon, "Hearings on Digital Movies and Piracy," *The New York Times*, March 1, 2002, p. C4.

47 Amy Harmon, "CD Technology Stops Copies, But It Starts a Controversy," *The New York Times*, March 1, 2002, p. C1.

48 Harmon, "Hearings on Digital," p. C4.

Rethinking the Digital Entertainment Business Model

The development of a strategic approach would be consistent with the actions taken by the film industry in the mid-1970s, when it dropped its opposition to the commercialization of VCR technology. The studios relented because they found a business model (i.e. video sales and rentals) that allowed them to profitably capitalize on the equipment. The adoption of a strategic approach, as applied to the copy protection problem in the digital age, might embrace some of the following elements.[49] First, the studios should abandon the fiction that they can exercise absolute control over their content. No matter what content protection system is introduced, someone will inevitably figure out a way to defeat it. What is needed is a copy protection system good enough to defeat the average pirate, without being so heavy-handed that it places the content owner in direct conflict with legitimate needs of paying customers. Owners of legal material have the right to make copies for their own use and have grown accustomed to doing so. Any copy protection system that abridges that right will be met with an angry customer reaction in the market.

Any new media business model must also look to reward customers, not punish them. Customers are usually happy with some combination of product choice, convenience, and reasonable pricing. Perhaps a way can be developed to make secure, pay-per-view delivery of first-run movies via the Internet while they are still playing in the local theater. Given the broad theater distribution of films today, a large dropoff in ticket sales typically occurs after the first two to three weeks following the initial release date. With theater ticket prices averaging $8, a pay-per-view delivery system in the same price range may be an excellent way to generate new sales without cannibalizing theater sales. Home viewing and theater viewing are good but not perfect substitutes because the viewing quality of the film seen at home may be less than that of a theater offering a night out, stadium seating, and a giant screen. Home viewing also allows the content owner to tap another market segment that may not be able to physically or financially access the theater showing. Media advertising expenditures that go into a theater release, along with the theater buzz, may pay additional dividends by stimulating a sizable near-term home demand.

Finally, the content owners should be encouraged to think outside the box, rather than rely on a government-imposed copyright protection model. Government rules are, by their nature, rigid and unable to respond to the full range of existing as well as evolving demands or technologies. A one-size-fits-all approach based on absolute control over content is unrealistic in today's consumer market and with today's technology. The digital recording of music and video offers enhanced opportunities for entertainment quality and creativity. Consumers clearly prefer the new products and are willing to make reasonable payments to receive them. The task for the content owners is to package, price, and deliver the digital products in convenient ways that also satisfy the consumer's desire for choice in different market segments.

SUMMARY AND PROSPECTS

This chapter completes the journey through the digital world of e-commerce and the Internet. Even though the Internet offers enormous benefits both today and in the future, the technology, in many areas, must still evolve to realize its full potential. Several of the tensions identified in this final chapter lay out a variety of competitive struggles between alternative technical directions or courses of action. When will universal broadband arrive, and will it be delivered via a hard-wired or wireless technology? Will wireless broadband be dominated by cell telephony or by a Wi-Fi connection? What sort of regulation or control will emerge over the Internet? Will it

---

49 The material in this section has been adapted from Thomas E. Weber, "E-World: To Avoid Napterization, Hollywood Must Move Beyond Copy Protection," *The Wall Street Journal*, March 18, 2002, p. B1.

be through private or governmental means? How will the issue of piracy of intellectual property be resolved, through technical controls on equipment or through a change in the business model adopted by the content owners? Will the appearance of smart code alter how the Web is used and the degree of usage? How will the growing use of the Web by people of the developing world alter the quality of their lives? As the technology of the Web grows and usage spreads, will its current structure, influenced by U.S. culture and values, evolve into something more global in nature? Will the Web accept leadership and learn from those outside of North America, or will the rest of the world become more like the United States in its preferences for markets, freedom of expression, language, and cultural values?

The first dozen or so chapters in this book laid out the technology and economic structure of e-commerce and the Internet. The chapters developed an economic history and discussion of the forces that described how e-commerce arrived at its current position. The discussion was intended to identify the group of firms that succeeded and why. It also tried to explain why so many firms failed with a substantial loss of investor funds. The economics of e-commerce and the Internet have yet to achieve an equilibrium. They are still changing, propelled onward by the force of the technology and the imagination of the users. The path of change and its results are uncertain. However, the consequences of the future evolution will have a decidedly economic character, as well as social, political, behavioral, and technical dimensions. Harnessing these changes for both economic efficiency and the benefit of future generations are the real challenges that lie ahead.

KEY TERMS AND CONCEPTS

antipiracy standard
extensible markup language (XML)
hybrid government-private governance
   model
hypertext markup language (HTML)
IEEE 802.11b (Wi-Fi)
interaction of scale and diversity in
   Web sales
Internet Corporation for Assigned
   Names and Numbers (Icann)
Internet version 2.0
m-commerce
semantic Web
short message service (SMS)
smart code

smart technology
SMS interoperability
strategic market-based approach to
   antipiracy
technology approach to standard setting
time shifting
visitor demand consolidation
Web version 2.0
Wi-Fi free riders
Wi-Fi hotspots
wired fidelity (Wi-Fi)
wireless applications protocol (WAP)
wireless cloud
wireless local area networks (WLAN)
wireless mesh network

DISCUSSION AND REVIEW QUESTIONS

1. Identify and discuss what you consider to be the three most important concerns facing the future of the Internet and e-commerce as identified in the introductory case. What makes them more important than the remaining five topics?

2. Who will be the Internet users of tomorrow? Where will they reside geographically? Why? What types of challenges does this new group of Internet users create?

3. What is visitor demand consolidation? Why may it be taking place? How can this trend work to reduce the overcapacity problem?

4. Explain how supplier consolidation in both the product delivery and technology delivery portions of the Internet and e-commerce are working to ease the overcapacity problem.

5. Under what conditions can the Web become a profitable environment in which firms can do business? How do issues of scale and diversity affect this profit potential? How does the leveraging of assets, along with multichannel customer contract influence the profit picture?

6. What is the nature of Tim Berners-Lee's vision of the Web version 2.0? How might the use of smart code and digital agents boost the use of the Web for an even greater range of activity?

7. Identify and explain the Wi-Fi version of the wireless Web. How and why does Wi-Fi challenge the telephony-based system of connecting to the Web?

8. Who governs the Internet today? Why? Why is future governance of the Web an important Internet challenge? What are some of the Internet governance options and tensions?

9. What is the nature of the tension between the owners of intellectual property and the manufacturers of electronic equipment regarding the protection of intellectual property in a digital world?

10. What is your assessment of the future evolution of the Web and e-commerce? Will the Web fulfill its early promise? Will B2C e-commerce become profitable and grow in its range of services delivered? How will the system evolve technologically?

WEB EXERCISES

1. Check for any updated information on global Internet usage through comScore Networks, available at **http://www.comscore.com/news/press_release.htm**.

2. To see names of locations such as airports, hotels, and coffee shops where your properly equipped laptop will be able to make connections with commercial Wi-Fi services link to **http://www.boingo.com**, **http://www.wayport.com**, and **http://locations.hotspot.t-mobile.com**. Use the HotSpot map at the T-mobile site, or the locations link at Boingo and Wayport to see whether a commercial Wi-Fi location is available in your hometown.

3. Visit the number one geographic location site, **http://www.mapquest.com/**, and the number five site, **http://www.randmcnally.com/**, to see whether you can discern why Web users might favor one site over the other. Which site is easier to use and gives the quickest access to location information? Which site is less cluttered? Why?

4. To learn more about the semantic Web link to the article by Tim Berners-Lee, James Hendler, and Ora Lassila entitled, "The Semantic Web," in *Scientific American*, available at **http://www.sciam.com/article.cfm?articleID= 00048144-10D2-1C70-84A9809EC588EF21**.

1G first generation cell phone technology, allowing the user to make a simple telephone call using wireless, cell-based, analog connections

2G second generation cell phone technology that includes a digital screen to communicate information as well as voice signals

2.5G interim solution that offers improvements in cell network technology, data compression, and faster data transfer speeds than the 2G

3G third generation cell phone system intended to offer transmission speeds 40 times faster than those of today

A

ability to pay the buyer's income relative to the price of the item

absolute cost advantage the situation that exists when an existing firm is able to produce and sell the product or service at a lower than average cost than any potential entrant or existing firm

accelerated depreciation a depreciation option, such as sum of the year's digits or double-declining balance, which assigns a greater proportion of the depreciation charges to the earlier years of the asset's life

accounting breakeven the accountant's term involving an output volume that demonstrates equality between total revenue and total cost measured in terms of expenses

accounting expenses costs in the form of cash outlays for labor, material, advertising, and any product acquisition costs paid to a previous stage of production

accounting profit revenues in excess of accounting expenses; measured by cash received or owed to the firm in exchange for the sale of its product minus the costs of doing business

acquisition cost the historical or original cost of starting the business

advanced-services rule the FCC directive that said that before AOL could add additional capabilities to AIM, AOL must make its system accessible to other IM services

advertising strategy the scheme of creating a brand name and image in the mind of the consumer

album mentality the view that the most profitable way to sell music was to bundle popular tunes together with other songs and sell them all in one album or CD

allocation efficiency the measure of how well society allocates the correct relative amount of resources to each product as is desired by consumers

allocative efficiency the situation in which the price the consumer pays for the unit is just equal to the extra costs the firm must pay to attract the resource away from its next best use

all-optical Internet systems technology that would eliminate need for costly, bulky converters and routers when signal changes direction

almost-on-demand music servers the system that allows listeners to select specific songs whenever they want

amortization a cost of business that does not require an outlay of cash

anticircumvention provision makes it a criminal offense to circumvent antipiracy measures built into commercial software

antidevice provision prohibits the manufacture or distribution of any device designed to circumvent technological copyright protections

antipiracy standard standards that effectively protect intellectual property

antitrust laws federal statutes limiting the competitive behavior of individual firms

any line of business a clause within Section 7 of the Clayton Act defining any type of economic activity that is adversely affected by a merger

any section of the country a clause within Section 7 of the Clayton Act defining the geographical scope of an economic activity that is affected by a merger

application service provider firms that host catalog services for widely used industrial products.

application-programming interfaces (API) software functions that allow easy access into parts of the operating system

arbitrage activity takes advantage of small price spreads for a given stock among different markets or within different time spans. The goal is to make a profit

ARPANET the first network, between UCLA and Stanford Research Institute

asset-light companies companies that set up markets and earn profits by facilitating the trades in those markets, but which own very little or none of the product being traded

attribute space the location and clustering of customers depending on their individual tastes and preferences

auction aggregation site a site that collects and centralizes bids on a specific item from a number of diverse and independent Web auctions

auction pricing a pricing scheme in which customers set the value of the service or product

audience clustering grouping listeners/viewers together according to common characteristics

Audio Home Recording Act (AHRA) of 1992 explicitly granted legitimate owners of music the right to make copies for their personal, noncommercial use

auditor a professional who certifies that the accountant keeps the financial records of the firm according to generally accepted accounting principles

avatar an animated Internet character that serves as an electronic "face" for a firm or activity

B

B2B exchange systems Web-based business exchanges that bring together major assemblers and parts firms in the global industry.

backend architecture firms firms that provide essential e-commerce services, such as web hosting and data center firms

bandwidth measure of carrying capacity of transmission system

banner ads Internet advertising which appears on Web portal sites to help fix the name of the product or firm in the mind of the consumer

barriers to entry obstacles that allow existing firms to earn economic profits, while keeping potential competition at bay

Berners-Lee, Tim Swiss physicist most closely associated with origins of the World Wide Web

beta test a method for testing and evaluation, usually of computer software, prior to general release

bilateral exchange a one-to-one business model, in which a single seller sets up a Web site listing products and prices in a form similar to a traditional catalog

bilateral marketplace a site that can offer both professional services for sale and projects open to bid

biometric data results in the creation of user silhouettes that can provide important information for advertisers

bondholder person who lends money to the firm in exchange for a predictable interest payment and the eventual return of the loaned funds

boolean search tools search tools used to efficiently search complex databases

brain drain the best and brightest entrepreneurs from foreign nations leave to set up their businesses in another country

brand awareness information designed to tell the buyer who the firm is, what it does, and the bundle of attributes that it stands for

brand equity value created by customer recognition of and satisfaction with a particular product or service

brand proliferation numerous variations of the same product

branding information designed to tell the buyer who the firm is, what it does, and the bundle of attributes that it stands for

brick-and-click operations a combination of sales via physical businesses and the Internet

brick-and-mortar channel physical sales locations and facilities for retail sellers

brick-and-mortar outlets a physical sales facility

broadband interconnect firms firms that supply high-speed Internet links through cable modems or DSL connections

build-to-order business model a model in which customers can design a product with options and color combinations (product attributes) that better fit their tastes, and for which they might pay a small price premium

bundling the combined selling of potentially/formerly independent products such as computer hardware or software products, or the grouping of popular tunes together with other songs and selling them together in a single album or CD

burn rate a measure of how fast a firm is using up its available funds

business failures occurs when the value of the firm's financial liabilities exceeds the value of its current and long run financial as well as physical assets

business incubators locations offering both physical and managerial support for the firm in which venture capitalists have invested funds

business methods patent legal protection of a method of doing business

business risk the risk of failure prior to reaching the IPO stage

business-to-business (B2B) e-commerce use of the Web by producers to sell directly to other businesses

business-to-business (B2B) exchange a Website that brings together at a single Internet location independent buyers and sellers of a given product

business-to-consumer (B2C) e-commerce use of the Web by producers to sell directly to end users

C

cable concentration cap rules regulations that limit a single cable operation to control no more than 30 percent of total U.S. cable subscribers, and limit the channels carrying programming produced by an affiliated company to 40 percent

cable Internet access Internet connection provided by cable TV firms

Cable Television Consumer Protection and Competition Act of 1992 a regulation that vests certain rights and options in local broadcast TV stations relative to their signals being carried by the local cable TV systems

cannibalization the advancement of one form of sales at the expense of another, such as the substitution of legal music downloads of individual songs in place of the purchase of the entire CD

capitalism an economic system driven by markets, prices, profits and rewards

carry a fee that investing partners charge (anywhere from 20 to 35 percent of the profits of the VC firm) as compensation for their expertise in investing the money of the funding partners

cartel pricing illegal coordination of product pricing by firms that are conspiring with one another to exploit market demand

Case 1 market a market that contains one or a few highly concentrated sellers of a product and a large number of smaller disorganized and fragmented buyers

Case 2 market a market that involves the opposite market structure of one or a few dominant buyers and a large number of smaller, disorganized, intensely competitive, and fragmented sellers

Case 3 market a market where both buyers and sellers are fragmented, small, numerous, and disorganized

catalog retailers experts in direct selling and remote order fulfillment such as Fingerhut, Lands' End, and J. Crew

category killer a retail situation in which a giant store, with a large amount of sales in a narrowly focused product line, severely limits the ability of other firms to sell that type of product for a profit

category of scarce resources the unique and valuable skills of the entrepreneur, along with labor, capital, and natural resources

caveat emptor a buyer-beware warning to potential product buyers or stock market investors

census industries collection of firms producing a similar product as defined by the U.S. Department of Commerce

channel conflict a set of problems that can arise when the manufacturer of a product tries to sell the item to the customer using different contact methods such as retail stores, Web sites, or direct marketing

Children's Online Privacy Act of 1998 a federal law that protects online privacy and prevents collecting data relating to children

circuit routing a multipath network used to send messages

clicks-and-bricks firms that have physical facilities and e-commerce outlets

clicks-and-catalogs firms that have e-commerce and catalog outlets

click-through rate the fraction of views of an electronic e-commerce advertisement that go immediately to the Web site that sponsors the ad

cluster a group of firms or customers that are closely linked by production characteristics, geography, or common attributes

co-branded site a Web site sponsored by two firms united in an e-commerce joint venture

code division multiple access (CDMA) one of a number of competing cell phone technologies that translates voice conversations into tiny packets of data and sends them out over the airwaves

collaborative filtering system additional purchase suggestions made by a seller to a purchaser based on purchases of other buyers who bought similar products

collaborative product development two or more firms working jointly on the development of the same product

commodities homogenous products sold by different producers

Communications Act of 1934 legislation that allowed for the creation of the Federal Communications Commission (FCC)

comparative static technique the process of taking one equilibrium position and comparing it to another

competition through price sales take place on the basis of the lowest possible price a seller will set in order to draw buyers from competitors, a typical method for selling commodities

competition through product differentiation selling on the basis of the creation of a distinct image or brand by a producer for its product

competition to become the standard a market competition between two different technologies with the goal of establishing the winner as the dominant technology for the product

competitive advantage a distinct or key advantage that a leading firm has over competitors

competitive advertising advertising designed primarily to place the name of the firm or product in front of the customer

competitive local exchange carriers (CLECs) new competitors to the existing phone company encouraged by the provisions of the Telecommunications Act of 1996

composition rights the rights of a firm to distribute melodies and lyrics

compounding the process of earning interest on interest

computer emergency response team (CERT) a federally funded coordination center located at the Software Engineering Institute on the campus of Carnegie Mellon University near Pittsburgh

computer intrusion incidents attempts to gain unauthorized access to a computer system

computer worms worms are self-propagating and spread rapidly across the Internet, locking up computers and blocking other forms of Web traffic, which, unlike viruses, do not need human intervention to spread

concentration ratio a quantitative approach to the measurement of the number of firms and their size within an industry

conduct remedy an agreement that would correct past behavior of a possible monopolist

conglomerate merger a merger between firms that either sell unrelated products or the same product in different geographic markets

consent order a negotiated agreement, in this case, between the FTC and merging forms

constant dollar terms value expressed in terms of money holding a steady purchasing power over a specific time period; current value minus the rate of inflation

consumer sovereignty the determination of products and prices based on buyer demand

consumer surplus uncompensated value of a product

content scrambling system an encryption technology used by the film industry to protect movies recorded in the DVD format

contribution margin revenues that cover the costs and allow a company to earn a normal profit

conversion rate to turn page viewers into e-tail buyers

cookies digital identifiers triggered when a computer revisits a sit

copy-and-skip system use of online entertainment where the user does not pay and accesses only free, peer-to-peer file sharing technologies

copyright legal protection prohibiting the unauthorized copying of intellectual property

cost minimization targeting a fixed output level and employing the least costly combination of fixed price inputs that will allow a firm to achieve the output target

cost-minimizing rule appropriate ratio for the combined employment of abundant and scarce inputs

cost-of-service pricing tallying up all of the explicit costs associated with producing a targeted volume of output and then taking on a per-unit charge. Also called standard-volume pricing

CR4 numbers equivalent value the oligopolic situation which indicates the number of firms of equal size that can exist in a market exhibiting the current concentration ratio

creative destruction the view, usually attributed to the economist Joseph Schumpeter, that markets are places of constant turmoil and new firms, ideas, products, and ways of doing business arise to replace old ones

credible threat an existing rival to an entrant that poses more than the normal challenges of entry and which will usually cause the potential entrant to seek an easier challenge

critical mass the stage in a business operation at which the volume of its operations allows for the profitable creation of highly specialized services

crony capitalism a system of resource allocation based upon favoritism and insider dealing rather than impersonal market decisions

cross promotion the selling of one type of product or process to a different or separate audience

cross-ownership rules the rule that no cable TV system was allowed to own a broadcast television station in the same market where it provided bale services

cross-subsidization when a merged company uses profits gained in one market to subsidize losses in another market

cultural infiltration the dominance of U.S. Web design, sights, and sounds, along with English as the de facto Web language, such that it leads to a digital invasion of U.S. ideas and culture into a foreign nation

cultural turbulence the appearance of the Internet today threatens to turn a global mix of distinct and diverse cultures into a single bowl of homogenized soup

current dollar terms value expressed in terms of present market prices

customer loyalty the situation that exists when buyers are insensitive to price increases and will purchase a particular product only

customer switching costs the costs associated with switching from one product or supper to another such as from one ISP to another

cybercrime the use of the Internet for illegal activities, transactions, unauthorized intrusions, or other breaches of computer security

cybersquatters persons who purchase a considerable volume of common government, personal, and business names which they have no intention of using themselves but hope to be able to sell later at huge profits

cyberterrorism using the Internet in a criminal way to engage in attack planning and communication

D

day traders stock participants who gave up their day jobs to become full-time Web stock traders

de facto standard the standard system for the majority of desktop and laptop computers

de novo entry the appearance of a new competitor in an existing industry without merging with a firm that is currently part of the industry

decentralized network a network that no one owns

DeCSS video encryption-cracking program

deep discount e-brokers electronic brokerage firms spawned by the Web with extremely low brokerage rates

default risk the risk that a business will fail of its own accord and be unable to repay its outstanding debts

delay (versioning) over time the practice of releasing the most sophisticated and expensive version of the product first, followed by stripped down and cheaper models at a later date

demand-based model of product differentiation differentiation based upon variations in product attributes desired by consumers

denial-of-service attacks a form of electronic attack that paralyzes a Web site by overloading it with bogus traffic and requests for information

dependence effect the demand for most goods grows out of the process of production itself. If production is to increase, the wants must be effectively contrived. In the absence of the contrivance the increase would not occur

depreciation a cost of business that does not require an outlay of cash. Strict rules in the IRS tax code define the time span over which specific pieces of capital equipment must be depreciated

dial-up connections Internet connection through standard telephone lines

digital cash an electronic form of cash used for bill payment or transactional purposes via the Internet

digital copying problem the issues occurring because of the ease with which most material, copyright-protected or not, can be digitized, copied, and transmitted

digital divide a gap between those who have regular access to the Internet and Internet information and those whose access is limited or non-existent

Digital Millennium Copyright Act (DMCA) a 1998 act passed by Congress that spells out the boundaries for electronic copyright protection

digital rights management owners of usually copyrighted electronic entertainment material using their power to protect illegal copying and to maximize the flow of revenues from the product

digital soul a metaphysical reference to the inner location where an individual's personal electronic records and transactions are recorded

digital subscriber line (DSL) Internet service provided through existing telephone system

digital watermark an electronic signal imbedded throughout a work signifying copyright protection

direct control model of Internet music distribution joint ventures of recording companies that will allow them to control both the content and distribution systems, including over the Internet

direct marketing sending an advertising message directly to a customer such as through surface mail or e-mail

direct subscriber lines (DSL) a form of broadband interconnection supplied by telephone companies using the existing copper wire technology

discount brokerage firms a brokerage firm whose fee schedule for transactions is below the industry standard

discount rate a rate of interest such that funds received in the future are worth less than an equal amount of money received today

discounted cash flow model a model to evaluate the flow of expected future income

discounting the process of taking an expected flow of future income and estimating its value in current dollar terms

diseconomies of scale the higher unit cost experienced in the long run resulting from larger firm size

disequilibrium approach views and analyzes the marketplace as being in constant flux and turmoil as opposed to being susceptible to analysis in equilibrium with competitive forces in balance

disintermediation the act of eliminating an intermediary between the buyer and seller from the system of purchase

disruptive technology an innovation, such as the Internet, that brings a radical change to the way in which firms compete in the marketplace

distressed tickets airline tickets that sell for reduced prices when they would normally remain unsold

distributed computing the breaking up of complex problems into smaller parts that can be worked on independently and recombined later

diversification of portfolio risk the spreading of investment dollars across different projects such that losses on a few projects would be more than compensated for by gains on the majority of investments

domain name suffixes suffixes such as .com, .edu, .gov, or .org used to indicate the type of site to which messages are being sent

downstream firms businesses such as retailers or product resellers that follow a given firm's stage in production

dual-network rule the rule that prohibited one firm from owning more than one of the four major broadcast networks

due diligence requirements the regulations that call for a full review of the potential conditions and consequences of a proposed mega-merger before it is completed

due diligence review a process whereby the investment banker determines the quality of the business plan and the soundness of the financial footing of the start-up before bringing it public

duopoly an industry in which there are only two intense rivals

dynamic competition competition involving technological change, product differentiation and constant changes in efficiency

dynamic efficiency the enhanced use of resources over time

dynamic pricing a form of price discrimination that continually charges different prices to different customers usually based upon some unique characteristic(s) of buyer demand

E

eBay modified English auction the scheme of bidding in which the seller receives a cost-of-service price plus a portion of the buyer's consumer surplus

e-books online books

e-Commerce joint venture putting two firms together on the Web allowing the union of complementary assets. The strengths of one firm tend to reinforce those of the other, while simultaneously eliminating the greatest weakness of the two firms. (For example, Amazon.com and Toys "R" Us)

e-commerce taxonomy the structure of the technology pyramid that allows for e-commerce transactions

economic breakeven the volume of output where the firm is earning a dollar amount just equal to a normal profit

economic concentration the concept that helps define and quantify the number and/or size dispersion of the firms in a given product market

economic Darwinism the concept that only the fittest survive in highly competitive markets

economic efficiency the measure used by economists to determine how well society is using its scarce resources

economic firms entities that transform raw resources into finished goods and services. They are impersonal, intellectual abstractions that are potentially ephemeral or fleeting in nature, achieving permanency only if they use resources efficiently

economic industry a collection of firms producing products that consumers regard as similar to one another and serve as good substitutes

economic loss the state in which a firm's average total cost measured in terms of opportunity cost exceeds it revenue per unit

economic pluralism the fact that the marketplace offers a wide variety of potential solutions to an economic problem

economic profits revenues earned in excess of all opportunity costs, including a normal profit

economic tensions the competitive pressures pulling e-firms in different and sometimes mutually exclusive direction

economics the social science that studies the choices concerning the use, production, and distribution of scarce resources to satisfy relatively unlimited human desires for goods and services

economics of diversification firms broaden their product lines to reduce the risks associated with excessive exposure in a single market; can be accomplished through merger with another firm

economics of search a branch of economics that identifies both clock time and distance as two market frictions that hold implications for consumer behavior and market efficiency

economies of scale the lowest production costs obtainable for a given size of production capacity; the situation that exists when the per-unit cost of production declines as the firm increases its production volume or scale of output in the long run

economies of scope use of a fixed resource for more than one activity to exploit its productive value

education as an interpersonal process exposure to and transfer of information from one person to another through direct contact

eduCommerce mixes the delivery of noncredit courses with the sale of products and services

efficiency consequences the assessment of how well scarce resources are being used in market equilibrium

efficiency paradox the Internet as a vehicle for creating opportunities for intermediation as opposed to triggering disintermediation

efficiency within the firm the owners of the firm want to use the available resources to their maximum benefit

efficiency within the marketplace the fact that competitive markets will usually lead to the most valuable use of scarce resources

e-finance Web version of traditional financial activities such as banking and stock brokerage

e-health information Internet based information that helps individuals to improve how they care for themselves

e-insurance insurance that you purchase electronically

elastic demand a relatively strong consumer response to a price change

elasticity coefficient numerical measure of the responsiveness of consumer demand to a change in the price of an item

electronic bill presentation a potential killer application for the Internet that involved easy online payments, but that has so far failed to capture the imagination of a large volume of either creditors or bill payers

electronic colonialism the assertion that leadership in setting standards for and accelerating the spread of national values and culture via the Internet is the intellectual counterpart to physical occupation of another country

electronic commerce (e-commerce) the act of doing business electronically over the Internet

electronic construction portals help bring building projects to completion on time and under budget, providing cost saving and revenue enhancements greater than the fees allocated to the exchanges

electronic eavesdropping software that tracks, captures and listens in on Internet traffic

electronic firewall prevents unauthorized access and the leakage of information to rivals who may share the same B2B exchange

electronic funds transfer (EFT) electronic checks

electronic multitasking using two or more electronic devices, such as the television and the computer, simultaneously

electronic social interaction using the Internet with its tools of e-mail, attachments, and shared Web pages to move the process of knowledge creation from sharing a design to creating a design together

empire building mergers brought about primarily for the sake of size and/or leadership reputation

empowerment the ability to act and control transactions

encryption the scrambling or degrading of copyrighted digital content and making it available only to those who have an authorized password

encryption programs software that sends e-mails in scrambled code that blocks the ability of the software to read the intercepts without having access to the keys that unlock the code

English auction the type of auction in which the seller has a lowest price he or she will accept and the bidder has a maximum price he or she is willing to pay

enhanced connectivity the Internet as a medium as it allows a two-way tension of conversation and ideas

entrepreneur a risk-taking businessperson who perceives market gaps and seizes the opportunity for a potentially profitable response to the forces of disequilibrium

entrepreneurship a concept where the individual serves as an innovator or person who develops a commercial application of an invention and brings it to the marketplace

entry barriers conditions prohibiting entry of new firms into an industry regardless of the existence of positive profit incentives

equilibrium the state that exists when opposing forces are in balance and markets are at rest

equilibrium analysis views competitive markets as tending towards a position of rest were an analysis of economic consequences can be viewed

e-real estate firms listing and selling of homes and commercial property over the Internet

essential facilities a key form of private infrastructure, such as a bridge, whose economic function warrants special regulation, oversight, or supervision by a branch of government

e-tailing online retailing

ethical disconnect the view that exchanging copyrighted music files over the Internet is not ethically as wrong as stealing a CD from a store

excise tax a fixed amount of tax money levied per unit sold

exclusion actions taken by a dominant firm designed to keep competitors out of the marketplace

expected flow of economic profits the anticipated profits gained by a patent, or other property, over the lifetime of the property

expenses accounting term referring to the production-related cash outlays, as well as a charge for the depreciation of capital assets

explicit opportunity cost a tangible cash outlay or financial commitment

explicit opportunity costs economic costs that are comparable to the expenses recorded by an accountant

extensible markup language (XML) a new generation of more sophisticated computer code

external failure forces actions that originate from outside of the firm and threaten its continued existence, profitability, or competitive position

external security dimension protection from the Internet being used as a vehicle for terrorist attacks designed to cripple key parts of the U.S. economy such as financial services, energy delivery, and the operation of public infrastructure

externality a situation in which a normal market transaction between two individuals has either positive or negative third-party consequences

externally generated tensions tensions created by or relating to conditions of the external marketplace including governmental policy and legal, technical, or social forces

F

fair use doctrine legal exceptions to the unauthorized use of copyrighted materials

fast second strategy the ability of an imitator to focus on successful products and approaches without the delays of test markets, R&D efforts, and other risks and delays that accompany the introduction of a new product

Faustian bargain a decision that presents both a benefit and a burden

Fax and phone technology model a model of business information exchange that predates and competes with the efficiencies of electronic exchanges

federal regulatory approach actions that reflect the belief that government has the right to intervene in business activity

fiber-optic technology multiple strands of tiny, hair-thin, glass wires bundled into a cable

file-sharing technology technology that allows for the direct exchange of files

financial analysts technical specialists who undertake an independent, ongoing review of the financial health of firms or industries in their area of expertise. They write reports for clients detailing their findings, offering assessments of future earnings, and making stock purchase recommendations

financial planners formerly known as stockbrokers, they advise clients on managing their funds and market a wide range of investment vehicles to their customers

financing and syndication (Fin-Syn) rules regulations that prohibit television networks from taking a financial interest in the programs they air and profiting from the syndication of those programs

first-mover advantage the rewards or gains that come with being among the initial firms to provide a new product or enter a new market

first-price auction an auction bidding format where the winner bids the highest price and pays the amount of the bid

fixed access fee a lump-sum subscriber charge or a monthly fee a buyer must pay in order to participate in an activity or gain access

fixed costs charges such as depreciation on buildings and equipment and overhead that are constant and contribute to the cost of production

fixed-price strategy a scheme of pricing not open to negotiation between buyer and seller

float money earned in the form of interest on the premiums paid to insurance companies.

foreclosure the strategy in which a dominant firm controls one or more key stages of a market and uses that power to limit competition

four A's of media contact the linking of assets with audiences, advertiser opportunities, and providing access to tie the elements together

fragmented market no single firm or group of well-established firms dominates the marketplace

free rider problem the benefits received from a resource by those who do not pay for the resource

freeware any software program that is generally available free of charge

functional exchanges exchanges which offer a wide range of industrial products, used by business firms regardless of the buyer's product line

G

GAAP Rules generally accepted accounting principles

gatekeeper a firm that provides a general access point such as to the Internet

general information sites Web sites that provide news, weather, e-mail and other services usually attracting a higher number of visitors

get-big-fast strategy the goal of growing the market as fast as possible regardless of short-run cost, so as to take advantage of the economies of scale and scope that help to lower long-run unit cost

global system for mobile communications (GMS) one of several competing standards for the current use and future expansion of worldwide cell phone technology

globalization of the work effort firms in the developed world can use the Internet to outsource labor-intensive activity to other parts of the world, thereby lowering their labor costs while at the same time offering job opportunities to workers in remote developing nations thereby increasing their living standards

Gnutella an open source, free-to-all software program used to copy digital material

go-it-alone e-tail site an e-seller that does not have a physical retail or catalogue operation

goodwill accounting term reflecting the value assigned to a firm in excess of current market value, usually appears as a result of a merger between two firms

government franchise an exclusive license granted by the government to a local telephone or cable company, for example, allowing them to conduct economic activity within a specified geographic area

Gramm–Leach–Bliley Act of 1999 a federal law that requires financial institutions to notify their customers regarding the privacy policies of the institution

graphical user interface (GUI) the use of icons to organize the appearance of the computer screen and access instructions by mouse click rather than typed instructions

group aggregation model a business plan using Internet technology to form a group-buying scheme

group purchasing organizations the joining of several independent firms to form a larger organization in order to aggregate buying power and negotiate volume discounts

H

haggling negotiation between a buyer and seller over the price both are willing to accept

Health Insurance Portability and Accountability Act (HIPAA) federal legislation that requires health care providers to keep medical records in a form that is easily transferable. The Act is expected to drive physicians toward the use of WebMD type of electronic transactions model

health seekers someone who searches the Internet on a regular basis looking for information on diseases and treatment, clinical trials, and healthy diet programs

health supply-chain management coordinating the purchase and flow of medical supplies and equipment via the Internet

Herfindahl/Hirschman Index (HHI) a scale that makes use of market share data for all of the firms in an industry and incorporates information on their relative size dispersion

HHI numbers equivalent value equals 1/HHI and indicates the maximum number of firms of equal size permitted in an industry by a given HHI value

high-tech central distribution model deliveries made from automated warehouses

horizontal exchanges exchanges which offer a wide range of industrial products, used by most business firms regardless of the buyer's product line

horizontal Fin-Syn rule regulation that prohibits television networks from participating in the syndication of programs they air

horizontal merger a merger between two or more firms that sell the same product or products that are close substitutes in the same geographic market

horizontal TV-ownership limit the rule that no television network was allowed to own local stations that reached more than 35 percent of the nation's households

hybrid government-private governance model the number of board members is reduced to 15, with five being chosen by governments, and eliminating the five publicly elected posts

hypertext method of presenting information in a nonsequential manner

hypertext markup language (HTML) an easy to use, text based computer language used by Web browsers; original code of the Web

hypertext transfer protocol (HTTP) special search and retrieval protocol

I

identification of taxable items different jurisdictions apply different rules that vary widely in their tax treatment of items such as food, clothing, and health-related products

IEEE 802.11b the designation for interconnection standards developed by the technicians at the Institute for Electrical and Electronics Engineers

i-mode a popular Japanese cell-phone system that allows users to e-mail and perform a variety of wireless activities

implicit opportunity cost charges for the use of economic or scarce resources for which either no cash outlay is made or where the corresponding accounting charge differs from the true opportunity cost

implicit opportunity costs cost of using economic resources not associated with any comparable accounting expense

implicit price deflator (IPD) measures the price changes for all of the items that are part of GDP, including those bought by government, business, households, and through foreign exchange

incipiency the time before an act actually takes hold or becomes effective

increasing returns to scale a long-run increase in output that is achieved with a less than proportionate rise in physical inputs

increasing returns to scale increases in output volume achieved with less than a proportional increase in inputs

independent exchanges an autonomous business-to-business Internet intermediary that sells a service linking buyers and sellers in a given market

independent trading exchanges (ITE) a form of B2B trading vehicle that is a pure intermediary and not owned by any of the participants

industry-created exchange a collaboration of firms in an industry to buy resources and sell products

inelastic weak or insensitive consumer response to price change

infant industry argument the argument that a young and developing industry deserves protection from competition until it matures and is able to compete on an equal footing

infectious greed a phrase coined by Alan Greenspan describing the attitudes, atmosphere and uncontrolled lust for personal gain that gripped the U.S. stock market in the late 1990s

information asymmetries the parties on one side of a transaction have considerably less knowledge about a subject than do the parties on the other side

informational advertising advertising that is designed to convey information about the product such as price, conditions of sale, or product quality

informational Web sites Web sites that tell viewers about the firm and its products, but then require the viewer to contact the physical branches to obtain services

information-based system process to search, link, and access facts, pictures, sound, and animation at Web nodes

initial public offering (IPO) a legal activity that allows the firm to sell some of the ownership shares in the broader equity markets

innovator the person who turns the new product or process into a commercial application

instant message (IM) technology that allows two or more persons to carry on a real-time discussion

intangible asset nonphysical asset held by a firm that that contributes to the profitability of the firm in undefined ways, such as a patent or a recognizable brand name

intellectual capital resources invested to build up the information or knowledge assets of a firm or person

intellectual property the products produced by the creative efforts of authors, photographers, and songwriters etc.

intermediary an entity that stands between buyers and sellers in the marketplace, that usually charges a fee for supplying information or aiding in the exchange of a product or service

intermediary control model of Internet music distribution a system that allows third-party intermediaries to acquire the music distribution rights from recording firms

internal failure forces actions either taken or not taken by the owners of the firm

internally generated tensions tensions created by or relating to conditions of firm or industry structure, competitive behavior, or economic performance

Internet an electronic entity that links individual networks of computers together; a network of networks structured as a set of computer and cable connections

Internet access taxes a governmental charge levied on the money paid to access the Internet though an Internet service provider

Internet address a unique computer on a network

Internet backbone carriers the ten firms that carry the majority of the United States' high-speed Internet traffic

Internet browser the software package that links a personal computer to the Internet and allows the user to carry on e-commerce transactions

Internet censorship standards blocks the passage of what is deemed to be evil and offensive

Internet Corporation for Assigned Names and Numbers (Icann) a private, not-for-profit firm in charge of the IP address assignment function

Internet hardware and infrastructure firms the firms that produce the cable, equipment, hardware, and other physical components that make up the Internet

Internet job boards deal with fragmented markets on both sides of the job search process, working to focus the search process onto a single, centralized electronic site

Internet privacy to make sure that no unauthorized entity gains access to and/or uses personal information that has been transmitted over and stored on the Web

Internet security to protect the technical integrity of the Internet against unauthorized and/or illegal intervention

Internet security dimension to protect the Internet against a variety of criminal dangers including intrusions by hackers, the planting of viruses or worms, and attempts to shut down parts of the network through the introduction of denial-of-service attacks

Internet service provider (ISP) a firm that provides the Web user with the connection to the Internet

Internet synergy the collaborative intelligence of the Internet whole, which makes it greater than the sum of its individual parts

Internet Tax-Freedom Act (ITEA) created a three-year moratorium on the application of a variety of new Internet related taxes

Internet telephony using the Internet as a vehicle for the transmission of telephone voice calls

Internet version 2.0 a fully broadband, wireless system that will employ the IP V.6 and link just about every electronic appliance or product with a transmitter to the Web

interoperability the ability to communicate between differing systems

Interstate Commerce Act legislation that initially controlled the behavior of railroads that transported passengers or property between two or more states

Interstate Commerce Clause a section of the U.S. Constitution that allows the federal government to intervene in the market to rebalance the competitive process and defend the public interest in areas involving economic transactions between or among the states

inventor the person who comes up with a new product or method of doing business

investing partners persons who are passive participants in a venture capital firm, entrusting their money to the skills and experience of the managing partners

investment banker (IB) a firm, such as Goldman Sachs, Merrill Lynch, Morgan Stanley, or Credit Suisse First Boston that underwrites the IPO

investor roulette the serendipitous and unorganized meeting of potential investment partners and owners of new investment ideas through business seminars or social contacts

investors someone who buys shares of stock and holds them for the dividends and capital gains to be earned over an extended period of time

i-publishing the direct transfer of artistic material from the creator to the consumer via the Web

IPv6 enhanced version of existing Internet Protocol

irrational exuberance a phrase coined by Alan Greenspan describing the mob psychology, the human capacity for denial and getting rich quick mentality, which contributed to the speculative frenzy of the stock market in the 1990s

isocost lines lines that represent the combinations of capital and labor that can be purchased given the fixed price of each resource and a targeted amount of money (TC) to be expended on the purchase of resources

isolating technology the use of the Internet when it takes time away from the time spent interacting with real human beings, including friends, family members, and coworkers

isoquant curves curves that are convex to the origin and represent a constant level of output that can be produced with varying combinations of resource inputs

J

Java a computer programming language that can operate on normally incompatible computer platforms and across incompatible operating systems

judicial activism court decisions that led to great growth of patents to protect software and business methods

jurisdictional issues determining which jurisdiction's sales tax rate applies if an online sale takes place across the borders of different taxing districts

just and reasonable terms a legal term used in regulatory cases where product prices or tariffs are set without being arbitrary or capricious

just-in-time inventory deliver system placing retail orders electronically, with the parts requirements totaled electronically and daily (or hourly if needed), and then transmitted to the suppliers for immediate productions as well as deliver

K

kaizen a Japanese term signifying small, continual product improvement and upgrading

killer application (killer apps) Internet applications that require lots of bandwidth and high-speed Internet connections well beyond the 56 K speed of most dial-up modems

knowledge-based barriers technical expertise, management, innovation, and other intangible assets that help prevent competitors from luring a firm's customers away

L

laddering an alleged way of attracting a larger IPO allocation by having a fund manager pledge a certain level of additional aftermarket purchases of the stock

laser creates light impulses for use in fiber-optic cables

last-mile problem slow connection of the computer to the Internet, mainly in homes and some office locations

late-stage venture capitalists purchasers of premature IPO stocks who may unknowingly assumed more risk than might normally be associated with a traditional IPO

launch-and-learn strategy the idea of getting a Web site up quickly, and making improvements and modifications based on customer feedback experience

law of diminishing marginal returns a physical law that states that as an extra unit of a variable resource is added to the fixed input, the size of the resulting addition to output will eventually decline

learning curve traces out the reduction in costs associated with a firm's ability to make the flow of a new process run smoothly

left bids an auction bidding system where the bidders maximum price is identified prior to the auction, with increments to be bid up to the maximum as necessary by a representative of the auction house at the time of the auction

legal approach to enhanced Internet privacy involves the introduction of governmental laws requiring a site to obtain the informed consent of a visitor before collecting, exchanging, or aggregating information

legal life of a patent the length of time the subject of a patent is legally protected

legal or institutional entry barriers barriers to entry created by government power

legalistic frictions franchise laws and protectionist regulations that slow the spread of e-commerce in the protected markets

legislative inaction the refusal or inaction of Congress and other legislative bodies to pass regulations concerning Internet activity

leverage the potential ability to extend market power from one area of the market to another

limit pricing pricing of a product or service by the dominant firm below that allowed by its current market power so as to forestall future entry by one or more new competitors

limited partnership a business arrangement where partners are responsible for losses only to the extent of their financial participation in the firm

limited-menu third-party delivery model a business model where only nonperishable items are sold online and the delivery is scheduled via a private delivery service

linguistic intrusion the technical language of the Internet seeps into a traditional language to create hybrid words

liquidation preference in the event of the termination of the firm the start-up must pay a fixed amount of funds to the VC before other investors receive any funding

local TV station ownership rules FCC rules limiting the number of TV stations that can be owned by a single firm within a local market

lock-in effect a situation that deters customers from switching to another ISP

lock-up period the period of at least six months from the date of the IPO when the stock held by an insider cannot be sold

long run the situation in which all resources are variable

loss minimization a firm loses money but continues to produce in the short run because doing so will limit its losses to a level that is below its fixed costs

M

macroeconomic productivity a measure of overall output per worker

maintaining excess capacity the preemptive strategy of maintaining excess capacity as a deterrent to competitors' entry

managing partners persons who organize the VC firm and use their business experience as well as investment expertise to actively run the enterprise

manufacturer's suggested retail price (MSRP) a price suggested by a manufacturer to cover the production costs of the vehicle and earn some profit, also known as the sticker price

market capitalization the full current market value of a firm's outstanding common stock

market extension mergers mergers between two firms that produce the same product but sell it in different and noncompeting markets

market failure a situation where the market process fails to accurately allocate scarce resources efficiently; usually associated with externalities or an imbalance of information

market foreclosure a condition where actions taken by the existing dominant firm(s) limit the ability of a new competitor to enter the market

market frictions barriers such as lack of information or geographic distance that interfere with smooth, continuous, and efficient exchange in the market

market heroes people who often introduce substantial efficiencies in directing the flow of risk capital and the advancement of technology

market risk the risk of investing in an IPO

market segments distinct groups of buyers differentiated by age, income, sex, buying preferences and other characteristics

market villains people who sometime succeed in twisting the process of firm creation to favor their own personal gain at the expense of others

"may substantially lessen competition" a phrase from Section 7 of the Clayton Act halting anti-competitive mergers that are potentially capable of reducing competition in the marketplace

MC = MR marginal cost equal to marginal revenue, the rule for profit maximization

m-commerce the buying of products or services over the wireless Internet

merger a combination of two or more separate firms into a single legal entity

message-based system sends and receives messages, including text, data, voice and images

methods of doing business techniques for business operations that have become subject to possible patent protection

mezzanine financing the last stage of financing which raises the last round of venture money just prior to embarking upon an IPO

microeconomic theory the body of information and study of how markets work to organize and influence the actions of individual consumers and firms

microeconomics the branch of economics that looks at the behavior of individual units, including firms and consumers, as they deal with the resource scarcity problem

minimum efficient scale (MES) the state at which the firm achieves all possible scale economies in the long run

monopolist myth identifies the Internet as a vehicle to concentrate economic power and social dominance in the hands of a few large firms

monopoly a single-firm industry in which the producer makes a product for which no good substitutes are available and where entry barriers prohibit the appearance of new competitors

monopsony single-buyer market power

Moore's Law predicts that computing power on microprocessors would double every 18 months

mortgage-backed security part or all of a bank's mortgagte portfolio is packaged together as a single financial instrument to be sold to investors

MP3 files technology that allows users to compress music into files that are close to CD quality

multichannel sellers firms that have multiple sources of buyer contact, such as catalogs, e-commerce, and physical facilities

multimedia listings advertisements across print, film, cable, and Internet outlets

must-carry provision the regulation that requires the cable operator to retransmit the local TV station's signal in the cable basic tier, but without paying compensation to the local station for carrying the signal

mutual interdependence the situation that arises when an action taken by one firm has a direct, immediate, and perceptible effect on the sales and revenue received by the firm's rivals; usually found in an oligopoly market

N

narrow topic sites a site whose topic is closely related to that of the advertiser

national sales tax plan a tax plan where both the sales tax rate and base would be set at the national level, which would limit the e-tail versus retail sales tax distortion and stem some of the loss of tax revenues

natural monopoly the situation that occurs when one firm can satisfy the entire market at the lowest possible cost

Negroponte's development leverage hypothesis the Internet will help developing nations to connect to markets, train labor, educate children, teach governance skills, and generally expand horizons while raising living standards

net income an accounting measure of revenue minus all expenses including interest payments, taxes, and depreciation

Netscape Navigator an early commercial browser that combined text and graphics on the same page

network a situation in which diverse consumers, groups, or locations are served by the same connection

network externalities situations that convey positive benefits on both the supply and demand sides of the marketplace; where the cost of e-commerce transactions are reduced and the value of the flow of information to all users are increased with the number of members in the network

neutral common carrier an operating system that is required to treat all users equally

new economy Internet firms an e-commerce business model that lets the customer order items and pay for them via the Internet

nexus a connection between the state and the merchant

niche seller a firm that sells to only a well defined subset of the full buyer market for a given product

niche strategy production for a segment of the market that is not being satisfied by the market leader, or selling into a highly specialized segment of the buyer marketplace

nonprice competition competition based on product differentiation and factors other than price

normal profit an implicit cost that equals the dollar profits the resources could earn in their next best alternative use. It is where average revenue just equals average cost as defined in terms of opportunity cost

normal profits the revenues received by the entrepreneur that could be earned if the entrepreneurial resources were directed away from their current use and into their next best use

O

offshore tax havens any place, such as Bermuda, where a business might locate its headquarters for the purpose of avoiding taxes

old economy firms any business model where the business receives orders and conducts business by means other than the Internet

oligopoly an industry dominated by a few large rivals

oligopsony market power in the hands of a few buyers

one-click ordering a patented purchasing method developed at Amazon that combines use of a password with previously obtained information to save time and typing

one-stop telecommunications shopping a bundling of various communication services, such as telephone service, broadband Internet, and cable television connections

online hygiene habits regular use of antivirus software, establishing and changing passwords, and disconnecting from the Internet when not in use

online micropayment system the method of online payment of very small fees, possibly amounting to less than $1

online profiling tracking the actions, keystrokes, or otherwise keeping a record of the Web sites that an individual visits on the Internet

online security security for firms and computer systems connected to the Internet

online/off-line privacy threat the move to link Web behavior with names, addresses, and other forms of personal information

opaque auction process the bidding process in which much of the information is hidden from the bidder until the binding offer is accepted

open access open, unbiased access to any and all competitors or customers

open network a network that anyone can join who will abide by a few membership rules

opportunity cost a measure of resource value in the next best alternative use for that resource unit

opportunity cost the value of a resource in its next best alternative use. The value forgone where the resource is used elsewhere

optimal level of search the point where the value of the additional resources spent on the search process just match the value of the information obtained

opt-in policy a default computer setting that denies a site the right to exchange or collect personal information about a visitor unless it has been specifically permitted to do so by the Web user

opt-out policy a default computer setting that permits a site to collect and exchange personal information about a visitor unless the site has been specifically denied the right to do so by the individual

order book contains the names of potential institutional and individual buyers, along with the amount of their share purchase requests for a given IPO

origin-based transaction tax system the taxes are paid at the location of the principal place of business rather than at the destination end of the transaction

output maximization getting the highest volume of production with a targeted amount of dollar cost expended on resource inputs at fixed prices

overhead charges costs that remain constant and do not vary with output

P

packet switching technology a method for sending parts of messages to geographically dispersed computers

partnership a joining of persons in a business activity with each specializing in what he or she does best

passport a Microsoft project which is a centralized program of consumer identification designed to store personal information, including credit card data, in exchange for greater security and simplification of Web shopping, communication, and collaboration

patent a legal, governmental grant of protection from copying for machines, products, and processes

patent criteria three characteristics (useful, novel, and unobvious) the subject of a patent application must fulfill in order to qualify for patent protection

pay-for-play system the requirement that a user must pay for each use of online entertainment

pecuniary economies of scale a shifting of revenues and profits among firms based upon merger-created size or power disparities

peering arrangements an agreement between firms that allow for the exchange of communications traffic among each other at no charge

peer-to-peer (P2P) e-commerce use of the Web by individuals to communicate with each other for the purpose of undertaking transactions

penetration pricing strategy the strategy of selling products at an amount below today's full costs in an attempt to build sufficient sales volume and revenue to cover tomorrow's expected lower full cost

performance rights the rights to produce the public performance of a work

persistent economic profits profits that persist into the long run and distort the efficiency-creating aspects of the market

personal digital assistants handheld electronic devices that often combine some of the properties of an appointment calendar, calculator, computer and/or Internet connection appliance

pick-pack-deliver (PPD) strategy an approach to grocery sales where the seller removes items from shelves in a warehouse and delivers them to the customers location

piracy of intellectual property illegal duplication of copyrighted material such as music, books, or films; legally equivalent to the theft of tangible property

platform for Privacy Preferences (P3P) a code-based privacy system developed by the World Wide Web Consortium

polarizing tendency the reader filters out unwanted information and opinions and sees only pre-selected, like-minded viewpoints

political fragmentation a situation of information filtering that distorts the ideal embodied within the U.S. motto *E Pluribus Unum* (From many, one)

pooling of funds no single VC investor has all of its money tied up in a start up

populist myth identifies the Internet as a force that liberates and empowers the individual

pop-up ads Internet advertising which appears on Web portal sites to help fix the name of the product or firm in the mind of the consumer

potential entrant a firm that exists on the fringe of an industry that is attracted to that market, and which may actually enter the industry if expected profits become sufficient

prebuild business model a model in which the product is produced in anticipation of sales

predatory pricing selling a product at a price below average variable cost

pre-IPO investor an investor who puts money into a firm just prior to the IPO; often a less risky stage of the start-up's development

presence technology new technology that will allow others to monitor the usage or location of desktop, laptop, and handheld computers, cell phones, wireless Web pads, auto communications systems, and virtually any other device connected to the Web

price discrimination the tactic of selling a product with a single unique cost at different prices to different consumers in the same market

price elasticity of demand the relative sensitivity of consumer purchases to a change in the price of an item

price leadership model the situation in which the dominant firm sets a market price that is subsequently adopted by the smaller firms

price per unit of use a pricing scheme that encourages customers to optimize their usage up to the point where they equate the per-unit price with the additional value received from consuming one more, or the last, unit

price-to-earnings (P/E) ratio a measure of the expected earnings of an issue to its selling price

prior art previous or prior invention or idea that the subject of a patent application cannot patent

private label brand products that the e-tailer orders directly from the manufacturer, thereby giving the e-tailer considerable control over the design, quality, and cost of the product

pro forma **profits** profits derived using a name-your-own-accounting-rules system of financial record keeping used many e-commerce firms

problem of multiple tax jurisdictions arises if the county and/or city of residence also levy their own sales taxes in addition to the state

process innovation change that creates new ways of performing existing economic activities more efficiently

product attributes individual characteristics embodied within a specific product.

product differentiation the designing of a new product or modifying of an existing one for the purpose of selling it to the customer

product extension mergers mergers occurring between two firms selling products complementary to each other

product innovation change that yields new products or services for consumers

production-based product differentiation model the demand for goods depends upon the ability of firms to create products and then market them to an impressionable public, whose tastes and preference can be led and shaped by advertising

productive efficiency when goods and services are produced in the long run at the right volume, at the lowest cost, using the best technology

professional certification process standards set by the American Accreditation Health Care Commission to measure the quality of information, the disclosure about funding and advertising sources, the linkage to related sites, and other issues covering privacy and security of the online health care site

profit markup an amount added to the selling price of a product or service, above accounting expenses, to compensate the efforts of the entrepreneur

profit maximizing rule (MC = MR) to produce to the point where marginal cost is equal to marginal revenue

profit rule of competitive markets rule which states that all firms must earn a competitive return, or new resources will cease to flow into its activity, investors will disappear, and the resources already held by the firm will slip away, drawn by better opportunities elsewhere

profits the residual of total revenue minus total costs

programmer lock-in when software programmers become more reluctant to write new program applications for another operating system

project extranets a site that holds information available via the Web to any authorized source outside the host firm

proprietary Web site a highly efficient and cost effective way to build customer relationships

prospectus a statement that spells out in some detail the risks and uncertainties associated with the company and its future

protectionist legislation legislation used by traditional retail distributors which guards against new competitors or other changes in the status quo

psychological switching barrier a decision a consumer makes to stay with a particular seller based on perceptions of convenience, trust, price, and other factors

public forum doctrine individuals who have access to an audience and where listeners ought to be exposed to a diversity of view

public good existing facility or general knowledge that is available to everyone

pump-and-dump stock scam the act of acquiring shares of inexpensive stocks with low trading volumes and then talking them up with false messages left on stock trading boards for the purpose of selling the stock at a profit

pure competition a collection of firms that form an industry and is defined by large numbers of firms, homogenous products, price taking, no nonprice competition, and easy entry and exit

pure conglomerate mergers mergers between two firms that operate in totally separate product markets

pure Webcasters Internet-only music stations that provide songs on an almost-on-demand basis

Q

quasi-judicial body a government body such as the FCC that can hear cases, set industry rules, and render decisions that can be challenged later in a court of law

R

rachet provision a provision which states that in the event the start-up needs another round of financing before going to an IPO, the present late-stage investors would maintain their current ownership share in the firm, even if they were not participants in the later financing round

racing behavior the wasteful activity of rivalrous firms when they spend resources extravagantly to become the first to achieve a goal such as receiving a government patent

real gross domestic product (RGDP) the final value of all newly produced goods and services for a nation within one year. It is calculated minus any changes in value caused by fluctuations in product prices

reciprocity the situation that arises when one level of a vertically integrated firm purchases goods or services from an independent firm on the condition that the independent buy a portion of its supplies from another division of the vertical firm

recording rights the rights of a firm to produce the sound of the music

regressive tax persons with lower income levels generally pay a higher percentage of their income in the form of a tax

regulated encryption key escrows or encryption backdoors that allow law enforcement agencies to read encrypted files

related industries firms in one industry that share activities with or provide complementary products or services to firms in another industry

remote sales transactions out-of-state mail-order firms that sell product to in-state residents

rental rate what it would cost in today's dollars to lease the equipment from an independent owner

replacement cost what it would cost in today's dollars to buy the equipment from an independent owner

reserve price a price below which a seller will not complete a transaction

residual demand curve represents the amount of consumer demand left to a second seller after the first seller has captured her segment of market demand

retention fee a follow-on or monthly fee that must be paid in order to retain a particular service

retransmission consent provision the terms on which the local TV station will permit the cable operator to rebroadcast the TV station's signal

retroactive repricing provision a provision that allows the number of shares a venture investor receives to fluctuate with the value of the IPO

return-on-investment (ROI) a profit level that is consistent with the opportunity cost of acquiring capital funds if a project is to be economically viable

reverse auction pricing process the bidding scheme that places the pricing initiative in the hands of the buyer. The seller can either accept or reject the buyer's binding offer

RIAA v. Napster a copyright infringement case involving copyright-protected music and free digital distribution

ripping of CDs copying tracks from CDs to make MP3 files

rounds of VC financing the various stages of money infused into a new firm by a venture capital supporter up to the time of the initial public offering

routers transmitters located at the beginning and end of a cable to transfer signals to and from light impulses

ruinous competition vigorous competition that eventually proves impoverishing and self-canceling for some sellers

S

sales tax a tax levied according to the value of the item being purchased

sales tax administration in the industrial age the merchant collected the sales tax at the time and place of sales

sales tax administration in the information age a much more intricate and uncertain way to collect taxes on the sales of products or services

sales tax base list of items subject to the sales tax

sales tax rate the percentage tax rate at which the sales tax is levied

salvage rate the revenue that a firm could receive reflecting an implicit opportunity cost for equipment that contributes productive value here and elsewhere as scrap

scalable output a product or service whose volume of output can be increased quickly and efficiently at a lower cost per unity

Schumpeterian market gap the theory that says markets are in constant turmoil, creating gaps that can be filled by an entrepreneur if there is a potential for profit

science of photo optics light management

seasonal shutdowns shutdowns due to times of slow demand, model changeover, or company-wide vacations

second-price auction process the scheme of bidding in which the winning bid equals the second highest bid price plus a predetermined increment

seed financing earliest stage of financing before the management team or firm comes together

seed money the initial money need by entrepreneurs to begin their business adventure

selective and secret price concessions the process by which a reduction price is negotiated directly with a buyer, with the terms and possibly the existence of the deal being hidden from other potential buyers

self-organizing Web site a highly cost effective business model where the users of a Web site create the site's content

self-selection consumer choosing from possible offerings and prices rather than having the firm use market power to strategically restrict the range of choices and accessories

seller-posted pricing model the market scheme in which multiple buyers react to a price set by the seller of the product or service

semantic Web the smart code controlling the Web is able to understand the human language

sensitivity analysis an analysis to see what happens to the results under different assumptions

server farms systems designed to hold customer data in large e-warehouses

Sherman Antitrust Act of 1890 the first antitrust act; it prohibited contract, combination, and conspiracy in restraint of trade, along with attempts to monopolize a product or market

shopping bots robot shopping search engines that constantly send out searches for prices for a specific product at different sites on the Internet to determine the lowest price

short message service (SMS) an application popular in Europe and Japan

short run the situation in which at least one resource is fixed in supply while others are variable

short run profit-maximizing rule (MC = MR) to produce to the point where marginal cost is equal to marginal revenue

shutdown case the firm responds to its losses by ceasing operations in the short run, because to do so limits the loss to the amount of their fixed costs

silent blocking a form of Internet censorship which is done without any indication to the customers.

simulcast retransmission or simultaneous broadcasting of radio signals over the Web

simultaneous multiple version strategy the introduction simultaneously of several versions of the same product

sin tax an excise tax on alcohol or cigarettes

single-site cookies generally benign cookies in that they have certain privacy protections built into their structure

slotting fees revenue-sharing agreements with the wireless service providers to locate firm names or advertising on the cell phone screen

smart code combined with smart technology will be part of the new Internet application which will be more powerful and allow users to accomplish more tasks with less effort

smart technology combined with smart codes will be part of the new Internet application which will be more powerful and allow users to accomplish more tasks with less effort

SMS interoperability cell phone subscribers using one Internet connection standard could not easily send text messages to subscribers who use a different system

social firms the view that firms are analogous to living, breathing organisms that are valued for their own sake. They possess physical assets and develop corporate culture

socialism an economic system that downplays the importance of profits as a guiding force for the use of resources, and involves some mix of public and private ownership for the means of production

Sony Betamax case 1984 U.S. Supreme Court decision that held that if a new technology had substantial, noninfringing uses, it could not be held accountable for illicit uses

spillover costs adverse environmental consequences resulting from the production or market exchange process

spoiling the market the tendency for sellers to repeatedly offer last minute discounts thereby encouraging buyers to wait to the last minute to make a purchase exemplified by airline customers waiting until the last minute to buy plane tickets because they know the airline will offer large discounts to avoid flying with empty seats

stakeholders the collection of workers, investors, entrepreneurs, managers, customers, and suppliers, each of which has an interest in the operation of a firm

Standard Industrial Classification (SIC) code a U.S. Department of Commerce classification system that groups firms by their technical process of production or the raw materials used to make the finished good

standard volume (SV) the expected annual output for a product; used in establishing the list price of a product or service

standard-volume pricing tallying up all of the explicit costs associated with producing a targeted volume of output and then taking on a per-unit charge to cover profits. Also called cost-of-service pricing

start-up valuation problem the entrepreneur wants to set as high a value for the firm, with as small a share of ownership being given to the investor as possible in return for a fixed amount of money. Conversely, the VC firm wants to place a low value on the start-up at the time of funding commitment, and thereby receive a high fraction of the firm's equity value in trade for the given dollar investment

state franchise laws protectionist legislation designed to block the spread of e-commerce sales

State Street Bank case a 1998 court case that determined that business methods as applied to computerized business practices could be protected by patent

static efficiency a notion of productive and allocative efficiency at a moment in time so that society gets the most value out of a given technology set and fixed amount of resources

stock manipulation an illegal action affecting the value of common stock, such as executives from the investment bank ordering or coercing an analyst to make a buy recommendation of a stock and thereby placing the valuation of the firm in a false light

stockholders people who invests some or all of their wealth in exchange for part ownership of the firm

store-based delivery model the model where pick-pack-deliver tasks are undertaken from the shelves of local supermarkets

straight-line depreciation depreciating a fixed percentage of the asset's value each year over its projected useful life

strategic behavior barriers that are artificial in nature, and are created by deliberate actions of the firms

strategic partnership the relationship between retailing and e-tailing as a way to differentiate their product and try to establish themselves as a viable, profitable e-commerce entity

Streamlined Sales Tax Project a group of 30 states who meet regularly to try to come to an agreement on a simplified Internet transactions taxing system by the year 2003

strengths of a Web-based exchange system the first strength is the ability to gather, process, and transmit large amounts of information cheaply, while the second is the ability to provide ready access to that information on a 24/7 basis

structural approach the examination of markets as defined by their characteristics, such as the nature of their products, there degree of price control, height of entry barriers, and others

structural remedy an antitrust decision that would break up a possible monopolist into two or more competing firms

structure-conduct-performance (SCP) paradigm the view that competition and efficiency flow in a fairly linear and deterministic way from market structure to firm behavior to competitive performance

sunk cost a price that was paid in the past and cannot be altered on the basis of the degree of usage

supply-chain management controlling the purchase and flow of materials that go into the production process with the goal of limiting material cost and flow delays

support industries businesses that serve as suppliers to the industry leader

sword and shield a firm's use of a patent as a sword to intimidate competitors, and as a shield to protect assets from the suits of other

SWOT analysis an analysis that looks at the combination of the business's strengths, weaknesses, opportunities, and threats

symbiotic agreement an agreement between two parties in which both benefit by the association

symbiotic antagonism a small amount of cooperation between two rivalrous and conflicting firms

synergy the situation in which a combined firm can carry out a production activity in a less costly or more effective manner than if it were undertaken separately by the two firms

system vulnerabilities the extent to which a computer system is open to external attack or internal disruptions

T

target market the market to which an information pitch can be offered in greater detail and depth

target marketing campaign a form of online advertising directed at a market subset, which increases the likelihood that the surfer will click through to the advertising site and purchase its product

tax asymmetry arises when a tax is levied on only a subset of similar market transactions

tax avoidance a legal method to keep from paying a particular tax.

tax avoidance shell game a way for retailers as e-tailers to hide the sales transactions from the taxing jurisdictions by locating in a zero sales tax state or physically off-shore outside the boundaries of the U.S.

Tax burden Financing the state government via the sales tax

tax evasion an illegal scheme to keep from paying taxes, punishable by incarceration

tax incidence financial burden borne by the buyer

tax-induced behavioral gymnastics creating methods to avoid the creation of a nexus for purposes of taxation

technical barriers to entry barriers associated with the supply or production of the product

technological change the introduction of a new type of capital equipment or method of doing business with the usual effect of increasing productive efficiency

technology approach to enhanced Internet privacy; involves the use of a code-based solution to achieving privacy in cyberspace

technology approach to standard setting creating and installing imbedded copyright protection technology

"tend to create a monopoly" a clause within Section 7 of the Clayton Act prohibiting a merger before the result rises to the level of a monopoly

third-party collection solution the adoption of a national sales tax rate and base for online sales

third-party cookies electronic consumer identifiers placed on computers by a third party who then sells the information to advertisers who tailor the content of display ads to better suit the personal characteristics and buying patterns of an online surfer

tight oligopoly the situation that exists when CR4 reaches or extends beyond 60 percent

time division multiple access (TDMA) one of a number of competing cell phone technologies that slices phone conversations into segments of time on a given frequency and pieces it back together at the destination

time shifting individual viewing at a time and date that is convenient for the viewer rather than for the program scheduler

total fixed cost a cost that remains constant and does not vary with output

total variable cost a cost that changes directly with the volume of output

trade secret private information that a firm holds that benefits its competitive position

traders someone who purchases a stock with the intent of reselling or flipping it within a very short period of time in response to a favorable price movement

trading hub the final organizational form for a B2B exchange

transactional Web sites financial services Web sites that allow retail customers to check bank balances and move funds between accounts, as well as apply for loans and credit cards. Business customers can also apply for loans, wire transfer funds, and access cash management, along with payroll services.

transmission control protocol/internet protocol (TCP/IP) common language allowing different networks to communicate with each other

transparency uniform financial reporting allowing the comparison of accounting reports across the entire spectrum of ongoing firms, regardless of their line of business

transparent auction process an auction in which the participants are usually physically together and can hear and see each other as they participate

TV-duopoly rule the rule that limited the number of TV stations that a single company can own in a specific market

two-part tariff a pricing scheme by which buyers are charged both a fixed access fee and a price per unit of use

U

underwrite the process where the Investment banker lines up the legal and financial aspects of an IPO as well as finds buyers for the stock

undifferentiated commodity product a product that is identical to that produced by competitors

uneven playing field a problem between tax-exempt e-tailers and retailers, who must charge their customers a higher price for the same product because they collect sales taxes on the item

uniform resource locator a filename that allows access to a particular site on the Web

uniform tax solutions the adoption of a common sales tax rate and list of taxable items for online sales

universal interoperability standards the ability to communicate among all systems

upstream firms manufacturers and other businesses that precede a given firm's stage in production

user lock-in when it becomes less attractive for the user to switch computers that use a rival operating system

V

value added the portion of product worth that is added at a particular stage of the production process

value added tax a tax, similar to the ones that exist in Europe, placed on the value of the item at different stages of the production process. It can serve as a substitute for and have the same revenue-raising capacity as a national sales tax

value-of-service pricing setting the price for a product based on the worth of the product or service to the consumer

variable costs production costs that may vary due to adding additional amounts of resources

VC-IPO model of firm creation an efficient vehicle for the creation of new companies, which is also a way to create and sell stocks at a profit for the early investors

venture capital firm typically structured as a limited partnership in that partners are responsible for losses only to the extent of their financial participation in the firm. VC firms make high risk, early stage investments in new start-up firms and firm ideas

venture capitalist an intermediary who unites risk takers and innovators

versioning developing multiple levels of the same product with different components and different prices

vertical cable content limitation the rule that no single cable operator was allowed to have more than 40 percent of it channels carry programming produced by an affiliated company

vertical Fin-Syn rule regulation that prohibits television networks from taking a financial interest in the programs they air

vertical merger a combination of firms at different stages of the supply chain such as in a buyer-supplier relationship to one another

virtual (Internet only) e-tailer a seller that has only an Internet identity, and has no physical sales facilities

virtual banks internet banks that exist only in electronic as opposed to physical space

virtual colleges online colleges that exist only in electronic as opposed to physical space

virtual locker service technology that allows owners of CD music to store their songs on a provider's service

virtual supermarkets internet supermarkets that exist only in electronic as opposed to physical space.

visitor demand consolidation a growing number of users being attracted to an ever-decreasing number of sites

W

wave division multiplexing process of combining many colors of light, each carrying separate streams of data, in a single fiber-optic strand and sorting them at the other end

Web bugs devices invisibly added to Web pages to gather information about the visitors to a particular Web site

Web spiders search programs that survey the offering prices for a specific product at different sites on the Internet

Web version 2.0 a semantic Web, where the smart code controlling the Web is able to understand human language

Web-based collaboration where individual engineers or teams of individual specialists can engage in remote collaboration on a specific project via the Internet

Webcasters providers of online music services

Wi-Fi free riders proximate external users who access the unsecured private WLANs created by others

willingness to pay the buyer's personal circumstances (such as preferences and income) and the price of the current item versus the prices of substitute items

wired fidelity (Wi-Fi) a wireless Internet alternative to cell phone technology

wireless applications protocol (WAP) dominated today's 2G wireless Internet which is slow and lists few applications

wireless cloud individual base stations chained together in a series of interconnected Wi-Fi links

wireless local area networks (WLANs) individual computer networks

wireless mesh network the interconnection of individual computer networks

World Wide Web a technology carried by the Internet by which individuals can access a variety of Internet sites to carry on e-commerce and other activity

X

X-inefficiency functioning at a cost level that is above the minimum unit cost associated with the current output rate

Y

yield management when firms alter their prices depending on the time of day, number of vacancies, or other variables with the goal of maximizing their total profits

LIST OF TENSIONS